THE ENGLISH BIBLE IN AMERICA

The English Bible in America

A Bibliography of Editions of the Bible
& the New Testament Published
in America 1777-1957

Edited by

MARGARET T. HILLS

Librarian, American Bible Society

New York

American Bible Society

and

The New York Public Library

1961

Library of Congress Catalog Card Number: 61–12303

Printed at The New York Public Library

form p688 [iii-31-61 1m]

FOREWORD

NOW and again some relatively small knot in the wide fabric of human affairs gathers into itself a surprising number of diverse strands out of the long historical patterns and holds them still for us to look at and to marvel. Such a "knot" is this modest venture in bibliography. Here in these pages one may trace a history of the art of printing in America, or a development of American industry. One sees the long roll of American scholars engaged in most meticulous study of ancient languages and the art of translating them. The movement of American life may be traced from the colonies on the Atlantic seaboard to its western shores. Here there is documented a small but important aspect both of commercial enterprise and of benevolent initiative. More than all these, one may trace the power of religion and a great religious book to mold the life and ideas of a nation as it rose from small beginnings to greatness.

In considering the problem of the selection of entries from among Scriptures published in the United States to be entered in the anticipated revision of the first volume of "Darlow and Moule," * the Library of the American Bible Society adopted the writer's suggestion of preparing (primarily for local reference) a loose-leaf bibliographical catalogue. Upon this basis the skilled and accurate labors of Miss Dagny Hansen drew together the considerable material in the Society's library, the entries in O'Callaghan, Editions of the Bible; Evans, American Bibliography 1639–1800; Simms, The Bible in America; Wright, Early Bibles in America; and Pope, English Versions of the Bible; and the records of the Library of Congress's Union Catalog. The considerably more than five-foot shelf resulting has been enlarged and elaborated by Mr Robert D. Allenson, and all has been overseen and re-edited by the exceptional experience of Miss Margaret T. Hills, M.A., the Society's Librarian.

* Historical Catalogue of the Printed Editions of Holy Scripture in the Library of The British and Foreign Bible Society, compiled by T. H. Darlow, M.A. and H. F. Moule, M.A., London 1903.

[v]

Discovering that the result was of keen interest to other libraries and librarians, the possibility of publication was raised. Here, the Bible Society turned to its fellow-citizen of New York, The New York Public Library. The present collaboration in publication has resulted. This is particularly appropriate because The New York Public Library was for many years the caretaker of the Society's collection while the latter occupied a building not adequately fireproof. For this counsel and collaboration the Society wishes to thank in particular Dr David V. Erdman and, for much professional editorial skill, Mrs Elin Wolfe.

ERIC M. NORTH
for the American Bible Society

TABLE OF CONTENTS

INTRODUCTION

AS DR NORTH has stated in his Foreword this bibliography began as a working basis for the selection of matter to be added in a new edition of the Darlow and Moule *Historical Catalogue of the Printed Editions of Holy Scripture in the Library of the British and Foreign Bible Society.* As it grew in bulk and scope, it seemed more worthy of elaboration and publication. The work could have been done quite differently if we had had in mind the publication of this material in its present form.

The bibliography is based on the American Bible Society's collection of American printings of the Scriptures in English, checked against similar holdings in The New York Public Library and a microfilm (secured in 1956) of the English Bible section of the Library of Congress Union Catalog of Bibles. These entries were further checked against E. B. O'Callaghan's *A List of Editions of the Holy Scriptures . . . Printed in America previous to 1860,* John Wright's *Early Bibles of America,* P. Marion Simms's *The Bible in America,* and Hugh Pope's *English Versions of the Bible* (Revised and Amplified by Rev Sebastian Bullough). In each entry the copy described is either one owned by the American Bible Society (NNAB) or, lacking that, a New York Public Library copy (NN). Descriptions of books in neither of these collections were often obtained by correspondence, although Robert Allenson also examined personally a good many volumes at the American Antiquarian Society, Yale, Harvard, and several libraries in Philadelphia. All the items in Part I and many in Part II were either examined personally or checked by correspondence. Other items in Part II were taken directly from the Union Catalog microfilm. Efforts were made to locate some items in Part I through writing to libraries and historical societies. Where no location could be found for a copy listed in O'Callaghan or Wright, the page reference to that source is given. We have relied heavily on O'Callaghan and Wright for much valuable information incorporated into descriptions of items, and it seems appropriate that this new bibliography should appear exactly a century after the publication of Dr O'Callaghan's most valuable work.

We have included in this work only Scriptures in English but hope that a similar publication covering editions in other languages may eventually be prepared.

It sometimes happened that an entry ascribed in the Union Catalog to a particular library could not be located, in which case the symbol was removed from the entry or a note added.

ARRANGEMENT is chronological by year. Within each year Bibles are given first, by size (largest to smallest), then Old Testaments and Old Testament parts, then New Testaments and New Testament parts. In general only complete Bibles or Testaments are listed. When a new translation appeared in parts, however, the separate parts have usually been listed as issued, although in some cases the later parts have been listed under the first entry. Undated books have not been included without some evidence for ascribing a possible date. Books issued over several years have been entered under their earliest date, the entry date usually being that of the main title, and the second date, where differing from the main title, that of the New Testament (e. g. 1782/81). Books issued in volumes are entered under the date of the earliest volume.

TITLES as given do not reproduce exactly the type style, line breaks, punctuation, or capitalizations of the title-pages except for a few such important books as the first New Testament and the first Bible printed in America (Nos 1 and 11). The name of the publisher is always given before the place of publication and is preceded by the name of the printer or plate maker. Square brackets enclosing a name indicate that it appears not on the title-page but on its verso.

PAGINATION is usually given in totals, though for some important editions a summarized collational formula is given. In a formula such as "(10) (1276) 1277–1310 (89)" (No 30) the first sum within parentheses represents the number of pages containing preliminary matter, the second the number containing Old and New Testaments with intervening matter; the page numbers in series indicate a group of paginated additional matter (pages 1277–1310 Index and Tables); the third sum the number of pages containing another unpaginated or separately paginated group (89-page Concordance). When the sum is one, it is enclosed in square brackets if that page is unnumbered, thus [1]. When totals are given simply as "555 p" they signify pagination from page 1; parentheses "(555 p)" mean total pages of text *not* beginning on page 1. The statement "Reported as 555 p" is used for books not directly examined.

Where a book is indicated as a reprint of an earlier entry, pagination is not repeated.

MEASUREMENT in Part I (usually taken from page 3 of the text) covers the type page, including marginal material, folios, etc, and is given in millimetres. It is recognized that such measurement for books of this period may for various reasons not always be dependable. In Part II the measurement is of the height of the spine, in centimetres.

Where measurements could not be obtained, as for unlocated items in O'Callaghan, the listed size is given — e. g. "12mo."

LOCATION of copies is indicated by the symbols in the Eighth Edition Revised of *Symbols used in the National Union Catalog of the Library of Congress*. A table of the symbols with identification appears on p xxix.

In some cases we have included descriptions of privately owned copies or of copies found only in a publisher's office collection. Inquiries about these should be addressed to the American Bible Society.

VERSIONS: Unless otherwise indicated the text is that of the King James or Authorized Version, first published in 1611. No history of this version is given here nor of the Rheims-Douay Version of 1582–1609/10, as both these standard versions and their histories are well known. Nor is mention made of the revision of the Rheims-Douay text by Dr Challoner in the middle of the eighteenth century. For identification of such editions up through 1860 we have depended on Father Parsons' study, "First American Editions of Catholic Bibles." The reader is referred to Pope's *English Versions of the Bible* for much interesting and valuable information on Roman Catholic editions. For other translations or revisions we have attempted to give details as to the translator or translators and the background, purpose, and scope of the work.

DESCRIPTIONS: After version or edition identification (if not AV text), comes first a descriptive list of the make-up, contents, and arrangement of the text if it is not in normal double-column, verse-paragraph form. This is followed by any additional information.

APOCRYPHA: If the word Apocrypha appears in the title, its inclusion is not always given in the description of a King James Bible. The pagination is usually separate and stands out where full pagination is given. This material was very often included in quarto and folio Bibles through the first half of the nineteenth century but appears less and less in recent editions and in general is not included today. Exceptions are specifically indicated.

REPRINTS: In the case of frequently reprinted editions from the same plates or series of plates, we have listed later printings under the first entry (see Scott's Bible, 1827 No 583; Family Expositor, 1833 No 837). In Part I we have included all the reported printings of American Bible Society editions, but in Part II we have listed only new formats, recording in some instances the number of copies that have been printed from some of the more popular forms during the life of the plates or the series of related plates.

ILLUSTRATIONS: We have not been very systematic in dealing with illustrations. We were interested in Alexander Anderson and a few other American artists, who are listed in the general index, but have made no attempt to list all the artists, engravers, etc whose works appear in the books described.

INDICES: The following indices have been provided to enable the user of the bibliography to find various kinds of material:

GEOGRAPHICAL INDEX: Publishers listed by towns, the towns being grouped by states.

INDEX OF PUBLISHERS AND PRINTERS: A list of firms and individuals with the reference numbers of related items. Figures in parentheses refer to instances in which a printer or firm is referred to in relation to a publication which does not bear his name.

INDEX OF TRANSLATIONS AND OF TRANSLATORS AND REVISERS: A list of translations and versions, and a list of individuals who have revised or translated afresh the actual text. This may involve simply changes in English wording or different readings or renderings of the basic Hebrew or Greek texts.

INDEX OF EDITORS AND COMMENTATORS: A list of people who have added introductions, concordances, dictionaries, notes, and other material supplemental to the Bible text.

INDEX OF EDITION TITLES, such as the Dartmouth and Polyglott Bibles.

GENERAL INDEX: Lists artists, individuals, first appearances of special items such as the 1611 "The Translators to the Reader," and various other points of information.

We have not included in the indices all the editions with Canne's marginal references, Brown's or Cruden's Concordance, William Stone's plan for Reading the Bible through in a year, or other often-reprinted supplementary matter, though there is usually a note at the first appearance of such matter.

ACKNOWLEDGMENTS: In addition to the words of Dr North, it is fitting here to repeat recognition for the contribution of Miss Dagny Hansen in the original spade work on this project, including days spent in the Annex of The New York Public Library amid the unavoidable dust from thousands of aging leather-bound Scriptures, stultifying hours examining the DLC Union Catalog microfilm, and organizing a welter of material. Robert D. Allenson spent only four months on the project but his knowledge of and interest in the field were invaluable. Miss Kathleen M. Davidson of the American Bible Society staff has been a constant help in all phases of the work.

We are also greatly indebted to many patient librarians who have answered our many specific inquiries, to name only a few, the staff of the Alderman Library, University of Virginia; Miss Elizabeth Hughey of the Methodist Publishing House, Nashville; Mr Yeatman Anderson III of the Public Library of Cincinnati and Hamilton County; Miss Dorothy C. Barck, New York State Historical Society, Cooperstown; Mr Robert H. Haynes, Harvard; and the long-suffering staff of The New York Public Library. Miss Marjorie Peabody of Brattleboro supplied helpful material on the Holbrook & Fessenden firm; Miss Mary C. Urquhart of the Canadian Bible Society has given material on Canadiana.

It was Mrs Elin Wolfe who devoted meticulous editorial care to the preparation of our manuscript for publication. David H. Stam has shared the proofreading chore. To the Library's skilled compositor, Paul A. Arbucho, the Composing Room, and the Press Room, we are deeply indebted for the care, accuracy, and patience with which this material has been set and printed.

But we pay special tribute to the Reverend Eric M. North, D.D., long a General Secretary of the American Bible Society and now Consultant, who originally proposed the project and whose wise guidance and encouragement at every step have been invaluable.

As to myself, I accept responsibility for all the errors and inadequacy of the work. I have been over it many times in various stages, always finding something that I would like to add or reword and too often finding something to correct. Corrections, omissions, and amplifications will always be welcome.

Margaret T. Hills

THE ENGLISH BIBLE IN AMERICA

ENGLISH BIBLES came to America with many of the settlers at James-town and Plymouth and for many years thereafter they came with arriving colonists as cherished treasures from home and as sustaining supplies for a new life. Fires and other disasters inevitably related to frontier life as well as the needs of expanding families created demands for new Bibles among people whose life was traditionally Bible-oriented. The ships were small and the ocean wide in those days, but Bibles from England and Holland were often listed in the goods advertised in local newspapers as "just arrived" along with textiles and household necessities. Among other locally developing industries were printing and book making, but even a New Testament, to say nothing of a whole Bible, required a great deal of type, skilled labor, and paper, all scarce items. A very real obstacle was the Crown monopoly restricting the publication of the King James Bible to the King's printers.

William Bradford, the pioneer printer of Philadelphia and New York, late in the seventeenth century had issued a prospectus for an annotated Bible to cost 20 shillings (half to be paid in silver and half in produce). A few years later Cotton Mather sought subscriptions to finance his *Biblia Americana,* an annotated edition on which he had worked for years, but was unable to find a publisher either in America or England. (John Eliot's Massachusetts Indian Bible and Christopher Saur's German Bibles belong to another story.)

Sole witness for the first English Bible printed in America is Isaiah Thomas. When he was six years old he went to work for a Boston printer, Zechariah Fowle, to whom he was apprenticed a year later. While he was learning to set type he heard compositors talking about a Bible and New Testament on which they had previously worked. When, after half a century in the business, Thomas wrote his *History of Printing in America,* he told of a New Testament printed in Boston by Gamaliel Rogers and Daniel Fowle (brother of Zechariah), and also of a Bible printed by Kneeland and Green. He stated specifically that of a 12mo New Testament 2,000 copies were printed and of a Quarto Bible 700 to 800. Funds seem to have been supplied by a relative of Governor Hancock, Daniel Henchman, who was then interested in several publishing ventures. From the known dates of the two partnerships the New Testament must have been printed about 1749 and the Bible before 1752. Thomas, however, says the Bible was printed with the London imprint of Mark Baskett, whose dated imprint does not appear before 1761 although the Baskett family was printing Bibles from 1713 through 1769. When writing his book Thomas did not know of the location of any copies of either the Bible or Testament but said that Governor Hancock had owned one of the Bibles. Hancock's library seems to have been destroyed by fire, and no copies of either book have since been successfully identified. Presumably a volume printed in Boston with a London imprint could be distinguished from an actual London product by, as Thomas says, "the niceties of typography."

It is true that Isaiah Thomas was a very young boy when he heard the compositors' tale; yet Clifford K. Shipton, who has written a most interesting book on Thomas, says that he "was a marvelously accurate reporter; whenever I doubted him, I was proved wrong." Thomas may easily have got the first name of the imprint wrong. But who can say whether the Boston Baskett Bible is really fact or fiction?

The *Massachusetts Gazette* for 7 December 1770 carried an advertisement by John Fleeming of Boston for "The First Bible ever printed in America," in two folio volumes, with annotations, etc by the Rev Samuel Clark, to be printed from new type. Mr John Alden of the Boston Public Library tells us that in the Massachusetts Historical Society there is a four-page sheet with a sample of the text. This is not recorded in Evans or in Ford's *Massachusetts Broadsides*, but it is quoted in O'Callaghan (p xvii, 27). Printing was to begin as soon as 300 copies had been subscribed for, but the required subscriptions did not come in and the work was not begun.*

With the opening of the war with England the colonies were cut off from supplies of Scriptures from England, although some came in from Holland. The importance of English Bibles to the leaders of the country is evident in the concern of the Continental Congress, which voted on 11 September 1777 (by a majority of one) to import at government expense 20,000 Bibles from Holland. Without waiting for our struggling government to take this proposal from the shelf, several American printers undertook to provide Testaments printed in Philadelphia, Trenton, Boston, and Wilmington. Even these small books, in view of the scarcity and poor quality of paper and ink, were ambitious undertakings. It was not until toward the end of the war that the printer to the Congress, Robert Aitken, undertook a whole Bible. (See 1782/81 Bible, No 11.)

---

* Our account of these early publications is given only as background for our present work. For detailed studies the reader is referred to O'Callaghan, to Rumball-Petre's *America's First Bibles,* and to the following: Clifford K. Shipton, *Isaiah Thomas* (Rochester, Leo Hart 1948); Isaiah Thomas, *The History of Printing in America* (2d ed Albany 1874); Charles L. Nichols, *The Boston Edition of the Baskett Bible* (Worcester, American Antiquarian Society 1927); and Harry M. Lydenberg. "The problem of the Pre-1776 American Bible," *Papers* of the Bibliographical Society of America XLVIII (1952) 183–194 (an excellent summary).

After the Revolution American printers felt no compunction to heed the British monopoly of the printing of the King James Bible, although there was hesitancy about including the flowery seventeenth-century dedication to King James (first included in 1809 Bible, No 168). In 1791 Isaiah Thomas, now 42 years old, an experienced printer and business man, and in some sense a scholar in spite of complete lack of formal schooling, went into the Bible business extensively with folios, quartos, and smaller books, frequently reprinted from standing type (Nos 29 and ff). Also in 1791 Isaac Collins, a Quaker, began in Trenton a series carried on by his sons in New York. Both Thomas and the Collins family were particularly concerned for the accuracy of the Bible text, getting the best Bibles from England for copy and employing clergymen to read proof. They also provided introductions which they felt more appropriate to American use than the old Dedication to King James.

One of the most interesting of the early Bible printers was the Irish political refugee, Mathew Carey, who in 1790 printed the first American Douay Bible, but who ten years later went into publication of King James Bibles, of which he issued thousands during the following fifteen years. He specialized in quarto Bibles on several grades of paper, with varying kinds of maps and illustrations, and with or without the Apocrypha, a Concordance, and/or the Metrical Psalms (these particularly for Scotch Presbyterians). All of these men and their successors in the early nineteenth century were ambitious printers and good business men who had "on their lists" many other books, and were also concerned about economical methods of printing. Hugh Gaine (1792 Bible, No 40) imported type set in Scotland and shipped tied up in pages.

The invention of stereotyping (see 1812 Bible, No 213) begins a story that has not yet been fully told, particularly as it relates to the circulation of stereotype plates among New England and New York state printers during the early nineteenth century. O'Callaghan has some information on this, but to carry it further would require minute examination of hundreds of editions in addition to those represented in the Bible Society's own large collection. The Rev Wilfrid Parsons, S.J., covers early Roman Catholic editions in his "First American Editions of Catholic Bibles" (Historical Records and Studies, Vol xxvii). Many of the editions of the Phinney firm have similar pagination but have been reset page for page and often nearly line for line, and Bibles with other imprints are closely related to these. The plates used by most of the printers and publishers before 1860 were stereotyped by only two or three firms. The same paginations occur even well into the later decades of the nineteenth century. The Phinney and Holbrook and Fessenden firms were developed by enterprising frontier publishers. John Holbrook was a capable business man who had done well for himself in several lines before taking over his son-in-law's publishing business on that young man's sudden death. Neither Cooperstown nor Brattleboro in the early 1800s would seem natural centers for publishing enterprises, but the number of entries for these firms in the index of publishers and printers will show something of the extent of their activities in Bible publishing. The Connecticut Valley seems to have been a particularly active region in addition to Lunenburg, Mass, Windsor, Vt, Claremont, N. H., Concord, N. H., and Hartford. The geographical index includes many towns no longer associated with printing at all.

The geographical index also shows some interesting editions with Canadian imprints, which present a fascinating problem. For not only was it illegal to print the King James Bible in Canada, but according to a law passed by Parliament in 1825 it was illegal to import into Canada books whose publication in Great Britain was illegal. On 26 July 1827 the *Colonial Advocate* (published in York [now Toronto], Upper Canada, by William Lyon Mackenzie) carried a story about a "most noteworthy and revered preacher of the Presbyterian persuasion (of and from the United States of America)" having solicited subscriptions for a quarto Bible to be printed in Canada on Canadian-made paper and to be bound by Canadian bookbinders. Soon some 800 copies had been subscribed for at five dollars in sheep and six in calf. Mr Mackenzie had cooperated with this Rev Mr Thompson in his inquiry about printers, for he himself was most interested in fostering domestic industries. Now he had learned that "his reverence" had made up his mind to get his Bible printed "on the second hand stereotype plates of some country printer (whose name we have forgotten) in that portion of his late majesty's domains now known as the state of New York." On 9 August Mackenzie printed a story headed "Beware of Wooden Nutmegs," warning again of the imminent importation of these books, and calling as witnesses to his previous claim of misrepresentation Mr John Eastwood, papermaker; Francis Collins, printer; and Mr Maxwell, cabinet maker (among others), and referring to the law of 1825.

In the Toronto Public Library there is a broadside (*Bibliography of Canadiana*, No 1445) dated 6 August 1827 warning the public of this nefarious plot. The English Bible of 1827 (No 580), published in Cooperstown by E. and H. Phinney, seems to be the book that disturbed him. One copy at least got into Canada, for it is now in the Toronto Public Library — *Printed by H. and E. Phinney for S. Thompson, York (U. C.).*

The fiery Mackenzie was leader of a rebellion in 1837 and in the same year printed an edition of the New Testament (No 987) in Toronto, not in the King James Version but in Dickinson's translation (see 1833, No 839) against which there was no prohibition. He had hoped to publish the English Bible in Canada in the King James Version, for O'Callaghan (p xlix) quotes letters from Mackenzie stating that he purchased in 1835 or 1836 from the "Bible Society in New York" a set of Bible plates from which he intended to print a Bible, securing new titles with his own imprint, that instead he sold the plates to Mr Eastwood, who printed one edition on Canadian paper. Both Mackenzie and the Eastwood sons, however, told O'Callaghan in 1858 that one edition had been printed, about 1839 or 1840, but that they could find no copies; none are reported currently in the Canadian libraries consulted. While the American Bible Society disposed of some worn plates at about this time, it has no record of having sold any to Mackenzie. Other Bibles and Testaments with Canadian imprints were actually printed in the United States, but we have come upon no further record of opposition to their importation. It is fascinating to speculate on whether they were smuggled in or some later ordinance permitted their entry. As records now stand, no edition of the Authorized Version was legally printed in Canada until the World War II emergency edition of 1944 (No 2427).

That editions published by the Bible Societies south of the border were admitted is indicated in an article in the *Colonial Advocate* of 6 April 1826. In the course of a letter from Peter Russell Grant on printing in North America, reference is made to the need for importing Bibles from the "British and United States Societies" and to $211 remitted to the American Bible Society by a society in Niagara. This is recorded as from the Niagara Bible Society, in the American Bible Society report for 1826, page 101.

The Bible Societies, non-commercial publishers, appeared early in the nineteenth century. Earliest was the Philadelphia Bible Society, in 1808, inspired by the British and Foreign Bible Society founded in London in 1804. Its first edition (No 213) was printed from stereotyped plates made in England. Soon other local Societies were formed, most of them purchasing their Bibles from local printers (see Nos 168, 181, 234). In 1816 many of these joined in founding the American Bible Society. The need for inexpensive Bibles and Testaments on the expanding frontier made such a national Society necessary, and it has carried on its traditions ever since by supplying Scriptures far and wide in America and abroad and to such special groups as people in hospitals, prisons, and the armed forces, and refugees from fire and flood; also Scriptures in various languages for European immigrants and migratory workers.

In spite of the care with which Isaiah Thomas and Isaac Collins prepared their Bibles, many minor discrepancies had crept into the text at the hands of compositors and editors, so that in the 1830s the American Bible Society was often looked to as the protector of the text and many editions of sundry publishers bore on their title pages the statement: "Text . . . to the standard of the American Bible Society . . ." (see for example 1828, No 614). The Society made extra efforts for an accurate text in 1833 (No 822) and in 1834 (No 869).

In addition to providing accurate texts, the Society has sought to help young people by introducing into its editions American spelling and by changing some of the now obsolete forms of the King James version, as well as correcting punctuation, etc. This was first done in the 1850s (Nos 1443, 1504, 1643) and more recently in 1932 (No 2328).

Many of the early publishers printed Bibles for other firms, while usually keeping their own names in the imprints. (See 1822 Phinney B, No 439). Later in the century appeared the practice of using local distributor imprints with no indication of the actual publisher or printer. This practice is only sketched in these entries, but we find St Louis and Alabama imprints on books that were obviously not printed there but closely resemble issues of A. J. Holman and Co or the National Publishing Company. Each of these firms used emblems or trade marks by which their editions can be identified. National Publishing editions also usually carry copyrights by J. R. Jones, the founder of that firm.

By the second half of the century, Bible publishing began to settle down in New York and Philadelphia and firms active today began to appear, such as A. J. Holman and Co and J. B. Lippincott.

Also by the middle of the century some English Bibles appeared with the names of Thomas Nelson and Sons, Oxford University Press, and William Collins and Company of Scotland, all with American addresses. These editions were all printed in Great Britain until late in the century, when some were printed from plates imported from England or were imported in sheets and bound in the United States. All these processes have been carried on for some time, and the practice of each company has varied a great deal over the years. It has therefore been impossible to get a clear picture of the American printing history of such firms even for a particular format. We have entered books from our own collection in which American printing is indicated, but we are sure this is not a complete picture. Many of the twentieth-century Bibles sold by Harper and Bros are also printed in England and many copies of the Rheims-Douay Bible, such as those sold by the C. Wilderman Co, have been printed in Belgium, and so do not appear in these pages.

To give a true picture of the editions *sold* in America, one would need fuller data on these imported publications. One of the most frequently asked questions in the library of the American Bible Society is "How many Bibles were sold in the United States last year?" or "How many Bibles have been sold since the invention of printing?" As there is no complete list of printings, and certainly not of the number of copies printed, such questions cannot be answered; commercial publishers do not often issue their statistics.

During the 150 years of English Bible printing the physical appearance of the book has gone through many changes. In the eighteenth century, Bibles were generally bound in some grade of brown calf or sheep. Cloth appeared occasionally in the 1830s, but black leather was not general until about twenty years later, and limp, "divinity circuit" not until the late nineteenth century, though "envelope flaps" were common on small Bibles in the mid-nineteenth century. (Bindings, however, are seldom included in the descriptions in the following pages.)

Illustrations followed two streams — the imaginative, to make the book more attractive, and, as interest in archaeology developed, the more factual. The earliest were woodcuts and engravings based on the work of European artists. Even before the end of the eighteenth century, however, American artists were creating their own interpretations of Bible scenes, some perhaps rather crude. Alexander Anderson was one whose lively woodcuts were widely used in the 1820s and 1830s.

An engraving that appeared in many Bibles of the 1830s was *The Peaceable Kingdom*, illustrating Isaiah 11:1–9. This was from a drawing by Richard Westall and is said to have influenced several representations of the subject by the Pennsylvania "primitive" Edward Hicks (see No 717). Then came colored illustrations and lithographs, particularly for special title pages. Of particular interest is the "Illuminated Bible" published by Harper and Brothers about 1843 (No 1161) with hundreds of small engravings scattered through the text "to help and encourage the reader." Fine steel engravings decorated some of the large Bibles. There was another series of "Illuminated" Bibles toward the end of the century with half-tones "cut in" to the text on almost every page. Some of these were from photographs and some from drawings. The Doré illustrations vividly interpreted many of the family Bibles from about 1870 on. Reflections of changing social ideas are the chained African slave in an engraving *The Redeemer of the World* in a Douay Bible of 1858/57 (No 1673) and the allegorical frontispiece by Thomas Nast for Hitchcock's Analysis (1871 No 1868) showing a frock-coated missionary helping "heathen" and other sinners struggling toward "the Light." Early in the twentieth century appeared sepia reproductions of famous paintings and more recently still excellent colored reproductions of the world's most famous Biblical masterpieces. Various publishers have used colored paintings which seek to reproduce dramatic scenes in accurate detail.

As archaeologists began to report on actual scenes and discoveries in Bible lands there appeared first engravings and then half-tones from photographs of scenes in the Near East (No 2070) or from the paintings of Tissot in the 1880s based on life in Bible lands, or, more recently, from excellent color photographs of Bible lands. A fully illustrated modern edition is The Good News, a New Testament published by the American Bible Society in 1955 (No 2554) with more than 500 black and white photographs of Bible lands with brief archaeological notes.

The first American pronouncing New Testament appeared in 1814 (No 264), although a more popular edition was that of 1822 (No 452) "to which is applied, in numerous words, the orthoepy of the Critical pronouncing dictionary . . . by John Walker. By which the Proper Names are accented and divided into syllables exactly as they ought to be pronounced, according to the rules drawn from analogy and the best usage with an explanatory key by Israel Alger, Jun. . . ." A similar Bible was published in 1825 (No 531). These were often reprinted and have been followed by many other "Self-pronouncing" editions.

A number of optimistic people have published Testaments in revised spelling systems. There was Comstock's "perfect alphabet" (New Testament, 1848 No 1388) and a different but anonymous system (New Testament, 1855 No 1596). See p 202 and 234 for title pages.

Of course large English Bibles from 1535 had contained marginal references and these had continuously been elaborated and revised. Most of the early American quarto Bibles had references, often, as described in title pages, "those copious marginal References, known by the name of Canne's" (1807 B, No 143), or later simply as "Canne's Marginal Notes and References" (1816 B, No 296). Later the "Reference Bible . . . with References . . . Key Sheet of Questions . . . by Hervey Wilbur" had an extensive reprinting for thirty years (1823 NT, No 482; 1826 B, No 559). Another encouragement to easy reading was John H. Wilkins' "Revised Testament . . . in which the text of the common version is divided into paragraphs, the punctuation in many cases altered, and some words, not in the original expunged" (1824 NT, No 511). The printer Robert Estienne in the sixteenth century had popularized breaking the text into little numbered segments, but in the nineteenth century the process was reversed. In 1834 James Nourse prepared a Paragraph Bible (No 873) with verse numbers in the margins. It was many times reprinted, and the form was adopted in more and more new editions. A Testament probably of 1858 (No 1685) printed the text without any chapter or verse numbers and introduced quotation marks.

In the twentieth century there appeared a considerable number of abridged editions of which a few of the more interesting have been included. See General Index, abridgments.

Annotated Bibles, originating in England in the seventeenth and eighteenth centuries (and not protected even there by Crown monopoly), soon became very popular, in spite of the discouraging experiences of William Bradford and Cotton Mather. Scottish Presbyterians were particularly fond of John Brown's Self-interpreting Bible, first printed in New York in 1792 (No 37) and reprinted for a hundred years. There were also Thomas Scott's Bible, first printed in New York in 1804/09 (No 113), and the Matthew Henry Bible. Some of the founders of the Bible Society were particularly fond of Thomas Scott's Bible. Thomas Jefferson also had one (see No 113).

In mid-century, Case and Coffin and others printed many editions of the smaller, annotated Cottage Bible (No 818). Perhaps the most interesting from a publishing point of view is the Polyglott Bible (first American edition 1831, No 753). Not a polyglot Bible at all, nor even an annotated edition, it was an edition of the King James Bible with a full set of center references (Bibles earlier had references in outer margins). Originally it was published in England by S. Bagster and Son as a part of a true polyglot, with matching text in seven other languages, printed on two large facing pages from plates that could be used separately for each language or arranged in various combinations. There seems to have been some magic in the title, for by 1871 there had been published, apparently without any permission or any acknowledgment to Bagster, at least 100 erroneously titled "Polyglott" editions, mostly in small size but sometimes in fine quarto (e. g. Holbrook & Fessenden, 1833 No 820).

There have been many Bible commentaries. We have listed only those which were published as annotated Bibles, with complete text and usually copious notes (often Brown's or Scott's), or those which contained independent translations (such as The Speaker's Commentary, No 1893), or certain early twentieth-century editions in which the text was rearranged and annotated, following changes in the orientation of biblical scholarship and interest (such as Kent's Student's Old Testament, 1904–27, No 2158).

For hundreds of years people have been entering on blank Bible leaves records of weddings, births, and deaths, but it was not until the 1820s that publishers provided special pages for the purpose, usually two or four leaves between the Old and New Testaments. Starting out rather simply, these became increasingly elaborate, with appropriate figures and symbols. In 1858 (No 1670) a wedding certificate as part of a "Perpetual Genealogical Family Record" appeared in a Family Bible published by the Methodist Publishing House, Nashville, and this in various forms appeared later in many Bibles. Holman for years used one in color with doves, wedding bells, and bride and groom. In the 1880s there were included also "illuminated" Temperance pledges and albums for family photographs. During World War II, pages for service records were added.

In addition to maps and charts and pictures, for hundreds of years Bibles have contained concordances and explanations of terms. Popular in the early nineteenth century were lists of the offices and conditions of men, and tables of kindred. With the growing study of archaeology and manuscript discoveries of the late nineteenth century, the sections of helps grew bulkier and more elaborate. The Family Bibles contained illustrated dictionaries and all sorts of informational matter. Lithographed "illuminated" pages with the Lord's Prayer appeared in the late nineteenth century, and in the mid-twentieth century there were decorative pages for the Beatitudes, reproductions of Hoffman paintings, and pictures of Thorwaldsen statues. Some Roman Catholic editions had illustrated sections explaining the Rosary and the Stations of the Cross. Lists of prophecies, parables, and miracles and harmony outlines were common.

Late in the nineteenth century appeared Bibles (1899, No 2103) with the words of Jesus printed in red; one publisher tried putting them in italics, but in a bolder italics than were used traditionally for added words. Then there were Bibles with stars beside Old Testament verses that contain prophecies fulfilled in the New. One called the "Rainbow Bible" over-printed in various colors passages relating to Prophecy, Salvation, etc.

An important part of this story is the desire of scholars to make the writers of the Bible speak more directly to their contemporaries. The basically simple sixteenth-century English of the AV seemed less dignified than the elaborately balanced sentences of the eighteenth century and some of the terminology offended Victorian sensibilities. Such editions were prepared in Great Britain and soon after in this country. Noah Webster's (1833, No 826) was an interesting example and Rodolphe Dickinson's version (1833, No 839) was perhaps the most extreme (Luke 1:53: "but the affluent he has dismissed destitute").

The first English translation of the Greek Septuagint (a translation made from the Hebrew perhaps 200 years before Christ) was made by Charles Thomson, ex-Secretary of Congress, and printed by Jane Aitken, the daughter of Robert Aitken (1808, No 153).

These and other scholars were also often concerned about the Greek and Hebrew texts underlying the AV. Not all of them lived up to the principles stated in their prefaces, for some made relatively few changes in readings or renderings. One of the more effective was Alexander Campbell who based his work on that of James Macknight and Philip Doddridge and of George Campbell (whose rather modern views on translation were set forth in volume 1 of the first edition of his translation of the Gospels, London 1789). Jonathan Morgan (1848, No 1389) solved the problem of different translations for certain Greek words by leaving them in Greek. Julia E. Smith (1876, No 1918) the first woman to translate the whole Bible, was a staunch rights-for-women leader who sought to translate every Greek or Hebrew word in every instance by the same English word. As scholarship advanced during the nineteenth century with researches in archaeology and the discoveries of such ancient manuscripts as the Codex Sinaiticus and, later, the even earlier papyri, competent American scholars were available to contribute richly to the English and American Revisions of 1881–1885 and 1901, the Revised Standard Version of 1946–1952, the Jewish Publication Society Version (1903, No 2151), and the Confraternity Version, some of them such as Dr Goodspeed (1923, No 2260) and Dr Moffatt (1917, No 2235), even publishing their own translations.

During the early nineteenth century translators usually worked alone. In the entry for L. A. Sawyer's New Testament (1858, No 1687) there is quoted from his preface a plea for the value of the work of an individual translator: ". . . there are great works which individuals can perform better than multitudes or councils. Councils did not make the Bible at first. It was made by individuals each man acting for himself, and giving utterance to the mighty thoughts that God had given him . . . . nor has a council ever produced any immortal work of genius or learning, unless it is the English Bible of King James. . . ." This was written while the American Bible Union Committee (1862, No 1764) was working and may be a reflection of Sawyer's attitude toward that project. But the advantages of group scholarship have been demonstrated by the American Bible Union Version, and the other committee versions referred to above.

Another aspect of the results of developing Biblical scholarship was the change in the traditional order of the books. Dr Moulton's Modern Reader's Bible illustrates this as does also Kent's Shorter Bible (1918 NT, No 2242; 1921 OT, No 2253). Dr Moffatt in his Old Testament (1924–25, No 2275) tried to indicate the various sources of the Hexateuch by the use of different types.

Bible printing on a large scale, once under way, seems to have been generally a profitable business, but the fact that it continues to be profitable is due not to the ubiquity and number of its publishers, nor to their use of special features and promotion schemes, but to the continuous ability of the Bible to make a place for itself. Its physical coverings may change from brown calf to red fabricoid, its appurtenances from Tables of Offices and Affinities to Bible dictionaries and concordances, its illustrations from fanciful representations of the Dragon Chained to beautiful photographs of the Sea of Galilee, and even its words from sixteenth to twentieth-century vocabulary. Its pages may glow with texts printed in red, it may appear in unadorned style on poor paper in poor binding or be printed in beautiful type on the best paper for a fine church; it may be simply produced for missionary purposes or elaborately prepared and promoted for "status seekers." It may be the most published and even the most unread book, but a good proportion of the copies printed, somewhere, sometime, meet a heartfelt need of some man, woman, or child.

Commercial publishers have of course played a very large part in keeping this Book on the market and in adapting its appearance to changing tastes, and its publication has indeed been good business. The Bible Societies and other non-profit publishers have also had a great share in getting copies into homes, hotels, and institutions. There are thousands of homes in the United States with shelves of unused Bibles and there are thousands of homes still without any copy at all. But there are also hundreds of thousands of well-used Bibles and Testaments in homes all across the country and hundreds of thousands of thumbed Testaments in pockets and handbags of American men and women. All of these Bibles still carry the same history of a great people and the message of a changeless God and His love for mankind.

REFERENCE WORKS CONSULTED

Burr, Frederic M. *Life and Works of Alexander Anderson, M.D.* New York, Burr Bros., 1893.

Cheek, John Lambuth. "New Testament Translation in America," *Journal of Biblical Literature* LXXII Part II (1953) 103–114.

—— *The Translation of the Greek New Testament in America: A Phase of the History of American Criticism and Interpretation.* . . . Univ of Chicago dissertation, 1938. (Diss No 1846 microfilm)

Darlow, T. H. and Moule, H. F. *Historical Catalogue of the Printed Editions of the Holy Scripture in the Library of the British and Foreign Bible Society.* Vol I. London, 1903.

[Duyckinck, E. A.] *A Brief Catalog of Books Illustrated by Dr. Alexander Anderson with a Biographical Sketch of the Artist.* New York, 1885.

Evans, Charles. *American Bibliography, 1639–1800.* 14 vols. 1903–1959. Vol 13 edited by C. K. Shipton. Vol 14 Index.

Hall, Isaac H. *American Greek Testaments.* Philadelphia, Pickwick and Co., 1883.

New York Public Library. Stark, Lewis M. and Cole, Maud D. *Checklist of Additions to Evans' American Bibliography in the Rare Book Division of The New York Public Library.* New York, The New York Public Library, 1960.

O'Callaghan, E. B. *A List of Editions of the Holy Scriptures . . . Printed in America Previous to 1860.* . . . Albany, Munsell and Rowland, 1861.

Parsons, Wilfrid, S.J. "First American Editions of Catholic Bibles," *Historical Records and Studies* XXVII (1937) 89–98.

Pope, Hugh. *English Versions of the Bible.* Revised and Amplified by Rev. Sebastian Bullough. St Louis, B. Herder Book Co., 1952.

Rumball-Petre, Edwin A. R. *America's First Bibles.* Portland, Maine, Southworth-Anthoensen Press, 1940.

—— *Rare Bibles. Second Edition Revised.* New York, Philip C. Duschnes, 1954.

Shaw, Ralph R. and Shoemaker, Richard H. *American Bibliography . . . 1801–1805.* 5 vols. New York, Scarecrow Press, 1958.

Shea, John Gilmary. *A Bibliographical Account of Catholic Bibles, Testaments . . . Printed in the United States.* New York, Cramoisy Press, 1859.

Simms, P. Marion. *The Bible in America, Versions that have Played Their Part in the Making of the Republic.* New York, Wilson-Erickson, 1936.

Skeel, Emily E. *A Bibliography of the Writings of Noah Webster.* Edited by Edwin H. Carpenter, Jr. New York, The New York Public Library, 1958.

Strong, Raymond Lee. "English Translations of the Greek New Testament from 1611 to 1775," Princeton Theological Seminary dissertation, 1955.

Thomas, Isaiah. *History of Printing in America.* Second edition. Albany, Munsell, 1874.

Wright, John. *Early Bibles of America.* Third edition revised and enlarged. New York, Thomas Whittaker, 1894.

LOCATION SYMBOLS

Alabama

AB   Birmingham Public Library
AU   University of Alabama, University

Arkansas

ArCH   Hendrix College, Conway

England

BM   British Museum, London

California

C   California State Library, Sacramento
CBPac   Pacific School of Religion, Berkeley
CLCM   Los Angeles County Museum Library, Los Angeles
CLSU   University of Southern California, Los Angeles
CO   Oakland Public Library
CS   Sacramento City Library
CSaT   San Francisco Theological Seminary, San Anselmo (also CSfT)
CSmH   Henry E. Huntington Library, San Marino
CU   University of California, Berkeley

Canada

CaBVi   Victoria Public Library, Victoria, British Columbia
CaNSHK   University of King's College, Halifax, Nova Scotia
CaOH   Hamilton Public Library, Hamilton, Ontario
CaOKQ   Queen's College, Kingston, Ontario
CaOOSJ   Scolasticat St Joseph, Ottawa, Ontario
CaOTAr   Ontario Archives, Toronto, Ontario
CaOTP   Toronto Public Library, Toronto
CaOTU   University of Toronto, Toronto
CaOTV   Victoria University, Toronto
CaQMBM   Bibliothèque Municipale, Montreal, Quebec

Colorado

Co   Colorado State Library, Denver
CoD   Denver Public Library
CoHi   Colorado State Historical Society, Denver

Connecticut

Ct   Connecticut State Library, Hartford
CtHC   Hartford Seminary Foundation, Hartford
CtHT-W   Trinity College, Hartford, Watkinson Library
CtHi   Connecticut Historical Society, Hartford
CtW   Wesleyan University, Middletown (also CtMW)
CtY   Yale University, New Haven

District of Columbia

DCU   Catholic University of America Library
DCU-H   Hyvernat Collection
DGU   Georgetown University
DLC   U. S. Library of Congress
DW   U. S. Army War College Library (Fort McNair)
DWP   Public Library of the District of Columbia

Delaware

DeU   University of Delaware, Newark
DeWI   Wilmington Institute and the New Castle County Free Library,
               Wilmington

Florida

FT   Tampa Public Library, Tampa
FU   University of Florida, Gainesville

Georgia

GEU   Emory University, Atlanta
GMM   Mercer University, Macon

Illinois

ICBS   Chicago Bible Society, Chicago
ICHi   Chicago Historical Society, Chicago
ICL   Loyola University, Chicago
ICMcC   McCormick Theological Seminary, Chicago
ICN   Newberry Library, Chicago
ICU   University of Chicago, Chicago
IJI   Illinois College, Jacksonville
IMunS   Saint Mary of the Lake Seminary, Mundelein
IU   University of Illinois, Urbana

Iowa

IaB   Burlington Free Public Library, Burlington
IaCfT   Iowa State Teachers College, Cedar Falls
IaDaM   Davenport Public Museum, Davenport
IaDuU   University of Dubuque, Dubuque
IaU   State University of Iowa, Iowa City

Idaho

IdIf   Idaho Falls Public Library, Idaho Falls

Indiana

In   Indiana State Library, Indianapolis
InHi   Indiana Historical Society, Indianapolis
InNovJ   Jennings County Public Library, North Vernon
InRE   Earlham College, Richmond
InU   Indiana University, Bloomington
InUpT   Taylor University, Upland

Kansas

K	Kansas State Library, Topeka
KAS	St Benedict's College, Atchison
KBB	Baker University, Baldwin City (also KKB)
KU	University of Kansas, Lawrence
KWi	Wichita City Public Library
KXSM	St Mary College, Xavier

Kentucky

KyLo	Louisville Free Public Library
KyLoS	Southern Baptist Theological Seminary, Louisville
KyU	University of Kentucky, Lexington
KyWAT	Asbury Theological Seminary, Wilmore

Louisiana

LN	New Orleans Public Library
LU	Louisiana State University, Baton Rouge

Massachusetts

M	Massachusetts State Library, Boston
MA	Amherst College, Amherst
MAJ	Jones Library, Amherst
MAnP	Phillips Academy, Andover
MB	Boston Public Library
MBAt	Boston Athenaeum
MBC	Congregational Library, Boston
MBS	Social Law Library, Boston
MBU	Boston University
MBU-NE	Methodist Historical Society Library
MBU-T	School of Theology
MBrZ	Zion Reseach Library, Brookline
MBtS	St John's Seminary Library, Brighton
MH	Harvard University, Cambridge
MH-AH	Andover-Harvard Theological Seminary Library
MHi	Massachusetts Historical Society, Boston
MMeT-Hi	Tufts University, Medford, Universalist Historical Society
MQ	Thomas Crane Public Library, Quincy
MS	City Library Association, Springfield
MW	Worcester Free Public Library
MWA	American Antiquarian Society, Worcester
MWelC	Wellesley College, Wellesley
MWiW	Williams College, Williamstown

Maryland

MdBJ	Johns Hopkins University, Baltimore
MdBP	Peabody Institute, Baltimore
MdBS	St Mary's Seminary and University, Roland Park, Baltimore

Maine

MeHi	Maine Historical Society, Portland
MeWC	Colby College, Waterville

Michigan

Mi	Michigan State Library, Lansing
MiAlbC	Albion College, Albion
MiD	Detroit Public Library
MiDP	Providence Hospital, School of Nursing, Detroit
MiHi	Michigan Historical Commission, Lansing
MiU	University of Michigan, Ann Arbor
MiU-C	William L. Clements Library

Minnesota

MnM	Minneapolis Public Library
MnSJ	James Jerome Hill Public Library, St Paul
MnU	University of Minnesota, Minneapolis

Missouri

MoU	University of Missouri, Columbia

Mississippi

MsLE	Eastman Memorial Library, Laurel

New York

N	New York State Library, Albany
NAtt	Stevens Memorial Library, Attica
NB	Brooklyn Public Library, Brooklyn
NBP	Pratt Institute, Brooklyn
NBuDD	Delancy Divinity School, Buffalo (now Episcopal Theological Seminary of the Southwest, Austin, Texas)
NBuG	Grosvenor Reference Division, Buffalo and Erie County Public Library, Buffalo
NBuHi	Buffalo Historical Society, Buffalo
NCH	Hamilton College, Clinton
NCooHi	New York State Historical Association, Cooperstown
NGlf	Crandall Library, Glens Falls
NHi	New-York Historical Society, New York
NN	New York Public Library
NNAB	American Bible Society, New York
NNC	Columbia University, New York
NNFM	Grand Lodge of New York, F. & A. M. Library & Museum, New York
NNPM	Pierpont Morgan Library, New York
NNQ	Queens Borough Public Library, New York
NNU	New York University, New York
NNU-W	Washington Square Library
NNUT	Union Theological Seminary, New York
NPV	Vassar College, Poughkeepsie

NRAB	Samuel Colgate Baptist Historical Library of the American Baptist Historical Society, Rochester
NRU	University of Rochester, Rochester
NSchU	Union College, Schenectady
MSyOHi	Onondaga Historical Association, Syracuse

Nebraska

| NbHi | Nebraska State Historical Society, Lincoln |

North Carolina

NcAS	Sondley Reference Library, Asheville
NcBe	Belmont Abbey College Library, Belmont
NcC	Public Library of Charlotte and Mecklenburg County, Charlotte
NcD	Duke University, Durham
NcDaD	Davidson College, Davidson
NcRS	North Carolina State College of Agriculture and Engineering, Raleigh
NcU	University of North Carolina, Chapel Hill
NCWfC	Wake Forest College, Wake Forest
NcWs	Public Library of Winston-Salem and Forsythe County, Winston-Salem

New Hampshire

| NhD | Dartmouth College, Hanover |

New Jersey

Nj	New Jersey State Library, Archives and History, Trenton
NjHi	New Jersey Historical Society, Newark
NjM	Madison Public Library
NjMD	Drew University, Madison
NjMo	Morristown Public Library
NjN	Newark Public Library
NjNbS	Gardner A. Sage Library, New Brunswick
NjP	Princeton University, Princeton
NjPT	Princeton Theological Seminary, Princeton
NjPasHi	Passaic County Historical Society, Paterson
NjT	Trenton Free Library, Trenton

Ohio

OC	Public Library of Cincinnati and Hamilton County, Cincinnati
OCH	Hebrew Union College, Cincinnati
OCHP	Historical and Philosophical Society of Ohio, Cincinnati
OCU	University of Cincinnati, Cincinnati
OCl	Cleveland Public Library, Cleveland
OClW	Western Reserve University, Cleveland
OClWHi	Western Reserve Historical Society, Cleveland
ODW	Ohio Wesleyan University, Delaware
OGK	Kenyon College, Gambier
OHi	Ohio State Historical Society, Columbus
OO	Oberlin College, Oberlin

Ohio, continued

OSW   Wittenberg College, Springfield
OT   Toledo Public Library
OU   Ohio State University, Columbus
OYo   Public Library of Youngstown and Mahoning County, Youngs-
          town (Also OY)

Oregon

OrP   Library Association of Portland, Portland
OrPR   Reed College, Portland
OrPW   Western Conservative Baptist Theological Seminary, Portland

Pennsylvania

PBMC   Moravian College and Theological Seminary, Bethlehem
PChW   Wilson College, Chambersburg
PH   Haverford Public Library
PHC   Haverford College, Haverford
PHi   Historical Society of Pennsylvania, Philadelphia
PL   Lancaster Free Public Library
PLF   Franklin and Marshall College, Lancaster
PLatS   Saint Vincent College and Archabby Libraries, Latrobe
PMA   Allegheny College, Meadville
PMck   Carnegie Free Library, McKeesport
PNazMHi   Moravian Historical Society Museum, Nazareth
PP   Free Library of Philadelphia
PP-W   H. Josephine Widener Memorial Branch (inquire at PP)
PPABP   American Baptist Publication Society, Philadelphia
PPAmP   American Philosophical Society, Philadelphia
PPL   Library Company of Philadelphia
PPL-R   Ridgeway Branch
PPPD   Divinity School of the Protestant Episcopal Church, Philadelphia
PPPrHi   Presbyterian Historical Society, Philadelphia
PPeSchw   Schwenckfelder Historical Library, Pennsburg
PPi   Carnegie Library of Pittsburgh
PPiU   University of Pittsburgh, Pittsburgh
PPiW   Western Theological Seminary, Pittsburgh
PSC   Swarthmore College, Swarthmore
PSC-Hi   Friends Historical Library
PSt   Pennsylvania State University, University Park
PU   University of Pennsylvania, Philadelphia
PU-Ross   Ross Collection
PWb   Osterhout Free Library, Wilkes Barre

Rhode Island

RPB   Brown University, Providence
RPJCB   John Carter Brown Library, Providence

South Carolina

ScGrvF   Furman University, Greenville

Tennessee

THi	Tennessee Historical Society, Nashville
TNDC	Disciples of Christ Historical Society, Nashville
TNJ-R	Joint University Libraries (Vanderbilt University, George Peabody College for Teachers, and Scarritt College) Nashville Vanderbilt School of Religion
TNMB	Methodist Board of Missions, Nashville
TNMPH	Methodist Publishing House, Nashville
TNS	Scarritt College Library, Nashville
TU	University of Tennessee, Knoxville

Texas

TxDaM	Southern Methodist University, Dallas
TxU	University of Texas, Austin

Utah

USl	Free Public Library of Salt Lake City

Virginia

Vi	Virginia State Library, Richmond
ViLxW	Washington & Lee University, Lexington
ViRU	University of Richmond, Richmond
ViU	University of Virginia, Charlottesville
ViU-L	Law Library
ViW	College of William and Mary, Williamsburg

Vermont

VtHi	Vermont Historical Society, Montpelier
VtMiS	Sheldon Art Museum, Middlebury
VtU	University of Vermont, and State Agricultural College, Burlington

Wisconsin

WBB	Beloit College, Beloit
WKenHi	Kenosha County Historical Society, Kenosha
WRac	Racine Public Library
WU	University of Wisconsin, Madison

Washington

WaPS	State College of Washington, Pullman

Wyoming

WyHi	State of Wyoming Historical Department, Cheyenne

A BIBLIOGRAPHY OF EDITIONS OF THE BIBLE

AND THE NEW TESTAMENT PUBLISHED

IN AMERICA 1777–1957

PART I
1777 through 1825

1777 The New | Testament | Of our Lord and Saviour | Jesus Christ: | Newly Translated out of the | Original Greek; | And with the former | Translations | Diligently compared and revised. | Appointed to be read in Churches. | Philadelphia: | Printed and Sold by | R. Aitken, | Printer and Bookseller, | Front Street. | 1777. | Spectamur agendo.   *1*

1 vol: 353 [1] p   140 × 80 mm   NN, PHi
Signatures: [A]⁶, B–2F⁶, 2G³.

Evans 15243. Title page has imprint and motto set in designed border; verso has Order of Books. A vignette — hat, flute, etc. — appears on p 353. Last page has Books Printed and Sold at R. Aitken's Printing-Office, opposite the London Coffee-house, Front Street. Error in 1 Tim 4:16, *thy* doctrine, for *the* doctrine.

This is the first English NT printed in America. Since is was forbidden to print Bibles in English in America during the colonial period, and their importation from England was cut off during the Revolutionary War, a serious need arose for making the Scriptures available to the people of this country. This matter was brought before Congress by a select Committee in 1777, and a resolution was passed to import 20,000 Bibles from Holland and Scotland. However, the project did not materialize (see Wright, p 54–56). At this time Robert Aitken, printer to Congress, undertook the printing of a NT in English which appeared in 1777. Other editions were published in 1778, 1779, and 1781. For Aitken's Bible, see 1782, No 11.

1778 The New Testament . . . R. Aitken: Philadelphia   *2*

                                                          Not Located
    Evans 15743. O'Callaghan (p 30) says the only source for this NT seems to be a notice in the *Pennsylvania Packet* for Nov 3, 1778.

1779 The New Testament . . . R. Aitken: Philadelphia   *3*

    Not in Evans. O'Callaghan (p 30) lists a school edition.   Not Located

1779 The New Testament . . . Printed and Sold by Isaac Collins, Printer to the State of New Jersey: Trenton   *4*

Reported as 348 p   150 × 88 mm   PHi
    Not in Evans. Appears to be first NT printed in New Jersey. Most of the Epistles have material at end stating where they were written. Pages 325 to end misnumbered 345–368. For Collins' first Bible, see 1791, No 31.

1780 The New Testament . . . Massachusetts-Bay . . . Printed by Thomas and John Fleet, at The Bible and Heart in Cornhill: Boston   *5*

Reported as 397 unnumbered p   151 × 92 mm   MB
Signatures: A–2B⁸. Cited copy lacks T2–T7 and 2B⁸.
    Not in Evans. This is the first English NT printed in Massachusetts. Isaiah Thomas reported of these printers: "They were correct printers, very attentive to their concerns, punctual in their dealings, good citizens, and much respected." (Thomas, p 123)

1780 The New Testament . . . Hall and Sellers: Philadelphia   *6*

Unpaged   152 × 90 mm   PP
Evans 16715.

[1]

1780   The New Testament . . . Francis Bailey: Philadelphia   **7**

151 × 85 mm   NN

NYPL 717. Cited copy incomplete from end of John (p 161) through Revelation.

PHi has undated copy (298 p, 155 × 90mm) imprinted *Pennsylvania: Printed by F. Bailey, Lancaster, and J. Steele, at the Printing-Office, Octorara.* Octorara is in Lancaster County. See 1801 NT, No 83.

1780   The New Testament . . . Isaac Collins: Trenton   **8**

Not Located

NYPL 717. DLC has card with reference to Nelson (William Nelson, *Check-List of the Issues of the Press of New Jersey, 1725, 1728, 1754–1800,* Paterson, N. J., 1899) but no location. The Nelson entry reads "n 1780. New Testament, Trenton. Isaac Collins." The n indicates that the compiler desired full, lined-off titles and collation.

1781   The New Testament . . . Printed and sold by James Adams: Wilmington, Delaware   **9**

408 p   153 × 85 mm   DeWI, DLC

Signatures: [A]⁶, B–U⁶, W–2K⁶.

Evans 17102. The first NT printed in Delaware.

1781   The New Testament . . . R. Aitken: Philadelphia   **10**

Unpaged   143 × 80 mm   CSmH

Evans 17101. Appears to be same as NT of the 1782/81 Aitken Bible (No 11).

1782/81   The | Holy Bible. | Containing the Old and New | Testaments: | Newly translated out of the | Original Tongues; | And with the former | Translations | Diligently compared and revised. | [Device — Arms of the State of Pennsylvania] | Philadelphia: | Printed and Sold by R. Aitken, at Pope's | Head, Three Doors above the Coffee | House, in Market Street. | M.DCC.LXXXII   **11**

1 or 2 vols: 143 × 80 mm   960 leaves   CSmH, DLC, ICN, MH, MWA, MiU–C, NN, NNAB *

Signatures: π¹, [A]¹², B–2Z¹², 3A⁶ (-3A6), ²[A]⁶, B–2D⁶. (W used in NT signatures.)

Evans 17473. Has two preliminary leaves: title, within border; verso blank (1 leaf). Second leaf has on recto and half of verso "By the United States in Congress Assembled: September 12, 1782," a request by Congress that the Chaplains of Congress, Dr. Wm. White and Mr. George Duffield, examine the text, with their report and the action by Congress, signed by Charles Thomson, approving the publication and recommending the edition to the inhabitants of the United States. Order of Books also appears on recto of second leaf. NT title has *The New | Testament | Of our Lord and Saviour | Jesus Christ; | Newly Translated out of the | Original Greek; | And with the former | Translations | Diligently compared and revised.* | [Vignette — hat, flute, etc.] | *Philadelphia: | Printed and Sold By R. Aitken, Bookseller, | opposite the Coffee-House, Front-Street.* | *M.DCC.LXXXI.* Verso has Order of Books followed by initials R. A. in script letters. No Apocrypha. Error in ı Tim 4:16, *thy* doctrine, for *the* doctrine.

1782   The New Testament . . . Joseph Crukshank: Philadelphia   **12**

Reported as 440 p   154 × 86 mm   OC

Signatures: A–2N⁶, 2O⁴.

Evans 17477. Has catchwords.

Another copy privately owned by Mr. Kirke Bryan, Norristown, Pennsylvania.

* For other locations and further information, see Rumball-Petre, *America's First Bibles,* p 81 ff.

1782 The New Testament . . . Printed and Sold by Isaac Collins, Printer to the
State of New Jersey: Trenton   **13**

Reported as 348 p   150 × 88 mm   CtY
Not in Evans. Appears to be reprint of the Collins 1779 NT (No 4) with pagination
corrected.

1786 The New Testament . . . J. Crukshank; F. Bailey; Young, Stewart, and Mc-
Culloch; and T. Dobson: Philadelphia   **14**

Text ends O12   162 × 88 mm   NN, NNAB
Evans 19511. Has Order of Books on verso of title page. Error in 1 Tim 4:16, *thy* doctrine,
for *the* doctrine.
NN has second copy with imprint *J. Crukshank: Philadelphia.*

1787 The New Testament . . . Printed and Sold by James Adams . . . : Wilmington
15

Reported as 335 p   140 × 76 mm   DeWI
Not in Evans.

1788 The Christian's New and Complete Family Bible: Or Universal Library of
Divine Knowledge . . . With the Apocrypha at Large; Illustrated with Annotations and Commentaries . . . By Those Eminent Divines, Henry, Doddridge, Gill, Brown, &c. &c. . . . Printed for the Proprietors; And Sold by all
the Booksellers in the United States: Philadelphia   **16**

Unpaged: 568 leaves   374 × 210 mm   NN, NNAB, OC, PHi
Signatures: [A]², B–9O², 2A–2I², 3[A]², B–3H². 32H missigned '2G'. 32K missigned '2L'.
Not in Evans. Has four preliminary leaves: frontispiece; title page with verso blank; To
the Christian Reader, with Order of Books on verso; and an engraving. Commentaries are
arranged in form of footnotes. NT title, undated, imprinted *Berwick* [England]; *Printed By
And For John Taylor.* 28 plates.
   The general title imprint would indicate that the OT was printed in Philadelphia even
though the wording "Printed for the Proprietors" is somewhat indefinite. However, there seems
to be some evidence that the whole Bible was printed in England. Rumball-Petre in the
Antiquarian Bookman for March 8, 1952 (ix, no 10, p 972) states that the paper used in both
Testaments is the same, the type of both title pages is from the same font, the columns of text
are the same width, and the plates are all by British engravers.
   The theory has also been advanced by Whitman Bennett that this may be the folio Bible
published by William Woodhouse, Philadelphia, in 1788 (see Evans 20960). Since a copy of
the Woodhouse Bible of this date has never been located, any relationship between these two
Bibles cannot be definitely established. (See also *Antiquarian Bookman* ix, no 6 [Jan 19 and 26
and Feb 9, 1952] p 640–641.)

1788 The New Testament . . . Isaac Collins: Trenton   **17**

Unpaged: 232 leaves   186 × 102 mm   MWA, NjT, NN, NNAB, PHi
Evans 20968. Order of Books appears on verso of title page. Error in 1 Tim 4:16, *thy*
doctrine, for *the* doctrine.

1788 The New Testament . . . Benjamin Edes & Son: Boston   **18**

Unpaged   "12mo"   MWA
Evans (20966) notes that this NT was printed with new type of superior quality. Added
material includes A Dictionary of Proper Names and A Table of Kindred. Cited copy is
incomplete.

1788   The New Testament . . . Shepard Kollock: Elizabethtown [New Jersey] *19*

Unpaged: 192 leaves   150 × 84 mm   NN
Signatures: [A]⁶, B–2I⁶. Signed variously, some quires also signed with §, *, †, ‡.
Evans 20967. Has Order of Books on verso of title page. Table of Kindred at end of NT
followed by two blank leaves. Errors in Matthew 7:6, *least* they trample them, and Matthew
20:1, for the kingdem of heaven.
NN copy lacks Heb 12:29 to II Peter 1:18.

1788   The New Testament . . . Printed and sold by Isaac Collins: Trenton   *20*

Reported as 359 [1] unnumbered p   148 × 87 mm   PU–Ross
Signatures: A–2F⁶.
Not in Evans. PU–Ross says this is the only copy known today. Another copy, since untraced,
was sold in 1915 at the auction of the library of William Nelson.

1789   The New Testament . . . Hugh Gaine: New York   *21*

Unpaged: 168 leaves   151 × 87 mm   NN
Signatures: A–O¹².
NYPL 914. Title has initials H. G. in script letters in oval design; Order of Books on
verso. Table of Kindred at end. Errors in Acts 8:9, *sorcercy,* for *sorcery;* Phil 4:15, *begginning,*
for *beginning.*
This in the first New Testament printed in New York.

1789   The New Testament . . . Joseph Crukshank: Philadelphia   *22*

                                                                           Not Located
Evans 21690.

1790   The | Holy Bible, | translated from the | Latin Vulgate; | Diligently compared
         with the | Hebrew, Greek, and other editions, | in divers languages; | And first
         published by | the English College at Doway, Anno 1609. | Newly revised,
         and corrected, according to | the Clementine edition of the Scriptures. | With
         Annotations for elucidating | the principal difficulties of Holy Writ. | Hau-
         rietis aquas in gaudio de fontibus Salvatoris. Isaiah xii. 3 | Philadelphia: |
         Printed and Sold by Carey, Stewart and Co. | M.DCC.XC   *23*

2 vols in 1: Vol I, (viii) (487); Vol II, (280) 281–488 488–490   223 × 158 mm
             CSmH, DGU, DLC, MWA, MiU, NjMD, NN, NNAB, OC, RPJCB
Evans 21681 (1789); 22349 (1790). Rheims-Douay Version, based on Bishop Challoner's
second edition, 1763–64. Vol I preliminary matter includes Order of Books, Approbations, and
Names of Subscribers (page v has designation "Vol I" at foot); text: Genesis-Proverbs. Vol II
(no title) text: Ecclesiastes-Maccabees; NT — Matthew-Apocalypse; and Tables of References,
Chronological Table, Order and Distribution of Books, and a Table of the Epistles and Gospels.
      This is the first American edition of the Douay translation of the Vulgate Bible, and is
alleged to be the first quarto Bible published in the United States.
      Mathew Carey (1760–1839) was a journalist in his native Ireland and in his zeal for
exposing injustice — especially the persecution of the Irish Catholics — he at one point found
it expedient to seek temporary refuge in France where he was befriended by Benjamin Franklin
and the Marquis de Lafayette. About two years later he returned to Ireland and continued his
journalistic career. This time his attacks on the English government brought him a jail sentence
of one month. After his release in 1784 at the age of 24, and still facing a libel suit, he escaped
to America in disguise. With the aid of Lafayette, then in America, he established himself as a
printer and publisher in Philadelphia.
      In 1789, Mr. Carey announced plans to publish a translation of the Vulgate Bible if he
could secure 400 subscribers. The actual number secured was 471. The total number of the
edition printed is not known; however, it could not have been much over the number of sub-

scriptions as the demand for a Catholic Bible was small in the United States at that time. The undertaking was therefore an expensive one for the size of the edition, and it was first decided to print the Bible in 48 parts, to be issued weekly. Though it is generally assumed that a few parts were printed (the designation "Vol 1" does not appear on any signatures on the first 89 pages of text), Carey abandoned the scheme and formed the publishing firm of Carey, Stewart & Co., which published the Bible on Dec 1, 1790. The type was specially cast by Baine and Co., Philadelphia. It is now the rarest of the notable early American editions of the Bible. (See Rumball-Petre, *America's First Bibles* p 97–106.)

In the course of a few years, Carey's firm became one of the largest bookselling and printing firms and the largest and most important Bible printing house in the country. Eventually he was to publish three editions of the complete Rheims-Douay Bible (one in 1790, and two issues in 1805), three Catholic English Testaments (1805, 1811, and 1816), and over sixty editions of the Bible according to the King James Version. See note under 1801, No 77, for further information concerning Carey's printing of the King James Version.

In 1817 his eldest son, Henry, became associated with his father and four years later Mathew's son-in-law, Isaac Lea, joined the firm. Carey retired in 1824. In 1833 William Blanchard, who had worked for the firm, became a partner and the firm was known as Carey, Lea and Blanchard. On Henry's retirement it became known as Lea and Blanchard. It later was known as Henry C. Lea and Company and, from 1907, as Lea and Febiger.

In the graveyard adjoining Old St. Mary's Church in Philadelphia, originally a Catholic edifice, there is a plaque listing "Matthew [sic] Carey, The leading publisher of the early years of the Republic and the chief force in the creation of early American literature. . . . " He had first been buried here but in 1918 his remains were removed by his descendant, Edward Carey Gardiner, to Holy Sepulchre Cemetery, Montgomery County, Pennsylvania.

Carey was the first president of the American Company of Booksellers, organized in 1801 in New York, which in 1802 held a Book Fair in New York. The next year the fair was held in Philadelphia and thereafter alternately in the two cities for some years.

1790   The Christian's New and Complete Family Bible. Published by William
         Woodhouse: Philadelphia   **24**

                                                                        Not Located

Evans 20960 (1788), 21680 (1789), 22347 (1790). O'Callaghan (p 35) quotes advertisements from the *Pennsylvania Packet* for Nov 15, 1788 and Jan 3, 1789 and the *Pennsylvania Gazette* for May 26, 1790 announcing publication of various numbers of this work, for which there had been 1,000 subscribers. It may be the 1788 edition (No 16).

1790   The Holy Bible . . . William Young: Philadelphia   **25**

Unpaged: 443 leaves   153 × 88 mm   MWA, NN, NNAB, OC, PP
Signatures: [A]¹², B–2C¹², [2D]¹², 2E–2L¹², [²A]⁶, B–E⁶, F⁵.
Evans 22345 ("12mo"); 22346 ("24mo"). Has To the Reader (related to but different from that in No 31), Account of the Dates or Time of Writing the Books of the New Testament, and Order of Books on leaf following title. Tables at end of both Testaments. At end are The Psalms of David in Metre (Scotch version . . . 1790). Error in 1 Tim 4:16, *thy* doctrine, for *the* doctrine.
Also issued without Metrical Psalms.
This appears to be the first Bible with American imprint which contains the Metrical Psalms. It was advertised as a school edition at "five-eighths of a dollar" (Wright, p 323).

1790   The New Testament . . . Abel Morse: New Haven   **26**

"12mo"   Not Located

Evans 22358. O'Callaghan (p 36–38) lists this item with many errors but does not give location. A copy was reported at Madison College, Madison, Tennessee; however, correspondence has brought no reply.

1790   The New Testament . . . Hugh Gaine: New York   **27**

151 × 87 mm   CtY, DLC, ICBS, MWA, NN
Evans 22359. Same as 1789 NT (No 21) with errors continued.

1790   The New Testament . . . John McCulloch: Philadelphia   **28**

Reported as 357 unnumbered p   133 × 76 mm   ICBS
Not in Evans.

1791   The Holy Bible . . . Isaiah Thomas: Worcester   **29**

   2 vols: Vol ɪ, (4) 5–460; Vol ɪɪ, (6) 461–635 (3) 637–786 (4) 789–991 992–1012
362 × 190 mm   ICBS, CtY, MB, MBC, MWA, MdBP, MiU, NN, NNAB, OC

Evans 23186. This is Thomas' folio edition, issued in two volumes. Vol ɪ has two preliminary
leaves (frontispiece and title), text to end of Proverbs, and 14 plates. Vol ɪɪ has three pre-
liminary leaves (frontispiece, title same as above, and blank leaf), text beginning with
Ecclesiastes, Apocrypha (colophon reads: This Folio Edition of the Bible, and one In Royal
Quarto, were printed by Isaiah Thomas, at Worcester, Massachusetts, in the year ᴍᴅᴄᴄxᴄɪ),
NT followed by Index, and 23 plates. All plates are executed by American engravers: J. H.
Seymour, J. Norman, S. Hill, and A. Doolittle.

   Division of material in volumes differs in some copies; also the number and position of plates
vary. NN has two copies: one with 48 copperplates (two are missing), and another in one vol.
Also issued without Apocrypha.

   Isaiah Thomas, whom Benjamin Franklin called "the Baskerville of America," was one of
the notable publishers of the Bible during the early days of the Republic. He began his publishing venture in Boston, together with Zechariah Fowle, in 1770. Shortly thereafter he became
sole owner of the firm. At this time he published the newspaper *Massachusetts Spy,* in which
he supported the colonial cause. During the Revolutionary War he moved his presses and types
to Worcester, Massachusetts, where he built up a large business. He also established branches in
other cities: Thomas & Andrews, Boston; Thomas, Andrews & Penniman, Albany; Thomas,
Andrews & Butler, Baltimore; and Thomas & Co., Walpole, New Hampshire.

   In 1790, Mr. Thomas announced his plan for the publication of a folio Bible and also
for one in Royal quarto (see following entry, No 30). He made a special effort to procure a
correct text for his Bible and examined about thirty editions of the King James Version printed
at various dates by different publishers. His text was further examined by a number of clergymen of Worcester and by other qualified people who compared it with no less than eight
copies. (O'Callaghan, p 40.) It has the correct reading in ɪ Tim 4:16, *the* doctrine.

   Thomas published one folio edition and several quarto, octavo, and duodecimo editions.
See 1797, No 57, for note on Thomas' standing type for his duodecimo editions.

1791   The Holy Bible . . . Isaiah Thomas: Worcester   *30*

   1 vol: (10) (1276) 1277–1310 (89)   250 × 195 mm   CtY, DCL, ICBS, MB, MWA,
                                                               MiU, NcD, NN, NNAB, ViU

Evans 23185. This is Thomas' Royal quarto edition issued in one volume. Has five preliminary leaves: frontispiece; title with verso blank; To Christians of Every Denomination; To
the Publick with Order of Books on verso; and OT title with "The Property of   " inscribed
within border. With Apocrypha followed by Family Record pages. Text has marginal references. NT followed by Index and Tables (p 1277–1310) and A Brief Concordance to the
Holy Scriptures by John Brown (89 p). NT colophon reads: This Royal Quarto Edition of
the Bible, and likewise one in Folio, with Fifty Copperplates were printed by Isaiah Thomas,
at Worcester, Massachusetts, ᴍᴅᴄᴄᴄxᴄɪ.

   Number of plates varies with different copies and some copies do not have Concordance.
Also found bound in two vols.

   In order to make the quarto edition more generally available, Mr. Thomas made special
arrangements for payment. "The price to subscribers . . . shall be only Seven Dollars, although
the English Editions of the same size, and of an inferior quality are sold for eight or nine
dollars. . . . For those who are not able to pay for one all in Cash — from such the Publisher
will receive one half of the sum, or twenty-one shillings, in the following articles, viz. Wheat,
Rye, Indian Corn, Butter, or Pork, if delivered at his store at Worcester, or at the store of
himself & Co. in Boston by the 20th day of December 1790, the remaining sum of 21 shillings,
to be paid in Cash" on delivery of the books. (Wright, p 76.)

1791 The Holy Bible . . . Isaac Collins: Trenton   *31*

Unpaged: 658 leaves   247 × 177 mm   CSmH, CtY, MiU-C, NjT, NN, NNAB, OC, PPL-R, ViU

Signatures: [A]^4, B–4Q^4, 4R^2, A*–U*^{4}, ^{2}[A]^4, B–T^4, U^2, [‡A]^4, ‡B–‡2G^4, ‡2H^2, ^{3}[A]^4, B–I^4. P* missigned '*P'.

Evans 23184. Has four preliminary leaves: title with verso blank; To the Reader [by Dr. John Witherspoon]; Account of the Dates with verso blank; and Order of Books with verso blank. With Apocrypha. Index, Tables, and A Brief Concordance by John Downame (1790) follow NT. Error in ı Tim 4:16, *thy* doctrine, for *the* doctrine.

Material added to the text varies with copies. NN and NjT copies have Practical Observations on Old and New Testaments by Reverend Mr. Ostervald. The Observations are in smaller type and follow the Apocrypha.

NNAB copy lacks the Observations. PHi has copy without Apocrypha. Also found bound in two vols.

This is the first Bible printed in New Jersey and the first to be printed by Isaac Collins, a Quaker and native of Delaware. He later moved to Trenton where he was a printer to the State of New Jersey. He remained there until 1795, when he moved to New York where he carried on his business for another ten years. Collins' first printing of the Scriptures was a New Testament which appeared in 1779 (No 4).

In 1789 Collins issued a proposal to publish the Holy Bible on receipt of 3000 subscriptions, at a cost of Four Spanish Dollars; One dollar to be paid at the time of subscribing, the remainder on the delivery of the book. He later announced that Downame's Concordance would be included at no extra cost. This Bible was published in 1791 in an edition of 5000 copies. (Simms, p 130.)

In the Advertisement to his second edition, 1807, Collins gives the following information about his first edition of 1791. In order to comply with the various sentiments regarding the inclusion of the Apocrypha and commentaries, Collins offered to print the Bible with the Apocrypha or Ostervald's Notes — or both or neither — providing subscribers made their wishes known in advance. An address To the Reader by Dr. Witherspoon was substituted for the Dedication to King James, and an Account of the Dates or Time of Writing the Books of the New Testament, also by Dr. Witherspoon, was published for the first time in this Bible. Both were later used by many other printers in their editions. Similar material is found in W. Young's 1790 duodecimo printed in Philadelphia (No 25).

"As the Dedication of the English translation of the Bible to King James the first of England seems to be wholly unnecessary for the purposes of edification, and perhaps on some accounts improper to be continued in an American edition, the Editor has been advised by some judicious friends to omit it, and to prefix to this edition a short account of the translations of the Old and New Testaments from the original Hebrew and Greek in which they were written." "The Publisher has only further to add, that he has made the following impression from the Oxford edition of 1784 by Jackson and Hamilton — and has been particularly attentive in the revisal and correction of the proof-sheets with the Cambridge edition of 1668 by John Field — with the Edinburgh edition of 1775 by Kincaid, and, in all variations, with the London edition of 1772 by Eyre and Strahan — that where there was any difference in words, or in the omission or addition of words, among these, he followed that which appeared to be most agreeable to the Hebrew of Arias Montanus, and to the Greek of Arias Montanus and Leusden, without permitting himself to depart from some one of the above-mentioned English copies, unless in the mode of spelling, in which he has generally followed Johnson." (From To the Reader, first and last paragraphs.)

This edition of Collins' Bible is particularly known for its accurate text. A number of eminent authorities in the field, including Dr. Witherspoon, superintended the work. Recourse was had to the most authentic copies of the Bible in the original languages and to the best English versions. The typography was thoroughly checked and it was said that only two errors were found after its publication — one a broken letter, the other a punctuation mark. Collins also notes that Mathew Carey, Wm. Durell, and other printers adopted this edition as their standard of correctness.

A copy of this edition was used by Noah Webster as printer's copy for the sections in which he followed the King James text, including the error in ı Timothy 4:16; see 1833, No 827.

1791/92   The Holy Bible . . . W. Young: Philadelphia   *32*

1 or 2 vols   130 × 70 mm   ICU, MiU, MWA, NN, NNAB, PPL

Evans 23183, 24110 (NT only). Preliminary matter includes To the Reader and Order of Books. With Metrical Psalms (1793). Error in 1 Tim 4:16, *thy* doctrine, for *the* doctrine. NT title dated 1792.

Also published without Metrical Psalms. NNAB copy has signatures misbound at end of NT.

1791   The New Testament . . . John McCulloch: Philadelphia   *33*

"12mo"   Not Located

Evans 23201; O'Callaghan, p 43; Wright, p 412. A school edition.

1791   The New Testament . . . John Mycall: Newbury-port [Massachusetts]   *34*

Unpaged: 162 leaves   163 × 90 mm   NN
Signatures: A–2C⁶.

Evans 23200. Has Order of Books on verso of title page. At end is An Alphabetic Etymological Explanation of Many Names of Persons, Places, &c. Which are Mentioned in the New Testament. Error in 1 Tim 4:16, *thy* doctrine, for *the* doctrine.

1791   Explanatory Notes upon the New Testament by John Wesley . . . The First American Edition. Printed by J. Crukshank, sold by J. Dickins: Philadelphia
                                                                          35

3 vols: Vol I, 416 p; Vol II, 348 p; Vol III, 347 p   154 × 78 mm   NjMD, TNJ–R

Evans 23976; 25011 (1792 edition). Index (4 p) at end of Vol III.
TNJ–R has Vols I and III only, the latter printed by Pritchard and Hall.
This is the first appearance in the United States of the Wesley Version. As a result of his intensive study of the Greek text (particularly the Bengel edition) begun in 1729, John Wesley, the founder of the Methodist Church, felt the AV could be improved by the use of a better Greek text and by better renderings into English. He made 12,000 deviations from the AV, a very considerable number of which were adopted by the ERV and some by the RSV. The text appeared first in 1755 in London, with explanatory notes; a standard edition was issued in 1760 and a pocket edition, without notes, in 1790. This is the first American edition, many times reprinted with and without the notes. The title pages generally do not indicate that the text is not that of the AV. See the edition of the 1790 text, without notes, prepared by George C. Cell in 1938 (No 2369).

1791   The New Testament . . . Hall and Sellers: Philadelphia   *36*

Reported as 331 unnumbered p   151 × 89 mm   MWA, ViU
Not in Evans.

1792   The Self-Interpreting Bible . . . | To Which are Annexed, | Marginal References And Illustrations, | An Exact Summary Of The Several Books, | A Paraphrase On The Most Obscure Or Important Parts, | An Analysis Of The Contents Of Each Chapter, | Explanatory Notes, | And Evangelical Reflections. | By The Late Reverend John Brown, | Minister Of The Gospel At Haddington. | [Five lines of Scripture texts] | New-York: | Printed by Hodge and Campbell, | and Sold at their respective Book Stores. | M.DCC.XCII   *37*

Unpaged: 520 leaves   376 × 213 mm   CSmH, CtY, ICBS, MiU–C, MWA, NN, NNAB
Signatures: π², [A]², b–k², 2A–T², 3[A]², B–3X², *2.

Evans 22348 (1790); 24099 (1792). Has twenty-three preliminary leaves: frontispiece — patriotic motif showing woman representing America who is holding the Constitution in her hand and is receiving a Bible (1 leaf); title with verso blank (1 leaf); The Author's

Address, with To the Reader on verso (1 leaf); An Introduction to the Right Understanding of the Oracles of God (18 leaves); Appendix of Tables and the Order of the Books (2 leaves). Tables follow NT. Contains 20 plates, each labelled *Engraved for the American Edition of Brown's Family Bible.* Apocrypha wanting?

NNAB has a second copy, with title page and frontispiece missing, which has Apocrypha. Following NT are Table of Proper Names, List of the Subscribers [headed by] George Washington, Esq. President of the United States of America, and an Acknowledgment to the Subscribers by the publisher. Wright (p 387) lists a Royal folio NT which is probably made up of the NT parts, but no copy has been located.

This is the earliest edition of the Bible printed in New York. It was published by subscription, George Washington being the first subscriber, and was printed in forty parts over a period of two years. See O'Callaghan, p 45; also Wright, p 104–109. John Brown (1722–1787) was a Scottish weaver who became a Presbyterian minister. Although self-educated he prepared an annotated Bible, Bible dictionary and concordance, and a metrical version of the Psalms. His Self-Interpreting Bible appeared first in 1778 in Edinburgh and was many times reprinted in Scotland and in America.

1792 The Holy Bible . . . Hodge and Campbell: New York   **38**

Unpaged: 542 leaves   238 × 182 mm   CtY, ICU, MBU–T, MWA, NN, NNAB, OCIW
Signatures: π², [A]⁴, B–4R⁴, ⁵A–⁶Z⁴, ²²A–2F², a–i².
Evans 23097. Has three preliminary leaves: frontispiece; title with verso blank; and To the Reader with Order of Books on verso. Malachi to end of Apocrypha is in smaller type. Following NT are Index, Tables, etc. (36 p). Metrical Psalms at end (49 p).
NT has its own title page and may be found separately.

1792 The Holy Bible . . . T. Allen: New York   **39**

237 × 182 mm   NNAB
Evans 24096. Appears identical with the 1792 Hodge and Campbell Bible (No 38) but lacks Metrical Psalms. Has 14 plates, mostly signed by C. Grignion.

1792 The Holy Bible . . . Hugh Gaine: New York   **40**

Unpaged: 408 leaves   148 × 88 mm   CSmH, CtY, ICBS, MiU, NN, NNAB
Evans 24098 (also separate NT under this number). With Apocrypha. Preliminary matter includes Order of Books with Account of Dates on verso. Table of Kindred and Table of Time follow OT. A Table of Offices follows NT.
Also issued with Metrical Psalms and an Index of the Bible. NNAB copy lacks title page and Apocrypha.
The ruby type for this edition is said to have been set up in Scotland and imported in page form, ready for printing. The type was apparently kept standing. In 1803, the forms were sold to Mathew Carey of Philadelphia (see No 106). Because of the delay on his own school edition, Thomas is said to have purchased 500 copies of this Bible in sheets in 1792.

1792 The New Testament . . . Benjamin Johnson: Philadelphia   **41**

Reported as 276 p   "12mo"   MWA
Evans 24109.

1792 The New Testament . . . Printed by William Spotswood: Philadelphia   **42**

Reported as 282 unnumbered p   157 × 87 mm   MWA
Not in Evans. Has chapter headings but no catchwords. Text is followed by advertisements for Robert Campbell of Philadelphia and W. Spotswood. Colophon reads "Printed and sold by W. Spotswood."
Another copy is privately owned by Mr. Kirke Bryan, Norristown, Pennsylvania.

1793/94   The Holy Bible . . . Isaac Collins: Trenton   **43**

Text ends 7B2   192 × 115 mm   CSmH, DLC, ICBS, MWA, NjT, NN, NNAB
Evans 25171; 26666 (NT only). Preliminary matter includes Order of Books with Account of the Dates on verso, and To the Reader. NT, dated 1794, has Tables at end.

1793   The Holy Bible . . . Isaiah Thomas: Worcester   **44**

960 p   187 × 106 mm   MiU, MWA, NN, NNAB, OClWHi
Signatures: [1A]⁸, 2B–22Z⁸, 23A–45Z⁸, 46A–590⁸. Each quire numbered by one in
ascending power.
Evans 25172. Leaf following title has Advertisement to the Folio and Quarto Editions,
To Christians of every Denomination; and To the Publick. Apocrypha is unpaged. A Table of
Offices follows NT.
NN copy lacks Apocrypha. MWA has second copy with NT dated 1801.
This is Thomas' octavo edition which was carefully copied from his folio and quarto
editions; see 1791, No 29 and No 30. In the Advertisement to this edition, Thomas announced
that he was putting to press two other editions — one in Demy quarto; the second in duo-
decimo, or the Common School Bible.

1793   The New Testament . . . J. Bailey and W. Dickson: Lancaster [Pennsylvania]
45

Unpaged: 150 leaves   162 × 88 mm   MWA, PHi
Signatures: A–M¹², N⁶.
Evans 25191.

1794   The Holy Bible . . . translated from the original Greek . . . Printed by William Young: Philadelphia   **46**

152 × 87 mm   CSmH, MWA, NNAB, TNS
Evans (26648) notes that the type and signatures agree with Hugh Gaines's Bible of 1792
(No 40) and with Carey's 1803/02 edition (No 106). The format is similar to Young's 1790
edition (No 25). See also 1808, No 154. The general title seems to be a rearrangement of the
NT title, in which the word "Greek" is used instead of "tongues."
MWA has second copy with Metrical Psalms.

1794   Expository Notes with Practical Observations upon the New Testament . . .
Wherein the whole of the . . . text is recited . . . by William Burkitt . . .
Printed by Abel Morse for the Rev. David Austin of Elizabethtown   **47**

1 vol: (vi) 7–1168   229 × 178 mm   CtHi, MWA, NNAB
Evans 26668. William Burkitt (1650–1703) was a minister of the Church of England
who is remembered particularly for his often reprinted *Expository Notes* of which the Gospels
were first published in London in 1700 and Acts through Revelation in 1703.

1794   The New Testament . . . Printed By Alexander Young and Thomas Minns,
for J. Boyle, B. Larkin, J. White, Thomas and Andrews, D. West, E. Larkin,
W. P. Blake, and J. West: Boston   **48**

Unpaged: 144 leaves   "12mo"   MBAt, MWA
Signatures: A–Z⁶.
Evans 26664. Verso of title has Order of Books. Table of Kindred follows text.

1794? The New Testament . . . First Edition. Peter Brynberg and Samuel Andrews
. . . : Wilmington   **49**

Reported as 306 unnumbered p   162 × 92 mm   DeWI

Not in Evans. Undated, but cited copy has pencil notation at bottom of title page: "1794 or prior"; however no information as to when or by whom the entry was made. "A Checklist of Delaware Imprints up to and including 1800," by Dorothy L. Hawkins (Master's thesis, Columbia University, 1928) mentions the firm of Brynberg and Andrews which printed books in Wilmington from 1791 to 1793, after which date Brynberg worked alone. So 1794 is a possible publication date for this NT.

1794 The New Testament . . . Henry Ranlet: Exeter [New Hampshire] **50**

Evans 26665. Not Located

1795 The New Testament . . . Printed . . . For Henry Ranlet, Thomas Odiorne, Jun., Samuel Parker and William Stearns: Exeter [New Hampshire] **51**

Reported as 336 unnumbered p 153 × 88 mm MdBP, MWA
Not in Evans. Has Table of Kindred at end.

1795 The New Testament . . . Parker & Robinson: Newburyport **52**

"12mo" MWA

Evans 28285. Contains An Alphabetic Etymological Explanation of the Names and Persons. See 1791 Mycall NT, No 34; also 1801 Parker & Robinson NT, No 85.

1796 The Holy Bible . . . Berriman & Co., by Jacob R. Berriman: Philadelphia **53**

Unpaged: 376 leaves 363 × 216 mm CSmH, ICBS, MiU, MWA, NN, NNAB, OC, PPL
Signatures: [A]², B–9D².
Evans 30065. Has four preliminary leaves: frontispiece; title page with verso blank; Order of Books with verso blank; and A Correct Map of the Countries surrounding the Garden of Eden. Has marginal notes. Index, Tables, and a List of Subscribers follow NT. 16 plates and 2 maps.
Also issued without plates and with general title reset in different fonts of type, without date.
Wright (p 325) says this Bible is valued as a collector's item, as the illustrations give excellent examples of the work done by several American engravers of this period.

1796 Expository Notes . . . New Testament . . . by William Burkitt . . . First American Edition. Printed by T. Dunning and W. W. Hyer: New York **54**

631 p 383 × 205 mm Not Located
Evans 30084, 30085; O'Callaghan, p 52. Actually this is the second American edition of Burkitt's commentary; see 1794 NT, No 47.
NNAB has copy agreeing with the description in O'Callaghan but with imprint of William W. Woodward, Philadelphia.

1796 The New Testament . . . J. Bailey and W. & R. Dickson: Lancaster **55**

"12mo" Not Located
Evans 30080.

1796 The Four Gospels, translated from the Greek. With Preliminary Dissertations, and Notes Critical and Explanatory. By George Campbell . . . Printed by Thomas Dobson . . . : Philadelphia **56**

1 vol: (viii) (xvi) (488) (196) (16) 215 × 152 mm MWA, NNAB
Evans 30086. Pages 277–278 incorrectly numbered 275–276, disturbing subsequent pagination.
This is the first of several American editions of the George Campbell Version. George Campbell (1719–1796), a Scottish Presbyterian theologian who was long principal of Mari-

schal College, Aberdeen, made a translation of the Gospels which was first printed in 1778 in England and many times reprinted. It was also published with James Macknight's Epistles (1845) and included in Alexander Campbell's 1826 NT (No 567).

1797   The Holy Bible . . . United States of Columbia. Isaiah Thomas: Worcester **57**

Unpaged: 396 leaves   154 × 90 mm   NN
Signatures: [A]¹², B–2K¹².
Evans 31806. Leaf following title has Advertisement, To Christians of every Denomination signed by Isaiah Thomas; To the Publick; and Order of Books. Tables of Scripture Measure and Table of Time follow OT. Error in Acts 6:3, whom *ye* may appoint, for whom *we* may appoint.
MWA has copy with NT dated 1800.
This is Thomas' duodecimo Bible, advertised in his 1793 octavo edition (No 44) as a Common School Bible to be printed on beautiful new type cast particularly for the purpose to be completed with all speed. The first edition was not published until 1797. It is known as Thomas' Standing Edition as the type was kept undistributed or standing ready for the press. During this period it was common practice for printer-publishers to reset and reprint a standard work again and again, in order that the type could be released for other work as soon as any printing was accomplished. This process was very expensive in terms of labor and time. With such an extensive book as the Bible and with a continuous sale, the problem was a serious one. Isaiah Thomas conceived the idea of buying sufficient type to set up the entire Bible at one time, so that it could be reprinted at convenience. Negotiations were undertaken with the Fry Foundry in London, and in 1791 Thomas agreed to the terms of £1444 for nonpariel type for a duodecimo Bible, to be completed in "not less than 12 months." See *The Isaiah Thomas Standing Bible* by Douglas C. McMurtrie (pamphlet privately printed, 1928). See also *Isaiah Thomas* by Clifford K. Shipton (Rochester, The Printing House of Leo Hart, 1948).

1797/92   The Holy Bible . . . Hugh Gaine: New York   **58**

150 × 88 mm   MiD, MiU, MWA, NN, NNAB
Evans 31807. Same as Gaine's 1792 edition (No 40). NT title page dated 1792.

1797   The New Testament . . . J. Bailey and W. & R. Dickson: Lancaster [Pennsylvania]   **59**

Unpaged: 150 leaves   165 × 89 mm   MWA, NN
Signatures: A–M¹², N⁶.
Evans 31817. Order of Books appears on verso of title.

1797   The New Testament . . . Printed and Sold by Edward O'Brien: New-Haven. Also Sold Wholesale and Retail by John Turner, Printer: Philadelphia   **60**

Unpaged   152 × 87 mm   MWA, PHi
Evans 31818. Has Table of Kindred added.

1797   New Testament . . . Printed and Sold by Peter Brynberg: Wilmington   **61**

Reported as 336 p   149 × 89 mm   DeWI
Not in Evans. This is the first NT printed by Brynberg alone; see 1794 NT, No 49.

1798   The Holy Bible . . . together with the Apocrypha . . . Printed for John Thompson & Abraham Small, [from the hot-press of John Thompson]: Philadelphia   **62**

2 vols: 614 leaves   332 × 180 mm   CBPac, DLC, ICBS, ICN, MB, MWA, NN,
                                            NNAB, OClWHi, PPL, ViU
Signatures: [A]², B–10D², 10E³, 2A–2L², χ¹, ³A–3T². 9C missigned 'C9'.

Evans 30066 (1796); 33408 (1798). Vol I has three preliminary leaves: frontispiece by Alexander Lawson is inscribed *Published by J. Thompson & Abm. Small for the Hot-pressed Bible Philadelphia Nov. 1798*; general title with heraldic eagle surmounted by a Bible, verso blank; and Order of Books, verso blank. Vol II begins with Proverbs; Apocrypha printed in italics; Index and Tables at end of NT which has its own title page.

NNAB copy is incomplete. Also published with List of Subscribers.

This is the first hot-press edition of the Bible printed in America. In the advertisement (April 30, 1796) it was "proposed to deliver the whole in forty numbers, at one half dollar each; one of which will be completed every two weeks." The finished work was completed in 2 vols in November 1798.

1798 The Holy Bible . . . Isaiah Thomas: Worcester **63**

151 × 87 mm ICBS, MWA, NN, NNAB

Evans 33409. Same as Thomas' 1797 edition (No 57) from standing type. Error in Acts 6:3 continued.

1798 The New Testament . . . Peter Brynberg: Wilmington **64**

280 p 162 × 90 mm NN, NNAB

Evans 33416. Has Order of Books on verso of title. Verso of last leaf of NT contains list of Books Printed and Sold by Peter Brynberg. Last page numbered 291 as pagination skips 12 pages from 229 to 240.

1798 The New Testament . . . Printed and sold by Edward O'Brien: New-Haven. Also, sold wholesale and retail by David Dunham: New York **65**

152 × 87 mm MWA

Evans 33415. Same as 1797 O'Brien NT (No 60).

1799 The Holy Bible . . . Thomas Dobson: Philadelphia **66**

367 × 214 mm ICU, MWA, NNAB, PHi, ViU

Evans 35188. Format is similar to Berriman & Co. folio of 1796 (No 53). John Adams heads the List of Subscribers.

Has map by A. Anderson, assumed to be Alexander Anderson (1775–1870) who, according to Wright, was the first American wood-engraver. The following entries from his diary (Burr, p 207) are of interest: "Dec. 7, 1798 I intended to confine myself to wood-engraving; but C. Tiebout wishes me to undertake a map, and I cannot resist the offer. . . ." "23rd, Sunday I infring'd upon my general rule and labour'd at the map all day — except in the afternoon. . . ." Anderson was educated for medicine at his parents' insistence, but abandoned the medical profession in 1798. Many of his woodcuts and engravings appear in Bibles of the first half of the 19th century.

1799 The Holy Bible . . . Isaiah Thomas: Worcester **67**

153 × 89 mm IU, MWA

Evans 35189. Same as Thomas' 1797 edition (No 57) from standing type. *United States of Columbia* appears in imprint.

NN and NNAB have copies with NT title dated 1800. IU also has NT (1799) bound separately.

1799 The New Testament . . . Octoraro: Printed by Francis Bailey, and to be sold at his Bookstore . . . : Philadelphia **68**

Unpaged: 150 leaves 164 × 87 mm MWA
Signatures: A–M^{12}, N^6.
Not in Evans.

1799   The New Testament . . . Appointed to be read in Churches and Families. Printed for Isaac Pearson: Philadelphia   **69**

Unpaged: 138 leaves   163 × 85 mm   MWA
Signatures: A–U⁶, X–Z⁶.
Evans (35198) lists imprint as *Philadelphia: Printed* [by Charles Cist] *for Isaac Pearson.* . . .

1799   The New Testament . . . Charles Cist: Philadelphia   **70**

Unpaged: 120 leaves   145 × 85 mm   MWA, NN
Signatures: A–U⁶.
Evans 35197. Verso of title has Order of Books. Error in 1 Tim 4:16, *thy* doctrine, for *the* doctrine.

1799   The Four Gospels, translated from the Greek. With Preliminary Dissertations and Notes Critical and Explanatory. By George Campbell . . . Printed by A. Bartram: Philadelphia   **71**

Reported as (viii) (xvi) (488) (196) (16)   215 × 152 mm   MBU–T, MWA, PP
Evans 35200. George Campbell Version; see 1796, No 56.

1800   The Holy Bible . . . Isaiah Thomas: Worcester   **72**

153 × 89 mm   MH–AH, MWA
Evans 36955. Reprint of Thomas' 1797 edition (No 57) from standing type.

1800   The Holy Bible . . . Hugh Gaine: New York   **73**

Reported as 404 leaves   146 × 87 mm   DLC
Evans (36954) reports 696, 192 p.
MWA has NT only.

1800   The New Testament . . . Printed and sold by Benjamin Gomez, Bookseller and Stationer . . . : New York   **74**

Unpaged   151 × 88 mm   MWA
Evans 36957. Appears to be same as Hugh Gaine's 1789 NT (No 21). The errors in Acts 8:9 and Philippians 4:15 are continued.

1800   The New Testament . . . Hugh Gaine: New York   **75**

Reported as 192 p   148 × 87 mm   CtY, DLC, MWA
Not in Evans. Appears to be same as Hugh Gaine 1792 NT (No 40) from standing type.

1801   The Holy Bible . . . Correctly copied from Collins's Quarto Edition . . . Printed for William Durell . . . by George F. Hopkins: New York   **76**

1 vol: (4) 5–868 (2) 3–212   321 × 203 mm   CSmH, KBB, MWA, NCooHi, NN, NNAB, VtHi
Shaw 170; O'Callaghan, p 57. With Apocrypha. Error in Acts 10:26; *Saying stand up,* for *saying, Stand up.* Issued in parts.
NN copy has Dr. Witherspoon's Preface and 16 plates. NNAB copy has 14 plates but number and position of plates vary with copies. Vignette on title page signed A. Anderson shows Adam and Eve, and there is a full page engraving, also signed, of Jonah under a huge gourd. O'Callaghan lists 15 engravings copied from W. Heptinstall's Bible (London, 1794–95).

1801 The Holy Bible . . . Printed for Mathew Carey . . . by Joseph Charless: Philadelphia   **77**

Text ends 5G2   245 × 199 mm   NN, NNAB, PHi, ViU

Shaw 171. Preliminary matter includes Order of Books on verso of title, Subscribers' Names (2 leaves), and Preface by Mathew Carey (2 leaves). Apocrypha, set in smaller type, has preliminary page with "This Bible is the Property of   " inscribed within border which is surmounted by two vases. Family Record pages precede and follow NT. An Errata follows NT colophon. At end are An Index to the Holy Bible; A Table of Offices; Tables of Scripture Measures; Tables of Proper Names; Table of Time; A Clergyman's Address to Married Persons at the Altar; The Old and New Testaments Dissected; Portrait of an Apostolic Preacher, from Cowper; A Table of Kindred and Affinity; and Judea, Palestine or the Holy Land (a description). 9 historical engravings are included but the Map of Palestine mentioned on title page is omitted.

NN copy has woodcut in place of Errata and the Map of Palestine is included.

This appears to be the first edition of the King James Version to be published by Mathew Carey. Carey was the foremost printer and publisher of the Bible in America during the first quarter of the nineteenth century and published over sixty duodecimos and quartos of the King James Version (see note under 1790, No 23). As his business expanded, much of the work was transferred to other printers, as can be noted from the above imprint and imprints of many subsequent editions.

The distinctions among the various quarto editions are in the number and arrangement of materials added to the text in the form of tables, indexes, commentaries, plates (maps and historical scenes), and the quality of the paper on which they are printed. According to Carey's Advertisement of 1816 (quoted in O'Callaghan, p 131–134), prices varied from $3.75 for a Bible printed on coarse paper without Apocrypha, plates, etc., to $20 for a Bible printed on superfine paper with Apocrypha, Concordance, 100 plates, etc., and done in Morocco gilt with gilt edges.

1801 The Holy Bible . . . Printed By M. L. & W. A. Davis, For Gaine & Ten Eyck, S. Campbell, John Reid, John Broome & Son, E. Duyckinck, T. & J. Swords, T. S. Arden, P. A. Mesier, S. Stevens, and T. B. Jansen & Co.: New York   **78**

1 or 2 vols   241 × 195 mm   CSmH, NN, NNAB, PHi, ViU

Shaw 169. With Apocrypha. Index follows NT.
NN copy in 2 vols.

1801 The Holy Bible . . . First Philadelphia Edition. Printed for Mathew Carey . . . Joseph Charless, Printer: Philadelphia   **79**

Unpaged   157 × 100 mm   OClW, PSC, PSt

Preliminary matter includes Order of Books and Account of Dates. A Table of Offices follows NT.

This appears to be the first duodecimo edition of the Bible published by Mathew Carey.

1801 The Holy Bible . . . I. Thomas and E. T. Andrews: Boston   **80**

151 × 88 mm   MWA, NN

Shaw 168. Same as Thomas' 1797 edition (No 57) from standing type with error in Acts 6:3 continued. An Account of the Dates is added to the preliminary material.

O'Callaghan (p 60) notes that the standing type for Thomas' duodecimo was removed from Worcester to Boston at this time.

1801 The New Testament . . . Correctly copied from Collins's Quarto Edition . . . Printed for William Durell: New York   **81**

212 p   368 × 252 mm   NN

Shaw 173. This is the NT of Durell's folio Bible of this year (No 76) with new title page. Error in Acts 10:26 continued. 2 plates.

1801   The New Testament . . . Thomas Dobson: Philadelphia   **82**

"12mo"   Not Located

O'Callaghan (p 61): "Not seen; mentioned in *Portfolio*, 4to I, 51."

1801   The New Testament . . . Octoraro: Printed by Francis Bailey, and to be sold
         at his Bookstore, No. 116 Highstreet, Philadelphia   **83**

Unpaged: 150 leaves   165 × 89 mm   MWA, NN, NNAB
Signatures: A–M¹², N⁶.
Shaw 174. See also 1780 NT, No 7.

1801   The New Testament . . . Printed and sold by Peter Brynberg: Wilmington **84**

Unpaged   163 × 90 mm   MWA
Shaw 175. Cited copy lacks Rev 22:10 to end. Some pages of text defective.

1801? New Testament . . . Printed and sold by Parker & Robinson: Newburyport
                                                                          85

163 × 90 mm   MBU–T
Reprint of 1791 Mycall NT (No 34) with Alphabetic Etymological Explanation. Dated
by O'Callaghan (p 61).

1801   The New Testament . . . Benjamin Gomez: New York   **86**

150 × 87 mm   MWA, NN
Shaw 172. Identical with 1800 Gomez NT (No 74) which in turn agrees with the 1789
Hugh Gaine edition (No 21). Errors in Acts 8:9 and Philippians 4:15 are continued.

1802   The Holy Bible . . . Printed for M. Carey by Robert Cochran: Philadelphia **87**

2 vols in 1   285 × 230 mm   MiHi, NN, PSC–Hi
Shaw 1876.

1802   The Holy Bible . . . Printed for Mathew Carey: Philadelphia   **88**

1 vol: (913) (118)   245 × 199 mm   CSmH, CtHT–W, MWA, NcAS, NcD, NN,
                                                                NNAB, PHi, ViU
Shaw 1878 (?). Materials appended to text are same as those in Carey's 1801 edition
(No 77) except Preface and Errata are omitted and A Concise View of the Evidences of the
Christian Religion by J. Fletcher and A Brief Concordance to the Holy Scriptures by John
Brown (Thomas Manning, Printer, 1802 — 118 p) are added. Index, Tables, etc. are unpaged.
6 maps and 24 historical engravings. Note at bottom of p 591 has "Joseph Charless, Printer."
Also issued without Concordance. NN copy has 22 plates.

1802/01   Holy Bible . . . Printed for & sold by T. B. Jansen & Co. . . . . New York **89**

Unpaged   239 × 169 mm   Privately Owned
NT dated 1801 with imprint *Printed by M. L. & W. A. Davis for Gaine and Ten Eyck, S.*
Campbell, John Reid, John Broome & Son, E. Duyckinck, T. & J. Swords, T. S. Arden, P. A.
Mesier, S. Stephens and T. B. Jansen & Co.: New York. See 1801, No 78.

1802/01   The Holy Bible . . . together with the Apocrypha . . . Second Worcester
            Edition . . . Isaiah Thomas: Worcester   **90**

1 vol: (736) 737–960   189 × 106 mm   DLC, MBU–T, MiU, MWA, NN, NNAB,
                                                                          TxU

Shaw 1879. Apocrypha follows p 736 and is unpaged. Preliminary matter includes Advertisement to Thomas' folio and quarto editions (see 1791, No 30), To the Public, and Order of Books. OT has own title page and generally resembles that of Thomas' 1793 octavo (No 44). NT imprinted *Printed . . . by Isaiah Thomas, Jun. for Isaiah Thomas . . . 1801.*

1802/01 The Holy Bible . . . Second Worcester Edition. Printed at Worcester, Massachusetts, for West & Greenleaf: Boston   **91**

189 × 105 mm   NNAB

Reprint of Isaiah Thomas' octavo of this year (No 90) with a new general title page. NT title dated 1801.

1802 The Holy Bible . . . Printed for William Young: Whitehall. Philadelphia   **92**

Text ends Ll 2   175 × 98 mm   CSmH, NN, PPL–R

Preliminary matter includes Order of Books and To the Reader. Tables follow both Testaments. Metrical Psalms (1805) at end. NNAB has copy with NT dated 1805 and text ending on Ll2a with Table of Offices . . . on verso.

Whitehall is a town in the neighborhood of Philadelphia. In 1802 William Young sold his business on Chestnut Street to W. W. Woodward but he continued to print to some extent from his establishment on Bank Street. (Wright, p 324.)

1802 The Holy Bible . . . Isaiah Thomas & E. T. Andrews: Worcester   **93**

151 × 88 mm   MB, MWA

Shaw 1875 (?). Reprint of Thomas' 1797 edition (No 57) from standing type. NN has copy with NT imprinted *Printed by I. Thomas, jun., 1801.*

1802 The New Testament . . . Printed for Benjamin Johnson and Jacob Johnson: Philadelphia   **94**

Reported as 362 unnumbered p   184 × 105 mm   CSmH, DLC, MWA
Shaw 1883.

1802 The New Testament . . . Peter Brynberg: Wilmington   **95**

279 [1] p   160 × 90 mm   MWA, NN

Agrees with 1798 Brynberg edition (No 64) but pagination has been corrected. Publisher's advertisement appears on last page.

1802 The New Testament . . . Isaiah Thomas, Jun.: Worcester   **96**

Text ends Cc6   154 × 87 mm   MBU–T, MWA, NN, NNAB
Separate issue of NT from Thomas' 1797 duodecimo Bible (No 57).

1802 The New Testament . . . Printed by E. Merriam & Co., For the Booksellers: Brookfield, Massachusetts   **97**

Unpaged   151 × 89 mm   GEU, MWA

Has Table of Kindred at end. GEU copy lacks first seven chapters of Matthew and the last page of Revelation.

Shaw lists copy (1887) imprinted *For Isaiah Thomas and Ebenezer Andrews* (320 p, located at DLC and MB).

Ebenezer Merriam (1777–1858) had served as apprentice to Isaiah Thomas.

1802 The New Testament . . . Printed and sold by Benjamin Gomez, Bookseller and Stationer . . . : New York   **98**

151 × 88 mm   MWA

Same as Gaine's 1789 NT (No 21) and Gomez' 1800 edition (No 74) with errors continued.

1802 The New Testament . . . printed by Robert Carr for Mathew Carey: Phila-
        delphia   **99**

Unpaged   DLC, NPV, ODW, PSt
Shaw 1884.

1803 The Holy Bible . . . with . . . the explanatory notes of Ostervald. Printed by
        Sage and Clough, for William Durell: New York   **100**

Unpaged   248 × 194 mm   MWA
Shaw 3793. Text is same as that in the Sage and Clough edition of this year (No 103)
but type has been shifted to allow space for Ostervald's notes at the foot of the page. NT title
imprint identical with general title of No 103 except Sage & Thompson appears in place of
M'Dermut & Thompson. Has Index and Concordance (Published by William Durell . . . T. Kirk,
Printer — 72 p) at end.
    Privately owned copy contains illustrations "Engraved for Durell's Edition of the Bible."

1803 The Holy Bible . . . Printed by and for Samuel Etheridge; and for J. White &
        Co., Thomas & Andrews; West & Greenleaf; E. Larkin; and J. West, Boston:
        Charlestown, Massachusetts   **101**

Text ends 5G2   245 × 199 mm   CSmH, DLC, MB, MBU–T, MWA, NN, NNAB,
                                                                              PSt
Shaw 3789. Appears to be reset from Carey's 1801 edition (No 77) with same plates.
With Apocrypha. A Summary History of the Bible is added to preliminary matter. Brown's
Concordance (1803) follows NT.
    DLC also has copy without Concordance.

1803 The Holy Bible . . . Printed by John Adams and William Hancock, for
        Mathew Carey: Philadelphia   **102**

1080 p   245 × 185 mm   MWA, NcD, NN, NNAB, PHi
    Preliminary matter includes Order of Books and an Index of Articles Annexed. With
Apocrypha in smaller type. NT title imprinted *Third Philadelphia Edition.* Has same added
materials as in Carey's 1801 quarto (No 77) except the Subscribers' Names, Preface, and A
Clergyman's Address to Married Persons are omitted. Added are A Concise View of Evidences
of the Christian Religion by J. Fletcher and A Table of Passages in the Old Testament quoted
by Christ and His Apostles in the New Testament. Colophon: T. S. Manning, Printer.
    NN copy has Brown's Concordance. PHi copy has 10 maps, 20 historical engravings, and
Concordance.

1803 The Holy Bible . . . Printed by Sage and Clough, for S. Campbell, E. Duyck-
        inck, T. & J. Swords, P. A. Mesier, T. S. Arden, and M'Dermut & Thompson:
        New York   **103**

Text ends 5K2   240 × 192 mm   DLC, NN, NNAB
Shaw 3788. See also Durell edition of this year, No 100. Has Apocrypha in smaller type
with separate signatures. Index to the Bible follows NT.
    NNAB copy lacks general title page and Gen 1–3, and has only 5 leaves of Index.

1803/04 The Holy Bible . . . Fourth Philadelphia Edition . . . Printed by John
           Adams for Mathew Carey: Philadelphia   **104**

913 p   243 × 185 mm   NN
    Has same materials appended to text as Carey's 1803 edition (No 102) and, in addition,
has Metrical Psalms (no date). With Apocrypha in smaller type. Pagination is scrambled fol-

lowing p 92 and the signatures are inconsistent throughout. NT imprinted *Printed by William Hancock . . . 1804.*

O'Callaghan (p 68) suggests that this Bible was made up of odd signatures left over from other editions which were connected by resetting portions of the text.

1803 The Holy Bible . . . I. Thomas and E. T. Andrews: Boston **105**

151 × 88 mm   MB, MWA, NN, NNAB

Shaw 3790. Same as 1797 Thomas edition (No 57) but with a rule after each book. Error in Acts 6:3 continued.

1803 / 02 The Holy Bible . . . Seventh Philadelphia Edition . . . Robert Cochran, Printer . . . Mathew Carey: Philadelphia **106**

Text ends Ll 12   150 × 88 mm   MWA, NN

Order of Books and Account of Dates precede text. A Table of Kindred and Table of Time follow OT. NT, dated 1802, is followed by a Table of Offices.

MWA copy has Metrical Psalms (Charless, 1801). NN has another copy for this year with *Eighth Philadelphia Edition* on title page.

About 1803, Mathew Carey purchased the standing type of the duodecimo published by Hugh Gaine in 1792 (No 40), which this edition closely resembles, and which his subsequent duodecimos follow. See also 1794, No 46.

1803 The New Testament . . . Whitehall: Printed for William Young . . . : Philadelphia **107**

Unpaged   171 × 95 mm   MWA

Last leaf, bottom of recto, has "Carefully read five times, by five different persons from the most correct Editions"; verso has Table of Offices and Conditions of Men. Error in I Tim 4:16 has been corrected.

1803 The New Testament . . . Bonsal & Niles: Wilmington **108**

279 [1] p   158 × 87 mm   NNAB

Resembles 1802 Brynberg edition (No 95). List of Books sold by Bonsal & Niles, who also had a bookshop in Baltimore, appears on last page.

1803 The New Testament . . . Samuel Etheridge: Charlestown, Massachusetts **109**

547 p   158 × 86 mm   CSmH, MWA, NN

Shaw 3797. Verso of title has Order of Books. List of books sold by Samuel Etheridge appears on last page.

MWA copy has two leaves of unsigned advertising following text.

1803 The New Testament . . . Samuel Bragg, Jun'r: Dover [New Hampshire] **110**

Text ends Dd6   152 × 92 mm   MWA, NN, NNAB

Shaw 3759. The initials S. B. appear on title page within ornate border.

1803 The New Testament . . . Printed by Samuel Green, New-London: For Thomas S. Arden, Book-Seller . . . : New-York **111**

Unpaged   148 × 88 mm   MWA

Shaw 3796. Has Table of Kindred on last page. Cited copy lacks two leaves from Matt. 2:20 to 6:5.

1804   The Holy Bible ... page for page with that of Isaac Collins ... Fourth Philadelphia Edition ... Printed by John Adams, For Mathew Carey: Philadelphia
112

1 vol: (1080) (72)   243 × 185 mm   NN

Shaw 5848. With Apocrypha. Verso of OT title page has Order of Books, Index to
Articles Annexed, and List of Maps and Plates. A Table of Offices, Index of Years and Times,
Analysis of the Old and New Testaments, and Family Record follow OT. NT title imprinted
Fourth Philadelphia Edition ... Printed by William Hancock ... 1804. Following NT are
Judea, Palestine or the Holy Land; Index to the Holy Bible; Table of Time; Table of Proper
Names; Table of Kindred; A Concise View of the Evidences of the Christian Religion by J.
Fletcher; Table of Passages in the Old Testament quoted by Christ and His Apostles in the
New Testament. Has Brown's Concordance (T. Kirk, Printer, 1804) at end — 72 p. Text has
marginal notes and references. 10 maps and 20 historical engravings.

In 1803 Mathew Carey decided to publish a new edition of the Bible in quarto and keep
the type standing; the above appears to be the first printed from this standing type. It has
certain typographical variations which appear here for the first time and are repeated in
subsequent editions. The format of the text — 1046 p, with added material to 1080 p — is
consistent in Carey's quartos after 1804. This is the first Carey edition in which the Apocrypha
is printed in the same type as the Testaments. The reference in the title to the Collins 1791
Bible should also be noted; this latter is remarkable for its accurate text and typography and
Carey and other printers of the time adopted it as a standard of correctness (see 1791, No 31).

1804–09   The Holy Bible ... With Original Notes, Practical Observations, and
Copious Marginal References. By Thomas Scott ... The First American, from
the Second London Edition, Improved and Enlarged ... Printed By and For
William W. Woodward: Philadelphia
113

4 or 5 vols   232 × 174 mm   DLC, MnM

Shaw 5847, 7990. Vol i (1804) preliminary matter includes To the Reader and Introduction; text: Genesis-Samuel. Vol ii (1805) Kings-Solomon's Songs. Vol iii (1806) Isaiah-Malachi.
Vols iv and v (1809, sometimes bound together) Preface (Printer's note reads "The American
publisher did not receive the General Preface of the Author, until the whole work was completed
in London ...") followed by complete NT text; at end is List of Subscribers, including Elias
Boudinot (first President of ABS) and Thomas Jefferson, and 2 leaves of Family Record.

DLC has the copy owned by Thomas Jefferson, which is No 1471 in E. Millicent Sowerby's
Catalogue of the Library of Thomas Jefferson (ii, Washington, The Library of Congress,
1953). Miss Sowerby quotes Jefferson as writing that in 1807 Scott was awarded a Doctor of
Divinity diploma from "Dickinsonian College," Carlisle, "by persons whose names I never
before heard." She also quotes a letter from the publisher asking if he wants the last volume
bound as one or two, adding that the price will be $1.75 more than the original subscription of
$20 for the set.

NNAB has copy with Vol ii lacking, Vols iv and v bound together, and Vol i imprinted
The Second American Edition ... 1807. Printer's note in Vol i (1804) reads "The call for the
work was so great, that after I proceeded with about 200 pages of Vol. second, I found it
necessary to increase the number of copies; and in Vol. third to proceed with that increased
number, which of course called for the reprinting of all the first volume and part of the
second...." Consequently, there are two editions of Vol i only.

Vol i of the second printing contains Scott's note to the revised edition (London 1809)
stating that the proper Preface will be written after the completion of the revision. This
Preface is followed by a Recommendation signed by six "respectable Ministers of the Gospel in
Philadelphia ..." including Ashbel Green and Jacob J. Janeway who were active in founding
the Philadelphia Bible Society in 1808. In addition to the text there are long chapter summaries,
copious references in both margins and a great amount of commentary in smaller type in the
lower part of the page.

This is the first appearance in the United States of the popular family commentary known
as Scott's Bible. Thomas Scott (1747–1821), a Church of England clergyman with Calvinist
leanings, prepared a commentary for the English publisher Bellamy, which was planned to
appear in 100 weekly numbers (a procedure popular at that time). Scott was to receive a

guinea a number and the first number appeared in March 1788. But because of financial difficulties when the work was completed (in 174 numbers, in June 1792) Bellamy was bankrupt and Scott not only lost his money but was saddled with a debt from which he was relieved by friends in 1813 (Darlow and Moule I, 309). Wright (p 202) quotes Horne (*Manual of Biblical Bibliography* p 259) with the statement that "twenty-five thousand two hundred and fifty copies were sold in the United States of America from 1808 to 1819." Its popularity lasted well into the middle of the century. The last London edition seems to be the sixth, published in 1823.

1804   The Holy Bible . . . Robert Carr, Printer . . . Published by Benjamin Johnson: Philadelphia   **114**

4 vols   184 × 112 mm   CSmH, MB, MWA, NN, NNAB, PP

Shaw 5850. Vol I, Genesis-Ruth. Vol II, Samuel-Psalms. Vol III, Proverbs-Malachi. Vol IV, complete NT text. Each volume contains title page followed by Table of Contents.

1804   The Holy Bible . . . Printed for Thomas & Andrews, By J. T. Buckingham: Boston   **115**

151 × 88 mm   MWA, NcBe, NN

Shaw 5849. Same as Thomas's 1797 edition (No 57) with error in Acts 6:3 continued. NN copy lacks general title.

1804   The New Testament . . . Published by Jacob Johnson & Co.: Philadelphia *116*

Reported as 347 p   163 × 95 mm   DLC, PU

Shaw 5854. This is the edition used by Thomas Jefferson for his *Life and Morals of Jesus of Nazareth*. See 1904, No 2162.

PU copy has note on verso of flyleaf: "The Cover of this Book is part of the Skin of a Favourite *Dog* which belonged to my Brother John Wallace during my Apprenticeship, and was Bound in the Year 1804 — by myself-." On the title page is the autograph of Thomas Wallace.

1804   The New Testament . . . Bonsal & Niles: Wilmington   **117**

158 × 87 mm   MWA, NN

Shaw 5855. Same as 1803 Bonsal & Niles edition (No 108).

1804   The New Testament . . . Eighth Edition . . . Evert Duyckinck and Peter A. Mesier: New York   **118**

Text ends O12   151 × 87 mm   NNAB

Shaw 5853. See 1798, No 21; also 1800, No 74.

NN has copy dated this year with *Sixth Edition* on title page (168 p).

1804   The New Testament . . . E. Merriam & Co. for the Booksellers: Brookfield, Massachusetts   **119**

334 p   148 × 83 mm   MWA, NN

Has Order of Books on verso of title. Pages 239–240 misnumbered 237–238 and the error in pagination continues so that text ends on p 332. MWA copy is incomplete.

1805   The Holy Bible, translated from the Latin Vulgat . . . first published by the English College at Doway, A.D. 1609. And The New Testament, first published by the English College at Rhemes, A.D. 1582 . . . with Annotations . . .

1805, continued

First American, from the Fifth Dublin edition. Newly Revised and corrected
to the Clementin edition of the Scriptures . . . Mathew Carey: Philadelphia
120

1 vol: (12) 1–772 (4) 1–214 (6)   245 × 188 mm   AU, CSmH, DGU, DLC, NN,
NNAB, PLatS

Shaw 7991. Rheims-Douay Version. The term in the title, *First American, from the Fifth
Dublin edition,* means only that this is the first appearance in the United States of Dr. Troy's
1791 Dublin edition of the Bible.

Preliminary matter includes Subscribers' Names, Historical and Chronological Index to
the Old Testament, Order of Books, and Directions for Placing Plates. Following NT title is An
Admonition and Prayer before the Reading, with a translation of the Decree of the Council of
Trent and Order of Books on verso. At end are An Historical Index to the New Testament,
A Table of References, and A Table of the Epistles and Gospels. Has 3 maps, chart of Scheme
of the Lives of the Patriarchs, and 6 engravings. Inserted between p 384 and 385 of the OT
are *385, 386* and *387, 388*; and in the NT *41, 42*, *43, 44*, *45, 46*, and *47, 48* are
inserted between p 40 and 41.

NN copy has different arrangement of supplementary material and a different series of
illustrations.

1805 The Holy Bible . . . Seventh Philadelphia Edition . . . Mathew Carey: Philadelphia
121

1080 p   243 × 185 mm   CtY, MB, NN, PHi

Shaw 7988. Same as Carey's 1804 edition (No 112) from standing type but with 4 maps
only which are not the same as those mentioned in the title. Each signature of the OT and
Apocrypha is marked "7" in addition to letter and number. Concordance (T. Kirk, Printer, 1803).

1805 The Holy Bible . . . Printed by Mann and Douglass, for themselves: For J.
Tiebout . . . S. Stephens . . . S. Gould & Co. . . . Ronalds & Doudon . . . Sage &
Thompson . . . D. D. Smith . . . C. Flanagan . . . J. Harrison . . . G. B. Waite
. . . T. Kirk . . . C. Brown . . . D. Longworth . . . R. M. M'Gill . . . G. Sinclair,
New York. David Brewer, Jun. Taunton, Massa. S. Kollock, Elizabeth-Town.
J. Oram, Trenton: Morris-Town, New Jersey
122

1142 p   185 × 104 mm   DLC, MWA, Nj, NjHi, NjM, NjMo, NN, PP

Shaw 7987. With Apocrypha. Has Table at end of each Testament.

1805 The Holy Bible . . . Sixteenth Philadelphia Edition. Printed by Mathew Carey: Philadelphia
123

151 × 88 mm   MWA

Reprint of Carey's 1803/02 16mo (No 106).

1805/06 The Holy Bible . . . Twentieth Philadelphia Edition . . . Mathew Carey:
Philadelphia
124

Text ends Ll12   151 × 88 mm   NN, NNAB

Same as Carey's 1803/02 seventh edition (No 106) from standing type with a few minor
variations in spacing of text. NT dated 1806.

MWA has twenty-fourth Philadelphia edition with general title dated 1806.

1805 The Holy Bible . . . Printed for Thomas & Andrews, By J. T. Buckingham:
Boston
125

151 × 87 mm   NN, NNAB

Shaw 7986. Same as Thomas' 1797 edition (No 57) with error in Acts 6:3 continued.

1805   The New Testament ... translated from the Latin Vulgat ... first American, from the fifth Dublin edition ... Mathew Carey: Philadelphia   **126**

214 p   245 × 188 mm   NN, PPL-R

Shaw 8001. From Dr Troy's edition of the Rheims text. 10 plates and 2 maps.
O'Callaghan (p 80) says this was issued previous to Carey's 1805 Bible (No 120). It was reissued in 1811 and 1816 (Nos 196 and 309).

1805   The New Testament ... William Young: Whitehall [Philadelphia]   **127**

Unpaged   Not Located

Shaw 8002. Supposedly held by PNazMHi but not found, 1959. See No 92. This may be NT in NNAB copy.

1805   The New Testament ... Peter Brynberg ... : Wilmington   **128**

160 × 87 mm   NN

Shaw 8003. Agrees with Brynberg editions of 1798 (No 64) and 1802 (No 95).

1805   The New Testament ... Printed by T. Kirk for Campbell and Mitchell, Sage and Thompson, S. Stansbury, D. Smith and B. Dornin: Brooklyn   **129**

Unpaged: 130 leaves   151 × 87 mm   MWA, NN

Signatures: [A]^6, B-W^6, X^4.
Shaw 7999; 7998 (Kirk only).
NN has three copies, one of which has Greek text interleaved with English text (432 p, signed A-E^6, [F]^6, G-NN^6).

1805   The New Testament ... E. Duyckinck ... and P. A. Mesier: New York   **130**

151 × 87 mm   NN

Shaw 8000. Agrees with Duyckinck's eighth edition of 1804 (No 118).

1806   The Self-Interpreting Bible ... references ... notes by the late John Brown ... Second American Edition ... Printed by Sage & Clough for Robert Mc-Dermut ... : New York   **131**

Unpaged: 520 leaves   376 × 215 mm   CSmH, MH, MWA, NcD, NN, NNAB, PPL–R, ViU

Signatures: π^2, π[A]^2, B–K^2, A–8A^2, ^{9}[A]^2, B–T^2, ^{10}[A]^2, B–Z^2, ^{22}A–3Y^2. 5T missigned '5F'.
Format resembles that of the 1792 Self-Interpreting Bible of Hodge & Campbell (No 37). OT, Apocrypha, and NT all have separate signatures. Apocrypha in smaller type. NT imprinted *Printed by Hopkins and Seymour for Robert McDermut.*
PPL–R copy has plates. O'Callaghan (p 82) describes a copy with 24 engravings from Thomas' 1791 folio (No 29), from which the references have been erased but the engraving numbers have in most cases been retained. This has the added imprint of J. & T. Ronalds.

1806   The Holy Bible ... Mathew Carey: Philadelphia   **132**

243 × 185 mm   DLC, MWA, NcD, NNAB, NHi, TNMPH

Same as Carey's 1804 edition (No 112) from standing type. Concordance (Printed by Thomas Kirk, Brooklyn, 1807).
NN has copy with general and OT titles dated May 8th, 1805. NT title is dated 1806 with statement *Tenth Philadelphia Edition*. Has 3 maps and 27 historical engravings. O'Callaghan (p 83) notes that NT title is sometimes found with date 1807.

1806   The Holy Bible ... Fielding Lucas: Baltimore   **133**

"12mo"   Not Located

Wright, p 389.

1806   The Holy Bible . . . Printed for Thomas & Andrews, by J. T. Buckingham:
Boston   *134*

154 × 88 mm   DLC, MWA, NNAB
Same as Thomas' 1797 edition (No 57) with error in Acts 6:3 continued.

1806   The Holy Bible . . . W. W. Woodward: Philadelphia   *135*

1 or 2 vols   120 × 61 mm   MWA, NN, NNAB, ViU
Vol I preliminary matter includes To the Reader and Order of Books; text: Genesis-
Proverbs 13:10. Vol II (no title page) text: Proverbs 13:11-Revelation; Table of Offices and
Metrical Psalms (1806) follow NT. NN copy in 2 vols.

1806   The New Testament . . . Duyckinck & Miller: New York   *136*

"16mo"   Not Located
Wright, p 389.

1806   Explanatory Notes Upon the New Testament. In Two Volumes. By John
Wesley, M.A. . . . The Second American Edition . . . William C. Robinson,
Printer. Published by Ezekiel Cooper and John Wilson: New York   *137*

2 vols: Vol I, 368 p; Vol II, 400 p.   178 × 95 mm   MBU–NE, NjMD, NNAB
Wesley Version; see 1791 NT, No 35. Vol I has Preface dated 1754 followed by Gospels
and Acts. Vol II, Romans-Revelation; Index of Words Explained on p 400.
NNAB has Vol I only.

1806   The New Testament . . . Merriam & Co.: Brookfield, Massachusetts   *138*

148 × 83 mm   MB, MWA
Same as 1804 Merriam edition (No 119).

1806   The New Testament . . . First Hartford Edition, printed from the Second
Edition of Collins's Bible . . . Printed by Lincoln and Gleason: Hartford *139*

336 unnumbered p   143 × 85 mm   Ct, CtY, MWA, NNAB
Has Table of Kindred added. O'Callaghan (p 84) notes that the type from which this
Testament was printed was cast expressly for it in Philadelphia, set up in Hartford, and
distributed as fast as each form was worked off. The edition consisted of 10,000 copies.

1807   The Holy Bible . . . Edinburgh, Printed for W. Swan & S. Allinson, New York;
And Sold by them, and by the Principal Booksellers in the United States *140*

Text ends 5G2   256 × 201 mm   NN, NNAB
Probably not printed in U.S., but O'Callaghan (p 85) lists this because title page wording and added materials follow Carey's 1801 quarto (No 77). Contains Apocrypha, Index
of the Bible, Cowper's Portrait of an Apostolic Preacher, Clergyman's Address to Married
Persons, Account of Judea, Tables, and Brown's Concordance (1807). One map and 9 historical
engravings.
      NN copy has imprint *Printed for W. Swan et S. Allinson, New York, And Sold at Paris,
by Truchy, Bookseller, 18 Boulevart des Italiens . . . Edinburgh.* The general title page was
printed separately and pasted in. The mistake of *et* for *&* in the title seems to point to Paris
as the place of printing, but both Testament titles, though foreign in typographical appearance,
are printed with signatures and the NT title reads *&*.

1807   The Holy Bible . . . Mathew Carey: Philadelphia   *141*

243 × 185 mm
                                                    MiU–C, MWA, NN, NNAB, PHi

Similar to Carey's 1804 edition (No 112) from standing type except plates consist of 10 maps only. Error on NT title, line 10, *Comared* should be *Compared*. Concordance (1805).

PHi copy has Concordance printed by Thomas Kirk, Brooklyn, 1807. NN has second copy with OT title dated 1806, NT title dated 1807.

1807 The Holy Bible . . . With Marginal Notes and References; and the Explanatory Notes of Ostervald . . . Collins, Perkins, and Co.: New York   *142*

Unpaged: 690 leaves   242 × 171 mm   CSmH, CtHi, CtY, DLC, MB, MWA, NN, NNAB, NHi, PP, PSt

Signatures: [A]⁴, B–4Z⁴, A*–U*⁴, ‡A–‡2G⁴, ‡2H³, 2I⁴ (=‡2I), ⁵[A]⁴, B–U⁴, ⁶[A]⁴, B–I⁴.

Collins' second edition, based on his 1791 edition (No 31). Preliminary matter includes frontispiece (*Providence* by Carracci), Advertisement to the Second Edition, Dr. Witherspoon's To the Reader and Account of the Dates, List of Maps and Historical Engravings, and Order of Books. With Apocrypha, followed by Ostervald's Notes and Family Record pages. NT followed by Index to the Holy Bible, A Table of Time, Tables of Scripture Measure, Table of Offices, Table of Kindred, Table of Proper Names, and Brown's Concordance (1806). Plates are labelled *Engraved for Collins's Quarto Bible, Second Edition*. Plate of St. John the Evangelist, before John's Gospel, signed by A. Anderson.

NNAB has another copy with Apocrypha and plates omitted.

In the above-mentioned Advertisement to the Second Edition, Collins makes the following statements: "The admirers of engravings in their Bibles, will be pleased with those introduced into this edition. The great price paid for the engravings, the plan of procuring a single plate from each of the first artists of our country, and some from an eminent engraver lately from London, and the exciting a competition by the reward of a gold medal for the best, have produced a set of plates, which may be regarded a specimen of the degree of perfection to which the art of line engraving has advanced in the United States. . . . As some persons may prefer their Bibles without plates, copies may be had without them. The same regard to the accomodation of individuals will also be observed with respect to the Apocrypha, and the Notes of Ostervald."

In 1796, Isaac Collins moved his business from Trenton to New York and in 1802 his son became a partner in the firm. When in 1805, Benjamin W. Perkins, Jr also became a partner, the firm became known as Collins, Perkins and Co.

1807 The Holy Bible . . . With those copious marginal References, Known by the name of Canne's Notes . . . Jacob Johnson, and Kimber, Conrad and Co.: Philadelphia   *143*

Text ends 6H4   203 × 117 mm   MBU–T, MWA, NjMD, NN, NNAB, PP, ViU

Apocrypha lacking? Preliminary matter includes Order of Books and Tables of Scripture Weights, Money, and Time. Following NT are A Table of Offices, Table of Passages, and Table of Kindred. The references and notes appear in both margins and historical dates at the head of each column of text.

This is the first appearance in the United States of Canne's Bible. John Canne (d. 1667?), a leader of the English Independents in Amsterdam, prepared marginal notes or references which were described on the title as "shewing the Scriptures to be the best interpreters of Scripture." They first appeared in a small Bible probably printed in Amsterdam in 1662 (and possibly even as early as 1644) and were many times reprinted. These references, more for the purpose of commentary and explanation than for scholarly understanding, are often suggestive and carefully selected. In their many reprintings they became full of typographical errors and were often added to by later editors.

1807/06 The Holy Bible . . . Printed for Thomas & Andrews, by J. T. Buckingham: Boston   *144*

151 × 88 mm   NN

Similar to Thomas' 1797 duodecimo (No 57) with error in Acts 6:3 continued. NT title dated 1806.

Also published with NT title dated 1808.

1807   The Holy Bible ... M. Carey: Philadelphia   **145**

151 × 88 mm   MB, NN, PSt

Similar to Carey's duodecimo of 1803/02 (No 106). Has Tables at end of both Testaments. NN copy lacks general title page as well as first three chapters of Genesis.

1807   The Holy Bible ... With Original Notes, Practical Observations, and Copious Marginal References. By Thomas Scott ... The Second American Edition ... Printed By and For William W. Woodward: Philadelphia   **146**

Vol I only. See 1804–09, No 113.   NNAB

1807–08   The Family Expositor; or a Paraphrase and Version of the New Testament; With Critical Notes, and a Practical Improvement of each Section. In Six Volumes ... by P. Doddridge, D.D. To which is prefixed, A Life of the Author, by Andrew Kippis ... Etheridge's Edition, from the Eighth London Edition. Sold by him at Washington Head Bookstore. Sold also by said Etheridge and Company, in Boston. S. Etheridge, Printer: Charlestown, Massachusetts   **147**

6 vols: Vol I, 492 p; Vol II, 636 p; Vol III, 468 p; Vol IV, 484 p; Vol V, 502 p; Vol VI, 516 p   177 × 105 mm   M, MHi, MWA, TNMPH, ViU

Vols IV–VI are dated 1808 and have Etheridge and Bliss in place of Etheridge and Company. This is the first American edition of the Doddridge Version, first published in England in 1739–1756. A two-volume edition was also extracted from the original Family Expositor (see 1807, No 148; also 1836, No 935). The Rev. Philip Doddridge D.D. (1702–1751) was a Congregational minister and hymn writer. He received the degree of D.D. from both universities at Aberdeen. One of his best known hymns is "Awake, my soul, stretch every nerve." Strong (p 109–133) says Doddridge was particularly careful in translating verb tenses, demonstrative pronouns, and the definite article, producing a rather flat text but providing a paraphrase which assured pleasurable and profitable reading. The notes show the "warm evangelical spirit of the man." In England at least 13 editions of the Family Expositor (in 4 or 6 vols) were published by 1824.

1807   The Family Expositor Abridged ... P. Doddridge ... by S. Palmer. Printed by Lincoln & Gleason: Hartford   **148**

2 vols: Vol I, 482 p; Vol II, 416 p   170 × 100 mm   MWA

Doddridge Version; see previous entry, No 147. Has frontispiece.

1807   The New Testament ... T. Kirk, Printer, Brooklyn ... for Campbell and Mitchell, R. M'Dermutt, Brisban and Brannan, Thompson, Hart & Co., J. Tiebout, M. Ward, S. Wood, S. Stephens, and S. Stansbury, Booksellers: New York   **149**

Reported as 260 unnumbered p   164 × 105 mm   CSmH, MWA

Has Table of Kindred at end.

1807   The New Testament ... E. Duyckinck ... and P. A. Mesier: New York   **150**

151 × 87 mm   NN

Agrees with Duyckinck's editions of 1804 (No 118) and 1805 (No 130).

1807   The New Testament ... Printed by E. Merriam & Co.: Brookfield, Massachusetts   **151**

332 p   150 × 83 mm   NNAB

1808 The Holy Bible ... Mathew Carey: Philadelphia   **152**

1 vol: (4) (676) (6) 835–1080 (40)   242 × 182 mm   DLC, MWA, NNAB
                                                                        PHi, TxU

Similar to Carey's 1804 quarto (No 112) except Apocrypha and Concordance are omitted and Metrical Psalms are added.

NN has copy with NT date 1809 and Metrical Psalms omitted. DLC has second copy dated 1808/10.

1808 The Holy Bible, Containing the Old and New Covenant, Commonly Called the Old and New Testament: Translated from the Greek, by Charles Thomson, Late Secretary to the Congress of the United States ... Printed by Jane Aitken ... : Philadelphia   **153**

4 vols: Vol i, 252 leaves; Vol ii, 245 leaves; Vol iii, 222 leaves; Vol iv, 240 leaves
188 × 105 mm   CtY, DLC, MBAt, MWA, MWiW, NjMD, NN, NNAB, OC, PBMC, ViW

Signatures: All signatures in each volume preceded by volume designation. Vol i, π^2, A–Z^4, Aa–Zz^4, 3A–3Q^4, 3R^2. Vols ii–iv have identical scheme but end with following signatures: Vol ii, 3P^3; Vol iii, 3I^4, Vol iv, 3N^2.

Vol i, Genesis-i Samuel. Vol ii, ii Samuel-Psalms. Vol iii, Proverbs-Malachi, followed by note about the translation, and Errata. Vol iv, NT. Each volume has general title page as well as its own part title page. Text is printed in single-column paragraph form, with verse numbers in left margin. Italics are rarely used except for emphasis, words supplied to complete the sense being bracketed. Has a few footnotes. Without Apocrypha. Copyright Pennsylvania, Sept. 12, 1808.

Charles Thomson (1729–1824) made the first translation of the Septuagint into the English language, and the first English translation of the NT in the western hemisphere. He emigrated to this country from his native Ireland in 1739. By chance he met a patroness who provided his early education. After receiving the degree of Master of Arts, he served as a tutor at the College of Pennsylvania, which later became the University of Pennsylvania. He adopted the patriot cause, and was unanimously elected secretary to the Continental Congress upon its organization in 1774. He held this post until 1789 when he resigned in order to pursue his scholarly interests. His first acquaintance with the Septuagint came when he purchased one part of Bp. Pearson's edition as a curiosity at an auction. After his inquisitiveness had turned to fascination, he found the other part in the same store. This edition, including also a reprint of Thomas Buck's printing of the Greek NT (1632), was published by John Field at Cambridge, England in 1665.

Thomson spent twenty years in making the translation. The books called Apocrypha, which are included in the canon of the Greek OT but not in the Hebrew, were omitted in his translation. After copying the MS four times, he had it published at Philadelphia by Jane Aitken, the first woman to print any part of the Holy Scriptures in America, and the daughter of the printer Robert Aitken. It is of interest that the name "Cha. Thomson" appears as the signer of the Congressional resolution in the front of the 1782 Aitken Bible (No 11).

A manuscript copy in three volumes of Thomson's translation of the Septuagint (and NT?) is in the Reis Library, Alleghany College, Meadville, Pa. NNAB has a portion of the autograph translation of the work. It has many textual changes in the original hand on 305 numbered foolscap sheets. Leaves 1–32 are lacking, 305 is in fragments. The MS seems to have included Job to Malachi; leaf 33 begins with Psalm 22:20. Thomson's own printed copy of the translation with his last MS corrections is owned by the Library Company of Philadelphia. The Pennsylvania Historical Society's library has his translation from the Greek NT, *The New Covenant Commonly Called the New Testament*, one volume. PHi also has the *Synopsis of the Four Evangelists, and Interpretations of Biblical Words and their translation from Greek into English*, 3 vols, in his handwriting.

In addition to the translations, a *Synopsis of the Four Evangelists; or, A regular history of the conception, birth, doctrine, miracles, death and resurrection of Jesus Christ in the words of the Evangelists* was published for the editor by Wm. M'Culloch, Philadelphia (iv, 200, 50 p. 23 cm, NNAB and PMA). PMA also has the MS of this work.

Thomson's OT was printed in London in 1904 in 2 vols by S. F. Pells. It was followed by the NT in 1929.

1808?   The Holy Bible ... William Young: Philadelphia   *154*

151 × 86 mm   NNAB

Similar to the Young editions of 1790 (No 25) and 1794 (No 46) with general title page dated 1794 but now correctly worded. However many of the signatures scattered throughout are from another book and do not have page headings; book titles and Tables at end are set in a different type. The printing on the newer signatures is much sharper and blacker. NT, imprinted *Whitehall: Printed for William Young . . . Philadelphia. 1808,* with wreath enclosing "This Book is the Property of   " on verso of title, later appears in several Carey Bibles. See 1816/08, No 305, and 1817, No 333.

1808   The Holy Bible . . . Printed for Thomas & Andrews, By J. T. Buckingham: Boston   *155*

151 × 88 mm   MB, MWA, NN, NNAB

Similar to Thomas' duodecimo of 1797 (No 57) from standing type with error in Acts 6:3 continued.

1808   The Holy Bible . . . Mathew Carey: Philadelphia   *156*

148 × 88 mm   MWA, NCooHi, NN, NNAB, PPL–R

Similar to Carey's 1803/02 edition (No 106) from standing type with error in 1 Tim 4:16 corrected.

1808   The New Testament . . . Abel Dickinson: Whitehall, Philadelphia   *157*

Text ends Z2   173 × 97 mm   NN

Has Table of Offices at end.

1808   The New Testament . . . E. Duyckinck and P. A. Mesier: New York   *158*

151 × 87 mm   NN, NNAB

Similar to Duyckinck's editions of 1804 (No 118), 1805 (No 130), and 1807 (No 150).

1808   The New Testament . . . E. Merriam & Co.: Brookfield   *159*

148 × 83 mm   NN

Similar to Merriam 1804 edition (No 119).

1808   The New Testament . . . Printed and sold by Peter Brynberg: Wilmington *160*

Reported as 402 p   149 × 86 mm   DeWI

1809   The Holy Bible . . . Printed by M. Carey . . . Published by Johnson and Warner: Philadelphia   *161*

243 × 183 mm   NN

Similar to Carey's 1804 edition (No 112) from standing type, except plates consist of one map (Plan of Jerusalem) and 19 historical engravings. Concordance wanting?

O'Callaghan (p 93) notes that the engravings (except nos. 3 and 7) are from Thomas' folio of 1791 (No 29) with references to his edition erased. The engravings are by J. Norman, J. Seymour, J. H. Seymour, G. Love, Negalle, and S. Hill.

1809   The Holy Bible . . . Mathew Carey: Philadelphia   *162*

243 × 182 mm   IU, NN, NNAB, NHi, PHi

Similar to Carey's 1804 quarto (No 112) but without Apocrypha or Concordance. Plates consist of two hand-colored historical engravings.

NN has another copy with Apocrypha, Concordance (Mathew Carey, 1810), and 10 maps. MWA has copies with NTs dated 1808, 1810, and 1812.

1809   The Holy Bible . . . Printed by M. Carey . . . Published by Kimber and Con-
         rad: Philadelphia   **163**

1046 p   242 × 182 mm   NN
Similar to Carey's 1804 quarto (No 112) but without plates or any appended matter fol-
owing NT.

1809   The Holy Bible . . . Printed by M. Carey . . . Published by William Elliot:
         New-Brunswick   **164**

2 vols   242 × 182 mm   CtY, MWA, NNAB
Similar to Carey's 1804 quarto (No 112) but without plates. Vol i: Genesis to Malachi.
Vol ii: Apocrypha, NT, and same supplementary matter as in Carey edition. Concordance
dated 1808.
CtY and MWA copies have general title imprint *W. Elliot and R. Eastburn: New-York.*

1809   The Holy Bible . . . Apocrypha . . . Printed by Greenough and Stebbins, for
         Hastings, Etheridge and Bliss, E. Larkin, Thomas and Andrews, D. West,
         Andrews and Cummings, Manning and Loring, J. West and Co., and O. C.
         Greenleaf: Boston   **165**

1 vol: (735) [1] (2) 739–959 [1]   189 × 105 mm   MWA, NN, NNAB
Apocrypha (84 leaves) is unpaged, in smaller type, and follows p [736]. Preliminary
matter includes To the Reader [by Dr. Witherspoon], Account of Dates, and Order of Books.
Tables of Scripture Measures follow OT and A Table of Offices follows NT.
NN and second MWA copy lack Apocrypha.

1809   The Holy Bible . . . Printed by Greenough and Stebbins: Boston   **166**

151 × 88 mm   MWA, NNAB
Similar to Thomas' 1797 edition (No 57) but with error in Acts 6:3 corrected. Error in
i Tim 4:16, *thy* doctrine, for *the* doctrine, occurs here and in subsequent issues printed by
Greenough and Stebbins. An Account of the Dates is included in the preliminary matter.
NN has copy with NT title dated 1810. NNAB has second copy with correct reading in
i Tim 4:16.

1809   The Holy Bible . . . Printed by Mathew Carey: Philadelphia   **167**

151 × 88 mm   MWA
Similar to Carey's editions of 1803/02 (No 106) and 1807 (No 145).

1809   The Holy Bible . . . Hudson & Goodwin: Hartford, Connecticut   **168**

Text ends Ll12   146 × 87 mm   CSmH, Ct, CtHC, CtW, CtY, NcWs, NjPasHi,
                                                      NN, NNAB, NNPM, NSchU
Title page has "H" and "G" in script letters. Preliminary matter includes Dedication to
King James and Order of Books. OT followed by Table of Kindred and Table of Time; NT
followed by Table of Offices. Error in i Tim 4:16, *thy* doctrine, for *the* doctrine.
Also published with NT dated 1810.
This is the first Bible printed in Connecticut and was referred to by the publishers as the
"School Bible." The firm of Watson and Goodwin, Hartford, Connecticut, published the well-
known *Connecticut Courant.* In 1779 Watson died and Barsillai Hudson became the publishing
partner of Goodwin, establishing the firm of Hudson and Goodwin. The following (from
O'Callaghan, p 96) appeared in the *Connecticut Courant* of 18 October 1809: "Hudson and
Goodwin have the satisfaction to announce to the public that they have this day completed
their *first edition of the School Bible.* The type is entirely new, imported at heavy expense (from
the foundry of Wilson and Sons, Glasgow, at a cost of 6000 crowns), and the paper is so good
a quality that it is asserted with confidence to be the best of the kind offered for sale in this

country." The type was apparently kept standing and O'Callaghan notes that it was sold for old metal about 1837.

Between 1809 and 1813 copies of this Bible were purchased at about sixty cents each for distribution by the following newly formed organizations: Albany Bible Society, Bible Society of Charleston, South Carolina, Auxiliary Bible Society of the County of Cayuga, New York, Connecticut Bible Society, Fairfield County Bible Society, Connecticut, New Jersey Bible Society, New York Bible Society, Bible Society of the State of Rhode Island and Providence Plantations. A copy in the Library of the British and Foreign Bible Society, London, was presented by the Connecticut Bible Society as a sample of the books they were purchasing for distribution. No copies have been located with the Connecticut Bible Society imprint.

1809 The New Testament . . . Dickinson, Printer . . . Published by Solomon Wiatt: Philadelphia   *169*

Text ends Z2   170 x 93 mm   NN
Has Table of Offices at end.

"This book is not to be sold, but given away" appears on verso of title. An explanation follows which relates that the expense of printing this Testament was met by the donation of a $1000 legacy by John Hancock of Burlington, N. J., for gratuitous distribution of the New Testament and other religious books among the poor.

1809 The New Testament . . . Benjamin Johnson: Philadelphia   *170*

347 p   161 × 92 mm   NN

1809 The New Testament, in an Improved Version, upon the Basis of Archbishop Newcome's New Translation: with a Corrected Text, and Notes Critical and Explanatory. Published by a Society for Promoting Christian Knowledge and the Practice of Virtue, by the Distribution of Books . . . From the London Edition . . . Printed by Thomas B. Wait and Company . . . for W. Wells: Boston   *171*

1 vol: (xxx) (612)   151 × 86 mm   ICU, MB, MBS, MWA, NN, NNAB, PMA

Preliminary matter includes Introduction, Order of Books, and Table of Undisputed and Disputed Books According to Eusebius. Text is printed in paragraph form, with verse numbers in left margin and notes at foot of page.

This seems to be the only American edition of Belsham's "Improved Version" of Newcome's translation. Archbishop William Newcome of the Church of Ireland was one of the eighteenth century British scholars concerned with improving the English Bible. He published an edition of the Minor Prophets in London in 1785, of Ezekiel in 1788, and a New Testament in 1796. Newcome's NT was taken as a basis for one prepared by a group of London scholars, chief of them being Thomas Belsham, a Unitarian. Variations from the Textus Receptus were indicated in the margin where there were also placed passages from Newcome's text that had been changed in this new text, first printed in London in 1808. A London edition of 1817 contains some changes made after comparison with Griesbach's second edition.

In 1809 there was printed in Philadelphia by Kimber and Conrad an edition of *An English Harmony of the Four Evangelists, Generally disposed after the Manner of the Greek of William Newcome* (NNAB). This had first appeared in London in 1802, arranged by Richard Phillips using the AV, and was arranged in parallel columns (xiii, 476, 4 p). Newcome's Greek Harmony had been published in Dublin in 1778.

1809 The New Testament . . . Printed and sold by E. Duyckinck . . . and P. A. Mesier . . . : New York   *172*

151 × 87 mm   MWA

See 1789, No 21; also 1804, No 118. The error in Acts 8:9 still stands, but Philippians 4:15 has been corrected to *beginning.*

1809 The New Testament . . . E. Merriam & Co . . . : Brookfield **173**

148 × 83 mm MB

Similar to 1804 Merriam edition (No 119).

1810 The Holy Bible . . . Mathew Carey: Philadelphia **174**

243 × 185 mm MiU, MWA, NCooHi, NN, NNAB, NHi

Same as Carey's quarto of 1804 (No 112) from standing type, with same materials added to text. Concordance (Carey, 1810).

NNAB has three copies: one printed on inferior paper with Concordance omitted and with only 10 historical engravings (a Map of Canaan mentioned in the List of Engravings is missing, as is the Table of Passages at the end of the Bible); another on inferior paper with no plates; and a third on medium quality paper from which preliminary and first two pages of text are missing, but with 5 maps and 22 historical engravings, and Concordance imprinted *Brooklyn: T. Kirk, Printer, 1805.* MiU copy has added imprint *Sold by Donald Fraser, New York.*

1810/12 The Holy Bible . . . with Notes by Thomas Scott . . . in six volumes . . . A new American, from the last London edition, improved by a more conspicuous insertion and arrangement of the marginal references, on an original plan of the present publishers . . . J. Seymour, Printer . . . Published by Williams and Whiting: New York **175**

6 vols 212 × 120 mm CtHi, CtY, IaU, MiU, MWiW, NcAS, NN, NNAB, ViW

The new American edition of Scott's Bible with references between text and notes. See 1804–09, No 113.

Vol I (1810) preliminary matter includes Preface, Introduction, and To the Reader; text: Genesis-Joshua. Vol II (1811) Judges-Esther. Vol III (1811) Job-Solomon's Song. Vol IV (1812) Isaiah-Malachi. Vol V (1812) Matthew-Acts. Vol VI (1812) Romans-Revelation; four pages of Tables at end. Vol II imprinted *Samuel Whiting & Co.* Vols III–VI imprinted *Whiting and Watson.*

Privately owned set has Vol II imprinted *Whiting and Watson.*

1810/12 The Holy Bible . . . [with Scott's preface, preliminary remarks to the several Books, and marginal references] . . . J. Seymour, Printer . . . Williams and Whiting: New York **176**

1 or 2 vols 212 × 120 mm MWA, NN

Has Scott's introductory material but not his notes; see 1804–09, No 113. All Books have Introduction; historical dates at head of each column of text. Preliminary matter ([i]–xxii) includes frontispiece, title, Preface, and Introduction to OT. Family Record follows OT. NT, dated 1812 with imprint *Whiting and Watson* . . . , followed by Order of Books; Tables of Scripture Measures, Money and Kindred; and Brown's Concordance (Thomas Kirk, Printer, 1812). Maps wanting?

NN has another copy bound in 2 vols, without Brown's Concordance.

1810 The Holy Bible . . . Printed by Greenough and Stebbins: Boston **177**

151 × 88 mm MB, MWA, NN

Agrees with Greenough and Stebbins edition of 1809 (No 166). Error in I Tim 4:16 continued.

1810 The Holy Bible . . . Mathew Carey: Philadelphia **178**

150 × 88 mm N, NN, NNAB

Same as Carey's duodecimo of 1803/02 (No 106). Copies of Carey's 1803 duodecimo were purchased at fifty-six cents for distribution by the Bible Society of Philadelphia, organized in 1808. Similar NTs were purchased at twenty-five cents.

1810   The Holy Bible . . . Hudson and Goodwin: Hartford   **179**

2 vols   146 × 87 mm   MWA, NN

Identical with Hudson and Goodwin 1809 duodecimo (No 168) except bound in 2 vols. Vol I, OT. Vol II, NT. There are no volume designations on title pages. At end of NT is a Dictionary of the Bible imprinted *First American Edition from the Second London Edition, Enlarged. Printed at the Press of and for Isaiah Thomas, Jun. . . . Worcester, January, 1798.*

1810   The Holy Bible . . . William W. Woodward: Philadelphia   **180**

1 or 2 vols   129 × 61 mm   KBB, KyLo, MB, MiU, MWA, NcD, NN, NNAB, NNC
Preliminary matter includes To the Reader and Order of Books.

MWA and second NN copies have Memorandum pages following NT. NNAB copy with general title dated 1810, NT title dated 1811, and Metrical Psalms (1811). MB copy in 2 vols. MiU copy lacks NT.

1810   The New Testament . . . The first American, from the Cambridge Stereotype
          Edition . . . Printed for Williams and Whiting, and the New York Bible So-
          ciety: New York   **181**

"12mo"   Not Located
O'Callaghan, p 102.

"Particular inquiries were made for the purpose of ascertaining whether it would be eligible for the Society to purchase types; and considering the delay, expense, and uncertainty incident to any proceedings for importing stereotype from Europe, the idea was entirely relinquished. Means were also employed to ascertain where the best and cheapest Bibles could be procured at home; and those printed by Messrs. Hudson, Goodwin, & Co. Hartford, were, on the whole, preferred. From them have been procured two thousand copies, and two thousand more have been ordered. All Bibles procured for the use of the Society, are stamped on the cover and upper edge of the leaves with the name of the New-York Bible Society, and deposited in the Book-store of Messrs. Williams & Whiting, who have generously offered, without any compensation, to take the trouble of delivering them as the Managers shall direct." ([First] *Annual Report of the New-York Bible Society* 1810, p 4ff.) See also 1809, No 168.

1810   The New Testament . . . Abel Dickinson: Philadelphia   **182**

171 × 95 mm   NN, NNAB

Identical with Wiatt edition of 1809, printed by Dickinson (No 169). Has Table of Offices at end.

1810   The New Testament . . . Mathew Carey: Philadelphia   **183**

Unpaged   150 × 88 mm   ViU
Appears to be NT of Carey's 1803/02 duodecimo (No 106) from standing type.

1810   The New Testament . . . E. Merriam & Co.: Brookfield   **184**

148 × 83 mm   MWA, NN
Same as Merriam edition of 1804 (No 119).

1810   The New Testament . . . Brook W. Sower, Printer . . . John Hagerty: Balti-
          more   **185**

Unpaged   120 × 61 mm   MiU, NN, ViU
Has historical dates at head of text and references at foot of page. Bound in pocket folder. Error in I Tim 4:16.

NN copy lacks pages following last signature, P6. MiU and ViU copies have An Alphabetical Table of Sundry Proper Names at end.

1810 A New Literal Translation from the Original Greek of all the Apostolical
Epistles with a Commentary and Notes, Philological, Critical, Explanatory
and Practical. To which is added, A History of the Life of the Apostle Paul.
By James Macknight, D.D., Author of a Harmony of the Gospels, &c. In Six
volumes. To which is prefixed, An Account of the Life of the Author . . .
T. B. Wait & Co., printers . . . Published by W. Wells and T. B. Wait & Co.:
Boston   *186*

    6 vols   175 × 91 mm   MBAt, MWA
O'Callaghan, p 103. Text covers Romans through Jude, Greek and English texts.
    James Macknight (1721–1800) was a Presbyterian divine and Biblical critic, born in
Ireland of Scottish ancestors. He studied at the Universities of Glasgow and Leyden and in
1769 served as Moderator of the General Assembly of the Church of Scotland. In 1756 he
published in London a Harmony of the Gospels with the King James Version. In 1787 he
published his own version of Thessalonians, which was followed in 1795 by an edition with
the rest of the Epistles. His text was several times reprinted in England and in the United States.

1811 The Holy Bible . . . Mathew Carey: Philadelphia   *187*
    241 × 187 mm   DLC, MWA, NNAB, NHi, PHi, PSt
    Same as Carey's 1804 quarto (No 112) from standing type except it is printed on inferior
paper and Apocrypha, Concordance, and plates are omitted. Error in Esther 1:8, *to* the King,
for *so* the King occurs here for the first time.
    NN has copy on superior paper with Apocrypha, Concordance (1809), and only 2 maps;
NT title dated 1812. NNAB has another copy with NT dated 1815, which has one map and
18 historical engravings. The plates mentioned in the List of Engravings on verso of OT title
are not the ones included. The engravings in this Bible are different from those usually found
in Carey editions and are by Mola, Coning, Guercino, Craig, Marillier, Le Brun, Bloemart, Le
Clerc, Corbould, West, Northcote, B. Picart, Thurston, L. Caracci, and Pietro da Cartonna.
Concordance title reads *A New Edition, Corrected Throughout, and Carefully Compared with
those of Cruden, Brown, Taylor, &c . . . Second Edition.. London . . . 1817.*

1811–25 The Holy Bible . . . with a Commentary and Critical Notes . . . by Adam
Clarke, LL.D. . . . Printed by D. & G. Bruce . . . Published by Ezra Sargeant:
New York   *188*

    6 vols   220 × 172 mm   CtHi, NN, NNAB, TNMPH, ViU
    Vol I (1811) preliminary matter includes Advertisement and General Preface by Clarke;
text of OT: Genesis-Joshua. Vol II (*Third American Edition . . . Published by Daniel Hitt and
Abraham Paul . . . Abraham Paul, Printer, 1821*) Judges-Job. Vol III (*Printed and Published
by Abraham Paul, 1825*) Psalms-Isaiah. Vol IV (1825) Jeremiah-Malachi. Vol I of NT (*Published by Daniel Hitt and Abraham Paul . . . Abraham Paul, Printer, 1818*) Matthew-Romans.
Vol II of NT (1818) Corinthians-Revelation.
    Adam Clarke, LL.D. (1763–1832) was born in Ireland but became very active in Eng-
land in the Methodist Church. He was an Honorary Governor for Life of the British and
Foreign Bible Society. The most important of his numerous works is this commentary on the
Bible, first printed in England in 8 vols, 1810–1825. In the *Panoplist* for October 1810 (1811
vol, n.s. III, p 239a) an edition in parts at $1.50 each by John T. Watson, Philadelphia, and
Daniel Fenton, Trenton, was listed under proposed works but there is no record of its publication. Clarke's commentary is still being published by the Methodist Publishing Concern.

1811–12 The Holy Bible . . . with Notes by Thomas Scott . . . Woodward's Second
American, from the Second London Edition . . . Five Volumes . . . Dickinson,
Printer . . . William W. Woodward: Philadelphia   *189*

    5 vols   201 × 120 mm   CtY, NcU, NN, RPB
    The third American edition of Scott's Bible; see 1804–09, No 113. Vol I (1811) pre-
liminary matter includes Preface by Thomas Scott, Recommendations from Ministers of the

Gospel in Philadelphia, General Preface, and Appendix to General Preface; text: Genesis-Samuel. Vol II (1812) Kings-Proverbs, Chapt. XIX. Vol III (1812) Proverbs, Chapt. xx-Malachi. Vol I of NT (1811) Matthew-Acts. Vol II of NT (1812) Romans-Revelation. Predictions Contained in the Revelation of St. John, followed by Tables (3 p). Each Testament and each Book has an Introduction. Historical dates are included at the head of each column.

1811   The Holy Bible . . . Greenough & Stebbins, Printers: [Boston] . . . Published
       by Daniel Cooledge . . . : Concord, New Hampshire   *190*

Reported as 659 [1] p   170 × 96 mm   MWA

1811   The Holy Bible . . . Greenough & Stebbins, Printers . . . Thomas and Andrews,
       J. West and Co., William Andrews, West and Blake, and Edward Cotton:
       Boston   *191*

959 p   170 × 96 mm   MBU–T, MWA, NN

With Apocrypha. Preliminary matter includes To the Reader (from Collins' edition . . . 1807, No 142), Account of the Dates, and Order of Books. Tables at end of both Testaments.

    MBU–T copy has distributor's imprint pasted over original: *Published by Daniel Cooledge. Sold at his wholesale and retail bookstore. Greenough & Stebbins, printers: Concord, N. H.*

1811   The Holy Bible . . . Printed by Greenough and Stebbins . . . Thomas and An-
       drews, John West and Co., West and Blake, and William Andrews: Boston
                                                                      192

151 × 88 mm   IU, MWA, NN, NNAB

Agrees with the 1809 edition printed by Greenough and Stebbins (No 166). Error in I Tim 4:16 continued.

    "24 dozen common duodecimo Bibles were procured of William Andrews, agent for the Boston Bible Proprietors . . ." (*Report of The Bible Society of Salem and Vicinity . . . 1812,* p 5).

1811   The Holy Bible . . . Mathew Carey: Philadelphia   *193*

150 × 88 mm   MiU, MWA, NN, ViU

Same as Carey's duodecimo of 1803/02 (No 106).

1811   The Holy Bible . . . Hudson & Goodwin: Hartford   *194*

146 × 87 mm   CLCM, Ct, CtY, MWA, NCH, WKenHi

Same as Hudson & Goodwin edition of 1809 (No 168).

1811/10   The Holy Bible . . . William W. Woodward: Philadelphia   *195*

129 × 62 mm   NN

Similar to 1810 Woodward edition (No 180) but without Metrical Psalms. OT title dated 1811, NT title dated 1810.

1811   The New Testament . . . Translated from the Latin Vulgate . . . M. Carey:
       Philadelphia   *196*

245 × 118 mm   DGU

Rheims Version, reprinted from 1805 Bible (No 126).

1811   The New Testament . . . George Long, Printer . . . Samuel A. Burtus: New
       York   *197*

Unpaged: last signature Yy4   180 × 103 mm   NN

Printed on excellent quality paper and in clear attractive type.
NN has another copy with imprint *George Long: New York*.
MWA has copy imprinted *Published by Whiting and Watson:* New York.

1811 The New Testament . . . Printed and sold by E. Duyckinck . . . and P. A.
Mesier . . . : New York   **198**

151 × 87 mm   MWA
Same as 1809 edition (No 172) with error in Acts 8:9 continued. See also 1789, No 21.
Verso of title has *G. Bunce, Print*.

1811 The New Testament . . . Printed and Sold by Peter Brynberg: Wilmington
199

Reported as 274 [1] p   149 × 89 mm   DeWl, MWA
Last page has list of books for sale by Peter Brynberg.

1811 The New Testament . . . E. Merriam & Co.: Brookfield   **200**

148 × 83 mm   MBAt
Appears to be same as Merriam NT of 1804 (No 119).

1811 The New Testament . . . Printed by W. W. Woodward . . . : Philadelphia **201**

129 × 61 mm   MWA, PLF
Agrees with NT of Woodward's 1810 Bible (No 180). The first pages of signatures D
through S carry an * after the letter, apparently to distinguish NT from OT signatures. Three
leaves for Memorandums follow text.

1811 The New Testament . . . Brook W. Sower, Printer . . . John Hagerty: Baltimore   **202**

120 × 61 mm   MWA, NN
Agrees with Hagerty 1810 edition (No 185). Has An Alphabetical Table of Sundry Proper
Names at end.

1811 The New Testament . . . Sweeny & McKenzie, Printers . . . Published and Sold
by Solomon Wiatt: Philadelphia   **203**

Unpaged   120 × 60 mm   ICU, MWA

1811 The New Testament . . . Sweeny & M'Kenzie, Printers . . . Published and Sold
By Benjamin C. Buzby: Philadelphia   **204**

Text ends Ff6   117 × 60 mm   NN, NNAB
Errors in Acts 6:3, whom *ye* may appoint, for whom *we* may appoint, and 1 Tim 4:16, *thy*
doctrine, for *the* doctrine.

1811 The New Testament . . . Paul & Thomas, Printers . . . Published By S. Whiting & Co., 96 Broadway: New-York   **205**

443 p   97 × 55 mm   CtY, NcD, NNAB
Has Table of Names at end of NT. This may be the 32mo printed by Whiting and
Watson which is listed by O'Callaghan (p 111).
MWA has copy with imprint *Daniel Hitt: New York*.

1811?   The New Testament . . . Asahel Brown, Charlestown, Massachusetts   **206**

Not Located

Mentioned under "works proposed" in the *Panoplist* for November 1810 (1811 vol, n.s. III, 288b).

1811   The Four Gospels, translated from the Greek. With Preliminary Dissertations, and Notes Critical and Explanatory. By George Campbell . . . In four
volumes. With the Author's Last Corrections . . . T. B. Wait & Co., Printers
. . . Published by W. Wells and Thomas B. Wait and Co.: Boston   **207**

Vol III: (xxxv) (412)   167 × 101 mm   MWA

George Campbell Version; see 1796, No 56. Vol III contains complete text of the Gospels.
MWA holds the 4 vols complete.

1812/11   The Holy Bible . . . Mathew Carey: Philadelphia   **208**

242 × 182 mm   DLC, KKB, MWA, NjMD, NN, NNAB

Appears to be the same as Carey's 1804 edition (No 112) and has identical maps and
historical engravings. In most respects the typography has the variations of the Carey standing
type, but it is possible that parts of the type were reset at this time. The error in Esther 1:8,
to the King, for *so* the King, which occured in the 1811 edition (No 187) is continued
here. The error in Lev 19:12, *the* God, for *Thy* God, occurs in this edition for the first time. NT
title dated 1811.

NNAB has another copy in which NT is dated 1812 and the plates consist of 5 maps
and 6 historical engravings; and a third printed on inferior paper with Concordance and plates
omitted. O'Callaghan (p 108) lists copy with 10 maps and 15 historical engravings, and another
with 2 maps only.

1812   The Holy Bible . . . John Cunningham, Printer . . . Published by Merrifield
and Cochran: Windsor [Vermont]   **209**

1 vol: 5–956 957–964 (25)   228 × 176 mm   ICN, ICU, MBU–T, MH, MWA,
                                                                        NNAB, OC, VtHi

This is the first Bible printed in Vermont. With Apocrypha. Preliminary matter includes
general and OT titles and Order of Books. Following NT are A Clergyman's Address to Married Persons, Analysis of the Old and New Testaments, Chronological Index, Summary History
of the Bible (in smaller type), Family Record, Index of the Holy Bible, Table of Proper
Names, Tables of Scripture Measures, Table of Kindred, and Table of Time. Continuously
paged through Family Record (p 957–964 are scrambled); Index and Tables (25 p) are
unpaged.

O'Callaghan (p 108) lists copy with 7 engravings which are labelled *First Vermont
Edition,* of which 6 are by Isaac Eddy, Weathersfield, Vt., and one by James Hill. VtHi has
copies with map.

1812   [The Holy Bible] The New Testament . . . with the learned and excellent
Preface of the Rev. Thomas Scott, D.D., Author of the commentary on the
Bible, etc. Illustrated with maps . . . J. Seymour, Printer . . . Whiting and
Watson: New-York   **210**

Unpaged   204 × 120 mm   Quincy, Mass. Hist. Soc.

Has Scott's introductory material but not his notes. See 1804–09, No 113; also 1810–12,
No 175. This is a complete Bible but has NT bound before OT. There is no OT title page but
there are introductions to the OT and to the Five Books of Moses, followed by full OT text.

1812   The Holy Bible . . . First New-York Edition . . . George Long, Printer . . . Published by E. Duyckinck, Smith and Forman, Collins and Co., J. Tiebout, S. A.
Burtus, and B. Crane: New-York   **211**

1 vol: 7–735 739–959   195 × 110 mm   CtY, DLC, MWA, NB, NN, NNAB

With Apocrypha (unpaged). Preliminary matter includes To the Reader [by Dr. Wither-spoon], and Order of Books. Tables follow both Testaments. P 735 misnumbered 765.

NN copy has Brown's Concordance (Thomas Kirk, Printer, 1812) and 4 woodcuts; pagination is correct. MWA copy has A. Anderson engravings: *David at his Early Devotions* (facing p 455); *The Wise Men Worshipping Christ* and *The Vision of Simeon* (?) (frontispieces to NT); *Jesus in the Corn Field* (facing p 792).

NT issued separately? (O'Callaghan, p 109).

1812 The Holy Bible ... M. Carey: Philadelphia   **212**

152 × 88 mm   MWA, NN, NNAB

Same as Carey's 1803/02 edition (No 106) except for minor changes. Does not have subject headings. Has doubled ruled lines at head of first text page of each Testament. Initial letter of each signature is in larger type.

Title page and Chapters i to xxxv of Genesis are missing in NN copy.

1812 The Holy Bible ... Stereotype Edition ... Stereotyped by T. Rutt, Shackle-well, London, for the Bible Society of Philadelphia   **213**

1 vol: (633) (192)   152 × 83 mm   CSmH, ICHi, MiU–C, MWA, NN, NNAB, PP

Preliminary matter includes Order of Books and Account of Dates. Tables of Scripture Measures and Table of Time follow OT.

This is the first stereotyped Bible to be printed in the United States. The plates were imported from England by the Philadelphia Bible Society. The British and Foreign Bible Society donated £500 toward the cost and the United States government admitted the plates free of duty. They were received in October 1812, and were immediately turned over to the printer, William Fry of Philadelphia. His initial print run of Bibles was 1050 copies; of NTs, 750 copies (see 1812, No 222A). The sixth printing in May 1814 brought the total number of Bibles to 14,125 copies; the total number of NTs to 3,250.

The Bible Society of Philadelphia, the first in the United States, was organized in December 1808. Its first president was Bishop White, who, as one of the chaplains to Congress, reported on the Aitken Bible in 1792.

1812 The Holy Bible ... Greenough & Stebbins, Printer ... Printed for Thomas and Andrews, West and Richardson, West and Blake: Boston   **214**

151 × 90 mm   MWA

Same as Thomas' 1809 edition (No 166) with error in 1 Tim 4:16 continued.

MH and NN have copies with NT title dated 1811.

1812 The Holy Bible ... Hudson & Goodwin: Hartford   **215**

148 × 87 mm   MWA, NCooHi, NN, NNAB

Same as Hudson & Goodwin edition of 1809 (No 168).

1812 The Holy Bible ... Printed for the New York Bible Society ... by Hudson and Goodwin: Hartford   **216**

146 × 81 mm   Ct, CtY, MWA, NN, OYo, PPL, RPB, WyHi

Same as Hudson & Goodwin 1809 edition (No 168) except for new title pages. The New York Bible Society was organized in Nov 1809; see 1810 NT, No 181.

1812 The Holy Bible ... First American Diamond Edition ... B. W. Sower & Co., Printers ... Published and Sold by John Hagerty: Baltimore   **217**

Text ends Q3   120 × 67 mm   CSmH

Text is prefixed by a Synopsis of the Holy Bible (7 p). Double ruled lines precede text of each Testament and each Book.

MWA and PMA have copies with NT dated 1810. MB, NNAB, and PHi have copies with NT dated 1811. NN has two copies: one with NT dated 1810; another with NT dated 1811.

1812   The Holy Bible . . . Wilmington, Delaware   **218**

Not Located

Wright (p 348), Rumball-Petre (*Rare Bibles* 1st ed, p 34 and *America's First Bibles*, p 161), and Simms (p 130) refer to such an edition but it is not listed in O'Callaghan.

1812   The New Testament . . . J. Seymour, printer . . . Published by Whiting and
         Watson: New York   **219**

Reported as 146 leaves   202 × 120 mm   DLC

1812   The New Testament . . . First New-York edition . . . George Long, Printer . . .
         E. Duyckinck, Smith and Forman, Collins and Co., J. Tiebout, S. A. Burtus,
         and B. Crane: New-York   **220**

Reported as 739–959 [1]   195 × 110 mm   CtHT–W

1812   The New Testament . . . Printed by W. B. & G. Allen, and sold, wholesale and
         retail, at their Bookstore, and by the Principal Booksellers in New-England:
         Haverhill [Massachusetts]   **221**

Unpaged   178 × 104 mm   MBU–T

1812   Explanatory Notes Upon the New Testament. By John Wesley . . . 3d Amer-
         ican Edition. John C. Totten, Printer. Published by Daniel Hitt and Thomas
         Ware, for the Methodist Connection in the United States   **222**

Reported as (vi) (400)   "8vo"   ICU, MB
Wesley Version; see 1791 NT, No 35.

1812   The New Testament . . . Stereotyped by T. Rutt, Shacklewell, London, for
         the Bible Society at Philadelphia: [Philadelphia]   **222A**

Reported as (192)   152 × 83 mm   MWA
Separate issue of NT from 1812 Bible (No 213).

1812   The New Testament . . . Printed and Published by Mathew Carey: Phila-
         delphia   **223**

Reported as 300 p   "12mo"   ViU

1812   The New Testament . . . Hudson and Goodwin: Hartford   **224**

Reported as 334 p   146 × 83 mm   MWA, NjMD

1812   The New Testament . . . Fielding Lucas: Baltimore   **225**

"24mo"   Not Located
Wright, p 390.

1813?   The Holy Bible . . . with references, etc., by the late Rev. John Brown . . .
          Embellished with a series of beautiful engravings. Printed and published by
          T. Kinnersley: New York   **226**

Reported as i-li (1216) 1217–1222 [1]   400 × 210 mm   CO

Preliminary matter includes To the Reader by J. Brown; Introduction; Calculation of Number of Books, Chapters, Verses, Words, etc.; and Order of Books. Following NT are A Collection of Similes, Tables of Scripture Measures, and Table of Offices.

No date appears on the title pages but two of the engravings have "Published as the Act directs by T. Kinnersley, August 1, 1812" and ". . . April 20, 1812." The engravers are Wallis, Charles P. Harrison, J. Barlow, I. Brown, Neagle, and J. Bragge. These engravings are also found in an 1816 London edition (NNAB). It is possible that this book was not printed in America.

1813   The Holy Bible . . . Apocrypha . . . arguments prefixed to the different books . . . by the Reverend Mr. Ostervald . . . Index . . . table . . . Brown's concordance . . . maps . . . elegant historical engravings: George Long, printer . . . Published by Smith & Forman: New-York   **227**

Reported as (viii) (1048) (72)   275 mm   DLC

1813   The Holy Bible . . . Saml. Etheridge, Junr.: Charlestown, Massachusetts **228**

Not Located

O'Callaghan (p 113) reports that he has not seen this Bible, but inferred its publication from having found a "Biblical Map of the Land of Canaan, shewing the situation of principal places mentioned in the Histories of Joshua & the Judges," with the above imprint on it.

1813   The Holy Bible . . . with Observations . . . by . . . Ostervald . . . George Long, Printer . . . Published by Evert Duyckinck, John Tiebout, G. & R. Waite, and Websters and Skinners of Albany: New York   **229**

Text ends 6B4   245 × 187 mm   NN, NNAB

Practical Observations by Rev. Ostervald appear at foot of page throughout text. Preliminary matter (p i-viii) includes frontispiece; The Preliminary Discourse, Giving Some Directions Concerning the Reading of the Holy Scriptures; and Order of Books. Apocrypha has separate signatures and is in smaller type. Family Record follows. Index, Table of Kindred, Table of Time, Table of Offices, and Brown's Concordance (1813) follow NT. Has 2 maps and 9 historical engravings (A. Anderson).

1813   The Holy Bible . . . Mathew Carey: Philadelphia   **230**

242 × 181 mm   InHi, MWA, NN, NNAB, PHi

Same as Carey's 1812/11 quarto (No 208) from standing type, except the plates consist of 10 maps and 13 historical engravings. Concordance (Brooklyn: Thomas Kirk, 1812). Errors in Esther 1:8 and Lev 19:12 are continued.

The copy owned by InHi is said to be the first Bible brought to Indianapolis and was used in the first religious service there (Nowland family). NN has three copies: one on inferior paper with Concordance omitted but with 6 maps and 5 historical engravings; another on inferior paper with Concordance omitted and no plates; a third, with Concordance omitted but with 9 maps and 16 historical engravings, has OT title dated 1813 and NT title dated 1814.

1813   The Holy Bible . . . Printed for Johnson & Warner [by Mathew Carey]: Philadelphia   **231**

1080 p   242 × 181 mm   NN, NNAB

Agrees with 1809 edition printed for Johnson & Warner by Mathew Carey (No 161).

1813/12   The Holy Bible . . . with Scott's preface, preliminary remarks to the several Books, and copious marginal references . . . J. Seymour, Printer . . . Whiting and Watson: New York   **232**

Text ends 6X2   236 × 162 mm   NN

With Apocrypha. Preliminary matter includes a Note by the Publishers. NT, dated 1812, is followed by Index and Tables. Has historical engravings. Maps and Concordance wanting? O'Callaghan (p 111) lists separate edition of NT, dated 1812, with maps. No copy located.

1813 The Holy Bible . . . with Scott's preface, preliminary remarks and marginal references . . . J. Seymour, Printer . . . Whiting and Watson: New York   **233**

212 × 120 mm   NN

Same as Whiting and Watson 1812 edition (No 210).

1813 The Holy Bible . . . Corrected from the Oxford Stereotype Text . . . Printed by E. W., Wm. B., and H. G. Allen: Newburyport [Massachusetts]   **234**

Text ends 3M6   162 × 93 mm   MBAt, MWA, NcWfC, NNAB

Text has subject captions but no catchwords. Verso of title has Order of Books. Tables of Scripture Measures, Money, and Time follow OT. NT, imprinted *E. W. & W. B. Allen . . .*, has Account of Dates and Analysis of the Old and New Testaments on verso.

MWA has another copy with *For the Merrimack, Maine, New Hampshire and other Bible Societies,* in place of *Corrected . . . Text.*

1813 The Holy Bible . . . W. Mercein: New York   **235**

"12mo"   Not Located

Wright, p 391.

1813 The Holy Bible . . . W. Greenough, Printer . . . Printed for Thomas & Andrews, West and Richardson, and West and Blake: Boston   **236**

154 × 90 mm   MWA

Similar to Thomas' 1797 edition (No 57) from standing type.

NN and NNAB have copies with NT dated 1814.

1813 The Holy Bible . . . Printed by Hudson & Goodwin: Hartford   **237**

148 × 87 mm   Ct, MWA, NGlf, NjPT, NN, NSyOHi, OC, PPL

Same as Hudson & Goodwin edition of 1809 (No 168).

1813 The Holy Bible . . . Printed by Mathew Carey: Philadelphia   **238**

147 × 88 mm   MiU, MWA

Same as Carey's 1803/02 duodecimo (No 106) from standing type.

1813? The Holy Bible . . . Stereotype Edition . . . Stereotyped by B. and J. Collins for R. P. and C. Williams: Boston   **239**

Reported as 810 p   145 mm   Not Located

DLC Union Catalog lists location as NBuG but copy was not located there. This seems to be an erroneous date as it is too early for a Collins sterotyped edition; on the other hand pagination does not match the 1818 Williams Bible (No 355).

1813 The Holy Bible . . . W. W. Woodward: Philadelphia   **240**

1 or 2 vols   129 × 62 mm   CSmH, NcD, NN, ViU

Agrees with the 1810 Woodward edition (No 180) without Metrical Psalms.

MWA has copy with 1816 NT; NNAB has copy with 1811 NT. NN has two other copies: one with 1815 NT; another in 2 vols with Metrical Psalms dated 1813.

1813   The New Testament . . . Lincoln & Edmands, Printers . . . Published by E. Larkin . . . and Lincoln & Edmands: Boston   **241**

Unpaged   189 × 109 mm   .   CtHi, MB, MWA
Added are An Account of the Dates and Table of Offices.

1813   The New Testament . . . J. Bouvier, Printer . . . Benjamin Johnson: Philadelphia   **242**

Text ends Z6   170 × 93 mm   NN

1813   The New Testament . . . Mathew Carey: Philadelphia   **243**

Unpaged   "12mo"   DCU

1813   The New Testament . . . J. Bouvier, Printer . . . Published by Thomas M. Longstreth: Philadelphia   **244**

Reported as 271 unnumbered p   "12mo"   PLatS
Title page has Order of Books on verso.

1813   The New Testament . . . John Shryock: Chambersburg, Pennsylvania   **245**

"12mo"   Not Located
Wright, p 391.

1813   The New Testament . . . Second American from the Cambridge Stereotyped Edition . . . Revised and Corrected by Rev. J. McDonald . . . H. C. Southwick: Albany   **246**

"12mo"   Not Located
O'Callaghan (p 116) reports a copy at N but correspondence has failed to confirm this. Error in 1 Tim 4:16. The type was kept standing for several years. See 1816 NT, No 316. NN copy is missing.

1813   The New Testament . . . Corrected from the Oxford Stereotype Text . . . Printed by E. W. & W. B. Allen: Newburyport   **247**

162 × 93 mm   NNAB
Identical with NT of 1813 Allen Bible (No 234).

1813   The New Testament . . . Printed by Todds, Clark & Crandal, for Themselves, and for H. & E. Phinney, Jun.: Hartwick [New York]   **248**

Reported as 271 unnumbered p   157 × 89 mm   CSmH, MWA

1813   The New Testament . . . First American Stereotyped Edition . . . From the Foundry of Joseph D. Fay: New York   **249**

Reported as 311 unnumbered p   155 × 88 mm   ICBS
Has A Table of Kindred.

1813   The New Testament . . . W. Greenough, Printer . . . Thomas and Andrews, West and Richardson and West and Blake: Boston   **250**

Text ends Kk2   154 × 90 mm   NN
Appears to be NT of Thomas' 1797 duodecimo Bible (No 57) from standing type.

1813   The New Testament . . . John Fitch: Westfield, Mass.   **251**

152 × 85 mm   NNAB

NNAB copy ends p 332 — Revelation 21:13 to end missing.

1813   The New Testament . . . E. Duyckinck: New York   **252**

151 × 87 mm   MH, MWA, NN

Agrees with Duyckinck edition of 1804 (No 118). G. Long, Printer appears on verso of title page. Acts 8:9 "corrected" to *sorcecy*. Table of Kindred at end.

1813   Evangelical History: or a Narrative of the Life, Doctrines and Miracles of Jesus Christ, Our Blessed Lord and Saviour, and of His Holy Apostles: Containing the Four Gospels and the Acts: with a General Introduction, and Prefatory Remarks to each Book and Notes, Didactic, Explanatory and Critical. Designed chiefly for those who have not leisure to peruse the larger Works of Voluminous Commentators. By Alden Bradford. [text of John 20:20] Published by Bradford & Read: Boston, and for sale by J. Brewer: Providence; A. Sherman, Jr.: New Bedford; J. Avery: Plymouth; J. Dabney: Salem; J. Babson: Wiscasset; E. Goodale: Hallowell; Varney & Co.: Dover; A. Finley: Philadelphia; Eastburn, Kirk & Co.: New-York   **253**

Reported as (526) 527–528 [1]   145 × 81 mm   DLC, MBAt, MeWC, MWA, NjHi

P 527–528 contain publisher's catalogue and [529] errata. 2 maps. Printed by Watson and Bangs of Boston.

Alden Bradford (1765–1843), a descendant of Governor Bradford and John Alden, graduated from Harvard in 1786, served as Congregational Minister in Wiscasset, Maine, and later was clerk of court there. His experience as a bookseller in Boston was financially unsuccessful. For a time he edited the *Boston Gazette* and served as Secretary of the Commonwealth from 1812 to 1824. His strong anti-Mason activity resulted in his loss of the secretaryship. He had already become a Unitarian and was a man of strong upright character, public spirit, and cultivated tastes. (DAB) See also "Memoir of Alden Bradford" by Samuel Eliot Morrison, in the *Massachusetts Historical Society Proceedings* LV (Oct 1921–June 1922) 153–164.

1813   The New Testament . . . Appointed to be read in churches and families . . . Jonathan Pounder: Philadelphia   **254**

114 × 60 mm   KXSM

Agate type, last signature Ff (V and W not used). The number of leaves in a signature varies.

1813   The New Testament . . . Published by Benjamin & Thomas Kite . . . : Philadelphia   **255**

114 × 60 mm   MWA

1814   The Holy Bible . . . Apocrypha . . . Third Edition . . . Collins and Co.: New-York   **256**

Text ends Dd3   253 × 177 mm   CtY, ICN, MWA NN, NNAB, OCU, ViU

Reprint of Collins' second edition of 1807 (No 142) with minor changes. Concordance (1814).

NN copy has 3 maps and 9 historical engravings; plates are labelled *Engraved for Collins' Quarto-Bible, Third Edition*. NN has another copy without Concordance. CSaT and second ViU copies have engraved illustrations and maps, Ostervald's Practical Observations (1814), and at end, Index and Brown's Concordance (1814).

1814 The Holy Bible . . . M. Carey: Philadelphia **257**

243 × 185 mm   DCU–H, ICN, MB, MdBJ, MWA, NN, NNAB, NHi, PHi, PP

Same as Carey's 1812/11 edition (No 208) but without plates or Concordance. Errors in Lev 19:12 and Esther 1:8 are continued.

NN has four copies: one with 10 maps and 15 historical engravings, Concordance (Thomas Kirk . . . 1812); a second on inferior paper with Concordance omitted but with 6 maps and 5 historical engravings; a third on inferior paper with Concordance and plates omitted; and a fourth on inferior paper with Apocrypha, Concordance, and plates omitted (omission of Apocrypha accounts for break in pagination from 676 to [835]).

1814–16 The Holy Bible . . . with Original Notes, Practical Observations, and Copious Marginal References. By Thomas Scott . . . In Five Volumes. The Fourth American Edition . . . J. Seymour, Printer . . . Dodge and Sayre: New York **258**

5 vols   236 × 178 mm   IaB, MWA, NcD, NjMD, NNAB, OT

The fourth American edition of Scott's Bible (see 1804–09, No 113) was published over the period 1814 to 1816 in 36 numbers at seventy-five cents each. Volume designation appears on each number.

Vol i, Nos i–viii (1814) preliminary matter includes Author's First Preface, General Preface, and Appendix to the General Preface ([i]–xx); Introduction to OT and Books of Moses; text: Genesis–Samuel. Vol ii, Nos ix–xvi (1814) Kings–Proverbs, Chapt. xix. Vol iii, Nos xvii–xxiv (1815) Proverbs, Chapt. xx–Malachi. Vol iv, Nos xxv–xxxi (1816) Matthew–i Corinthians, Chapt. v. Vol v, Nos xxxii–xxxvi (1816) i Corinthians, Chapt. v–Revelation.

NNAB copy is still unbound and in original paper covers. NN and IU have NT only, bound in 2 vols.

1814 The Holy Bible . . . with Copious marginal references, also introductions to all the books and chapters . . . with the general preface . . . of Thomas Scott . . . W. W. Woodward's plan of publishing . . . Griggs & Dickinsons, Printers . . . Printed for, and published by William W. Woodward: Philadelphia **259**

210 × 125 mm   CSmH, CU, ICU, MB, MWA, NcAS, NN, NNAB, PP, PSC–Hi

Scott's Bible; see 1804–09, No 113. Preliminary matter includes Family Record (2 p) before title, Author's First Preface signed by Scott (2 p), and General Preface (v–xx). Entered by the Clerk of Pa. 1814.

1814 The Holy Bible . . . W. Greenough, Printers . . . Printed for Thomas & Andrews, West and Richardson, and West and Blake: Boston **260**

154 × 90 mm   MWA, PWb

Same as Thomas' 1797 duodecimo (No 57) from standing type.

1814 The Holy Bible . . . Mathew Carey: Philadelphia **261**

151 × 87 mm   DLC, MWA, NN

Same as Carey's 1803/02 edition (No 106) from standing type.

1814 The Holy Bible . . . Printed for the Massachusetts Bible Society . . . Hudson and Goodwin: Hartford **262**

148 × 87 mm   Ct, CtY, IaB, IU, MWA, NN, NNAB, NNPM

Same as Hudson and Goodwin edition of 1809 (No 168). Has Tables at end of both Testaments.

The Massachusetts Bible Society was organized in July 1809.

1814   The New Testament . . . taken from the most correct copies of the present
         authorized version. With the marginal readings . . . by Adam Clarke. Printed
         by D. & G. Bruce . . . Published by Eastburn, Kirk & Co.: New York   **263**

Vol I: Reported as 1002 unnumbered p   223 × 175 mm   PMA

For Adam Clarke, see 1811–25, No 188. Preliminary matter includes An Introduction to
the Four Gospels, and to the Acts of the Apostles; and Preface to Matthew. Vol I contains
Gospels and Acts only. Each book is preceded by a preface and there are 3 Chronological
Tables at end. Has one folded map.

Title page has note *Subscriptions received by the publishers; Jonathan Pounder, Philadel-*
phia; Munroe & Francis, and Lincoln & Edmands, Boston; E. F. Backus, Albany; E. Morford, and
John Mill, Charleston; Howe & Deforest, New-Haven; Thomas & Whipple, Newburyport;
Henry Whipple, and Cushing & Appleton, Salem; and Seymour & Williams, Savannah.

1814   The New Testament . . . with an Introduction giving an account of Jewish
         and other sects; with Notes illustrating obscure Passages and explaining
         obsolete Words and Phrases; for use of Schools, Academies, and Private
         Families. By J. A. Cummings, Author of Ancient and Modern Geography . . .
         Flagg and Gould, Printers, Andover [Massachusetts] . . . Published and sold
         by Cummings and Hilliard: Boston   **264**

Unpaged   "12mo"   CSmH, MBAt, MH, MWA

P iv–v and 7–13 only are numbered. Tables of Offices, Tables of Scripture Measures etc.,
and Rules for Pronouncing Scripture Names and Sacred Geography are added to text.

1814   The New Testament . . . Isaac & W. R. Hill, Printers . . . D. Cooledge: Con-
         cord [New Hampshire]   **265**

Text ends Dd5   166 × 93 mm   MWA, NcD, NN, NNAB

Has advertisement on recto of last leaf. NNAB and NcD copies imprinted *I. and W. R.*
Hill.

1814   The New Testament . . . E. Merriam & Co.: Brookfield   **266**

336 p   153 × 86 mm   MWA, NNAB

The type for this edition was apparently set with the edition of 1804 (No 119) as copy.
The first page of text is numbered 3 instead of 1, and the error in pagination at p 237–240 has
been corrected. P 236 is wrongly numbered 226.
MWA copy lacks p 5–8.

1814   The New Testament . . . Hudson and Goodwin: Hartford   **267**

334 p   151 × 84 mm   MBC, MWA, NN

1814   The New Testament . . . William B. Allen & Co.: Newburyport [Massachu-
         setts]   **268**

Text ends O8   122 × 63 mm   CtHi, MB, MiU–C, MWA

Order of Books appears on verso of title.

MWA also has copies with imprints (1) . . . *sold by them, (bound or in sheets) wholesale*
and retail, and by various other Booksellers in New-England, and (2) . . . *Sold wholesale*
and retail by H. G. Allen, Haverhill, Ms. and by the various Booksellers in New-England.

1815   [The Holy Bible] . . . Paul and Thomas, Printers . . . Published by D. Hitt and
         T. Ware, for the Methodist Connexion in the United States: New York   **269**

Reported as (886) (40)   270 × 215 mm   PHi

Above imprint taken from NT title as this copy lacks general title page. Has Anderson
engravings.

1815/14   The Holy Bible . . . Collins & Co.: New York   **270**

253 × 177 mm   NN

Reprint of the 1814 third edition of Collins' Bible (No 256) with same plates and maps. NT and Concordance, dated 1814, have imprint *Collins's third edition*.

1815   The Holy Bible . . . M. Carey: Philadelphia   **271**

242 × 182 mm   MWA, NN, NNAB, PP, ViU

Same as Carey's 1812/11 edition (No 208) except plates consist of 10 maps and 15 historical engravings. Errors in Lev 19:12 and Esther 1:8 are continued. Concordance (1815).

NNAB has another copy with different engravings. NN has second copy with Concordance and plates omitted, NT dated 1816; and a third with Concordance (1812, but without Apocrypha and plates. MB has copy with NT dated 1816.

1815   The Holy Bible . . . Second New York Edition . . . G. Long, Printer . . . E. Duyckinck, Collins & Co., T. & J. Swords, Peter A. Mesier, Samuel A. Burtus, T. A. Ronalds, and G. & R. Waite: New York   **272**

195 × 110 mm   CSmH, MWA, NN

Same as 1812 edition (No 211).

1815   The Holy Bible . . . Apocrypha . . . First Brookfield Edition . . . E. Merriam and Co.: Brookfield   **273**

960 p   192 × 110 mm   CtY, MWA, NN, NNAB

Closely resembles the E. Duyckinck, etc. edition of 1812 (No 211). Preliminary matter includes To the Reader [by Dr. Witherspoon] and Account of the Dates. Apocrypha is unpaged. Tables follow both Testaments.

This edition consisted of 12,000 copies (O'Callaghan, p 124).

1815   The Holy Bible . . . Stereotype Edition. Stereotyped by T. Rutt, Shacklewell, London, for the Bible Society at Baltimore. Edes, Printer: Baltimore   **274**

968 p   191 × 108 mm   DLC, NNAB, ViU

Order of Books and Account of Dates precede text.

The Bible Society of Baltimore was founded in September 1810. In its Sixth Report, presented at a meeting in September 1816, the Society reported that "the Brevier octavo Stereotype plates," part of which had arrived the year before, were now all in hand and an edition of 500 copies was being printed. It was also reported that plans were under way for a second edition of 2,500 copies. These plates were later sold to the American Bible Society; see 1829, No 673.

1815   The Holy Bible . . . Apocrypha . . . Anson Whipple: Walpole [New Hampshire]   **275**

1 vol: (735) 740–959 [1]   188 × 105 mm   CSmH, ICN, KyLo, MB, MBU–T, MWA, NN, NNAB

Preliminary matter includes To the Publick, Account of Dates, Order of Books, Tables of Scripture Measures, and Table of Time. Apocrypha (88 leaves) is unpaged. Table of Offices appears on last leaf.

This is the first Bible printed in New Hampshire. O'Callaghan (p 125) says that Whipple was Isaiah Thomas' son-in-law and that Thomas owned the press on which the Bible was printed. Typesetting began about 1810 and the printing progressed to Deuteronomy 26 when the project was suspended and not resumed until 1812. Rumball-Petre (*Rare Bibles* p 29) says 8,000 copies were printed on coarse paper.

1815   The Holy Bible . . . Munroe, Francis and Parker: Boston   **276**

720 p   161 × 94 mm   NN

Has Order of Books on verso of title. Table of Scripture Measures and A Chronological Index of Years and Times follow OT.

1815   The Holy Bible . . . Cummings and Hilliard: Boston   **277**

720 p   161 × 95 mm   MWA, NN

Follows exactly the Munroe, Francis, and Parker duodecimo of this year (No 276).

1815   The Holy Bible . . . Wm. B. Allen & Co.: Newburyport [Massachusetts] **278**

720 p   160 × 95 mm   CtY, MWA, NN

Appears to be from same type as Munroe, Francis, and Parker edition of this year (No 276).

1815   The Holy Bible . . . Stereotyped and Printed by D. & G. Bruce: New-York **279**

684 p   160 × 89 mm   MB, MWA, NN, NNAB, NNC, NjMD

Nonpareil type. Has Tables at end of both Testaments.

This is the first Bible printed from stereotype plates cast in the United States. Verso of title page reads "This first American stereotype Bible has been copied from the Edinburgh edition printed under the revision of the General Assembly of the Kirk of Scotland, and carefully compared with the Cambridge, Oxford, Hartford and New York editions."

David Bruce emigrated from Scotland to America in 1770, and pursued his trade as a printer. In 1804 he and his brother established the printing firm of D. & G. Bruce in New York. In 1812 David Bruce went to England and there learned what he could of the stereotyping process. On his return he introduced a number of improvements in the process, which soon came into wide use in America. (*American Dictionary of Printing and Bookmaking* p 72–73.) See also 1816 Collins Bible, No 296.

1815   The Holy Bible . . . W. Greenough, Printer . . . Printed for Lincoln and Edmands: Boston   **280**

Reported as 814 unnumbered p   151 × 89 mm   MWA, PMA
PMA copy lacks general title page.

1815   The Holy Bible . . . Hudson and Goodwin: Hartford   **281**

148 × 87 mm   MWA, NN, NNAB

Same as 1809 edition (No 168) but has new title pages.

1815   The Holy Bible . . . Printed by Mathew Carey: Philadelphia   **282**

147 × 88 mm   MiU

Same as Carey's 1803/02 duodecimo (No 106) from standing type.

1815   The New Testament . . . Hudson and Goodwin: Hartford   **283**

344 p   "12mo"   Not Located

O'Callaghan, p 127. Errors in Acts 6:3 and 1 Tim 4:16.

1815   The New Testament . . . Printed by George Hough . . . : Concord [New Hampshire]   **284**

Reported as 336 p   190 × 109 mm   MWA
Has Table of Kindred on last page.

1815   The New Testament . . . Robert Patterson: Pittsburgh   **285**

Unpaged   165 × 80 mm   PPi
Printed by S. Engles.

1815   The New Testament . . . Carefully examined and corrected, by the Rev. S. Payson, D.D. Printed, published, and sold by Simeon Ide: New-Ipswich, N. H.   **286**

Unpaged   158 × 89 mm   MWA
Strip pasted across title, and, originally, over "Carefully . . . Payson, D.D.": *First New-Ipswich Edition.*

O'Callaghan (p 137) quotes from Kidder and Gould's *History of New Ipswich* (Boston 1852, p 237): "Mr. Ide, having purchased a small Ramage press and a font of bourgeois type which had already been pretty well worn on an edition of Shakespeare, placed them in the blacksmith's shop on his father's farm, and undertook to print an edition of the New Testament in duodecimo form. By the assistance of a sister, about twelve years old, in setting type, it was accomplished in about six months. That this, his first publication, might be as free from errors as possible, he engaged the Rev. Dr. Payson, of Rindge, to read the proof sheets. As there was only type enough to set twelve pages at a time, he walked to his house, a distance of four miles, twice a week, to read proofs with him; and to give greater currency to the edition, he prevailed on Dr. Payson to allow him to insert on the title page, 'Revised and corrected by Rev. S. Payson, D.D.' Some of the Doctor's friends having got the impression that he had been making a new Translation of the Testament, it gave him no little uneasiness. To relieve him of this, Mr. Ide printed the words 'first New-Ipswich edition,' and pasted the slip over the obnoxious line. An edition of 5000 was worked off, and 1000 copies, in full binding, were sold to the New Hampshire Bible Society, for $280, which was less than cost, in order to raise money to purchase paper. The others were retailed at fifty cents a copy."

1815   The New Testament . . . First American Stereotyped Edition . . . Published by West and Richardson: Boston   **287**

Reported as 312 p   156 × 87 mm   MB
Added is A Table of Kindred.

1815   The New Testament . . . Stereotyped and printed by D. & G. Bruce . . . : New-York   **288**

Reported as 529–684   155 × 90 mm   CtHT–W

1815   The New Testament . . . E. Duyckinck: New York   **289**

151 × 87 mm   MWA
Reprint of the Duyckinck and Mesier NT of 1804 (No 118). See also 1809, No 172. The error in Acts 8:9 "corrected" from *sorcercy* to *sorcecy.*

1815   The New Testament . . . Hudson and Goodwin: Hartford   **290**

Reported as 334 p   146 × 81 mm   NjMD

1815   The New Testament, with an Analysis of the several books and chapters. By the Rev. J. Wesley, M.A. A. Paul, Printer. Published by D. Hitt and T. Ware for the Methodist Connexion in the U. States: New York   **291**

Reported as 459 p   102 × 54 mm   MWA, PH, TNMB
This seems to be the AV text with Wesley introductions. For Wesley Version, see 1791 NT, No 35.

1816   Exposition of the Old and New Testaments. By Matthew Henry . . . Hogan
         & Towers: Philadelphia   **292**

6 vols   Not Located

O'Callaghan, p 134. This is said to be the first American edition of the commentary by
Matthew Henry, first published in London, 1708–10, in 5 vols. Matthew Henry (1662–1714)
was a Presbyterian minister at Chester. He died after completing the Gospels and the rest was
prepared by several ministers. While not a critical commentary, it was long celebrated as the
best of English commentaries for devotional purposes and is still in print.

1816   The Holy Bible . . . together with the Apocrypha . . . J. Holbrook's Stereo-
         type Copy. First Edition. : Brattleborough [Vermont]   **293**

Reported as (8) 9–683 (160) (2) 687–930 (2) 243 × 181 mm   CtY, MAnP, MWA, VtHi

Format agrees with that of the Collins 1816 quarto (No 296). *J. Holbrook's Stereotype
Copy. First Edition.* appears inside octagonal device on title page. NT title imprinted *Stereotyped by B. & J. Collins: New York.* Plates.

VtHi copy has added engraved titles (1816). VtHi has another copy dated 1816 but
imprinted *Second Edition.*

This is the first of many editions printed in Brattleborough (or Brattleboro).

In 1803 William Fessenden (1779–1815), a young printer from New Hampshire, came to
Brattleboro and a year later established a newspaper and printing business. Among his pub-
lications was Webster's spelling book, the plates and rights to which he had secured from
Anthony Haswell at Bennington. His business flourished and he married a daughter of John
Holbrook (1761–1838), a successful business man who had built up a considerable business
in shipping meat and other products down the river to Connecticut. In 1815 Fessenden died
very suddenly, and his father-in-law, then living at Warehouse Point, Conn., returned to
Brattleboro to take over Fessenden's business which he successfully developed into an industry
that was an important factor in the growth of the town. He immediately undertook the publication of the above Bible. "For undertaking to publish a large family Bible, by subscription, in
this obscure town so far away from the great centers of trade, Mr. Holbrook was ridiculed
by the greatest publishers of the day in New York and Boston, and certain failure of the
enterprise was by them confidently predicted." To secure an adequate supply of paper Mr.
Holbrook set up a paper mill, which in itself was quite a project in an area with no machine
shop, no iron foundry, nor engine lathe. The iron castings were brought by horse from
Rhode Island. William Fessenden's brother, Joseph, joined the firm but died in 1834. Deacon
Holbrook withdrew from the firm in 1832 when he became president of the bank. John C.
Holbrook and others then bought out the old firm. The company failed during the financial
crisis of 1836 but was reorganized as a joint stock concern as the Brattleboro Typographic
Company which "died a gradual lingering death." (Henry Burnham, *Brattleboro . . . Early
History with Biographical Sketches of Some of Its Citizens,* D. Leonard: Brattleboro, 1880,
p 34–35. See also Mary R. Cabot, *The Annals of Brattleboro,* Press of E. L. Hildreth and Co.:
Brattleboro, 1921, Vol I, p 232–235 and 1681–1895.)

In 1837 the Brattleboro Typographic Company approached the ABS with proposals for printing but the ABS Managers considered the matter "inexpedient."

The number of entries for this firm in its various forms during the 1820s and early 1830s is
indication of its success.

1816   The Holy Bible . . . M. Carey: Philadelphia   **294**

242 × 182 mm   NN

Same as Carey quarto of 1812/11 (No 208). With Apocrypha and Concordance (1816).
Errors in Esther 1:8 and Lev 19:12 continued. 70 maps and historical engravings.

This Bible was published originally at $12.50, $15, and $18 (O'Callaghan, p 130).

1816 – 18   The Holy Bible . . . with Thomas Scott's Notes . . . In three volumes . . .
            The Fourth American quarto edition, on a new and cheap plan: arranged in

a different manner from any former edition . Griggs & Co., Printers…Printed for and published by William W. Woodward: Philadelphia   **295**

3 vols: Vol I, (4) (15) (854) (8); Vol II, (2) (932); Vol III, (2) (800) (16)
242 × 178 mm   MWA, NcU, NN, NHi, ViU, ViRU

Scott's Annotated Bible; see 1804–09, No 113. Vol II dated 1817 and Vol III dated 1818.

VRU copy has Family Records, Prefaces, and Recommendations preceding text and 8 p of advertisements of religious books at end of Vol I. OC has Vol II only. NNAB has Vol III only, lacking all after end of Philippians.

1816 The Holy Bible . . . Collins's Stereotyped Edition . . . Apocrypha . . . With Canne's Marginal Notes and References . . . Stereotyped by B. & J. Collins . . . Printed and Sold by Collins and Co. . . . : New-York   **296**

1 vol: (8) 9–682 (160) 678–898 899–932 (56)   241 × 178 mm   ICN, MB, MWA, NjMD, NN, NNAB

Preliminary matter includes frontispiece (*The Murder of Abel*), Advertisement to the Stereotype Edition, To the Reader [by Dr. Witherspoon], and Account of the Dates with Order of Books on verso. Family Record follows OT. Index, Tables, and Concordance (1815) follow NT.   20 historical engravings and 4 maps.

MBU–T has undated copy which lacks Brown's Concordance and is imprinted *Published by Charles Ewer: Boston. Stereotyped by B. & J. Collins.*

This is the first stereotyped quarto edition of the Bible printed in the United States. To do the stereotyping, the publishers employed John Watts, who introduced the art into the United States about 1813, having learned about the process from Richard Watts and Andrew Wilson in London. It was issued with and without Apocrypha: with Apocrypha and Concordance; with Concordance; with Ostervald's Notes; with Ostervald's Notes and Concordance; and with Ostervald's Notes, Apocrypha, and Concordance. Prices ranged from $3.50 to $18.50 according to contents, paper, and binding. See O'Callaghan, p 129–130.

1816/18 The Holy Bible . . . with Thomas Scott's Notes. In Five Volumes . . . The Sixth American, from the Second London Edition . . . S. L. Loomis, Hart and Lincoln, Printers . . . Published by Sheldon & Goodrich, and Simeon L. Loomis: Hartford   **297**

5 vols: Vol I, 953 p; Vol II, 1014 p; Vol III, 913 p; Vol IV, 704 p; Vol V, 720 p.
240 × 178 mm   AU, MWA, NN, NNAB, NRU

This is the first Connecticut edition of Scott's 1804–09 Bible (No 113). Vol I (1816) Prefaces followed by OT text, Genesis-Samuel. Vol II (1817) Kings-Proverbs. Vol III (1818) Ecclesiastes-Malachi, followed by Family Record. Vol I of NT (1816) Matthew-Acts. Vol II (1817) Romans-Revelation, with Tables, Etc., and Concordance (Printed . . . by John Holbrook, Brattleborough, Vt., n. d.) at end.

NNAB copy has each volume bound in two parts, thus making ten books. Each has separate title page, but volume designations I to V only are used. Part designations are labelled on the spine of each book. No Concordance. K has copy with all volumes dated 1817; no Concordance.

1816 The Holy Bible . . . with Original Notes and Practical Observations. By Thomas Scott. In Six Volumes. Fifth American Edition . . . Published by Samuel T. Armstrong: Boston   **298**

6 vols   210 × 123 mm   MH, MWA, NjP

Scott's Bible; see 1804–09, No 113. Also known as Armstrong's first Boston edition. Vols I–IV, preliminary matter includes Preface, Introduction to OT and to the Book of Moses; OT text. Vols V–VI, preliminary matter includes Introduction to NT; NT text. At end of Vol VI are Retrospective Review of the Predictions Contained in the Revelation of St. John, Tables of Scripture Measures, Table of Offices, Family Record, and Names of Subscribers. Text has footnotes throughout and each book has an Introduction. Each volume has separate signatures.

NT sometimes dated 1815. MAnP has set with Vols I–III dated 1816, Vols IV and VI dated 1817, and Vol V dated 1815.

MB, MWA, and NN have Armstrong's second Boston edition, variously dated 1817 or 1818; NcD has NT only. MWA and ViU have Armstrong's third Boston edition, Armstrong with Crocker & Brewster, Boston, and J. P. Haven, New York, 1823; NRU has Vols II, III, and IV only without New York imprint.

1816 The Holy Bible . . . Stereotype Edition. Stereotyped by T. Rutt, Shacklewell, London, for The Bible Society at Philadelphia: [Philadelphia]   **299**

1 vol: (968) (303)   200 × 110 mm   NNAB
Order of Books precedes each Testament. Tables at end.

1816 The Holy Bible . . . Stereotyped by B. & J. Collins . . . Printed and Published by E. F. Backus: Albany   **300**

1 vol: (756) (181) (234)   190 × 106 mm   MWA, N, NN, NNAB
Preliminary matter includes Address to the Reader [by Dr. Witherspoon], and Order of Books. Family Record follows Apocrypha.

1816 The Holy Bible . . . Printed and published by W. Mercein: New York   **301**

684 p   160 × 89 mm   NN
Tables between OT and NT.

1816 The Holy Bible . . . [no publisher given]: Hudson, New York   **302**

"8vo"   Not Located
Wright, p 391.

1816 The Holy Bible . . . Stereotyped by E. & J. White, for "The New-York Bible Society," and "The Auxiliary New-York Bible Society": New York   **303**

1 vol: (832) (254)   155 × 87 mm   DLC, MiAlbC, MWA, NN, NNAB
Brevier Duodecimo Bible. Preliminary matter includes Order of Books. NT imprint reads *Published by the American Bible Society*. Tables on verso of NT title. Length of printed matter on page varies.

NNAB and MWA copies have imprint of New York Bible Society on both general and NT title pages.

The imprint of the American Bible Society is seen for the first time on this Bible. The ABS was founded in May 1816 "to encourage the wider circulation of the Holy Scriptures without note or comment," using "the version now in common use." Managers of the new organization felt that their first exertions ought to be directed toward the procurement of well-executed stereotype plates, for accommodation of large areas of the American continent. They accordingly contracted for three sets of stereotype plates of duodecimo size and three sets of octavo size for the English Bible to be ready in the spring of 1817. During the interim when the plates were in preparation, the New York Bible Society, which was founded in 1809, and the New York Auxiliary Bible Society united in presenting the American Bible Society with the stereotype plates of a duodecimo size Bible in brevier type which they had had made with funds contributed by other societies and individuals in different parts of the country. The ABS printed its first edition of 10,000 copies from these plates of which the above described Bible is a copy. It was issued in November 1816 and sold for $1 to $1.85.

By the end of 1820, the ABS had the following sets of plates for the whole Bible and for separate NTs:

BIBLE: 1 set — Brevier Duodecimo, stereotyped by E. & J. White, priced at 85¢ to $1. See 1817, No 332.

> 3 sets — Minion Duodecimo, stereotyped by D. & G. Bruce, priced at 64¢ to 73¢. See 1819, No 377.
>
> 3 sets — Long Primer Octavo, stereotyped by E. & J. White, priced at $1.25 to $3. See 1818, No 347.
>
> NT: 1 set — Bourgeois Duodecimo, stereotyped by D. & G. Bruce, priced at 30¢ to 35¢. See 1819, No 388.
>
> 2 sets — Brevier Octodecimo, stereotyped by A. Chandler, priced at 22¢ to 25¢. See 1820, No 412.

The prices given above were current in 1821 and the variations in cost were due to differences in paper and binding.

In 1824, one set of plates for a New Testament of octavo size in pica type, stereotyped by A. Chandler, was acquired. This sold for 56¢ to $1.13. See 1824, No 503.

Of the above plates, two sets for the whole Bible (one Minion Duodecimo, and one Long Primer Octavo) were loaned to the Kentucky Bible Society which was to be responsible for printing editions for distribution west of the Alleghanies. See 1819, No 376. (See also *American Bible Society Reports*, 1817–1825.)

1816   The Holy Bible . . . Stereotyped by E. & J. White. Published by the American Bible Society: New-York   **304**

1 vol: (832) (254)   155 × 87 mm   MWA, NN, NNAB

This Brevier Duodecimo is the first Bible which carries the imprint of the American Bible Society on both general and NT title pages. It is from the same plates as the 1816 edition (No 303) printed by the ABS bearing imprint of the New York Bible Society.

The *ABS Report* for 1842 (p 30) says a new book is being prepared to take the place of the Brevier Duodecimo, for the plates are worn out. See 1844, No 1209.

1816/08   The Holy Bible . . . Printed by Mathew Carey: Philadelphia   **305**

151 × 90 mm   NN

Same as Carey's seventh edition of 1803/02 (No 106) from standing type. NT imprinted *Whitehall. Printed for William Young. 1808.* See 1808 NT, No 154.

1816   The Holy Bible . . . W. Greenough, Printer . . . Printed for Lincoln and Edmands: Boston   **306**

Text ends Kk12   151 × 87 mm   MWA

1816   The Holy Bible . . . Printed by Hudson and Co.: Hartford   **307**

147 × 88 mm   MWA, NNAB

Reprint of Hudson & Goodwin edition of 1809 (No 168). Error in 1 Tim 4:16 continued. CtY and NN have copies with NT imprinted *Hudson and Goodwin, 1815.*

1816   The Holy Bible . . . W. W. Woodward: Philadelphia   **308**

Unpaged: last signature S[3]*   131 × 62 mm   CSmH, MWA, NN

NT followed by pages for Memorandums and Metrical Psalms (1811).

MWA copy lacks Metrical Psalms.

1816   The New Testament . . . Translated from the Latin Vulgate . . . Mathew Carey: Philadelphia   **309**

Reported as 214? p   245 × 188 mm   DGU

Rheims Version, reprinted from 1805 Bible (No 120). A school edition, with Psalms.

1816 The New Testament . . . Stereotype Edition . . . Stereotyped by T. Rutt, Shacklewell, London, for the Bible Society at Philadelphia: [Philadelphia]
                                                                            310

303 [1] p   202 × 110 mm   MWA, NN, NNAB, PP
Appears to be NT from the Bible Society of Philadelphia edition of the Bible of this year (No 299). Has Tables at end of text.

1816 The New Testament . . . P. M. Lafourcade: Philadelphia   **311**

Unpaged   198 × 118 mm   NN, PHi, PP
NN copy interleaved with manuscript translation of NT by P. Doddridge, with his autograph on title page.

1816 The New Testament . . . Robert Ferguson & Co., Printers . . . Published by Cramer, Spear and Eichbaum: Pittsburgh   **312**

Reported as 249 p   180 × 102 mm   CSmH

1816 The New Testament . . . Robert Porter: Wilmington, Delaware   **313**

Reported as 276 p   170 × 100 mm   DeU

1816 The New Testament . . . Stereotyped by B. & J. Collins . . . Printed and Sold by Sheldon & Goodrich: Hartford   **314**

290 p   164 × 93 mm   NN

1816 The New Testament . . . Printed by John Mann . . . : Dover [New-Hampshire]
                                                                            315

Unpaged   161 × 93 mm   MWA

1816 The New Testament . . . The Second American, from the Cambridge Stereotype Edition; Carefully revised and corrected, by the Rev. John M'Donald, of Albany. Printed and sold by S. Southwick: Albany. Sold, also, wholesale and retail, by S. Wood: New-York   **316**

Unpaged   159 × 84 mm   MWA
See 1813 NT, No 246. On last page of text, "Finis" is enclosed in a design of feathers and pearls.

1816 The New Testament . . . Stereotyped by D. & G. Bruce, New York . . . Printed by Thomas Desilver: Philadelphia   **317**

335 p   158 × 87 mm   MWA, NN, NNAB
Has Order of Books and Table of Kindred, etc.

1816 The New Testament . . . Printed by Jesse Cochran: Windsor, Vt.   **318**

Text ends Dd5   156 × 90 mm   CSmH, MWA, NjMD, NNAB, NNU–W, VtHi
Some signatures are in different size type.

1816 The New Testament . . . E. Merriam and Co. . . . Brookfield [Massachusetts]
                                                                            319

Reported as 336 p   153 × 86 mm   MWA

1816   The New Testament . . . W. Greenough, Printer . . . Lincoln and Edmands: Boston   **320**

Text ends Kk12   152 × 91 mm   NN

1816   The New Testament . . . E. Duyckinck: New York   **321**

151 × 87 mm   MWA

Reprint of 1804 NT (No 118). See also 1815, No 289. The "corrected" error still stands in Acts 8:9.

1816?   The New Testament . . . Isaac Collins: Trenton   **322**

"16mo"   Not Located

Wright, p 392. This must be a wrong date, for Isaac Collins moved to New York in 1796 and took his son into partnership.

1816   The New Testament . . . George Goodwin & Sons: Hartford   **323**

140 × 83 mm   DLC

DLC copy ends on p 324 with Rev 13:13.

1816   The New Testament . . . William B. Allen & Co.: Newburyport   **324**

122 × 63 mm   MWA, NNAB

Appears to be a reissue of Allen NT of 1814 (No 268).

1817/18   The Holy Bible . . . Including marginal readings and parallel texts. With a commentary and critical notes . . . By Adam Clarke . . . Second American Edition . . . Abraham Paul, Printer . . . Published by Daniel Hitt and Abraham Paul: New York   **325**

4 vols: unpaged   284 × 227 mm   ICN, MWA

For Adam Clarke, see 1811–25, No 188. Vol i (1817) and Vol ii (no title page or date), OT text. Vol i (1818) and Vol ii (1818), NT text. Length of printed matter on page varies.

1817   The Holy Bible . . . M. Carey & Son: Philadelphia   **326**

243 × 185 mm   DCL, MWA, NjPT, NN, NNAB, PHi, ViU

Same as Carey's 1812/11 quarto (No 208) from standing type. No Apocrypha or Concordance. Error in Lev 19:12 continued. 9 maps and 16 historical engravings.

1817/16   The Holy Bible . . . with marginal notes and references . . . Apocrypha . . . Brown's Concordance . . . an account of the lives and martyrdom of the Apostles and Evangelists . . . J. Holbrook's Stereotype Copy. Seventh Edition.: Brattleborough, Vt.   **327**

1 vol: (8) 8–683 [1] (160) (2) 687–898 (2) 899–930 (2) (56)   242 × 178 mm
                                                                               NNAB

Appears to be same as Collins' stereotype quarto of 1816 (No 296) except for a few differences in material added to text. See also Holbrook's first edition, 1816, No 293. Preliminary matter includes frontispiece (chart), added engraved title dated 1816, To the Reader, Account of Dates, and Order of Books. Family Record follows OT. Preceding NT are frontispiece, engraved title (1816), and NT title dated 1816 with imprint *Stereotyped by B. and J. Collins, Printed and sold by John Holbrook, Brattleborough, Vermont*. Index, Tables, etc., An Account of Lives of Apostles, and Concordance (1816) at end. Illustrated with 5 single- and 2 double-page maps and charts and 17 additional engravings and woodcuts. Three of these, *Angel with Book, Absalom,* and *Creation,* are signed by Anderson.

Union Catalog has card locating copy at DLC "dated 1816–1818 with 1816 NT and Concordance." No explanation is given as to where 1818 date appears. MWA has copies marked Third Edition and Ninth Edition, both dated 1817 but with 1816 engraved titles.

1817/16   The Holy Bible . . . with Canne's marginal notes and references . . . Stereotyped by B. & J. Collins . . . Printed and Sold by Collins and Co. . . . : New-York   **328**

240 × 178 mm   CSmH, CtY, MnU, N, NN, NNAB

Reprint of Collins' stereotype quarto of 1816 (No 296) except Family Record follows Apocrypha. With frontispiece, maps, and plates. NT and Concordance dated 1816.
NN copy has Concordance dated 1818.

1817   The Holy Bible . . . with Marginal Notes and References . . . John Brown's Concordance, &c. &c. Embellished with twenty-five maps and historical engravings. Published by D. & E. Fenton: Trenton   **329**

Reported as (1080) (72)   234 × 183 mm   MWA, NjT

Concordance paged separately and bears imprint *Printed and Published by Mathew Carey & Son: Philadelphia, 1817.*

1817   The Holy Bible . . . Stereotyped by D. & G. Bruce, New York . . . W. E. Norman: Hudson   **330**

837 p   168 × 93 mm   NN

MWA has copy with imprint *Stereotyped for the American Bible Society by D. & G. Bruce . . . Printed by Daniel Fanshaw, 8th edition.*

1817/18   The Holy Bible . . . Stereotyped by B. & J. Collins, New York . . . Printed by Websters and Skinners: Albany   **331**

792 p   160 × 90 mm   NNAB, NNC

Preliminary matter includes Order of Books and Account of Dates. Tables of Scripture Measures follow OT. Error in 1 Tim 4:16 *thy* doctrine, for *the* doctrine. NT dated 1818.
O'Callaghan (p 139) notes copy with double set of signatures — one in 12s and one in 6s.

1817   The Holy Bible . . . [Daniel Fanshaw, Printer]. Stereotyped by E. & J. White for the American Bible Society: New-York   **332**

155 × 87 mm   NN

Reprint of 1816 ABS Brevier Duodecimo (No 303).
MWA has copy with NT dated 1816.
Daniel Fanshaw, of 20 Sloat Lane, obtained a ten-year contract with the ABS which was twice renewed. In 1826 he put into the Bible House on Nassau Street the first power presses (Treadwell) ever used in a book office in New York and soon acquired nine more. His contract was not renewed in 1844, partly due to his refusal to put in larger presses. His printing business then shrank but he had invested in real estate uptown and at his death in 1860 was reputed to be a millionaire. Among his eccentricities were his refusal to wear an overcoat and an item in his will that would disinherit his son should he ever use tobacco. (Wright, p 334.)

1817   The Holy Bible . . . M. Carey & Son: Philadelphia   **333**

152 × 90 mm   NN

Same as Carey's 1803/02 duodecimo (No 106) from standing type. Has Metrical Psalms added (Wm. Young, 1815).

PHi and second NN copies have NT imprint *Whitehall. Printed for Wm. Young . . . 1808.* See 1808, No 154.

1817   The Holy Bible . . . W. Greenough, Printer . . . Printed for Lincoln and Edmands: Boston . . . sold also by Collins & Co.: New York   **334**

Text ends Kk12   151 × 87 mm   MB, MWA, NN, NNAB, ViU

"The Property of   " appears in ornamented border on verso of title; Order of Books follows with Account of Dates on verso. Tables follow OT. Error in 1 Tim 4:16, *thy* doctrine, for *the* doctrine.

MWA also has NT bound separately.

1817   The Holy Bible . . . Printed by Hudson and Co.: Hartford   **335**

147 × 87 mm   CtY, MWA, NN, NNAB

Reprint of Hudson & Goodwin edition of 1809 (No 168). Error in 1 Tim 4:16 continued.

1817/18   The Holy Bible . . . Stereotyped by B. & J. Collins . . . Printed and sold by Collins & Co.: New York   **336**

1 vol: (690) (209)   129 × 64 mm   NNAB

Preliminary matter includes To the Reader and List of Books. NT title dated 1818 with imprint *Published by Collins and Hannay . . . J. & J. Harper, Printers.*

1817   The New Testament . . . [Daniel Fanshaw, Printer] . . . Stereotyped by E. and J. White for "The American Bible Society": New-York   **337**

215 p   196 × 110 mm   MWA, NN, NNAB

Same as Long Primer Octavo NT accompanying ABS Bible of 1818 (No 347).

1817   The New Testament . . . Printed by H. & E. Phinney, and sold by them wholesale and retail, at their Bookstore: Cooperstown, N. Y.   **338**

Unpaged   165 × 90 mm   MBU–T, MWA, NjMD

Vignette on title page (*Christ crucified*).

First NT issued by this firm. See 1822 Bible, No 439.

1817   The New Testament . . . Stereotype Edition . . . Stereotyped by B. and J. Collins, New-York. Printed and sold by L. Lockwood: Bridgeport [Connecticut]   **339**

Reported as 290 [1] p   159 × 91 mm   DLC, MWA

Tables of Kindred on last page.

1817   The New Testament . . . translated out of the Latin Vulgate . . . And first puplished [sic] by the English College of Rhemes, Anno 1582 . . . Newly revised and corrected according to the Clementin edition of the Scriptures . . . Printed by W. Duffy: Georgetown, D. C.   **340**

516 p   156 × 80 mm   DGU, DLC, NjMD, NN

Rheims Version, from 1811 Dublin edition. Preliminary matter includes Admonition with Letter of Pope Pius VI on verso. Approbations, which follows, has on verso "Georgetown, February 20, 1817. Having had this edition of the New Testament printed in Georgetown, by Wm. Duffy, examined; it has been found strictly conformable to the Dublin Edition of the same work printed in 1811, and also that printed in 1814. Hence I permit it to be published.

[signed] Leonard [Neale], Archbishop of Baltimore." Tables and List of Subscribers follow text.

MWA has a portion only, with title *The Holy Gospels . . . Printed by W. Duffy, bookseller and stationer: Georgetown, D. C.*, (8) (234) p, with the Acts of the Apostles beginning on p 230 and running to chapter 3, verse 4. The Approbation on p [8] reads as above.

1817   The New Testament . . . Printed and sold by Robert Porter: Wilmington   *341*

Reported as 276 p   155 × 90 mm   DeWI

1817   The New Testament . . . Printed by George Goodwin and Sons: Hartford   *342*

334 p   148 × 87 mm   NN, NNAB

Appears to be NT of Hudson and Goodwin Bible of 1809 (No 168) with error in 1 Tim 4:16 continued.

1817   The New Testament . . . Stereotyped by B. and J. Collins . . . Published by
                Sheldon and Goodrich: Hartford   *343*

210 p   129 × 64 mm   NN, NNAB

Same as NT of Goodrich Bible of 1818 (No 354). Frontispiece has notation *Engraved for S. G. Goodrich's Pearl Bible.*

1818–20   The Holy Bible . . . with Notes . . . Together with appropriate Introductions, Tables and Indexes. Prepared and arranged by the Rev. George
                D'Oyly, B.D., and the Rev. Richard Mant, D.D. . . . Under the direction of
                the Society for Promoting Christian Knowledge . . . The first American Edition, with Additional Notes, selected and arranged by John Henry Hobart,
                D.D., Bishop of the Protestant Episcopal Church in the State of New York
                . . . Printed and Published by T. and J. Swords: New-York   *344*

2 vols   244 × 186 mm   DLC, FU, MH, MWA, NN, NNAB, NHi, ViW

Vol I (1818) preliminary matter includes Advertisement to the American Edition, Dedication to the Archbishop of Canterbury, General Introduction to Bible, Introduction to OT, Dedication to King James, and Order of Books; text: Genesis-Isaiah. Vol II (1820) text: Jeremiah-Revelation; at end are Index, Tables, List of Authors, and Family Record.

O'Callaghan (p 143) notes that this Bible was originally to have been issued in numbers. Each signature has volume number to which it belongs.

Thomas and James Swords established their printing business about 1786, printing periodicals and general literature and gradually increasing their theological publications until they practically became the unofficial printers to the Protestant Episcopal Church. Thomas was for 30 years vestryman of Trinity Church. James retired in 1832, becoming president of the Washington Fire Insurance Company, and Edward Stanford joined the firm, which was then known as Swords and Stanford and Company. After Thomas died in 1843, his sons Edward and James joined the firm, which was known as Stanford and Swords until 1855 when it ceased. (C. E. Butler, "T. and J. Swords, Publishers," *NYPL Bulletin* xxv, No 2 [Feb 1954] 89–93.)

1818   The Holy Bible . . . M. Carey & Son: Philadelphia   *345*

242 × 182 mm   CSmH, DCL, NjHi, NN

Same as Carey quarto of 1812 / 11 (No 208) except it has 100 maps and historical engravings. The plates included here previously appeared in Carey's quarto of 1816 (No 294) with 32 different ones added. Concordance (1818).

Number of plates varies in copies for this year. NN has another copy with NT imprint *Published by H. C. Carey & I. Lea . . . 1822* and Concordance imprint *Mathew Carey & Son . . . 1821.*

1818   The Holy Bible . . . J. Holbrook's Stereotype Copy: Brattleborough   **346**

242 × 178 mm   MWA, VtHi

Reprint of Holbrook quarto of 1816 (No 293) from the Collins stereotype plates.

NNAB has a copy with engraved titles for both Testaments dated 1816. Engraved frontispiece (*Scheme of the Births, Ages and Deaths of the Patriarchs*) has hand-colored hemispheres. One engraving on thin paper, *The Creation* signed by Anderson, appears before OT; another *(Sampson* [sic] *killing the lion . . . Exertions for a wife*) faces p 213. There are 15 other engravings, some signed by other engravers, and 3 single-page and 2 folded maps, hand-colored. Family Record (1 leaf) for marriages and children's marriages with engraving and border follows OT; a second leaf may have been removed. Concordance (Holbrook 1816, 56 p) is preceded by An Account of the Lives, Sufferings, and Martyrdom of the Apostles and Evangelists (1 leaf).

NNAB also has a copy dated 1823, imprinted Holbrook & Fessenden.

1818   The Holy Bible . . . [Third Edition]. Stereotyped by E. and J. White, for
      "The American Bible Society": New York   **347**

1 vol: (705) (215)   196 × 110 mm   NN, NNAB

Long Primer Octavo printed by Daniel Fanshaw. Tables follow OT. The first edition has not been located but it may have been published in 1817. The *ABS Report* for 1817 contains a specimen page of this Bible. See 1816, No 303.

MWA and NNAB have copies marked fifth edition. CSmH, MiU, NN, and NNAB have copies marked sixth edition. NNAB has a third copy with NT dated 1819.

1818   The Holy Bible . . . M. Carey & Son: Philadelphia   **348**

"12mo"   Not Located

O'Callaghan (p 143): "Though at first view this edition would seem to be a Carey 12mo of 1808, with only new title pages, yet the text has evidently been recomposed. Like the editions of 1812, 1814 and 1817, there are no headlines to the columns. In many places the short s is used where the long ſ is found in the other editions. There are no signature figures to the edition of 1808. In Exodus 19:11, 'Sinai' is printed 'Sinia:' (an error to be found also in the editions of 1814 and 1817) and in I Kgs 4:29, 'the sea shore,' is printed 'these ea shore'."

1818   The Holy Bible . . . Stereotyped by B. and J. Collins, New-York . . . Printed
      and Sold by Cramer and Spear: Pittsburg   **349**

792 p   157 × 90 mm   InU, NNAB

Preliminary matter includes space for owner's name, Order of Books, and Account of Dates. Tables follow OT.

1818   The Holy Bible . . . Stereotyped by B. and J. Collins, New York . . . J. H. A.
      Frost, Printer . . . Published by West and Richardson: Boston   **350**

792 p   157 × 90 mm   CSmH, MWA, NNAB

Preliminary matter includes Account of the Dates, with Order of Books on verso. Tables follow OT.

1818   The Holy Bible . . . [16th Edition]. Stereotyped by E. & J. White . . . Amer-
      ican Bible Society: New York   **351**

155 × 87 mm   MWA, NN

Reprint of 1816 ABS Duodecimo Brevier (No 303). Daniel Fanshaw, Printer appears on verso of title page.

MWA copy marked 14th edition.

1818   The Holy Bible . . . Printed by Hudson and Co.: Hartford   352

147 × 87 mm   MWA, NNAB

Reprint of Hudson & Goodwin 1809 edition (No 168). Error in ı Tim 4:16 continued.
CtY has copy with NT dated 1819; NN has copy with NT dated 1824 imprinted *Printed by Hudson and L. Skinner.*

1818   The Holy Bible . . . Stereotyped by B. and J. Collins . . . J. & J. Harper, Print-
         ers . . . Published by Collins and Hannay: New York   353

129 × 64 mm   MWA, NN, NNAB

Appears to be same as Collins edition of 1817/18 (No 336).
Also published with Metrical Psalms (1818).

1818/17   The Holy Bible . . . Stereotyped by B. & J. Collins . . . Published by S. G.
            Goodrich: Hartford   354

129 × 64 mm   DLC, MWA, NN

Appears to be same as Collins edition of 1817/18 (No 336). NT imprinted *Published by Sheldon and Goodrich . . . 1817.*

1818   The Holy Bible . . . Stereotyped by B. & J. Collins . . . Published by R. P. & C.
         Williams: Boston   355

1 vol: (690) (209)   129 × 64 mm   IMunS, MB, MWA, NN, NNAB

Appears to be from same plates as Collins edition of 1817/18 (No 336) except it has engraved frontispiece with inscription. NN copy does not have frontispiece.

1818   Explanatory Notes Upon the New Testament, by John Wesley. 4th Amer-
         ican Edition . . . Published by J. Soule and T. Mason for the Methodist Epis-
         copal Church in the United States: New York   356

Reported as 766 p   179 × 92 mm   DLC, MBU–NE, NjMD
Wesley Version; see 1791 NT, No 35.
NjMD copy bound in 2 vols; marked Abraham Paul, printer.

1818   The New Testament . . . Printed and sold by Robert Porter: Wilmington 357

Reported as 243 p   168 × 97 mm   DeWI, DLC

Additional leaf contains A Table of Kindred and Affinity, wherein whosoever are related are
forbidden in Scripture, and by our Laws, to marry together.

1818   The New Testament . . . Stereotyped by B. and J. Collins . . . Published by
         L. and F. Lockwood: New-York   358

290 p   164 × 93 mm   NNAB
Has Table of Kindred at end.

1818   The New Testament . . . Stereotyped by B. and J. Collins . . . S. A. Morrison
         & Co.: Keene [New Hampshire]   359

381 p   163 × 95 mm   MH, MWA, NNAB, ViU
Has Table of Kindred on last page.

1818   The New Testament . . . Stereotyped by B. and J. Collins . . . Printed by Web-
         sters & Skinners: Albany   360

609–792 p   160 × 90 mm   NN, OHi
Appears to be NT of Websters and Skinners Bible of 1817 (No 331).

1818   The New Testament . . . The Second American, from the Cambridge Stereotype Edition; Carefully revised and corrected. Printed and Published by
William Williams: Utica [New York]   **361**

Reported as 334 p   158 × 85 mm   MWA

Appears to be same as S. Southwick 1816 edition (No 316). "Finis" on last page appears
in the same design.

This is the first edition published by William Williams who came from Framingham, Mass.,
in 1787 and made Utica an important center of book production and distribution. He served his
apprenticeship with his brother-in-law, Asahel Seward (who had been apprenticed to Isaiah
Thomas), and became his partner in 1807. Williams executed many woodcuts, some for local
banknotes. He took part in the War of 1812, was an elder in the Presbyterian church, a delegate
to the convention that established the American Bible Society in 1816, and superintendent of the
Utica Sunday Schools and teacher of a class as well. He also published books for the Mohawk
and Choctaw Indians and two Hawaiian tracts for E. Loomis, contributing the cost of paper,
press, and binding. During the cholera epidemic of 1832 he personally attended the sick. He published both Protestant and Catholic Testaments. His activities in the anti-Masonic movement and
financial losses connected with the publication of the American edition of the Edinburgh Encyclopedia caused his financial ruin in 1833. A head injury from a fall in 1840 seriously impaired his
activities and he died in Utica in 1850. He was the father of S. Wells Williams, American missionary and Chinese scholar, who was president of the ABS from 1881 to 1884. (Madelaine B. Stern,
"Books in the Wilderness," *NYHA New York History* xxxi, No 3 [July 1950] 266–270).

1818   The New Testament . . . Stereotyped by E. and J. White . . . Published by the
American Bible Society: New-York   **362**

254 p   157 × 86 mm   NN, NNAB

Has Tables on verso of title page.

1818   The New Testament . . . E. Duyckinck: New York   **363**

151 × 87 mm   MWA

Reprint of 1804 NT (No 118). The "corrected" error still stands in Acts 8:9. See also
1815 NT, No 289.

1818   The New Testament . . . Printed by George Goodwin and Sons: Hartford **364**

Reported as 334 p   148 × 87 mm   MWA

See 1809 Bible, No 168; also 1817 NT, No 342.

1818   The New Testament . . . Printed and Sold by Samuel G. Goodrich: Hartford
365

321 p   134 × 77 mm   MWA, NNAB

Title page has *Owner*   within ornamented border.

1818   The New Testament . . . Sold by Oliver D. Cooke and Sons: Hartford **366**

321 p   131 × 76 mm   NN

1818   The New Testament . . . Stereotyped by B. & J. Collins. R. P. & C. Williams:
Boston   **367**

209 p   129 × 64 mm   NN

Frontispiece and text from same plates as NT of Williams' 1818 Bible (No 355).

1818   The New Testament . . . Stereotyped by B. & J. Collins . . . J. & J. Harper,
Printers . . . Published by Collins and Hannay: New York   **368**

Reported as 209 p   129 × 64 mm   IU

Same as NT of Collins 1818 Bible (No 353).

1818   The New Testament . . . Griggs & Co., Printers . . . Published by Benjamin C.
          Buzby: Philadelphia   *369*

Reported as 445 p   97 × 55 mm   MWA

1818   The New Testament . . . Patterson & Lambden: Pittsburg   *370*

"12mo"   Not Located
Wright, p 392.

1819   The Holy Bible . . . with Canne's notes and references. Printed and sold by
          Collins & Co.: New-York   *371*

242 × 178 mm   CtY, NN
Collins' stereotype edition, same as 1816 quarto (No 296). With Apocrypha, Index, Tables,
etc., and Brown's Concordance (1819).
NN copy has 19 historical engravings and 3 maps.

1819   The Holy Bible . . . Apocrypha . . . Index . . . J. Holbrook's Stereotype Copy:
          Brattleborough   *372*

Reported as (683) (160) 685–930 (2) (56) (123)   242 × 178 mm   VtHi
Reprint of Holbrook quarto of 1816 (No 293). With 1816 engraved title, Apocrypha, and
Brown's Concordance.
VtHi has another copy with different plates.

1819   The Holy Bible . . . M. Carey & Son: Philadelphia   *373*

241 × 185 mm   NN
Same as Carey's quarto of 1812/11 (No 208). Has Apocrypha and Brown's Concordance
(1818). Error in Lev 19:12 continued; error in Esther 1:8 corrected. 8 maps and 17 historical
engravings.

1819   The Holy Bible . . . Apocrypha . . . Index . . . Concordance . . . account of the
          lives . . . plates. J. Holbrook's Stereotype Copy: Brattleborough   *374*

Reported as (930) (2)   238 × 178 mm   VtHi
Without engraved titles, plates, etc., but with Family Record pages. Printed on cheaper
paper than 372. Although the same material appears on the page the letterpress measures shorter
than 372.

1819   The Holy Bible . . . 7th Edition. Stereotyped by E. & J. White, for "The Amer-
          ican Bible Society": New-York   *375*

196 × 109 mm   IU, NN, NNAB
From same plates as ABS Long Primer Octavo of 1818 (No 347).

1819/17   The Holy Bible . . . [1st Edition]. Stereotyped for the American Bible
             Society, by D. & G. Bruce, New York . . . Printed for the Kentucky Auxiliary
             Bible Society, William G. Hunt: Lexington   *376*

837 p   169 × 93 mm   NN, NNAB
Minion Duodecimo. Verso of title has Order of Books. NT dated 1817.
2,000 copies of this edition were printed from plates sent by the ABS to the Kentucky Bible
Society to provide Scriptures west of the Alleghenies. See 1816, No 303.

1819   The Holy Bible . . . [17th Edition]. Printed by D. Fanshaw . . . Stereotyped
for the American Bible Society by D. & G. Bruce: New-York   **377**

837 p   167 × 93 mm   KKB, NN, NNAB , VtMiS

Minion Duodecimo. Verso of title page has Order of Books. Tables at end of OT.
NNAB also has 20th edition and MWA has 21st edition, both dated 1819.

1819   The Holy Bible . . . [21st Edition]. Stereotyped by E. & J. White for the
American Bible Society. D. Fanshaw. Printer: New-York   **378**

1 vol: (832) (254)   155 × 87 mm   MWA

Reprint of 1816 ABS Brevier Duodecimo (No 303).
NNAB has 23rd edition dated 1819; NN has 23rd and 24th editions, both of this year.

1819   The Holy Bible . . . W. Greenough, Printer . . . Printed for Lincoln and Edmands: Boston   **379**

152 × 90 mm   MWA, NN, NNAB

Appears to be reprint of Lincoln and Edmands 1817 Bible (No 334). Error in 1 Tim 4:16
continued.
Also issued with NT dated 1817.

1819   The Holy Bible . . . Printed and sold by Hudson and Goodwin: Hartford,
Connecticut   **380**

147 × 87 mm   NN

Appears to be reprint of Hudson & Goodwin edition of 1809 (No 168) of which the type
was apparently kept standing.

1819   The Holy Bible . . . Printed by John H. A. Frost . . . for West, Richardson and
Lord: Boston   **381**

"12mo"   Not Located

A stereotyped edition. O'Callaghan (p 382) quotes Melvin Lord: "Many large editions were
printed from these stereotype plates in succeeding years."

1819   The Holy Bible . . . W. Hill Woodward, Printer . . . Printed for W. W. Woodward: Philadelphia   **382**

128 × 65 mm   MWA, NNAB

Agrees with 1816 Woodward edition (No 308) except OT and NT have separate signatures.
Metrical Psalms (1819).
MWA copy lacks Metrical Psalms.

1819   The New Testament . . . Stereotyped by E. and J. White, for "The American
Bible Society": New-York   **383**

195 × 109 mm   NNAB, ViU

Same as NT of 1818 ABS Long Primer Octavo Bible (No 347).

1819   The New Testament . . . Stereotyped by B. and J. Collins. Published by Isaac
Peirce . . . : Philadelphia   **384**

Reported as 290 p   166 × 63 mm   MWA

1819   The New Testament . . . Long's Stereotype Edition . . . Stereotyped by B. and
J. Collins, N. York. Printed and Published by Isaac Long, jun.: Hopkinton
[New Hampshire]   **385**

381 p   163 × 93 mm   MWA, NN, NNAB

Appears to be same as Morrison edition (Keene, N. H.) of 1818 (No 359) from plates
stereotyped by B. & J. Collins. Has Table of Kindred at end.

NNAB copy has cover stamp and label of the Massachusetts Bible Society pasted inside
cover, p 155–194 lacking, and name of stereotyper mutilated on title page.

1819   The New Testament . . . Stereotyped by B. & J. Collins. Published by L. & F.
Lockwood: New York   **386**

Reported as 290 p   161 × 93 mm   DLC

1819   The New Testament . . . Stereotyped by B. and J. Collins, New-York. Printed
and published by John I. Williams: Exeter [New Hampshire]   **387**

312 p   161 × 90 mm   MWA, NhD, NNAB

Has Tables at end.

1819   The New Testament . . . [2nd Edition]. Printed by D. Fanshaw . . . Stereotyped for "The American Bible Society," by D. & G. Bruce: New York   **388**

312 p   160 × 90 mm   DLC, MiU, NN, NNAB

Bourgeois Duodecimo from separate ABS plates for the NT. Sold at 30¢ to 35¢.
MWA has tenth edition of this year.

1819   The New Testament . . . The second American, from the Cambridge Stereotype Edition . . . Published by William Williams: Utica   **389**

334 p   157 × 85 mm   N, NNAB

O'Callaghan (p 155) lists a similar edition for 1821; no copy located.

1819   The New Testament . . . First American Stereotype Edition. John H. A. Frost,
Printer . . . Published by West, Richardson & Lord: Boston   **390**

Reported as 312 p   156 × 87 mm   MWA

Reprint of 1815 NT (No 287).

1819   The New Testament . . . Printed by Hori Brown: Leicester   **391**

Reported as 336 p   155 × 86 mm   MWA

Appears to be same as E. Merriam's edition of 1814 (No 266). MWA copy lacks p 3–11,
covering Mat 1–7:16.

1819   The New Testament . . . S. G. Goodrich: Hartford   **392**

321 p   130 × 76 mm   NjMD, NN

Has engraved frontispiece and Order of Books.

1819   The New Testament . . . Published by J. Holbrook: Brattleborough   **393**

335 [1] p   120 × 62 mm   DLC, MWA, NNAB, PPL

Has title page with all-over design and frontispiece. Order of Books precedes text; at end
are An Account of Lives of Apostles and Evangelists and Table of Kindred. 4 unsigned historical
engravings, possibly by A. Anderson.

1820   The Self Interpreting Bible; with an evangelical commentary by the late Revd. John Brown . . . embellished with elegant engravings. S. Walker: New York   **394**

Reported as (xlix) (7) 5–1222 [1]   400 × 221 mm   MS

For contents, see 1822, Nos 432 and 433. With Apocrypha. Has engraved title by J. Palmer, Alby., from an original painting by B. West. Illustrated with wood-engravings and one map.

MWA has Vol I only of a 2-vol set.

1820   The Holy Bible . . . with Canne's marginal notes and references . . . Stereotyped by E. White. D. D. Smith: New York   **395**

770   252 × 193 mm   NN

With Apocrypha (112 p). Preliminary matter includes To the Reader [by Dr. Witherspoon], List of Books, and Contents of both Testaments. Index, Tables, etc. follow NT. 9 historical engravings and one map.

This is the first of many editions with Canne's marginal notes and references issued by Smith. A 54 p Concordance was often included.

1820/16   The Holy Bible . . . J. Holbrook's Stereotype Copy: Brattleborough **396**

242 × 178 mm   NNAB

Same as Holbrook quarto of 1817 (No 327) from the Collins stereotype plates. With Concordance. 8 historical engravings and 2 maps. NT dated 1816.

1820   The Holy Bible . . . Stereotyped by B. & J. Collins . . . Printed by W. Greenough, Lunenburg [Mass]. Sold also by Lincoln & Edmands: Boston   **397**

241 × 178 mm   DLC, MWA, NNAB

Same as Collins' stereotype edition of 1816 (No 296) but does not have Concordance and has no engravings except frontispiece.

MWA copy has two frontispieces by Dr. A. Anderson: *Jonah Preaching to the Ninevites* and *Touch Me Not*. MWA has another copy with NT dated 1822. NN has copy with Concordance, 19 historical engravings, and 3 maps.

1820/19   The Holy Bible . . . [10th Edition]. Stereotyped by E. and J. White for "The American Bible Society": New-York   **398**

196 × 110 mm   MB, MBtS, NNAB

Same as ABS Long Primer Octavo of 1818 (No 347). NT title dated 1819.

1820   The Holy Bible . . . Printed by D. Fanshaw . . . Stereotyped for The American Bible Society by D. and G. Bruce: New York   **399**

166 × 94 mm   NNAB

From same plates as ABS Minion Duodecimo of 1819 (No 377).

1820/18   The Holy Bible . . . Stereotyped by B. & J. Collins, New York . . . Printed by John H. A. Frost . . . for West, Richardson and Lord: Boston   **400**

792 p   160 × 90 mm   NN

Tables at end of OT. NT dated 1818.

1820   The Holy Bible . . . [28th Edition]. Stereotyped by E. & J. White . . . Published by the American Bible Society: New-York   **401**

155 × 87 mm   NNAB, NHi

Reprint of ABS Brevier Duodecimo of 1816 (No 303).

MWA has 30th edition, also dated 1820.

1820   The Holy Bible . . . W. Greenough, printer . . . Lincoln and Edmands: Boston. Sold also by Collins and Co., Newyork [sic]   **402**

Text ends Kk12   150 × 90 mm   MWA, NbHi, OCHP, ViW
Same as 1817 edition, No 334.

1820   The New Testament . . . Printed and Sold by Robert Porter: Wilmington **403**

Reported as 240 p   168 × 100 mm   DeWI

1820   The New Testament . . . George W. Mentz: Philadelphia   **404**

"12mo"   Not Located
Wright, p 392.

1820   The New Testament . . . Printed by E. Merriam and Co.: Brookfield [Massachusetts]   **405**

Reported as 336 p   167 × 100 mm   MBU-T

1820   The New Testament . . . Stereotyped by B. & J. Collins . . . Printed for the Booksellers: Philadelphia   **406**

290 [1] p   166 × 94 mm   NN
Table follows text.

1820   A Translation of the New Testament: By Gilbert Wakefield . . . From the Second London Edition. Printed by the University Press, by Hilliard and Metcalf: Cambridge [Massachusetts]   **406A**

1 vol: (xii) (450) (2) (163)   166 × 91 mm   ICU, MB, MH-AH, MWA, NN, NNAB
Preliminary matter includes Advertisement to this first American edition, dated 1820; Errata; Dedication to Rev. Robert Tyrwhitt, dated 1791; and Preface. Text is printed in paragraph form, single column, with verse numbers in left margin. Notes at end.
Gilbert Wakefield (1756–1801) was a classical scholar and controversial writer who became a Unitarian after serving as an Anglican clergyman. His alterations in the AV consist mostly in regard to "some low obsolete or obscure word, some vulgar idiom, etc." He made use of Walton's Polyglott Bible. His NT was first published in London in 1791 and again in 1795, although Thessalonians had been privately printed in 1781 and Matthew in 1782.

1820   The New Testament . . . Stereotyped by B. and J. Collins. Published by Oliver D. Cooke: Hartford   **407**

Reported as 290 [1] p   164 × 92 mm   MWA
Table of Kindred on last page.

1820   The New Testament . . . [14th Edition]. Stereotyped for "The American Bible Society," by D. & G. Bruce. Printed by D. Fanshaw . . .: New-York **408**

160 × 90 mm   MB, NN, NNAB, ViU
Bourgeois Duodecimo. From same plates as 1819 edition (No 388).
MWA has 20th edition and NN also has 23rd edition, both for this year.

1820   The New Testament . . . The second American, from the Cambridge Stereotype Edition . . . Published by William Williams: Utica   **409**

Reported as 334 p   157 × 85 mm   DLC, MWA
Reprint of 1818 NT (No 361).

1820   The New Testament . . . Printed by Hori Brown: Leicester [Massachusetts]
410

336 p   156 × 83 mm   NN

1820   The New Testament . . . Published by Richardson & Lord: Boston   *411*
"12mo"   Not Located
O'Callaghan (p 382) quotes Melvin Lord: "Large numbers were continued to be printed from the stereotype plates of this edition."

1820   The New Testament . . . [5th Edition]. Printed by D. Fanshaw. Stereotyped by A. Chandler and Co. for "The American Bible Society": New-York   *412*

352 p   137 × 75 mm   NNAB
Brevier Octodecimo. This appears to be the first publication of the octodecimo NT. See 1816, No 303.
NNAB has another copy which does not have edition number.

1821   The Holy Bible . . . with Canne's marginal notes and references . . . Stereo-typed by E. White, New York . . . Published and sold by Daniel D. Smith: [New York]   **413**

253 × 194 mm   CtY, NNAB
Same as Smith quarto of 1820 (No 395).

1821   The Holy Bible . . . with Canne's marginal notes and references . . . Apocrypha . . . Stereotyped by B. & J. Collins . . . J. & J. Harper, Printers . . . Published by Collins and Co.: New York   **414**

1 vol: (744) (138) 745–1010 (56)   245 × 191 mm   NN
Preliminary matter includes Advertisement dated 1819, To the Reader [by Dr. Witherspoon], and List of Books. Index, Tables, Lives of Apostles and Evangelists, etc., follow NT. Brown's Concordance. 8 historical engravings and 4 maps.

1821   The Holy Bible . . . Holbrook & Fessenden's Stereotype Edition . . . Apocrypha . . . Index . . . Brown's Concordance . . . account of the lives . . . Holbrook & Fessenden: Brattleborough   **415**

Reported as (930) (2) (56) (124)   242 × 179 mm   VtHi
With engraved titles dated 1816.

1821   The Holy Bible . . . Stereotype Edition . . . Abraham Paul, Printer . . . Published by E. White and E. Bliss: New-York   **416**

1 vol: (705) (215) (12)   197 × 110 mm   NNAB
Same format as ABS Long Primer Octavo of 1818 (No 347). Has 12 p of Contents at end.

1821   The Holy Bible . . . [12th Edition]. Stereotyped by E. and J. White, for "The American Bible Society": New-York   **417**

196 × 110 mm   NNAB
Same as ABS Long Primer Octavo of 1818 (No 347).

1821   The Holy Bible . . . Stereotyped by D. and G. Bruce: New York   **418**

837 p   169 × 93 mm   MB, NN
Tables follow OT.

1821/18   The Holy Bible . . . Stereotyped by B. and J. Collins, New York; J. H. A.
Frost, Printer. Richardson and Lord: Boston   *418A*

792 p   159 × 91 mm   NNAB
NT, dated 1818, is from West and Richardson Bible of that year (No 350).

1821/22   The Holy Bible . . . Stereotype Edition . . . Stereotyped by B. and J. Collins, New-York. Printed and published by John I. Williams: Exeter [New
Hampshire]   *419*

Reported as 792 p   158 × 89 mm   MWA
NT, dated 1822, has imprint *Printed by Cushing and Appleton: Salem, Mass.* See 1822,
No 444.

1821   The Holy Bible . . . Published by the American Bible Society. Stereotyped
by E. & J. White: New-York   *420*

157 × 88 mm   NNAB
Reprint of ABS Brevier Duodecimo of 1816 (No 303).

1821   The Holy Bible . . . Stereotyped by E. and J. White for the Auxiliary New-
York Bible and Common Prayer-Book Society: New York   *421*

1 vol: (676) (208)   156 × 98 mm   NNAB

1821   The Holy Bible . . . Printed and Sold by W. Greenough: Lunenburg [Mas-
sachusetts]   *422*

Text ends Kk12   152 × 90 mm   CSmH, MB, NN, WBB
Preliminary matter includes "Property of   ," List of Books, and Account of Dates.
Tables at end of OT.

1821/23   The Holy Bible . . . Stereotype Edition . . . Stereotyped by B. & J. Collins
. . . J. & J. Harper, Printers . . . Published by Collins and Hannay: New York
                                                                         423

Reported as (690) (209) [1]   129 × 64 mm   NHi
To the Reader appears on p 3–4. NT dated 1823.
O'Callaghan (p 153) lists with NT dated 1818 in some copies (see 1817/18, No 336) and
with Metrical Psalms (undated) included.

1821   The Holy Bible . . . Printed by Hudson and Goodwin: Hartford   *424*

"12mo"   Not Located
O'Callaghan, p 154. Possibly a reprint of 1809 edition (No 168).

1821   The Holy Bible . . . First Stereotype Edition . . . Published and Sold by E.
White: New-York   *425*

1 vol: (705) (216)   104 × 55 mm   MWA, NNAB
Preliminary matter includes Dedication to King James.

1821   The New Testament . . . Patterson and Lambdin: Pittsburgh   *426*

"8vo"   Not Located
LC Union Catalog lists this octavo NT from a 1935 second hand book dealer.

1821 The New Testament . . . Stereotyped by B. & J. Collins . . . Oliver D. Cooke: Hartford **427**

290 [1] p   165 × 94 mm   NNAB
Has Table of Kindred at end. See 1820 NT, No 406.

1821 The New Testament . . . Stereotype Edition. Printed and Published by Miller & Hutchens: Providence **428**

Reported as 312 p   162 × 90 mm   DLC, MWA
Stereotyped by B. & J. Collins.
Rumball-Petre (*America's First Bibles* p 161) gives 1821 for the first *Bible* printed in Rhode Island but no copy has been located.

1821 The New Testament . . . Gray & Bunce, Printers . . . Published and sold by James A. Burtus: New York **429**

312 p   160 × 89 mm   NN

1821 The New Testament . . . Printed by George Goodwin and Sons: Hartford **430**

344 p   150 × 84 mm   NN, NNAB
See 1818 NT, No 364.

1821 The New Testament . . . 15th Edition. Printed and Sold by Samuel G. Goodrich: Hartford **431**

136 × 76 mm   NN
Appears to be same as Goodrich edition of 1818 (No 365).

1822 The Holy Bible . . . [Self Interpreting Bible]. By the Late Rev. John Brown . . . Published by S. Walker, Newbury-Street: Boston **432**

Reported as (li) (876) (158) 877–1222 (2)   400 × 221 mm   MB
With Apocrypha. Preliminary matter includes frontispiece; preliminary engraved title page dated 1820 (*The Self Interpreting Bible . . . Printed & Published by S. Walker, 148 Cherry Street: New-York*); An Introduction to the Right Understanding of the Oracles of God; Order of Books; To the Reader; and A Calculation of the Number of Books, Chapters, Verses, Words, Letters, Etc. in the Old and New Testaments, and the Apocrypha. NT has folded map, frontispiece, and title page. At end are A Collection of Similes Contained in the Scriptures, Arranged Alphabetically; A Table of Scripture Measures; and A Table of Offices and Conditions of Men. Illustrated with engravings. See 1792, No 37.

1822 The Holy Bible . . . [The Self Interpreting Bible]. By the Late Rev. John Brown . . . Printed and Published by T. Kinnersley: New-York **433**

1 vol: (8) (li) (1) 3–1222 (2)   393 × 206 mm   MWA, NNAB
Text, appended materials, and pagination agree with the S. Walker edition for this year (No 432) but without Apocrypha. Frontispiece has notation *Published by S. Walker . . . New-York*; added engraved title page has *The Self Interpreting Bible . . . Printed & Published by S. Walker . . . New-York . . . 1820*. All other titles dated 1822. Colophon reads: Stereotyped and printed by J. McGowan, London. This Bible was published in 162 parts. Part numbers appear at foot of page of each new part. 38 historical engravings and one map.
Number of engravings varies with copies. Also published with Apocrypha.
T. Kinnersley published the Self Interpreting Bible with London imprint in 1816 (first printed 1814) and it was also stereotyped and printed by J. McGowan with the same pagination (NNAB). It would seem that both this and the Walker editions of 1820 and 1822 may be made up of imported sheets or else were printed from imported plates. See 1792, No 37.

1822 The Columbian Family and Pulpit Bible: being a corrected and improved
American edition of the popular English Family Bible; with . . . notes and
annotations . . . from Poole, Brown, Doctors A. Clarke, Coke, Scott, Dodd-
ridge, &c. With numerous additions, in the present work, from . . . Michaelis,
Lowth, Newcome, Blaney, Horsely, Campbell, Gerard, Macknight, &c . . .
First American Edition . . . Printed by J. H. A. Frost, Published by Joseph
Teal: Boston   *434*

1 or 2 vols   381 × 214 mm   DLC, MiU, MWA, NN, NNAB

Vol i preliminary matter includes frontispiece with notation *Engraved for Fowler's Family
Bible*, added engraved title page, Preface by the American Editor, Introduction, and List of
Books; text: Genesis-Proverbs, Apocrypha. At end are An Account of the Apostles and engraved
Family Record. Vol ii has frontispiece but no title page; text: Ecclesiastes-Revelation. At end
are Indexes, Tables, etc. Notes to text appear on lower part of page. An illustrative argument is
prefixed to each Book. 36 engravings by J. Chorley, T. Kelly, O. H. Throop, W. B. Annin,
A. Bowan, and Gregory.

This Bible was issued in numbers and had more than 3,000 subscribers. The Rev. Jonathan
Homer, D.D., of Newton, Mass., revised some of the notes and enlarged others. Also published
in one volume. See Wright, p 208–209.

1822–24 The Holy Bible . . . [according to the present authorized English ver-
sion] with notes, critical, explanatory and practical, all the marginal readings of the most approved printed copies . . . with such others as appear to
be contenanced by the Hebrew and Greek originals . . . parallel texts . . . the
date of every transaction . . . by the Rev. Joseph Benson. J. & J. Harper
Printers, Published by N. Bangs and T. Mason, for the Methodist Episcopal
Church: New York   *435*

5 vols   290 mm   TNMB

Vol iii dated 1823 and Vol v dated 1824, with J. Emory replacing T. Mason in imprint. For
pagination, see 1839, No 1038.

1822/20 The Holy Bible . . . Canne's marginal notes and references . . . Index
. . . Tables . . . Stereotyped by B. & J. Collins, New-York. Printed and sold
by W. Greenough: Lunenburgh, Mass.   *436*

Reported as 932 p   270 × 210 mm   CaOTU

Has frontispiece, Witherspoon's To the Reader, and Account of the Dates. Order of Books
includes Apocrypha, but it is missing. Family Record follows OT. Indexes follow NT, which is
dated 1820.

1822/21 The Holy Bible . . . with Canne's marginal notes and references. Stereotyped by E. White . . . Published by Daniel D. Smith: [New York]   *437*

255 × 195 mm   NNAB

Same as Smith edition of 1820 (No 395) but with 10 engravings by R. Westall. Family
Record follows Apocrypha. NT dated 1821.

NNAB has another copy with 4 historical engravings by Mola, LeBrun, and Craig; NT dated
1823; no Apocrypha.

1822 The Holy Bible . . . With Canne's marginal notes and references. To which
are added, an index; an alphabetical table, &c . . . Published by Samuel Wood
& Sons . . . : New-York; and Samuel S. Wood & Co . . . : Baltimore   *438*

2 vols: (570) (112) 573–748 749–770   250 mm   NCooHi, ViU

Two leaves of Family Record follow OT. Illustrated.

Samuel Wood (1760–1844), a former teacher and bookseller, in 1806 began publishing children's books of his own compilation and authorship on a small press in the rear of his shop. The business thrived and was carried on by several sons. The office in Baltimore was opened in 1818 but as it was unsuccessful it was soon abandoned. (Harry B. Weiss, "Samuel Wood & Sons," *Bulletin of the NYPL* XLVI [Sept 1942] 755–771.)

1822 The Holy Bible ... With Canne's Marginal Notes and References ... Stereotyped, printed and published by H. & E. Phinney: Cooperstown [New York]
439

1 vol: (8) 9–574 575–576 (4) (2) 579–762 763–768   "4to"   Not Located

O'Callaghan, p 157–158. Has Witherspoon's To the Reader, Indexes, Tables, and Family Record, but no Apocrypha.

This is the first of a series of quarto Bibles published by H. and E. Phinney in Cooperstown between August 1, 1822, and the winter of 1848, when a fire destroyed their plant. O'Callaghan (p 158) quotes a letter from E. Phinney stating that the first edition consisted of 500 copies but that the last of the 138 editions (totalling 154,000 copies) printed during the latter part of 1848 was 4,475 copies. About 100,000 copies included the Apocrypha and 14,750 had Brown's Concordance. "The stereotype plates were made by H. and E. P. at Cooperstown. Two proofs were read with the greatest care, the text having been compared with other editions, and a premium offered to the men in the establishment for the discovery of errors, even after the plates were cast." (O'Callaghan, p 158.)

The Phinney brothers, Henry and Elihu, were the sons of an enterprising printer, Elihu Phinney, who came through the wilderness from Connecticut to Cooperstown in 1795 with press and type and established a press, bookshop, and newspaper serving much of western New York State. Yet he found time to serve as judge in the Court of Common Pleas. He died in 1813. James Fenimore Cooper, who in 1816 was a delegate to the convention that formed the American Bible Society, learned to set type in his shop, for fun. The Phinney's imported all sorts of books from New York and Philadelphia and distributed them with their own publications through towns and villages from large wagons with moveable tops and counters, even providing a canal boat book store on the Erie Canal. They established a stereotyping foundry in 1820 and by 1830 had the largest plant in the town, employing forty hands and five presses and were part-owners of a local paper mill. In 1839 the founder's grandson, Henry Frederick Phinney, joined the firm. Labor troubles arose when new power presses were installed and a number of men dismissed. At this time the fire occurred and the plant was moved to Buffalo. In 1854, H. F. Phinney, who had married a daughter of Cooper, moved to New York and joined Henry Ivison in educational publishing. (Madeleine B. Stern, "Books in the Wilderness," *NYHA New York History* XXXI, No 3 [July 1950] 261–266.)

Editions from similar plates were issued in 1833 by R. White & Co., Hartford (No 816) and G. M. Davison, Saratoga Springs (No 813); in 1842 by Jesper Harding, Philadelphia (No 1129); in 1852 by Alden, Beardsley and Co., Auburn (No 1488) — reprinted by Jesper Harding in 1857 (No 1639) and again by A. J. Holman in 1872 (No 1895); and in 1871 by William Harding (No 1867) — reprinted by Henry Altemus in 1890 (No 2037). The pagination in these editions is similar but the division of lines within the same verses occasionally varies, indicating that some must have been from other type-settings.

1822 The Holy Bible ... Stereotyped by B. & J. Collins ... Printed and sold by
W. Greenough: Lunenburg [Massachusetts]   *440*

240 × 178 mm   NNAB

Same as Collins' stereotype quarto of 1816 (No 296).

1822 The Holy Bible ... Stereotype Edition ... [A. Paul, Printer] ... Published
by E. Bliss & E. White: New York   *441*

Reported as (2) 3–705 [1] 1–151 (2) 3–215 (12)   198 × 111 mm   MWA, Church
Hist. Soc., Austin, Tex.; Thomas Cooke House and Museum, Edgartown, Mass.

Tables of Scripture Measures follow OT. Table of Contents at end. 11 illustrations, some signed by A. Anderson.

1822   The Holy Bible ... Stereotyped by D. & G. Bruce, New York ... Printed and
         published by E. & E. Hosford: Albany   **442**

837 p   169 × 93 mm   MWA, NcD, NN

1822   The Holy Bible ... Printed by D. Fanshaw ... Stereotyped for the American
         Bible Society by D. & G. Bruce: New-York   **443**

837 [1] p   165 × 92 mm   NNAB

1822   The Holy Bible ... Stereotyped by B. & J. Collins, New York ... Printed by
         Cushing and Appleton: Salem, Mass.   **444**

792 p   157 × 90 mm   NNAB
Tables follow OT.
MWA has copy with NT from this Bible bound with OT imprinted *John I. Williams: Exeter*
[New Hampshire] *1821*. See 1821, No 419.

1822/18   The Holy Bible ... Stereotyped by B. and J. Collins ... J. H. A. Frost,
            Printer, Published by Richardson and Lord: Boston   **445**

157 × 90 mm   NNAB
Same as West and Richardson 1818 edition (No 350). NT dated 1818.

1822   The Holy Bible ... W. Greenough: Lunenburg [Massachusetts]   **446**

152 × 90 mm   NN
Appears to be same as Greenough edition of 1821 (No 422).

1822   The Holy Bible ... Printed by Hudson and Goodwin: Hartford   **447**

148 × 87 mm   MWA, NN
Same as Hudson & Goodwin edition of 1809 (No 168).
MWA copy imprinted *Hudson and Company*.

1822   The Holy Bible ... Second Stereotype Edition ... [A. Paul, Printer]. Pub-
         lished by E. Bliss & E. White: New-York   **448**

1 vol: (704) (216)   105 × 54 mm   NNAB, PP
Has Dedication to King James and Order of Books.

1822   The Holy Bible ... Second Stereotype edition ... E. Bliss and E. White: New-
         York   **449**

Reported as (704) (216)   100 × 54 mm   CtHT-W, DLC
O'Callaghan (p 159) says this book has footnotes and that the one which appears on the NT
title, "This title of the book was put to it by the Evangelist himself," belongs on the first page
of Matthew.
CtHT-W copy has no footnotes.

1822   The New Testament. ... H. C. Carey and I. Lea: Philadelphia   **450**

242 × 182 mm   Not Located
O'Callaghan, p 159. See Carey's 1818 Bible, No 345.

1822   The New Testament ... Stereotyped by B. and J. Collins: N. York. Printed
         and published by Luther Roby ... : Amherst [New Hampshire]   **451**

Reported as 381 p   170 mm   MBU–T
This is the first edition printed by Luther Roby. Roby was born in Amherst on Jan 8, 1801.
At 15 he entered the office of the *Farmer's Cabinet* as an apprentice, where he remained for six

years. Early in 1822 he opened a printing and book shop on Amherst Plain but in December he moved to Concord where he issued the first number of the *Statesman* on Jan 6, 1823. He sold the paper in May but continued as its printer, in addition to producing school books, Testaments, Bibles, etc. With other colleagues he printed many editions during the next thirty years. It is said that his presses were at one time turned by a horse attached to a vertical shaft in the basement below the pressroom.

1822   The New Testament ... The Pronouncing Testament ... To which is applied, in numerous words, The Orthoepy of the Critical Pronouncing Dictionary; Also, the Classical Pronunciation of the Proper Names as they stand in the Text — Scrupulously Adopted From "A Key to the Classical Pronunciation of Greek, Latin, and Scripture Proper Names. By John Walker, Author of the Critical Pronouncing Dictionary, &c." ... To which is prefixed, An Explanatory Key ... By Israel Alger, Jun. ... Printed and Published by Lincoln & Edmands: Boston   **452**

304 p   166 × 88 mm   MB, MWA, NNAB

1822   The New Testament ... Appointed to be read in Churches ... Printed for the Booksellers: Philadelphia   **453**

335 [1] p   152 × 88 mm   NN
Table follows text.

1822   The New Testament ... Stereotyped by J. Howe, New York. Printed at Treadwell's Power Press: Boston   **454**

287 [1] p   152 × 94 mm   NN, NNAB

1822   The New Testament ... Printed by George Goodwin and Sons: Hartford **455**

150 × 84 mm   NN, NNAB
Reprinted from 1821 NT, No 430.

1822   The New Testament ... Stereotype Edition ... Printed and published by William Williams: Utica [New York]   **456**

324 p   136 × 77 mm   NBuG, NN, PPL-R

1822   The New Testament ... Stereotype Edition ... Printed by H. and E. Phinney, and sold by them wholesale and retail at their book-store: Cooperstown **457**

Reported as 324 p   135 × 75 mm   CtY

1822   The New Testament ... Holbrook and Fessenden: Brattleborough   **458**

120 × 62 mm   MWA, VtMiS
Same as 1819 Holbrook NT (No 393). Has frontispiece (*Good News* and a dove above a book) and 3 illustrations: *The Shepherds Glorify God.* Matt 2, signed "A"; *Transfiguration of Christ*, Mark 9; *Bearing the Cross*, Luke 23, signed "A."

1823   The Holy Bible ... together with the Apocrypha ... Canne's Marginal Notes and References ... Daniel D. Smith's Stereotype Edition ... Stereotyped by E. White: New-York. Published and sold by Daniel D. Smith ... : New York   **459**

Reported as (4) 5–570 (112) 573–770   252 × 194 mm   MWA
Has engravings.

[*1823*]   The Holy Bible ... With Canne's Marginal Notes and References ... Stereotyped by E. White, New-York ... Published and Sold by Kimber and Sharpless: Philadelphia   **460**

1 vol: (748) 749–770 (54) (18)   250 × 194 mm   NNAB

Preliminary matter includes Contents. Family Record follows OT. At end are Index, Tables, etc., Brown's Concordance (stereotyped by J. Howe, n.d.), and Metrical Psalms. Has straight double ruled lines between columns of text. Added materials vary. NNAB also has copy with Apocrypha (112).

NN has copy in which the name of E. White as stereotyper does not appear and NT is stereotyped by B. & J. Collins. It has single wavy lines between columns of text, Apocrypha, 30 engravings, and is paged to 1008 with Metrical Psalms at end. The edition in this format was also republished. See 1829, No 669. A privately owned copy contains wood engravings by Anderson.

This Bible is undated, but O'Callaghan (p 162) states that "The first edition of this Bible was printed in 1823. The stereotype plates of the OT were cast by Elihu White of New York; those of the NT by B. & J. Collins. Kimber and Sharpless continued the publication of large and numerous editions until 1844, when they sold the plates to Jasper Harding."

Publisher's address appears variously as 50 N. 4th Street, 93 Market Street (1824), and 8 So. 4th Street.

1823/22   The Holy Bible ... Printed by T. and J. Swords: New York   **461**

Unpaged: last signature 146^2 245 × 185 mm   NN

With Apocrypha. Preliminary matter includes Dedication to King James and List of Books. Memorandum pages follow OT. NT dated 1822, with Index, Tables, etc. at end.

1823/25   The Holy Bible ... With Canne's Marginal Notes and References ... Stereotyped for H. C. Carey and I. Lea, by B. & J. Collins ... Published by H. C. Carey and I. Lea: Philadelphia   **462**

243 × 182 mm   MH-AH, NNAB

Same as Carey's 1812/11 quarto (No 208) from standing type, but has no Concordance. With Apocrypha. Engravings throughout. Error in Lev 19:12 continued.

1823   The Holy Bible ... With Canne's Marginal Notes and References ... Stereotyped, Printed and Published by H. & E. Phinney: Cooperstown   **463**

Reported as 9–574, 575–576, 579–754, 755–768   "4to"   NNQ, NjPasHi

Preliminary matter includes Order of Books, To the Reader [by Dr. Witherspoon], and Contents. Tables follow OT. Account of Dates on verso of NT title. At end are Index, Tables, and Appendix. See 1822, No 439.

Also published with Apocrypha.

1823   The Holy Bible ... Printed and sold by W. Greenough. Edmund Cushing: Lunenburg, Mass.   **464**

Reported as (6) 9–683 (1) (165) (2) 687–932 (56)   230 × 180 mm   MWA

Wright (p 393) lists such a Bible under 1822, but no copy with this date has been located.

1823   The Holy Bible ... Printed and published by Holbrook and Fessenden: Brattleborough, Vermont   **465**

Reported as 684 p   190 mm   MW

Has frontispiece and two engravings.

1823   The Holy Bible ... [18th Edition]. Stereotyped by E. and J. White, for "The American Bible Society": New York   **466**

196 × 110 mm   MB, NNAB, ViU

Same as 1818 ABS Long Primer Octavo (No 347). NNAB also has fifteenth edition of this year.

A sixteenth edition was also issued this year.

1823/21 The Holy Bible . . . Sterotyped by D. & G. Bruce: Philadelphia **467**

837 p   169 × 94 mm   NN, NNAB

Tables at end of OT. NT title dated 1821.

1823/18 The Holy Bible . . . Stereotyped by B. and J. Collins, New-York . . . J. H. A. Frost, Printer . . . Published by Richardson and Lord: Boston **468**

Reported as (4) 5–605 (3) 609–792   159 × 90 mm   Privately Owned

Account of the Dates (1 p) and The Names and Order of the Books (1 p) follow title. Tables (1 p) follow OT. NT dated 1818, published by West and Richardson. See 1818, No 350.

1823 The Holy Bible . . . Printed and Sold by W. Greenough: Lunenburg **469**

152 × 89 mm   MWA, NNAB, ViU

Same as Lincoln and Edmands edition of 1817 (No 334) printed by Greenough. Error in I Tim 4:16 continued.

1823 The Holy Bible . . . Printed for Hudson and Co. by W. Hudson and L. Skinner: Hartford **470**

148 × 87 mm   NN

Same as Hudson and Goodwin 1809 duodecimo (No 168) from standing type.

1823 The Holy Bible . . . Stereotyped by B. & J. Collins. J. & J. Harper, Printer, Collins and Hannay: New York **471**

129 × 64 mm   NN

Same as the Collins 24mo of 1818 (No 353).

MWA has NT bound separately.

1823 The New Testament . . . with a Commentary and Critical Notes . . . by Adam Clarke . . . First American Royal Octavo Edition . . . Printed and Published by A. Paul: New York . . . Also published by N. Bangs and T. Mason . . . : New York; Martin Ruter: Cincinnati, Ohio; and Armstrong and Plaskitt: Baltimore **472**

2 vols: Vol I, 842 p; Vol II, 980, x p   219 × 125 mm   NNAB, ViU

Adam Clarke's Commentary: see 1811–25, No 188. NNAB has Vol I only: preliminary matter includes frontispiece (engraving of the Rev. Adam Clarke by J. B. Longacre from a painting by J. Jackson), Introduction to the Four Gospels, List of the Primitive Fathers and Ecclesiastical Works, General Observations, Chronological Table, Preface to the Gospel of St. Matthew, Account of Matthew the Evangelist, and Advertisement; text: Matthew-Acts. Gospel Harmony follows John; Tables, etc. follow text. ViU has Vol II only.

1823 The New Testament . . . to which is applied in numerous words, the orthoepy of the Critical Pronouncing Dictionary; also, the classical pronunciation of the proper names . . . scrupulously adopted from "A key to the classical pronunciation of Greek, Latin and Scripture proper names by John Walker . . ." proper names are accented and divided into syllables exactly as they ought to be pronounced according to rules drawn from analogy and the best usage; to which is prefixed an explanatory key by Israel Alger, Jun., Baltimore. Cushing & Jewett . . . Lincoln & Edmands: Boston **473**

Reported as 292 p   18 cm   CSaT, NcD

1823   The New Testament . . . Appointed to be read in Churches. Stereotyped by
         D. & G. Bruce, New-York . . . Published for the booksellers: Philadelphia **474**

Reported as 336 p   168 × 105 mm   DLC

1823   The New Testament . . . Second Pittsburgh Edition . . . Printed and Pub-
         lished by Cramer and Spear: Pittsburgh   **475**

Reported as 240 p   168 × 86 mm   MiU

1823   The New Testament . . . Stereotyped by B. and J. Collins, New York . . .
         Printed and published by Luther Roby: Concord [New Hampshire]   **476**

380 [1] p   164 × 94 mm   NN
Table follows text.

1823   Η ΚΑΙΝΗ ΔΙΑΘΗΚΗ   The New Testament, in Greek and English; the
         Greek According to Griesbach; the English upon the basis of the fourth
         London edition of the Improved Version, with an attempt to further im-
         provement from the translations of Campbell, Wakefield, Scarlett, Mac-
         knight, and Thomson. In Two Volumes. By Abner Kneeland, Minister of
         the First Independent Church of Christ, called Universalist, in Philadelphia
         . . . William Fry, Printer . . . Published by the Editor . . . and sold by him —
         Also by Abm. Small . . . : Philadelphia   **477**

2 vols: Vol I, (xvi) 17–358 359–360; Vol II, (x) (420) 421–443 (2)   158 × 87 mm
                                                                         ICN, NNAB
        Kneeland Version. Preface signed Abner Kneeland . . . April 1, 1822, Notes on the
Greek Alphabet, etc., Order of Books, Account of Times and Places of Writing Books, Disputed Books, and Contents precede text. Text is printed in parallel columns in paragraph
form, with verse numbers in text. At end of Vol I is Errata. At end of Vol II are Abstract Containing Some of the Most Important Articles in Parkhurst's Greek Grammar, Emendations,
To the Candid Reader, Greek Errata, and Publisher's Advertisement.
        O'Callaghan (p 160) lists both the diglot and the Greek text alone for 1822, and Hall
(p 30) describes an edition of the diglot with Vol I dated 1822 (and the final "r" in *printer*
omitted) but Vol II, 1823. Hall also lists separate Greek and English editions for 1823, as
well as this 1823 diglot. He adds that the Greek type seems to be the same as that used by Mathew
Carey in his edition of Epictetus, 1792. For the English text alone, see No 478.
        The Rev. Abner Kneeland (1774–1844) was originally a Baptist minister, but later be-
came a Universalist and then a Deist. During his ministry at the Universalist Church in Philadelphia he prepared this edition. While he originally planned to use Newcome's (Belsham)
"Improved Version," according to the "Emendations" he soon found he wished to make more
changes. He also lists further improvements he would like to make for a later edition.
        In January 1834, Mr. Kneeland was tried for "a certain scandalous, impious, obscene,
blasphemous and profane libel of and concerning God." Although conviction was secured, a long
series of hung juries and postponements in the appellate courts delayed his sentence until 1838.
Despite a protest petition signed by several eminent men, the sentence was enforced. Theodore
Parker's words gave vent to the feelings aroused by the case: "Abner was jugged for sixty days;
but he will come out as beer from a bottle, all foaming, and will make others foam." In 1839
Mr. Kneeland immigrated to "Salubria," on the Des Moines River in Iowa. His proposed
rationalist colony never materialized, and he died there in 1844. Among his other works was
A Brief Sketch of a New System of Orthography, 1807.

1823   The New Testament; Being the English Only of the Greek and English
         Testament; Translated from the Original Greek According to Griesbach . . .
         By Abner Kneeland . . . William Fry, Printer . . . Published by the Editor . . .
         and sold by him — Also by Abm. Small . . . : Philadelphia   **478**

1 vol: (xxiv) 25–416 417–423 (3)   158 × 92 mm   ICU, MMeT–Hi, NcAS, NN,
                                                                         NNAB, PPL–R

Separate issue of the English part of the Kneeland Greek-English edition of 1823 (No 477) from the same typesetting. P xvii–xxii misnumbered v–x. Has one leaf for Family Record with border. At end are Emendations and a page of Errata, followed by a list of other theological books of the publisher. Verso of title has Copyright (Pennsylvania), March 23, 1822. This edition was priced at $1.50.

1823 The New Testament . . . [26th Edition]. A. Paul, Printer . . . Stereotyped for "The American Bible Society," by D. & G. Bruce: New York   **479**

157 × 90 mm   MiU, N, NNAB

Reprint of 1819 ABS Bourgeois Duodecimo (No 388).

1823 The New Testament . . . Stereotyped by J. Howe, New York . . . Printed . . . by Johnstone and Van Norden: New York   **480**

288 p   152 × 94 mm   NN

1823 The New Testament . . . Stereotyped by Hammond Wallis, New-York. Printed by Simeon Ide: Windsor [Vermont]   **481**

Reported as 372 p   152 × 82 mm   MWA, VtMiS

Note dated Oct 7, 1875 in NNAB 1833 Windsor Bible, presented by S. Ide: "Simeon Ide of Claremont, N. H., says he bought the plates (new) of the 12mo NT in 1823 from H. Wallis, stereotyper of N. Y."

1823 The New Testament . . . with references and a key sheet of questions; historical, doctrinal and practical . . . by Hervey Wilbur. [Second Edition] . . . Stereotyped by T. H. and C. Carter . . . Published by Cummings, Hilliard & Co.: Boston   **482**

1 vol: (324) (18)   138 × 74 mm   NNAB

Preliminary matter includes frontispiece, Recommendations and Advertisement to This Edition, and Order of Books. Text is followed by key questions; then, with separate title page, Useful Tables . . . prepared to accompany the Reference Testament. By Hervey Wilbur . . . Published by Cummings, Hilliard & Co., Boston; Bliss & White, New York; and E. Littell, Philadelphia . . . 1824 (paged 1–18).

MWA has copy with imprint *Published by R. Bannister . . . Boston, stereotyped by T. H. Carter and Co.*; key sheet on p [3]; text begins on p 5 and ends p 321; no added matter at end.

The copyrights for Wilbur's Reference Testament and Reference Bible are dated 1822 and 1825 respectively. The Testament was published in 12mo and 32mo and the Bible in 4to and 12mo. Various stereotypers are listed in the imprints of subsequent editions and although their general format is similar, few seem to be printed from the same plates.

1823 The New Testament . . . Printed and sold by George Goodwin: Hartford **483**

1 vol: (412) 413–416   102 × 54 mm   NN, NNAB

Has frontispiece and added engraved title page. Order of Books precedes text; Contents at end.

1823 The New Testament . . . E. T. Scott: Philadelphia   **484**

445 p   96 × 54 mm   NN

1824 The Holy Bible . . . With Canne's Marginal Notes and References . . . Stereotyped, Printed and Published by H. and E. Phinney: Cooperstown [New York]   **485**

1 vol: 9–574 (99) 579–754 755–768   254 × 194 mm   NCooHi, NN, NNAB

Preliminary matter includes Map of the Journeyings of the Children of Israel, To the Reader [by Dr. Witherspoon], and Contents. With Apocrypha (paged 1–99). Family Record, frontispiece, and Account of Dates precede NT. At end are Index, Tables, etc. 7 engravings, signed by J. Seymour and S. Hill. See 1822, No 439.

NCooHi copy lacks Apocrypha.

1824   The Holy Bible . . . With Canne's Marginal Notes and References . . . Stereotyped by E. White . . . Published and Sold by Kimber and Sharpless: Phila-
delphia   *486*

1 vol: (570) (112) 571–770   250 × 194 mm   CtY, ICHi, MWA, MWelC, NNAB, PP

Same as Kimber and Sharpless 1823 edition (No 460) except Concordance and Metrical Psalms are omitted and Apocrypha and engravings are added.

1824   The Holy Bible . . . Apocrypha . . . with Canne's marginal notes and references . . . Stereotyped by E. White . . . Published and Sold by Daniel D.
Smith: New York   *487*

1 vol: (570) (112) 573–770   248 × 193 mm   NjPasHi, NN, NNAB

Same as 1820 Smith edition (No 395) except with engraved frontispieces to OT and NT, Family Record following Apocrypha, and Account of Dates preceding NT.

NN copy has no engravings; NNAB has second copy with different engravings and more of them.

1824   The Holy Bible . . . with Canne's Marginal Notes and References . . . Together with the Apocrypha . . . Stereotyped for Collins and Co. By B. & J.
Collins . . . Published by C. Ewer & T. Bedlington: Boston   *488*

1 vol: (6) 9–744 (138) 1009–1010 (4) 747–1008 (56) (2)   244 × 190 mm
                                                                                    ICU, MWA, NN, NNAB

Same as Collins 1821 quarto (No 414) except for a few changes in position of appended matter. Concordance (1824). 16 plates.

NN copy has 2 maps and 21 historical engravings.

1824   The Holy Bible . . . H. C. Carey & I. Lea: Philadelphia   *489*

243 × 183 mm   NNAB

Same as Carey's 1812/11 quarto (No 208) from standing type. Error in Lev 19:12 continued. 3 maps and 8 historical engravings. Cited copy has general title page missing.

1824   The Holy Bible . . . with Ostervald's Notes . . . Holbrook and Fessenden's
stereotype hot-press edition. Holbrook and Fessenden: Brattleborough *490*

242 × 180 mm   CtY, MWA, VtHi, VtU

Same as Holbrook stereotype quarto of 1817 (No 327) but with addition of Ostervald's Notes. Concordance. NT title imprinted *Stereotyped by B. & J. Collins . . . Printed and sold by John Holbrook.*

1824   The Holy Bible . . . commentary and critical notes by Adam Clarke. First
American Royal Octavo Edition . . . [Stereotyped by A. Chandler]. Printed
and published by Abm. Paul; also published by N. Bangs and T. Mason:
New York; Martin Ruter: Cincinnati, Ohio; and Armstrong and Plaskitt:
Baltimore   *491*

Reported as 948 p   210 × 120 mm   TNMPH

Vol ɪ only, Genesis-Joshua, of Clarke's Commentary; see 1811–25, No 188. Perhaps this goes with the 1823 NT (No 472).

1824   The Holy Bible, Translated from the Latin Vulgat . . . First Published by the English College at Doway . . . 1609. And the New Testament, First Published by the English College at Rhemes . . . 1582. With Annotations, References, and a Historical and Chronological Index. First Stereotype, from the Fifth Dublin Edition. Newly Revised and Corrected According to the Clementin Edition of the Scriptures . . . [Stereotyped by J. Howe]. Eugene Cummiskey: Philadelphia   **492**

Reported as (335) (444) (191) (3) (10)   195 × 107 mm   DGU

Rheims-Douay Version, from Dr. Troy's 5th Dublin edition. Preliminary matter includes added engraved title page dated 1827, Admonition, Prayer, Decree of the Council of Trent, and Order of Books. Approbation of Dr. Troy, 1791; Admonition; Prayer; Approbation of Henry Conwell, Bishop of Philadelphia, 1824; and Order of Books follow NT title. At end are A Table of References (p 190–191), A Table of All the Epistles (1 p), Index to NT (2 p), and Index to OT (10 p).

NNAB has copy with NT dated 1831, but otherwise matches this edition. DGU has another copy without Bishop Conwell's Approbation. DLC and NN have NT only, dated 1824. See O'Callaghan, p 165 and 166.

1824   The Holy Bible . . . [63rd Edition]. Printed by A. Paul. Stereotyped for The American Bible Society . . . by D. & G. Bruce: New York   **493**

166 × 94 mm   NNAB

From same plates as 1819 ABS Minion Duodecimo (No 377).

1824   The Holy Bible . . . Stereotyped by B. and J. Collins, New York . . . Printed by Websters and Skinners: Albany   **494**

160 × 90 mm   NNAB

Same as Websters and Skinners stereotype edition of 1817 (No 331) with error in 1 Tim 4:16 continued.

1824   The Holy Bible . . . Stereotyped by B. and J. Collins, New-York . . . J. H. A. Frost, Printer . . . Published by Richardson and Lord: Boston   **495**

157 × 90 mm   MB

Same as Richardson and Lord stereotyped edition of 1818 (No 350).

1824   The Holy Bible . . . H. C. Carey and I. Lea: Philadelphia   **496**

148 × 87 mm   NN

Format is same as Carey's 1803/02 duodecimo (No 106) from standing type.

1824   The Holy Bible . . . Printed by Hudson and Co.: Hartford   **497**

147 × 87 mm   NN

Reprint of Hudson & Goodwin edition of 1809 (No 168) from standing type. Cited copy has "For Louisa Webster, Jan. 1, 1828" written on fly leaf in the handwriting of Noah Webster.

1824?   The Holy Bible . . . Thomas Scott's Commentary . . . W. W. Woodward: Philadelphia   **498**

135 × 72 mm   Not Located

Scott's Annotated Bible; see 1804–09, No 113. NNAB has a flyer advertising Woodward's plan for a six volume pocket size edition of Scott's Bible, without marginal references but with full commentary, from the "last London Standard Edition"; to "contain about seven hundred pages" (in each volume?), to be delivered in boards at $1.75, in sheep at $2, and in calf at $2.50 per volume, successively in three months, payment on delivery. Those who secured four paid subscriptions would receive one set free. Woodward also planned a special deluxe edition on better paper, more elaborately bound.

1824   The Holy Bible . . . Stereotyped by B. and J. Collins, New York . . . Published
         by Silas Andrus: Hartford   *499*

1 vol: (690) (210)   128 × 65 mm   MWA, NN, NNAB
Preliminary matter includes frontispiece, added engraved title page (*Published by Silas Andrus, and Johnstone and Van Norden: New York and Hartford*), To the Reader [by Dr. Witherspoon], and Order of Books. Error in 1 Tim 4:16, *thy* doctrine, for *the* doctrine.
MWA copy omits printer's name on general title.
This is the first Bible issued by Silas Andrus who published numerous editions from 1824, joining with Judd about 1832 and with Judd and Franklin in 1837–39. The firm became known as S. Andrus and Son or William Andrus in the 1840s.

1824   The Holy Bible . . . Stereotyped by B. and J. Collins, New York . . . Johnstone
         and Van Norden, Printers . . . Published and sold by Johnstone and Van Nor-
         den: New York   *500*

Reported as (690) (210)   128 × 65 mm   MWA
Similar to Andrus edition of this year (No 499).

1824   The Holy Bible . . . Stereotyped by J. Howe, Philadelphia . . . Published by
         Daniel D. Smith: New-York   *501*

1 vol: (743) (238)   123 × 57 mm   NN, NNAB
The first edition of a new 32mo format. Preliminary matter includes two engravings by V. Brughel, Contents, added engraved title page, and Order of Books of OT. Two engravings by Maratti and Holbein follow OT; then Contents and Order of Books of NT.
Number and position of plates vary: also published without engravings.

1824   The New Testament . . . Published by David Watson: Woodstock [Vermont]
                                                                                    502

"8vo"   Not Located
Listed in NNAB card file from a dealer's catalogue, 1943.

1824   The New Testament . . . [1st Edition, A. Paul, Printer]. Stereotyped by A.
         Chandler for "The American Bible Society": New-York   *503*

429 p   185 × 112 mm   NNAB
This is the first Pica Octavo to be published from separate plates for the NT. Size of type is considerably larger than that of any former edition published by the ABS, and is set in a form more adapted to the circumstances of those whose sight has become impaired. (*ABS Report* for 1824, p 4.)
NN and MWA have third edition for this year; MWA also has sixth edition.

1824   The New Testament . . . Stereotyped by T. H. & C. Carter: Boston. Published
         by Jacob B. Moore: Concord, N. H.   *504*

Reported as (283) (4)   163 × 89 mm   MBU–T, MWA
Has An Alphabetical Table of Proper Names at end. MWA copy has on cover, stamped in a circle, *New Hampshire Bible Society*.

1824   The New Testament . . . The Pronouncing Testament . . . To which is applied
         . . . the Orthoepy of the Critical Pronouncing Dictionary . . . by John Walker

...to which is prefixed, An Explanatory Key ... by Israel Alger, Jun. ... Stereotyped by T. H. & C. Carter: Boston ... Published by Lincoln and Edmands: Boston. Sold also by Cushing & Jewett, Baltimore; Abraham Small, Philadelphia; John P. Haven, New York   **505**

Reported as (iv) 5–292   164 × 87 mm   MWA
Has vignette below center of title. See 1822 NT, No 452.

1824   The New Testament ... Stereotyped by B. and J. Collins, New York ... Published by Richardson and Lord, J. H. A. Frost: Boston   **506**

Reported as 312 p   "12mo"   MB
Added is *A Table of Kindred*.

1824   The New Testament ... Marot & Walker: Philadelphia   **507**

"12mo"   Not Located
Wright, p 393.

1824   The New Testament ... Stereotyped by B. & J. Collins, New York. Printed and Published by Josiah B. Baldwin: Bridgeport, Connecticut   **508**

290 [1] p   "12mo"   Not Located
O'Callaghan, p 169. Table follows text.

1824   The New Testament ... James Cunningham: New York   **509**

152 × 94 mm   Not Located
Wright, p 331. Same size as 1823 Johnstone and Van Norden NT (No 480).

1824   The New Testament ... [Stereotyped by B. and J. Collins, New York] ... Websters & Skinners: Albany   **510**

Reported as 609–792   151 × 91 mm   DLC

1824   Revised Testament ... The New Testament ... in which the common version is divided into paragraphs, the punctuation in many cases altered, and some words, not in the original, expunged. Stereotyped by T. H. Carter & Co. ... Published by Cummings, Hilliard & Co. ... : Boston   **511**

1 vol: (4) 3–297   149 × 81 mm   MB, MH–AH, MWA, NN, NNAB
    Printed in paragraph form, following Knapp's edition of the Griesbach text but with verse numbers in the outer margin. Verso of title page has record of registery by John H. Wilkins in the District Clerk's office, Massachusetts, May 1, 1824; followed by unsigned Preface, dated May 15, 1824 (2 p).
    MH–AH copy has note: "Possibly the author is John Hubbard Wilkins, 1794–1861, H. C. 1818."

1824   The New Testament ... Stereotyped for The Bible Society of Philadelphia: [Philadelphia]   **512**

352 p   136 × 75 mm   NN, NNAB

1824   The New Testament ... S. Andrus: Hartford   **513**

209 p   129 × 64 mm   NN, NNU
Has frontispiece and added engraved title page dated 1826.

1824   The New Testament . . . Stereotyped by B. and J. Collins . . . Published . . .
         by Johnstone & Van Norden: New-York   *514*

209 p   129 × 63 mm   NNAB
Appears to be same as NT of 1818 Collins and Hannay Bible (No 353) and 1817 Sheldon
and Goodrich NT (No 343), both from plates stereotyped by B. and J. Collins. See also No 513.

1824   The New Testament . . . Published by Holbrook & Fessenden: Brattle-
         borough, Vt.   *515*

120 × 62 mm   CSmH, CtHT–W, MWA, NN, NNAB, VtHi
Same as 1819 Holbrook NT (No 393).

1824   The New Testament . . . Darius Clark: Bennington, Vermont   *516*

335 [1] p   120 × 62 mm   MWA, NN
Table follows text.

1824   The Four Gospels, translated from the Greek. With Preliminary Disserta-
         tions, and Notes Critical and Explanatory. By George Campbell . . . In four
         volumes . . . With the Author's Last Corrections. True and Greene, Printers
         . . . Published by Timothy Bedlington and Charles Ewer: Boston   *517*

Vol III: (xxxv) (412)   171 × 104 mm   NNAB
George Campbell Version; see 1796, No 56. Reprint of the 1811 edition (No 207) with
Vol III containing complete text of the Gospels.

1825   The Holy Bible, Translated from the Latin Vulgate: Diligently Compared
         with the Hebrew, Greek, and Other Editions in Divers Languages . . . Douay-
         Rheims. With Useful Notes . . . Selected . . . By the Rev. Geo. Leo Haydock,
         and Other Divines . . . Embellished with Twenty Superb Engravings . . .
         Printed and Published by Eugene Cummiskey: Philadelphia   *518*

2 vols: Vol I, (812); Vol II, (409) (7) (xii) (367) (9)   360 × 199 mm   DGU, DLC,
                                                                                NN, NNAB
Rheims-Douay Version, from Haydock's folio Bible, Manchester, England, 1811–14. Preliminary matter includes frontispiece; Advertisement; Approbations; Admonition; Letter of
Pope Pius VI, Prayer; Decree of the Council of Trent; historical sketch; Approbation of Cummiskey's quarto and octavo Bibles, signed by Dr. Conwell, Dec 13, 1824, with Approbation
to the folio edition; Preface; List of Principal Commentators; and Order of Books. Index and
Family Record follow OT. Frontispiece and General Preface precede NT. At end are Publisher's Data, Index, Table, List of Readings, Theological History in Miniature, and List of
Subscribers.
    Also issued without engravings, without date, or with date of 1826 on back.
    1,000 copies were originally published in the United States, 1823–25, in 120 weekly
numbers of 16 pages each at 25¢.

1825   The Holy Bible . . . Apocrypha . . . Canne's marginal notes and references . . .
         Stereotyped, printed and published by H. & E. Phinney: Cooperstown   *519*

Reported as (576) (99) 579–768   254 × 194 mm   CoHi, CtY, MBC, MWA, N,
                                                                          OClWHi, VtMiS
See 1822, No 439.
NCooHi has 30 editions of Phinney quartos from 1824 to 1848. The number of engravings
varies but eight in addition to a frontispiece seems the most usual arrangement. This library has
4 varying copies of the above edition: (1) without Apocrypha and with illustrations like those
in the 1824 edition (No 485); (2) with Apocrypha and 20 wood engravings; (3) without

Apocrypha or illustrations but with NT dated 1826; (4) another dated 1825/26 without Apocrypha but with 10 engravings, signed by J. Seymour, Samuel Hill, and N. Haven (not all of these are the same as in the 1824 edition). NNAB has copy with 1826 NT.

NCooHi also has copies with varying imprints (. . . sold also by I. Tiffany, Utica) dated 1838, 1839, 1840, 1841, 1843, 1844, and 1848. The last has the I. Tiffany imprint on the NT title only; added to the general title is *Buffalo, — F. W. Breed.*

1825   The Holy Bible . . . Apocrypha . . . Stereotyped by E. White, New York; Published . . . by Daniel D. Smith: New-York   **520**

1 vol: (10) 5–570 (112) (6) 573–770 (54) (4)   253 × 193 mm   ICL, MB, MWA, NN, NNAB

Appears to be same as 1820 Smith quarto (No 395). Has concordance (stereotyped by J. Howe . . . 1825) 54 p, Family Record, and 17 engravings.

1825   The Holy Bible . . . Apocrypha . . . with Canne's marginal notes and references . . . Stereotyped by B. & J. Collins . . . J. H. A. Frost, Printer . . . Published by C. Ewer and T. Bedlington: Boston   **521**

1 vol: (1010) (56)   243 × 190 mm   MWA, NNAB

Similar to Collins edition of 1821 (No 414). Preliminary matter includes frontispiece, To the Reader, Order of Books, Account of Dates, and Advertisement to Collins' Stereotype Edition. Apocrypha followed by Family Record. At end are Index, Tables, etc., and Concordance (1824). 8 engravings by Butterworth-Livesey & Co.

NNAB has another copy without Apocrypha and Concordance, and with one engraving only which is labelled *For Rutter, Gaylord & Co., Edition, 1825.* See No 526.

1825   The Holy Bible . . . H. C. Carey & I. Lea: Philadelphia   **522**

1080 p   243 × 182 mm   NN

Same as Carey's quarto of 1812/11 (No 208) from standing type. Has Apocrypha but no Concordance. 8 historical engravings and 2 maps.

1825   The Holy Bible . . . with Ostervald's Notes. Stereotype Hot-Press Edition. Collins' Correct Stereotype Copy. Holbrook & Fessenden: Brattleborough   **523**

242 × 180 mm   MWA, NN, NNAB

Appears to be reprint of Holbrook & Fessenden stereotype quarto of 1824 (No 486) except it has 19 historical engravings by Chorly, Scoles, and others, and 7 maps and diagrams.

1825?   The Holy Bible . . . Charles Ewer: Boston   **524**

Reported as (744) (138) (8) 747–1010 (2) (56)   240 × 180 mm   MWA
Contains Apocrypha and Concordance.

1825?   The Holy Bible . . . Published by Charles Ewer: Boston   **525**

Reported as (683) (1) (160) (2) 687–932   240 × 180 mm   MBU–T, MWA
Appears to be same as Collins quarto of 1816 (No 296). With Apocrypha. Added engraved title imprinted *Published by Matthew Teprell. Sold by Freeman, Rutter & Co. at their Bookstore, wholesale & retail: Boston.*

1825   The Holy Bible . . . together with the Apocrypha . . . Stereotyped by B. & J. Collins, New-York. Published by Matthew M. Teprell. Sold wholesale and retail by Rutter, Gaylord & Co.: Boston   **526**

Reported as (683) (1) (160) (2) 687–932   240 × 180 mm   MWA
Appears to be same as 1816 Collins quarto (No 296). Has added engraved title page.

1825   The Holy Bible, Translated from the Latin Vulgate: Diligently Compared
with the Hebrew, Greek and Other Editions, in Divers Languages . . . With
Annotations, References, and a Historical and Chronological Index. First
Stereotype, from the Fifth Dublin Edition. Newly Revised and Corrected
According to the Clementin Edition . . . [Stereotyped by Hammond Wallis].
Published by Eugene Cummiskey: Philadelphia   **527**

Reported as (789) (228) (7) (2)   230 × 149 mm   DGU, MdBS
Rheims-Douay Version, from Dr. Troy's 5th Dublin edition. DGU copy has 10 engravings
and List of Subscribers.

1825/26   The Holy Bible. . . [with Clarke's Notes]. Royal Octavo Stereotype Edition. Stereotyped by A. Chandler. Azor Hoyt, Printer. Published by N.
Bangs and J. Emory for the Methodist Episcopal Church . . . : New York **528**

6 vols: Vol ɪ, 948 p; Vol ɪɪ, 888 p; Vol ɪɪɪ, 888 p; Vol ɪᴠ, 554 p; Vol ᴠ, 875 p; Vol ᴠɪ, 1015 p
23 cm   NN, ViU
For Adam Clarke, see 1811–25, No 188. Vol ɪ (1825) preliminary matter includes Adver-
tisement by A. Clarke, London, 1810 and General Preface; then OT text which runs through
Vols ɪɪ (1825), ɪɪɪ (1825), and ɪᴠ (1826) followed by appended material. NT text in last 2 vols,
Vol ɪ (1825) and Vol ɪɪ (1826). Each volume has own title page, some reading *First Royal
Octavo Stereotype Edition* or *First American Royal Octavo Edition.*
ViU has Vols ɪ–ᴠ only.
ViU reports four similar editions: (1) by N. Bangs and J. Emory, 1827; (2) by J. Emory
and B. Waugh, 1828; (3) by J. Emory and B. Waugh, 1831 (NT only); (4) by B. Waugh and
T. Mason, 1832. IU and MH have 1832/31 edition by J. Emory and B. Waugh (Vols ɪɪ and ɪɪɪ,
1831). TNMB has 1833 edition printed by J. Collord and published by B. Waugh and T.
Mason.

1825   The Holy Bible . . . with Canne's marginal notes and references . . . Stereotyped by J. Howe, Philadelphia. Published and Sold by Daniel D. Smith:
New York   **529**

811 p   205 × 120 mm   MB, NjMD, NNAB
Preliminary matter includes frontispiece, engraved OT title, Order of Books, To the
Reader [by Dr. Witherspoon], and Contents. Tables follow OT. NT has frontispiece, added engraved title, full NT title, and Account of Dates. 8 engravings drawn by R. Westall and engraved
by Wm. D. Smith.
NN has copy with Apocrypha (109 p), Metrical Psalms, and Concordance dated 1825
(103 p).

1825   The Holy Bible . . . Printed and published by Holbrook and Fessenden: Brattleborough, Vt.   **530**

Reported as 684 p   189 × 158 mm   VtHi

1825   The Holy Bible. [The Pronouncing Bible] . . . according to the orthoepy of
John Walker, as contained in his critical pronouncing dictionary and key to
the classical pronunciation of Greek, Latin, and Scripture Proper Names. By
Israel Alger, Jun., A.M. . . . Stereotyped by T. H. Carter & Co. Printed and
published by Lincoln & Edmands: Boston   **531**

1 vol: (714) (218) 219–220   189 × 101 mm   MWA, NN, NNAB
Preliminary matter includes engraved short and full title pages, Advertisement by the
Editor, Explanatory Key, and List of Books of the Testaments. NT title page imprinted *Stereo-
typed by S. Walker & Co.*, with Tables on verso. At end are Recommendations (by various
authorities from Boston and one from Pawtucket), and an Advertisement of Lincoln and
Edmands' Pronouncing Testament, Reader, etc. 30 small engravings, two to a page.
MWA copy has frontispieces and added engraved title.

1825 The Holy Bible . . . Stereotyped by B. & J. Collins . . . E. Cushing: Lunenburg, Mass.   **532**

792 p   160 × 90 mm   CSmH, MWA, NN
Tables follow OT.

1825 The Holy Bible . . . Holbrook and Fessenden's Stereotype Edition . . . Printed
and published by Holbrook and Fessenden: Brattleborough, Vt.   **533**

Reported as 3–526 (2) 529–684   159 × 60 mm   MWA, VtHi
Verso of title has statement: "This American stereotype Bible has been copied from the
Edinburgh edition printed under the revision of the General Assembly of the Kirk of Scotland,
and carefully compared with the Cambridge, Oxford, Hartford and New-York edition. D. & G.
Bruce. *New-York, June, 1815.*" See 1815, No 279.

1825 The Old and New Testaments; having a rich and comprehensive assemblage
of half a million parallel and illustrative passages, from those esteemed
authors Canne, Browne, Blayney, and Scott, and with those from the Latin
Vulgate, the French, and German Bibles, the whole arranged in scripture
order, and presenting, in a portable pocket volume, a complete library of
divinity. Bonus Textaurius est bonus Theologus. Printed for Thomas
Wardle: Philadelphia   **534**

Reported as (585) (188)   137 × 82 mm   PPPrHi
Half titles for Testaments read *The English Version of the Polyglott Bible.* Preliminary
matter includes Advertisement on verso of title; Praefatio in Biblia Polyglotta, in Latin (2 p);
Preface to the English Version of the Polyglott Bible, signed "T.C." [Thomas Chevalier] (5 p);
and Order of Books and Chronological Tables (1 p). The center reference column contains
different readings, indicated by Greek letters, from the folio and quarto Polyglott Bibles
Bagster was then editing in England, a series of references indicated by italic letters, and a
chronology at the top of the column. Interleaved with the text but paged separately is the
Scripture Harmony, or Concordance of Parallel Passages, etc.
    CSmH, ICU, and NNAB have undated copies with general title reading *The Old and
New Testaments; being the English Version of the Polyglott Bible; having a rich . . . divinity.
Printed for Samuel Bagster: London;* special NT title has *Philadelphia: printed for Thomas
Wardle, 1825.* It is possible that Wardle imported the books in sheets, supplying his own im-
print as the books were bound.
    This may be the first American edition of this small Bible and it was many times reprinted
in this country during the next twenty-five years. See 1831 B, No 753.

1825 The New Testament . . . Stereotyped by E. White. Daniel D. Smith: New-
York   **535**

573–748 p   254 × 194 mm   NN
NN copy interleaved with manuscript notes.

1825 The New Testament . . . Commentary and Critical Notes . . . by Adam Clarke
. . . Second American Stereotype Edition . . . Printed and published by A.
Paul: New York . . . Also published by N. Bangs and J. Emory . . . : New York;
Martin Ruter: Cincinnati, Ohio; Armstrong and Plaskitt: Baltimore   **536**

Reported as (863) (12)   210 mm   NcD, ViW
For Adam Clarke, see 1811–25, No 188. This is not from the same plates as the 1823
A. Paul edition (No 472). Vol ɪ only, Matthew through Acts. Text followed by Tables.

1825 The New Testament . . . Stereotype Edition. Stereotyped by T. H. & C. Carter: Boston. David Watson, Printer: Woodstock [Vermont]. Published by
Stevens & Blake: Claremont, New Hampshire   **537**

Reported as 283 p   163 × 88 mm   MWA

1825 The New Testament . . . Stereotyped by T. H. & C. Carter: Boston . . . David Watson, Printer: Woodstock [Vermont] . . . Published by Blake, Cutler & Co.: Bellows-Falls, Vt.   **538**
Reported as 283 p   163 × 88 mm   MB

1825 The New Testament . . . Stereotyped by B. & J. Collins . . . Published by Edmund Cushing: Lunenburg, Mass.   **539**
Reported as 609–792 p   160 × 90 mm   MiU
Separate issue of NT from Collins' stereotype Bible published by Cushing in 1825 (No 532).

1825 The New Testament . . . [The Pronouncing Testament]. Adopted from "A Key To The Classical Pronunciation of Greek, Latin, and Scripture Proper Names," by John Walker . . . To which is prefixed An Explanatory Key, by Israel Alger, Jun . . . Stereotyped by T. H. & C. Carter . . . Printed and Published by Lincoln & Edmands: Boston   **540**
Reported as (4) (292)   "12mo"   MB, MWA
Seems to be reprint of 1824 NT (No 505). Materials added to text include Key to Pronunciation, Table of Offices, Advertisement to This Edition, and Notice of Copyright. Has two illustrations.

1825 The New Testament . . . from which is selected an extensive vocabulary comprising the proper names and all other important words . . . arranged in columns over chapters from which they are selected . . . to which is prefixed Walker's Explanatory Key, governing the vocabulary . . . Jeremiah Goodrich . . . Published . . . by S. Shaw: Albany   **541**
1 vol: (6) 7–333 [1]   146 × 80 mm   NNAB
Preliminary matter includes frontispiece, Contents, Analysis of the Old and New Testaments, The Books of the NT, and A Table of Dipthongal Vowels, with note: "The observations at the heads of the books were taken from a Testament published in Edinburgh by Rev. William Brown." Words in the vocabulary are divided, defined, and pronounced, according to the authorities of John Walker. Has 3 historical engravings.

1825 The New Testament . . . Stereotype Edition . . . H. and E. Phinney: Cooperstown [New York]   **542**
Reported as 324 p   140 × 90 mm   CtHT–W

1825 The New Testament . . . [43rd Edition]. Stereotyped by A. Chandler and Co. for "The American Bible Society": New York   **543**
352 p   137 × 75 mm   NNAB
From same plates as 1820 Brevier Octodecimo (No 412).

1825 The New Testament . . . Stereotype Edition . . . Darius Clark: Bennington, Vermont   **544**
Reported as 335 p   120 × 62 mm   MWA, VtHi
Appears to have been printed from plates made from type of the 1824 edition (No 516).

1825 The New Testament . . . Published by Richardson and Lord: Boston   **545**
"18mo"   Not Located
O'Callaghan (p 386) quotes Melvin Lord: "This edition was designed for use of Schools. It was edited by Renselaer Bentley, and contained a Vocabulary of the words used in the book, alphabetically arranged, with their division, accentuation, part of speech, and definition; also, a list of all the proper names embraced in it, accented and pronounced."

PART II
1826 through 1957

1826? The Holy Bible [Self-Interpreting Bible] With References and Illustra-
tions . . . An Analysis of the Contents of Each Chapter, Explanatory Notes,
Evangelical Reflections . . . By the Late Rev. John Brown . . . T. Kinnersley:
New-York   **546**

    1 vol: (li) 3–1223   46 cm   NN, NNAB
    Reprint or reissue of Brown's 1822/20 Bible (No 433). Added engraved title page (dated
1826) has *The Self-Interpreting Bible with an Evangelical Commentary by the Late Revd.
John Brown . . . Brown's Splendid Bible.* Preliminary matter contains To the Reader by J. Brown;
Calculation of Number of Books, Chapters, Verses, etc. of the Testaments and the Apocrypha;
Introduction to the Right Understanding of the Oracles of God; and Order of Books. Family
Record follows OT. Tables at end. No Apocrypha. Engravings.

1826 The Holy Bible . . . Apocrypha . . . Canne's Marginal Notes and References
. . . Index . . . Printed and published by G. M. Davison: Saratoga Springs **547**

    Reported as (576) (96) 579–768   28 cm   NCooHi

1826 The Holy Bible . . . Canne's Marginal Notes and References . . . Stereotyped
by E. White, New York . . . Published and Sold by Kimber and Sharpless:
Philadelphia   **548**

    1 vol: (10) (570) 573–770   28 cm   NNAB
    Follows 1823 edition (No 460). Apocrypha wanting? Has To the Reader, Order of Books,
and Contents. NT title has Account of the Dates on verso. Index and Tables at end.

1826 The Holy Bible . . . Translated from the Latin Vulgat . . . With Annotations,
References, Indexes, etc . . . First Stereotype, from the Fifth Dublin Edition
. . . [Stereotyped by Hammond Wallis, New York] Published by Eugene
Cummiskey: Philadelphia   **549**

    28 cm   DGU, NN
    Appears to be Cummiskey's Bible of 1825 (No 527) with date altered. O'Callaghan
(p 176) says 1,000 copies of this edition were printed. Illustrated.

1826 The Holy Bible . . . [Daniel D. Smith's Stereotype Edition] With Canne's
Marginal Notes and References . . . Stereotyped by E. White, New-York . . .
Published and Sold by Daniel D. Smith: New York   **550**

    1 vol: (570) (112) 573–770 (34)   28 cm   NNAB
    Reprint of Smith's 1820 quarto (No 395) but with Apocrypha and Concordance.
NNAB has second copy with NT dated 1827 and Concordance dated 1825; Metrical Psalms;
frontispieces and engravings; OT title adds *Illustrated with engravings by Wright and Smith
from the designs of Richard Westall.*

1826–28 The Collateral Bible; or, A Key to the Holy Scriptures; in Which All the
Corresponding Texts are Brought Together Into One View, and Arranged
in a Familiar and Easy Manner. By William M'Corkle, Assisted by the Rev.
E. S. Ely, D.D., and the Rev. G. T. Bedell . . . J. Harding, Printer . . . Samuel
F. Bradford: Philadelphia; and E. Bliss and E. White: New York   **551**

    3 vols: Vol i, 809 p; Vol ii, 1012 p; Vol iii, 731 p   28 cm   NNAB

Vol ɪ (1826) preliminary matter includes Order of Books, Dr. Mill's Chronology of the NT, Account of the Translations of the Bible, Dedication to King James, Tables, Genealogy, and Preface; text: Genesis-Judges. Vol ɪɪ (Published by John Laval and Samuel F. Bradford, 1828) Ruth-Psalms. Vol ɪɪɪ (same imprint and date as Vol ɪɪ) Proverbs-Malachi.

The text is printed in three columns with that of related passages printed in smaller type after many verses. M'Corkle's name appears only on Vol ɪ title but is on the copyright in all three volumes. The NT text was never published.

1826?   The Holy Bible, in Three Volumes . . . Apocrypha . . . J. H. White's Stereo-
          type Edition. [Printed and Published by John H. White: Halifax]   552

3 vols: Vol ɪ, 787 p; Vol ɪɪ, (277) (139); Vol ɪɪɪ, 281–600   28 cm   ICN, NNAB
Format is similar to S. Walker's edition of 1826 (No 553). Vol ɪ, Genesis-Song of Solomon. Vol ɪɪ, Isaiah-Malachi; Apocrypha. Vol ɪɪɪ, NT text. Many of the engravings have *Eng. for Teal's Edition* and are similar to those in Teal's 1822 edition (No 434).
ICN copy catalogued 1830?. NNAB copy has Vol ɪɪ and ɪɪɪ bound together.
Above imprint taken from Vol ɪɪ. Correspondence with various Canadian and other bibliographical authorities and with Halifax in England has failed to produce any information about this edition or to locate other copies.

1826?   The Holy Bible . . . with References and various readings. Illustrated with
          engravings. In Two Volumes . . . Stereotyped at the Boston Type and Stereo-
          type Foundry. Late T. H. Carter & Co. . . . Printed and Published by S.
          Walker: Boston   553

2 vols: Vol ɪ, (4) (787) [1]; Vol ɪɪ, (2) 3–277 (2) (139) (3) 281–600   27 cm   NNAB
Frontispiece and added engraved title to each volume. With Apocrypha. Preliminary matter includes Order of Books and A Guide to a Regular Perusal of the Holy Scriptures by William Stones (for reading the NT and Psalms twice a year and the OT once). Family Record pages before NT have been removed. Issued in 116 numbers, not including Apocrypha. Some of the engravings (a few signed R. Campbell and J. B. Nagle) are dated 1826 and appeared previously in Walker's edition of Brown's 1822 Self-Interpreting Bible (No 432). NT has Stereotyped by James Conner.

1826   The Holy Bible . . . With Canne's Marginal Notes and References . . . M. M.
         Teprell: Boston   554

Reported as 932 p   27 cm   MB
Has engraved title-page, Brown's Concordance, etc. Apocrypha wanting?

1826   The Holy Bible . . . Stereotyped at the Boston Type and Stereotype Foundry,
         Late T. H. Carter & Co . . . Printed at Treadwell's Press . . . Published by Hil-
         liard, Gray, Little, and Wilkins, Munroe & Francis, Richardson & Lord, Lin-
         coln & Edmands, Crocker & Brewster, T. Bedlington, R. P. & C. Williams,
         Charles Ewer, Thomas Wells, and Josiah Loring: Boston   555

1 vol: (687) (134) (211)   23 cm.   NNAB
With Apocrypha, Tables, and Contents of Testaments.

1826   The Holy Bible [The Pronouncing Bible] . . . according to the orthoepy of
         John Walker . . . Stereotyped by T. H. Carter & Co. Printed and published
         by Lincoln & Edmands: Boston   556

21 cm   MBU–T
Reprint of 1825 edition (No 531).

1826? The Holy Bible . . . Translated from the Latin Vulgate . . . With Annotations by the Rev. Dr. Challoner; Together with References and an Historical and Chronological Index. With the Approbation of the Provincial Council. F. Lucas, jr.: Baltimore **557**

1 vol: (810) (214)   20 cm   NN

Rheims-Douay, from 5th Dublin edition. Has annotations at foot of page. Index wanting? This date may be wrong for Father Parsons lists the first edition of this Bible as 1837.

1826 The Holy Bible . . . Stereotyped by B. & J. Collins, New York . . . Johnstone and Van Norden, Printers . . . Published by Silas Andrus: Hartford **558**

"12mo"   Not Located

O'Callaghan, p 179.

1826 [The Holy Bible] The Reference Bible . . . With References . . . Key Sheet of Questions . . . Harmonies . . . Maps . . . Useful Tables . . . By Hervey Wilbur . . . Fourth Edition. [Power Press. — J. G. Rogers & Co.] Published by Cummings, Hilliard & Co., and Crocker & Brewster: Boston. Also by the American Sunday School Union: Philadelphia **559**

2 vols: Vol I, 736 p; Vol II, 737–1012 (324) (101)   19 cm   NN, NNAB

Wilbur's Reference Bible; for his NT, see 1823, No 482. Vol I preliminary matter includes added engraved title, Copyright 1825, Advertisement, Key, Order of Books, and Hints; text: Genesis-Ecclesiastes. Vol II has title and Key; OT text: Song of Solomon-Malachi, followed by Contents of OT; then NT title and Remarks; NT text: Matthew-Revelation. At end are Table of St. Paul's Journeys, Contents of NT, and Useful Tables including Harmonies of the Scriptures by Rev. G. Townsend. Both volumes illustrated with maps.

Also issued with *Stereotyped by T. H. Carter & Co.* in imprint of both vols or in Vol II only. Publishing information also varies in imprint: issued with *Cummings, Hilliard & Co.* only or with *Cummings, Hilliard & Co. and Crocker and Brewster* only.

1826 The Holy Bible . . . Printed and Sold by W. Greenough and Son: Lunenburg **560**

18 cm   NN

Reprint of Greenough edition of 1821 (No 422).

1826/18 The Holy Bible . . . [Stereotype Edition]. [Printed by] J. H. A. Frost [for] Richardson and Lord: Boston **561**

792 p   18 cm   NN, NNAB

Tables before and after OT. NT imprinted *West and Richardson, 1818.* See 1818, No 350.

1826/25 The Holy Bible . . . Stereotyped by B. and J. Collins, N. York . . . Published by Edmund Cushing: Lunenburg, Mass. **562**

792 p   18 cm   NN, NNAB

Has Order of Books. Tables follow OT. NT title, dated 1825, has Account of the Dates on verso. I Tim 4:16 reads *thy* doctrine, for *the* doctrine.

1826/24 The Holy Bible . . . Printed for H. Hudson by W. Hudson and L. Skinner: Hartford **563**

17 cm   NNAB

Reprint of Hudson and Goodwin edition of 1809 (No 168). NN has copy with NT dated 1826.

1826/25   The Holy Bible . . . Being the English Version of the Polyglot Bible.
Bagster: London   564

Reported as (585) (188)   14 cm   MBS
NT, dated 1825, has imprint of *T. Wardle, Philadelphia.* See 1825 Wardle edition, No 534;
also 1831 Polyglott Bible, No 753. Printed in the United States?

1826   The Holy Bible . . . [First Edition]. [A. Paul, Printer] . . . Stereotyped by
A. Chandler, for "The American Bible Society" . . . : New York   565

1 vol: (824) (251)   14 cm   NNAB
The first ABS Pocket Bible, sometimes referred to as the Nonpareil Pocket Bible (ABS
Annual Report 1827, price list) because it was printed in agate or nonpareil type. Has short
italic chapter summaries and running heads. Verso of title has Order of Books.

1826   The New Testament . . . With a Commentary and Critical Notes . . . by Adam
Clarke . . . W. Smith: New York   566

2 vols: Vol i, 940 p; Vol ii, 1088 p   25 cm   DeU
Adam Clarke's Commentary; see 1811–25, No 188.

1826   [The New Testament] The Sacred Writings of the Apostles and Evangelists
of Jesus Christ, Commonly Styled The New Testament. Translated from the
Original Greek, by George Campbell, James Macknight, and Philip Doddridge, Doctors of the Church of Scotland. With Prefaces to the Historical
and Epistolary Books; and an Appendix, Containing Critical Notes and Various Translations of Difficult Passages. Printed and Published by Alexr.
Campbell: Buffaloe, Brooke County, Virginia   567

1 vol: (478) (xlviii)   23 cm   CSmH, ICU, MiU, NN, NNAB, TNMPH
Preface signed by A. C. and Introduction to the Gospels precede text. Text in single-
column paragraph form, divided into sections. Hints to the Reader in smaller type follows the
Gospels. Introductions, also in smaller type, appear before Acts and Paul's Epistles. At end
are Errata, Appendix, Prefatory Hints to the Other Epistles, and Revelation. Aids to translation are at foot of page. Edited by the publisher. Copyright February 3, 1826.
    This is the first appearance of the Alexander Campbell Version of the NT which has been
in print for over a century. Alexander Campbell (1788–1866) was born in Ireland and educated
at the University of Glasgow. He came to America in 1809 as a Presbyterian minister, but soon
became a Baptist and later founded the Disciples of Christ. He was greatly impressed by a New
Testament published in London in 1818 which contained the Gospels translated by George
Campbell (see 1796, No 56), the Epistles by James MacKnight (see 1810, No 186), and the
Acts and Revelation from the Family Expositor of Doddridge (see 1807, No 147). He failed
in his attempt to arrange for its publication in America and undertook to produce an improved
version of that text. He admired the translation principles of George Campbell but also took
suggestions from the works of other scholars. However, he based his text mainly on Griesbach's
Greek NT, particularly the 1809/10 edition.
    A recent study of Alexander Campbell's work is Cecil K. Thomas' *Alexander Campbell and
His New Version* (The Bethany Press, St. Louis, 1959). In the foreword, Dr. Luther A. Weigle
says: "Campbell was an indefatigable student of Greek, honest in dealing with it, and coura-
geous in presenting its meaning. I agree with the author's statement that he 'was aware of the
basic principles of interpretation and translation which were accepted by the best scholars of
his day and which have been proved valid by the testing of over a century of critical study.' "
    Although Campbell substituted some ornate words of Latin derivation for the ordinary words
of common use, undue colloquialism in a modern (19th century) speech version would have
been less desirable. He was particularly concerned with the Greek readings considered spuri-
ous and the handling of these constitute important differences between later editions. In the
first and second editions they are printed in italics but in the third most are removed to an
appendix and the others printed in regular type.

Alexander Campbell also made a translation of Acts which was included in the American Bible Union Version (see 1862–63, No 1764).

1826 The New Testament . . . Stereotyped by T. & C. Carter . . . Printed and published by David Watson: Woodstock   **568**

Reported as 283 p   19 cm   VtHi

1826 The New Testament . . . P. Sheldon: Gardiner, Maine   **569**

290 p   19 cm   NNAB

1826 The New Testament . . . [Stereotyped by J. Howe, New York]. Published and
Sold by Mervin Hale: Elizabethtown [New Jersey]   **570**

288 p   18 cm   NN

1826? The New Testament . . . Stereotyped by H. Wallis, New-York. Manufacturing Company, Simeon Ide, Agent: Claremont, N. H.   **571**

372 p   17 cm   NNAB
NN has copy with imprint *Printed and sold by Simeon Ide: Windsor* [Vermont] *1826.*

1826 The New Testament . . . With References and a key sheet of Questions . . .
Designed to facilitate the acquisition of Scripture knowledge . . . by Hervey
Wilbur . . . Stereotyped by S. Walker & Co., Boston . . . Published by Cummings, Hilliard & Co., and Crocker & Brewster: Boston; also by the American Sunday School Union: Philadelphia   **572**

2 vols: (324) (83+)   15 cm   Not Located
O'Callaghan, p 180. Contains more supplementary material than the 1823 edition (No 482). Continuously paged but each volume has full title page.

1826 The New Testament . . . [Stereotyped by A. Chandler]. S. Andrus: Hartford
                                                                           573

251 p   15 cm   NNAB

1826 The New Testament . . . [Stereotyped by L. Johnson]. American Sunday
School Union: Philadelphia   **574**

288 p   15 cm   NNAB

1826 The New Testament . . . E. & T. Mills: Burlington, Vt.   **575**

Reported as 336 p   14 cm   VtHi

1826 The New Testament . . . Wells: Burlington, Vt.   **576**

Reported as 335 p   13 cm   VtU

1826 The New Testament . . . Printed by Samuel Marks: New-York   **577**

192 p   13 cm   NNAB
Text is printed in paragraph form with verse numbers in matching type. Engraved frontispiece.

1826 The New Testament ... Edwin T. Scott: Philadelphia **578**

447 p   12 cm   NNAB
Table at end.

1827? [The Holy Bible] An Exposition of the Old and New Testaments: Wherein
Each Chapter is Summed Up in its Contents; the Sacred Text Inserted at
Large in Distinct Paragraphs ... With Practical Remarks and Observations
by Matthew Henry ... with Prefatory Remarks, by Archibald Alexander and
Rev. Edward Bickersteth ... R. Carter and Brothers: New York   **579**

5 vols   29 cm   *ICMcC*   MiU
Has frontispiece and Introductory Remarks by Edward Bickersteth, dated Islington, May 21,
1827. The date is evidently supplied from this, but this firm seems to have begun Bible printing
in the 1850s. See 1816, No 292.

1827 The Holy Bible ... Apocrypha ... With Canne's Marginal Notes and References ... Stereotyped, Printed and Published by H. & E. Phinney: Cooperstown, N. Y.   **580**

28 cm   CDU
Reprint of Phinney's 1824 quarto (No 485).
CaOTP has copy imprinted *Printed by H. & E. Phinney for S. Thompson, York* [U.C.];
no Apocrypha. NCooHi has copy with 5 engravings, NT dated 1826, no Apocrypha. O'Callaghan
(p 182) lists copy with imprint *William Williams, Utica, N. Y.*

1827 The Holy Bible ... Canne's Marginal notes and references ... Index ...
Tables ... Stereotyped by James Conner, New-York ... Azor Hoyt, Printer
... N. Bangs and J. Emory, for the Methodist Episcopal Church ... : New-
York   **581**

Reported as (iv) (642) (92) (200) (12) (4) (47)   "4to"   CaOTP
Has Apocrypha, To the Reader, Family Record, Tables, and Concordance.

1827 The Holy Bible ... with Canne's Marginal Notes and References. Together
with the Apocrypha ... Stereotyped by B. & J. Collins. J. H. A. Frost, Printer.
Published by C. Ewer and T. Bedlington: Boston   **582**

"4to"   MBU–T
Reprint of Collins' 1821 quarto (No 414). Has Brown's Concordance at end.

1827 The Holy Bible ... [With Thomas Scott's Notes]. Stereotyped Edition from
the Fifth London Edition ... [Stereotyped by T. H. Carter & Co., Boston].
Published by Samuel T. Armstrong, Crocker and Brewster: Boston; J. Leavitt: New York   **583**

6 vols: Vol i, 756 p; Vol ii, 654 p; Vol iii, 654 p; Vol iv, 904 p; Vol v, 775 p; Vol vi, 807 p
23 cm   NNAB
Scott's Annotated Bible; see 1804–09, No 113. Vol i, Genesis-Judges. Vol ii, Ruth-Esther.
Vol III, Job-Solomon's Song. Vol iv, Isaiah-Malachi. Vol v, Matthew-Acts. Vol vi, Romans-
Revelation; Tables at end.
This Bible was planned by Crocker and Brewster in 1821 or 1820. Several Boston firms
rejected the project but Armstrong joined in having the first volume stereotyped. "It was so
successful that the rest of the set was also stereotyped within a year and a half at a cost of
twenty thousand dollars." Crocker and Brewster sold more than twenty thousand sets, each of
which cost about $6 to produce, went to the trade at $12, and sold at retail price of $24.

This was the firm's most successful book, and when Crocker and Brewster went out of business in 1876, the plates were sold to H. O. Houghton. (Rollo G. Silver, "The Boston Book Trade, 1800–1825," *Bulletin of The New York Public Library* LII, No 10 [Oct 1948] p 492.)

NN has copy with Vol VI dated 1824; NN also has reprints dated 1839, 1842, and 1844. NNAB has reprints dated 1831/30, 1835, 1842, and 1858. DLC and ViU have reprint dated 1830/32; DLC also has one dated 1855. USI has reprint dated 1849/61 and NSaSk has one dated 1864.

1827 The Holy Bible . . . Translated from the Latin Vulgat . . . Printed and Published by Eugene Cummiskey: Philadelphia   **584**

23 cm   DGU

Rheims-Douay, from 5th Dublin edition. Reprint of 1824 Cummiskey edition (No 492).

1827 The Holy Bible . . . With Canne's Marginal Notes and References . . . Stereotyped by J. Howe, Philadelphia . . . Published and Sold by Daniel D. Smith: New-York   **585**

23 cm   NNAB

Reprint of 1825 Smith edition (No 529) with Apocrypha and Concordance.

1827 The Holy Bible . . . [Stereotyped by D. & G. Bruce, New York]. Printed and Published by Holbrook and Fessenden: Brattleborough, Vt.   **586**

19 cm   NN

Information on verso of title indicates this is reprint of Bruce's 1815 stereotype edition (No 279).

1827 The Holy Bible . . . Stereotyped by D. & G. Bruce, New York . . . Printed and Published by Daniel D. Smith: New York   **587**

837 p   "12mo"   Not Located

O'Callaghan, p 183.

1827 The Holy Bible . . . Stereotyped by J. Howe, Philadelphia . . . Published by Silas Andrus: Hartford   **588**

Reported as 660 p   "12mo"   KyLo

O'Callaghan (p 184) lists a 681 p copy with Metrical Psalms.

1827 The Holy Bible . . . H. Hudson: Hartford   **589**

Text ends Ll12   17 cm   NN

Has Dedication to King James and Order of Books.

1827 The Holy Bible . . . Stereotyped by J. Howe . . . Philadelphia. Published by H. Holdship. Sold also by R. Patterson, Agent and by Johnston & Stockton . . . Pittsburgh   **590**

1 vol: (x) 11–743 (6) 7–238   14 cm   NNAB

Index and Order of Books precede each Testament.

1827 The Holy Bible . . . Published by Silas Andrus: Hartford   **591**

"18mo"   Not Located

O'Callaghan, p 184.

1827   An Amended Version of the Book of Job, with an Introduction, and Notes
Chiefly Explanatory. By George R. Noyes. Published by Hilliard and Brown:
Cambridge. From the University Press — By Hilliard, Metcalf & Co.: Cam-
bridge   **592**

1 vol: (xi) (116)   25 cm   NNAB

George Rapall Noyes (1798–1868) was born in Newburyport, Mass. He studied theology at
Harvard College, and thereafter was ordained a Unitarian minister. In 1840 he became professor of Hebrew and Oriental languages and lecturer on Biblical literature at Harvard. Early
in his career he became interested in translating parts of the Bible. He first translated the
above cited Book of Job, which was followed by the Psalms (1831), the Prophets (3 vols,
1833–37), and Proverbs, Ecclesiastes, and Canticles (1846). The second edition of the Book
of Job was published by James Munroe and Company, Boston, in 1838 (NNUT); the third
edition in 18??; and the fourth, revised, with Ecclesiastes and Canticles, in 1868 (No 1833).
Noyes's most extensive work was the translation of the NT from the text of Tischendorf, published in Boston in 1869 (No 1845). From 1866 on, all editions of the Noyes translations were
published by the American Unitarian Association, Boston.

1827   The New Testament . . . [Stereotyped by D. Hills]. F. Ingraham and J. Putnam: Boston   **593**

499 p   25 cm   MB, NjMD, NN, NNAB

Printed in paragraph form with chapter and verse indication only at the top of each page.
The paragraphing, following Griesbach, is taken from Reeve's London edition of 1802. The
punctuation follows Knapp's Greek Testament. The Advertisement on verso of title is signed
by B. G. Has Order of Books at end.

1827   The New Testament . . . Published by J. & B. Williams: Exeter, N. H.   **594**

299 p   "12mo"   Not Located
O'Callaghan, p 187.

1827   The New Testament . . . With an Introduction giving an Account of Jewish
and other Sects; with Notes illustrating obscure Passages, and explaining
obsolete Words and Phrases . . . By J. A. Cummings . . . Second Edition, revised and improved. Stereotyped at the Boston Type and Stereotype Foundry
. . . Hilliard, Gray, Little, and Wilkins: Boston   **595**

Reported as (305) 306–308   "12mo"   MB

Contains Introduction, Order of Books, and Prefatory Remarks. Tables at end. 3 maps.
See 1814 NT, No 264.
NN has reprint dated 1832.

1827   The New Testament . . . Mervin Hale: Elizabethtown [New Jersey]   **596**

"12mo"   Not Located
Wright, p 393.

1827   The New Testament . . . Richardson & Lord: Boston   **597**

312 p   "12mo"   Not Located
O'Callaghan, p 387.

1827   The New Testament . . . Stereotyped by Baker & Greele, Boston . . . Printed
for The American Bible Society by Abraham Paul: New-York   **598**

315 p   19 cm   NNAB

Verso of title page has first edition and Order of Books.
NN has second edition and MB has fifth edition, both of this year.

1827 The New Testament . . . Stereotype Edition . . . Published by Edmund Cushing: Lunenburg [Massachusetts]   **599**

310 p   18 cm   NNAB

1827 The New Testament . . . Stereotyped by J. Howe, New-York . . . Published and sold by Benjamin Olds: Newark   **600**

Reported as 288 p   18 cm   NjP

1827 The New Testament . . . With References and a Key Sheet of Questions . . . Designed to Facilitate the Acquisition of Scriptural Knowledge . . . By Hervey Wilbur . . . [Stereotyped at the Boston Type and Stereotype Foundry]. Hilliard, Gray, Little and Wilkins: Boston   **601**

16 cm   NN
Wilbur's Reference Testament; see 1823, No 482. Has Wilbur's Useful Tables at end.

1827 The New Testament . . . [Stereotype Edition]. G. J. Loomis: Albany   **602**

276 p   16 cm   NN
Leaves printed on one side only. Illustrated.

1827 The New Testament . . . Arranged in paragraphs, such as the Sense requires; the division of the chapters and verses being noted in the margin. By James Nourse, Student in the Theological Seminary, Princeton, N. J . . . Published by G. & C. Carvill: New York   **603**

1 vol: (373) (xxiii)   15 cm   NN, ViU
Tables at end. Printed at Princeton by D. A. Borrenstein.

1827 The New Testament . . . Stereotype edition. Stereotyped by James Conner, for "The American Bible Society": New-York   **604**

237 [1] p   15 cm   NNAB
Nonpareil Testament printed especially for Sunday Schools. Verso of title page has first edition and Order of Books.

1827 The New Testament . . . [Stereotyped by J. Conner] . . . A. Hoyt, printer . . . published by N. Bangs and J. Emory, for the Methodist Episcopal Church: New-York   **605**

237 p   15 cm   NNAB
Possibly printed from same plates as ABS 1827 NT (No 604).

1827 The New Testament . . . John H. Putnam: Concord, N. H.   **606**

"16mo"   Not Located
Wright, p 393.

1827 The New Testament . . . Stereotyped by J. Howe, Philadelphia . . . Published by E. Bliss: New-York   **607**

252 p   14 cm   NN
Has added engraved title page.

1827? The New Testament . . . Published by Holbrook & Fessenden: Brattleborough, Vt.   *608*

335 p   14 cm   NN

Reprinted from Holbrook & Fessenden Bible of this year (No 586). Account of Lives of
Apostles and Evangelists and Table at end. Illustrated.

1827 The New Testament . . . [Stereotyped by A. Chandler]. Published by Silas
Andrus: Hartford   *609*

251 p   14 cm   NN

1827 The New Testament . . . Published by Thomas Billings: Lowell [Massachu-
setts]   *610*

335 p   13 cm   NNAB

Has Account of the Lives of Apostles, etc., and Table.

1827 The New Testament . . . Third stereotype edition. White, Gallaher & White:
New-York   *611*

216 p   12 cm   NNAB
Frontispiece.

1827 The New Testament . . . Stereotype Edition . . . H. and E. Phinney: Cooperstown [New York]   *612*

Reported as 344 p   12 cm   MiU

NNAB has undated copy of this size. NCooHi has copy listed as 1832?. O'Callaghan
(p 351) quotes "E.P." that this NT was first published in 1832 "between which time and 1848,
they sold rising 200,000 copies, chiefly for Sunday Schools."

1828? The Holy Bible . . . Canne's Marginal References . . . Apocrypha . . . Concordance . . . The text corrected according to the Standard of the American
Bible Society. Stereotyped by James Conner, New-York . . . Printed and published by Holbrook and Fessenden: Brattleborough, Vt.   *613*

1 vol: (527) (78) (168) (14) (56) (124)   30 cm   NN, NNAB, OO, VtHi

Frontispiece, To the Reader, and Advertisement precede text. Last page of OT has Guide
to Reading by William Stones. NT has undated engraved title. At end are Tables, Lives of
Apostles, Concordance, and Ostervald's Practical Observations. Error in 1 Tim 4:16, *thy* doc-
trine, for *the* doctrine. Has a variety of engravings, some by L. Chorley and R. Westall. Four
Family Record pages with elaborate pictures and decorations which are attributed to Anderson.
Facing p 166 of NT is *The Dragon Chained* from which Anderson later did a woodcut (see
1829, No 670). Engraved maps and charts.
VtHi copy has Fessenden family records.

1828 The Holy Bible . . . With Canne's Marginal References, An Index, also Ref-
erences and a Key Sheet of Questions, Geographical, Historical, Doctrinal,
Practical and Experimental; Accompanied with Valuable Chronological
Harmonies of Both Testaments, and Highly Useful Tables . . . The Whole
Designed to Facilitate the Acquisition of Scriptural Knowledge in Bible
Classes, Sunday Schools, Common Schools and Private Families. By Hervey
Wilbur . . . The Text Corrected According to the Standard of the American
Bible Society . . . Stereotyped by J. Conner, New-York . . . Printed and Pub-
lished by Henry C. Sleight: New-York   *614*

1 vol: (527) (168) (31)   29 cm   NN, NNAB

A long list of dealers follows the publisher's name on title page. Apocrypha wanting? Copyright 1825.

This appears to be the first quarto edition of Wilbur's Reference Bible. For his duodecimo edition, see 1826, No 559 see also his 1823 NT, No 482. This is also the first appearance of the notation on the title page: *The Text Corrected According to the Standard of the American Bible Society.*

1828   The Holy Bible . . . With Marginal Notes and References . . . Apocrypha . . .
     Published and Sold by Edmund Cushing: Lunenburg, Mass.   **615**

1 vol: (683) (160) 687–898 899–930   28 cm   NNAB

To the Reader, Account of the Dates, and Order of Books precede text; Index, Tables, and Account of the Holy Land at end. Illustrated. On NT title *Stereotyped by B. and J. Collins: New York.*

1828   The Holy Bible . . . Stereotype Edition . . . Canne's Marginal Notes and ref-
     erences . . . Index . . . Printed and published . . . by G. M. Davison: Saratoga
     Springs   **616**

1 vol: (8) 9–574 575–576 (4) (2) 579–754 755–768   28 cm   NNAB

Preliminary matter includes Order of Books, Witherspoon's Preface, and Contents (5 p). Tables appear on p 575–576, followed by 2 leaves for Family Record. At end are Index and Tables. Apocrypha lacking and is not included on title page, although it is listed in Order of Books.

1828   The Holy Bible . . . with Canne's Marginal Notes and References . . . Apoc-
     rypha . . . Stereotyped by B. & J. Collins . . . Published by C. Ewer, T. Bed-
     lington, and J. H. A. Frost: Boston   **617**

1 vol: (744) (138) 747–1010 (56)   28 cm   NNAB

Has Advertisement to the Stereotype Edition (New York 1819) giving history of Collins editions — the stereotype edition being the firm's fourth edition — and To the Reader. At end are Index, Tables, Accounts of Judea and of the Apostles and Evangelists, and Concordance. Frontispiece (folded wood-engraving *Adam naming the Creation*).

1828   The Holy Bible . . . With Canne's Marginal Notes and References . . . Stereo-
     typed, printed and published by H. & E. Phinney: Cooperstown   **618**

768 p   28 cm   NCooHi, NN, NNAB

Includes frontispiece, Witherspoon's Preface, Tables, etc.
NN copy has 10 plates. NCooHi copy has Apocrypha and 8 woodcuts.

1828   The Holy Bible . . . Apocrypha . . . Canne's marginal references . . . Published
     and sold by Daniel D. Smith, . . . also by the principal booksellers in the
     United States: New-York   **619**

Reported as (574) (96) (4) 579–768 (54)   28 cm   NNQ

Has added engraved title page (1827). Brown's Concordance.

1828?   The Holy Bible . . . with Canne's Marginal Notes and References . . . M. M.
     Teprell: Boston   **620**

932 p   27 cm   NN

Collins Stereotype Edition. Has Apocrypha and Brown's Concordance. Frontispiece. NT title dated 1828.

1828   An Exposition of the Old and New Testaments . . . with practical Remarks and Observations by Matthew Henry, edited by the Rev. George Burder, and the Rev. Joseph Hughes, A.M. with the life of the author by the Rev. Samuel Palmer. First American Edition, to which is prefixed, a Preface, by Archibald Alexander, D.D. . . . John P. Haven: New-York; Robert Patterson: Pittsburgh; Towar & Hogan: Philadelphia   **621**

   6 vols: Vol i, 718 p; Vol ii, (919) (12); Vol iii, (882) (4); Vol iv, 1181 p; Vol v, 960 p; Vol vi, 934 p   25 cm   CoD
   Matthew Henry Commentary; see 1816, No 292. Vol ii has 12 p of Bibliography at end and Vol iii has 4 p of Publishers' Advertising.
   Cited copy has Vol v missing. NNAB has Vol i only and NN has Vols ii, iv, and v.
   DLC Union Catalog lists but does not locate a 6-vol edition dated 1828? imprinted *E. Barrington and G. D. Haswell, Philadelphia.*

1828   The Holy Bible . . . I. Ashmead & Co., Printers . . . McCarty & Davis: Philadelphia   **622**

   "4to"   ScGrvF
   This is Carey's quarto of 1812/11 (No 208) with new title pages but without Fletcher's Concise View. Error in Lev 19:12 continued; error in Esther 1:8 corrected. Contains 12 engravings by A. Anderson which are not those listed by O'Callaghan (p 189) for the edition he describes, then privately owned.

1828–26   The Holy Bible . . . [With Thomas Scott's Notes, etc.]. First American Stereotype Quarto Edition, In Five Volumes, from the London Standard Edition . . . Stereotyped by J. Howe, Philadelphia. Published by White, Gallaher & White: New-York   **623**

   5 vols: Vol i, 971 p; Vol ii, 1090 p; Vol iii, 1005 p; Vol iv, 803 p; Vol v, 850 p   23 cm NNAB
   Scott's Bible; see 1804–09, No 113. Vols i and v dated 1828. Vols ii and iv dated 1827. Vol iii, imprinted *W. W. Woodward, Philadelphia,* dated 1826. Vol i has as frontispiece an engraving of Scott, by G. B. Ellis, from a drawing by Cosse. At end of Vol v is A Retrospective View of the Predictions contained in The Revelation of St. John, and Tables.
   Wright (p 395) lists an 1834 edition. NN has 1834 edition.

1828   The Holy Bible, translated from the Latin Vulgat: With Annotations, References, &c. [Stereotyped by J. Howe] Published by Eugene Cummiskey: Philadelphia   **624**

   Reported as (335) (444) (191)   23 cm   DGU
   Rheims-Douay, from 5th Dublin Edition. O'Callaghan (p 190) says this is Cummiskey's 1824 edition (No 492) which consisted of 550 copies, with new titles.

1828   The Holy Bible . . . Stereotype Edition . . . [D. Fanshaw, Printer] . . . Stereotyped by James Conner, for The American Bible Society: New-York   **625**

   1 vol: (486) (162)   19 cm   NNAB
   Nonpareil Duodecimo with running heads and brief chapter summaries. First edition appears on verso of title, also Order of Books.
   Priced in 1828 at 55¢, or 50¢ in sheep. These could be sold to Auxiliary Societies at 20% discount if purchased specially for the use of Sunday Schools "as School stock exclusively, not to be given, or sold, or lent to the scholars." (*ABS Report* 1828, p ix.)

1828   The Holy Bible . . . D. Fanshaw, Printer. Stereotyped for the American Bible Society by D. & G. Bruce: New-York   **626**

   837 p   19 cm   NN

This is known as the Hornet copy. Note on last leaf reads "USS Hornet foundered at Sea in the Gale of Sep. V, 1829. And 199 Bibles like this went down with her. Simonds. This the only one saved. Myself the only person." This was Lieutenant L. E. Simmonds, U. S. Navy. For further details see David H. Clift, "The Hornet Bible," *The New York Public Library Bulletin* xxxix, No 6 (June 1935) 441–445. Although Lt. Simmonds actually seems to have been transferred from the ship about a month before the storm, the ship was lost with all hands.

In Nov 1817 the ABS donated sixty-five Bibles "to the United States ship, the *John Adams,* for its crew," thus beginning a long history of the supply of the Scriptures to the U. S. Navy and to the other branches of the Armed Forces. The *Hornet* had received several specific donations.

1828   [The Holy Bible] The Reference Bible . . . With References . . . Key Sheet of Questions . . . Harmonies . . . Maps, and Highly Useful Tables . . . By Hervey Wilbur . . . Sixth Edition. [Stereotyped by L. Johnson, Philadelphia] B. Perkins & Co.: Boston; American Sunday School Union: Philadelphia   **627**

19 cm   MWA

Reprint of Wilbur's 1826 duodecimo (No 559). Maps.
NN has eighth edition for this year.

1828/21   The Holy Bible . . . Stereotyped by D. & G. Bruce: Philadelphia   **628**

19 cm   NNAB

Same as ABS Minion Duodecimo of 1819 (No 377) and D. & G. Bruce edition of 1823 (No 467). NT title dated 1821.

1828   The Holy Bible . . . Printed and Published by Holbrook and Fessenden: Brattleborough, Vt.   **629**

684 p   19 cm   NN, PP

NT title lacks imprint. PP copy has Anderson engravings.

1828   The Holy Bible . . . [Stereotyped by James Conner] . . . published by N. Bangs and J. Emory, for the Methodist Episcopal Church: New-York   **630**

1 vol: (486) (162)   19 cm   NNAB

1828   The Holy Bible . . . Published by the Methodist Book Concern: New York   **631**

"12mo"   Not Located
O'Callaghan, p 191. Might be No 630.

1828   The Holy Bible . . . Stereotyped by E. & J. White, for the Auxilliary New York Bible and Common Prayer Society . . . : New York   **632**

"12mo"   Not Located
O'Callaghan, p 190.

1828   The Holy Bible . . . Stereotyped by B. and J. Collins, N. York . . . Published by Nahum Haskell: Woodstock, Vt.; and Timothy Bedlington: Boston   **633**

792 p   18 cm   NNAB, VtHi
Has Tables.

1828/27   The Holy Bible . . . Stereotyped by J. Howe, Philadelphia. Silas Andrus:
Hartford   **634**

660 p   18 cm   NN, NNAB

Tables (1 p) follow OT; Contents (5 p) follow NT. NT title, dated 1827, has Account
of the Dates on verso. 2 engravings.

1828   The Holy Bible . . . printed for the Bible Society, by the American Sunday
School Union: Philadelphia   **635**

1 vol: (599) (179)   17 cm   NNAB

Tables at end of OT.

1828   The Holy Bible . . . Published by Hudson and Skinner: Hartford   **636**

17 cm   NNAB

Format uniform with 1809 Hudson & Goodwin edition (No 168). Tables follow both
Testaments.

1828/26   The Holy Bible . . . . [Stereotyped by A. Chandler] Published by Silas
Andrus: Hartford   **637**

1 or 2 vols: (824) (251)   15 cm   NN, NNAB, ViU

Has engravings. NT dated 1826.
NN copy in 2 vols with engraved title. Also published with both titles dated 1828.

1828   The Holy Bible . . . Stereotyped by B. and J. Collins, New-York . . . Published
by Silas Andrus: Hartford   **638**

1 vol: (690) (209)   14 cm   NN

Contains Dr. Witherspoon's Preface. Added engraved title and frontispiece.

1828   The Holy Bible . . . Stereotyped by J. Howe. D. D. Smith: New-York   **639**

1 vol: (615)   13 cm   NNAB

This first edition of a new format has engraved title page and frontispiece; text arranged in
paragraph form, no introductions.

1828   The Holy Bible . . . Stereotyped by J. Howe, Philad. H. Adams: Philadelphia
640

1 vol: (852) (259)   12 cm   NN, NNAB

NN copy has engraved title. O'Callaghan (p 193) lists separate NT.

1828   The New Testament . . . Stereotyped by L. Johnson, Philadelphia. Towar &
Hogan: Philadelphia   **641**

238 p   26 cm   NN, NNAB

1828   The New Testament . . . Stereotyped by T. Rutt, Shacklewell, London, for
the Bible Society at Philadelphia: [Philadelphia]   **642**

23 cm   NNAB

Appears to be same as 1816 NT (No 310).

1828   The New Testament in the Common Version, Conformed to Griesbach's
Standard Greek Text. Press of the Boston Daily Advertiser. W. T. Lewis,
Printer: Boston   **643**

Unpaged   22 cm   DLC, MB, NN, NNAB

Text printed in paragraph form with verse numbers in the left margin and spaces within the line to indicate the beginning of a new verse. Copyright by Nathan Hale, District of Massachusetts, 1828.

The editor was John Gorham Palfrey (1796–1881), an ordained Unitarian minister and Dexter Professor of Sacred Literature at Harvard, 1831–39. In later years, he acted as politician, postmaster, lecturer, etc., as well as contributing to the *North American Review,* which he took over in 1835. The Advertisement (p [8]) of this NT states that "the editor . . . has exactly reprinted the Common Version, except in places where the Greek text, from which that version was made, is now understood to have been faulty. In other words, he has aimed to present the Common Version precisely as it would have been if the translators could have had access to the standard text of Griesbach, instead of the adulterated text of Beza. In the translations which he has introduced to correspond to the amended Greek, it has been his careful endeavor to imitate the style of the received version. . . ."

DLC, MB, MH, NN, and NNAB have 1830 reprint by Gray and Bowen, Boston, marked 3rd edition; copyright July 7, 1828 (491 p, 20 cm).

1828 The New Testament . . . Stereotyped by Baker & Greele, Boston . . . Timothy Bedlington: Boston; and William Greenough: Lunenburg [Massachusetts]
644

315 p   19 cm   NNAB

1828 The New Testament . . . To which is applied the Orthoepy of the Critical Pronouncing Dictionary . . . by J. Walker . . . An Explanatory Key. By I. Alger, Jun. Stereotyped by T. H. & C. Carter . . . Printed and Published by Lincoln & Edmands: Boston   **645**

19 cm   NN

Reprint of Lincoln and Edmands 1822 NT (No 452). With illustrated title page; Tables at end.

1828 The New Testament . . . [Stereotyped by J. Howe]. M'Carty & Davis' Edition: Philadelphia   **646**

Reported as 239 p   19 cm   PSt
Title page has vignette.

1828 [The New Testament] The Sacred Writings of the Apostles and Evangelists of Jesus Christ . . . Translated from the Original Greek by George Campbell, James Macknight, and Philip Doddridge . . . Second Edition. Printed and Published by Alexander Campbell: Bethany, Brooke County, Virginia **647**

1 vol: (lix) 61–389 390–456   18 cm   DLC, NN, NNAB, ViU

Alexander Campbell Version; see 1826 NT, No 567. This revised edition has added material before text.

1828 The New Testament. . . . Stereotyped by H. & H. Wallis, New-York . . . Rufus Colton: Woodstock, Vt.   **648**

Reported as 201 p   18 cm   VtHi

1828 The New Testament . . . Stereotyped by B. & J. Collins, New York . . . Miller & Hammond: Providence   **649**

Reported as 312 [1] p   18 cm   RPB
Table of Kindred and Affinity appears on p 312 after "Finis."

1828   The New Testament . . . Stereotyped by Hammond Wallis, New York . . .
Printed and sold by Simeon Ide: Windsor [Vermont]   *650*

Reported as 372 p   17 cm   MH

1828   The New Testament . . . J. B. & S. Baldwin: Bridgeport   *651*

270 p   17 cm   NN

1828   The New Testament . . . To which is added, a vocabulary of all the Words
Therein Contained . . . Adapted to the orthography and pronunciation of
Walker. Likewise, a catalogue of all the proper names . . . By Rensselaer
Bently . . . Printed and published by J. Adancourt: Troy, N. Y.   *652*

Reported as (226) (62)   16 cm   CSmH

1828   The New Testament . . . Stereotyped by J. Howe, Philadelphia. Printed & sold
. . . by R. Porter & Son: Wilmington   *653*

Reported as 240 p   16 cm   DeWI

1828   The New Testament . . . from which is selected an extensive vocabulary . . .
the proper names and all other important words . . . to which is prefixed
Walker's Explanatory Key governing the vocabulary . . . by Jeremiah Goodrich . . . Published . . . by S. Shaw: Albany   *654*

16 cm   NjMD
Reprint of 1825 edition (No 541).

1828   The New Testament . . . Published by James I. Cutler and Co.: Bellows
Falls: [Vermont]   *655*

Reported as 270 p   "16mo"   N

1828   The New Testament . . . Printed by Samuel Marks: New York   *656*

"24mo"   CSmH

1828   The New Testament . . . Stereotyped by L. Johnson . . . American Sunday
School Union: Philadelphia   *657*

288 p   15 cm   NN

1828   The New Testament . . . [Twelfth Edition]. With References and a Key Sheet
of Questions . . . Designed to Facilitate the Acquisition of Scriptural Knowledge . . . By Hervey Wilbur . . . Published by J. S. & C. Adams: Amherst,
Mass.   *658*

15 cm   MAJ, MWA, NN
Reprint of 1823 Wilbur's Reference Testament (No 482). Wilbur's Useful Tables at end.

1828   The New Testament . . . Stereotyped by James Conner: New York. Printed
and published by Horatio Hill & Co.: Concord, N. H.   *659*

Reported as 226 p   15 cm   MBU-T
NNAB has undated copy. O'Callaghan (p 227) also lists undated copy.

1828   The New Testament . . . Published by Luther Roby: Concord, N. H.   **660**

1 vol: (330) 331–335 [1]   14 cm   NNAB
At end are Lives, Sufferings, etc. of the Apostles and Evangelists and Table of Kindred.

1828   The New Testament . . . Published by H. C. Denison, Jr.: Castleton, Vt. **661**

Reported as 336 p   14 cm   VtHi
Blessed be he that readeth and they that hear the words of this book. Rev. 1.3 appears on
title page. Page 336 has Table of Kindred.

1828   The New Testament . . . Printed and Published by J. Sanderson: Elizabeth-
        Town [New Jersey]   **662**

13 cm   NN
Similar to Holbrook and Fessenden's 1827 NT (No 608). Has Account of Lives of Apostles,
etc.

1828   The New Testament, translated from the Latin Vulgat . . . Published by
        Eugene Cummiskey: Philadelphia   **663**

12 cm   Not Located
O'Callaghan (p 193) says 1250 copies of this Rheims Version were printed. See 1829 NT,
No 697.

1828   The New Testament . . . with references, and a key sheet of questions, his-
        torical, doctrinal, and practical . . . By Hervey Wilbur . . . 13th Edition, with
        a Harmony and Tables. B. Perkins & Co.: Boston   **664**

Reported as (463) (8) (64)   11 cm   CU
Has frontispiece and special title page. See Wilbur's Reference Testament (No 482).

1829   The Holy Bible. Self-Interpreting Bible with references and illustrations . . .
        by the Late John Brown . . . Printed and published by T. Kinnersley: New-
        York   **665**

46 cm   NNAB
Similar to 1826 Bible (No 546). Has engravings. Cited copy lacks general title page and
preliminary matter to p ix.

1829   The Holy Bible . . . With Canne's Marginal Notes and References . . . Stereo-
        typed by James Conner, New York . . . Printed and Published by Silas An-
        drus: Hartford   **666**

1 vol: (555) (82) (174)   42 cm   NNAB
    With Apocrypha. Preliminary matter includes Order of Books, Account of the Dates, Dr.
Witherspoon's To the Reader, and Lives of Apostles and Evangelists. Index and Tables at end.
Illustrations.
    "Mr. Conner manufactured the stereotype plates of this Bible as speculation. Mr. Andrus
purchased them readily for $5,000, the price first asked. It is said to be the first folio edition
of the Bible stereotyped in the United States — N. Y. Printer." (O'Callaghan, p 195.)

1829   The Holy Bible . . . With Canne's Marginal Notes and References . . . Stereo-
        type Edition . . . Published by Kimber and Sharpless: Philadelphia   **667**

1 vol: (744) (138) 747–1008 (54)   32 cm   NNAB
    With Apocrypha. Wavy line separates columns of text. Preliminary matter includes To the
Reader, Order of Books, Account of Dates, and Contents. At end are Index, Tables, Account
of Judea, and Concordance. NT stereotyped by B. & J. Collins. Engravings.

1829   The Holy Bible ... With Apocrypha ... With Canne's Marginal Notes and
         References ... Stereotyped, Printed and Published by H. & E. Phinney:
         Cooperstown   **668**

1 vol: (576) (99) 578–760   29 cm   NCooHi, NNAB
NNAB copy has 10 woodcuts. NCooHi has two copies: one with woodcut frontispiece
and 15 other woodcuts; another with two woodcut frontispieces and 8 other woodcuts.

1829   The Holy Bible ... With Canne's Marginal Notes and References ... Stereo-
         type Edition ... [Stereotyped by E. White]. Published by Kimber and Sharp-
         less: Philadelphia   **669**

1 vol: (570) 573–770   29 cm   NN, NNAB
Reprint of 1823 Kimber and Sharpless Bible (No 460). Lacks Apocrypha but has Metrical
Psalms. Frontispiece. Straight lines separate columns of text.

1829   The Holy Bible ... together with the Apocrypha ... with Marginal Notes and
         References ... Embellished with Maps and Historical Engravings. I. Ash-
         mead & Co. Printers. M'Carty & Davis: Philadelphia   **670**

28 cm   NNAB
Format same as Carey's 1812/11 quarto (No 208) but lacks Brown's Concordance at end.
Error in Lev 19:12 continued.
   The "Embellishments" included in the M'Carty & Davis 1828 edition (No 622) which are
enumerated by O'Callaghan (p 189) are not found in this copy. In their place are fourteen full
page wood engravings by Dr. Alexander Anderson: *Pharaoh's Sorcerers Turning the Rods into
Serpents* (frontispiece), *Moses Found in the Bulrushes, Samson Betrayed by Delilah, Daniel
Interpreting for Belshazzar, Daniel in the Lion's Den, Massacre of Innocents by Order of Herod,
The Flight into Egypt, John Baptizing Jesus Christ, Judas Casting away the Pieces of Silver,
Visit of the Virgin Mary to Elizabeth, Christ Raising the Son of the Widow of Nain, Incredulity
of Thomas, Bar-jesus Struck with Blindness,* and *St. John's Vision of the Dragon Chained.*

1829/28   The Holy Bible ... Published and Sold by Edmund Cushing: Lunenburg,
            Mass.   **671**

28 cm   NNAB
Reprint of 1828 Cushing quarto (No 615). NT dated 1828 in cited copy.

1829   The Holy Bible ... With Canne's Marginal Notes and References ... D. D.
         Smith: New York   **672**

Reported as 768 p   28 cm   PSt
Has Tables and Index. Illustrated with frontispiece, plates, and maps.

1829   The Holy Bible ... Stereotype Edition. Stereotyped by T. Rutt, London, and
         printed for The American Bible Society, by D. Fanshaw, Printer: New-York
                                                                              673

1 vol: (4) 5–746 (8) (2) 749–968   22 cm   NNAB
Marked fifth edition, which probably refers to several Baltimore editions as NNAB has no
record of earlier ABS editions. Leaf following title has Names and Order of the Books and
Account of the Dates. Contains running heads and chapter summaries.
   This was printed from plates made in London but purchased from the Baltimore Bible
Society "which could be paid for in Bibles and Testaments." (*ABS Report* 1829, p 8.) See
1815, No 274.

1829   The Holy Bible . . . Stereotype Edition . . . [Printed at the New-York Protestant Episcopal Press]. Published by the Auxiliary New York Bible Society and Common Prayer Book Society: New-York   **674**

"8vo"   Not Located

O'Callaghan, p 195.

1829   The Pronouncing Bible . . . According to the Orthoepy of John Walker . . . By Israel Alger, Jun. . . . Stereotyped by T. H. Carter & Co. . . . Printed and Published by Lincoln & Edmands: Boston   **675**

1 vol: (714) (214)   21 cm   NNAB

Copyright, Advertisement of Editor, 1825, Explanatory Key and Notes, and Order of Books appear on verso of title.

1829   The Holy Bible . . . [Sleight's Edition] . . . Stereotyped by James Conner. Printed by H. C. Sleight, and published at the American Tract Society's House: New York   **676, 677**

1 vol: (486) (162)   19 cm   NN

NN has another copy imprinted *Printed and Published by Henry C. Sleight: New-York.* O'Callaghan (p 196) notes an edition with NT dated 1828.

1829   The Holy Bible . . . Printed by Hudson and Goodwin: Hartford   **678**

"12mo"   Not Located

O'Callaghan, p 197.

1829   The Holy Bible . . . Stereotyped by J. Howe . . . Silas Andrus: Hartford   **679**

681 p   18 cm   NN, NNAB

Has frontispiece. Tables follow OT (1 p). Contents at end (p 656–681). Several leaves with two engravings each, after European painters, are inserted in NT.

1829   The Holy Bible . . . Published by Hudson and Skinner: Hartford   **680**

17 cm   NNAB

Similar to Hudson & Goodwin edition of 1809 (No 168). The Dedication to King James is omitted.

1829   The Holy Bible . . . Stereotyped by A. Chandler. Silas Andrus: Hartford **681**

Reported as (824) (251)   14 cm   ICN

Has added engraved title page.

1829   The Holy Bible . . . Stereotype Edition . . . Published by Charles Ewer: Boston   **682**

1 vol: (824) (251)   14 cm   NN

Also published with NT dated 1828.

1829   The Holy Bible . . . Stereotyped by J. Howe . . . Towar & Hogan: Philadelphia
                                                                        683

1 vol: (852) (259)   11 cm   NN, NNAB

Has added engraved title page and frontispiece.

1829   The New Testament . . . Arranged in Paragraphs, such as the Sense Requires
. . . By James Nourse . . . [Stereotyped by J. Howe]. Published by the American Sunday School Union: Philadelphia   **684**

1 vol: (vi) 3–272   22 cm   ICMcC, NNAB

Preliminary matter includes Recommendations to First and Second Editions and Preface
(most dated 1826). Copyright 1829. Printed in paragraph form with chapter and verse indications in margin; subject headings cut in at left. See 1827 NT, No 603.

1829   The Pronouncing Testament . . . to which is applied . . . the Orthoepy of the
Critical Pronouncing Dictionary . . . by J. Walker . . . to which is prefixed an
explanatory key, by Israel Alger, Jun. . . . Printed and published by Lincoln
and Edmands: Boston   **685**

Reported as 292 p   19 cm   IU

Has engraved title page and frontispiece.

1829   The New Testament . . . Translated out of the Latin Vulgate . . . and First
Published By the English College of Rhemes, Anno 1582. Newly Revised
and Corrected According to the Clementine Edition of the Scriptures . . . As
Approved by the Right Reverend John Dubois, Catholic Bishop of New-York
. . . Stereotype Edition . . . Printed for the Proprietors, by William Williams:
Utica   **686**

1 vol: (xii) 13–344   18 cm   DGU, NN, NNAB

Rheims Version. Preliminary matter includes Approbation by the Right Rev. John Dubois,
Bishop of New York (7 Sept 1828); Copyright (13 Sept 1828); A Table of Controversies (3 p);
A Table of Epistles and Gospels (3 p); A Chronological Table (3 p); and Order of the Books
(1 p). Error in James 5:17, a man *possible*, for a man *passible*.
"This is the first edition of what is called the Devereux Testament, from the fact that
Nicholas Devereux, Esq. of Utica owned the stereotype plates. At his expense were printed a
series of Testaments after Coyne's 1820 Dublin edition, for distribution among school children.
Cf. Thomas F. Meechan in *America*. Jan 15, 1937." (O'Callaghan, p 198–199.) The Dublin
edition contained no notes but this NT has a few. See Pope, p 425–427, for the 1820 Dublin NT.
Reprinted in 1831, 1833, 1835, and 1840. Reprinted in New York by Sadlier in 1842, 1845,
and 1847.

1829   The New Testament . . . Stereotyped by J. Howe, New York . . . B. Olds:
Newark, N. J.   **687**

287 p   18 cm   NN

1829   The New Testament . . . Stereotyped by J. Howe . . . Published by Silas
Andrus: Hartford   **688**

503–655 p   17 cm   NN

Separate issue from 1827 Bible (No 588).

1829   The New Testament . . . Published by William H. Niles: Middletown [Con-
necticut]   **689**

Reported as 288 p   16 cm   CtMW

Identical with 1836 Niles NT (No 962) and 1846 Noyes NT (No 1314). Cited copy lacks
p 3–10.

1829   The New Testament . . . Stereotyped by James Conner . . . Published by
J. Emory and B. Waugh, for the Methodist Episcopal Church: New York **690**

Reported as 237 p   16 cm   DLC

1829   The New Testament ... Stereotyped by James Conner, New-York ... Printed
and published by Daniel Neall: Philadelphia   **691**

226 p   16 cm   NN

1829   The New Testament ... Stereotyped by H. & H. Wallis, New-York. Printed
at the Protestant Episcopal Press. Published ... by the New York Protestant
Episcopal Press: [New York]   **692**

270 p   16 cm   NN

1829   The New Testament ... [Stereotype Edition]. With References and a Key
Sheet of Questions ... Designed to Facilitate the Acquisition of Scriptural
Knowledge ... By Hervey Wilbur ... Published by S. Wilson: Belchertown
693

324 p   15 cm   NN
Wilbur's Reference Testament; see 1823, No 482. Has Wilbur's Useful Tables at end.

1829   The New Testament ... Printed by A. Chandler: New York   **694**

352 p   15 cm   NN
Stereotyped by A. Chandler and Co.

1829?   The New Testament ... Stereotype Edition ... J. Wolcott, Jr., Printer: Lowell [Massachusetts]   **695**

1 vol: (330) 331–335   14 cm   NNAB
For matter at end, see 1828 Roby NT, No 660.

1829   The New Testament ... Printed and published by J. Sanderson: Elizabeth-
town [New Jersey]   **696**

335 p   13 cm   NN
For matter at end, see 1828 Roby NT, No 660.

1829   The New Testament ... Translated from the Latin Vulgat ... Newly Revised
... Stereotyped by J. Conner, New-York ... Published by Eugene Cummiskey: Philadelphia   **697**

1 vol: (406) 407–412   12 cm   DGU, NN
Rheims Version, from the 5th Dublin edition.
Pocket NT with a brief account of the writer before each book and chapter summaries. In-
cludes Admonition, Letter of Pope Pius the Sixth, Prayer, Tables, Subscribers' Names, and
Cummiskey's Catalogue of Catholic Publications for 1827–28.

1829   The New Testament ... Stereotyped by L. Johnson [for the] American Sunday School Union: Philadelphia   **698**

416 p   12 cm   NNAB

1830?   The Holy Bible, translated from the Latin Vulgate ... With annotations, by
the Rev. Dr. Challoner; together with References, and an Historical and
Chronological Index ... Fielding Lucas: Baltimore   **699**

Reported as (789) (235)   30 cm   MdBP,PLatS
Rheims-Douay, from 5th Dublin edition. Reprint of Cummiskey 1825 Bible (No 527). Has
frontispiece.

1830/29 The Holy Bible . . . With Canne's Marginal Notes and References . . .
Stereotyped, Printed and Published by H. & E. Phinney: Cooperstown **700**

Reported as 768 p   29 cm   NCooHi

Reprint of 1824 edition (No 485). With Apocrypha. Illustrations. NT dated 1829.

NNAB has copy with general title page dated 1829; added engraved title imprinted *Hartford, Published by Silas Andrus. 1830.*

1830 The Holy Bible . . . Stereotyped for Collins and Co. by B. & J. Collins . . . Published by Langdon Coffin: Boston **701**

Reported as (744) (138) 745–1010   29 cm   ViU

With Apocrypha and Brown's Concordance. Plates.

1830 The Holy Bible . . . With Canne's Marginal Notes and References . . . Stereotyped by E. White, New York . . . N. & G. Guilford and Morgan & Sanxay: Cincinnati **702**

Reported as (570) (112) 571–770   29 cm   OC

Has Apocrypha, Index, Tables, and Concordance (New York 1828, printed on quite different paper). Plates.

This would seem to be the first Bible printed in Ohio. In 1830 Morgan and Sanxay were the largest printers in the Western country and OC has no record of an earlier Ohio Bible.

1830 The Holy Bible . . . With Canne's Marginal References . . . Together with the Apocrypha and Index. Also References . . . Key Sheet of Questions . . . Harmonies . . . and Highly Useful Tables . . . By Hervey Wilbur . . . The Text Corrected According to the Standard of the American Bible Society. [Stereotyped by James Conner, New York] Published by White, Gallaher and White: New York **703**

"4to"   InNovJ

Reprint of Wilbur's 1828 Reference Bible (No 614) with Apocrypha (78 p).

1830 The Holy Bible . . . Stereotyped by L. Johnson . . . Towar & Hogan: Philadelphia **704**

1 vol: (750) (238)   26 cm   NN

Also published with Concordance, Apocrypha, and NT dated 1828. Both Bible and separate NT (the latter printed by C. Sherman & Co.) also issued with imprint *Towar, J. & D. M. Hogan; and Hogan & Co.: Philadelphia.*

1830? The Holy Bible . . . Stereotype Edition . . . Claremont Manufacturing Company's Power Press: Claremont, N. H. **705**

1 vol: (486) (162)   20 cm   NN, NNAB

Has Tables between Testaments.

MS note (Oct 7, 1877) in NNAB 1833 Windsor Bible: "Simeon Ide of Claremont, N. H. . . . says he bought . . . the Bible plates 2nd hand of Nahum Haskell, Woodstock Vt. in 1828." Although the 1833 Windsor Bible (No 828) is a reprint of this, the above is not from the plates used by Haskell in 1828.

1830? The Holy Bible . . . Stereotyped by J. Howe . . . Andrus and Judd: Hartford **706**

1 vol: (655) 656–681 (7)   19 cm   NNAB

Has Contents at end. Engravings.

Perhaps this should be dated 1832 as the joint imprint first appears then.

1830 The Holy Bible . . . Stereotype Edition . . . Printed by D. Fanshaw, for the
American Bible Society: New-York   **707**

1 vol: (508) (2) 511–669 [1]   19 cm   NNAB

Nonpareil 12mo appears at bottom of title page; verso has The Names and Order of the
Books and 106th edition. The last must refer to editions printed by Fanshaw or by the ABS
for this seems to be the first printing of this format and is different from the Nonpareil Duodecimo of 1828 (No 625). Verso of NT title has Tables. Stereotyped by A. Chandler.

1830 The Holy Bible . . . Stereotype Edition . . . Stereotyped by A. Chandler, For
The American Bible Society: New-York   **708**

1 vol: (650) (2) 653–852   19 cm   NNAB

Minion cc. 12mo. appears on bottom of title page; verso has 1st Edition, followed by
Names and Order of the Books and D. Fanshaw, Printer. NT title has *Minion, Cont: Chap:
12 mo.*, with Tables on verso. Printed with full chapter summaries and running heads.

1830 The Holy Bible . . . [Stereotype Edition]. Auxiliary New York Bible and
Common Prayer Book Society: New York   **709**

884 p   19 cm   NN
P 797–820 are numbered 121–144.

1830 The Holy Bible . . . Printed by Hudson and Goodwin: Hartford   **710**

"12mo"   Not Located
O'Callaghan, p 204.

1830 The Holy Bible . . . Stereotype Edition . . . R. Colton and G. W. Smith: Woodstock, Vt.   **711**

1 vol: (486) (162)   18 cm   NN
NN has second copy lacking last 8 pages.

1830 The Holy Bible . . . Published by George W. Mentz & Son: Philadelphia **712**

18 cm   NN
Appears to be from Carey's 1818 duodecimo (No 348).

1830 The Holy Bible . . . Stereotyped by B. and J. Collins, New-York . . . Richardson, Lord and Holbrook: Boston   **713**

792 p   18 cm   MH, NN
Has Account of the Dates, Order of Books, and Tables.

1830 The Holy Bible . . . R. Colton & G. W. Seeley: Woodstock, Vt.   **714**

"24mo"   Not Located
O'Callaghan (p 205) gives "G. L." as location.
Probably the same as Colton and Smith 1830 Bible (No 711) but both NN copies have no
mention of Seeley.

1830 The Holy Bible . . . Hudson and Skinner: Hartford   **715**

Text ends Ll 12   17 cm   NN

1830   The Holy Bible ... Stereotyped by J. Howe ... Published by Silas Andrus: Hartford   **716**

1 vol: (x) (729) (222) 223–225 (5)   14 cm   NN, NNAB
Has frontispiece and engraved title page (1828). Contents of Books of OT precede text, but follow text for NT.

1830   The Holy Bible ... [Stereotype Edition]. D. D. Smith: New-York   **717**

1 vol: (615) (192)   13 cm   NN, NNAB
Has added engraved title and frontispiece (*The Peaceable Kingdom of the Branch* by R. Westall). Illustrated.

1830   The Holy Bible ... Stereotyped by J. Conner, Published by J. Emory and B. Waugh for the Methodist Episcopal Church, at the Conference Office: New York   **718**

Reported as (814) (2) (247) (4)   12 cm   OC
Frontispiece for each Testament and Contents. James Collard, printer.

1830   The New Testament ... Stereotyped by B. & J. Collins: New York. Published by G. Clark: Boston   **719**

Reported as 312 p   22 cm   MBU–T, NNC
Table of Kindred and Affinity appears on bottom half of page 312.

1830   The New Testament ... [The Pronouncing Testament] To which is Applied, in Numerous Words, the Orthoepy of the Critical Pronouncing Dictionary ... By J. Walker ... To Which is Added an Explanatory Key. By I. Alger, Jun. ... [Stereotyped by T. H. & C. Carter] ... Printed and Published by Lincoln & Edmands: Boston   **720**

292 p   19 cm   NN
Illustrated title page. Tables at end.

1830   The New Testament ... Stereotyped by H. & H. Wallis, New-York ... Printed and published by Wm. F. Geddes: Philadelphia   **721**

201 p   18 cm   NN

183–   The New Testament ... Stereotyped by J. Howe. J. M'Dowell, and Kimber & Sharpless: Philadelphia   **722**

270 p   18 cm   NN

1830?   The New Testament ... S. Babcock: New Haven   **723**

288 p   16 cm   CtY, NN, NNAB
Woodcut on title page has two children singing a hymn; on verso another with two children reading, two sewing mottoes. Basket of flowers at foot of page.
NN copy catalogued 184–?.

1830   The New Testament ... Stereotype Edition ... Printed by Daniel Fanshaw, for the American Bible Society: New-York   **724**

226 p   15 cm   NNAB
Verso of title page has 1st Edition and Order of Books.
NNAB has another copy dated 1830 but marked ninth edition.

1830   The New Testament. . . S. Andrus: Hartford   **725**

222 p   13 cm   NN
Appears to be NT from 1830 Andrus Bible (No 716) without Contents at end.

1830   A Manual. The Apostolic Epistles with amendments in conformity to the
Dutch version. Published by the Translator: New York   **726**

1 vol: 189–295 [1] p   "12mo"   NN
   The translator was Egbert Benson (1746–1833) who was a leader in the Revolution and
representative in the Continental Congress, several succeeding conventions, and in Congress. He
served as judge of the New York Supreme Court, 1794–1812, and was considered an authority
on legal matters, second only to Alexander Hamilton. He was a trustee of Columbia University
and one of the founders and the first president of the New York Historical Society. He was
granted LL.D. degrees by Union, Dartmouth, and Harvard. His object in this edition seems
to have been to give the proper translation of the terms for charity and bishop, which he rendered as love and overseer.
   NN suggests that the pagination probably agrees with a copy of the NT in general use at
the time which he had marked up, as he prepared no further text.

1831   The Holy Bible . . . with references and illustrations . . . summary . . . paraphrase . . . analysis . . . by John Brown. Embellished with a series of . . . engravings. Printed and published by T. Kinnersley: New York   **727**

43 cm   NNAB
   Brown's Self-Interpreting Bible; see 1822, No 433. Added engraved title page imprinted
London, published by Thos. Kelly, 17 Paternoster Row, 1824. Before the text is an endorsement
for "This London Edition" by a number of British clergymen. This Bible was evidently issued
in parts and trimmed in binding, and page numbers do not appear before p 921. Has many
engravings, some 41 x 23 cm, and all done for Kelly. They may have been imported but the
book was probably manufactured in America.

1831   The Holy Bible . . . together with the Apocrypha . . . Canne's Marginal Notes
and References . . . Stereotype Edition . . . Printed and Published by G. M.
Davison: Saratoga Springs [New York]   **728**

Reported as (8) 9–576 (96) 579–754 755–768   30 cm   PHi
Has frontispiece and other engravings by Anderson.

1831   The Holy Bible . . . With Canne's Marginal Notes and References . . . D. D.
Smith: New-York   **729**

Reported as (576) (96) 579–768 (54)   29 cm   CtY
   Added engraved title page has imprint *Hartford, S. Andrus 1832.* With Apocrypha. Also
Index, Tables, and Concordance. Illustrated.
   NN has copy without engraved title, Apocrypha, Concordance or illustrations.

1831/32   The Holy Bible . . . with Canne's marginal notes and references . . . Stereotyped, Printed and Published by H. & E. Phinney: Cooperstown   **730**

768 p   29 cm   NNAB
Has Apocrypha inserted (99 p). NT dated 1832.
NCooHi has copy dated 1831/29, with 10 illustrations, no Apocrypha.

1831   The Holy Bible . . . with Canne's Marginal Notes and References . . . Stereotyped by B. & J. Collins . . . [Printed by J. H. A. Frost]. Published by Langdon
Coffin: Boston   **731**

29 cm   NjMD, NN, NNAB

Agrees with Collins & Co. 1821 quarto (No 414) but has added engraved title page and more illustrations. With Apocrypha and Concordance (1830).

NjMD copy has Concordance dated 1827 with imprint *Boston, printed for C. Ewer and T. Bedlington.* MB has separate NT.

1831/30 The Holy Bible . . . I. Ashmead & Co., Printers. McCarty & Davis: Philadelphia   732

1 vol: (676) 682–834 836–1076   28 cm   NN

From plates of Carey's 1812/11 quarto (No 208) but with Fletcher's Concise View omitted. Lev 19:12 is incorrect; see 1828, No 622. Metrical Psalms are added. Concordance (1833). Illustrated with Anderson engravings but from cancelled or split blocks. NT dated 1830.

1831 The Holy Bible . . . In Two Volumes . . . Published by Gray and Bowen: Boston   733

2 vols: Vol i, 915 p; Vol ii, 805 p   27 cm   NN, NNAB

Both volumes have title pages; Vol i has frontispiece. Verso of titles have Boston Press, Francis Jenkins, Proprietor; Stephen Foster, Printer.

NN copy printed on larger page (29 cm) with frontispiece for each volume.

1831 The Holy Bible . . . With Marginal Notes and References . . . [Stereotyped by B. & J. Collins]. Published and Sold by Edmund Cushing: Lunenburg, Mass.   734

27 cm   NN

Reprint of Cushing 1828 quarto (No 615).

1831 The Holy Bible . . . With Canne's Marginal References . . . Together with the Apocrypha and Index, also References . . . Key Sheet of Questions . . . Harmonies . . . and Highly Useful Tables . . . By Hervey Wilbur . . . The Text Corrected According to the Standard of the American Bible Society. [Stereotyped by James Conner, New York]. Published by White, Gallaher and White: New York   735

"4to"   DLC

Reprint of Wilbur's Reference Bible of 1828 (No 614). With Apocrypha (78 p).

1831 The Holy Bible . . . with Explanatory Notes . . . by Thomas Scott. Stereotype edition, with the Author's last Corrections and Improvement . . . C. Norris, Printer. Stereotyped by the Printer. Published by James Derby: Exeter, N. H.   736

26 cm   MBU–T

Scott's Annotated Bible; see 1804–09, No 113. MBU–T has Vols v–vi only, covering the NT.

1831 The Holy Bible . . . Stereotype Edition. Published by the Bible Association of Friends in America: Philadelphia   737

1 vol: (1061) (xxxiii) (92)   26 cm   NNAB

Tables, Index (with a few alternations, from Bagster's Comprehensive Bible), and Brown's Concordance at end.

Also issued bound in 2 or 3 vols.

1831 The Holy Bible . . . Bible Association of Friends in America: Philadelphia 738

1080 [1] p   25 cm   NNAB

Tables at end.

1831   The Holy Bible . . . Stereotyped at the Boston Type and Stereotype Foundry: Hilliard, Gray, Little, and Wilkins: Boston   **739**

1 vol: (687) (212) (iv)   25 cm   NN

1831   The Holy Bible . . . Translated from the Latin Vulgat . . . [Stereotyped by J. Howe]. Published by Eugene Cummiskey: Philadelphia   **740**

Reported as (335) (444) (191)   23 cm   DGU

Rheims-Douay, from 5th Dublin edition. 500 copies were reprinted from 1824 edition (No 492).
O'Callaghan (p 210) lists a separate NT, also 500 copies.

1831   The Holy Bible . . . With Canne's Marginal References . . . The Text Corrected According to the Standard of the American Bible Society. Stereotyped by James Conner, New York. Printed and Published by Holbrook and Fessenden: Brattleboro, Vt.   **741**

Reported as (527) (78) (168)   22 cm   NAtt

Reprint of 1828 Holbrook and Fessenden quarto (No 613).

1831   The Holy Bible . . . Printed and Published by George Clark: Boston, Mass.
                                                                               742

21 cm   NNAB, PP

Appears to be same as 1815 Bible by D. & G. Bruce (No 279) but with wider margins and engravings, supposed to be by Anderson.
NNAB copy has only 6 small engravings, although Anderson bibliography calls for 28.

1831/29   The Holy Bible . . . Stereotyped by James Conner. J. Collard, printer. Published by J. Emory and B. Waugh, for the Methodist Episcopal Church, at the conference office: New York   **743**

20 cm   TNMB

NT dated 1829.

1831   The Holy Bible . . . Boston Stereotype Edition. Waitt and Dow, sold . . . by Lincoln & Edmands: Boston   **744**

1 vol: (486) (162)   20 cm   NN, NNAB

Illustrated.

1831   The Holy Bible . . . Stereotyped by J. Howe, Philadelphia . . . J. B. Butler, Printer. Published by H. Holdship & Son: Pittsburgh   **745**

1 vol: (743) (238)   "12mo"   Not Located

O'Callaghan, p 210. Has Metrical Psalms.

1831   The Holy Bible . . . Printed by Hudson and Goodwin: Hartford   **746**
"12mo"   Not Located
O'Callaghan, p 210.

1831   The Reference Bible . . . By Hervey Wilbur . . . Carter Hendee & Co.: Boston
                                                                               747

321 p   "small 12mo"   Not Located

O'Callaghan (p 387) quotes Melvin Lord: "The references not being found very useful, were striken from the plates and the volumes subsequently published without them."
The pagination seems small for a Bible. See 1826 Bible, No 559.

1831   The Holy Bible . . . [Stereotype Edition] . . . Auxiliary New-York Bible and
Common Prayer Book Society, Printed at the New-York Protestant Episcopal
Press: New-York   **748**

884 p   19 cm   NN, NNAB

1831   The Holy Bible . . . Stereotype Edition . . . Rufus Colton: Woodstock [Ver-
mont]   **749**

Reported as (486) (162)   19 cm   VtHi

1831   The Holy Bible . . . [Stereotyped by L. Johnson]. Published by G. W. Mentz
& Son: Philadelphia   **750**

1 vol: (599) (179)   18 cm   NN

1831   The Holy Bible . . . Stereotyped by J. Howe . . . Published by Silas Andrus:
Hartford   **751**

655 p   18 cm   NN
Illustrated.

1831   The Holy Bible . . . Hudson & Skinner: Hartford   **752**

Text ends Ll12   17 cm   NN

1831   The English Version of the Polyglott Bible . . . With the Marginal Readings:
Together with a Copious and Original Selection of References to Parallel
and Illustrative Passages. Exhibited in a Manner Hitherto Unattempted.
Stereotyped by L. Johnson . . . Published by Key & Meilke: Philadelphia **753**

1 vol: (viii) (587) (190)   15 cm   NN, NNAB

Each Testament has frontispiece and added engraved title (with publisher spelled *Mielke*).
Order of Books and Preface to the English Version of the Polyglott Bible signed T. C. (Chevalier) precede text. Text has references in center column.

This is the first American edition of the frequently reprinted "Polyglott" Bible. It is actually
the English text from Samuel Bagster's genuine polyglot Bible which had originally been
printed in London in 1822 with the complete text in eight languages, four to a page. The whole
edition, except a few copies of the NT, was destroyed by fire. It was reprinted and issued in
1831, some copies with only six languages. The English text, first printed in 1816, was the AV
with a full reference column of over 60,000 references. See also 1825 Bible, No 534.

A large number of these "Polyglott" Bibles were printed in the United States, particularly
in New England, and in various sizes. The title and references must have been a sales "gimmick"
as indicated by the following quotations from Richardson Lought's *Hawkers and Walkers in
Early America, Strolling Peddlers, Preachers, Lawyers, Doctors, Players and others from the
Beginning to the Civil War* (Philadelphia, J. B. Lippincott Company, 1927): "The early peddler,
if contemporary documents are to be believed, was a lanky and hawk-beaked youth, an adven-
turous, brave, mercenary fellow, who had a rare understanding of human nature and a ready
tongue. His most effective salesmanship was the 'soft sawder' flattery. He was accused of pur-
veying wooden nutmegs and cucumber seeds, oak-leaf cigars, shoe-peg oats, polyglot Bibles (all
in English) and realistically painted bass-wood hams. He was, moreover, a commercial bird of
passage. He always left his customers convinced and satisfied with their share of the bargain,
but he usually managed to clear out after finishing his deal." (p 25) "It is said that the house of
every substantial farmer in the days following the Revolution had three ornaments — a polyglot Bible, a tin reflector and a wooden clock. . . . The polyglot Bible 'all in English' (one Yankee
peddler is alleged to have sold £16,000 worth of them) is a myth." (p 77)

1831 The Holy Bible . . . Stereotyped by J. Howe . . . Published by Silas Andrus: Hartford **754**

13 cm NNAB

Similar to 1830 Bible (No 716). Has frontispiece and engraved title dated 1830.

1831 A New Translation of the Book of Psalms, with an Introduction. By George R. Noyes. Published by Gray and Bowen. Boston **755**

1 vol: (xxviii) (232) 21 cm NNAB

Noyes Version; see 1827, No 592.

Reprinted in 1846 by James Munroe and Company, Boston. For third edition, revised, which includes Proverbs, see 1867, No 1819.

1831 The New Testament . . . Stereotype Edition . . . [Stereotyped by J. Howe, Philadelphia; Wm. Brown, printer]. Published by The Bible Association of Friends in America: Philadelphia **756**

386 p 21 cm NNAB

1831 The New Testament . . . Stereotype Edition . . . Published by Stimpson and Clapp: Boston **757**

20 cm NN, NNAB

Reprint of Paragraph NT of 1827 (No 593) but with new title page and wider margins. Advertisement (1831) states that approval of the edition has been expressed by the subscription of "almost all the clergymen, and those of every denomination in the city."

1831 The New Testament . . . Ludwig & Tolefree, Printers . . . Published by R. Schoyer: New York **758**

315 p "12mo" Not Located

O'Callaghan, p 212. Only II Peter, Chapt. 3 to Jude has column and chapter headings.

1831? The New Testament . . . translated from the Latin Vulgate . . . Published by Fielding Lucas, Jr.: Baltimore **759**

353 p 19 cm NN

Rheims Version. Has Tables on p 345–353.

"Mr. Cummiskey informs me that he sold the plates of his 12mo Testament . . . to Mr Lucas, in 1830 or 1831. I have not been able to find a copy of the Cummiskey 12mo, and am therefore unable to say how far that volume agrees with this; but on comparing it with the Devereux Testament of 1829, the text of both appears to be identical; even the error in James 5:17. . . . The preliminary matter of the Devereux Testament, included on pp. ii–xi, is, in the Lucas edition, transferred to the end of the volume where the 'Table of Controversies' is entitled 'Table of References.' " (O'Callaghan, p 211.)

1831 The New Testament . . . Stereotyped by H. & H. Wallis, New York . . . [Cook & Taylor, Printers]. Published by J. I. Cutler & Co.: Bellows Falls, Vt. **760**

Reported as 270 p 16 cm CSmH

1831 The New Testament . . . To which are added Explanatory Notes; embracing A Historical and Geographical Account of the Places mentioned in the New Testament; and Biographical Notices of Individuals; also Definitions of

1831, continued

Terms, References, &c. With an Outline of Jewish History; and a Historical and Geographical Sketch of Palestine. Prepared for the Instruction of Youth ... By J. Olney ... Published by Silas Andrus: Hartford, Conn.; Luke Loomis & Co.: Pittsburg, Penn.; A. B. Roff: Cincinnati, Ohio; J. S. Kellogg: Mobile, Ala.   **761**

378 p   16 cm   NN
Has maps.

1831   The New Testament ... Published by A. Colton: Middlebury   **762**

Reported as 336 p   "18mo"   C. F. Libbie & Co.

1831?   The New Testament ... Stereotyped by James Conner, New York ... Published by Luke Loomis: Pittsburgh   **763**

1 vol: (226) (6)   15 cm   NNAB
Has List of Proper Names and Contents at end.
O'Callaghan (p 212) notes copy dated 1831, marked sixth edition.

1831   The New Testament ... Stereotyped by A. Chandler. Printed by D. Fanshaw, for the American Bible Society: New York   **764**

1 vol: (340) 341–344   13 cm   NNAB
Verso of title page has 1st Edition and Order of Books. Contents at end (4 p). Has short chapter summaries and running heads.
   NNAB has NT dated 1837 with same format and pagination, marked first edition and stereotyped by Smith and Valentine.

1831   The New Testament ... Published by James Derby [Stereotyped by the Publisher]: Exeter, N. H.   **765**

259 p   12 cm   NN, NNAB

1831?   The New Testament ... Translated from the Latin Vulgat with Annotations and References ... Published by F. Lucas, Jr.: Baltimore   **766**

12 cm   NNAB
Rheims Version, from the 5th Dublin edition. Reprint of Cummiskey's 1829 32mo (No 697). Verso of title page has Approbation of James, Archbishop of Baltimore, Order of Books, and Note. Followed by an Admonition, Letter of Pope Pius vi, and Prayer (2 p). At end are Tables (6 p).

1831   The New Testament ... [Pocket Reference Testament]. With Original Selections of References to Parallel and Illustrative Passages; and Marginal Readings: ... to Facilitate Acquisition of Scripture Knowledge in Bible Classes, Sunday Schools, &c. Stereotyped by L. Johnson ... Published by Armstrong & Plaskitt: Baltimore   **767**

281 p   "24mo"   Not Located
O'Callaghan, p 212.

1831   The Polyglot New Testament ... With Marginal Readings, illustrated with numerous Engravings ... Published by J. C. Riker: New York   **768**

11 cm   WBB
See 1831 Bible, No 753; also 1833 NT, No 855.

1831? The New Testament . . . Stereotyped by Henry Wallis & Luther Roby . . .
Concord, N. H. . . . Claremont Manufacturing Co.: Claremont, N. H. **769**

Reported as 259 p   "48mo"   MBU–T
Has frontispiece. Dated by O'Callaghan (p 213).

1832 The Comprehensive Bible . . . With the Various Readings and Marginal
Notes Usually Printed Therewith: A General Introduction . . . Introductions
and Concluding Remarks to Each Book: The Parallel Passages Contained in
Canne's Bible; Dr. Adam Clark's Commentary . . . ; Rev. J. Brown's Self-
Interpreting Bible . . . ; Dr. Blayney's Bible; Bishop Wilson's Bible, Edited
by Crutwell; Rev. T. Scott's Commentary . . . ; and the English Version of
Bagster's Polyglott Bible . . . Philological and Explanatory Notes . . . Stereotyped by James Conner, New-York. Published by Andrus & Judd: Hartford
770

1460 p   30 cm   NNAB
Preliminary matter includes Order of Books followed by Chronological Order, Editor's
Preface (London 1826), General Contents, The Translators to the Reader, Contents of the
Old and New Testaments in Historical Order, Analysis and Compendium to the Sacred Scrip-
tures, and Introduction. A General Outline of the History of the Jews follows OT. Chronological
Index, Subject Index, and Index to Notes, etc. at end.
This Bible was originally edited by William Greenfield and published in parts in England
by S. Bagster between 1825 and 1827. A few years later, Isaac Pitman, the inventor of Pitman's
shorthand, offered to check all the 500,000 references but found very few misprints.

1832? The Holy Bible, Translated from the Latin Vulgate . . . With Annotations
by the Rev. Dr. Challoner; Together with References . . . Index. Revised and
Corrected According to the Clementine Edition of the Scripture . . . Published by Fielding Lucas, Jr.: Baltimore   **771**

1 vol: (4) 9–789 (3) (4) 5–222 223–235   30 cm   DGU, NN, NNAB
Rheims-Douay, from 5th Dublin edition. Has engraved Approbation of the Archbishop of
Baltimore (showing Cathedral at Baltimore), Original Approbations, Decree of the Council of
Trent, quotation from Pope Pius vi, Admonition, Prayer, and Order of Books. P [790] is blank,
followed by list of Lucas' publications (1 p), verso blank, and two leaves of Family Record.
After NT text, Tables and Indexes for OT and NT. Engraved frontispieces to both Testaments
and 7 other illustrations, most within architectural frames, engraved by Neagle, Woodruff, and
Hamm.
O'Callaghan (p 214) states that this edition is from the plates of Cummiskey's quarto of
1825 (No 527) which Mr. Lucas purchased in 1830 or 1831. He also says that the Approbation of the Bishop of Baltimore is missing from some copies.

1832 The Holy Bible . . . With Canne's Marginal Notes . . . Stereotyped by H. & E.
Phinney: Cooperstown   **772**

Reported as (576) (99) 577–768   29 cm   CSmH, NCooHi
With Apocrypha and Tables. Frontispiece and illustrations.
NCooHi has 4 copies: (1) 8 illustrations, no Apocrypha; (2) 10 illustrations, Apocrypha;
(3) 8 illustrations, Apocrypha, NT dated 1831; (4) 8 illustrations, Apocrypha, NT dated 1833.

1832 The Holy Bible . . . By Hervey Wilbur. The Text Corrected According to the
Standard of the American Bible Society . . . N. & J. White: New-York **773**

Reported as (527) (78) (168) (31)   29 cm   MiU
Has frontispiece and plates. With Apocrypha. At end are Index, Tables, etc., and Useful
Tables of Scripture Names Prepared to Accompany the Reference Bible by Hervey Wilbur,
which has separate title page with same imprint as above.

1832   The Holy Bible . . . The Text Corrected According to the Standard of the
American Bible Society . . . Stereotyped by James Conner, New-York. Published by the Brattleboro' Bible Company. Peck, Steen & Co. Agents: Brattleboro'   774

1 vol: (527) (168) (14)   29 cm   NNAB
Follows Holbrook and Fessenden 1828 edition (No 613) with same materials added to text
but without Apocrypha. Has different woodcut plates, from Anderson's older series, some of the
blocks being worn and split. One of these, *Samson wrestling with the lion,* is signed.

1832/31   The Holy Bible . . . Apocrypha . . . Published and Sold by Edmund Cushing: Lunenburg, Mass.   775

28 cm   NNAB
Follows 1828 edition (No 615) with some difference in engravings. Stereotyped by B. & J.
Collins. NT title dated 1831.
      NNAB has an edition imprinted *Boston: Printed and published by Charles Gaylord,* printed
from a related set of plates but the references are often missing although the reference number
appears in the text. Other references are missing from the Cushing edition.

1832   [The Holy Bible] The New Testament . . . With Canne's Marginal Refer-
ences. Stereotyped by James Conner, New-York . . . [J. Collord, Printer].
Published by B. Waugh and T. Mason, for the Methodist Episcopal Church:
New-York   776

1 vol: (642) (92) (200) (12) (4) (2) (48) (4)   28 cm   NNAB
General title page missing from cited copy; above imprint taken from NT title. Engraved
OT title page has *New-York, Published by N. Bangs & J. Emory: for the M. E. Church.* . . . To
the Reader and Order of Books precede text; Account of the Holy Land and Genealogy of
Patriarchs follow OT. With Apocrypha. Index, Tables, Concordance, and Guide to Perusal of
Scriptures by William Stones at end.

1832   The Holy Bible . . . [I. Ashmead & Co., Printers]. McCarty and Davis: Philadelphia   777

1 vol: (676) 836–1076   28 cm   NN
Reprint of Carey's quarto issued by McCarty and Davis in 1828 (No 622). Gap in paging
due to omission of Apocrypha. Does not have Concordance, Metrical Psalms, or engravings.

1832/31   The Holy Bible . . . Stereotyped at the Boston Type and Stereotype
Foundry, late J. H. Carter & Co. . . . [Hale's Steam Press]. Nathan Hale;
Sampson and Clapp; Hilliard, Gray, Little and Wilkins; Richardson, Lord
and Holbrook; Lincoln and Edmands; Crocker and Brewster; Munroe and
Francis; and R. P. and C. Williams: Boston   778

1 vol: (687) (134) (212) (xii)   24 cm   NN
With Apocrypha. Table of Contents. NT dated 1831.

1832   The Holy Bible . . . N. Hale: Boston   779

1 vol: (687) (134) (212) (xii)   24 cm   NN
Similar to preceding entry (No 778) but with short imprint. Has Apocrypha in smaller type.

1832   The Holy Bible . . . J. A. Ballard: Boston   780

"8vo"   Not Located
O'Callaghan, p 215.

1832   The Holy Bible [with Thomas Scott's Notes] . . . Stereotyped by A. Pell and
Brother, N. Y. E. Williams, Printer . . . Collins and Hannay: New York **781**

3 vols   23 cm   NNAB

Scott's Bible; see 1804–09, No 113. Has frontispiece and Brown's Concordance. NNAB has
Vol II only, Job-Mal, 965 p.

1832   The Holy Bible translated from the Latin Vulgat . . . Published by Eugene
Cummiskey, Stereotyped by J. Howe: Philadelphia   **782**

23 cm   DGU

Rheims-Douay Version. 500 copies reprinted from 1824 Bible (No 492).

1832/31   The Holy Bible . . . [Stereotype Edition]. Charles Gaylord: Boston **783**

1 vol: (486) (162)   22 cm   NN

Added engraved title page dated 1833. NT title dated 1831.

1832   The Holy Bible . . . with Canne's Marginal Notes and References . . . Stereotyped by J. Howe, Philadelphia . . . Published and Sold by Daniel D. Smith:
New-York   **784**

1 vol: (811) (3)   22 cm   NN, NNAB

Frontispiece, To the Reader, and Table of Contents precede text.
Wright (p 396) lists an edition of 1834.

1832?   The Holy Bible . . . [Stereotype Edition]. Published by Jas. B. Smith & Co.:
Philadelphia   **785**

1 vol: (436) (162)   "12mo"   Not Located

O'Callaghan, p 216.

1832   The Holy Bible . . . Stereotyped by B. & J. Collins, New York . . . Published
by Moses G. Atwood: Concord, N. H.   **786**

792 p   18 cm   MB, NN

Tables follow OT. NT does not have title page.
O'Callaghan (p 210) lists an edition dated 1831 in the Lenox Collection with the statement
"This is a wretchedly printed book." Although the Union Catalog locates this at NN, no copy
with the 1831 date could be found in 1959.

1832   The Holy Bible . . . Stereotyped by J. Howe . . . , Philadelphia . . . Published
by Silas Andrus: Hartford   **787**

1 vol: 3–499 503–655 656–660   18 cm   NNAB

Has two frontispieces and illustrations (two plates per page). Tables follow OT; Contents
of Books at end.

1832   The Holy Bible . . . Stereotyped by J. Conner, James Collard, Printer. B.
Waugh and T. Mason for the Methodist Episcopal Church at the Conference
Office, 14 Crosby Street: New York   **788**

Reported as (814) (10) (247) (4)   18 cm   KBB

Has frontispiece, *The Peaceful Kingdom of the Messiah*. Indexes follow OT and NT.
NN has NT only, without *for the Methodist Episcopal Church*. . . .

1832   The Holy Bible . . . Hudson & Skinner: Hartford   **789**

Text ends Ll12   17 cm   NN
O'Callaghan (p 217) also lists a duodecimo of this date by Hudson and Goodwin, but no
copy has been located.

1832   The English Version of the Polyglott Bible . . . With Marginal Readings . . .
         Selection of References to Parallel and Illustrative Passages. Exhibited in a
         Manner Hitherto Unattempted. Stereotyped by L. Johnson . . . Published by
         Edward C. Mielke: Philadelphia   **790**

1 vol: (587) (190)   15 cm   MBU–T, NjMD, NN
Frontispiece and added engraved title page to each Testament. Preface by T. C. The pub-
lisher's name is evidently misspelled in this edition; all other references have spelling *Meilke*.
See 1831, No 753.
Also published with engraved title page dated 1831 and with Metrical Psalms (Key and
Mielke 1831, 64 p).

1832   The Holy Bible . . . Published by Silas Andrus: Hartford   **791**

Reported as (729) (225) (70)   "24mo"   MB, MiU
Published with and without Metrical Psalms.

1832   The Holy Bible . . . [Stereotyped by A. Chandler]. Published by William H.
         Niles: Middletown [Connecticut]   **792**

1 vol: (824) (251)   14 cm   NN
Illustrated.

1832/31   Pocket Reference Bible. The English Version of the Polyglott Bible . . .
            With Original Selections of References to Parallel and Illustrative Passages;
            and Marginal Readings . . . Stereotyped by L. Johnson . . . Published by
            Armstrong & Plaskitt: Baltimore   **793**

1 vol: (viii) (920) (282)   13 cm   NN
Has added engraved title pages. Added matter includes Order of Books and Chronological
Order, Preface, Tables, Contents of Books, Discourses, Parables and Miracles of Jesus, Harmony
of the Gospels, and Proper Lessons for Sunday Mornings. NT dated 1831.
ViU has copy with imprints of *Armstrong & Plaskitt* and *Plaskitt & Co*.

1832   The Holy Bible . . . Stereotyped by L. Johnson. Alexander Towar; Also Hogan
         & Thompson: Philadelphia   **794**

1 vol: (819) (256) (82)   12 cm   NN, NNAB
Has added engraved title page and frontispiece. Metrical Psalms at end.
NN engraved title imprinted Hogan and Thompson only. O'Callaghan (p 217) notes some
copies have engraved title dated 1829 or 1834 with imprint of Towar & Hogan.

1832   The Holy Bible . . . Seventh Stereotype Edition . . . Published by N. and J.
         White: New-York   **795**

1 vol: (704) (216)   12 cm   NN
Has frontispieces to Testaments and engravings. Dedication to King James.

1832   [The New Testament] The Sacred Writings of the Apostles and Evangelists
         of Jesus Christ . . . Translated from the Original Greek by Drs. G. Campbell,

J. Macknight, and P. Doddridge . . . [Third Edition Revised and Enlarged].
Printed and Published by Alexander Campbell: Bethany, Brook County,
Va.   **796**

1 vol: (517) (100)   23 cm   CSmH, NcD, NN, OO, ViU
Alexander Campbell Version; see 1826 NT, No 567. Contains Preface, Emendations, Appendix, Notes, and Tables. Illustrated with maps.

1832 The New Testament . . . Stereotyped by B. and J. Collins, New York . . .
S. Andrus: Hartford   **797**

22 cm   NN
Seems to be similar to 1830 Clark NT (No 719). Has 8 plates.
NNAB has copy with undated imprint *Andrus and Judd: Hartford, Ct.*, which probably belongs here since Andrus and Judd imprint superseded that of S. Andrus in 1832. Table of Kindred on last page.

1832 The New Testament . . . Stereotyped by Hammond Wallis, New York . . .
Printed and Sold by Simeon Ide: Windsor [Vermont]   **798**

372 p   17 cm   NN

1832 The New Testament . . . Olds: Newark   **799**

17 cm   NcD
Has title in vignette. Cited copy lacks all after ɪɪ John 1:7.

1832 The New Testament . . . Ide and Goddard's Power Press: Windsor [Vermont]   **800**

372 p   17 cm   NN

1832 The New Testament . . . Stereotyped by J. Conner, New-York. Printed and
Published by William Williams: Utica   **801**

237 p   16 cm   NN, NNAB

1832 The New Testament . . . J. Harmstead: Philadelphia   **802**

"16mo"   Not Located
Wright, p 395.

1832 The New Testament . . . F. Lucas: Baltimore   **803**

12 cm   Not Located
Wright, p 395. Rheims Version. Probably a reprint of 1831 Lucas NT (No 766).

1832 The New Testament . . . Stereotyped by L. Johnson. Published by B. F.
Brookfield: Elizabethtown, N. J.   **804**

344 p   "32mo"   Not Located
O'Callaghan, p 218.

1832 The New Testament . . . Published by Luther Roby: Concord, N. H.   **805**

Reported as 335 p   "32mo"   MBU–T

1832 The New Testament . . . Stereotyped by J. Howe, Philadelphia. S. Andrus: Hartford   **806**

222 p   13 cm   NN
Has 16 plates.

1832 The New Testament . . . Stereotyped by J. Conner. James Collord, printer. Published by B. Waugh and T. Mason: New York   **807**

Reported as (247) (4)   12 cm   TNMB

1832 The New Testament . . . Stereotyped by L. Johnson. American Sunday School Union: Philadelphia   **808**

11 cm   NNAB
Uniform with 1829 edition (No 698).

1832 The New Testament . . . With Marginal Readings; and Illustrated by Original References . . . Carefully Chosen and Newly Arranged . . . John C. Riker: New York   **809**

1 vol: (ii) (350)   11 cm   CSmH, NN
Engraved title page, illustrations. See 1833 NT, No 855.

1832 The New Testament . . . Stereotyped by L. Johnson. Towar and Hogan: Philadelphia   **810**

256 p   11 cm   NNAB
Appears to be NT of 1832 Bible (No 794). Has frontispiece and engraved title page by R. W. Pomeroy.
Also published with imprints of Alexander Towar and Hogan & Thompson.

1832 [Polymicrian Testament] The New Testament . . . With Short Explanatory Notes, and Numerous References to Illustrative and Parallel Passages, Printed in a Centre Column . . . [Stereotyped by James Conner; D. Fanshaw, Printer]. Published by Jonathan Leavitt: New York; Crocker and Brewster: Boston   **811**

Reported as 546 p   10 cm   MB, MBU–T
New Testament in Greek appears at head of title. Added short title page has *New Testament* in 48 languages. Maps.
First published in London in 1831 by S. Bagster, this is another Bagster edition that was "pirated" in America. See 1831 Polyglott Bible, No 753; also 1832 Comprehensive Bible, No 770. Bagster published matching editions of the Greek NT edited by Greenfield and a Hebrew NT.

1833 The Holy Bible. [Self-Interpreting Bible]. With References and Illustrations . . . An Analysis of the Contents of Each Chapter, Explanatory Notes, Evangelical Reflections . . . By the Late Rev. John Brown . . . T. Kinnersley: New-York   **812**

1 vol: (li) 3–876 (158) 877–1216   48 cm   NNAB
Reprint of 1826? edition (No 546); see also 1822/20 Brown's Self-Interpreting Bible, No 433. With Apocrypha. Illustrated. Title page dated 1833; added engraved title, 1826.

1833 The Holy Bible . . . Stereotype Edition. Canne's Marginal Notes and References . . . Printed and Published . . . by G. M. Davison: Saratoga Springs **813**

1 vol: (576) (96) 579–754 755–768   29 cm   NNAB

Has same added material as H. and E. Phinney edition of 1823 (No 463). With Apocrypha. Contains some Anderson woodcuts.

O'Callaghan (p 220) says Davison used the plates a number of times and then sold them to S. and W. Ward, New York, who do not seem to have used them.

1833   The Holy Bible . . . [Stereotyped by J. Conner, New-York]. With Canne's Marginal References . . . Together with the Apocrypha and Index, also References . . . Key Sheet of Questions . . . Harmonies . . . and Highly Useful Tables . . . By Hervey Wilbur . . . The Text Corrected According to the Standard of the American Bible Society. Peck and Wood: Brattleboro, Vt.
814

29 cm   MB, NN
Reprinted from plates of Wilbur's Reference Bible of 1828 (No 614). Apocrypha wanting? Illustrated.

1833   The Holy Bible . . . with Canne's marginal references . . . Apocrypha . . . Index . . . Stereotyped by James Conner, New-York. Carter, Hendee, and Co., Brattleboro' Power Press Office: Boston   *815*

Reported as (528) (138) 1009–1010 (168) (56) (10) (4)   29 cm   VtHi
Undated added engraved title page has imprint *Boston Edition . . . Langdon Coffin.* Has frontispiece and woodcut illustrations.

1833   The Holy Bible . . . With Canne's Marginal Notes and References . . . Published by R. White & Co.: Hartford   *816*

1 vol: 9–574 (99) 579–768 (54) (18)   29 cm   NNAB
Set with slight variations from 1823 H. and E. Phinney stereotype edition (No 463) with same materials added to text. Has Brown's Concordance and Metrical Psalms.

1833   [The Holy Bible] The New Testament . . . Stereotyped, Printed and Published by H. & E. Phinney: Cooperstown   *817*

1 vol: (576) (99) 577–768   29 cm   NNAB
Reprint of 1823 edition (No 463) but with different illustrations. General title page missing from cited copy; above taken from NT title.

NCooHi has copy without Apocrypha or illustrations. THi has separate NT.

1833–34   [The Holy Bible] The Cottage Bible, and Family Expositor . . . With Practical Expositions and Explanatory Notes. By Thomas Williams . . . To Which are Added, the References and Marginal Readings of the Polyglott Bible . . . The Whole Carefully Revised, and Adapted to the Use of Sunday Schools, &c . . . Edited by Rev. William Patton . . . Complete in Two Volumes . . . [Stereotyped by Conner and Cooke. H. Mason, Printer]. Conner and Cooke: New-York   *818*

2 vols: Vol i, (736); Vol ii, 737–1440   28 cm   NNAB
Vol i (1833) Genesis-Solomon's Song; Vol ii (1834) Isaiah-Revelation, Index. Frontispiece and separate title page to each volume. Preliminary matter includes a Preface to London and American Editions, General Introduction, Introductory and Concluding Remarks on Each Book. Has Essay on the Historical Connexion between the Old and New Testaments (p 991–994) followed by Tables. Index to Principal Notes in the Cottage Bible and Chronological Index to the Bible (p 1421–1440). NT dated 1833. Copyright 1833. Maps and historical engravings throughout.

This Bible (first printed in London in 1825–27) was reprinted many times. The stereotype plates were sold by Mr. Conner to D. F. Robinson of Hartford, who published the work for several years. He sold them to Sumner of Hartford; they were later sold to Case, Lockwood & Co. of that city. (O'Callaghan, p 222.)

1833   The Holy Bible . . . With Canne's Marginal Notes and References . . . Stereotyped by James Conner, New-York . . . J. Collord, Printer. Published by B. Waugh and T. Mason, for the Methodist Episcopal Church: New-York   *819*

28 cm   NNAB
Reprint of 1832 edition (No 776).

1833   The English Version of the Polyglott Bible . . . With the Marginal Readings . . . References to Parallel and Illustrative Passages . . . To which are Added A Critical Introduction to the Holy Scriptures and to Each of the Books; An Essay on the Right Interpretations of the Writings in which the Revelations of God are contained, by James Macknight, D.D. Three Sermons on the Evidences of Christianity, by Philip Doddridge, D.D. A Geographical and Historical Index . . . A Concordance by Rev. J. Brown; A Complete Index and Concise Dictionary . . . and . . . Tables . . . Family Record . . . and Numerous Woodcuts . . . [Printed at the Brattleboro' Power Press Office]. Lincoln, Edmands & Co. and Pierce and Parker: Boston; . . . Peck & Wood: Brattleboro'   *820*

1 vol: (6) (82) (20) (48) 7–705 (54) 3–216 (48) (64) (84)   27 cm   NNAB
Verso of title has Recommendations. Text is preceded by Preface signed T. C. and Order of Books, A Concise Introduction by the Rev. Joseph Warne, Tables, and Illustrations of Scripture (the last, 48 p, printed on one side only). An Outline follows OT. At end are New Geographical and Historical Index by Thomas Starling, New and Complete General Index by the Rev. John Brown, and Brown's Concordance. The imprint of Peck and Wood appears on the Concise Introduction and the two indexes; Concordance imprint Lincoln, Edmands & Co. and William Pierce: Boston, and Fessenden & Co. and Peck & Wood: Brattleboro'. Engraved maps and charts. Copyright 1833 by Jos. Fessenden & J. C. Holbrook.

1833   The Holy Bible . . . With Marginal Notes and References . . . M'Carty and Davis: Philadelphia   *821*

29 cm   C, NNAB
Reprint of 1832 Bible, No 777. With Apocrypha and Tables, and Anderson engravings.

1833   The Holy Bible . . . Stereotype Edition . . . D. Fanshaw, Printer . . . Stereotyped by A. Chandler, For the American Bible Society: New-York   *822*

1214 p   26 cm   NNAB
Small Pica Octavo. The first ABS edition with marginal references (in two center columns) chronology, and chapter summaries. Has two leaves for Family Record before NT and Tables on verso of NT title.
NNAB has another copy on better paper with wide margins, 28 cm.
This was printed from a similar edition of the British and Foreign Bible Society. Preparation of the plates was hindered by the yellow fever raging in the city in 1832.

1833   The English Version of the Polyglott Bible . . . with the Marginal Readings and Original Selection of References to Parallel and Illustrative Passages . . . Carter, Hendee, and Co.: Boston   *823*

26 cm   DLC
Has frontispiece and added engraved title page. Preface signed T. C.

1833 The Holy Bible . . . A. Towar and Hogan & Thompson: Philadelphia; J. P. Haven: New York **824**

25 cm   DLC

With Apocrypha. Also Concordance (1830), Paraphrases, and Metrical Psalms.

1833 The Holy Bible, Translated from the Latin Vulgate . . . With Annotations, References . . . Index. From the Last London and Dublin Editions. The Whole Revised and . . . Compared with the Latin Vulgate. Published with the Approbation of the Right Rev. John DuBois . . . [Stereotyped by Conner and Cooke]. Published by John Doyle: New York **825**

1 vol: (752) (6) 755–959 960–968   25 cm   NN, NNAB

Rheims-Douay Version, from Murray's 1825 Dublin edition. Preliminary matter includes Approbations, Order of Books, Sketch of Principal Epochs, frontispiece, Admonition, Letter of Pope Pius VI, Prayer, and Decree of the Council of Trent. Family Record follows OT. Frontispiece, Order of Books, The Sum of the New Testament, and The Sum of the Four Gospels precede NT. At end are List of Readings, Index, and Tables. Illustrated.

This is the first of many editions of Doyle's Catholic Bible, published at prices ranging from $2.50 to $5. The plates subsequently were purchased by E. Dunigan & Brother, New York. (O'Callaghan, p 221 and 276.)

1833 The Holy Bible . . . In the Common Version. With Amendments of the Language, by Noah Webster, LL.D. . . . Published by Durrie & Peck & Co. . . . : New Haven **826**

1 vol: (xvi) (907)   23 cm   CtY, DLC, ICU, MA, MB, MWA, MiU, NjMD, NN, NNAB, PPL

Order of Books; Preface signed by N. W., New Haven, 1833; and Introduction (which lists principal alterations) precede text. Has references in center column. Copyright 1833, by Noah Webster, Printed by Hezekiah Howe & Co. Preface has note: "The copy used by the compositors was the quarto Bible, prepared by the late Isaac Collins, of New York. . . ." See 1791, No 31. The error in I Tim 4:16 is reproduced.

Also published in 2 or 3 vols.

Noah Webster (1758–1843), compiler of Webster's Dictionary and a Congregational layman, undertook a revision of the English Bible. As early as 1784, in his *Grammar,* he had pointed out an error in Mt 23:24. In 1822 he consulted Professor Moses Stuart at Andover and a group of scholars about revision. In 1831 he sent out a manuscript circular asking about its desirability. Only James Milnor, then one of the secretaries of the American Bible Society, seems to have replied (Jan 30, 1832) and that discouragingly.

In his interesting preface Webster points out that changes have taken place in the language in the past 200 years so that some words "are not understood by common readers, who have no access to commentaries, and who will always compose a great proportion of readers." Other words have changed meaning, thus causing false ideas and so "do not present to the reader the *Word of God.*" He corrected errors in grammar, substituted words and phrases now in good use "for those either wholly obsolete, or deemed below the dignity and solemnity of the subject," inserted "euphemisms, words and phrases which are not very offensive to delicacy," and corrected a few errors in translation in consultation with the original languages. Feeling that all denominations should use one Bible, he tried to avoid offending any group. Many whom he consulted seemed to feel that some revision of the common version was needed but "no person appears to know how or by whom such revision is to be executed." The revisions turned out to be quite minor — about 150 words and phrases were changed — and rendered little aid to a clearer presentation.

Webster was keenly hurt by the indifference of the public to what he considered "the most important enterprise of my life." When the Bible was issued in September 1833, it sold at $3. In 1836 he authorized N. and J. White in New York to sell it at $2 and later at $1.50. (*Webster Bibliography,* p 378–380.)

The Bible was republished in 1841 (No 1112) and the NT issued separately in 1839 (No 1061).

1833 [English Version of the Polyglott Bible] The Holy Bible . . . with Introductory and Concluding Remarks to each Book of the Old and New Testaments; and the References and Marginal readings of the Polyglott Bible, with numerous additions from Bagster's Comprehensive Bible . . . Conner & Cooke: New York   *827*

    1 vol: (937) 939–961   21 cm   Not Located
    O'Callaghan, p 223. *First Edition* appears on NT title. Illustrated Chronological Index at end.
    This edition is known as The Bible Annual. Being desirous that the Polyglott Bible should appear with a few wood engravings, Mr. Conner secured the services of J. A. Adams, Esq., to execute them in the highest and most finished style of the art. All the arrangements completed, he had the satisfaction of publishing a splendid edition of the Bible as an annual New Year's present. See 1834 Andrus and Judd edition (No 868).

1833   The Holy Bible . . . Stereotype Edition. Ide & Goddard's Power Press: Windsor [Vermont]   *828*

    1 vol: (486) (162)   20 cm   NN, NNAB
    Postcard in NNAB copy reads "Claremont, N. H. June 6 [1877?] My dear Sir — Some time ago you suggested my sending to the society's Library a copy of the Bible, from Stereotype plates, which I published in Windsor, Vt. — the 1st edit. in 1826, I think. I send by mail the earliest edit. I have succeeded in finding. It was printed from 3d or 4th-hand plates, originally owned, if my memory serves me, by Timothy Bedlington, Boston; which were made into [from?] moveable type a long time ago. — S[imeon] I[de]."

1833   The Holy Bible . . . Stereotyped by James Conner . . . Printed and Published by Edward Sanderson: Elizabeth-Town, N. J.   *829*

    1 vol: (486) (162)   19 cm   NN, NNAB

1833   The Holy Bible . . . Stereotyped by J. Howe, Philadelphia. Published by Andrus & Judd: Hartford   *830*

    1 vol: (655) 656–681 661–720   18 cm   NNAB
    Reprint of 1827 Andrus duodecimo (No 588) with new title pages and plates. Has Metrical Psalms. General Contents at end is of different format and paging.
    Also issued without plates.

1833   The Holy Bible . . . Stereotyped by A. Chandler . . . Published by Andrus & Judd: Hartford   *831*

    1 vol: (824) (251)   "12mo" or "24mo"   Not Located
    O'Callaghan, p 224. Has frontispiece with two engravings.

1833   The Holy Bible . . . Published by Gilman and McKillip: Hartford   *832*

    Text ends Ll12   "12mo"   Not Located
    O'Callaghan, p 224. Tables follow OT. NT imprinted *Hartford: Published by Hudson & Skinner.* Table of Offices at end. See 1832 Bible, No 789.

1833   The Holy Bible . . . Coffin, Roby, Hoag & Co.: Concord, N. H.   *833*

    "18mo"   Not Located
    Wright, p 395.

1833   The Holy Bible . . . Stereotyped by J. Howe . . . Philad . . . Published by
    Andrus & Judd: Hartford   **834**

1 vol: (729) (222) 223–225   13 cm   NNAB
Contents at end.

1833   The Holy Bible . . . Seventh Stereotype Edition . . . Published by N. & J.
    White: New York   **835**

12 cm   ViU
Same as 1832 ediiton (No 795). Has 2 plates.

1833–37   [The Old Testament] A New Translation of the Hebrew Prophets, Ar-
    ranged in Chronological Order. By George R. Noyes. Three Volumes. Vol. I,
    containing Joel, Amos, Hosea, Isaiah, and Micah . . . Charles Bowen: Boston,
    1833. Vol. II, containing Nahum, Zephaniah, Hababbkuk, Obadiah, Jeremiah,
    Lamentations . . . James Munroe and Company: Boston, 1837. Vol. III, con-
    taining Ezekiel, Daniel, Haggai, Zechariah, Jonah, and Malachi . . . James
    Munroe and Company: Boston, 1837   **836**

3 vols: Vol I, (xii) (250) 251–252 253–288; Vol II, (vi) 3–239 243–293; Vol III, (238)
241–295   21 cm   MH
Noyes Version; see 1827, No 592.
MH has another set with Vol I dated 1843 (xi, 3–249, 253–304) but Vols II and III are
dated 1837.

1833   The Family Expositor; or, A paraphrase and version of the New Testament
    . . . by Philip Doddridge, D.D. American edition. With a memoir of the
    author, by N. W. Fiske . . . an introductory essay by Moses Stuart . . . With
    a portrait, engraved from an original picture in Wymondley house. [Stereo-
    typed at the Boston Type and Stereotype Foundry, printed by J. S. & C.
    Adams] J. S. & C. Adams, and L. Boltwood: Amherst   **837**

Reported as (xx) 17–1006 (6)   26 cm   MA, MWA, TU
Doddridge Version; see 1807–08 NT, No 147. Has frontispiece and plates.
MA reports a 1-vol edition by Jonathan Leavitt, New York, 1831, but no copy has been
located. Other similar editions were published in 1834 (MA, MH, MWA, OO, PPDrop), 1844,
fourteenth edition, J. S. & C. Adams (MAJ), 1845, J. S. & C. Adams (IaFairP, LRul, MShM),
1846, sixteenth edition, J. S. & C. Adams (CChi, ICMBI, KyLoP), and 1857, Robert Carter &
Brothers, New York (O'Callaghan, p 361, not located).

1833   The New Testament . . . With Marginal Readings, a Collection of Parallel
    Texts, and Copious Summaries to Each Chapter with a Commentary and
    Critical Notes . . . by Adam Clarke. J. J. Harrod, Book agent from the Meth-
    odist Protestant Church: Baltimore   **838**

2 vols: Vol I, (940); Vol II, (1088)   25 cm   NNAB, TNMB
For Adam Clarke, see 1811–25, No 188. Has portrait, engraved by Durand from a portrait
by Partridge.
NNAB has Vol II only.

1833   A New and Corrected Version of The New Testament; or, a Minute Revision,
    and Professed Translation of the Original Histories, Memoirs, Letters, Proph-
    ecies, and Other Productions of the Evangelists and Apostles . . . A Few . . .
    Notes. By Rodolphus Dickinson . . . Published by Lilly, Wait, Colman, &
    Holden: Boston   **839**

1 vol: (xl) 41–381 [1] 383–499 [1]   25 cm   DLC, MB, NcAs, NN, NNAB, ViU

Fly title, frontispiece (portrait of Dickinson), Dedication, Preface, References, Divisions, and Subdivisions precede text. Appendix and list of some of the subscribers (dated 1833) at end. Copyright 1831, by Rodolphus Dickinson, South Carolina. Published by subscription.

Rodolphus Dickinson (1787–1863), a rector of the Episcopal Church of St. Paul's parish in the District of Pendleton, South Carolina, sought to make the text more readable both in content and form. It was based on the Greek version of Griesbach. In the Preface, Dickinson states: "The lapse of centuries has produced a revolution in the English language, requiring a correspondent change in the version of the scriptures; and I may add, that the errors in grammar and rhetoric, the harsh and indelicate expressions, dispersed through the generally adopted text, demand amendment." The Testament was printed in paragraph form with no other material on the page than the text and headings. The titles of the several books were changed. The translation was for the most part a mere substitution of words which did not always enhance the readability of the text. See O'Callaghan, p 225f; also Simms, p 232.

The left-hand page heading throughout the NT is "Apostolic Productions." In i Tim 4:16 Dickinson translates "Attend to yourself, and to your doctrine," continuing the error which has been noted in many AV editions since 1791. His translation of the Lucan canticles is remarkable: "And it happened, that when Elizabeth heard the salutation of Mary, the embryo was joyfully agitated . . . ; and she exclaimed with a loud voice, and said Blessed are you among women! and blessed is your incipient offspring!" (Luke 1:41–42) . . . "He has precipitated potentates from their thrones, and has exalted the lowly. He has satisfied the necessitous with benefits; but the affluent he has dismissed destitute." (Luke 1:52–53.)

1833 The New Testament . . . Stereotype Edition . . . Lilly, Wait, and Company: Boston   *840*

453 p   20 cm   NNAB
Tables at end.

1833 The New Testament . . . [Stereotyped by J. Howe, New-York]. Johnstone and Van Norden: New-York   *841*

Reported as 288 p   "12mo"   Not Located
Union Catalog lists copy at NN, but none has been found, 1959.

1833 The New Testament . . . Published by Daniel Cooledge: New-York   *842*

324 p   "12mo"   Not Located
O'Callaghan, p 227. Title page has woodcut. Table and Historical Facts follow text.

1833 The New Testament . . . Hale: Boston   *843*

Reported as 315 p   "12mo"   MB

1833 The New Testament . . . Stereotype Edition. S. C. Stevens: Dover, N. H. *844*

Reported as 283 p   19 cm   PSt

1833 The New Testament . . . Stereotype Edition . . . Printed and Published by Charles Gaylord: Boston   *845*

162 p   19 cm   NN, NNAB
Frontispiece *(Resurrection)*.

1833 The New Testament . . . Stereotyped by H. Wallis, New-York . . . Ide and Goddard's Power Press: Windsor [Vermont]   *846*

372 p   18 cm   NN, NNAB, VtHi
NN and NNAB copies are undated.

1833 The New Testament, Translated Out of the Latin Vulgate . . . and First Published by the English College of Rhemes . . . 1582. Newly Revised . . . As Approved by J. Dubois, Catholic Bishop of New York . . . [Stereotype Edition]. Printed by W. Williams: Utica **847**

1 vol: (xii) (344)   17 cm   NNAB

See Devereux Testament originally published by Williams in 1829, No 686.

1833 The Village Testament . . . with Notes, Original and Selected; Likewise Introductions and Concluding Remarks to Each Book, Polyglott Reference and Marginal Readings, Chronological Table, Geographical Index, and Maps . . . By Rev. William Patton. Two Volumes in One . . . Published by Conner & Cooke: New York **848**

1 vol: (12) 13–710 711–718   16 cm   Not Located

O'Callaghan, p 226. Has text in paragraphs, references in the outer margin, and notes at foot of page. The several pages are within parallel rules. Preface has statement: "This Commentary contains much that is found in the Notes upon the New Testament of the Cottage Bible." See 1833, No 818.

1833 The New Testament . . . S. W. Neall: Philadelphia **849**

Reported as 191 p   16 cm   DLC

1833 The New Testament . . . Stereotyped by Henry Wallis & Luther Roby, Concord, N. H. Published by Coffin, Roby, Hoag & Co.: Concord, N. H.   **850**

190 p   15 cm   NN

Engraved title, with same imprint, has *The English Version of the Polyglott Bible, with Marginal Readings . . . and References. . . .*

1833 The New Testament . . . [Stereotype Edition]. Andrus and Judd: Hartford
851

Reported as 251 p   14 cm   ViU
Frontispiece.

1833 The New Testament . . . Stereotyped by J. Howe, Philadelphia . . . Bishop Davenport: Trenton, N. J.   **852**

252 p   14 cm   NN

1833 The New Testament . . . [Stereotyped by L. Johnson, Philadelphia]. Published by R. White: Hartford   **853**

259 p   13 cm   NN

1833 [The New Testament] The Sacred Writings of the Apostles and Evangelists of Jesus Christ . . . Translated from the Original Greek, by Doctors George Campbell, James Macknight, and Philip Doddridge. With prefaces, various emendations, and an Appendix, by Alexander Campbell. Stereotyped from the 3d ed. rev. A. Campbell: Bethany, Va.   **854**

Reported as 336 p   12 cm   ICU, NjMD, TNMPH

Alexander Campbell Version; see 1826 NT, No 567. Known as the Pocket Edition. Preface headed to "the Fourth or Stereotyped Edition." The Appendix is not as extensive as in earlier editions but it contains explanatory notes. There are also minor changes from previous editions.

1833 The New Testament . . . With the Marginal Readings and Illustrated by Original References both Parallel and Explanatory and a Copious Selection Carefully Chosen and Newly Arranged . . . [Stereotyped by James Conner]. John C. Riker: New York   **855**

350 p   11 cm   MB, NNAB

Polyglott Testament on cover title. While the preface reads much like that for the Polyglott Bibles it does not follow it exactly nor do the references. Has frontispiece, added engraved title, Order of Books, and Preface. Also has sterling currency reduced to dollars and cents. Full-page steel engravings; wood engravings heading each book, some of the latter initialed "A.A.," possibly A. Anderson.

1833 The New Testament . . . Hogan & Thompson: Philadelphia and Tuscumbia, Ala.   **856**

Not Located

Wright, p 395, but no copy known by A-Ar. Probably a regular Hogan & Thompson edition with added imprint. See 1835, No 898.

1834 The Holy Bible . . . Stereotype Edition . . . Stereotyped by A. Chandler and printed by D. Fanshaw, for the American Bible Society: New-York   **857**

1043 p   31 cm   NNAB

Pica Quarto, based on an edition of the British and Foreign Bible Society. It is the first Reference Quarto published by the ABS and was sold at $5 in embossed calf. Other editions with cheaper paper and binding followed. Has two reference columns in center, with chronology, and italic chapter summaries.

1834 The Holy Bible . . . with the Apocrypha . . . Canne's marginal notes and references . . . index . . . table . . . Published by R. White & Co.: Hartford   **858**

Reported as 768 p   29 cm   NjMD

Has Concordance dated 1833 (54 p) and Metrical Psalms (18 p).

1834/31 The Holy Bible . . . With Canne's Marginal Notes and References . . . Stereotyped by B. & J. Collins . . . Published by Langdon Coffin: Boston **859**

1 vol: 9–744 (138) 747–1010 (56)   29 cm   NNAB

With Apocrypha. Preliminary matter includes frontispiece, added engraved title (1831), Advertisement to the Stereotype Edition, To the Reader, Order of Books, and Account of Dates. Index, Tables, Account of the Holy Land, and Brown's Concordance (1830) follow text. Illustrated. NT title has imprint *Stereotyped for Collins and Co. By B. & J. Collins. 1831.*

1834–38 The Comprehensive Commentary on the Holy Bible; Containing the Text According to the Authorized Version; Scott's Marginal References; Matthew Henry's Commentary, Condensed . . . the Practical Observations of Rev. Thomas Scott, D.D., with Extensive Explanatory, Critical, Philological Notes, Selected from Scott, Doddridge . . . and Many Other Writers on the Scriptures . . . The Whole Designed to be a Digest . . . of the Best Bible Commentaries . . . Edited by Rev. William Jenks . . . Re-edited and Adapted to the Views of the Baptist Denomination of Christians, by Rev. Joseph A. Warne . . . Fessenden and Co.: Brattleboro'; Shattuck and Co.: Boston   **860**

5 vols: Vol I, 830 p; Vol II, 852 p; Vol III, 924 p; Vol IV, 838 p; Vol V, 734 p   28 cm
MB, NN, NNAB, NRAB

Baptist Edition appears at head of title page. Vol I (1835, Stereotyped by Thomas G. Wells and Co.: Boston) Genesis-Judges. Vol II (1836, Fessenden and Co.: Brattleboro') Ruth-Psalm

LXIII. Vol III (1837, Brattleboro' Typographic Co. Stereotyped by Folsom, Wells and Thurston . . . : Cambridge) Psalm LXIV–Malachi. Vol IV (1834, Stereotyped by Shepard, Oliver, Lancaster and Co., Lancaster, Mass.) Matthew-John and elaborate Family Record pages. Vol V (1838, imprint same as Vol III) Acts-Revelation. Vol IV is the first volume of the NT and was published first according to the Preface. Each volume has frontispiece and numerous plates. Copyright dates are same as imprint dates.

Also published in 6 vols, Vol VI containing a Supplement to the Commentary dated 1838 (see No 894). Range of dates varies, e. g. 1834–39, 1834–46, 1835–38, 1834–40. Vol IV of the 1834–46 set (NN) imprinted *J. B. Lippincott and Co.: Philadelphia*.

For non-denominational edition, see 1835–38, No 894. The only difference seems to be that some pages were reset for the Baptist edition (Vol IV: 14, 16, 17, 18, 310, etc.) with slight changes, each such page being identified by the addition of BAPTIST EDITION at the bottom. These two editions are reported in *American Baptist Magazine* for Aug 1834 (p 336).

William Jenks (1778–1866) graduated from Harvard in 1797 and became a reader in Christ Church Cathedral, 1797–1805. He was ordained a Congregational minister in 1805, serving at First Church, Bath, Maine, for thirteen years. He served as an Army Chaplain in the War of 1812. After several years as professor of Oriental Languages and English Literature at Bowdoin College, he returned to Boston where he devoted himself to work among seamen. The immediate sale of the Comprehensive Commentary was over 20,000 copies. (DAB)

James A. Warne was born in England in 1795. At an early age he became associated with the Little Wild Street Baptist Church in London. After coming to America he served pastorates in Newbern, North Carolina, Providence, Rhode Island, South Reading and Brookline, Mass., and Philadelphia. He died in 1881.

1834 The Holy Bible . . . Apocrypha . . . with Canne's marginal notes and references . . . tables . . . Published by Joseph Wilson: Hollowell [U. C.] **861**

1 vol: (574) (99) 576–768   28 cm   CaOTAr, CaOTP

Same as 1827 Phinney edition printed for S. Thompson, York, U. C. (No 580) except with Apocrypha and many illustrations. Probably not printed in Canada.

NN and NCooHi have copies of 1834 with Phinney imprint, the latter with frontispiece and 7 woodcuts.

1834 The Holy Bible . . . With Canne's Marginal Notes and References . . . Stereotyped by James Conner, New York. B. Waugh and T. Mason, for the Methodist Episcopal Church: New-York **862**

Reported as (642) (91) (200) (12) (4)   28 cm   CtY
With Apocrypha. Index at end.

1834 The English Version of the Polyglott Bible . . . to which are added A Critical Introduction . . . By Rev. Joseph A. Warne . . . [Printed at the Brattleboro' Power Press Office.] Fessenden & Co. and Peck & Wood: Brattleboro'. Sold by Lincoln, Edmands & Co. and William Peirce: Boston **863**

27 cm   CSmH, DLC, NcD, NNAB, PP, VtHi

Fessenden & Co's Edition appears at head of title page. Identical with Lincoln, Edmands & Co. . . . Peck & Wood edition of 1833 (No 820).

NNAB has another copy with part title in place of general title: *A Concise Introduction . . . By the Rev. Joseph A. Warne*; NT title same as above.

1834 [The Holy Bible] The Cottage Bible and Family Expositor . . . With Practical Expositions and Explanatory Notes. By Thomas Williams . . . The References and Marginal Readings of the Polyglott Bible . . . Notes . . . from Bagster's Comprehensive Bible . . . The Whole Carefully Revised, and Adapted to the Use of Sunday Schools . . . Edited by Rev. William Patton . . . Com-

plete in Two Volumes . . . [Stereotyped by Conner & Cooke]. D. F. Robinson
and H. F. Sumner: Hartford   *864*

2 vols   27 cm   NNAB
Reprinted from 1833 Conner and Cooke edition (No 818) Illustrations.

1834   The Holy Bible . . . Stereotype Edition . . . With Canne's Marginal Notes and
References . . . C. Alexander & Co.: Philadelphia   *865*

Reported as (829) (xxi)   "4to"   PMA
Has frontispiece, Index, Tables, and plates. See 1838 Cincinnati edition, No 1002.

1834   The Holy Bible . . . Guilford: Cincinnati, Ohio   *866*

Reported as (735) (176) 739–959   23 cm   DLC
With Apocrypha.
Wright (p 395) lists a Cincinnati quarto, with no publisher, for 1833.

1834   The Holy Bible . . . Stereotyped, printed and published by H. and E. Phinney: Cooperstown, N. Y.   *867*

Reported as 569 p   29 cm   IaDaM

1834   The Holy Bible . . . With Introductory and Concluding Remarks to Each
Book of the Old and New Testaments; and the References and Marginal
Readings of the Polyglott Bible with Numerous Additions from Bagster's
Comprehensive Bible . . . [Stereotyped by Conner & Cooke]. Published by
Andrus & Judd: Hartford   *868*

1 vol: (70) (937) 939–962 (108)   21 cm   MBU–T, NNAB
General title not dated; NT title, dated 1834, has Andrus only in imprint and First Edition.
Has frontispiece to each Testament and references in center columns. Preliminary matter includes Tables, Advertisement, Introduction, Historical Connexion between Testaments, Introduction to New Testament, and Introductory and Concluding Remarks to Each Book. At end
are Chronological Index and Concordance.
Andrus published a New Year's edition which became known as *The Annual* of which the
above appears to be the first edition. See 1833 Conner and Cooke Bible, No 827.

1834   The Holy Bible . . . Stereotype Edition . . . Stereotyped by A. Chandler,
Printed by D. Fanshaw, for the American Bible Society: New York   *869*

984 p   19 cm   NNAB
Reference Duodecimo Bible. The first ABS small reference Bible, set from "a new and elegant pattern copy, just prepared by the British and Foreign Bible Society . . . Eminently
calculated for the use of Bible classes and teachers of Sunday schools." Has double reference
columns with chronology and italic chapter summaries. Tables appear on p 750 and there are
eight blank pages before NT title.

1834   [The Holy Bible] The New Testament . . . Arranged in Paragraphs and
Parallelisms, With Philological and Explanatory Annotations, by T. W. Coit
. . . Printed By and For Manson and Grant: Cambridge . . . Published By
William Peirce: Boston   *870*

1 vol: (963) (230)   19 cm   NNAB
General title page missing from cited copy; above from NT title. Preliminary matter
includes Editor's Preface by Coit, The Translators to the Reader (from the first edition of the
AV, 1611), and Tables. Alternative readings and renderings appear at foot of page.

O'Callaghan (p 231) quotes the *American Baptist Magazine* with the statement that this is the first printing in an American Bible of the 1611 Translators' Preface, but see No 770.

Dr. Coit was Rector of Christ Church, Cambridge.

1834 The Right-Aim School Bible; comprising the Holy Bible . . . and an Annexment containing the Free-Debt-Rule Petitions, addressed the First to the twenty-four states, the Second to the Congress, the Third to the President, of the United States of America, and affixed Memorials; the Fourth Petition to three high offices of the Government of England; also the Declaration of Freedebtism, In view of a humble and earnest Call on all People to "Search the Scriptures" and to heed the analogy and application of Freedebtism to Religious Principle and Scripture Text instancing from the Lord's Prayer and Precepts, in His Sermon on the Mount, "Forgive us our Debts as we forgive our Debtors," "All things whatsoever ye would that men should do to you, do ye even so to them: for this is the law and the Prophets." Entered . . . in the year 1834, by Rufus Davenport, In the Clerk's Office of the District of Massachusetts. Stereotype Print: [Boston]   *871*

1 vol: (510) (162) (6)   19 cm   NN
Order of Books appears on verso of title. Regular AV text.
Not a school Bible but a Bible of the Right-Aim School:
    The main FREE-DEBT RULE is, "All persons shall become free from debt by surrendering, at the place of their inhabitance, all their estate to the use of all their creditors, in ratable proportion." The RIGHT-AIM example of Dealing on Free-Debt Rules, is "Any nonfulfillment from unexpected innocent inability shall not subject a party to imprisonment, nor to more payment than ability shall afford in ratable proportion to all creditors. . . ."
    The author, in publishing this annexment, in the binding with Scripture, by the name of the RIGHT-AIM SCHOOL BIBLE, adds no preface, more than is contained in the title page; but refers to the preceding forms of the FREE-DEBT-RULE DEALING-BILL, with the FREE-DEBT-RULE ACCOUNT, and gives notice, that details may be expected, in a separate publication, soon after measures shall be sufficiently advanced, with the organization of the Right-Aim School, whereof is herein contained the preliminary brief.

Respectfully,

RUFUS DAVENPORT.

1834 The Holy Bible . . . Cook & Schoyer: Pittsburg   *872*
"18mo"   Not Located
O'Callaghan, p 388.

1834 The Holy Bible . . . Arranged in Paragraphs, Such as the Sense Requires . . . By James Nourse . . . [Stereotyped by J. Howe, Philadelphia]. Perkins, Marvin & Co.: Boston; Henry Perkins: Philadelphia   *873*

1 vol: (xii) (942) (322)   16 cm   MWA, NN, NNAB, OO
    Advertisement, Preface, Order of Books, and Chronology of Books precede text. Divisions of chapters and verses are noted in margin. Poetry in metrical form in smaller type. Recommendations at end. Copyright 1834. Misprint in Romans 4:5, his faith is counted for *unrighteousness*, for *righteousness*. This has been corrected in a separate NT (NNAB).

1834 The English Version of the Polyglott Bible . . . With the Marginal Readings . . . With a Copious and Original Selection of References . . . Exhibited in a

1834, continued

Manner Hitherto Unattempted. Stereotyped by L. Johnson . . . Published by Desilver, Jr. & Thomas: Philadelphia **874**

15 cm   NN, NNAB

Similar to 1831 Key & Meilke edition (No 753). Engraved title page and frontispiece to each Testament.

1834 [The Holy Bible] The New Testament . . . [Stereotyped by B. & J. Collins, New York]. Published by Johnston and Stockton: Pittsburgh **875**

1 vol: (743) (2??)   14 cm   NNAB

General title and up to p 22 missing from cited copy; above from NT title. Also p 219 to end missing.

1834 The Holy Bible . . . Stereotyped by J. Howe . . . Philad . . . Published by Andrus & Judd: Hartford **876**

1 vol: (729) (222)   14 cm   NNAB

Contents follow each Testament. 16 engravings.

1834 The Holy Bible . . . Published by Nathan Hale . . . Cottons and Barnard: Boston **877**

1 vol: (510) (162)   14 cm   MB, NNAB

Has maps as frontispieces to both Testaments; 8 other maps. Stereotyped at the Boston Type and Stereotype Foundry on verso of NT title.

MB copy has general title imprint *Printed for the Publisher;* NT title same as above.

1834 The Holy Bible . . . Stereotyped by L. Johnson. J. S. & C. Adams: Amherst, Mass. **878**

1 vol: (856) (259) [1]   13 cm   MA, MAJ, NN

1834 The Holy Bible . . . Stereotyped by Henry Wallis & Luther Roby . . . Concord, N. H. . . . Published by C. & A. Hoag: Concord, N. H. **879**

1 vol: (852) (259)   12 cm   NNAB

Added engraved title page. With or without frontispiece.

1834 The Holy Bible . . . Hogan & Thompson: Philadelphia **880**

Reported as (819) (256)   11 cm   MB

Reprint of Alexander Towar's 1832 Bible (No 794). Has engraved title page; plates.

1834 The New Testament . . . Translated Out of the Latin Vulgate . . . First Published by the English College of Rheims . . . with the Original Preface, Arguments and Tables, Marginal Notes, and Annotations. To Which are Now Added, an Introductory Essay and a complete Topical and Textual Index . . . [John H. Turney's Stereotype]. Published by Jonathan Leavitt: New York; Crocker and Brewster: Boston **881**

458 p   23 cm   DCU, ICU, NcD, NN, NNAB

Preliminary matter includes Notice, containing a list of ministers recommending the publication and a list of subscribers (2 p); Introductory Address to Protestants (4 p); Preface to the 1582 edition (18 p). Following text are Notes Omitted (1 p), Explication of Certain Words (1 p), and Index (p 441–458). Copyright 1833.

Also published without date or with imprint of J. Leavitt alone.

This is a reprint in modernized spelling of the original edition of the Rheims NT, prepared for Protestants. O'Callaghan (p 233–236) points out a good many errors in spite of the certificate by six clergymen that "it is an exact and faithful copy of the original work without abridgment or addition, except that the Latin of a few phrases which were translated by the annotators, and some unimportant expletive words were undesignedly omitted" (p iv).

1834   The New Testament . . . Stereotype Edition . . . Published by W. & S. B. Ives: Salem   *882*

315 p   20 cm   NNAB

1834   The Right Aim School Testament . . . [Stereotype Print]. And an Annexation of the Preliminary Brief of the Right-Aim School, the Declaration of Free-debtism, and the Free-Debt Rules, with Some Appurtances . . . By R. Davenport: Boston   *883*

315 p   19 cm   MB, NN

The NT of the Right Aim School Bible of this year (No 871).

1834   The New Testament . . . Stereotype Edition. Ide and Goddard's Power Press: Windsor, Vt.   *884*

162 p   18 cm   NN

Last page misnumbered 182.

1834   The New Testament . . . James Macfarland & Co. Printers and Publishers: Kingston [U. C.]   *885*

Reported as 270 p   17 cm   CaOTP, CaQ, MBM

P 68 misnumbered 69; 101 appears as "01." This edition of the King James Version does not appear to have been printed with royal permission.

CaOTP has another copy, undated, with imprint *Printed and published by R. Stanton, York* [U.C.] that would seem to have been printed from the same plates. BM lists NT of 270 p with Macfarland imprint dated 1829.

1834   [The New Testament] The Village Testament . . . with Notes . . . Introduction and Concluding Remarks to Each Book, Polyglott References and Marginal Readings . . . Index . . . Tables . . . By W. Patton. Second Edition. H. C. Sleight: New York   *886*

718 p   16 cm   NN, NNAB

Has 2 folded maps. See 1833 NT, No 848.

1834   The New Testament . . . Arranged in Paragraphs . . . By James Nourse . . . [Stereotyped by J. Howe, Philadelphia]. Perkins, Marvin & Co.: Boston *887*

1 vol: (vii) (322)   16 cm   ICN, ICU, NN, NNAB

1834   The New Testament . . . Stereotyped by Henry Wallis and Luther Roby, Concord, N. H.   C. & A. Hoag: Concord, N. H.   *888*

263 p   12 cm   MBU–T, NN

Has added engraved title page and frontispiece.

1834   [Polymicrian Testament] The New Testament . . . with Short Explanatory Notes, and Numerous References to Illustrative and Parallel Passages,

1834, continued

Printed in a Centre Column ... [Stereotyped by James Conner]. Published
by Jonathan Leavitt: New-York; Crocker & Brewster: Boston   *889*

1 vol: (viii) (546)   11 cm   NNAB

Greek title at top of title; book titles in Greek. Has two added title pages, one with *The
New Testament* printed in 48 languages. Also A Key to the Languages. Advertisement following
full title has statement: "This edition of the English Testament, is printed in the same form,
and with the same care and diligence, as the Greek Testament published some time since of
this size. ... In the centre column of the English Testament are inserted the Various Readings,
and a new and very copious selection of really Parallel Passages, being, with some additions,
the same as are found in the volume containing the English Version of the Polyglott Bible. ..."
Illustrated with maps. See 1832 NT, No 811.

1834   The New Testament ... Stereotyped by J. A. James, Cincinnati. [Printed
by F. S. Benton, Cincinnati] Published by Corey and Fairband, and Jonathan
Leavitt: New York   *890*

469 [1] p   9 cm   ICBS, NN

1835?   The Devotional Family Bible ... with Practical and Experimental Reflections on each Verse of the Old and New Testaments ... By Rev. Alexander
Fletcher ... Virtue, Emmins and Company: London and New York   *891*

Reported as (iv) (1622)   37 cm   CtHi

References in center column; Reflections at foot of page. Has Address, Tables, etc. 57 plates.
Published in numbers.

NNAB has four copies: one imprinted *Virtue and Yorston, New York* which lacks Address
but has engraved titles and plates and Concordance (80 p); another bound in 2 vols, with
Apocrypha; a third set unbound; and an undated edition imprinted *National Publishing Co.,
Philadelphia*, which has inscription showing a gift in 1884. This Bible seems to have been
reissued a good many times, for NNAB has record of the following imprints: *Emmins and Co.,
Virtue and Company,* and *George Virtue,* all undated.

1835   The Holy Bible ... With Canne's Marginal References ... Text Corrected
According to the Standard of the American Bible Society. Stereotyped by
James Conner, New York. Andrus and Judd: Hartford   *892*

1 vol: (527) (78) (168)   29 cm   NN

With Apocrypha. Frontispiece and engraved title have imprint *Published by Silas Andrus,
1835.* Added are Index, Tables, Lives and Martyrdom of Evangelists, etc. Illustrated.
Also published with Metrical Psalms.

1835   The Holy Bible ... With Canne's Marginal Notes and References ... Stereotyped by E. White, New York. Kimber and Sharpless: Philadelphia   *893*

Reported as (570) (112) 573-770   29 cm   DLC

With Apocrypha, Tables, and Brown's Concordance. Plates.

Wright lists 1840 (p 398) and 1847 (p 401) editions, the first, with Apocrypha, held by NN.
IU has 1845 edition, but Family Record has entries indicating publication before 1845. NN has
185-? edition with Concordance and Metrical Psalms. All of these editions of uniform pagination are undated and the ascribed dates are probably much later than when the books were
actually issued.

1835-38   The Comprehensive Commentary on the Holy Bible: Containing the text
According to the Authorized Version; with Marginal References; Matthew
Henry's Commentary, condensed ... the Practical Observations of Rev.

Thomas Scott, D.D., with Extensive Explanatory, Critical, and Philological
notes, selected from Scott, Doddridge, [etc.] . . . Edited by Rev. William
Jenks . . . Brattleboro' Typographic Company: Brattleboro'   *894*

6 vols   28 cm   DLC, IaU, MiU, OO

Similar to 1834–38 Baptist Edition re-edited by Warne (No 860). Publishers of volumes
vary. Vol i has frontispiece and added engraved title page. Illustrated with plates and maps.
   Also published in 5 vols, with Vols iii–v imprinted *Fessenden: Brattleborough*. The 5-vol
set is sometimes dated 1835–40.
   NNAB has 6-vol set of this non-denominational edition dated 1836–46. Vols i, iii, and iv
dated 1845; Vol ii (imprinted Fessenden & Co.), 1836; Vol v (imprinted J. B. Lippincott & Co.,
Philadelphia and Joseph Steen & Co., Brattleboro'), 1846. Vol vi is the Supplement (Brattle-
boro Typographic Co., stereotyped at the Boston Type and Stereotype Foundry, Incorporated
October 26, 1836) and contains Concordance (1838, 280 p), Guide (198 p), Biographies of
Biblical Writers (227 p), Index (20 p), Tables (26 p), Symbolic Dictionary (56 p), and
General Index (58 p).
   Joseph Steen (1797–1881) served as an apprentice with William Fessenden remaining
with Holbrook and Fessenden until 1828 when he became associated with paper-making and
later bookselling and binding. He was the object of ridicule from his fellow workers in the
printing trade because of his abstemiousness (a whiskey distillery from which they seemed
to draw their strength was next to the Brattleboro printing house) and was active in organizing
a temperance Society in 1830. He shared in many phases of community life, serving variously
as pension agent for soldiers of the Revolution, assignee in bankruptcy for Windham County,
justice of the peace, selectman, member of the school board and newspaper proprietor and
editor. From the Holbrook-Fessenden plates Steen published "eleven thousand royal octavo
Bibles, one thousand five hundred pages each, two thousand school books and one thousand
pocket Testaments." Mary R. Cabot, *Annals of Brattleboro, 1681–1895*, Brattleboro, 1921.
p 244–245, 312–314.

1835   The Holy Bible, Containing the Old Testament; Translated out of the Orig-
          inal Hebrew . . . and the Greek New Testament; Printed from the Text and
          with the Various Readings of Knapp; Designed for the Use of Students . . .
          [Stereotyped by A. Chandler]. Published by Charles Starr: New-York   *895*

1 vol: (766) (xix) (234) 235–248   28 cm   NNAB
First American wide-margin Bible. Printed on ruled paper. NT in Greek only.
ScGrvF has copy with NT in English included.

1835/34   The Holy Bible . . . with Canne's Marginal Notes and References . . .
            Stereotyped and Published by H. & E. Phinney: Cooperstown   *896*

Reported as (576) (99) 577–768 (35)   28 cm   CtY
NT title dated 1834.
O'Callaghan (p 248) also lists copy with NT dated 1836. NCooHi has 1835 copy with
Apocrypha and 9 illustrations; another with Brown's Concordance and 16 illustrations.

1835   The Holy Bible . . . With the References and Marginal Readings of the Poly-
          glott Bible, and Numerous Additions from Bagster's Comprehensive Bible.
          Stereotyped by Conner & Cooke. Published by Charles Gaylord: Boston *897*

1 vol: (581) 585–762   28 cm   NN
Has frontispiece and Tables. References in center column. Copyright 1833.
MB has copy with Apocrypha, Brown's Concordance, and plates.

1835   The Holy Bible . . . Thomas Scott . . . Samuel T. Armstrong: Boston   *898*

6 vols   28 cm   NNAB
A reprint of the 1827 Scott Bible (No 583).

1835   The Holy Bible . . . Stereotyped by L. Johnson, Philadelphia . . . Alexander
          Towar . . . and Hogan & Thompson: Philadelphia . . . ; J. P. Haven: New-
          York; Pierce & Parker: Boston; D. M. Hogan: Pittsburgh; D. Woodruff:
          Tuscaloosa [Alabama]   *899*

25 cm   NNAB

Same as Towar & Hogan edition of 1830 (No 704) but without Concordance. Probably a
standard Hogan & Thompson edition. Apocrypha wanting? Cited copy lacks NT and binding
does not allow space for Apocrypha.
DLC has copy with 1833 NT. See 1833 NT with Tuscumbia, Ala. imprint, No 856.

1835   The Holy Bible . . . Published by Robinson, Pratt & Co.: New York   *900*

Reported as 773 p   "8vo"   CtHi
O'Callaghan, p 241.

1835   The Holy Bible . . . with References and Marginal Readings of the Polyglott
          Bible with Numerous Additions from Bagster's Comprehensive Bible . . .
          [Stereotyped by Conner & Cooke; Kingsland & Baptist, Print.]. Published
          by J. P. Peaslee: New York   *901*

937 p   22 cm   NNAB

Has frontispiece to each Testament. NT title has *First Edition*. P 351 misnumbered 251;
p 658 misnumbered 558.
    O'Callaghan (p 242) says this was printed from a duplicate set of Conner & Cooke plates.
See 1833, No 827.

1835   The Holy Bible, translated from the Latin Vulgat: with Annotations, Ref-
          erences and Indexes . . . Published by Eugene Cummiskey: Philadelphia *902*

1 vol: (335) (444) (191)   21 cm   Not Located

Rheims-Douay Version. O'Callaghan, p 241.   500 copies were reprinted from Cummiskey's
1824 edition (No 492).

1835   [The Holy Bible] The English Version of the Polyglott Bible . . . with the
          Marginal Readings: Together with a Copious and Original Selection of
          References, Parallel and Illustrative Passages. Exhibited in a Manner Hither-
          to Unattempted. J. H. Butler: Northampton [Mass.]; T. & M. Butler: Buffalo
                                                                                 903

"12mo"   RPB

1835   The Holy Bible . . . Printed by Hudson & Goodwin: Hartford   *904*

"12mo"   Not Located
O'Callaghan, p 242.

1835   The Holy Bible . . . Stereotyped by James Conner . . . Printed and Published
          by Edward Sanderson: Elizabethtown, N. J.   *905*

1 vol: (486) (162)   19 cm   NN
Has frontispiece.

1835   The Holy Bible . . . Stereotyped by J. Howe, Philad. . . . Published by Andrus
          & Judd: Hartford   *906*

                                                                            Not Located
O'Callaghan, p 243. Same as Andrus duodecimo of 1832 (No 787).

1835   The Holy Bible ... Published by Hudson & Skinner: Hartford   **907**

17 cm   NN

Same as 1828 edition (No 636) except with "The property of   " in border on verso of title page.

1835   The Holy Bible ... The text of the common version arranged in paragraphs
         ... By James Nourse ... Perkins, Marvin & Company: Boston; ... Henry
         Perkins: Philadelphia   **908**

16 cm   NNAB

Reprint of 1834 edition (No 873). Binder's title has *Paragraph Bible.* A Table of the Chronology of the Psalms (5 p) follows OT.

1835   The English Version of the Polyglott Bible ... Stereotyped by L. Johnson
         ... Published by Desilver, Thomas & Co.: Philadelphia   **909**

15 cm   NN, NNAB

Reprint of 1834 edition (No 874) published by Desilver, Jr., and Thomas. Has added engraved title page. Issued with or without plates.

1835   The Holy Bible ... Stereotyped by J. Howe, Philadelphia ... Published by
         Andrus & Judd: Hartford   **910**

"24mo"   MB

1835   The Holy Bible ... Zeigler: Philadelphia   **911**

No further information given.   ScGrvF

1835   The New Testament ... Designed for the Use of Students. Stereotyped by
         A. Chandler. Charles Starr: New-York   **912**

234 p   31 cm   NN

Text printed in small type on ruled paper, with space on page for manuscript notes. See 1835, No 895.

1835   A New Literal Translation, from the Original Greek, of all the Apostolical
         Epistles. With a Commentary, and Notes, Philological, Critical, Explanatory,
         and Practical. To which is added, A History of the Life of the Apostle Paul.
         By James Macknight ... A New Edition, to which is prefixed, An Account
         of the Life of the Author. Desilver, Thomas & Co.: Philadelphia   **913**

1 vol: (viii) (776)   27 cm   NNAB

Macknight Version; see 1810, No 186. Text and commentary printed in parallel columns with many notes and introductions.

1835   The New Testament ... With a commentary and critical notes ... by Adam
         Clarke. New Edition, improved ... Peter D. Meyers, and sold by the Prin-
         cipal booksellers in the United States: New York   **914**

2 vols in 1: (12) 9–456; (546)   25 cm   ICU

For Adam Clarke, see 1811–25, No 188. Has frontispiece. Introductions to each book and Chronological Table to the books of the NT.

Later editions published by Thomas, Cowperthwait and Co., Philadelphia in 1844 (DLC), 1848 (ViU), 1850 (TNMPH), and 1852 (MB). O'Callaghan (p 293) lists 1846 edition but gives no publisher. Also published by Charles Desilver, Philadelphia in 1857.

1835   The Sacred Writings of the Apostles and Evangelists of Jesus Christ, Commonly Styled The New Testament. Translated from the Original Greek, by Doctors George Campbell, James Macknight, and Philip Doddridge. With Prefaces, Various Emendations, and an Appendix. By Alexander Campbell. Fourth Edition . . . Printed and Published by M'Vay & Ewing: Bethany, Brooke Co., Va.   **915**

1 vol: (51) 52–401 (80)   23 cm   CSmH, MiU, NN, NNAB

Alexander Campbell Version; see 1826 NT, No 567. General Preface dated Jan 29, 1826, Preface to the Gospels, Hints to Readers, Introductions and Prefaces to Acts-Revelation, and Introduction to the 3rd and 4th Editions precede text. Appendix at end. Text is printed in paragraph form, single column, with verse numbers in left margin. Copyright undated.

In January of this year Campbell turned over the publication to M'Vay and Ewing. There are a few changes in this edition.

1835   The New Testament . . . Stereotyped by J. Howe, New-York. B. Olds: Newark   **916**

287 p   18 cm   NN

Has illustrated title page.

1835   The New Testament . . . Translated from the Latin Vulgat . . . Published by Eugene Cummiskey: Philadelphia   **917**

"8vo"   Not Located

Rheims Version. O'Callaghan, p 243.

1835   The New Testament . . . Translated from the Latin Vulgat . . . Printed by William Williams for the Proprietors: Utica   **918**

1 vol: (xii) 13–344   17 cm   NN

Rheims Version. This is the Devereux Testament originally published in 1829 (No 686).

1835   The New Testament . . . Stereotyped by J. Howe, Philadelphia. J. R. and A. Lippitt: Zanesville [Ohio]   **919**

Reported as 270 p   17 cm   OC

1835? The New Testament . . . Stereotype Edition . . . Published by Andrus & Judd: Hartford   **920**

257 p   "12mo"   Not Located

Rheims Version. O'Callaghan, p 243.

1835   The New Testament . . . Stereotype Edition. Andrus and Judd: Hartford **921**

251 p   15 cm   NN, NNAB

1835   The New Testament . . . Printed and sold by H. Ludwig: New-York   **922**

259 p   13 cm   NNAB

1835   The New Testament . . . Brattleboro', Vt.   **923**

Reported as 416 p   12 cm   VtHi

No printer or publisher given.

1836 The Holy Bible . . . With References and Illustrations; an Exact Summary of the Several Books . . . By the Late Rev. Brown . . . Printed and Published by T. Kinnersley: New York **924**

"folio" CSmH

Reprint of 1826? Brown's Bible (No 546). See also 1822, No 433. With Apocrypha. Has frontispiece; added engraved title page with *The Self Interpreting Bible*, dated 1826. Illustrated.

1836 The Comprehensive Bible . . . With the Various Readings and Marginal Notes Usually Printed Therewith. A General Introduction . . . Introductions and Concluding Remarks to Each Book: The Parallel Passages Contained in Canne's Bible; Dr. Adam Clarke's Commentary . . . Rev. J. Brown's Self-Interpreting Bible . . . Dr. Blayney's Bible . . . Bishop Wilson's Bible, Edited by Crutwell; Rev. T. Scott's Commentary . . . and the English Version of Bagster's Polyglott Bible, Systematically Arranged: Philological and Explanatory Notes . . . Third Edition Corrected . . . Stereotyped by James Conner . . . New York . . . Published by Judd, Loomis & Co: Hartford **925**

1 vol: (92) 93–1090 (8) 1097–1460 30 cm NNAB

Reprint of 1832 Bible (No 770). Has frontispieces to both Testaments.

1836 The Holy Bible . . . With Canne's Marginal References. Together With the Apocrypha and Concordance. To Which are Added an Index, A Table of Texts, and What has Never Before Been Added, An Account of the Lives and Martyrdom of the Apostles and Evangelists . . . The Text Corrected According to the Standard of the American Bible Society. Stereotyped by James Conner, New-York. Published by Judd, Loomis & Co.: Hartford **926**

1 vol: (527) (78) (168) (12) (4) (56) (19) [1] 30 cm NNAB

Preliminary matter includes frontispiece, To the Reader, Advertisement, Order of Books. A Reading Guide by William Stones follows OT. Frontispiece and title page precede NT. Index, Tables, Account of Lives, Concordance, and Metrical Psalms at end.

1836 The Holy Bible . . . With Marginal Notes and References . . . R. P. Desilver: Philadelphia **927**

Reported as (676) 681–1076 (24) 29 cm DLC

With Apocrypha. Index, Tables, Metrical Psalms, and Brown's Concordance at end. Illustrated.

1836 The Holy Bible . . . with Canne's Marginal Notes and References. Together with the Apocrypha. To Which are Added an Index . . . Stereotyped by B. and J. Collins, New-York. Published by Kimber and Sharpless: Philadelphia **928**

29 cm NNAB

Reprint of Kimber and Sharpless stereotype edition of 1829 (No 667). Wavy lines separate columns of text. Has Index, Tables, etc.; also Metrical Psalms and Brown's Concordance.

1836 The Holy Bible . . . with Canne's Marginal Notes and References . . . Index . . . Tables . . . Published by R. White, and Hutchison and Dwier: Hartford **929**

1 vol: (574) (96) 579–768 (54) 29 cm NNAB

With Apocrypha. Order of Books, To the Reader (from the Collins Bible), and Contents precede text. Frontispiece and added engraved title to OT. Brown's Concordance at end. Engraved title calls for engravings by Wright and Smith from the work of R. Westall but cited copy contains only the frontispieces. While this is similar to the Phinney edition of 1831–32, it does not match line for line.

1836   The Holy Bible ... with Canne's Marginal Notes & References ... Stereotyped, Printed and Published by H. & E. Phinney: Cooperstown   **930**

Reported as 768 p   28 cm   NjPasHi

1836   The English Version of the Polyglott Bible ... with Marginal Readings ... References, to which are Added ... Introduction ... by Rev. Joseph A. Warne ... Essay ... by James MacKnight ... Sermons ... by Philip Doddridge ... Bible Gazetteer. A Concordance by Rev. J. Brown ... Index ... Dictionary ... Together with ... Tables ... Family Record ... Maps and Engravings on Steel ... and ... Woodcuts ... Published by Fessenden & Co.: Brattleboro'   **931**

28 cm   NNAB
Reprint of 1833 Polyglott Bible (No 820) but with material arranged differently. Preface signed T. C.   Copyright 1833 by Fessenden and Holbrook.

1836   The Holy Bible ... With Canne's Marginal Notes and References ... Haskell: Woodstock, Vt.   **932**

Reported as 927 p   28 cm   MB, VtHi
With Apocrypha. Has added engraved title dated 1837 and reproduction of 1611 title. Index and Tables at end. Illustrated.

1836–46   The Comprehensive Commentary on the Holy Bible; Containing the Text According to the Authorized Version. Scott's Marginal References ... Edited by William Jenks ... Fessenden & Co.: Brattleboro'   **933**

6 vols   28 cm   IJI
See 1834–38 Baptist Edition, No 860; also 1835–38 nondenominational edition, No 894. Vol ɪ missing from cited copy. Vols ɪɪ (1836), ɪᴠ (1845), and ᴠɪ (Supplement) imprinted Brattleboro; Vols ɪɪɪ (1846) and ᴠ (1846) imprinted *Lippincott & Co., Philadelphia.*

1836–37   The Cottage Bible, and Family Expositor ... With Practical Expositions and Explanatory Notes, by Thomas Williams ... To which are Added the References and Marginal Readings of the Polyglott Bible ... Edited by Rev. William Patton. Complete in Two Volumes ... D. F. Robinson and H. F. Sumner: Hartford   **934**

2 vols   27 cm   NN
Reprint of 1833–34 Conner and Cooke Cottage Bible (No 818). Each volume has frontispiece and illustrations. Vol ɪ dated 1836; Vol ɪɪ, 1837.

1836   The Holy Bible, Translated from the Latin Vulgat ... The Old Testament, First Published ... at Doway ... 1609. And the New Testament ... at Rhemes ... 1582. With Annotations, References, and a Historical and Chronological Index. First Stereotyped from the Fifth Dublin Edition. Newly Re-

vised and Corrected According to the Clemintin Edition . . . [Stereotyped
by J. Howe]. Published by Eugene Cummiskey: Philadelphia   **935**

1 vol: (691) (191)   24 cm   NN

Rheims-Douay, from the 5th Dublin edition. Printed from new type set from 1824 Cummiskey Bible (No 492). Family Record follows OT. Tables at end.

1836/33   The Holy Bible, Translated from the Latin Vulgate . . . With Annotations, References . . . Index. Published with the Approbation of the Right Rev. John DuBois . . . [Stereotyped by Conner & Cooke]. Published by John Doyle: New York   **936**

24 cm   NN, NNAB

Rheims-Douay. Reprint of 1833 edition (No 825) but with different illustrations and minor corrections. NT dated 1833.

1836   The Holy Bible . . . Published by Charles Lane: Sandbornton, N. H.   **937**

Text ends Ff6   19 cm   NNAB
Has frontispiece of two woodcuts to each Testament.

1836   The Holy Bible . . . Stereotyped by J. Howe, Philadelphia . . . Published by Judd, Loomis & Co.: Hartford   **938**

Reported as (655) 656–681   "12mo"   CSmH, CtY, ViU
Has Contents at end.

1836   The Holy Bible . . . Printed by Hudson & Goodwin: Hartford   **939**

"12mo"   Not Located
O'Callaghan, p 246.

1836/35   The Holy Bible . . . [Superfine Edition]. [Stereotyped by Conner & Cooke] Auxiliary New York Bible and Common Prayer Book Society: New York   **940**

1044 p   17 cm   NN
NT dated 1835.

1836   The Holy Bible . . . The Text of the Common Translation is Arranged in Paragraphs, such as the Sense Requires . . . By James Nourse. [Stereotyped by J. Howe, Philadelphia] . . . Published by Perkins and Marvin: Boston; Henry Perkins: Philadelphia   **941**

1 vol: (vii) (942) (322)   16 cm   MH–AH, NN, NNAB

Preface and Order of Books precede OT. NT title and Order of Books precede NT. List of OT quotations in the NT at end. Copyright 1834, by Perkins, Marvin & Co.

1836   The Holy Bible . . . From the Authorized Oxford Edition . . . Hogan and Thompson: Philadelphia   **942**

1 vol: (1098) (342)   16 cm   NN, NNAB
NT title has *Stereotyped and printed by Haswell and Barrington.*

1836   The English Version of the Polyglott Bible . . . With the Marginal Readings:
        Together with a Copious and Original Selection of References to Parallel
        and Illustrative Passages. Exhibited in a Manner Hitherto Unattempted.
        Stereotyped by L. Johnson, Published by Desilver, Thomas & Co.: Phila-
        delphia   **943**

15 cm   NNAB

Reprint of Key & Meilke edition of 1831 (No 753) previously published by Desilver and
Thomas in 1834 (No 874) and 1835 (No 909).

1836   The Holy Bible . . . [Printed by Brown and Sinquet, Philadelphia]. Stereo-
        typed by L. Johnson. Bible Association of Friends in America: Philadelphia
                                                                                     944

1 vol: (1098) (342)   15 cm   NNAB

NT also published separately this year (No 963).

1836   The English Version of the Polyglott Bible . . . Luther Roby, Printer . . .
        Stereotyped by Henry Wallis and L. Roby, Concord, N. H. . . . Published by
        Roby, Kimball and Merrill: Concord, N. H.   **945**

1 vol: (viii) (587) (190)   15 cm   NNAB

Has frontispiece and added engraved title to each Testament. Also Preface signed T. C.

1836   The Holy Bible . . . George Dearborn: New York   **946**

1 vol: (726) (221)   "24mo"   Not Located

O'Callaghan, p 248. Engraved title page has *The Diamond Bible*. Illustrated.

1836   The English Version of the Polyglott Bible, with Marginal Readings and
        References . . . [Stereotyped by T. G. Wells & Co., Boston]. J. B. & S. L.
        Chase & Co.: Woodstock, Vt.   **947**

1 vol: (867) (259) 260–267   14 cm   NN

Has frontispiece; Tables at end of each Testament. Illustrated.

1836   The Holy Bible . . . Stereotyped by L. Johnson. J. S. & C. Adams: Amherst **948**

13 cm   NNAB

Similar to 1834 Adams edition (No 878) from which above information was taken as cited
copy lacks general title page.
MAJ has a similar edition, undated.

1836   The Holy Bible . . . Stereotyped by J. Howe . . . Philad. Published by Judd,
        Loomis & Co.: Hartford   **949**

1 vol: (x) 11–729 (222)   13 cm   NNAB

Has two engravings before each Testament. Contents before OT (8 p) and after NT (6 p).

1836   The English Version of the Polyglott Bible: . . . With Marginal Readings;
        Together with a Copious and Original Selection of References to Parallel
        and Illustrative Passages. Exhibited in a Manner Hitherto Unattempted. J. H.
        Butler: Northampton [Mass.]; T. & M. Butler: Buffalo   **950**

1 vol: (856) (259)   12 cm   NNAB

    Has frontispiece. Added engraved title page and Tables precede each Testament. Preface
signed T. C.   Illustrated.

1836/34 The Holy Bible . . . Stereotyped by Henry Wallis and Luther Roby . . .
Published by Charles Hoag: Concord, N. H. **951**

1 vol: (852) (259)   11 cm   NN

Has frontispiece and added engraved title page. NT, dated 1834, and engraved title imprinted *C. and A. Hoag.*

O'Callaghan (p 247) lists a Bible of this pagination, stereotyped by Luther Roby, printed
by Allison and Foster, and published by Oliver L. Sanborn, Concord.

1836 The Holy Bible . . . Sanderson: Elizabethtown **952**

No further information available.   IaB

1836 the new testament . . . in raised letters for the use of the blind, by the american and massachusetts bible societies. Printed at the new-england institution: boston **953**

Reported as 147 leaves   31cm   PPAmP

The first of four volumes containing the NT in raised letters. Text ends with Luke 6:49.
This was the project of Samuel G. Howe, M.D. of the New-England Institution for the Education of the Blind, Boston, who had been investigating the problem for several years. He had purchased type and a press by March of 1835 and printed the Acts (100 copies). Mark and John
had been previously printed elsewhere, possibly in England. The ABS and the MBS each contributed $1,000 to the project and the New-York Female Bible Society, $800. (*ABS Report*
1835, p 27–28, 92–94.) In May 1836, Dr. Howe sent to the ABS a copy of the volume cited.
He hoped to have the other three in a few weeks. (*ABS Report* 1836, p 87.) Ever since this
time, the ABS has regarded the supply of Scriptures for the blind as part of its regular work.

The American Bible Society has issued English Scriptures for the blind in the versions and
systems indicated below. The date is that of the completion of the series cited; in most instances
the first volume of a series began to appear several years in advance. Reprintings frequently
followed.

DATE	SYSTEM	VERSION	PART	NO OF VOLS OR RECORDS
1836	Line Letter	AV	NT*	1
1843	Line Letter	AV	Bible	16
1894	New York Point (one side)	AV	Bible	11
1911	American Braille	ASV	Bible	19
1916	New York Point (Bi-page)	AV	Bible	11
1919	Revised Braille Grade 1½ (one side)	ASV	NT	7
1922	Revised Braille Grade 1½ (one side)	AV	Bible	21
1929	Revised Braille Grade 1½ Interpoint	ASV	OT	15
1930	Revised Braille Grade 1½ Interpoint	AV	Bible	20
1930	Revised Braille Grade 1½ Interpoint	ASV	Bible	20

* First vol only; this series was completed in 8 very large vols.

DATE	SYSTEM	VERSION	PART	NO OF VOLS OR RECORDS
1935	Braille Grade 2 Interpoint	ASV	Bible	18
1944	Talking Book Records 12"	AV	Bible	169
1950	Talking Book Records 10"	AV	Bible	170
1951	Braille Grade 2 Interpoint	AV	Bible	18
1953	Braille Grade 2	RSV	NT	4

The following editions of the Pocket Bible for the blind, containing favorite passages, were also issued by ABS:

DATE	SYSTEM	VERSION	NO OF VOLS OR RECORDS
1922	New York Point Bi-page	AV	1
1922	Braille 1½	AV	1
1935	Moon	AV	1
1935	Talking Book Records 12"	AV	2
1950	Talking Book Records 10"	AV	2
1954	Braille, Grade 2	AV	1

The New York point system was devised by W. B. Waite of the New York Institution for the Education of the Blind. The Gospel of John was printed by ABS in 1874 (99 leaves, 36 cm, NNAB). In 1915 Mr. Waite presented to the ABS a special press designed by him for printing in this system.

1836   The Family Expositor; or, A Paraphrase and Version of the New Testament; with Critical Notes, and a Practical Improvement to each Section. By Philip Doddridge, D.D. American Edition. With a Memoir of the Author, by N. W. Fiske . . . and an Introductory Essay, by Moses Stuart . . . J. S. & C. Adams, and L. Boltwood: Amherst   **954**

1 vol: (xx) 17–998 (8)   27 cm   MAJ, MWA, NN, OO
Doddridge Version; see 1807–08 NT, No 147, also 1833, No 837.
McKeon and Cowles (*Amherst, Massachusetts Imprints, 1825–1876*, p 58) report two variants, in both of which the Explanation of the Tables and the Index is tipped in between p xviii and xix on a full leaf. Verso of title page of one copy has Stereotyped at the Boston Type and Stereotype Foundry; on the other is Stereotyped at the Boston Type and Stereotype Foundry. J. S. and C. Adams, printer.

1836   The New Testament . . . Published for the Vermont Bible Society. E. P. Walton & Son: Montpelier   **955**

Reported as 336 p   24 cm   MH–AH

1836   Evangelical History; or the Books of the New Testament; with a General Introduction, a Preface to Each Book, and Notes Explanatory and Critical. In Two Volumes. By Alden Bradford Vol. I. Containing the Four Gospels. Joseph Dowe: Boston   **956**

Reported as 400 p   21 cm   ICU, MBAt
Bradford Version; see 1813 NT, No 253. In his preface, the translator states: "It is proposed soon to publish a second volume, on a similar plan, containing the historical book of Acts,

and the apostolic Epistles." There is no record of its publication. The translation is based on the Greek text of Griesbach.

1836 The New Testament . . . With an Introduction, Giving An Account of Jewish and Other Sects; with Notes Illustrating Obscure Passages, and Explaining Obsolete Words and Phrases; for the Use of Schools, Academies, and Private Families by J. A. Cummings, Author of Ancient and Modern Geography. Fourth Edition. Revised and Improved. Hilliard, Gray, and Company: Boston   **957**

20 cm   NNAB
Each chapter has prefatory remarks. Notes at foot of page. Tables at end. See 1827 NT, No 595.

1836 Pronouncing Testament . . . By Israel Alger . . . Crocker and Brewster: Boston   **958**

"12mo"   Not Located
O'Callaghan, p 248. See 1822 NT, No 452.

1836 The New Testament . . . In Which the Text of the Common Version is Divided into Paragraphs, the Punctuation in Many Cases Altered and Some Words, Not in the Original, Expunged. Stereotyped by T. H. Carter & Co. . . . Hilliard, Gray and Co.: Boston   **959**

297 p   18 cm   NNAB
Paragraph Testament appears at head of title instead of *Revised Testament* as in the 1824 NT (No 511).

1836 The New Testament . . . Published by John G. Tilton: Newburyport   **960**
450 p   17 cm   NNAB
Has woodcut on title page.

1836 The New Testament . . . Published by O. L. Sanborn: Concord, N. H.   **961**
226 p   16 cm   NNAB

1836 The New Testament . . . Published by William H. Niles: Middletown   **962**
288 p   16 cm   NNAB

1836 The New Testament . . . Stereotype Edition. Stereotyped by L. Johnson. Published by the Bible Association of Friends in America: Philadelphia **963**
342 p   15 cm   NNAB
Separate issue of NT from the Friends Bible of this year (No 944).

1836 Reference and pronouncing Testament, according to the standard of the A. . . B. . . S. . . ; with a copious and judicious selection of references . . . translated from the German and interspersed with the text. By John Winebrenner. The Gospel Publisher: Harrisburg, Pa.   **964**

Reported as (416) (47) (1) p   15 cm   DLC
Preliminary matter includes copyright (1836), explanatory preface and testimonials (1 p), a key to pronunciation and order of books (2 p). Printed in bold face type with references in

smaller type between verses and the pronunciation indicated not only for proper names but for many common words.

John Winebrenner (1797–1860), earlier a pastor of the German Reformed Church, in 1830 founded the General Eldership of the Church of God in North America.

The Memorial Public Library, Alexandria, Pa., has a copy without the Short Dictionary and Gazetteer at the end.

1836   The Polyglott New Testament . . . With Marginal Readings and References . . . [Stereotyped by T. G. Wells & Co., Boston]. J. B. & S. L. Chase & Co.: Woodstock, Vt.   **965**

264 p   14 cm   NN, NNAB

Has frontispiece. Order of Books on verso of title. At end are Contents of Books and the Discourses, Parables and Miracles of Jesus arranged in chronological order. Illustrated.

1836   The New Testament . . . with the Marginal Readings; and Illustrated by Original References, both Parallel and Explanatory, and a Copious Selection, Carefully Chosen, and Newly Arranged. Stereotyped by James Conner. John C. Riker: New-York   **966**

Reported as (ii) (350)   11 cm   MBU–T

Added engraved title page has *The Polyglot New Testament with Marginal Readings.*

1836   The New Testament . . . Printed by James Nelson, Jr. Published by George F. Richardson: Brunswick [Maine]   **967**

Reported as 259 p   "32mo"   MBU–T

1837   The Holy Bible . . . Apocrypha . . . Index and Concise Dictionary . . . embellished with several fine engravings. [Stereotyped by Henry W. Rees, New York] James Collord, Printer. Thomas Mason & George Lane, for the Methodist Episcopal Church: New York   **968**

1 vol: (16) (797) (120) (256) (10) (2) (53)   31 cm   NNAB

Engraved frontispiece and half-title for each Testament, plates. Family Record follows Apocrypha which is in smaller type. At end are Sayings of Jesus, NT Contents, Chronology, Stone's Daily Reading Plan, Barr's Index and Dictionary, and 7 blank p.

1837   The Holy Bible . . . With Canne's Marginal References . . . The Text Corrected According to the Standard of the American Bible Society. Stereotyped by James Conner, New-York . . . Andrus, Judd, & Franklin: Hartford   **969**

30 cm   DLC

With Apocrypha. Index, Tables, and Account of the Lives of Apostles and Evangelists. At end are Brown's Concordance and Metrical Psalms. Illustrated.

1837   The Holy Bible . . . With Canne's Marginal References . . . Text Corrected According to the Standard of the American Bible Society. Stereotyped by James Conner . . . Published by T. Mason & G. Lane, for the Methodist Episcopal Church: New York   **970**

1 vol: (528) (78) (168) (56) (19)   29 cm   NN

With Apocrypha. Frontispieces to both Testaments; 14 plates. Preliminary matter includes To the Reader [by Dr. Witherspoon], Advertisement, and Order of Books. Stone's Guide to Reading the Scriptures follows OT. Index, Tables, etc., Brown's Concordance, and Metrical Psalms at end.

NNAB has an undated copy with imprint: *New York: Published by L. Stebbins*, with the same added matter except that the Concordance has 35 p.

1837 The Holy Bible . . . with Canne's marginal references . . . Apocrypha . . . Index . . . References and a key sheet . . . Hervey Wilbur . . . text . . . standard of the American Bible Society . . . Stereotyped by James Conner . . . E. Sanderson, Printer, Elizabeth-town, N. J. Published by N. and J. White: New-York   **971**

Reported as (528) (78) (2) (168) (31)   29 cm   VtHi

1837? The Holy Bible . . . Stereotyped, Printed and Published by H. & E. Phinney: Cooperstown, N. Y.   **972**

1 vol: (576) 577–754 755–766   28 cm   NNAB

General title page missing from cited copy; above from NT title. Tables follow OT. Index at end. NCooHi has copy with woodcut frontispieces and 5 illustrations.

1837? The Holy Bible . . . With Canne's Marginal Notes and References . . . Nafis and Cornish: New York; Nafis, Cornish & Co.: St. Louis   **973**

1 vol: (829) (cxlvii) (xxi) (56) (19)   "4to"   Not Located

O'Callaghan (p 250) locates a copy in the Legislative Assembly Library in Canada but the National Library at Ottawa says this library was destroyed by fire a number of years ago. Preliminary matter includes To the Reader, Order of Books, and Contents of Books. With Apocrypha, followed by Family Record. Index, Tables, etc., Brown's Concordance, and Metrical Psalms at end. Wood engravings by Anderson.

1837 The Holy Bible . . . The text carefully printed from the most correct copies of the present authorized translation, including the marginal readings and parallel texts: with a commentary and critical notes . . . by Adam Clarke. A new edition with the author's final corrections . . . [Stereotyped by Henry W. Rees.]. James Collord, printer . . . Published by T. Mason & G. Lane, for the Methodist Episcopal Church: New-York   **974**

6 vols   27 cm   TNMPH

Revised edition of Clarke's Commentary; see 1811–25, No 188. Vol III contains Asiatic Proverbs (p 795–798), The Targum or Chaldee Paraphrase of the Song of Songs (p 872–889), and The Gitagovinda (p 890–902).

TNMPH has another set with Vol III dated 1840.

NN has the following reprints: Vols I–IV, Herrod, Baltimore, 1837; 6–vol set with Vols I–III dated and imprinted as above, Vol IV, G. Lane, 1840, Vols V–VI, Carlton and Phillips, 1854, 1853 (New Edition condensed and supplemented by the best modern authorities by Daniel Curry [1809–1887], 920 and 1070 p); G. Lane and P. P. Sandford, 1843–44; and two sets by Carlton & Porter dated 185– and 1856 (the latter with NT vols imprinted Carlton & Phillips). N and DeU have 1840–43 set with G. Lane. TNMPH has NT only of 1842 set by G. Lane and P. P. Sandford and first vol of NT of 1844 copy by G. Lane and C. B. Tippett. MdBJ has 1842–45 set by G. Lane and P. P. Sandford, with NT vols imprinted G. Lane and C. B. Tippett. NcD has 1848 and 1857 sets, both by Carlton. WaPS has 1850 set by Lane and Scott. ViLxW has 1853 set and PMA has 1855 set, both by Carlton & Phillips.

1837 The English Version of the Polyglott Bible . . . With the Marginal Readings, and . . . References to Parallel and Illustrative Passages . . . Introduction to the Holy Scriptures, and to Each of the Books; by Rev. Joseph A. Warne. An Essay on the Right Interpretations of the Writings in Which the Revelations of God are Contained, by James Macknight . . . Three Sermons . . . by Philip Doddridge . . . Brattleboro' Typographic Co.: Brattleboro', Vt.   **975**

27 cm   CtY

Reprint of Lincoln, Edmands & Co. 1833 edition (No 820) copyrighted by Fessenden and Holbrook. *Fessenden & Co's. Edition* appears at head of title.

1837   The English Version of the Polyglott Bible . . . Stereotyped by L. Johnson . . .
Published by Desilver, Thomas & Co.: Philadelphia   **976**

"12mo"   Not Located
O'Callaghan, p 252. *Philadelphia: Published by Thomas, Cowperthwait & Co.* appears on
engraved title page and frontispiece.

1837   The Holy Bible . . . Claremont Manufacturing Co.: Claremont, N. H.   **977**
"12mo"   Not Located
Wright, p 397.

1837?   The Holy Bible, Translated from the Latin Vulgate . . . With Annotations
by the Rev. Dr. Challoner . . . With the Approbation of the Provincial Council . . . Published by Fielding Lucas, Jr.: Baltimore   **978**

1 vol: (810) (214)   20 cm   IMunS, NN
Rheims-Douay, from the 5th Dublin edition. Has Challoner's Annotations arranged as
footnotes. Tables (p 809–810). See 1826? Bible, No 557.

1837   [Swedenborgian Bible] The Holy Bible . . . O. Clapp: Boston   **979**
1 vol: (510) (162)   20 cm   NN, NNAB
The Books of Ruth, Chronicles, Ezra, Nehemiah, Esther, Job, Proverbs, Ecclesiastes, Song
of Solomon, Acts of the Apostles, and the Epistles are omitted; but Bible is paged as if the
whole text were included. Second preliminary leaf has From the Arcana Coelestia of Emanuel
Swedenborg, followed by a list of the books which Swedenborg indicates as "having an internal
sense."

1837   The Holy Bible . . . Stereotyped by J. Howe . . . Philad. Judd, Loomis & Co.:
Hartford   **980**
1 vol: (x) 11–729 (225)   14 cm   NN, NNAB
Has frontispieces and Contents to both Testaments.
Also issued with illustrations throughout.

1837   The English Version of the Polyglott Bible . . . J. B. & S. L. Chase & Co.:
Woodstock, Vt.   **981**
Reported as (4) (867) (268)   13 cm   VtHi

1837   Pocket Reference Bible. The English Version of the Polyglott Bible . . . With
Original Selections of References to Parallel and Illustrative Passages; and
Marginal Readings . . . Stereotyped by L. Johnson . . . Published by Arm-
strong & Berry: Baltimore   **982**
1 vol: (viii) (920) (281)   12 cm   NN
Has frontispiece. Each Testament has added engraved title.

1837   The Holy Bible . . . Authorised Version. With Notes, Practical and Explanatory, by the Rev. Henry Stebbing . . . Allan Bell & Co.: London; T. Tegg &
Son and H. Washbourne, J. K. Herrick: New York   **983**
2 vols: (1084) (338)   "32mo"   Not Located
O'Callaghan (p 252) says "Copies of Stebbing's Diamond Bible had been smuggled for
a number of years into the United States. It was finally seized by the revenue officers and its
illegal introduction put an end to." Illustrated.
NNAB has an 1836 edition (different pagination, printed in three columns) with similar
imprint but without *J. K. Herrick: New York.*

1837 The Family Expositor; or, a Paraphrase and Version of the New Testament; with Critical Notes, and a Practical Improvement to Each Section. By Philip Doddridge . . . American Edition. With a Memoir of the Author, by N. W. Fiske . . . an Introductory Essay, by Moses Stuart . . . with a Portrait, Engraved from an Original Picture in Wymondley House . . . [Stereotyped at the Boston Type and Stereotype Foundry]. J. S. & C. Adams, and L. Boltwood: Amherst   **984**

1 vol: (4) (xx) 17–949 [1] (52)   27 cm   DLC, MA, NNAB, TNMPH
Doddridge Version; see 1807–08 NT, No 147. Preliminary matter includes portrait as frontispiece, Memoir of Philip Doddridge, Remarks on Doddridge's Family Expositor, Explanation of Tables and Index, Index of Sections, and Directions for Reading the Family Expositor. At end are Appendix, Tables, Index, etc., and Family Record. Text has inner column containing AV text. Doddridge's version, in italics, is interwoven with paraphrase, with an Improvement after each section. Chapter and verse numbers in outer margins; notes at foot of page. Gospels printed in Harmony form. Copyright 1833.

1837 The New Testament, Arranged in Historical and Chronological Order; with Copious Notes on the Principal Subjects in Theology; the Gospels on the Basis of the Harmonies of Lightfoot, Doddridge, Pilkington, Newcome, Michaelis; the Account of the Resurrection . . . The Epistles . . . Divided According to the Apostles' Arguments. By the Rev. George Townsend . . . The Whole Revised . . . Divided into Paragraphs, Punctuated . . . Italic Words Re-Examined . . . Passages & Words of Doubtful Authority Marked . . . Parallel Passages Given . . . By Rev. T. W. Coit, D.D. . . . [Vol ii, 1st American Edition]. Published [and Printed] by Perkins and Marvin: Boston; Henry Perkins: Philadelphia   **985**

1 vol: (48) (455) (472)   26 cm   ICU, MB, NcAS, NNAB
Marked Vol ii at foot of some pages; for OT companion volume, see 1838, No 1022. Has Introduction and Portions of Scripture for Daily Reading. Text, in single column, paragraph form, is divided into fifteen parts and then into sections. At end are Notes on the Canon, Christianity, and the Church; Notes on the Harmony of Gospels, Acts, Epistles; three Indexes; and The Gospels Harmonized. Stereotyped at the Boston Type and Stereotype Foundry. Copyright by Perkins and Marvin 1837.
Townsend's OT appeared first in England in 2 vols in 1821, and the NT in 1825. His arrangement is based mainly on J. Lightfoot's Chronicle of 1647, etc.

1837 The New Testament . . . Stereotyped by Redfield & Lindsay, for the American Bible Society, Instituted in New-York, in the Year 1816. Printed by D. Fanshaw: New-York   **986**

1 vol: (431) (112)   24 cm   NNAB
Pica Octavo. "This book being of large clear type, is designed for aged people, and such others as have imperfect vision." The first ABS NT issued with the Psalms.
Cited copy is marked third edition but the book was first issued in this year. This seems to be the first appearance of the phrase *Instituted in New-York, in the Year 1816*, from which *in New-York* later disappears.

1837 The Productions of the Evangelists and Apostles, a faithful and true translation of the Scriptures of the New Testament, with references, subdivisions and an appendix containing notes to the preface and notes on the text. To which is added the Apocrypha. William Lyon Mackenzie: Toronto   **987**

Reported as (xl) 41–499 (134)   23 cm   CaOKQ, CaOTP
Dickinson Version; see 1833 NT, No 839. Dickinson's name appears only at the end of the list of subscribers. A note on p iii states that the Canadian publisher has omitted the

Inscription and part of the Preface, asterisks taking the place of the omitted material. Portrait also omitted. All other material as in the original Boston edition.
W. L. Mackenzie was the leader of the Upper Canada rebellion of 1837.

1837   The New Testament . . . Published by T. Mason and G. Lane, for the Methodist Episcopal Church: New-York   **988**

Reported as 556 p   23 cm   NNUT
Has frontispiece.

1837   The New Testament . . . Fielding Lucas: Baltimore   **989**

Reported as 214 p   20 cm   DGU
Rheims Version. Issued separately from 1837 Bible (No 978). Without Approbations.

1837   The New Testament . . . By William Tyndale, the Martyr. The Original Edition, 1526, Being the First Vernacular Translation from the Greek. With a Memoir of his Life and Writings. To Which are Annexed, the Essential Variations of Coverdale's, Thomas Mathew's, Cranmer's, the Genevan, and the Bishops' Bibles, as Marginal Readings. By J. P. Dabney . . . Printed and Published by Gould & Newman, from the London Edition of Bagster: Andover [Massachusetts] and New York   **990**

1 vol: (viii) (2) 11–105 (490)   19 cm   CSmH, CU, DLC, MAnP, MiU, NcD, NjN,
                                                                                                     NN, NNAB
Has portrait of Tyndale.
NNAB has second copy without portrait.
The first printed English NT, translated by William Tyndale (1494–1536), appeared in 1525 in Worms, Germany. His Pentateuch was printed in 1530.

1837   The New Testament . . . Stereotype Edition . . . Published by A. J. Dickinson and C. Ward . . . : Philadelphia   **991**
453 [1] p   18 cm   NN
Appended are the Psalms and Hymns of the Presbyterian Church of America, imprinted Philadelphia 1836. Tables at end.

1837   The New Testament . . . [Stereotype Edition]. Judd, Loomis & Co.: Hartford   **992**
251 p   16 cm   NN

1837   New Testament . . . S. Babcock & Co.: Charleston   **993**
288 p   16 cm   NN

1837   The Polyglott New Testament . . . With Marginal Readings and References . . . J. B. & S. L. Chase & Co.: Woodstock, Vt.   **994**
14 cm   Not Located
O'Callaghan (p 255) lists this as separate issue from 1836 Bible (No 947).

1837   The New Testament . . . [Stereotyped by L. Johnson]. McCarty & Davis: Philadelphia   **995**
256 p   12 cm   NN

1837   The New Testament ... B. Olds: Newark   **996**

344 p   12 cm   NN

1837   The Four Gospels . . . by Rev. George Campbell . . . in two Volumes . . .
Printed and published by Gould and Newman: Andover and New York   **997**

"8vo"   Not Located

O'Callaghan, p 256. George Campbell Version; see 1796, No 56.

1838   The Holy Bible ... With Canne's Marginal Notes and References ... Stereotyped by James Conner, New-York ... Andrus, Judd, & Franklin: Hartford
998

44 cm   NNAB

Reprint of Silas Andrus 1829 folio (No 666). With Apocrypha.

1838?   The Holy Bible . . . references and various readings. Illustrated with engravings. In Two Volumes . . . Printed by John D. Toy. Joseph N. Lewis:
Baltimore   **999**

2 vols in 1: Vol I, 787 p; Vol II, (277) (139) 281–600   30 cm   NNAB

Vol I preliminary matter includes frontispiece, added engraved title, Order of Books,
Guide to Regular Perusal of the Scriptures by William Stones; text: Genesis to Song of Solomon.
Vol II has general title and NT title; text: Isaiah to Revelation, also Apocrypha. Illustrated.

O'Callaghan (p 256) lists an edition published in numbers by Lewis and Coleman, Baltimore, but gives the printer as John D. Fry. Ornamental title has *Published by Joseph N. Lewis,
Baltimore*. The copy reported to O'Callaghan has the date 1838 in MS on the cover. An undated
copy examined by the ABS in 1952, from the estate of the Collyer brothers, has the imprint
of *Phoenix N. Wood and Co., Baltimore* and gives the printer as John D. Toy.

1838   The Holy Bible ... With Canne's Marginal References ... The Text Corrected According to the Standard of the American Bible Society. Stereotyped
by James Conner, New-York ... Published by T. Mason & G. Lane, for the
Methodist Episcopal Church: New-York   **1000**

1 vol: (527) (78) (168)   29 cm   NNAB

With Apocrypha. Has frontispiece to each Testament and woodcuts (2 per page). References in center column. Preliminary matter includes To the Reader, Publisher's Note, and Order
of Books. Stone's Guide to Reading the Scriptures follows OT. Index and Tables at end.
Stereotyped at the Boston Type and Stereotype Foundry appears on verso of NT title.

1838   Holy Bible ... with Canne's marginal notes and references ... H. & E. Phinney: Cooperstown, N. Y. . . . sold also by I. Tiffany: Utica   **1001**

Reported as (576) (99) 577–768   28 cm   NCooHi

With Apocrypha. Has frontispiece and 8 woodcuts.
NCooHi has copy with NT dated 1837.

1838   The Holy Bible ... With Canne's Marginal Notes and References ... U. P.
James: Cincinnati   **1002**

1 vol: (8) 9–829 (xxi)   28 cm   NN, NNAB

Alexander's Stereotype Edition appears at head of title. With Apocrypha. Contains To
the Reader, Advertisement to Alexander's Stereotype Edition (1834), Order of Books, and
Contents. Index, Tables, etc. at end. Has several engravings before title page and in OT, and a
woodcut by Anderson before NT.
Also issued with Concordance (56 p).

1838   The Holy Bible . . . I. Ashmead & Co., Printers. Published by R. P. Desilver: Philadelphia   *1003*

1 vol: (1076) (72) (24) (4)   28 cm   NNAB

With Apocrypha. Engraved frontispieces to Testaments. Tables, Index, Concordance, and Metrical Psalms at end.

1838   The English Version of the Polyglott Bible . . . With the Marginal Readings . . . Brattleboro Typographic Co.: Brattleboro, Vt.   *1004*

Reported as (705) (216) (84)   27 cm   VtMiS
Fessenden & Co's. Edition appears at head of title.

1838   The Holy Bible . . . Bible Association of Friends in America: Philadelphia
                                                                            1005

Reported as (1061) (xxxiii) (92)   26 cm   NNUT
Includes Index and Concordance.

1838   The Holy Bible . . . Published by Robinson, Pratt & Co.: New York   *1006*
"8vo"   Not Located
O'Callaghan, p 389.

1838   The Holy Bible . . . Robert Barker: London . . . John Gray, Printer . . . Stereotyped by White & Hagar, for the American and Foreign Bible Society: New York   *1007*

"8vo"   Not Located
O'Callaghan, p 258. Reprinted from the 1833 Oxford reprint of 1611, which uses modern spelling. Although the American and Foreign Bible Society was formed in 1836 by Baptists who were dissatisfied with the attitude of the ABS on the matter of transliteration of the Greek word for "baptize" in missionary translations, they adopted the "version in common use" for use in English. See 1838 NT, No 1027; also 1839 Bible, No 1042.

The Society is still in existence in 1960, a board of Baptist ministers administering the remaining funds for Bible distribution but it no longer publishes. See also the American Bible Union (1862, No 1764) and the American Baptist Publication Society, (1891, No 2048).

1838   The English Version of the Polyglott Bible . . . Arranged in a Manner Hitherto Unattempted . . . Published by Brattleboro's Typographic Company, Incorporated October 26, 1836: Brattleboro, Vt.   *1008*

Reported as 850 p   "8vo"   MH-AH

1838   The Holy Bible . . . The Text Printed from the Most Correct Translation, Including the Marginal Readings and Parallel Texts. With a Commentary and Critical Notes . . . By Adam Clarke . . . [Stereotyped by F. Lucas, jr. and W. & J. Neal]. J. J. Harrod: Baltimore   *1009*

4 vols: Vol ɪ, (1032); Vol ɪɪ, (1005) (14) (46); Vol ɪɪɪ, (940); Vol ɪᴠ, (1088)   26 cm
                                                                              NN
Clarke's Commentary; see 1811–25, No 188. Vols ɪ–ɪɪ, OT. Vols ɪɪɪ–ɪᴠ, NT.

1838   The Holy Bible . . . Stereotyped by L. Johnson, Philadelphia. Haswell, Barrington & Haswell: Philadelphia   *1010*

1 vol: (750) (238)   26 cm   NN, NNAB
Apocrypha not included, although it is listed in the Order of Books.
Haswell, Barrington & Haswell were successors to Alexander Towar.

1838 The Holy Bible ... With the References and Marginal Readings of the Polyglott Bible, with Numerous Additions from Bagster's Comprehensive Bible.
First Edition ... [Stereotyped by Conner & Cooke]. Andrus, Judd & Franklin: Hartford   ***1011***

962 p   23 cm   NNAB
   Reprint of text of Andrus & Judd Polyglott edition of 1834 (No 868) with Index (p 939–
962) but not Concordance. Has 4 engravings.
   Also issued without Index.

1838 The Holy Bible ... Stereotype Edition ... Claremont Manufacturing Company's Power Press: Claremont, N. H.   ***1012***

20 cm   NN, NNAB
   Reprint of 1830? edition (No 705).

1838 The Holy Bible ... T. Mason & G. Lane: New York   ***1013***

Reported as (510) (162)   20 cm   DLC

1838 The Holy Bible ... Andrus, Judd & Franklin: Hartford   ***1014***

Reported as 681 p   18 cm   CtY
Has frontispiece and illustrations.

1838 The Holy Bible ... Stereotyped by Henry Wallis and L. Roby, Concord,
N. H. ... Published by Roby, Kimball & Merrill: Concord, N. H.   ***1015***

"24mo"   Not Located
O'Callaghan, p 259.

1838 The Holy Bible ... Stereotyped by J. Howe, Philadelphia ... Andrus, Judd
and Franklin: Hartford   ***1016***

1 vol: (x) (729) (225)   14 cm   NN
Illustrated.

1838 The Holy Bible ... Robinson and Franklin, Successors to Leavitt, Lord &
Co.: New York   ***1017***

1 vol: (852) (259) 261–263   "32mo"   Not Located
O'Callaghan, p 259. Has frontispieces to OT and Contents at end.

1838 The Holy Bible ... [Printed by D. Fanshaw]. Stereotyped by Smith and
Valentine for the American Bible Society ... : New-York   ***1018***

979 p   13 cm   NNAB
   32mo Diamond Pocket Bible. "Some delay has been experienced in procuring suitable
type from which to make the stereotype plates. It has been necessary to have punches cut
on purpose for this object, but which has resulted in a type of rare symmetry and beauty"
(*ABS Report* 1838, p 25). Plates made from these were used until well into the twentieth
century. They were finally scrapped in 1942, there having been no printing since before 1922.

1838 The English Version of the Polyglott Bible ... With the Marginal Readings:
Together with a Copious and Original Selection of References to Parallel

and Illustrative Passages. Exhibited in a Manner Hitherto Unattempted . . .
Published by G. & C. Merriam: Springfield   *1019*

1 vol: (856) (259)   12 cm   NNAB
Has Order of Books, Preface signed T. C., and engraved title page for NT.

1838   The Holy Bible . . . Hogan & Thompson: Philadelphia   *1020*

1 vol: (819) (256) (83)   11 cm   NNAB
Frontispiece; engraved title dated 1834. Has Metrical Psalms. Illustrated.

1838   The Holy Bible . . . Thomas, Cowperthwait & Co.: Philadelphia   *1021*

1 vol: (852) (259) 261–263 (81)   11 cm   NNAB
Has frontispiece. Added engraved title precedes each Testament. Order of Books. Contents and Metrical Psalms at end.

1838   The Old Testament, Arranged in Historical and Chronological Order, on the
Basis of Lightfoot's Chronicle, in such a Manner that the Books, Chapters,
Psalms, Prophecies, &c. &c. May be Read as One Connected History, in the
Words of the Authorized Translation. With Notes and Copious Indexes. By
the Rev. George Townsend . . . Revised, Punctuated, Divided into Para-
graphs and Parallelisms . . . By the Rev. T. W. Coit, D.D. [Vol. i. Stereotyped
at the Boston Type and Stereotype Foundry] Published [and Printed] by
Perkins and Marvin: Boston; Henry Perkins: Philadelphia   *1022*

1 vol: (viii) (1188) (24)   26 cm   CtY, MiU, NNAB
Marked Vol i at foot of some pages; for NT companion volume, see 1837, No 985. Preface
to American Edition, Introduction, and Portions of Scripture for Every Day in the Year precede
text. Text, in single column, paragraph form, is divided into eight periods and further sub-
divided into parts. Indexes at end. Copyright by Perkins and Marvin 1838.

1838?   The New Testament, Arranged in Historical and Chronological Order; with
Copious Notes on the Principal Subjects in Theology . . . By the Rev. George
Townsend . . . The Whole Revised . . . by the Rev. T. W. Coit . . . Crocker
and Brewster: Boston   *1023*

Reported as (455) (472)   26 cm   ICU
See 1837 NT, No 985.

1838   The New Testament . . . London: Imprinted by R. Barker, 1611. Stereotyped
by White and Hagar, for the American and Foreign Bible Society: New
York   *1024*

252 p   19 cm   NN
Reprint of the 1611 AV in modern spelling. See 1838 Bible, No 1007.

1838   The New Testament . . . Stereotyped by J. Howe, New-York . . . Printed and
Published by Benjamin Olds: Newark   *1025*

288 p   "12mo"   Not Located
O'Callaghan, p 259.

1838   The New Testament . . . A. Dickinson: Philadelphia   *1026*

"12mo"   Not Located
Wright, p 398.

1838 The New Testament . . . London: Imprinted by Robert Barker, 1611 . . .
Stereotyped by White and Hagar, for the American and Foreign Bible Society: New-York   **1027**

236 p   16 cm   NN, NNAB

Reprint of the 1611 AV in modern spelling. On verso of title page, below Order of Books,
is a Table of the Meaning of Certain Words used in this Version, giving in three columns the
Greek, This Version, and Proper Meaning. Thus, Angel, Baptism, Baptize, Bishop, Charity,
Church, and Easter are, respectively, to be read as Messenger, Immersion, Immerse, Overseer,
Love, Congregation, and Passover. See 1838 Bible, No 1007; also 1850 Cone & Wykoff edition,
No 1444.

1838 The New Testament . . . Stereotyped by H. & H. Wallis, New-York. Published by Josiah B. Baldwin: Bridgeport   **1028**

270 p   16 cm   NNAB

1838 The New Testament . . . Stereotyped by J. Howe . . . Philad. Andrus, Judd
and Franklin: Hartford   **1029**

14 cm   NNAB

Same as 1830 Andrus NT (No 725).

1838 The New Testament . . . With Marginal Readings: and Illustrated by Original References . . . Carefully Chosen and Newly Arranged . . . J. H. Butler:
Northampton [Massachusetts]   **1030**

Reported as 259 p   12 cm   MB

From the 1836 Polyglot Bible (No 950). Illustrated.

1838 The New Testament . . . Haswell, Barrington & Haswell: Philadelphia **1031**

"32mo"   Not Located

Wright, p 398.

1839 The Comprehensive Bible . . . Robinson & Franklin: New York   **1032**

"Large 4to"   ViW

1839 The Holy Bible . . . With Canne's Marginal Notes and References . . . [Printed
by Jesper Harding]. Hogan & Thompson: Philadelphia   **1033**

1 vol: (576) (96) 579–743   29 cm   NN, NNAB

With Apocrypha. Brown's Concordance and Metrical Psalms at end.
Also issued with Index, etc. at end of text and paged to 768. Also with Apocrypha paged
to clxvii.

1839 The Holy Bible . . . Roby, Kimball & Merrill: Concord, N. H.   **1034**

29 cm   MBU–T

With Apocrypha; Family Record; illustrations.

1839 The Holy Bible . . . With Canne's Marginal Notes and References . . . Published and Sold by H. & E. Phinney: Cooperstown, N. Y. Also sold by I. Tiffany: Utica   **1035**

28 cm   NNAB, VtHi

Reprint of Phinney's 1824 quarto (No 485). With Apocrypha.
NCooHi has copy with woodcut frontispieces and 8 other woodcuts; no Apocrypha.

1839   The Holy Bible . . . [I. Ashmead & Co., Printers]. Published by McCarty and Davis: Philadelphia   *1036*

1 vol: (676) 836–1076   28 cm   NN

This is a continuation of the 1812/11 Carey edition (No 208). Apocrypha wanting? Has large woodcut frontispiece and 4 engravings. Lev 19:12 is incorrect.

1839   The Holy Bible . . . With Canne's Marginal Notes and References . . . The Text Corrected According to the Standard of the American Bible Society. Stereotyped by James Conner, New-York. Robinson & Franklin, Successors to Leavitt, Lord & Co.: New York   *1037*

28 cm   NN, NNAB

Reprint of 1835 Andrus and Judd edition (No 892) and of 1836 Judd, Loomis & Co. edition (No 926). With Apocrypha. Has Concordance, Tables, Metrical Psalms, etc.

1839   The Holy Bible . . . With Critical, Explanatory, and Practical Notes . . . by . . . Joseph Benson . . . T. Mason and G. Lane for the Methodist Episcopal Church: New York   *1038*

5 vols: Vol i, 953 p; Vol ii, 1155 p; Vol iii, 1088 p; Vol iv, 859 p; Vol v, 808 p   27 cm

Reprint of 1822–24 edition (No 435).   GEU

1839   The Holy Bible . . . Translated from the Latin Vulgat: with Annotations, References, and a Historical and Chronological Index. First Stereotype, from the Fifth Dublin Edition. Newly Revised and Corrected According to the Clementin Edition of the Scriptures . . . [Stereotyped by Eugene Cummiskey]. Published by Eugene Cummiskey: Philadelphia   *1039*

1 vol: (335) (444) (191)   "8vo"   Not Located

O'Callaghan, p 260. Rheims-Douay, from the 5th Dublin edition. Agrees with 1836 Cummiskey edition (No 936) but has Approbations of Archbishop Eccleston of Baltimore, Bishops Conwell and Kenrick of Philadelphia, and Dr. Hughes, coadjutor Bishop of New York. Has engraved title page. See also 1824 Bible, No 492.

1839   The Holy Bible . . . Printed by D. Fanshaw . . . Stereotyped by J. S. Redfield, for the American Bible Society, Instituted . . . : New-York   *1040*

1 vol: (939) (292)   24 cm   NNAB

Long Primer Octavo, the first printing of a new format. In 1839 this book sold for $2.25 in calf with gilt edges, $1.75 in embossed calf, and $1 in sheep. MS note on cover: "By advice of a special Committee, Dec. 1841, in view of the many inaccuracies of this ed. it was directed that the unbound sheets be destroyed." Corrections were made in the second edition, 1841.

1839   The Holy Bible . . . Published by Charles Lane: Sandbornton, N. H.   *1041*

Reported as 684 p   19 cm   NjMD

1839   The Holy Bible . . . London, 1611, imprinted by Robert Barker . . . John Gray, Printer . . . Stereotyped by White and Hagar, for the American and Foreign Bible Society: New York   *1042*

1 vol: (839) (252)   19 cm   NN, NNAB

Reprint of the 1611 AV in modern spelling. Verso of NT title has the list of words whose meaning has changed. See 1838, No 1007 and 1838 NT, No 1027.

1839   The Holy Bible . . . [Stereotyped by J. Howe, Philadelphia]. Robinson and
Franklin [Successors to Leavitt, Lord & Co.]: New York   *1043*

1 vol: (655) 656–660   "12mo"   Not Located
O'Callaghan, p 262. Has two frontispieces to OT with *Hartford, Andrus & Judd* at foot
of each.

1839   The Holy Bible . . . Stereotyped by J. Howe, Philadelphia . . . Andrus, Judd &
Franklin: Hartford   *1044*

655 p   "12mo"   Not Located
O'Callaghan, p 262. Has several woodcuts.

1839   The Holy Bible . . . With References and Marginal Readings of the Polyglott
Bible, with Numerous Additions from Bagster's Comprehensive Bible . . .
[C. Sherman & Co., Printers]. Published by Robert P. Desilver: Philadelphia
1045

Reported as (937) 939–982   "12mo"   NRU
With Metrical Psalms at end. Copyright 1833.

1839   The Holy Bible . . . With Marginal Readings and References . . . J. Collord,
Printer. Published by T. Mason and G. Lane, for the Methodist Episcopal
Church: New-York   *1046*

1 vol: (786) 787–804 (245) 246–249   15 cm   NNAB
Table of Names follows OT. NT has frontispiece, engraved title page, and general title
page. Tables at end.

1839   The Holy Bible . . . Armstrong and Berry: Baltimore   *1047*

1 vol: (1018) (328)   15 cm   NN
Table of Contents at end of each Testament.
Wright (p 398) lists separate NT for this year.

1839   The Holy Bible . . . [Stereotype Edition]. E. Hunt & Co.: Middletown, Conn.
1048

1 vol: (824) (251)   15 cm   NN

1839   The English Version of the Polyglott Bible . . . Together with a Copious and
Original Selection of References to Parrallel and Illustrative Passages. Ex-
hibited in a Manner Hitherto Unattempted. Stereotyped by L. Johnson . . .
Thomas, Cowperthwait & Co.: Philadelphia   *1049*

1 vol: (viii) (587) (190)   15 cm   NNAB
Has frontispiece and Preface signed T. C.   Engravings precede both Testaments.

1839/36   The English Version of the Polyglott Bible, containing the Old and New
Testaments; with the Marginal Readings . . . Stereotyped by Henry Wallis
and L. Roby: Concord, N. H.   Published by Roby, Kimball, and Merrill:
Concord, N. H.   *1050*

Reported as (viii) (587) (190)   15 cm   MBU–T
Has added engraved title and plates before each Testament. NT dated 1836.

1839   The Holy Bible . . . Stereotype Edition. Brattleboro' Typographic Company:
Brattleboro, Vt.   *1051*

1 vol: (824) (251)   14 cm   NNAB
Has frontispiece and engraved title page with imprint *Brattleboro Bible Company.* Stereotyped by Boston Type and Stereotype Foundry.

1839   The Holy Bible . . . Stereotyped by Henry Wallis & Luther Roby . . . Concord,
N. H. [N. A. Foster, Printer] Published by O. L. Sanborn: Portland [Maine]
1052

11 cm   NNAB
Reprint of 1834 Hoag edition (No 879). Frontispiece and added engraved title precede
text.

1839   The Holy Bible . . . Robinson & Franklin, Successors to Leavitt, Lord & Co.:
New York   *1053*

Reported as (852) (259)   "32mo"   DLC
Frontispiece; Contents at end; illustrated.

1839   The Holy Bible . . . Geo. Townsend . . . : Boston   *1054*

No publisher or other information available. Not found at ViW 1960.   ViW

1839   The Old Testament, Arranged in Historical and Chronological Order, on
the basis of Lightfoot's Chronicle, in such a Manner, that the Books, Chapters . . . &c. May be Read as One Connected History, in the Words of the
Authorized Translation. With Notes and Copious Indexes. By the Rev. G.
Townsend. Revised, punctuated . . . a Choice and Copious Selection of References Given, &c. by the Rev. T. W. Coit. Published by Perkins & Marvin:
Boston; Henry Perkins: Philadelphia   *1055*

27 cm   NNAB
Reprint of 1838 OT (No 1022) but with new title page. See also 1837 NT, No 985.

1839   The Family Expositor; or, A paraphrase and version of the New Testament
. . . By Philip Doddridge, D.D. American edition. With a memoir of the
author by N. W. Fiske . . . an introduction by Moses Stuart . . . With a portrait
. . . Twelfth edition. Published by Charles McFarland: Amherst, Mass. *1056*

Reported as (xx) 17–998 (6)   27 cm   MWA, NCH
Doddridge Version; see 1807–08, No 147. Frontispiece and plates. Stereotyped at the
Boston Type and Stereotype Foundry appears on verso of page following 998.
ArCH and GMM have thirteenth edition, 1839.

1839   The New Testament . . . Stereotyped, Printed and Published by H. & E.
Phinney: Cooperstown, N. Y.   *1057*

"4to"   Not Located
O'Callaghan, p 263. Has frontispiece and 4 woodcuts.

1839   The Sacred Writings of the Apostles and Evangelists of Jesus Christ, Commonly Styled the New Testament. Translated from the Original Greek by
Doctors George Campbell, James Macknight, and Philip Doddridge, with

Prefaces, Various Emendations, and an Appendix, by Alexander Campbell. Sixth Edition . . . Forrester & Campbell: Pittsburgh **1058**

Reported as (424) (80)   23 cm   DLC, KBB, OC, PPiU

Alexander Campbell Version; see 1826 NT, No 567.

This is a reprint of the 1835 edition (No 915) and the last published under Campbell's supervision. In 1842 Campbell reported that 35,000 copies of his NT had been sold and 5,000 given away.

1839 Explanatory Notes upon the New Testament by John Wesley, M.A. . . . J. Collord, Printer. Published by T. Mason and G. Lane for the Methodist Episcopal Church, at the Conference Office, 200 Mulberry-Street: New York   **1059**

Reported as 734 p   23 cm   NjMD

Wesley Version; see 1791 NT, No 35.

1839 The New Testament . . . Stereotyped by B. and J. Collins, New-York. Robinson and Franklin, Successors to Leavitt, Lord and Co.: New York   **1060**

312 p   23 cm   NNAB

1839 The New Testament in the Common Version, With Amendments of the Language, by Noah Webster, LL.D. . . . [Stereotyped by J. S. Redfield]. Published by S. Babcock: New Haven   **1061**

267 [1] p   20 cm   CtY, MB, NN, NNAB

Webster Version; see 1833, No 826. New format has Order of Books before text and Testimonials at end; no references or notes. Error in I Tim 4:16 is continued. Copyright 1833 by Noah Webster.

O'Callaghan (p 268) lists an 1840 NT in the Lenox Collection but this must refer to the above edition which is dated 1840 on the cover.

Also issued with two front fly leaves with "specimens of the emendations of language. . . ." A notice about the adoption of the text in the city schools in New Haven appeared in the New Haven *Daily Herald*, May 19, 1840.

1839 The New Testament . . . S. Colman: New York   **1062**

447 p   "12mo"   Not Located

O'Callaghan, p 264.

1839 The New Testament . . . Printed by D. Fanshaw . . . Stereotyped by J. S. Redfield for the American Bible Society, Instituted . . . : New-York   **1063**

371 p   17 cm   NNAB

First edition of a new format.

1839 The New Testament . . . Bible Society of Philadelphia: [Philadelphia]   **1064**

416 p   12 cm   NNAB

1839 [Polyglott Testament] The New Testament . . . With Marginal References to Parallel Passages: . . . [Stereotyped by Conner & Cooke, New York] J. & J. W. Prentiss: Keene, N. H.   **1065**

422 p   12 cm   NN

Has added engraved title. Copyright 1833.

1839   The New Testament . . . [Stereotyped by L. Roby]. Roby, Kimball, and Merrill: Concord, N. H.   *1066*

254 p   12 cm   MB, NN

1839   The New Testament . . . Haswell, Barrington & Haswell: Philadelphia *1067*

318 p   "24mo"   Not Located
O'Callaghan, p 264.

1839   The Polymicrian Testament. H. Perkins: Philadelphia; Perkins and Marvin: Boston   *1068*

"32mo"   Not Located
Wright, p 398.

1840   The Holy Bible . . . With Canne's Marginal Notes and References . . . Published by Roby, Kimball, and Merrill: Concord, N. H.   *1069*

1 vol: (574) (96) 579–768 (31) (5)   30 cm   NNAB
Preliminary matter includes Order of Books, engraved title page, frontispiece, To the Reader [Dr. Witherspoon], Contents, and Chart. Tables, Apocrypha, and Family Record follow OT. Verso of NT title has Account of Time of Writing NT Books. Index, Account of the Holy Land, Tables, and Concordance at end. Illustrated.

184–   The Holy Bible . . . together with the Apocrypha . . . to which is appended, A Concordance, the Psalms of David in Metre, an Index, Tables, and other Useful Matters. The Text conformable to the Standard of the American Bible Society. Hollowbush & Carey, Publishers, 218 Market Street: Philadelphia   *1070*

29 cm   PHi
PHi has title page only (in drawer with detached family Bible records, in folder marked "Brown Bible Record"). There is an 1843 date in an older hand than the later entries. Possibly 1840–50.

1840   The Holy Bible . . . with Canne's Marginal notes and references . . . Published and sold by H. & E. Phinney: Cooperstown, N. Y. . . . Sold also by I. Tiffany: Utica   *1071*

Reported as (576) (99) 577–768   28 cm   NCooHi
With Apocrypha. Has two woodcut frontispieces and one other woodcut.

1840/39   The Holy Bible . . . With Canne's Marginal Notes and References . . . Published and Sold by H. & E. Phinney: Cooperstown, N. Y.   *1072*

28 cm   NN
Reprint of Phinney quarto of 1824 (No 485). With Apocrypha and Concordance. Illustrated. NT title imprinted *Stereotyped, Printed and Published by H. & E. Phinney . . . 1839.*

1840   The Comprehensive Commentary on the Holy Bible; Containing the Text According to the Authorized Version . . . Matthew Henry's Commentary, Condensed . . . Edited by Rev. William Jenks . . . Published by the Brattleboro Typographical Company: Brattleboro, Vt.   *1073*

27 cm   IaDuU, MBC, OSW
See 1834–38 Bible, No 860; also 1835–38 Bible, No 894.

1840   The English Version of the Polyglot Bible . . . With Marginal Readings . . . A
Critical Introduction . . . by Rev. Joseph A. Warne . . . Brattleborough Typographic Company: Brattleborough   **1074**

   1 vol: (vi) (82) (68) (705) (216) (63) (84)   27 cm   Not Located
   Wright, p 399. Illustrated. See 1834, No 863.

1840   The Polyglot Bible . . . Charles Gaylord & William O. Blake: Boston   **1075**
   "4to"   Not Located
   Wright, p 399.

1840?   The Holy Bible . . . Stereotyped by L. Johnson, Philadelphia. Ed. Barrington and Geo. D. Haswell: Philadelphia   **1076**

   26 cm   NNAB
   Reprint of 1838 edition (No 1010) except with Apocrypha (120 p) and Concordance
(85 p). Editions of 1838 and 1839 carry the firm name as Haswell, Barrington and Haswell.
This is assumed to be a later edition.

1840   The Holy Bible . . . Munroe and Francis: Boston   **1077**
   1 vol: (687) (212) (xii)   24 cm   NN
   Has frontispiece.

1840   The Holy Bible . . . Translated from the Latin Vulgat: With Annotations,
References, and a Historical and Chronological Index. First Stereotype from
the Fifth Dublin Edition . . . [Stereotyped by J. Howe]. Published by Eugene Cummiskey: Philadelphia   **1078**

   23 cm   CSmH, DGU, NN, NNAB, ViLxW
   Rheims-Douay, from the 5th Dublin edition. Reprint of 1836 Bible (No 935).

1840   The Holy Bible . . . Stereotype Edition. Stereotyped by T. Rutt, London, for
the Pennsylvania Bible Society: [Philadelphia]   **1079**

   23 cm   PSt

1840   The Holy Bible . . . Joseph McDowell: Philadelphia   **1080**
   "12mo"   Not Located
   Wright, p 399.

1840   The Polyglott Family Bible . . . With Marginal Readings and References,
and Parallel Passages . . . J. and J. W. Prentiss: Keene, N. H.   **1081**

   "12mo"   Not Located
   O'Callaghan, p 266.

1840   The Holy Bible . . . Hogan & Thompson: Philadelphia   **1082**
   1 vol: (1096) (342)   "12mo"   Not Located
   O'Callaghan, p 265.

1840   The Holy Bible . . . Printed by D. Fanshaw. Stereotyped by Richard C. Valentine, for the American Bible Society, Instituted . . . : New-York   **1083**

1 vol: (805) (250)   16 cm   NNAB
   Pearl Reference 18mo, first edition. Has double center reference columns with chronology, and chapter summaries. Published to meet a frequent demand for a small Bible-class and Sunday-school Bible and sold at $1.75 in morocco, $1.12½ in calf, or 62½¢ in sheep.

1840   The English Version of the Polyglott Bible . . . With Marginal Readings . . . Together with a Copious and Original Selection of References to Parallel and Illustrative Passages. Exhibited in a Manner Hitherto Unattempted . . . Published by G. & C. Merriam: Springfield   **1084**

1 vol: (856) (259)   12 cm   NN
   Text corresponds with that of Chase's Woodstock edition of 1836 (No 947). Headings on p 212 and 213 are transposed. Has two engraved titles and a few etchings.

1840   The New Testament, Arranged in Historical and Chronological Order; with Copious Notes on the Principal Subjects in Theology; the Gospels on the Basis of the Harmonies of Lightfoot, Doddridge and others . . . The Account of the Resurrection on the Authorities of West, Townson, and Cranfield; The Epistles are Inserted in Their Places, and Divided According to the Apostles' Arguments. By the Rev. George Townsend . . . The Whole Revised . . . by the Rev. T. W. Coit . . . Perkins and Marvin: Boston; H. Perkins: Philadelphia
                                                                     1085

27 cm   DLC, MdBP
   Reprint of Perkins & Marvin 1837 edition (No 985).

1840   The New Testament . . . Stereotype Edition. Stereotyped by T. Rutt, Shacklewell, London, for the Pennsylvania Bible Society: [Philadelphia]   **1086**
303 [1] p   23 cm   NNAB

1840   The New Testament . . . Translated from the Latin Vulgate . . . First Published by the English College at Rheims, A. D. 1582. With Annotations, References, and an Historical and Chronological Index. From the last London and Dublin Edition. Published with the Approbation of the Right Rev. Francis Patrick Kenrick, and the Right Rev. J. Hughes . . . [Stereotyped by L. Johnson]. Eugene Cummiskey: Philadelphia   **1087**

429 p   20 cm   DGU, NjMD, NN
   Rheims Version, from Murray's 1825 Dublin edition. O'Callaghan (p 266) says the edition consisted of 2750 copies, some with Cummiskey's Advertisement of Catholic Publications at end (3 p). Approbations dated October 1, 1839.

1840   The New Testament . . . G. W. Mentz and Son: Philadelphia   **1088**
Reported at 240 p   20 cm   PHi
   Has engraving on title page signed "Gilbert."

1840?   The New Testament . . . John F. Brown: Concord, N. H.   **1089**
Reported as 310 p   19 cm   MB
   NhHi can supply no additional data about J. F. Brown except that he was active in local politics in 1853 and 1862 and quotes from Bouton's *History of Concord* (p 490, Sept 27, 1851):

"Mr. John F. Brown, of this town, the well known book-seller and publisher presented us on Wednesday with an apple raised by himself. . . ." See 1840 NT, No 1099.

1840   The New Testament . . . Translated from the Latin Vulgate . . . With Annotations to clear up the Principal Difficulties of Holy Writ, as Approved by the Right Reverend John Dubois, Catholic Bishop of New York. Stereotype Edition . . . Printed by Thomas Davis, for the Proprietors: Utica   *1090*

1 vol: (xii) (3) (344)   18 cm   DGU, NN
Rheims Version.
This is the 1829 Devereux Testament (No 686) with a new title page but without the certificate of copyright. The error in James 5:17 is continued.

1840   The New Testament . . . Stereotype Edition . . . Published by John G. Tilton: Newburyport   *1091*

450 p   18 cm   NN

1840   Polyglott School Testament. The New Testament . . . With the Marginal Readings, Compendious Annotations, and Copious References to Parallel and Illustrative Passages . . . [Stereotyped by Conner and Cooke]. J. & J. W. Prentiss: Keene, N. H.   *1092*

422 p   17 cm   NN, NNAB
Text in single column. Copyright 1833.
NN copy has headline *Polyglott Family Testament.*

1840   The New Testament . . . Stereotyped for the Bible Society of Philadelphia: [Philadelphia]   *1093*

352 p   16 cm   NNAB

1840   The New Testament . . . Wm. S. Young: Philadelphia   *1094*

259 p   15 cm   NN
P 181–192 are omitted and p 133–144 repeated.

1840   The New Testament . . . : Middletown [Connecticut]   *1095*

"24mo"   Not Located
Listed in Union Catalog, but no further information given.

184–   The New Testament . . . [Stereotyped by Richard C. Valentine]. S. Andrus & Son: Hartford   *1096*

344 p   12 cm   NN
Has engraved title page and illustrations.

1840   [The Polyglott Reference Testament] The New Testament . . . With the References and Marginal Readings of the Polyglott Bible . . . G. Wells: New York   *1097*

742 p   12 cm   NN
Table precedes text. Illustrated.

1840 The Polymicrian Testament. H. Perkins: Philadelphia; Perkins & Marvin: Boston   *1098*

"32mo"   Not Located
Wright, p 399.

1840 The New Testament . . . [Stereotyped by Jacob Perkins, Concord, N. H.]. Published by John F. Brown: Concord, N. H.   *1099*

383 p   MiU
See 1840? NT, No 1089.

1841 The Holy Bible . . . With Canne's Marginal Notes and References . . . Published and Sold by H. & E. Phinney: Cooperstown, N. Y. . . . and sold by I. Tiffany: Utica   *1100*

1 vol: (576) (99) 577–768   29 cm   NNAB
Reprint of 1822 Phinney quarto (No 439) but with Apocrypha. Has two frontispieces and 6 other woodcuts.

1841 The Holy Bible . . . with Canne's Marginal References. Together with the Apocrypha and Concordance. To which are Added, an Index, a Table of Texts, and What has Never Before been Added, An Account of the Lives and Martyrdom of the Apostles and Evangelists . . . The Text Corrected According to the Standard of the American Bible Society. Stereotyped by James Conner, New-York . . . Published by P. Canfield: Hartford   *1101*

1 vol: (527) (78) (168) (10) (6) (53) (19) (4)   29 cm   NNAB
Preliminary matter includes To the Reader [Dr. Witherspoon], Advertisement, and List of Books. Has Metrical Psalms and Family Record. Several engravings.

1841 The English Version of the Polyglott Bible . . . critical introduction by Joseph Warne . . . essay by James Macknight . . . Sermon by Philip Doddridge . . . Concordance . . . Index . . . engravings . . . The Brattleboro' Typographic Company: Brattleboro', Vt.   *1102*

Reported as (vi) (82) (20) 7–705 (54) (216) (46) (63) (84) 849–850 (2)   28 cm
                                                                          NNAB, VtHi
Has engraved and illustrated title page. Order of books, Introduction, tables and chronology, contents, and 20 plates lettered A–T and 24 other plates precede text. After OT, History from OT to NT, Evidences of Christianity (Doddridge), Introduction and Family Record. At end, Geographical and Historical Index, Index and Dictionary, Brown's Concordance, 1 leaf on geography, and 1 leaf of publisher's advertisement.

1841 The Cottage Bible, and Family Expositor . . . With Practical Expositions and Explanatory Notes. By Thomas Williams . . . References and Marginal Readings of the Polyglott Bible . . . Notes . . . from Bagster's Comprehensive Bible . . . The Whole Carefully Revised, and Adapted to the Use of Sunday Schools . . . Edited by Rev. William Patton . . . Complete in Two Volumes . . . [Stereotyped by Conner & Cooke]. Printed and Published by Case, Tiffany and Burnham: Hartford   *1103*

2 vols: 994 p   27 cm   NNAB
Printed from Conner & Cooke plates of 1833 Cottage Bible (No 818). Has new title page and some different engravings. Volumes paged continuously. Copyright 1833, by James Conner and William R. Cooke. Preface dated 1834.

1841   The Holy Bible . . . The References and Marginal Readings of the Polyglott Bible, with Numerous Additions from Bagster's Comprehensive Bible . . . [Stereotyped by Conner & Cooke]. Robinson, Pratt & Co.: New-York   *1104*

1 vol: (40) (580) 585–772   27 cm   NNAB

Reprint of Gaylord's 1835 edition (No 897). Has frontispiece to each Testament, Introduction, Introductory and Concluding Remarks to each Book. Chronological Index at end. Copyright 1833, by James Conner and William R. Cooke.

1841   The Holy Bible . . . With the References and Marginal Readings of the Polyglott Bible, and Numerous Additions from Bagster's Comprehensive Bible . . . Thomas, Cowperthwait & Co.: Philadelphia   *1105*

982 p   23 cm   NN

With Metrical Psalms. Illustrated.

1841   The Holy Bible . . . With Introductory and Concluding Remarks to Each Book . . . and the References and Marginal Readings of the Polyglott Bible, with Numerous Additions from Bagster's Comprehensive Bible . . . [Stereotyped by Conner & Cooke]. Robinson, Pratt & Co.: New York   *1106*

23 cm   NNAB

Seems to be reprint of the Andrus and Judd Annual of 1834 (No 868) but without Concordance. Frontispieces to both Testaments, Advertisement, and Introductory and Concluding Remarks to each book precede text. Chronological Index at end.

1841   The Holy Bible . . . Munroe and Francis: Boston   *1107*

1 vol: (687) (212)   "8vo"   Not Located

NT has undated imprint of Nathan Hale.

Union Catalog locates a copy at NN but book could not be found, 1959. O'Callaghan (p 268) lists an octavo by Munroe & Francis, Hilliard, Gray & Co., and Crocker & Brewster, with NT imprinted Mathew Hale . . . and Alex. Price. See 1840, No 1077.

1841   The Holy Bible . . . Stereotype Edition . . . Published by H. & E. Phinney: Cooperstown, N. Y.   *1108*

1 vol: (486) (162)   22 cm   NN

Has frontispiece to each Testament. Family Record follows OT. Tables on verso of NT title.

O'Callaghan (p 268) says the total number printed of this Bible was 2,000.

1841   The Holy Bible . . . [Stereotyped by A. Chandler]. William Andrus: Hartford   *1109*

1 vol: (824) (251) (70)   "12mo"   Not Located

O'Callaghan, p 269. Has frontispiece and engraved title to each Testament. Metrical Psalms.

1841   The Holy Bible . . . Stereotyped by D. & G. Bruce, New York . . . William Andrus: Hartford   *1110*

"12mo"   Not Located

O'Callaghan, p 269. Same as 1827 Smith edition (No 587). Has two engraved frontispieces.

1841   The English Version of the Polyglott Bible . . . Together with a Copious and Original Selection of References to Parallel and Illustrative Passages. Ex-

hibited in a manner Hitherto Unattempted. Stereotyped by L. Johnson.
Thomas, Cowperthwait & Co.: Philadelphia   *1111*

15 cm   NNAB

Appears to be from L. Johnson plates of Key & Meilke edition of 1831 (No 753), also
published in 1832 (No 790) and by Desilver in 1834 (No 874), 1835 (No 909), and 1836
(No 943). Has frontispiece and added engraved title to each Testament. Preface signed T. C.

1841   The Holy Bible . . . With Amendments of Language by Noah Webster . . .
         [Stereotyped at the Boston Type and Stereotype Foundry]. Published by
         N. Webster: New Haven   *1112*

1 vol: (852) (260)   13 cm   CtY, DLC, MB, MWA, NcAs, NN, OC

Webster Version; see 1833, No 826. There are minor changes in the Introduction. Tables
of Names on p 257–260.

NN copy has "Given by Noah Webster to his daughter Louisa Webster, New Haven,
May 4, 1842."

CtHT–W, MWA, and OC have separate NT.

1841   The Holy Bible . . . Thomas, Cowperthwait & Co.: Philadelphia   *1113*

Reported as (852) (263)   12 cm   MiU

1841   The Holy Bible . . . W. & H. Merriam: Greenfield, Mass.   *1114*

1 vol: (725) (220)   12 cm   NN

Illustrated.

1841   [The Holy Bible] The New Testament . . . William Andrus: Hartford   *1115*

1 vol: (852) (259) [1]   12 cm   NNAB

General title page missing from cited copy; above taken from NT title. Has two frontispieces to each Testament. Error in Prov 6:6, Go to the *aunt,* for Go to the *ant.*

1841/40   The Holy Bible . . . Hogan and Thompson: Philadelphia   *1116*

11 cm   NNAB

Similar to 1832 Towar and Hogan & Thompson edition (No 794). Frontispiece and added
engraved title dated 1834. Metrical Psalms at end. NT dated 1840.

1841   The Holy Bible . . . Stereotyped by Henry Wallis & Luther Roby, Concord,
         N. H. . . . [N. A. Foster, Printer]. Sanborn, Sherburne & Co.: Portland   *1117*

11 cm   NNAB

Appears to be reprint of 1834 Hoag edition (No 879), also published by Sanborn in 1839
(No 1052). Has frontispiece and added engraved title page.

1841   The New Testament . . . [Stereotyped by J. Fagan. Printed by T. K. and P. G.
         Collins, Philadelphia]. Grigg & Elliot: Philadelphia   *1118*

240 p   24 cm   NNAB

1841   The New Testament . . . Translated from the Latin Vulgate . . . Published by
         Eugene Cummiskey: Philadelphia   *1119*

"8vo"   Not Located

Rheims Version. O'Callaghan (p 269) says an edition of 2,000 copies was published.

1841   The New Testament . . . Roby, Kimball & Merrell: Concord, N. H.   *1120*

807 p   "12mo"   Not Located

O'Callaghan, p 269. The pagination seems too much for an NT but it does not match that of any Bible by this publisher. *Merrell* should probably be *Merrill*.

1841   The New Testament . . . Stereotyped by B. & J. Collins: New York. Benjamin
          Adams: Boston   *1121*

290 p   20 cm   NN
Table precedes text.

1841   The New Testament . . . Stereotype Edition. [Printed by King Baird] Pub-
          lished by Crolius & Gladding: Philadelphia   *1122*

453 p   19 cm   NN
Table at end.

1841   The New Testament . . . Stereotyped by James Conner, New York . . . J. W.
          Ely: Cincinnati   *1123*

Reported as 226 p   16 cm   OC

1841   The New Testament . . . H. & E. Phinney: Cooperstown   *1124*

Reported as 454 p   9 cm   NCooHi
Has preliminary title page and frontispiece.

1841   The Polymicrian Testament . . . H. Perkins: Philadelphia; Ives & Dennet:
          Boston   *1125*

"32mo"   Not Located
Wright, p 399.

1842   The Holy Bible . . . Stereotyped by James Conner, New York . . . Printed and
          Published by Silas Andrus: Hartford   *1126*

"folio"   Not Located
O'Callaghan, p 270.

1842   The Holy Bible . . . With Canne's Marginal Notes and References . . . E. Mor-
          gan and Co.: Cincinnati   *1127*

Reported as (4) (6) (570) (112) 573–770   30 cm   DLC
With Apocrypha. Has frontispiece. Index, Tables, etc. at end. Illustrated.

1842   The Holy Bible . . . With Canne's Marginal References. Together with the
          Apocrypha and Concordance. To which are Added an Index, A Table of
          Texts, and What has Never Before Been Added, An Account of the Lives
          and Martyrdom of the Apostles and Evangelists . . . The Text Corrected Ac-
          cording to the Standard of the American Bible Society. Stereotyped by James
          Conner, New York . . . Published by William Andrus: Hartford   *1128*

30 cm   NNAB
Reprint of 1836 Judd, Loomis & Co. edition (No 926).

1842   The Holy Bible . . . With Canne's Marginal Notes and References . . . J. Harding, Printer. Published by Jesper Harding: Philadelphia   **1129**

    1 vol: (8) 9–574 579–754 755–768   29 cm   NNAB
    Has To the Reader [by Dr. Witherspoon from Collins' Bible] and Contents of Books. Tables
follow OT. At end are Index, Tables, etc.

1842   The Holy Bible . . . With Canne's Marginal Notes and References . . . [H. &
E. Phinney's Stereotype Edition]. Published and Sold by H. & E. Phinney:
Cooperstown, N. Y.   **1130**

    "4to"   MWA
    Reprint of 1824 Phinney quarto (No 485), with Apocrypha. Illustrated.
Privately owned copy imprinted *I. Tiffany, Utica.*

1842   The Comprehensive Commentary on the Holy Bible . . . Scott's Marginal
References; Matthew Henry's Commentary, Condensed . . . the Practical Observations of Rev. Thomas Scott . . . with Extensive Explanatory, Critical,
and Philological notes, Selected from Scott, Doddridge, Gill, Adam Clarke
. . . and many other Writers . . . Edited by William Jenks . . . Brattleboro
Typographic Co.: Brattleboro, Vt.   **1131**

    28 cm   WaPS
    See 1835–38 Bible, No 894.

1842   The Holy Bible . . . Apocrypha . . . marginal notes and references . . . Index
. . . Tables . . . Embellished with maps and historical engravings. I. Ashmead
& Co., Printers. William M'Carty: Philadelphia   **1132**

    1 vol: (4) (674) 675–676 682–834 (4) 835–1046 1047–1076 (24) (72)   28 cm
                                                                              NNAB
    Unpaged Family Record appears before NT. Has usual material in M'Carty and Davis
editions at end; also Metrical Psalms and Brown's Concordance. 16 Anderson engravings, new
series, in ornamental frames.

1842   The Cottage Bible, and Family Expositor . . . with Practical Expositions and
Explanatory Notes. By Thomas Williams. . . . The References and Marginal
Readings of the Polyglott Bible, Together with Original Notes. . . . Bagster's
Comprehensive Bible, and other Standard Works . . . The Whole Carefully
Revised . . . Edited by Rev. William Patton . . . Complete in Two Volumes
. . . [Stereotyped by Conner & Cooke]. Printed and Published by Case, Tif-
fany & Burnham: Hartford   **1133**

    28 cm   NNAB
    Reprint from Conner and Cooke plates of the 1833 Cottage Bible (No 818). Copyright 1833,
by James Conner and William R. Cooke.
    NNAB has Vol I only.

1842   The Holy Bible; Being the English Version of the Old and New Testaments,
Made by Order of King James I. Carefully Revised and Amended, the mean-
ing of the sacred original being given, in accordance with the best transla-
tions and the most approved Hebrew and Greek lexicographers: By Several
Biblical Scholars . . . Stereotyped by L. Johnson. [Kay and Brothers, Printers]
Published for David Bernard, by J. B. Lippincott: Philadelphia   **1134**

    1 vol: (iv) (629) 630–632 (4) (iii) (192)   28 cm   NN, NNAB

Preface signed The Proprietor, 1842, precedes text. Tables and Family Record follow OT. NT has Preface by A. C. Kendrick. Index of Names and Places at end. References arranged in double center column. Reference columns in OT also contain readings of the AV displaced by this edition. Copyright by David Bernard 1842.

The signer of the Preface, The Proprietor, no doubt refers to David Bernard. No clue is given to the translators of the OT. However, Dr. Simms (p 249) notes that Dr. George Ripley Bliss was among them. The Preface sets forth the purpose of the translation as an attempt to achieve uniformity of spelling and rendering, to correct the grammar, and to change such terms as are indelicate, antiquated or left untranslated in the AV. The NT, an "immersion" version, was translated by Dr. A. C. Kendrick, a Baptist scholar of Greek language and literature. The edition is apparently based on the Greek OT of John Pearson and on the Greek NT editions of Buck (1632) and Field (1665), as well as the AV. A second edition was also published this year.

1842   The Holy Bible . . . The References and Marginal Readings of the Polyglott Bible, with Numerous Additions from Bagster's Comprehensive Bible . . . Robinson, Pratt & Co.: New-York   **1135**

Reported as (40) 3–773   27 cm   CSmH
Has frontispiece.

1842   The Holy Bible . . . Printed by D. Fanshaw for the American Bible Society . . . : New York   **1136**

1 vol: (968) (303)   24 cm   NNAB
Small Pica Octavo, first edition. Has Family Record (4 p) between Testaments. Tables appear on verso of NT title. Priced in 1842 at $1 in sheep.

1842   The Holy Bible . . . According to the Commonly Received Version. London, 1611: Imprinted by Robert Barker . . . American and Foreign Bible Society: New York   **1137**

2 vols   19 cm   ICU
Third edition. See 1838, No 1007; also 1839, No 1042.

1842   The Holy Bible . . . Stereotyped by J. Howe, Philadelphia . . . Published by William Andrus: Hartford   **1138**

1 vol: (655) 658–681   "12mo"   Not Located
O'Callaghan, p 271. Contents at end. Has plates (2 per page) and map of Cannaan.

1842   The English Version of the Polyglott Bible . . . The Marginal Readings: Together with a Copious and Original Selection of References to Parallel and Illustrative Passages . . . Stereotyped by L. Johnson . . . Thomas, Cowperthwait & Co.: Philadelphia   **1139**

15 cm   NNAB
Reprint of 1839 edition (No 1049) with similar engraved frontispiece and titles.

1842   The Holy Bible . . . Stereotyped by J. Howe, Philadelphia . . . Published by William Andrus: Hartford   **1140**

1 vol: (615) (192)   "24mo" or "32mo"   Not Located
O'Callaghan, p 271. Has engraved frontispiece and illustrations. The text is in double columns, but in paragraphs.

1842   The Holy Bible . . . Stereotype Edition. Published by William Andrus: Hartford   *1141*

1 vol: (824) (251)   14 cm   NN
Illustrated.

1842   The Holy Bible . . . Stereotyped by J. Howe, Philad . . . R. W. Pomeroy: Philadelphia   *1142*

1 vol: (819) (256) (83)   "32mo"   Not Located
O'Callaghan, p 271. Has frontispiece. Added engraved title with imprint *Hogan & Thompson . . . 1834*. Metrical Psalms at end.

1842   The Holy Bible . . . John Locken: Philadelphia   *1143*

"32mo"   Not Located
O'Callaghan, p 271. Has frontispiece and added engraved title with *The Everlasting Gospel*.

1842   The Holy Bible . . . Sanborn and Carter: Portland   *1144*

Reported as (852) (259)   "32mo"   MBU–T
Added engraved title has *The Everlasting Gospel*.

1842   The Holy Bible . . . Published by W. & H. Merriam: Greenfield, Mass. *1145*

1 vol: (725) (220)   12 cm   NN
Has engraved frontispiece and added engraved title with *The Diamond Bible*. NT also has engraved frontispiece and added engraved title with *Diamond New Testament*. Illustrated.

1842   The English Version of the Polyglott Bible . . . With Marginal Readings . . . References to Parallel Passages. Exhibited in a Manner Hitherto Unattempted . . . G. & C. Merriam: Springfield, Mass.   *1146*

1 vol: (856) (259) (76)   12 cm   NN
Has added engraved title page and illustrations.

1842?   The New Testament . . . Stereotyped by B. & J. Collins, New York . . . Published by Kimber & Sharpless: Philadelphia   *1147*

1 vol: (265) (15)   "4to"   Not Located
O'Callaphan, p 272. Has added engraved title. Metrical Psalms at end. Illustrated.

1842   Practical Observations on the New Testament. By the Rev. T. Scott . . . Arranged for Family Worship, with an Introduction, by A. Alexander . . . I. Ashmead & Co.: Philadelphia   *1148*

Reported as (xii) (532)   "4to"   DLC
Scott's Annotated Bible; see 1804–09, No 113. Has Recommendations to This Edition. Illustrated.

1842   The New Testament . . . With Brief Explanatory Notes. By Jacob Abbott & John S. C. Abbott. First Edition. Stereotyped by the Boston Type and Stereotype Co. . . . Published by Crocker and Brewster: Boston   *1149*

Reported as 586 p   20 cm   MB

1842 The New Testament ... Stereotype Edition. Griffith & Simon: [Philadelphia]
1150

453 [1] p   19 cm   NNAB
Has Tables at end.
O'Callaghan (p 272) lists a copy with printer on verso of title page, King & Baird ... Phila-
delphia, but it is not on NNAB copy.

1842 The New Testament ... Translated out of the Latin Vulgate. With Annota-
tions to Clear up the Principal Difficulties of Holy Writ. As Approved by the
Right Reverend John Dubois, Catholic Bishop of New York ... Stereotype
Edition ... D. & J. Sadlier: New York   *1151*

Reported as (xii) 13–344   18 cm   DGU, WBB
Rheims Version, from Coyne's 1820 Dublin edition. This is Sadlier's first NT from the
"Devereux" plates purchased from Williams. The original approbation by Bishop Dubois
appears on the verso of the title page.

1842 The New Testament ... [Stereotyped by J. Howe, New York]. B. Olds: Newark   *1152*

288 p   18 cm   NN
Has added engraved title.

1842 The New Testament ... Stereotyped by J. Howe, Philadelphia ... Published
by Charles Scott: Trenton   *1153*

Reported as 240 p   17 cm   NjT

1842 The New Testament ... Published by O. O. Wickham: Sagharbor, L. I. [New
York]   *1154*

Reported as 288 p   16 cm   N, NNQ

1842 The New Testament ... Stereotype Edition ... Bible Association of Friends
in America: Philadelphia   *1155*

Reported as 342 p   16 cm   PHC

1842 The New Testament ... [Stereotyped by Morrill, Silsby, & Co., Concord,
N. H.]. Peabody & Daniel: Franklin, N. H.   *1156*

368 p   15 cm   NNAB

1842 The New Testament ... [Stereotyped by R. C. Valentine]. N. Leonard: Lock-
port, N. Y.   *1157*

344 p   13 cm   NNAB

1842 New Testament ... Published by Benjamin Olds: Newark   *1158*

344 p   12 cm   NNAB

1842 The New Testament ... [Stereotyped by Richard C. Valentine]. W. Andrus:
Hartford   *1159*

453 p   9 cm   NN

1843   The Holy Bible ... With Canne's Marginal Notes and References ... Stereo-
         typed by James Conner, New York ... Printed and Published by Silas An-
         drus: Hartford   *1160*

40 cm   NN

Reprint of 1829 edition (No 666). With Apocrypha. Engraved frontispiece to each Testament. Preliminary matter includes Account of the Lives of the Apostles and Evangelists.

1843–46   The Illuminated Bible ... With Marginal Readings, References, and
            Chronological Tables ... Apocrypha ... Embellished with Sixteen Hundred
            Historical Engravings by J. A. Adams, more than Fourteen Hundred of
            Which are from Original Designs by J. B. Chapman ... Harper & Brothers,
            Publishers: New-York   *1161*

1 vol: (844) (128) (256) (4) (8) (14) (34)   34 cm   CSmH, IaU, IU, KBB, MB,
                                                            NN, NNAB, ViLxW, ViU

Dated 1846 with, at foot of title, *Entered ... in the year 1843 by Harper and Brothers.*
Frontispiece and illuminated title to each Testament. Tables, Index, and Concordance at end.
   NN copy has no date on title pages. NN has another copy (Arents Collection) in 54 fasci-
cles, as originally issued.
   This work was originally announced in 1843, and was issued in 54 numbers at 25¢ each.
J. A. Adams, the engraver, is credited with having taken the first electrotype in America from
a woodcut. Many in this Bible are so done. Artists were engaged for more than six years
in the preparation of the designs and engravings included in this Bible, at a cost of over $20,000.
(O'Callaghan, p 288.)
   Frank Weitenkampf writes in *The Boston Public Library Quarterly* (July 1958, p 154–
157): "The engravings after Chapman carefully reproduced the prim line-work of the drawings.
There was very little of the tone-work made possible by the 'white line' method of the Englishman Bewick, introduced here by Alexander Anderson. ... However, this Harper publication
was a remarkable production for its time and place, and retains its importance in the annals of
American book-making. W. J. Linton, noted wood-engraver and author, knew 'no other book
like this, so good, so perfect in all it undertakes.' The illustrations are like picturings of history,
as are so many of the old European Biblical paintings and illustrations."

1843   The Holy Bible ... With Canne's Marginal Notes and References ... [Phin-
         ney's Stereotyped Edition]. Published and Sold by H. & E. Phinney: Coopers-
         town, N. Y. Also sold by I. Tiffany: Utica   *1162*

29 cm   NNAB

Reprint of Phinney's quarto of 1824 (No 485).
   NCooHi has two copies: one with Apocrypha, 2 woodcut frontispieces and 8 other woodcuts; the second without Apocrypha or illustrations, but with NT dated 1844.

1843   The Holy Bible ... Stereotyped by E. White, New-York. ... Published by
         E. Morgan and Co.: Cincinnati   *1163*

29 cm   OC

Similar to 1842 edition (No 1127) but without Apocrypha.

1843   The Cottage Bible, and Family Expositor ... With Practical Expositions and
         Explanatory Notes. By Thomas Williams. The References and Marginal
         Readings of the Polyglott Bible, Together with Original Notes ... Bagster's
         Comprehensive Bible ... Edited by Rev. William Paton. Complete in Two
         Volumes ... [Stereotyped by Conner & Cooke]. Printed and Published by
         Case, Tiffany and Burnham: Hartford   *1164*

2 vols   28 cm   NNAB

Reprint from plates of the 1833–34 Cottage Bible (No 818) with new title page and some different engravings. NNAB has Vol I only. Preface dated 1833. Copyright 1833, by James Conner and William R. Cooke.

1843 The Holy Bible . . . [With Scott's notes . . . observations . . . References]. From the latest London Edition . . . W. E. Dean, Printer and Publisher: New York **1165**

3 vols: Vol I, (874) 875–876; Vol II, (965); Vol III, (973) 974–1042   27 cm   NNAB

Scott's Annotated Bible; see 1804–09, No 113. Vol I preliminary matter includes frontis-piece, Preface, Postscript followed by Advertisement to the London Stereotype Edition (dated 1822), and Introduction to OT; text: Genesis-Esther, followed by Epitome of the History of the Jews. Vol II, Job-Malachi, followed by Family Record. Vol III, NT text, followed by Retro-spective View of the Revelation of St. John, and Brown's Concordance.

Other editions were issued in 1844, 1848, 1850 (all NN, the last from DLC Union Catalog, Vols II–III only). Also by J. B. Lippincott & Co., Philadelphia: 1857 (GEU), 1866 (IU), 1868 (ViLxW), and 1871 (MQ). See also 1832 edition by Collins and Hannay, No 781.

1843 The English Version of the Polyglott Bible . . . Marginal Readings . . . Ref-erences . . . Critical Introduction . . . by Rev. Joseph Warne. An Essay on the Right Interpretation of the Writings . . . by James Macknight . . . Three Ser-mons . . . by Philip Doddridge . . . A Geographical and Historical Index . . . A Concordance by Rev. J. Brown. A Complete Index and Concise Diction-ary to the Bible . . . Peabody & Daniel, and D. Kimball: Franklin, N. H. *1166*

1 vol: (705) (216)   27 cm   MBU–T, NN, NNAB

Has frontispieces and added engraved titles. Preface, introductions and other supplementary matter. Engravings and woodcuts. At end, Index (46 p), Dictionary (84 p), Concordance (84 p), and geography (6 p). Copyright 1833 by Holbrook & Fessenden.

1843 The Holy Bible . . . The References and Marginal Readings of the Polyglott Bible, With Numerous Additions from Bagster's Comprehensive Bible . . . Robinson, Pratt & Co.: New York *1167*

Reported as 773 p   27 cm   MH
Illustrated.
ICU lists copy bound with Chronological Index; stereotyped by Conner & Cooke, 1843.

1843/44 The Pictorial Bible . . . Illustrated with More than One Thousand Engrav-ings, Representing the Historical Events, After Celebrated Pictures; the Landscape Scenes from Original Drawings; and the Subjects of Natural His-tory, Costume, and Antiquities, from the Best Sources: J. S. Redfield: New York *1168*

1 vol: (1102) (vi) (ii) (348)   26 cm   DCU, NN

Has added engraved title. References arranged in form of footnotes. NT title, dated 1844, has Tables on verso. One map.

NN has another copy with 1846 NT; paged (ii) (1124) (348), with Table of Ancient Chronology on p 1103–1124; references at foot of page. O'Callaghan (p 273) describes a Lenox copy with *J. S. Redfield* alone on engraved title; *J. S. Redfield, Thomas, Cowperthwait & Co., Philadelphia and Price & Co., Boston* on general title; and NT, dated 1846, with Redfield alone.

1843 The Holy Bible . . . With Canne's Marginal Notes and References . . . Stereo-typed by J. Howe, Philadelphia . . . S. Andrus and Son: Hartford *1169*

24 cm   NNAB

Similar to 1825 Daniel Smith edition (No 529). Preliminary matter includes To the Reader and Contents. Tables and Family Record follow OT. NT has frontispiece, title, and Account of the Dates. Illustrated.

Also published with Apocrypha (109 p), Concordance (136 p), and Metrical Psalms (39 p).

1843   The Holy Bible . . . Stereotyped by D. & G. Bruce, New York . . . S. Andrus
and Son: Hartford   *1170*

1 vol: (637) 641–837 656–681   20 cm   NNAB
General Contents of the Books at end. Illustrated.

1843   [The Holy Bible . . . Fourth Edition] The New Testament . . . According to
the Commonly Received Version. London, 1611: Imprinted by Robert Barker . . . Stereotyped by White and Hagar, for the American and Foreign
Bible Society: New-York   *1171*

20 cm   ICU, NNAB
Seems to be reprint of 1838 (No 1007), 1839 (No 1042), and 1842 (No 1137) editions.
General title page missing from NNAB copy; above taken from NT.
Fifth edition also issued this year.

1843   The Holy Bible . . . Stereotyped by James Conner . . . Printed and Published
by Edward Sanderson: Elizabeth-town, N. J. Sold in New York by Turner,
Hughes & Hayden   *1172*

Reported as (486) (162)   19 cm   NjPT

1843   The Holy Bible . . . Stereotyped by D. & G. Bruce, New York. William Andrus: Hartford   *1173*

1 vol: (637) (337)   "12mo"   Not Located
O'Callaghan, p 274.

1843   The Holy Bible . . . Published by Mentz & Rovoudt: Philadelphia   *1174*

1 vol: (599) 601–606 (179) 181–182   18 cm   NN
Contents follow both Testaments. Tables.

1843   The Holy Bible . . . Stereotyped by J. Howe, Philadelphia . . . S. Andrus &
Son: Hartford   *1175*

681 p   17 cm   NN
Tables are at end of OT; Contents at end of NT. Illustrated.

1843   The English Version of the Polyglott Bible . . . With the Marginal Readings:
Together with a Copious and Original Selection of References to Parallel and
Illustrative Passages, Exhibited in a Manner Hitherto Unattempted . . . Pub-
lished by R. H. Sherburne: Boston   *1176*

1 vol: (856) (259)   13 cm   NNAB
Has frontispiece and added engraved title. Order of Books followed by Chronological
Order. Preface signed T. C.   Chronology of Our Saviour's Life at end.

1843   The Holy Bible . . . S. Andrus and Son: Hartford   *1177*

1 vol: (852) (259)   12 cm   NNAB
Frontispieces to both Testaments.

1843 The Holy Bible . . . W. & H. Merriam: Troy, New York   *1178*

12 cm   ViU

Diamond Bible appears on added engraved title page. Illustrated.

1843 The Holy Bible . . . J. B. Lippincott & Co.: Philadelphia   *1179*

1 vol: (824) (251)   "24mo"   Not Located

O'Callaghan, p 274. Bound up with Book of Common Prayer.

1843 The Holy Bible . . . John Locken: Philadelphia   *1180*

Reported as (852) (259) 261–263   "32mo"   NBuG

Both Testaments have frontispieces; also added engraved titles headed *The Everlasting Gospel*. Contents at end. Illustrated.

O'Callaghan (p 274) lists copy bound with the Book of Common Prayer printed by Lippincott, 1842.

1843 The English Version of the Polyglott Bible . . . Published by G. & C. Merriam: Springfield   *1181*

"32mo"   Not Located

O'Callaghan, p 274. Has frontispiece. Illustrated.

1843 The Holy Bible . . . Hogan & Thompson: Philadelphia   *1182*

No other information given.   ScGrvF

1843 The New Testament . . . Stereotyped by L. Roby. Luther Roby: Concord, N. H.   *1183*

1 vol: (390) (iv)   22 cm   NNAB

Table of Contents at end.

1843 The New Testament . . . Published by Wm. W. Nason: Newburyport, Mass.   *1184*

"12mo"   Not Located

O'Callaghan p 275.

1843 The New Testament . . . London, Imprinted by Robert Barker, 1611. Third Edition . . . John Gray, Printer . . . Stereotyped by White and Hagar, for the American and Foreign Bible Society: New York   *1185*

252 p   19 cm   Not Located

O'Callaghan, p 275. See 1838 Bible, No 1007.

1843 The New Testament . . . Stereotyped by J. Howe, Philadelphia . . . Published by Charles Scott: Trenton   *1186*

240 p   19 cm   NNAB

1843 The New Testament . . . Stereotype Edition . . . The Bible Association of Friends in America: Philadelphia   *1187*

Reported as 342 p   16 cm   PSt

1843 The New Testament . . . [Stereotyped by James Conner, N. Y.]. Ira White: Wells-River, Vt. **1188**

226 p   15 cm   NN, VtHi

1843? The New Testament . . . William Stewart: Hagerstown, Md. **1189**

344 p   13 cm   NN

Annexed is an edititon of the Shorter Catechism (Hagerstown: Published by William Stewart. Edwin Bell. Printer. 1843).

1843 The New Testament . . . Benjamin Olds, Publisher: Newark **1190**

Reported as 318 p   12 cm   Privately Owned

1843 The New Testament . . . [Stereotyped by Richard C. Valentine . . . New York]. H. & E. Phinney: Cooperstown **1191**

Reported as 454 p   9 cm   NCooHi

Has frontispiece and added engraved title. Other engravings.

"5300 copies of this Testament have been issued from the Cooperstown press, from 1832–1848. *E.P.*" (O'Callaghan, p 275.)

1843 The New Testament . . . S. Andrus: Hartford **1192**

"48mo"   Not Located

O'Callaghan, p 275.

1844 The Holy Bible . . . With Marginal Readings, References, and Chronological Dates . . . James Collord, Printer. Published by G. Lane & P. P. Sandford, for the Methodist Episcopal Church: New-York **1193**

1 vol: (xiii) (797) (253) 254–256 (11) (39)   30 cm   NNAB

Frontispiece, engraved OT title page, Account of the Authorized Version, Divine Authority of Scriptures by Rev. J. Fletcher, Contents of Books of OT, Tables and Order of Books precede text. Family Record follows OT. Frontispiece and engraved title to NT, followed by Discourses, Parables and Miracles of Jesus, and Contents of Books of the NT. Text has central column of references. Reading Guide and Concordance at end.

Note on p 2: "In this edition of the Bible, the chronology of Dr. Clarke has been followed at the beginning of the Books, and that of the standard edition of the American Bible Society in all other places. This will account for the discrepancy in the dates."

1844 The Holy Bible . . . With Canne's Marginal References . . . And What Has Never Before Been Added, An Account of the Lives and Martyrdom of the Apostles and Evangelists . . . The Text Corrected According to the Standard of the American Bible Society . . . Stereotyped by James Conner . . . S. Andrus and Son: Hartford **1194**

1 vol: (527) (78) (168) (12) (35) (19)   29 cm   NNAB

Has frontispieces to Testaments. To the Reader, Advertisement, and Order of Books precede text. Following OT is a Reading Guide by William Stones. With Apocrypha, followed by Family Record. Index, Tables, etc., Concordance, and Metrical Psalms at end. Engravings and maps.

1844 The Holy Bible . . . [Phinney's Stereotype Edition]. Published by H. & E. Phinney: Cooperstown **1195**

29 cm   NN, NNAB

Reprint of 1824 edition (No 485) with Apocrypha, but with plates of the 1829 edition (No 668).

NCooHi has two copies: one with Apocrypha and 10 illustrations; another with NT dated 1843, no frontispieces but 9 illustrations, and with added imprint *Sold also by I. Tiffany, Utica.*

1844 The Holy Bible... With Canne's Marginal Notes and References... J. Harding, Printer. Jesper Harding: Philadelphia   **1196**

1 vol: (574) (96) 579–768   29 cm   CtY, NNAB

With Apocrypha. Each Testament has frontispiece. Tables follow OT. Family Record. Illustrated.

1844 The Holy Bible... With Notes, Explanatory and Practical; Taken Principally from the Most Eminent Writers of the United Church of England and Ireland; Together with Appropriate Introductions, Tables and Indexes. Prepared and Arranged by Rev. George D'Oyly... and the Rev. Richard Mant ... Under the Direction of the Society for Promoting Christian Knowledge. For Use of Families. With Additional Notes Selected and Arranged by John Henry Hobart... Stanford & Swords: New-York   **1197**

2 vols   28 cm   NN

Notes at foot of page. NN has Vol i only. See Swords's 1818–20 edition, No 344.

1844 The Cottage Bible, and Family Expositor... Notes, by Thomas Williams ... Edited by Rev. William Patton... Case, Tiffany and Burnham: Hartford   **1198**

2 vols   28 cm   KBB

KBB has Vol i only, Gen-Solomon's Song, 736 p.

1844 The Holy Bible, Translated from the Latin Vulgate... The Old Testament First Published by the English College, at Douay, A.D. 1609; and the New Testament, First Published by the English College, at Rheims, A.D. 1582. With Annotations, References, and an Historical and Chronological Index. From the Last London and Dublin Editions... Published with the Approbation of the Most Reverend John Hughes, Archbishop of New York... Edward Dunigan: New York   **1199**

28 cm   NN, PPiW

Rheims-Douay Version. Reprinted from Doyle's 1833 edition (No 825).

1844 The Holy Bible... The References and Marginal Readings of the Polyglott Bible, with Numerous Additions from Bagster's Comprehensive Bible... Robinson, Pratt & Co.: New York   **1200**

Reported as 773 p   27 cm   ViLxW

1844 The Holy Bible, Translated from the Latin Vulgate;... With Annotations, References, and an Historical and Chronological Index. From the Last London and Dublin Editions. The Whole Revised and Diligently Compared with the Latin Vulgate. Published with the Approbation of the Right Reverend John Hughes, D.D., Bishop of New York... Published by Edward Dunigan: New York   **1201**

26 cm   DGU, NN, NNAB

Rheims-Douay Version. From the plates of Doyle's 1833 edition (No 825). Issued in several forms and with varying number of engravings and also in parts as The Illustrated Bible. Has lithoprinted titles in color to each Testament and engraved frontispiece, with Approbation of Bishop Hughes (1844) and an engraving of old St. Patrick's Cathedral. Engraved Family Record (4 leaves) at end of OT. 6 engravings.

Later editions published by Excelsior Catholic Publishing House, New York, 1844? (KAS) and by P. J. Kennedy, New York, 1892? (NN).

1844   The Holy Bible . . . Stereotyped by R. C. Valentine, for the American and Foreign Bible Society: New York   *1202*

1 vol: (938) 939–940 (288)   24 cm   ICU, NNAB

Has Order of Books followed by Chronological Order. Tables and Family Record follow OT. Verso of NT title has Order of Books, etc.

1844   The Holy Bible . . . With Canne's Marginal Notes and References . . . Stereotyped by J. Howe, Philadelphia. S. Andrus & Son: Hartford   *1203*

1 vol: (10) 11–619 [1] (109) 623–811   24 cm   NN

With Apocrypha. Order of Books, To the Reader, and Contents precede text. Tables follow OT. Account of Dates on verso of NT title.

Also issued with Brown's Concordance (139 p) and Metrical Psalms (39 p).

1844–46   The Holy Bible . . . With . . . Notes . . . Observations, and . . . References. By Thomas Scott . . . 1st American Stereotype Quarto Edition . . . from the London Standard Edition, with the Author's Last Corrections and Improvements . . . J. M. Campbell: Philadelphia; Saxton & Miles: New York   *1204*

5 vols   "4to"   DLC

Scott's Annotated Bible; see 1804–09, No 113. Vol i, Genesis-Samuel. Vol ii, Kings-Proverbs. Vol iii, Ecclesiastes-Malachi. Vol iv, Matthew-Acts. Vol v, Romans-Revelation. Vols ii–v imprinted *Philadelphia, J. Harding*.

1844?   The Holy Bible . . . Isaac M. Moss: Philadelphia   *1205*

"4to"   Not Located

Wright, p 257, 400. Contains 20 illustrations by A. Anderson.

1844   The Holy Bible . . . J. B. Lippincott & Company: Philadelphia   *1206*

1 vol: (1098) 1101–1440   "4to"   Not Located

"This edition is without notes or engravings. The pages are included within double rules; it is a beautiful specimen of typography." (O'Callaghan, p 275.)

1844   The Holy Bible . . . Stereotype Edition . . . Published by The Bible Association of Friends in America: Philadelphia   *1207*

"8vo"   Not Located

O'Callaghan, p 276. Reprint of 1831 Bible (No 738).

1844   The Holy Bible . . . Published by R. S. H. George: Philadelphia   *1208*

"8vo"   Not Located

O'Callaghan, p 276.

1844   The Holy Bible . . . American Bible Society, Instituted . . . : New York *1209*

1284 p   21cm   NNAB

Bourgeois Duodecimo. The first edition of a book planned to take the place of the first ABS edition; see 1816, No 304. Has Family Record (4 p) between Testaments, Tables on verso of NT title, and Contents of the NT. Error on p 1256, i Peter should read II Peter. "From its compact form and fair type, it is well calculated for ordinary reading, particularly for the supply of pews in churches." (*ABS Report* 1845, p 29.) Priced in 1844 at $2.50 in morocco, $1.62½ in calf with gilt edge, $1.25 in embossed calf, and 75¢ in sheep.

1844   The Holy Bible . . . With the References and Marginal Readings of the Polyglott Bible, with Numerous Additions from Bagster's Comprehensive Bible.
[C. Sherman and Co., Printers.] Lindsay & Blakiston: Philadelphia   *1210*

937 p   20 cm   NN, NNAB

The text corresponds in all respects with that of the 1833 Bible Annual (No 827). Has frontispiece to each Testament, Names and Order of Books, and Chronological Order of Books. Copyright 1833, by James Conner and William R. Cooke.

Also issued with illuminated title or without any year on title page.

"Mr. Conner having decided on stereotyping an elegant edition of the Polyglott Bible (12mo), he got up a new size and style of type called Agate, cut in a condensed and compressed manner; the intention being to admit of a certain number of figures and points coming within a given space — the whole included within a center column of notes. Of this Bible he made several sets of plates from the same composition; then took out the references and center column of notes, and completed many sets of an 18mo Bible, and a proportionate number of plates for the New Testament. N. Y. Printer." (O'Callaghan, p 277.)

1844   The English Version of the Polyglott Bible . . . With Marginal Readings,
References . . . Published by Sanborn & Carter: Portland   *1211*

"12mo"   Not Located

O'Callaghan, p 278. Added engraved title and frontispiece to each Testament.

1844   The Holy Bible . . . Published by R. S. H. George . . . For the Bible Committee of the Society of the Protestant Episcopal Church for the Advancement
of Christianity in Pennsylvania: Philadelphia   *1212*

1044 p   "12mo"   Not Located

O'Callaghan, p 278.

1844   The Holy Bible . . . [Stereotyped at the Boston Type and Stereotype Found-
ry]. Luther Roby: Concord, N. H.   *1213*

1 vol: (824) (251)   "12mo"   Not Located

O'Callaghan, p 278.

1844   The Holy Bible . . . [Stereotyped by A. Chandler]. S. Andrus & Son: Hartford   *1214*

1 vol: (824) (251)   "12mo"   Not Located

O'Callaghan, p 278. Has engraved title and frontispiece.

1844   [The Holy Bible] The New Testament . . . New York Bible and Common
Prayer Book Society: New York   *1215*

1034 p   19 cm   NNAB

General title page missing from cited copy; above taken from NT.

1844   The Holy Bible . . . Stereotyped by D. & G. Bruce, New York . . . S. Andrus
         & Son: Hartford   *1216*

1 vol: (837) 656–681 (31)   19 cm   NN
Has frontispiece to each Testament. Contents and Metrical Psalms at end. P 837 misnumbered 337.

1844   The Holy Bible . . . From the Authorized Oxford Edition . . . Hogan and
         Thompson: Philadelphia   *1217*

15 cm   NNAB
Reprint of 1836 edition (No 942).

1844   The English Version of the Polyglott Bible . . . Stereotyped by L. Johnson . . .
         Thomas, Cowperthwait & Co.: Philadelphia   *1218*

Reported as (vi) (587) (190)   "24mo"   MB
Has added engraved title to each Testament. Illustrated.

1844   The Holy Bible . . . Thomas, Cowperthwait & Co.: Philadelphia   *1219*

1 vol: (852) (259)   "24mo"   Not Located
O'Callaghan, p 279. Contents and Metrical Psalms follow text.

1844   The English Version of the Polyglott Bible . . . Published by S. H. Colesworthy: Portland [Maine]   *1220*

Reported as (587) (190)   "24mo"   MBU–T
Added engraved title imprinted *Sanborn & Carter and S. H. Colesworthy: Portland.*

1844   The Holy Bible . . . Stereotyped by J. Howe, Philadelphia . . . Hogan &
         Thompson: Philadelphia   *1221*

"32mo"   Not Located
O'Callaghan, p 279.

1844   The Holy Bible . . . [T. K. & P. G. Collins, Printers, Philadelphia]. Sorin &
         Ball: Philadelphia   *1222*

1 vol: (852) (263) (81)   12 cm   NNAB
The Everlasting Gospel. J. Locken. Philadelphia appears on added engraved titles to Testaments. For Locken edition, see 1843 Bible, No 1180. Contents and Metrical Psalms at end.
Illustrated.

1844   The Holy Bible . . . [T. K. & P. G. Collins, Printers]. R. S. H. George: Philadelphia   *1223*

1 vol: (852) (259)   "32mo"   Not Located
O'Callaghan, p 279. NT imprinted *Philadelphia: Sorin & Ball, 1844*; see No 1222. With
Book of Common Prayer imprinted *Philadelphia: J. B. Lippincott, 1842.*

1844   The Holy Bible . . . Stereotyped by J. Howe, Philad . . . Published by Silas
         Andrus & Son: Hartford   *1224*

1 vol: (729) (224)   "32mo"   Not Located
O'Callaghan, p 279. Contents at end (p 223–224).

1844   The Polyglott Bible . . . G. & C. Merriam: Springfield   **1225**

"32mo"   Not Located

Wright, p 401.

1844   The Holy Bible . . . Stereotyped by Henry Wallis & Luther Roby . . . N. A.
Foster, Printer. Sanborn & Carter: Portland   **1226**

1 vol: (852) (259)   12 cm   NNAB

Added engraved title page dated 1843. NT imprinted *Grigg and Elliot: Philadelphia*.

1844   The Holy Bible . . . Stereotyped by Henry Wallis & Luther Roby . . . Concord,
N. H. . . . Published by R. H. Sherburne: Boston   **1227**

1 vol: (6) (viii) (721) (225)   12 cm   NNAB

Has added engraved title page (1843), frontispiece, and Contents of the Books of the OT.

1844   The English Version of the Polyglott Bible . . . With the Marginal Readings:
Together with a Copious and Original Selection of References to Parallel
and Illustrative Passages. Exhibited in a Manner Hitherto Unattempted . . .
Published by G. & C. Merriam: Springfield   **1228**

12 cm   NNAB

Uniform with 1838 Bible (No 1019).

1844   The Holy Bible . . . Published by W. & H. Merriam: Troy, N. Y.   **1229**

1 vol: (734) (224)   12 cm   KBB, NNAB

Has frontispieces and added engraved titles to both Testaments (with *Diamond Bible* and
Diamond Testament respectively at head of each title). Contents of Books follow OT and NT.
Illustrated.

1844   The Holy Bible . . . S. Andrus and Son: Hartford   **1230**

1 vol: (852) (259) 260–263 (81)   12 cm   NN

Has two frontispieces. Contents of Books follows NT. Metrical Psalms at end. Illustrated.

1844   Practical Observations on the New Testament. Arranged for Family Worship. With an Introduction by A. Alexander . . . Lindsay & Blakiston: Philadelphia   **1231**

Reported as (xii) (532)   28 cm   ViU

Engravings from Westall's designs. With Scott's annotations.

1844   The New Testament, arranged in historical and chronological order . . . by
the Rev. George Townsend . . . revised, divided into paragraphs punctuated
according to the best critical texts . . . by the Rev. T. W. Coit, D.D. . . . Published by Crocker and Brewster . . . : Boston   **1232**

Reported as (455) (472)   27 cm   NB

The notes occupy 472 p, with indexes, See 1837 NT, No 985.

1844   The New Testament . . . Illustrated with Several Hundred Engravings, Representing The Historical Events . . . The Landscape Scenes . . . and the Subjects of Natural History, Costume, and Antiquities . . . with a New and Beau-

1844, continued

tiful Map of Palestine in the Time of our Savior . . . Stereotyped by Redfield and Savage . . . J. S. Redfield: New York   *1233*

348 p   27 cm   NNAB
Pictorial NT, similar to Knight's Pictorial Bible, London, 1836–38, but without commentary. Seems to have been reset; see 1843–44 Bible, No 1168. Has added engraved title page,
Tables, List of Illustrations, and map. References at foot of page. Initial letter of each chapter
and most books is in ornate design.

1844   The New Testament . . . Stereotyped by R. C. Valentine for the American
and Foreign Bible Society: New York   *1234*

1 vol: (288) (74)   "8vo"   N
With Metrical Psalms.

1844   [The New Testament] Expository Notes with Practical Observations on the
New Testament . . . Wherein the Sacred Text is at Large Recited, and the
same Explained . . . by William Burkitt . . . Sorin & Ball: Philadelphia *1235*

2 vols: Vol i, 725 p; Vol ii, 847 p   23 cm   NjMD
Preceded by Dedications and a Prayer. For William Burkitt, see 1794, No 47.

1844   Explanatory Notes upon the New Testament, by John Wesley . . . G. Lane
and P. P. Sandford: New York   *1236*

Reported as 734 p   23 cm   NcAS
Wesley Version; see 1791 NT, No 35.

1844   The New Testament . . . Stereotyped by J. Howe, Philadelphia . . . Published
by Alfred L. Dennis . . . : Newark   *1237*

Reported as 11–240   12 cm   DLC
Lacks p 1–10.

1844   The New Testament . . . Stereotype Edition . . . Jesper Harding: Philadelphia   *1238*

312 p   19 cm   NNAB
Verso of title has Order of Books. Table follows text.

1844   The Polyglott New Testament . . . [Printed by Thurston, Ilsley and Co., Port-
land]. S. H. Colesworthy: Portland   *1238A*

432 p   17 cm   NNAB
Has Tables on verso of title page. Geographical and other Indexes on p 423–432. Copyright
by Conner and Cooke 1833.

1844   The New Testament . . . Ticknor: Boston   *1239*

Reported as 450 p   "12mo"   MB

1844   The New Testament . . . To Which are Added, Sketches of the Lives of Christ
and the Twelve Apostles . . . Knowlton and Rice: Watertown, N. Y.   *1240*

237 [1] p   16 cm   NN
Table at end.

1844 The New Testament . . . Stereotyped by Luther Roby, Concord, N. H. . . .
Published by Luther Roby: Concord, N. H. **1241**

254 p   12 cm   NN

1844 The New Testament . . . Translated from the Latin Vulgat. With Annotations
and References . . . Published by Fielding Lucas, Jr.: Baltimore **1242**

412 p   12 cm   Not Located
O'Callaghan, p 281. Rheims Version. Reprint of 1831? NT (No 766).

1844 The New Testament . . . With the Marginal References, Both Parallel and
Explanatory, and a Copious Selection, Carefully Chosen, and Newly Ar-
ranged . . . And the sterling currency reduced to dollars and cents . . . J. C.
Riker . . . : New York **1243**

12 cm   NNAB
Reprint of the Riker 1833 NT (No 855). Engraved title has *The Polyglott New Testament*
(with symbolical figures).

1844 The Polymicrian Testament . . . Perkins & Purves: Philadelphia **1244**

"32mo"   Not Located
Wright, p 400. See 1834 NT, No 889.

1844 The New Testament . . . Translated from the Latin Vulgate . . . Published by
Eugene Cummiskey: Philadelphia **1245**

Rheims Version. Edition of 1,000 copies (O'Callaghan, p 280).   Not Located

1845 The Holy Bible . . . With Canne's Marginal Notes and References . . . Stereotyped by James Conner . . . S. Andrus & Son: Hartford **1246**

"folio"   Not Located
O'Callaghan (p 281) says collation agrees with the edition of 1829 (No 666). With
Apocrypha. Index and Tables.

1845 The Holy Bible . . . together with the Apocrypha. In two Volumes . . . Published by Butler and Williams: Philadelphia **1247**

2 vols in 1: (iii) (787) (277) (139) 281–600   30 cm   NNAB
Vol ı, Genesis-Song of Solomon, and Vol ıı, Isaiah-Revelation, bound together. Added
engraved title has *Solomon's Temple*. Frontispiece depicts *The Descent of the Holy Ghost*,
with tongues of fire appearing over the worshippers. Following the title appears A Guide to a
Regular Perusal of the Holy Scriptures by William Stones; verso blank.

1845 The Holy Bible . . . With Canne's Marginal References . . . The Text Corrected According to the Standard of the American Bible Society. Stereotyped by James Conner: New York. S. Andrus & Son: Hartford **1248**

1 vol: (527) (78) (168) (34)   29 cm   NN
With Apocrypha. Has An Account of the Lives and Martyrdom of the Apostles and
Evangelists. Index, Tables, and Concordance at end. See Andrus and Judd 1835 Bible, No 892.

1845? The Holy Bible, Translated from the Latin Vulgate . . . The Old Testament
. . . First Published . . . at Doway . . . 1609; and the New Testament . . . at
Rheims . . . 1582. With annotations, by the Rev. Dr. Challoner; Together

1845?, continued

with References, and an Historical and Chronological Index. Revised and
Corrected According to the Clementine Edition of the Scriptures. With the
Approbation of the Right Rev. Bishop Hughes . . . Published by D. and J.
Sadlier, 58 Gold Street and 221 Bleeker Street: New York   *1249*

1 vol: (793) (228)   29 cm   DGU, MB, NNAB

Rheims-Douay Version, from the 5th Dublin edition. Reprinted verbatim from Cummiskey's
1824 quarto (No 492). Has added engraved title pages (the first with 58 Gold Street only),
Approbations for the Original Old and New Testaments, the Decree of the Council of Trent,
Letter from Pope Pius VI, Admonition, Prayer, and Order of Books of the OT. Index at end of
OT (787–793, 1 p blank) and Family Record (2 leaves). Preceding NT are Admonition, Letter
from Pope Pius VI, Prayer, Approbation (1582), and Order of Books for the NT. Tables and
Index at end (p 223–228). Engravings by Jordan and Halpin, J. Rogers, A. L. Dick, and others
from paintings by Copley, Mola, Westall, and others.

Also published with Ward's Errata of the Protestant Bible, dated 1845 (118 p).

1845/44   The Holy Bible . . . Canne's Marginal Notes and References . . . Published
by H. & E. Phinney: Cooperstown, N. Y.   *1250*

28 cm   NNAB

Reprint of Phinney quarto of 1822 (No 439) with addition of Apocrypha, Concordance,
and woodcuts. NT dated 1844.

1845   The Cottage Bible and Family Expositor . . . With Practical Expositions and
Explanatory Notes. By Thomas Williams . . . To Which are Added the References and Marginal Readings of the Polyglott Bible, Together with Original Notes, and Selections from Bagster's Comprehensive Bible, and Other
Standard Works . . . The Whole Carefully Revised . . . Edited by Rev. William Patton . . . Complete in Two Volumes . . . [Stereotyped by Conner and
Cooke]. Printed and Published by Case, Tiffany and Burnham: Hartford
                                                                 1251

2 vols   28 cm   NNAB

Reprint of the Cottage Bible from Conner & Cooke plates of 1833 (No 818) previously
published by Case in 1841 (No 1103), but with different illustrations. Copyright 1833, by
Conner & Cooke.

1845   The English Version of the Polyglot Bible . . . With Marginal Readings . . .
References . . . Critical Introduction to Each of the Books . . . Essay . . . by
James McKnight . . . Sermons by Philip Doddridge . . . Index and Bible Con-
cordance . . . Dictionary to the Bible . . . Tables. Peabody & Daniell: Franklin
[New Hampshire]   *1252*

Reported as (vi) (82) (20) 7–705 (54) (4) (216) (46) (63) (84)   28 cm
                                                                        MH–AH

Has twenty-four numbered plates. Also two frontispieces, engraved title pages, and two
other wood-engravings.

1845   The Holy Bible . . . With Canne's Marginal Notes and References . . . J. Harding, Printer. Published by Jesper Harding: Philadelphia   *1253*

28 cm   NNAB

Reprint of 1842 Harding quarto (No 1129) with addition of frontispiece to each Testament
and Family Record following OT.

NNAB also has a copy with general title dated 1846 but NT title 1845. Has different frontispieces.

1845 The Holy Bible Containing the Old Testament . . . and the Greek New Testament; Printed from the Text and with Various Readings of Knapp: Together with the Commonly Received English Translation. Designed for the Use of Students . . . Stereotype Edition . . . J. C. Riker: New York   *1254*

1 vol: (775) (xix) (234) 235–248   28 cm   CSmH, NjMD, NN, NNAB

Text printed in single narrow column (1¼") on ruled paper at inner edge. NT has separate title page and is paged in duplicate with Greek and English on facing pages. Greek text from the fourth German edition, revised by Roediger; R. B. Patton prepared the American edition. Latin Glossary at end.

NNAB and NjMD copies do not have Greek text and Glossary. NjN and PL have NT only.

1845 The Holy Bible, Translated from the Latin Vulgat: With Annotations, References and Index . . . [Stereotyped by J. Howe]. Published by Eugene Cummiskey: Philadelphia   *1255*

27 cm   WU

Rheims-Douay Version. Similar to Doyle's 1833 edition (No 825). Has frontispiece and illustrations.

1845 The Holy Bible . . . With Canne's Marginal Notes and References . . . Thomas, Cowperthwait, & Co.: Philadelphia   *1256*

"4to"   AB

1845 The Holy Bible . . . With the References and Marginal Readings of the Polyglott Bible, with Numerous Additions from Bagster's Comprehensive Bible . . . [Stereotyped by Conner & Cooke. Kingsland and Baptist, Printers]. Published by H. & E. Phinney: Cooperstown   *1257*

"8vo"   Not Located

"Mr. E. Phinney informs me that their firm printed only 1000 copies of this Polyglott Bible. It is at present [1861] entirely out of the market, the issues of the Bible Society having rendered its further publication unprofitable. It was from a duplicate set of Conner & Cooke's plates. See 1833." (O'Callaghan, p 283.) Copyright by James Conner & William R. Cooke, New York, 1833.

1845 The Holy Bible . . . Stereotyped by T. B. Smith, for the American and Foreign Bible Society: [New York]   *1258*

"8vo"   Not Located

O'Callaghan, p 283. Small Pica type.

1845 The Holy Bible . . . Stereotyped by T. B. Smith for the American and Foreign Bible Society: New York   *1259*

"12mo"   Not Located

O'Callaghan, p 283. Brevier type.

1845 The Holy Bible . . . Stereotyped by D. and G. Bruce, New York. S. Andrus and Son: Hartford   *1260*

Reported as (837) 656–681   "12mo"   CtY

Frontispiece to each Testament. General Contents at end.

O'Callaghan (p 284) lists a similar edition stereotyped by J. Howe, Philadelphia.

1845 The Holy Bible . . . The Text of the Common Translation is Arranged in
        Paragraphs, Such as the Sense Requires . . . By James Nourse . . . [Stereo-
        typed by J. Howe, Philadelphia]. S. Andrus & Son: Hartford   *1261*

1 vol: (vii) [1] (942) (324)   17 cm   NN
Illustrated.

1845 The Holy Bible . . . American and Foreign Bible Society: New York *1262*

"18mo"   N

1845 The English Version of the Polyglott Bible . . . Sanborn and Carter: Port-
        land   *1263*

15 cm   NNUT
Same as S. H. Colesworthy edition of 1844 (No 1220). Has added engraved title and
frontispiece to each Testament. Preface.

1845 [The Holy Bible] The New Testament . . . With the Marginal Readings; and
        Illustrated by Original References . . . and a Copious Selection . . . Newly
        Arranged . . . Stereotyped by J. C. D. Christman & Co., Philada. . . . Published
        by S. Andrus & Son: Hartford   *1264*

1 vol: (824) (256) (73)   15 cm   NNAB
General title and some preliminary pages missing from cited copy; above taken from NT
title. Has part of Preface of the Polyglott Bible signed T. C. Chronological Table at end of OT.
Frontispiece, title, and Order of Books to NT. Center References. Metrical Psalms at end.

1845 The Holy Bible . . . [Stereotyped by A. Chandler]. S. Andrus & Son: Hart-
        ford   *1265*

1 vol: (824) (251) (72)   15 cm   NNAB
Reprint of S. Andrus edition of 1828/26 (No 637) but with Metrical Psalms. Illustrated.

1845 The Holy Bible . . . Thomas, Cowperthwait & Co.: Philadelphia   *1266*

"24mo"   Not Located
O'Callaghan, p 284. Frontispiece to each Testament.

1845 The English Version of the Polyglott Bible . . . With the Marginal Readings
        . . . Biddle: Philadelphia   *1267*

"24mo"   ScGrvF

1845 The Holy Bible . . . Stereotyped by Henry Wallis & Luther Roby . . . Concord,
        N. H. . . . Sanborn & Carter: Portland   *1268*

12 cm   DLC
The Everlasting Gospel appears on added engraved title.

1845 The Holy Bible . . . Uriah Hunt & Son: Philadelphia   *1269*

12 cm   NNAB
Similar to Cowperthwait's 1838 edition (No 1021) but with different illustrations. Each
Testament has frontispiece, added engraved title (with *The Everlasting Gospel* at head and
imprinted *G. Eckendorff, Philadelphia*), and Order of Books on verso of title. Contents and Metrical Psalms at end.

Fly leaf of cited copy inscribed to Edwin Francis Hyde by his mother, Elizabeth Alvina Hyde, Jan. 1st, 1848. Mr Hyde was associated with the American Bible Society as a member of the Board of Managers (1894–1919), as a vice-president (1919–1924), and as president (1924–1933).

1845 The English Version of the Polyglott Bible . . . With the Marginal Readings: Together with a Copious and Original Selection of References to Parallel and Illustrative Passages. Exhibited in a Manner Hitherto Unattempted . . . Published by G. & C. Merriam: Springfield   **1270**

1 vol: (856) (259)   12 cm   NNAB

Has added engraved title, frontispiece, and Preface signed T. C.

1845 The Holy Bible . . . Published by W. & H. Merriam: Troy, N. Y.   **1271**

Reported as (8) (726) (221) 222–224   "32mo"   N

Has Contents to both Testaments. With Book of Common Prayer imprinted *Philadelphia, Lippincott & Co., 1842* (O'Callaghan, p 285).

1845 The English Version of the Polyglott Bible . . . [Stereotyped by J. C. D. Christman & Co.]. Sorin and Ball: Philadelphia   **1272**

Reported as (vii) [1] (824) (256)   "32mo"   MiU

Has added engraved title and frontispiece. Preface signed T. C.

[5605–06] 1845–46 [The Torah in Hebrew and English] The Law of God . . . Edited, and with Former Translations diligently Compared and Revised, by Isaac Leeser. Printed by C. Sherman, for the Editor: Philadelphia   **1273**

5 vols: Vol I, (x) (175); Vol II, 168 p; Vol III, 153 p; Vol IV, 149 p; Vol V, (135) 136–147
23 cm   NNAB

Volume First, The Book of Genesis, preceded by Preface. Volume Second, The Book of Exodus. Volume Third, The Book of Leviticus. Volume Fourth, The Book of Numbers. Volume Fifth, The Book of Deuteronomy, with Contents of the five volumes, Directions for the Reading of the Law, and a Postscript at end. A mock title page for the Pentateuch (lacking in cited copy) precedes the individual title to each volume. The Hebrew text is on the right opening, and the parallel English version on the left, both in paragraph form. The facing pages are numbered separately (the Arabic figures one ahead of the Hebrew). A few notes are placed at the foot of the English pages. The Haphtoroth to the text, and also for various Sabbaths and festivals, are given at the end of each volume. Entered in the year 1845, by Isaac Leeser. The Postscript to Vol V is dated Tebeth 10th, 5506/January 8th, 1846.

Issued in two formats, octavo and duodecimo.

Rabbi Isaac Leeser (1806–1868) received Talmudic instruction and linguistic training in his native Germany. After coming to this country at the age of 17, he assisted his uncle, a merchant at Richmond, Va. When some articles he had written in defense of Judaism attracted attention, he was invited in 1829 to become hazzan, or precentor, of the Congregation Mikveh Israel at Philadelphia. The next year he began to deliver sermons and became recognized as the pioneer of the Jewish pulpit in this country. His *Collected Discourses* were published in ten volumes in 1867.

Rabbi Leeser had long hoped to prepare an English version of the Holy Scriptures for his fellow Jews. About 1838 he announced his project, and began publishing at his own expense seven years later. Concerning the style of his translation, Rabbi Leeser wrote (in Postscript to Deuteronomy, p 147) that "it has been the Editor's endeavor to furnish as nearly as possible, a literal transcript of the Hebrew, and any harshness which may have hence resulted, he trusts, will be kindly overlooked for the fidelity to the original. . . ."

While he made full use of the works of German writers from Mendelssohn on, he refrained from consulting with English-speaking Jews. His only acknowledgment among English writers is to the editor of Bagster's Comprehensive Bible, William Greenfield. He adopted the German and Hebrew text of Wolf Heidenheim, published between 1818–1821, for his edition of the Pentateuch.

In addition to the translation, he also produced, with the help of Joseph Jaquett, an Episcopal priest, an edition of the Hebrew Bible in 1849, the first American edition with Masoretic notes.

1845   The New Testament . . . Stereotyped by T. B. Smith for the American and
         Foreign Bible Society: New York   **1274**

"8vo"   Not Located
O'Callaghan, p 285. Small Pica type.

1845   The New Testament . . . Stereotyped by B. & J. Collins, New York. Benjamin
         Adams: Boston   **1275**

"8vo"   Not Located
O'Callaghan, p 285.

1845   The Cottage Polyglott Testament . . . With Notes, Original and Selected . . .
         Polyglott References and Marginal Readings . . . Adapted to Bible Classes,
         [etc.] by William Patton, D.D. . . . Published by Sumner & Goodman: Hart-
         ford   **1276**

1 vol: (12) (718)   19 cm   NjMD, NNAB
Preliminary matter includes added engraved title, Tables, Preface, and Introduction to the Cottage Testament. Each book has Introductory and Concluding Remarks. All printed matter on page enclosed in double rule border, with references at one side of text only and notes at foot of page. Geographical and Chronological Indexes at end. Maps. Copyright by Sumner & Goodman, 1845.

1845   The New Testament . . . Translated out of the Latin Vulgate: With Annota-
         tions. As Approved by the Right Rev. John Hughes, Catholic Bishop of New
         York . . . [Stereotype Edition]. D. & J. Sadlier: New York   **1277**

19 cm   MBtS, NcAS, NN
Rheims Version. Reprint of 1842 Devereaux NT (No 1151).

1845   The New Testament . . . W. D. Ticknor: Boston   **1278**

450 p   "12mo"   Not Located
O'Callaghan, p 286.

1845   The New Testament . . . Stereotyped by T. B. Smith for the American and
         Foreign Bible Society: New York   **1279**

346 p   "12mo"   Not Located
O'Callaghan, p 285. Brevier type.

1845   The New Testament . . . Stereotyped by T. B. Smith for the American and
         Foreign Bible Society: New York   **1280**

"16mo"   Not Located
O'Callaghan, p 285. A Nonpareil 18mo was also issued the same year.

1845   The New Testament . . . American Bible Society . . . : New York   **1281**

250 p   16 cm   NNAB
Pearl Reference 18mo NT from the 1840 Bible (No 1083), now issued separately for the first time.

1845   The New Testament . . . Translated from the Latin Vulgate: With Annotations, a Chronological Index, Table of References, etc., etc. Approved by the Right Rev. John Hughes, D.D. Bishop of New York. Edward Dunigan: New York   *1282*

1 vol: (4) 5–349 350–356   "18mo"   Not Located
Rheims Version. O'Callaghan, p 286. Has letter of Pius VI. At end are Index and Tables.
Shea (p 36) says this is from plates of a Belfast edition.

1845   The New Testament . . . Luther Roby: Concord, N. H.   *1283*

254 p   12 cm   NN
Stereotyped by L. Roby.

1845   The New Testament . . . Stereotyped by T. B. Smith, for the American and Foreign Bible Society: New York   *1284*

346 p   12 cm   NNAB
Contains Order of Books and Chronological Order of Books. Price list at end.

1845   The New Testament . . . S. Andrus and Son: Hartford   *1285*

Reported as 454 p   10 cm   CSmH, CtY
Has frontispiece and other plates.

1845   The New Testament Translated Out of the Original Greek; The Four Gospels by G. Campbell, the Epistles by J. Macknight, and the Acts and Revelations of the Common Version . . . J. G. Wells: Hartford   *1286*

419 p   12 cm   NN
George Campbell and J. Macknight Versions; see 1796, No 56, and 1810, No 186.

1846   The Holy Bible . . . Canne's marginal notes and references . . . index . . . tables . . . J. B. Perry; Philadelphia; Nafis and Cornish: New York   *1287*

Reported as (632) (cxlvi) (2) 635–829 (xxi) (56) (19)   30 cm   PHi
Contains engravings by Anderson.

1846   The Holy Bible . . . With Canne's Marginal References. Together with Apocrypha . . . To Which are Added an Index, and References, and a Key Sheet of Questions . . . The Text Corrected According to the Standard of The American Bible Society . . . Published by Thomas, Cowperthwait & Co.: Philadelphia   *1288*

1 vol: (527) (78) (168) (31) (56) (24)   30 cm   NNAB
Has frontispiece to each Testament, Order of Books, To the Reader, and Key Questions.
Family Record follows Apocrypha. Index, Tables, Wilbur's Useful Tables, Guide to Perusal of
the Scriptures by William Stones, Brown's Concordance (stereotyped by C. Alexander & Co.),
and Metrical Psalms follow NT. Engravings, mostly signed by Anderson, are similar to 1842
William M'Carty edition (No 1132) but in different frames.

1846   The Holy Bible . . . With Canne's Marginal References . . . To Which are Added an Index, and a Key Sheet of Questions . . . The Text Corrected According to the Standard of the American Bible Society . . . Published by Merriam, Moore & Co.: Troy, N. Y.   *1289*

30 cm   NNAB

Similar to preceding Bible by Thomas, Cowperthwait & Co. (No 1288) but without engravings. *Troy Edition* appears at head of title.

O'Callaghan (p 289) says the plates were originally stereotyped in Philadelphia [by Thomas, Cowperthwait and Co.? — see No 1288], then sold to a Baltimore printer who sold them to Homer Merriam. Merriam later sold them to a printer in Dayton, Ohio, who was still publishing from them in 1860. See 1856, No 1606.

1846   The Holy Bible . . . With Canne's Marginal Notes and References . . . Published by Luther Roby: Concord, N. H.   *1290*

29 cm   NNAB
Reprint of Roby, Kimball, and Merrill 1840 edition (No 1069).

1846   The Holy Bible . . . With References and Various Readings . . . Butler's Edition . . . : Philadelphia   *1291*

2 vols in 1   29 cm   CU, OU
Illustrated. See 1845 Bible, No 1247.

1846   The Holy Bible . . . with Canne's Marginal Notes and References . . . Apocrypha . . . Sumner and Goodman: Hartford   *1292*

1 vol: (576) (96) 579–768 (31)   29 cm   NN
Has frontispiece. Index, Tables, etc. at end.

1846   The Holy Bible . . . Canne's Marginal Notes and References . . . Published by H. & E. Phinney: Cooperstown, N. Y.   *1293*

1 vol: (8) 9–574 (2) (99) (5) 579–754 755–768   28 cm   NNAB
Reprint of 1822 Phinney edition (No 439) but with Apocrypha. Illustrations, some signed by J. and J. H. Hall.
Copy with ten wood engravings by A. Anderson owned by Thomas Cooke House and Museum, Edgartown, Mass.

1846   The Holy Bible . . . J. B. Lippincott & Co.: Philadelphia   *1294*

26 cm   NN
Reprint of 1844 Bible (No 1206).

1846   [The Holy Bible] The New Testament . . . Stereotyped by J. Howe . . . Philadelphia . . . S. Andrus and Son: Hartford   *1295*

1 vol: (620) (2) (109) (15) 623–811 (136)   25 cm   NNAB
Reprint of 1843 Andrus octavo (No 1169) but with Apocrypha and Concordance. General title page missing from cited copy; above taken from NT title.

1846   The Holy Bible . . . Translated from the Latin Vulgat: With Annotations, References and Indexes . . . [Stereotyped by J. Howe]. Published by Eugene Cummiskey: Philadelphia   *1296*

"8vo"   Not Located
O'Callaghan, p 289. Rheims-Douay, from the 5th Dublin edition. An edition of 1,000 was printed. See 1824 Bible, No 492.

1846?   The Comprehensive Bible . . . A General Introduction . . . Introductory and Concluding Remarks to Each Book: The Parallel Passages Contained in Rev.

T. Scott's Commentary; Canne's Bible; Rev. J. Brown's Self-Interpreting Bible; Dr. Adam Clarke's Commentary; and the English Version of Bagster's Polyglot Bible, Systematically Arranged; Etc., Etc. . . . Samuel Bagster and Sons: London; J. B. Lippincott and Co.: Philadelphia   **1297**

1 vol: (12) (96) (998) 999–1002 1005–1338 (xlv) (45)   24 cm   NNAB
Editor's Preface (London, 1846), General Contents, Dedication to King James, Translators to the Reader, Order of Books, Chronological Table, Analyses of Contents, Index to Introduction, and Introduction precede text. Indexes at end. Printed in U. S.?

1846 The Holy Bible . . . According to the Commonly Received Version. London, 1611: Imprinted by Robert Barker . . . American and Foreign Bible Society: New York   *1298*

20 cm   ICU, ScGrvF
OT marked eighth edition; NT marked seventh edition.

1846 The Holy Bible . . . Stereotype Edition . . . S. Andrus & Son: Hartford   *1299*

1 vol: (824) (251) (70)   "12mo"   Not Located
O'Callaghan, p 290. With Metrical Psalms.

1846 The English Version of the Polyglott Bible . . . [Stereotyped by J. C. D. Christman & Co., Philada.]. Published by S. Andrus & Son: Hartford   *1300*

1 vol: (823) (256) (73)   "12mo"   Not Located
O'Callaghan, p 290. With Metrical Psalms.

1846 The Holy Bible . . . [Piercy & Reed, Printers]. New York Bible and Common Prayer Book Society: New York   *1301*

798 p   "12mo"   Not Located
O'Callaghan, p 290.

1846 The Holy Bible . . . Published by James B. Smith: Philadelphia   *1302*

648 p   "12mo"   Not Located
O'Callaghan, p 290.

1846 The Holy Bible . . . American Bible Society, Instituted . . . : New York   *1303*

691 [1] p   18 cm   NNAB
Has Tables on last page. There seems to be no record of when this format was first issued, but this is the earliest copy NNAB has.

1846 The Holy Bible . . . American Bible Society, Instituted . . . : New York   *1304*

1278 p   16 cm   NNAB
Minion 18mo, first edition. The plates were prepared "after a well known Oxford Bible of that size. From the compact form and yet bold and distinct letter there is little doubt that this book will soon have an extensive circulation." It was in 1845 that the ABS began a new practice of owning its own steam presses and doing its own printing. Formerly it had paid a printer even though the work was done in its own building. "The new presses procured are six in number and of two sorts, three of Adams (a Boston press) and three of Hoe & Co., of New-York . . . . The former is best adapted to nice, fine work; the latter executes with great rapidity, at the rate of 28 tokens each per day, enough for 392 nonpareil Bibles or 1260 small Testaments. It is computed that the six presses, running twelve hours a day, can print of the various sizes and qualities of books issued by the Society not far from 200,000 Bibles and 380,000 Testaments per annum." (*ABS Report* 1846, p 26–28.)

1846   The Holy Bible . . . S. Andrus & Son: Hartford   *1305*

1 vol: (726) (324)   "24mo"   Not Located
O'Callaghan, p 389. 4 plates.

1846/45   The English Version of the Polyglott Bible . . . with Marginal Readings
. . . References to Parallel Passages and Illustrative Passages, Exhibited in
a Manner Hitherto Unattempted . . . E. C. & J. Biddle: Philadelphia   *1306*

1 vol: (ii) (824) (256)   14 cm   NN
Has added engraved titles to both Testaments. Table at end of OT. Illustrated. NT dated
1845.

1846   The Holy Bible . . . [Stereotyped by J. C. D. Christman & Co., Phila.]. Silas
Andrus & Son: Hartford   *1307*

1 vol: (932) (292)   "32mo"   Not Located
O'Callaghan, p 290. Frontispiece to OT.

1846   A New Translation of the Proverbs, Ecclesiastes, and the Canticles, with Introductions, and Notes, chiefly Explanatory. By George R. Noyes . . . Chapman Brothers: London; James Munroe and Company: Boston   *1308*

1 vol: (xix) (290)   20 cm   NNAB
Noyes Version; see 1827, No 592. Copyright 1846 by James Munroe and Co.; Metcalf
and Company, printers.
In subsequent editions Proverbs are included with the Psalms (see 1867, No 1819);
Ecclesiastes and Canticles with Job (see 1868, No 1833).

1846   The Cottage Polyglott Testament . . . With Notes, Original and Selected . . .
Polyglott References and Marginal Readings . . . by William Patton . . . Sumner & Goodman: Hartford   *1309*

Reported as 718 p   "12mo"   MB
Has engraved title page and maps.

1846   The New Testament . . . Published by Henry Oliphant: Auburn   *1310*

299 p   "12mo"   Not Located
O'Callaghan, p 293. Error in i Tim 4:16 continued; Luke 20:25 marked 26.

1846   The New Testament . . . Stereotyped by Baker & Greele, Boston . . . Published by H. & E. Phinney: Cooperstown   *1311*

315 p   "12mo"   Not Located
"We printed 1000 of the 12mo Testament and subsequently condemned the plates to
metal. E. P." (O'Callaghan, p 293.)

1846   The New Testament . . . Robins & Smith: Hartford   *1312*

Reported as 288 p   "12mo"   MB

1846   The New Testament . . . [Stereotype Edition]. Jesper Harding: Philadelphia
1313

312 p   19 cm   NN
Table at end.

1846   The New Testament . . . E. Noyes: Middletown, Conn.   *1314*

288 p   17 cm   NNAB
Uniform with William H. Niles edition of 1829 (No 689).

1846   The New Testament . . . A. H. Rowand: Philadelphia   *1315*

1 vol: (321) 322–324   16 cm   NN
Table, NT History, and Reasons Why the Christian Religion is Preferable follow text.

1846   The New Testament . . [Stereotyped by J. Conner, N. Y., A. B. F. Hildreth,
         Printer]. Published by A. Low: Bradford, Vt.   *1316*

226 p   16 cm   NN

1846?   The New Testament . . . Stereotype Edition . . . Printed and Published by
          Alpheus Richardson: Groton, Mass.   *1317*

Reported as 335 p   15 cm   CSmH

1846   The New Testament . . . William S. Young: Philadelphia   *1318*

259 p   15 cm   NN
NN has another copy with *J. Gladding, Philadelphia* as bookseller and bookbinder on
leather cover. O'Callaghan (p 294) refers to Lenox Collection copy as printed by Gladding.

1846   The New Testament . . . [Stereotyped by L. Roby, Concord, N. H.]. A. Rich-
         ardson: Groton, Mass.   *1319*

254 p   12 cm   NN

1846   [Polymicrian Testament] The New Testament . . . With Short Explanatory
         Notes, and Numerous References to Illustrative and Parallel Passages,
         Printed in a Centre Column . . . Published by A. S. Barnes & Co.: New York
                                                                               1320

12 cm   NB, NNAB
Reprint of the 1834 Polymicrian Testament published by Leavitt and Crocker & Brewster
(No 889). Stereotyped by James Conner appears at end of text.

1846   The New Testament . . . Published by H. and E. Phinney: Cooperstown,
         N. Y.   *1321*

187 p   Not Located
This book was not among those transferred by NBuDD to the Episcopal Theological Seminary of the Southwest, Austin, Texas.

1847–51   The Holy Bible . . . [Self Interpreting Bible with Brown's Notes]. Pub-
            lished by Joseph Neal: Baltimore   *1322*

1 vol: (876) 877–1216 1217–1222 [1]   40 cm   NN
Probably a reprint of Walker's 1820 (No 394) and 1822 (No 432) editions and of
Kinnersley's 1822 edition (No 433). Title pages are undated. The Bible was published by
subscription and issued in 40 parts. Bound with this copy are cover sheets to Parts 1 (containing Recommendations to this Edition) and 39–40. Part 1 imprinted *Published by John Wallace . . . : Baltimore;* and note reads "The cheapest Family Bible ever published. A new and
superb edition of Brown's Self Interpreting Bible. . . ." Preliminary matter includes frontispiece,
added illustrated title page, Introduction, Order of Books, and To the Reader by J. Brown.

Also A Calculation of the Number of Books, Chapters, Verses, Words, Letters, etc. of the Old and New Testaments and the Apocrypha. Family Record follows OT. At end are A Collection of Similes and Tables of Scripture Measures and Offices. Illustrated with numerous steel engravings.

O'Callaghan (p 312) describes an unlocated copy in parts, with Neal imprint dated 1847, but with slip pasted over it: *Published by John Cathers & Co. . . .* MDCCCLI. Parts 21–40 also have Wallace's address on the slip. He adds the type is badly worn.

1847   The Holy Bible . . . Canne's Marginal Notes and References . . . Apocrypha . . . Published by B. B. Mussey: Boston   *1323*

1 vol: (744) (133) 747–1010 (56)   30 cm   NNAB
Preliminary matter includes frontispiece, added engraved title, Advertisement to the Stereotype Edititon (dated 1819), To the Reader, and Order of Books. Family Record follows OT. Index, Tables, etc. at end. Also Brown's Concordance (stereotyped by B. &. J. Collins).

1847   The Holy Bible . . . Canne's marginal references . . . Apocrypha and concordance . . . index . . . table of texts . . . Lives and martyrdom of the apostles and evangelists. With plates. The text corrected according to the standard of the American Bible Society. Stereotyped by James Conner, New York . . . S. Andrus and Son: Hartford   *1324*

Reported as (527) (78) (168) (12)   30 cm   NcDaD
Stones's Guide to a Regular Perusal of the Holy Scriptures follows OT. Engraved titles and plates.

1847   The Comprehensive Bible . . . With Introduction . . . Introductions and Concluding Remarks to Each Book: The Parallel Passages . . . Philological and Explanatory Notes . . . Printed for Samuel Bagster: London . . . [Printed by T. K. and P. G. Collins]. Republished by the American and Foreign Bible Society: New York   *1325*

1 vol: (92) 93–1090 1091–1096 1097–1430 1431–1460   30 cm   NNAB
Editor's Preface (1826), General Contents, Translators to the Reader (1611), Contents, and Introduction precede text. History and Family Record follow OT. Tables and Indexes at end.
TNMPH has copy imprinted *London, printed for Samuel Bagster: Philadelphia, republished by J. B. Lippincott and Co.* See 1832 edition, No 770.

1847   The Holy Bible . . . Stereotyped by E. White, New-York . . . Published by E. Morgan and Co.: Cincinnati   *1326*

29 cm   OC
Similar to 1842 edition (No 1127) but without Apocrypha.

1847   [The Holy Bible] The New Testament . . . With Canne's Marginal References . . . The Text Corrected According to the Standard of the American Bible Society . . . Published by James A. Bill: Philadelphia   *1327*

1 vol: (527) (78) (168) (31) (54)   29 cm   NNAB
General title page missing from cited copy; above taken from NT title. With Apocrypha. Family Record follows OT. Frontispiece to NT. Index, Tables (by Hervey Wilbur), Guide to Daily Scripture Reading by William Stones, and Brown's Concordance at end. Illustrated.

1847   The Holy Bible . . . With References and Various Readings . . . In Two Volumes . . . Published by E. H. Butler & Co.: Philadelphia   *1328*

2 vols in 1: Vol I, 787 p; Vol II, (277) (139) 281–600   28 cm   NN

Butler's Edition appears at head of title. Vol I, Genesis-Song of Solomon, and Vol II, Isaiah-Malachi, Apocrypha, and NT, bound together. Colored frontispiece to each Testament. References arranged as footnotes. Published in 116 numbers. Illustrated.

This edition is notable for its very heavy black verse numbers, capitals, and italics. Reprinted in 1848, in 1857 by Harding (*Harding's Superfine Edition*), and in 187–? by Holman (*Holman's Imperial Quarto, English type*).

1847   The Holy Bible . . . Joseph Steen and Co.: Brattleboro, Vt.; J. B. Lippincott and Co.: Philadelphia   **1329**

Reported as (2) (vi) (2) (82) (46) 7–705 (54) (8) (216) (46) (63) (2) (53) (3) 27 cm   MWA

Polyglott edition. Has frontispiece and added engraved title page imprinted *Peabody and Daniell, Franklin, N. H.*

1847   The Holy Bible . . . The References and Marginal Readings of the Polyglott Bible, with Numerous Additions From Bagster's Comprehensive Bible . . . Published by Pratt, Woodford & Co.: New-York   **1330**

1 vol: (40) (581) 585–773   27 cm   NNAB

Frontispieces to Testaments. General Introduction; Introduction to NT and to each Book. Tables at end. Copyright by Conner & Cooke, 1833.

1847   The Holy Bible . . . Bible Association of Friends in America: Philadelphia
1331

Reported as (1062) (xxxiv) (92)   26 cm   InRE

Tables (some from Bagster's Comprehensive Bible) and Brown's Concordance (with separate title page) at end.

1847   The Holy Bible, translated from the Latin Vulgat . . . [Stereotyped by J. Howe]. Published by Eugene Cummiskey: Philadelphia   **1332**

"8vo"   DGU

Rheims-Douay Version, from the 5th Dublin edition. O'Callaghan (p 296) says this edition consisted of 500 copies. See 1824 Bible, No 492.

1847–48   The Holy Bible . . . [Thomas Scott's Notes, Observations, and References] . . . Silas Andrus & Son: Hartford   **1333**

4 vols: Vol I, (874) 875–876; Vol II, 965 p; Vol III, 828 p; Vol IV, (855) 856–872   23 cm
NNAB

A new edition of Scott's Bible; see 1804–09, No 113. Vol I (1847) Genesis-Esther; Epitome of History of the Jews at end. Vol II (1847) Job-Malachi; Family Record at end. Vol III (1848) Gospels & Acts, with Introduction and Postscript (notes in text and references at foot of page); Family Record at end. Vol IV (1848) Romans-Revelation; Accounts and Tables at end.

CtMW and NcD have NT only, the first dated 1845–55 and the second 1853.

1847   The Holy Bible . . . Stereotyped by J. Howe, Philadelphia . . . S. Andrus & Son: Hartford   **1334**

720 p   "12mo"   Not Located

O'Callaghan, p 297. Has two frontispieces; Metrical Psalms; illustrations.

1847   The Holy Bible . . . Stereotype Edition . . . Jesper Harding: Philadelphia **1335**

1 vol: (486) (162)   "12mo"   Not Located
O'Callaghan, p 296.

1847/45   The Holy Bible . . . Hogan and Thompson: Philadelphia   *1336*

"12mo"   Not Located

O'Callaghan (p 297) says this is a reprint of 1836 edition (No 943). NT dated 1845.

1847   The Holy Bible . . . J. B. Lippincott & Co.: Philadelphia   *1337*

"12mo"   Not Located

O'Callaghan, p 297. With Book of Common Prayer (1845).

1847   The Holy Bible . . . The Text of the Common Translation is Arranged in
Paragraphs, Such as the Sense Requires: the Divisions of Chapters and
Verses Being Noted in the Margin for Reference. By James Nourse . . . Amer-
ican and Foreign Bible Society: New York   *1338*

Reported as (vii) [1] (942) (324)   17 cm   Not Located
Listed in LC Union Catalog.

1847   The English Version of the Polyglott Bible . . . With the Marginal Readings;
Together with a Copious and Original Selection of References to Parallel
and Illustrative Passages, Exhibited in a Manner Hitherto Unattempted . . .
Sorin & Ball: Philadelphia   *1339*

15 cm   ViU
Has frontispiece, plates, and maps.

1847   The English Version of the Polyglott Bible . . . With the Marginal Readings
. . . A Copious and Original Selection of References to Parallel and Illustra-
tive Passages, Exhibited in a Manner Hitherto Unattempted: Hyde, Lord &
Duren: Portland   *1340*

1 vol: (viii) (587) (190)   15 cm   NNAB
   Has added engraved title pages (Sanborn and Carter, Portland, 1845), frontispieces, Order
of Books, and Preface signed T. C.

1847   The Holy Bible . . . Marginal Readings and References . . . Index of Scripture proper names . . . Joseph Longking, printer . . . Published by Lane &
Tippett, for the Methodist Episcopal Church: New York   *1341*

Reported as (804) (249)   14 cm   NjMD

1847   The English Version of the Polyglott Bible . . . With a Copious and Original
Selection of References to Parallel and Illustrative Passages, Exhibited in a
Manner Hitherto Unattempted. Stereotyped by Henry Wallis and L. Roby,
Concord, N. H. . . . Published by Grigg, Elliot & Co.: Philadelphia   *1342*

"24 mo"   Not Located

   O'Callaghan, p 297. Engraved title imprinted *Portland: Sanborn & Carter, 1845*. NT imprinted *Portland: Hyde, Lord & Duren, 1847*. Preface signed T. C. Each Testament has frontispiece and vignette. J. Roby may be misprint for L. Roby.
   Grigg, Elliot & Co. was succeeded by Lippincott, Grambo & Co.; see 1850, No 1435.

1847   The Holy Bible . . . G. Eckendorff: Philadelphia   *1343*

1 vol: (852) (259) 261–263 (81)   "24mo"   Not Located
O'Callaghan, 297. Contents and Metrical Psalms at end.

1847   The English Version of the Polyglott Bible . . . with Marginal Readings: Together with . . . References . . . Exhibited in a Manner Hitherto Unattempted
. . . Published by G. & C. Merriam: Springfield   *1344*

1 vol: (856) (259)   12 cm   NNAB
Order of Books and Preface signed T. C. precede text. Each Testament has frontispiece
and added engraved title imprinted *Geo. & Chas. Merriam.* Illustrated.

1847   The Holy Bible . . . Published by Merriam, Moore & Co.: Troy, New York
                                                                       1345

1 vol: (726) (8) (221) 222–224   11 cm   DLC, NNAB
Contents follow each Testament. NT has frontispiece and added engraved title with
Diamond New Testament . . . W. & H. Merriam. See 1836 Diamond Bible, No 946.
O'Callaghan (p 298) lists copy with Metrical Psalms (76 p).

1847   The Holy Bible . . . [Stereotyped by Thurston & Co., Portland, Me.]. Sanborn
& Carter: Portland   *1346*

1 vol: (817) (259)   "32mo"   Not Located
O'Callaghan, p 298. With Book of Common Prayer imprinted *Lippincott, Grambo & Co.:*
Philadelphia, 1850.

1847   The English Version of the Polyglott Bible . . . Published by the American
and Foreign Bible Society: New York   *1347*

"32mo"   Not Located
O'Callaghan, p 297. Each Testament has frontispiece and added engraved title with imprint *Springfield, Published by Geo. & Chas. Merriam.*

1847/46   The Holy Bible . . . Sanborn & Carter: Portland   *1348*

1 vol: (852) (259) [1]   11 cm   NNAB
Reprint of 1839 Sanborn edition (No 1052). Has frontispiece and added engraved title.
NT title dated 1846.

1847   The Holy Bible . . . Published by Jesper Harding: Philadelphia   *1349*

1 vol: (819) (256) (87)   11 cm   NNAB
Has frontispiece and added engraved title page. Metrical Psalms at end.

1847   The New Testament . . . Collins & Brother: New York   *1350*

Reported as 386 p   20 cm   ICU

1847   The New Testament . . . Translated Out of the Latin Vulgate . . . First Published by the English College of Rhemes . . . 1582. Newly Revised and Corrected According to the Clementine Edition . . . With Annotations . . . D. &
J. Sadlier: New-York   *1351*

1 vol: (xii) (344)   19 cm   NN, NNAB
Rheims Version. See 1842 NT, No 1151.

1847   The New Testament . . . Published by Henry Oliphant: Auburn   *1352*

299 p   18 cm   NN

1847   The New Testament . . . The Text of the Common Translation is Arranged
         in Paragraphs, Such as the Sense Requires . . . By James Nourse . . . American
         and Foreign Bible Society: New York   *1353*

  322 p   17 cm   ICU, NN

1847   The New Testament . . . [Stereotyped by R. C. Valentine . . . New York].
         H. & E. Phinney: Cooperstown   *1354*

  1 vol: (340) 341–344   "16mo"   Not Located
  O'Callaghan, p 298. Has Contents at end. Illustrated. MBU–T has copy dated 1848.

1847   The New Testament . . . [Printed by Reed and Cunningham]. Stereotyped
         by T. B. Smith for the American and Foreign Bible Society: New York *1355*

  12 cm   NNAB
  Fifth edition, same as 1845 NT (No 1284).

1847   The New Testament . . . With the Marginal Readings; and Illustrated by
         Marginal References, both Parallel and Explanatory, and a Copious Selec-
         tion, Carefully Chosen, and New Arranged . . . J. C. Riker: New-York   *1356*

  11 cm   NN
  Has frontispiece and illustrations. See 1833 NT, No 855.

1848   The Holy Bible . . . With Canne's Marginal Notes and References . . . Sum-
         ner & Goodman: Hartford   *1357*

  1 vol: (768) (96) (31) (28)   30 cm   NNAB
  Reprint of H. & E. Phinney quarto of 1824 (No 485). With Apocrypha, Concordance, and
  Metrical Psalms.
  Also issued without Metrical Psalms.

1848   The Holy Bible . . . With References and Various Readings . . . In Two Vol-
         umes . . . Published by E. H. Butler & Co.: Philadelphia   *1358*

  2 vols in 1   30 cm   NNAB
  Reprint of Butler's 1847 edition (No 1328). *Butler's Edition* appears at head of title. Has
  colored frontispieces, etc.

1848   The Holy Bible . . . [Printed by Thurston & Co., Portland, Maine]. Published
         by Hyde, Lord & Duren: Portland   *1359*

  1 vol: (574) 575–576 (96) 579–768 (31)   29 cm   NNAB
  With Apocrypha. Has frontispiece to each Testament, To the Reader [by Dr. Witherspoon],
  and Contents, Tables, Index, etc., and Concordance at end.

1848   The Pictorial Bible . . . Illustrated with More Than One Thousand Engrav-
         ings Representing the Historical Events . . . The Landscape Scenes . . . and
         the Subjects of Natural History, Costume and Antiquities . . . Published by
         Robert Sears . . . J. S. Redfield: New York   *1360*

  1 vol: (12) (1102) 1103–1124 (12) (348)   29 cm   NNAB
  Has added engraved title page and List of Illustrations. Chronology follows OT. NT has
  frontispiece and added engraved title. Illustrated.

1848   The Holy Bible . . . With Canne's Marginal References . . . and a Key Sheet of Questions . . . The Text Corrected According to the Standard of the American Bible Society. Merriam, Moore & Co.: Troy [New York]   *1361*

1 vol: (527) (78) (168) (31) (56) (24)   29 cm   NN

1848   The Holy Bible . . . With Canne's Marginal Notes and References. Together with the Apocrypha . . . Published by H. & E. Phinney: Cooperstown, N. Y.; F. W. Breed: Buffalo   *1362*

Reported as 768 p   29 cm   NCooHi, PPeSchw

Has frontispiece to each Testament and 6 other illustrations in OT. Family Record precedes Apocrypha (99 p); Tables precede NT. NT title imprinted *Sold also by I. Tiffany, Utica.* See 1824 Bible, No 485.

NCooHi copy has frontispieces and 4 other illustrations.

This is the last of the Cooperstown imprints as the plant burned down in 1849.

1848   The Holy Bible . . . [Stereotyped by J. Fagan, T. K. & P . G. Collins]. J. B. Lippincott & Co.: Philadelphia   *1363*

1 vol: (10) (1440)   28 cm   NNAB

Has frontispiece and colored fly leaf. Entire page of text is boxed in double rules. Illustrated.

1848–49   Comprehensive Commentary on the Holy Bible; Containing the Text According to the Authorized Version; Scott's Marginal References; Matthew Henry's Commentary, Condensed . . . The Practical Observations of T. Scott, with Extensive Explanatory, Critical and Philological Notes, Selected from . . . Writers on the Scriptures . . . Edited by W. Jenks . . . J. B. Lippincott & Co.: Philadelphia   *1364*

28 cm   OCH

OCH has Vols i and iii and Supplement (1849) only. See 1835–38, No 894.

1848   The English Version of the Polyglott Bible . . . With Marginal Readings . . . Published by Joseph Steen & Co., and G. H. Salisbury: Brattleboro, Vt.   *1365*

Reported as (705) (54) (216) (84)   28 cm   Privately Owned

Has frontispiece. Index at end. Illustrated. See 1847, No 1329.

1848   The Holy Bible . . . [Printed by T. K. and P. G. Collins]. American and Foreign Bible Society: New York   *1366*

Reported as 1440 p   27 cm   ICU

See Lippincott edition of this year, No 1363.

1848   The Holy Bible . . . Stereotype Edition . . . [Printed by Kite & Walton]. Printed for the American and Foreign Bible Society by the Bible Association of Friends in America: Philadelphia   *1367*

27 cm   NN, NNAB

Reprint of 1831 Bible Association of Friends in America edition (No 737). Has Tables, Index, etc., and Brown's Concordance at end.

1848   The English Version of the Polyglott Bible . . . Stereotyped by Conner & Cooke. Phillips and Sampson: Boston   *1368*

1 vol: (11) (16) (581) (106) 585–762 (78)   27 cm   NN

With Apocrypha. Has added engraved title pages, Preface signed T. C., and Tables. Frontispiece to NT. Index and Concordance at end. Illustrated.

1848   The Cottage Bible, and Family Expositor . . . With Practical Expositions and
        Explanatory Notes. By Thomas Williams . . . To which are Added, the Ref-
        erences and Marginal Readings of the Polyglott Bible, together with Orig-
        inal Notes and Selections from Bagster's Comprehensive Bible . . . The Whole
        Carefully Revised . . . Edited by Rev. William Patton . . . Complete in Two
        Volumes . . . Case, Tiffany & Burnham: Hartford   *1369*

        2 vols   27 cm   NN
        NN has Vol II only (737–1440 p). Has frontispiece, maps, plans, and historical engravings.

1848   The Holy Bible . . . Stereotyped by E. White, New York . . . Published by
        E. Morgan and Co.: Cincinnati   *1370*

        27 cm   OC
        Similar to 1842 Morgan edition (No 1127).

1848   The Holy Bible . . . [Printed by T. K. and P. G. Collins]. Stereotyped by L.
        Johnson, Philadelphia . . . Published by J. B. Lippincott & Co.: Philadelphia
                                                                              1371

        1 vol: (750) (238)   26 cm   NNAB
        Does not have supplementary matter or references.

1848   The Comprehensive Commentary on the Bible . . . Acts. Revelation. Edited
        by William Jenks . . . J. B. Lippincott & Co.: Philadelphia; Joseph Steen &
        Co.: Brattleboro   *1372*

        25 cm   PSC–Hi
        PSC–Hi has Vol v only. See 1835–38, No 894.

1848   The Holy Bible . . . With Canne's Marginal Notes and References . . . Pub-
        lished by Miller & Burlock: Philadelphia   *1373*

        829 p   "4to"   Not Located
        O'Callaghan (p 299) says this Bible was issued for the first time in November 1846, and
        by November 1859, 33,800 copies had been printed, some with Apocrypha, Brown's Concord-
        ance, and the Metrical Psalms. Those issued after 1851 are without date. Though represented
        by the publishers as a "new edition," this corresponds in text and other parts with the 1837?
        edition of Nafis & Cornish (No 973) and with that of James of Cincinnati, 1838 (No 1002).
        With Index and Tables at end.
        O'Callaghan (p 302) lists a separate NT with imprint of Edward W. Miller.

1848   The Holy Bible . . . With Canne's Marginal Notes and References . . . Harvey
        Griffith: Philadelphia   *1374*

        "4to"   Not Located
        O'Callaghan, p 299. Agrees with previous entry by Miller & Burlock (No 1373) except that
        Index and Tables are wanting and Concordance is added.

1848   The Holy Bible . . . The Proper Names of Which . . . Being Accurately Ac-
        cented in the Text . . . According to the Orthoepy of John Walker. By Israel
        Alger, Jun. . . . B. B. Mussey and Company: Boston   *1375*

        23 cm   ICU
        The Pronouncing Bible appears at head of title page. Has added engraved title page.

1848 The Holy Bible . . . Stereotyped by C. Davison & Company. [Printed by Leavitt, Trow & Co.] American and Foreign Bible Society: New York **1376**

1 vol: (508) 509–510 (161)   19 cm   NNAB

1848 The Holy Bible . . . Stereotyped by J. Howe . . . S. Andrus & Son: Hartford
1377

820 p   "12mo"   Not Located

O'Callaghan, p 301. Has frontispiece to OT. Contents and Metrical Psalms at end. Illustrated.

1848 The English Version of the Polyglott Bible . . . Stereotyped by L. Johnson . . . [Printed by Smith and Peters]. Thomas, Cowperthwait & Co.: Philadelphia   **1378**

1 vol: (587) (190)   "12mo"   Not Located

O'Callaghan, p 301. Has engraved frontispiece and added title to each Testament.

1848 The Holy Bible . . . The Text of the Common Translation is Arranged in Paragraphs, Such as the Sense Requires . . . By James Nourse . . . [Printed by John J. Reed]. American and Foreign Bible Society: New York   **1379**

18 cm   NNAB

Reprint of Perkins, Marvin and Co. 1834 edition (No 873). Copyright by Perkins, Marvin and Co., 1834.

1848 The Holy Bible . . . American Bible Society, Instituted . . . : New York **1380**

1 vol: (591) [1] (184)   18 cm   NNAB

Nonpareil or Sunday School Bible first printed this year, although cited copy is marked seventh edition. Has Tables on p [592].

1848 The Holy Bible . . . S. Andrus & Son: Hartford   **1381**

1 vol: (852) (259) 261–263 (81)   "24mo"   Not Located

O'Callaghan, p 301. Has frontispiece and added engraved title. Contents and Metrical Psalms at end.

1848 The Holy Bible . . . American Bible Society, Instituted . . . : New York **1382**

16 cm   NNAB

Pearl Reference 18mo Bible from a new set of plates, with slight differences from the 1840 edition (No 1083) although with same pagination.

1848 [The Holy Bible] The New Testament . . . J. B. Lippincott & Co.: Philadelphia   **1383**

1 vol: (856) (259) (77)   13 cm   NNAB

General title page missing from cited copy; above taken from NT. Metrical Psalms at end.

1848 The Holy Bible . . . Sanborn & Carter: Portland [Maine]   **1384**

1 vol: (818) (259)   12 cm   NN

The Everlasting Gospel appears on added engraved title. Frontispiece.

ΔE

NW TESTAMENT

OV WR

LORD AND SEVYWR

JYZUS KRIST,

TRANSLETED ΦT OV

ΔI WRIDINAL GRIK,

AND WIΔ

ΔE FORMUR TRANSLECUNZ DILIJENTLI
KOMPΘRD AND RXVIZD.

IN KOMSTOK'S PURFEKT ALFABET.

FILADELFIA:
PUBLICT BI A. KOMSTOK, M.D.,
Nu. 100 MULBERI STRYT.
1848.

Komstok's Purfekt Alfabet New Testament. No 1388.

1848   The Holy Bible . . . Published by Jesper Harding: Philadelphia   *1385*

Reported as (819) (256) (87)   "32mo"   MB
With Metrical Psalms.

1848   The Holy Bible . . . Thomas, Cowperthwait & Co.: Philadelphia   *1386*

"32mo"   Not Located
O'Callaghan, p 301. Has frontispiece and engraved title.

1848   The English Version of the Polyglott Bible . . . With Marginal Readings . . .
A Copious and Original Selection of References . . . Published by Chapin
Bridgman & Co.: Springfield   *1387*

11 cm   NN, NNAB
Reprint of the 1838 Merriam Bible (No 1019) but with Metrical Psalms at end (76 p).
NN copy lacks Metrical Psalms. NNAB copy has 1856 added engraved title imprinted
G. and C. Merriam.

1848   The New Testament . . . In Komstok's Purfekt Alfabet. [Stereotyped by
J. Fagan. Printed by Smith and Peters.] Publict bi A. Komstok . . . : Fila-
delphia   *1388*

1 vol: (8) 9–397 (4)   23 cm   NNAB
Preliminary matter (in roman type) includes Recommendations; Preface; A Phonetic Alphabet of the English Language, Graphic and Typic, by Andrew Comstock, M.D.; and Remarks on
the Phonetic Alphabet. The text is printed in a phonetic alphabet from a specially cut font
of type. The transliteration of the title, as above, is only an approximation.

1848   The New Testament . . . Translated from the Greek, Into Pure English; with
Explanatory Notes, on Certain Passages, Wherein the Author Differs from
Other Translators. By Jonathan Morgan . . . S. H. Colesworthy: Portland;
B. B. Mussey: Boston; P. Price: New York; J. Gihon: Philadelphia; A. T.
Ames: Cincinnatti [sic]; Noble and Dean: Louisville   *1389*

Reported as (ix) 11–307   19 cm   ICU, MeHi, NBuG, NcAS
Stereotype edition. The orthography is reported to be somewhat curious.
Jonathan Morgan was a lawyer and inventor in Portland, Maine, best remembered as an
eccentric who wore a weird wide hat, a long cloak, and huge goggles. A printer who had set
type for his Testament wrote that he was a constant attendant of the Universalist Church and
possibly one of its founders. He loved to ask questions that were very difficult to answer. He
seems to have been inactive as a lawyer and while his inventions were ingenious, he did not
perfect them or profit from them. He patented a coffee grinder with a long handle and devised
a brick steamboat. When his NT was being set he became interested in the plate-making
process — at that time a plaster cast was submerged for nearly a whole day in molten type
metal — and invented a "chemical card of *papier maché*" which, unfortunately, was consumed
in the hot metal. In his translation, he modified some of the language of the AV and left in
Greek some words on which translators differed. (*Post Scrapbook* iv, p 105.) This is a sample of
his work: "Ye are the salt of the earth: but if the salt hath perished, with what shall it be
salted? thenceforth it is good for nothing, if not to be outcast and downtrodden of men." —
Mt. 5:13. While Morgan made several attempts at spelling reform, the only instances appearing
on two pages examined (p 14 and 15) is the use of ä to separate vowels in *Judeä* and *liäble.*

1848   The Cottage Polyglot Testament . . . Sumner & Goodman: Hartford   *1390*

"12mo"   Not Located
Wright, p 402.

1848   The New Testament . . . The Text of the Common Translation is Arranged in
Paragraphs such as the Sense Requires . . . by James Nourse . . . American
and Foreign Bible Society: New York   *1391*

    324 p   17 cm   NNAB

1848   The New Testament . . . E. Hunt: Hartford, Conn.   *1392*

    288 p   16 cm   NN

1848   The New Testament . . . American Bible Society, Instituted . . . : New York
                                                             1393

    1 vol: (349) (3)   12 cm   NNAB
    Pocket Testament, first edition 1848. Contents at end.

1848   Polymicrian Testament . . . H. Perkins: Philadelphia   *1394*

    "32mo"   Not Located
    Wright, p 402.

1849   The Holy Bible . . . With Canne's Marginal References . . . Apocrypha . . .
The Text Corrected According to the Standard of the American Bible Society. Stereotyped by James Conner, New York . . . S. Andrus & Son: Hartford   *1395*

    1 vol: (527) (78) (168)   30 cm   NN

1849   The Holy Bible . . . With Marginal Readings, References and . . . Dates . . .
Joseph Longking, Printer. Published by George Lane and Levi Scott, for the
Methodist Episcopal Church: New York   *1396*

    30 cm   NNAB
    Reprint of 1844 Lane & Sandford edition (No 1193) with addition of Apocrypha (120 p)
and Barr's Dictionary of the Bible (53 p).

1849   The Holy Bible . . . With Canne's Marginal Notes and References . . . [Stereo-
typed by E. White, New York]. E. Morgan and Co.: Cincinnati   *1397*

    1 vol: (4) (6) (570) 573–770   28 cm   NNAB
    Has frontispiece to both Testaments. Preliminary matter includes To the Reader [by Dr.
Witherspoon], Order of Books, and Contents. Apocrypha wanting? Family Record precedes NT.
Verso of NT title has Chronology. Index and Tables at end.

1849   The Holy Bible . . . With Critical, Explanatory, and Practical Notes . . . A
Copious Collection of Parallel Texts; Summaries to Each Book and Chapter
. . . By Rev. Joseph Benson . . . G. Lane & L. Scott: New York   *1398*

    5 vols   27 cm   NN
    Reprint of 1822–24 Bible (No 435) with NT in Vols IV–V. NN has Vols II–IV only.

1849   The Cottage Bible, and Family Expositor . . . With Practical Expositions and
Explanatory Notes, by Thomas Williams. To Which are Added, the References and Marginal Readings of the Polyglott Bible, Together with Original
Notes, and Selections from Bagster's Comprehensive Bible, and Other Standard Works. Carefully Revised. Edited by Rev. William Patton . . . J. W. Bradley: Philadelphia   *1399*

    2 vols   "4to"   ICN

1849 The Holy Bible . . . With Canne's Marginal Notes and References . . . Published by Phinney & Co.: Buffalo; Ivison & Phinney: New York **1400**

"4to" Not Located

O'Callaghan, p 303. After the destruction of H. & E. Phinney's plates by the fire in 1849, Messrs. Phinney & Co. of Buffalo purchased from Sumner & Goodman, Hartford, Conn., the plates from which this Bible was printed. See 1822, No 439; also 1848, No 1362.

1849 The Holy Bible . . . Sanborn & Carter: Portland **1401**

"18mo" Not Located

O'Callaghan, p 390. Has added engraved title headed *The Everlasting Gospel* and dated 1847.

1849 The English Version of the Polyglott Bible . . . With Marginal Readings; Together with a Copious and Original Selection of References to Parallel and Illustrative Passages Exhibited in a Manner Hitherto Unattempted . . . J. B. Lippincott & Co.: Philadelphia **1402**

Reported as (vii) [1] 9–824 (256) 14 cm ViU
Illustrated.

1849? The Holy Bible . . . Miller & Burlock: Philadelphia **1403**

12 cm NNAB

Size and pagination of text are same as in Cowperthwait edition of 1838 (No 1021) and editions of numerous publishers after that date, but this Bible is from different plates. Has frontispiece and added engraved title. Metrical Psalms at end.

Also issued with *I. Ashmead* as printer on title page; with Contents (p 261–263); or with Apocrypha and imprint of Edward W. Miller.

O'Callaghan (p 305) says the first edition of this Bible was published in July 1849. At least twenty editions totalling 61,000 copies were issued.

1849 The Holy Bible . . . Published by Jesper Harding: Philadelphia **1404**

"32mo" Not Located
O'Callaghan, p 304.

1849 The Holy Bible . . . Leavitt & Allen: New York **1405**

Not Located

Wright, p 402.

1849 The New Testament . . . With Numerous Illustrations by W. Croome and J. H. Brightly . . . S. Augustus Mitchell, Jr.: Philadelphia **1406**

1 vol: (vi) (399) 26 cm NNAB

Has frontispiece, added engraved title, List of Illustrations, and Order of Books. Tables and Map of Palestine by Ira S. Drake at end.

Dr. Frank Weitenkampf ("American Bible Illustrations," *The Boston Public Library Quarterly*, July 1958, p 155) says the unsigned steel engravings "lack the lighter touch of Croome's drawings on the wood-blocks of other books, and are not especially inspired picturings."

1849 The New Testament . . . Stereotyped by C. Davison & Co., for the American and Foreign Bible Society: New York **1407**

406 [1] p 24 cm NNAB
Verso of title has Order of Books and Chronological List.

NNAB copy is interleaved with plain paper on which appear manuscript notes, probably by James J. Woolsey, whose name is written on the flyleaf. These consist of suggested changes, mostly from "baptize" to "immerse."

1849   The New Testament . . . American Bible Society . . . : New York   *1408*

670 p   19 cm   NNAB

This is the first of a series of diglot NTs published to meet the needs of great numbers of immigrants reaching this country in mid-century. It has facing title in German, Luther Version, and is printed in parallel columns with German on the left. Similar editions were printed this year with Danish and Dutch.

1849   The Pronouncing Testament. The New Testament . . . To Which is Applied
. . . the Orthoepy of the Critical Pronouncing Dictionary; Also, the Classical
Pronunciation of the Proper Names . . . Adopted from "A Key to the Classical
Pronunciation of Greek, Latin, and Scripture Proper Names. By John Walker
. . ." Prefixed, an Explanatory Key. By Israel Alger, Jun. . . . Crocker & Brewster: Boston   *1409*

"12mo"   MB

1849   The Cottage Polyglott Testament . . . With Notes Original and Selected . . .
Polyglott References and Marginal Readings . . . By William Patton . . . Sumner & Goodman: Hartford   *1410*

Reported as 718 p   "12mo"   MB
Has added engraved title page; maps.

1849   [The New Testament] The Good News of Our Lord Jesus, the Anointed;
from the Critical Greek Text of Tittmann . . . [Stereotyped by Hobart & Robbins, New England Type and Stereotype Foundry, Boston]. Published by
Joshua V. Himes: Boston   *1411*

484 p   17 cm   DLC, MB, MH–AH, NjMD, NN, NNAB

Preface signed by N. N. Whiting, Williamsburgh, Long Island. Text in paragraph form, with "controverted" texts printed in brackets.

Rev. Nathan N. Whiting was an Adventist. His translation is based on the Greek text of J. A. H. Tittmann as revised by Aug. Hahn and edited by Prof. Edward Robinson, 1842. The variations from the common version are few. In the Preface Whiting states: "Where the language of the common English version was not obscure, and where it gave the proper signification of the original it has been adopted." This is an "immersion" version.

1849   The New Testament . . . [Twelfth Edition]. Stereotyped by T. B. Smith, for
the American and Foreign Bible Society: New York   *1412*

1 vol: (344) (124)   12 cm   NNAB
Has Metrical Psalms (Arranged in Paragraphs and Parallelisms . . . , 1847) at end of text.

1849   The New Testament . . . Published by Phinney & Co.: Buffalo   *1413*

"32mo"   Not Located
O'Callaghan, p 305. First Buffalo edition; see No 1400 of this year.

1849   The Four Gospels, Translated from the Latin Vulgate, and Diligently Compared with the Original Greek Text, Being a Revision of the Rhemish Trans-

lation, with Notes Critical and Explanatory. By Francis Patrick Kenrick.
Bishop of Philadelphia ... Edward Dunigan & Brother: New-York   **1414**

572 p   24 cm   DGU, NN, NNAB

The Four Gospels: Map of Palestine, Dedication to the Bishops of the seventh Provincial
Council, Synopsis of the Gospels; Explanations; half title; General Preface; and Preface to St.
Matthew precede text. Notes below text. Preface to each Gospel. No Approbation.

"A few years ago, a new version of the four gospels, made directly from the Greek ... was
published in England by ... Dr. [John] Lingard ... I have freely availed myself of his
labors. ..." (General Preface, p 29.)

This is the first appearance of the Kenrick Version. Francis Patrick Kenrick (1797–1863)
was born in Ireland and received his theological training at the College of the Propaganda in
Rome. He came to the United States about 1820 to assume the chair of theology at Bardstown
Seminary in Kentucky. He was consecrated Bishop of Philadelphia in 1830 and was transferred
to the See of Baltimore in 1851. His brother, Peter Richard, became Archbishop of St. Louis.
Dr. Kenrick undertook a revision of the Rheims-Douay Bible, after it was decided at the
Provincial Council of Baltimore in 1829 to prepare a revision of that translation. His work was
published in parts over the period 1849–1860: The Four Gospels (1849); Acts-Revelation
(see 1851, No 1484); Psalms, Books of Wisdom, and Canticle of Canticles (see 1857?,
No 1665); Job-Prophets (see 1859, No 1708); Pentateuch (see 1860, No 1729); The Historical
Books (see 1860, No 1730). The complete New Testament (revised) (see No 1761) was published in one volume in 1862. The revision is based on the Latin Vulgate and Rheims-Douay
version. In the Introduction to the Pentateuch (p ix) Dr. Kenrick notes: "In revising the Douai
translation I have constantly had in view the Hebrew original, which, however, I did not always
feel at liberty to render closely where it would imply a departure from the Vulgate."

1850? The Holy Bible, Translated from the Latin Vulgate ... Published by Tallis,
Willoughby & Co.: London and New York   **1415**

"folio"   Not Located

O'Callaghan, p 306: "This is a copy of the engraved title page of an edition of the Douay
Bible proposed to be published in thirty parts by the above house, with thirty-one beautiful
engravings. In a cross in the centre of the paper cover, the following title was printed:
*The Holy Bible ... With Annotations, References, and Historical and Chronological Index.
The Whole Revised by the Rev. George L. Haydock. The Inaccuracies of Former Editions are
Corrected by the Very Rev. Dr. Hamell* [Hamill], *V. G.*"

"Only six numbers of this edition were issued and, the house having dissolved, the plates
were bought by D. & J. Sadlier and suppressed. The edition bore the approbations of the
Most Rev. the Archbishop of New York, the Bishops of Albany, Philadelphia, and many other
Catholic Divines in the United States."

1850 The Holy Bible ... The Text Conformable to the Standard of the American
Bible Society ... [Printed by Collins]. Whilt & Yost: Philadelphia   **1416**

1 vol: (574) 575–576 (88) 579–754 755–768 (22) (41)   30 cm   NNAB

With Apocrypha. Preliminary matter includes colored frontispieces, To the Reader, and
Contents. Tables follow OT. Family Record precedes NT. Index, Tables, Metrical Psalms, and
Concordance at end. Illustrated.

NNAB has second copy, undated.

1850 The Holy Bible ... With Canne's Marginal References, Together with the
Apocrypha ... To Which are Added an Index, and References, and a Key
Sheet of Questions ... The Text Corrected According to the Standard of the
American Bible Society ... Published by Thomas, Cowperthwait, & Co.:
Philadelphia   **1417**

30 cm   NNAB

Reprint of 1846 edition (No 1288) but with different frontispiece.

1850   The Holy Bible . . . The Apocrypha . . . Canne's Marginal notes and References . . . Index . . . [J. Harding, Printer]. Published by Jesper Harding: Philadelphia   *1417A*

30 cm   NNAB

A reprint of 1844 B (No 1196) but with added preliminary matter: Order of Books, To the Reader, and Contents. Index, tables, Brown's Concordance (54 p) and Metrical Psalms (18 p) at end.

1850   The Holy Bible . . . With the Marginal Readings, References and Chronological Dates . . . [Joseph Longking, Printer]. Published by George Lane and Levi Scott, for the Methodist Episcopal Church: New-York   *1418*

30 cm   NNAB

Reprint of the 1849 Lane and Scott edition (No 1396) including Barr's Dictionary.

1850   The Holy Bible . . . With Canne's Marginal References . . . Apocrypha . . . To Which are Added an Index, and References, and a Key Sheet of Questions . . . Accompanied with Valuable Chronological Harmonies of Both Testaments . . . The Text Corrected According to the Standard of the American Bible Society . . . Merriam, Moore & Co.: Troy, N. Y.   *1419*

30 cm   NNAB

Reprint of 1846 Merriam edition (No 1289). Includes wood engravings by Alexander Anderson.

1850   The Holy Bible . . . Canne's marginal references . . . Apocrypha . . . Concordance . . . Index . . . Lives and Martyrdom . . . Plates . . . Text corrected according to the . . . American Bible Society. Stereotyped by James Conner . . . S. Andrus and Son: Hartford   *1420*

Reported as (528) (78) (2) (168) (10) (2) (35) (19)   30 cm   VtHi

1850   The Holy Bible . . . Published by Phinney & Co.: Buffalo   *1421*

Reported as 768 p   29 cm   NBuHi
With Apocrypha.

1850   The Holy Bible . . . Apocrypha . . . Canne's Marginal Notes and References . . . Index . . . John B. Perry, J. W. Bradley, W. A. Leary: Philadelphia *1421A*

1 vol: (632) 146 635–829 (1) 22 57 19   29 cm   NNAB

Perry's New Stereotype Edition appears at head of title. Frontispiece, To the Reader, Order of Books, and Contents precede text. Family Record, with colored scenes, follows Apocrypha. Index, Concordance, and Metrical Psalms at end. Maps and 26 woodcuts, mostly by Anderson, in elaborate frames.

1850   The Holy Bible . . . With Canne's Marginal Notes and References . . . Luther Roby: Concord, N. H.   *1422*

1 vol: (576) (96) 579–768   29 cm   NNAB

Engraved frontispiece to each Testament. Preface from Collins' Bible. Tables (p 575–576). With Apocrypha followed by Family Record. Chronology on verso of NT title. Index, Tables, and Brown's Concordance at end. Illustrated.

1850   The Holy Bible . . . With References and Various Readings . . . Apocrypha
        . . . In Two Volumes . . . Published by E. H. Butler & Co.: Philadelphia *1423*

2 vols in 1   29 cm   NBuG, NNAB

Butler's Edition appears at head of title; see 1847, No 1328. Has illuminated frontispiece
and fly title.

1850   The Holy Bible . . . With Canne's Marginal Notes and References . . . Pub-
        lished by Wanzer, Foote & Co.: Rochester, N. Y.   *1424*

29 cm   NN

Corresponds to H. & E. Phinney 1824 edition (No 485) but has Concordance added (31 p).

1850   The Cottage Bible and Family Expositor . . . With Practical Expositions and
        Explanatory Notes. By Thomas Williams . . . The References and Marginal
        Readings of the Polyglott Bible, . . . With Original Notes, and Selections from
        Bagster's Comprehensive Bible . . . The Whole Carefully Revised . . . Edited
        by Rev. William Patton . . . Complete in Two Volumes . . . Printed and Pub-
        lished by Case, Tiffany and Company: Hartford   *1425*

2 vols   28 cm   NNAB

Reprint of 1833–34 Conner and Cooke edition (No 818).

1850   The Holy Bible . . . With Canne's Marginal References . . . Published by John
        B. Perry: Philadelphia; Nafis & Cornish: New-York   *1426*

1 vol: (632) 634–829 (xvi) (19)   28 cm   NN

Apocrypha and Concordance wanting. NT imprint has Perry's name only. Tables, etc.,
and Metrical Psalms at end. Illustrated.

1850   The Holy Bible, translated from the Latin Vulgate. Published with the Ap-
        probation of the Most Rev. John Hughes, D.D., Archbishop of New York,
        Most Rev. Samuel Eccleston, D.D., Archbishop of Baltimore, and the Right
        Rev. Bishop of Boston. With Parallel References . . . Edward Dunigan &
        Brother: New York   *1427*

Reported as 968 p   28 cm   NcU

Rheims-Douay Version, from Murray's 1825 Dublin edition. Reprint of Dunigan's 1844
Bible (No 1199) with new illuminated titles and 15 plates. Called "The Illustrated Family
Edition."

1850   The Holy Bible . . . With Canne's References . . . Published by A. C. Good-
        man & Co.: Hartford   *1428*

1 vol: (744) (138) 747–1010   28 cm   NN

With Apocrypha. Frontispiece to each Testament. Has Collins' Advertisement of 1819, Dr.
Witherspoon's Preface, Order of Books, and Account of Dates of Writing NT. At end are Index,
Tables, etc., Brown's Concordance, and Metrical Psalms.

1850   The Holy Bible . . . With Critical, Explanatory, and Practical Notes . . . A
        Copious Collection of Parallel Texts; Summaries to Each Book and Chapter
        . . . by Rev. J. Benson. G. Lane & L. Scott: New York   *1429*

5 vols   27 cm   NN

NN has Vols i–iii only; NT vols missing. See 1822–24, No 435.

1850 The Holy Bible . . . With Canne's Marginal Notes and References . . . S. Andrus: Hartford   **1430**

Reported as (811) (136) (39)   25 cm   ViU
Has a Concise Table of Contents of the Books of the Old and New Testaments.

1850 The Holy Bible . . . New York Bible and Common Prayer Book Society: New York   **1431**

"8vo"   Not Located
Wright, p 403.

1850 The Holy Bible, translated from the Latin Vulgat: With Annotations, References, and a Historical and Chronological Index . . . [Stereotyped by J. Howe]. Published by Eugene Cummiskey: Philadelphia   **1432**

"8vo"   Not Located
O'Callaghan (p 308) lists an edition of 500 copies of this Rheims-Douay Version. With Approbations of Archbishop Eccleston of Baltimore, Bishops Conwell and Kenrick of Philadelphia, and Bishop Hughes of New York. See 1839 Bible, No 1039.

1850 The Holy Bible . . . Lippincott, Grambo & Co., Successors to Grigg, Elliot & Co.: Philadelphia   **1433**

"12mo"   Not Located
O'Callaghan, p 308.

1850 The Holy Bible . . . Published by Hogan and Thompson: Philadelphia   **1434**

1 vol: (1098) (342)   "12mo"   Not Located
O'Callaghan, p 308.

1850 The English Version of the Polyglott Bible . . . With a Copious and Original Selection of References to Parallel and Illustrative Passages, Exhibited in a Manner Hitherto Unattempted . . . [C. Sherman, Printer]. J. B. Lippincott & Co.: Philadelphia   **1435**

1 vol: (viii) (824) (256)   15 cm   NNAB
Has colored frontispiece and added title page imprinted *Lippincott, Grambo & Co.* Preface to the English Version of the Polyglott Bible signed T. C.   Tables.

1850 The Holy Bible . . . American and Foreign Bible Society: New York   **1436**

15 cm   ICU

1850 The Holy Bible . . . Published by John Ball: Philadelphia   **1437**

1 vol: (x) 11–729 (225) (81)   13 cm   NNAB
Each Testament has frontispiece and added engraved title. Contents and Metrical Psalms at end.

1850 The Holy Bible . . . [Printed by C. Sherman]. Lippincott, Grambo & Co., Successors to Grigg, Elliot & Co.: Philadelphia   **1438**

1 vol: (726) (221) (76)   11 cm   NNAB
With Metrical Psalms.

1850   The Holy Bible . . . Published by Jesper Harding: Philadelphia   *1439*

"32mo"   Not Located

O'Callaghan, p 309.

1850   The New Testament . . . Translated from the Latin Vulgate . . . Newly Revised and Corrected, with Annotations, Explanatory of the most Difficult Passages. Illuminated after Original Drawings. By W. H. Hewett, Esq. . . . [John J. Reed, Printer]. Hewett & Spooner: New York   *1440*

1 vol: (389) 391–396   25 cm   NN

Rheims Version revised by the Rev. James McMahon. Presentation plate, Letter of Pius vi, Approbations (1847, 1848), Family Record, Preface, and Order of Books precede text. Index and Tables at end. Illustrated.

This is called "The Pictorial Catholic New Testament." It was originally published in numbers, the first in 1848. It is embellished with nearly 150 fine woodcuts. The edition was purchased in 1854 by John Murphy & Co., Baltimore, by whom the work was later issued, and this copy, though retaining the imprint of Hewett & Spooner, has Baltimore, Murphy & Co. on the back cover. (O'Callaghan, p 310.)

1850   The New Testament . . . Published by Thomas, Cowperthwait & Co.: Philadelphia   *1441*

"4to"   Not Located

O'Callaghan, p 309.

1850   Explanatory Notes Upon the New Testament by John Wesley . . . Lane & Scott: New York   *1442*

Reported as 734 p   24 cm   MiU, NcD, ODW

Wesley Version; see 1791 NT, No 35.

1850   The New Testament . . . American Bible Society . . . : New York   *1443*

1 vol: (447) [1] (112)   23 cm   NNAB

Pica Octavo, the first of a series of "standard editions." In 1847 the attention of the Committee on Versions had been called to the fact that there were minor variations among the English Bibles issued by the ABS and also by other publishers, mainly in the matter of the use of italics, punctuation, and capitalization. Italics had been used in the King James Bible to show that certain words not actually appearing in the Hebrew or Greek text were inserted to make sense in English; in black letter editions these were in small roman letters. The page headings also varied somewhat as it was necessary to revise them with most new settings since the Biblical material appearing on any page would be different. Changes seem to have been made by various printers, although American printers such as Isaac Collins claimed to have based their texts on the best Oxford and Cambridge editions, particularly the Oxford University Press edition of 1769 edited by Dr. Benjamin Blayney.

In 1847, the Board charged a committee to investigate the matter and prepare for the ABS a more accurate text, one in which the page headings and chapter summaries used only words and expressions found in the text. The Society's Royal Octavo Bible of 1833 (No 822) was to be compared with recent copies from London (BFBS?), Oxford, Cambridge, and Edinburgh, and with the original 1611 edition. The results of a 3½ years' study were published in the *Annual Report* for 1852 (p 28–37). The Committee's report pointed out that although 24,000 variations had been found among the six copies examined, "there is not one, which mars the integrity of the text, or affects any doctrine or precept of the Bible" (p 36).

The New Testament cited above was the first result of the report. It was followed in 1852 by the Bourgeois Octavo Reference Bible (No 1504) which was voted at the annual meeting of May 1851 to be the Society's standard.

1850   The Commonly Received Version of the New Testament . . . With Several
         Hundred Emendations. Edited by Spencer H. Cone and Wm. H. Wyckoff
         . . . Sold by Lewis Colby . . . Also by E. H. Tripp: New York. Duncan, Hurl-
         butt & Co.: New Orleans   *1444*

Reported as 394 p   22 cm   ICU, NcAS
Preface signed by C. & W., New York, April 1850.

The Rev. Spencer H. Cone, D.D. (1785–1855) had been a teacher, actor, and journalist
before being converted in 1814, after which he became a Baptist preacher. He was a Corresponding Secretary of the American Bible Society from 1833 to 1836 (when he became involved
in the controversy over "immerse" editions) and was active in the founding of the American
and Foreign Bible Society, serving as its president. In 1850, he was influential in founding the
American Bible Union, an organization of Baptists interested in the publication of an improved
version of the New Testament in English, and of which he was also president. (See 1862–63,
No 1764.) The Rev. Henry William Wyckoff (1807–1876) was editor of *The Baptist Advocate*
and minister of the Laight Street Baptist Church in New York. He was also active in the organization of the American and Foreign Bible Society and the American Bible Union.

The Cone-Wyckoff revision of the NT was based on the original Greek and the work of
numerous commentators during the previous 200 years. The editors claimed to "have removed
many of the most objectionable blemishes and so far made a good translation better," along
with having made "several hundred emendations." It was an "immersion" version.

Dr. Cone was eager to have the version made available and in 1851 it was published "at
the expense of a few benevolent individuals." Its publication at private expense grew out of
the controversy then existing regarding the refusal of organizations, such as the ABS, to print
sectarian versions. The revision was to serve until a more satisfactory work could be provided
and the plates were to be offered to the AFBS for wide distribution for purposes of criticism
and correction of the text.

ICN, NN, and NNAB have 1851 reprints by E. H. Tripp, New York (iv, 394 p). O'Callaghan (p 361) lists 1857 reprint, also by Tripp.

1850   The New Testament . . . Translated from the Latin Vulgate . . . With Anno-
         tations, etc. . . . Edward Dunigan & Brother: New York   *1445*

15 cm   PLatS
Rheims Version. Reprint of 1845 NT (No 1282) with new title page.

1850   The New Testament . . . H. S. & J. Applegate: Cincinnati   *1446*

344 p   12 cm   NN

1850   The New Testament . . . Miller and Burlock: Philadelphia   *1447*

"32mo"   Not Located
O'Callaghan, p 311. With Psalms. The publishers informed O'Callaghan that between
June 1850 and 1860 (?) they had issued seven editions of this NT amounting to 11,000 copies.

1850   The Polymicrian Testament . . . H. Perkins: Philadelphia   *1448*

"32mo"   Not Located
Wright, p 403.

1850? The New Testament . . . Published by J. H. Butler: Northampton   *1449*

384 p   9 cm   MBU–T, NNAB, ViU
Illustrated.
Privately owned copy, also undated, noted with four wood engravings signed "A.A." but
they do not seem to be up to Anderson's usual standard.

1851 The Holy Bible . . . The Text Conformable to the Standard Edition of the American Bible Society . . . Published by Lippincott, Grambo & Co., Successors to Grigg, Elliot & Co.: Philadelphia *1450*

30 cm NN

Has same pagination as old Phinney editions; see 1824, No 485. Frontispiece. Tables follow OT. Apocrypha and Family Record. Index, Tables, Concordance, and Metrical Psalms at end. References in central double column. Illustrated.

Also issued without woodcut illustrations.

1851 The Holy Bible . . . Leavitt & Allen: New York *1451*

30 cm NN

Similar to old Phinney editions; see 1824, No 485. Has colored frontispiece. Tables. With Apocrypha followed by Family Record. Concordance and Metrical Psalms at end.

1851 The Holy Bible . . . Apocrypha . . . Canne's Marginal Notes and References . . . Index . . . Tables . . . Concordance . . . Psalms of David in metre. Published by John B. Perry . . . for sale by Wm. A. Leary & Co.: Philadelphia *1452*

Reported as (574) (88) (4) 579–768 (41) (22) 30 cm PSt
Illustrated.

1851 The Comprehensive Bible . . . With the Various Readings and Marginal Notes Usually Printed Therewith . . . Introductions and Concluding Remarks to Each Book . . . The Parallel Passages Contained in Canne's Bible . . . Philological and Explanatory Notes . . . A Chronological Index . . . Lippincott, Grambo & Co.: Philadelphia *1453*

Reported as (1460) (24) 30 cm PMA
See 1832, No 770.

1851 The Holy Bible . . . With Canne's Marginal References . . . To Which are Added, an Index, a table of texts, and . . . An Account of the Lives and Martyrdom of the Apostles and Evangelists . . . The Text Corrected According to the Standard of the American Bible Society. Stereotyped by James Conner . . . S. Andrus and Son: Hartford *1454*

Reported as (527) (78) (168) (10) (35) (19) 30 cm CtY
With Apocrypha. Frontispiece and other illustrations. Family Record. Index, Tables, and Concordance at end.

1851 The Holy Bible . . . Apocrypha . . . With Canne's Marginal Notes and References . . . Jesper Harding: Philadelphia *1455*

1 vol: (570) (112) 573–748 749–770 (35) (18) (10) 30 cm NNAB
Reprint of Kimber & Sharpless 1823 Bible (No 460) with appended materials. *Kimber & Sharpless' Edition* appears at head of title. The Kimber & Sharpless plates were sold to Jesper Harding in 1844.

1851 The Holy Bible . . . Lippincott, Grambo & Co.: Philadelphia *1456*

1 vol: (1098) 1101–1440 28 cm NN
Has frontispiece and added engraved title page. Family Record follows NT.

1851   The Holy Bible . . . With . . . Canne's Marginal Notes and References . . .
         Published by A. C. Goodman & Co.: Hartford   *1457*

   1 vol: (744) (138) 747–1010   28 cm   NN
   With Apocrypha followed by Family Record. Each Testament has engraved frontispiece.
Preliminary matter includes Advertisement to Collins' stereotype edition of 1819, Dr. Wither-
spoon's Preface, Order of Books, and Account of Dates. Historical Accounts, Concordance, and
Metrical Psalms at end.

1851–52   Comprehensive Commentary on the Holy Bible . . . Scott's Marginal Ref-
            erences, Matthew Henry's Commentary . . . Edited by William Jenks. Lip-
            pincott & Co.: Philadelphia   *1458*

   5 vols   28 cm   ODW
   See 1835–38, No 894.

1851   The Holy Bible . . . With References and Marginal Readings of the Polyglott
         Bible, with Numerous Additions from Bagster's Comprehensive Bible . . .
         Published by Pratt, Woodford & Co.: New York   *1459*

   1 vol: (40) (581) 585–762 763–773   27 cm   NN
   Each Testament has engraved frontispiece. Introduction, various tables, and Family
Record. Index and Tables at end.

1851   The Cottage Bible, and Family Expositor . . . With Practical Expositions and
         Explanatory Notes. By Thomas Williams . . . The References and Marginal
         Readings of the Polyglott Bible . . . Notes . . . from Bagster's Comprehensive
         Bible . . . The Whole Carefully Revised . . . Edited by Rev. William Patton
         . . . Complete in Two Volumes . . . [Stereotyped by Conner & Cooke]. Printed
         and Published by Case, Tiffany and Company: Hartford   *1460*

   2 vols   27 cm   NN, NNAB
   Printed from plates of Conner & Cooke 1833–34 Bible (No 818) but with different illustrations. NN has Vol I only; NNAB has Vol II only. Copyright 1833 by James Conner and William R. Cooke.

1851   The Holy Bible . . . With a Commentary and Critical Notes . . . By Adam
         Clarke . . . Super Royal Octavo Stereotype Edition . . . H. S. & J. Applegate &
         Co.: Cincinnati   *1461*

   4 vols   27 cm   ICU
   Adam Clarke's Commentary; see 1811–25, No 188. Vol I, Genesis-Esther. Vol II, Job-
Malachi. Vol III, Matthew-Acts. Vol IV, Romans-Revelation. Has frontispiece.
   TNMPH has Vol IV only.
   Reprinted in 1854 (IaU, Vol IV only), 1855 (In, Vols I–III only), 1856 (MiU, InUpT),
1858 (FT), 1860 (C), and in 1861 by Applegate, Pounsford & Co. (ViU).

1851   The Holy Bible . . . With Canne's Marginal Notes and References . . . James
         M. Alden: Auburn   *1462*

   "4to"   Not Located
   O'Callaghan, p 315. Printed from duplicate plates of Phinney's edition; see 1824, No 485.
With Apocrypha. Index, Tables, and Concordance at end.

1851   The Holy Bible . . . With the Marginal References and the Usual Various
         Readings . . . Notes; Reflections; Questions; Improved Readings; Improved

Divisions of Chapters; the Chronological Order; Metrical Portions Distinguished; and Various Other Advantages, Without Disturbing the Usual Order of the Books, Verses and Chapters. By the Rev. Ingram Cobbin . . . Samuel Hueston: New York   **1463**

1 vol: (1000) (376) (xii)   "4to"   Not Located

O'Callaghan, p 314. *The Illustrated Domestic Bible* appears on added title page. Preliminary matter includes Preface (dated Camberwell, August 15, 1847) and Key to This Work. Historical Connexion of the Old and New Testaments and Family Record follow OT. Supplementary illustrations, selected chapters adapted for reading on particular occasions, and indexes at end. Illustrated.

Issued in 25 numbers. The work first appeared in London in 1837. See 1856 Bible, No 1613.

1851   The Holy Bible . . . Translated from the Latin Vulgate: With Annotations by the Right Rev. Dr. Challoner: Together with References . . . and Corrected According to the Clementine Edition of the Scriptures. With the Approbation of the Most Rev. John Hughes . . . Archbishop of New York . . . Published by D. & J. Sadlier & Co.: Boston . . . Montreal   **1464**

"4to"   DGU

Rheims-Douay Version, from the 5th Dublin edition. Reprint of Sadlier's 1845 Bible (No 1249).

1851   The Holy Bible . . . With References and Various Readings, and Apocrypha . . . In Two Volumes . . . Published by E. H. Butler & Co.: Philadelphia **1465**

2 vols   "4to"   ViU

Butler's Edition; see 1847, No 1328.

[*1851*]   The Holy Bible . . . With Canne's Marginal Notes and References . . . James A. Bill: Philadelphia   **1466**

"4to"   Not Located

O'Callaghan (p 313) says this is Miller and Burlock's 1848 edition (No 1373) with Apocrypha, Brown's Concordance (56 p, published by Edward W. Miller, Philadelphia, 1850), and Metrical Psalms (19 p).

1851   The Holy Bible . . . American Bible Society . . . : New York   **1467**

1 vol: (1026) (6) 5–320   26 cm   NNAB

Pica Royal Octavo, the first whole Bible with the standardization changes, but not all of them. See 1850 NT, No 1443; also 1852 Bible, No 1504.

1851   The Holy Bible . . . New York Bible and Common Prayer Book Society: New York   **1468**

"8vo"   Not Located

Wright, p 403.

1851?   The Holy Bible . . . Published by Richard & George S. Wood: New York **1469**

1 vol: (486) (162)   "12mo"   Not Located

O'Callaghan, p 316. Verso of title has Richard and George S. Wood, Proprietors, New York printed in an oval border, and inside the oval is Woodvale Water-power Press, Morristown, N. J. Error in ɪ Tim 4:16.

1851   The Holy Bible . . . Lippincott, Grambo & Co., Successors to Grigg, Elliot &
         Co.: Philadelphia   *1470*

1044 p   "12mo"   Not Located
O'Callaghan, p 316.

1851   The English Version of the Polyglott Bible . . . With . . . Marginal Readings,
         . . . References to Parallel and Illustrative Passages . . . Illustrated . . . Lip-
         pincott, Grambo & Co.: Philadelphia   *1471*

1 vol: (viii) (824) (256)   15 cm   NNAB, ViU
With Tables and maps.

1851   The English Version of the Polyglott Bible . . . Stereotyped by L. Johnson
         . . . Thomas, Cowperthwait & Co.: Philadelphia   *1472*

"24mo"   Not Located
O'Callaghan, p 316. Reprinted from 1839 Bible (No 1049).

1851   The Holy Bible . . . Sanborn & Carter: Portland   *1473*

1 vol: (818) (259)   12 cm   NNAB
Has frontispiece. *The Everlasting Gospel* appears on added engraved title which is dated
1847.

1851   The Holy Bible . . . Lippincott, Grambo & Co., Successors to Grigg, Elliot &
         Co.: Philadelphia   *1474*

1 vol: (726) (221) (81)   "32mo"   Not Located
O'Callaghan, p 316. Has Metrical Psalms.

1851   The Holy Bible . . . Lippincott: Philadelphia   *1475*

Reported as (856) (259) (77)   12 cm   ICN
Has Metrical Psalms.

1851?   The New Testament . . . With Brief Notes and Instructions, By Rev. Justin
          Edwards . . . Containing the References and Marginal Readings of the Poly-
          glott Bible. Published by the American Tract Society: New York and Boston
                                                                                1476

425 p   24 cm   ICU, NB, NjMD, NN, NNAB, PHi
Family Bible appears at head of title. Has references below text between single rules, with
notes below. Copyright by O. R. Kingsbury, 1851.
Also issued with maps and with Psalms of David (paged 665–766) bound in. See 1853–56
Bible, No 1530.

1851   The New Testament; or, The Book of the Holy Gospel of our Lord and our
         God, Jesus the Messiah. A Literal Translation from the Syriac Peshito Ver-
         sion. By James Murdock, D.D. [Stereotyped by Billin & Brothers. M'Gown,
         Printer.] Published by Stanford and Swords, No. 137 Broadway: New York
                                                                                1477

1 vol: (ix) (471) 473–515   23 cm   NNAB
Title in Syriac characters appears at head of title page. Text in single column, paragraph
form, with verse numbers in text. Variant notes and Syriac words (in Jacobite characters) in

outer margin. Appendix I, Distribution of the Syriac New Testament into Lessons, and Appendix II, The Syriac Translations of the Scriptures, at end. Copyright 1851 by James Murdock.

James Murdock (1776–1856) graduated from Yale College and entered the Congregational ministry. He was later professor of Ancient Languages at the University of Vermont, and professor of Sacred Rhetoric and Ecclesiastical History at Andover Theological Seminary. In 1828 he retired to devote himself exclusively to the study of church history, orientalia, and philosophy. Among his many undertakings was the translation of the NT into English from the Syriac. In the Preface, Mr. Murdock states that his aim was to accomplish a literal translation in idiomatic English (modelled after the AV) in Saxon rather than Latin phraseology, using English forms of proper names from the Peshito. The translation was considered a faithful and scholarly one, and was well and widely received.

Reprinted in 1852 with portrait of translator (NNAB) and in 1855. Issued with imprint of Robert Carter & Brothers: New York, various years from 1858 to 1879 (NNAB has 1859 copy). Horace L. Hastings of Boston reprinted it in 1892 (BM). In an 1893 "sixth edition" he contributed a historical introduction and sketch of the translator; a bibliographical appendix by Dr. Isaac H. Hall takes the place of Murdock's Appendix II (xlviii, 507 p, 23 cm, NNAB).

1851? The New Testament . . . R. & G. S. Wood: New York   **1478**

   310 p   19 cm   NNAB

1851? The New Testament . . . Translated out of the Latin Vulgate: With Annotations . . . D. & J. Sadlier: New York   **1479**

   344 p   17 cm   NN
Rheims Version. See 1842 NT, No 1151.

1851 The New Testament . . . American Bible Society . . . : New York   **1480**

   1 vol: (371) 372–376 (100)   17 cm   NNAB
Brevier 18mo with Psalms. Contents (p 372–376). First printed in 1839, without Contents.

1851 The New Testament . . . Translated from the Latin Vulgate; With Annotations . . . Approved by the Most Rev. John Hughes . . . Archbishop of New York . . . Edward Dunigan & Brother: New York   **1481**

   356 p   "18mo"   Not Located
O'Callaghan, p 318. Rheims Version. See 1845 Dunigan NT, No 1282.

1851 The New Testament . . . American Bible Society . . . : New York   **1482**

   1 vol: (353) 354–356   13 cm   NNAB
Agate 32mo, eleventh edition, probably first printed in 1850. Has Contents on p 354–356.

1851 The New Testament . . . American Bible Society . . . : New York   **1483**

   384 p   11 cm   NNAB
Diamond 64mo, ninth edition, probably first printed in 1850. New ABS standard text; see 1850 NT, No 1443.
Also issued with Psalms (100 p).

1851 The Acts of the Apostles, the Epistles of St. Paul, the Catholic Epistles, and the Apocalypse. Translated from the Latin Vulgate, and diligently compared with the Greek text, being a revision of the Rhemish Translation, with Notes, Critical and Explanatory, By Francis Patrick Kenrick, Bishop of Philadelphia . . . Edward Dunigan and Brother: New York   **1484**

   Reported as 680 p   "8vo"   DGU, NN
Bishop Kenrick's Version; see 1849, No 1414. This completes Kenrick's NT.

1852 The Holy Bible, translated from the Latin Vulgate . . . With Useful Notes
. . . by the Rev. George Leo Haydock . . . Edward Dunigan and Brother:
New York   **1485**

Reported as 1671 p   36 cm   DGU, DLC
Rheims-Douay Version. Haydock text edited by the Rev. James McMahon. With Approbation of the Most Rev. Archbishop Hughes, May 1852. Engravings.
NN has copy with 1854 NT.
First issued in 38 parts. Editing was begun by the Rev. J. R. Bayley, later Bishop of Newark,
but carried on and completed by the Rev. J. McMahon. While many corrections were made,
some errors remained. One is at Gen 1:16, note: light is said to "be nearly 3000 years in coming to us from the remotest star in our *stratum*," for *system*. (O'Callaghan, p 320–322.)

1852 The Holy Bible . . . With Marginal Readings, References, and Chronological
Dates . . . Joseph Longking, Printer. Published by George Lane & Levi Scott:
New York   **1486**

1 vol: (xii) (2) (757) (237) 238–240 (11) (39)   31 cm   NNAB
Preliminary matter includes frontispiece, Brief Account of the Authorized Version by
Adam Clarke, Divine Authority of the Scriptures by Rev. John Fletcher, Contents of the OT,
Tables, and Order of Books followed by Chronological Order. Family Record pages follow OT.
Contents of Books; Discourses, Parables, and Miracles of Jesus; Chronology of the Holy Bible;
and Concordance at end.

1852 The Holy Bible . . . The Text Conformable to the Standard of the American
Bible Society . . . Stereotyped by L. Johnson. Published by John B. Perry:
Philadelphia   **1487**

1 vol: (574) (2) (88) 579–754 755–768 (41) (22)   30 cm   NNAB
Names of six agents follow publisher on title page. With Apocrypha. Has frontispiece to
each Testament. To the Reader and List of Contents of Books precede text. Tables follow OT.
Verso of NT title has Dates of Writing NT. Index, Tables, etc., Concordance, and Metrical
Psalms at end. Illustrated.
Pagination follows that of old Phinney editions (see 1824, No 485), but this is apparently
the first issue in this format with double column center references. The 1852 James edition
(No 1491) is probably from the same molds, as the impression is far less clear than in this
Johnson-Perry edition.
Reprinted in 1855 and 1856. Jesper Harding printed a similar edition (Harding's Fine
Edition) from his own plates in 1857 (No 1639). These plates passed to his successor, A. J.
Holman, who printed from them in 1872 (No 1875) and later. Other similar editions were
issued by John Edwin Potter, Philadelphia, in 1865 (No 1789); by William Flint, Philadelphia,
in 1869 (No 1838); and by C. F. Vent, New York and Cincinnati, and others, J. Fagan & Son,
Stereotypers, in 1871 (No 1866).

1852 The Holy Bible . . . With Canne's Marginal Notes and References . . . Published by Alden, Beardsley & Co.: Auburn; Wanzer, Beardsley & Co.:
Rochester   **1488**

1 vol: (574) (2) (96) 576–754 755–768   30 cm   NNAB
With Apocrypha. Frontispiece to each Testament. Verso of title has Order of Books. To
the Reader [by Dr. Witherspoon from Collins' Bible] and Contents precede text. Index, Tables,
etc. follow each Testament.

1852 The Holy Bible . . . Canne's Marginal References . . . Index, a table of texts
. . . an account of the lives and martyrdom of the apostles and evangelists
with plates. The text corrected according to the standard of the American
Bible Society. Published by E. T. Day: Hartford   **1489**

Reported as (527) (168)   30 cm   NjMD
With Metrical Psalms (19 p).

1852   The Holy Bible . . . With Canne's Marginal Notes and References . . . Published by Edward W. Miller: Philadelphia   **1490**

1 vol: (632) 635–829 (xxi) (10)   29 cm   NNAB
Has frontispieces to Testaments. To the Reader, Order of Books, and List of Contents. Family Record follows OT. Verso of NT title has Dates of Writing NT. Index, Tables, etc., and Metrical Psalms at end.

1852   The Holy Bible . . . with the Apocrypha . . . a Concordance, the Psalms of David in Metre, an Index, Tables, and Other Useful Matters. The Text Conformable to the Standard of the American Bible Society . . . [Stereotyped by A. C. James]. Published by J. A. & U. P. James: Cincinnati   **1491**

1 vol: (574) (88) 579–768 (41) (22)   29 cm   NNAB
Frontispiece, Order of Books, To the Reader, and Contents precede text. Illustrated. See Perry Bible of this year (No 1487).

1852   The Holy Bible . . . Apocrypha . . . Canne's marginal notes and references . . . Index . . . tables . . . Phinney & Company: Buffalo   **1492**

768 p   29 cm   Privately Owned

1852   The Holy Bible . . . The Text Conformable to the Standard of the American Bible Society . . . T. K. Collins, Jr.: Philadelphia   **1493**

Reported as (768) (22) (41)   29 cm   In
Similar to old Phinney editions; see 1824, No 485. Family Record precedes NT.

1852   The Holy Bible, Translated from the Latin Vulgate . . . With Annotations, by The Rev. Dr. Challoner; Together with References and . . . Index. Revised and Corrected According to the Clementine Edition . . . With the Approbation of the Most Rev. John Hughes . . . Published by D. & J. Sadlier & Co.: New York . . . Boston . . . Montreal   **1494**

1 vol: (12) (793) (11) (228) (2) (4) (118) (6)   29 cm   DGU, NNAB
Rheims-Douay Version. Each Testament has frontispiece and added engraved title. Approbations precede text. Family Record and Index follow OT. Admonitions, Prayers, etc. precede NT. Tables, Index, and Ward's Errata to the Protestant Bible at end. See 1845?, No 1249.

1852   The English Version of the Polyglott Bible . . . critical introduction by Joseph Warne . . . essay by James Macknight . . . Sermons by Philip Doddridge . . . Concordance . . . Index . . . engravings . . . Published by Joseph Steen & Co. and G. H. Salisbury: Brattleboro', Vt.   **1495**

28 cm   VtHi
Pagination same as in 1841 Brattleboro Typographic Co. edition (No 1102), but with insertion of 82-page section before the twenty plates.

1852   The Holy Bible . . . Translated from the Latin Vulgate: With Annotations, References, and Index. From the Last London and Dublin Editions. Published with the Approbation of the Most Rev. John Hughes . . . Archbishop of New York . . . Published by Edward Dunigan & Brother: New York   **1496**

27 cm   DGU
Rheims-Douay Version. Has colored title and frontispiece to each Testament. See 1844, No 1199.

1852   The Holy Bible . . . [Stereotyped by J. Fagan. Printed by T. K. & P. G. Collins]. Lippincott, Grambo & Co., Successors to Grigg, Elliot & Co.: Philadelphia   *1497*

27 cm   NNAB

Reprint of Lippincott's 1848 edition (No 1363) but with different engravings.

1852   The Holy Bible . . . With the References and Marginal Readings of the Polyglot Bible. With Numerous Additions from Bagster's Comprehensive Bible . . . Pratt, Woodford and Co.: New York   *1498*

27 cm   CEU

See 1851, No 1459.

1852   The Holy Bible, Translated from the Latin Vulgate . . . With Annotations and References, and . . . Index. P. Donahoe: Boston   *1499*

1 vol: (4) 5–681 682–691 [1] (2) (2) (4) 5–189 190–191 [1]   26 cm   DGU, NNAB

Rheims-Douay Version. Each Testament has engraved frontispiece and Index. Family Record follows OT. Tables at end. Approbation of Bishop of Boston added. See Cummiskey's 1836 edition, No 935.

MBtS, NN, and NNAB have copies on cheaper paper, without rules, Family Record, or frontispieces (22 cm).

O'Callaghan (p 324) says this was printed from the plates of Cummiskey's 1824 edition, Lucas having sold the plates to Donahoe, and quotes an advertisement of the small edition: "The Unrivalled dollar edition of the Douay Bible."

1852   The Holy Bible . . . Translated from the Latin Vulgate . . . With Annotations, References and Indexes . . . [Stereotyped by J. Howe]. Published by Eugene Cummiskey: Philadelphia   *1500*

26 cm   DGU

Rheims-Douay Version. See 1836, No 936.
O'Callaghan (p 323) says 500 copies were printed.

1852–53   Annotations upon the Holy Bible; Wherein the Sacred Text is Inserted, and various Readings Annexed, Together with the Parallel Scriptures . . . by Matthew Poole . . . R. Carter and Brothers: New York   *1501*

3 vols   26 cm   Not Located

Matthew Poole (1624–1679), an English Nonconformist theologian, had completed the notes through Isaiah 58 at his death. The work was carried on by his colleagues and first published about 1685.

1852   The Cottage Bible and Family Expositor . . . With Practical Expositions and Explanatory Notes, by Thomas Williams; To Which are Added the References and Marginal Readings of the Polyglott Bible, Together with Original Notes and Selections from Bagster's Comprehensive Bible . . . The Whole Carefully Revised . . . Edited by Rev. William Patton . . . Case: Hartford
1502

2 vols   "4to"   MnM

With plates and maps.

1852   The Holy Bible . . . Published by Carlton & Phillips: New-York   *1503*

1 vol: (872) (268)   25 cm   NNAB

Tables, Order of Books, and Family Record are included between OT and NT.

1852 The Holy Bible . . . American Bible Society . . . : New York   **1504**

1 vol: (839) (7) 843–1100   24 cm   NNAB

Bourgeois Reference Octavo, the first official edition with the new ABS standard text. See 1850 NT, No 1443.
NNAB also has an 1868 corrected copy.

1852 The Holy Bible . . . American Bible Society . . . : New York   **1505**

1 vol: (835) (5) (260)   20 cm   NNAB

Brevier Duodecimo, the first in this size printed with new ABS standard text. Composition of this book began before that for the 1850 NT (No 1443) but printing did not take place until 1852. This contains the earliest changes for a whole Bible. The chapter summaries are like those in the Pica Royal Octavo of 1851 (No 1467).
NNAB also has 1866 copy with corrected headings and chapter summaries.

1852 The Holy Bible . . . Lippincott, Grambo & Co., Successors to Grigg, Elliot & Co.: Philadelphia   **1506**

Reported as 1044 p   20 cm   NcWfC

1852 The Holy Bible . . . Published by the New York Bible and Common Prayer Book Society: New York   **1507**

"12mo"   Not Located
O'Callaghan, p 325.

1852 The Holy Bible . . . Stereotyped by J. Howe, Philadelphia . . . S. Andrus and Son: Hartford   **1508**

1 vol: (499) 503–655 (26) 661–720   18 cm   NNAB

Frontispiece and Contents precede text. Tables between Testaments. General Contents and Metrical Psalms at end. Illustrated.

1852 The Holy Bible . . . Thomas, Cowperthwait & Co.: Philadelphia   **1509**

1 vol: (852) (259) (3) (81)   "32mo"   Not Located

O'Callaghan, p 325. Has frontispiece and added engraved title. Contents and Metrical Psalms at end.

1852 The New Testament . . . Expounded and Illustrated According to the Usual Marginal References in the Very Words of the Holy Scriptures, with Notes and a Complete Marginal Harmony of the Gospels . . . By Clement Moody . . . [Joseph Longking, Printer]. Published by George Lane and Levi Scott: New York   **1510**

Reported as (viii) (655)   27 cm   DLC

1852 The Cottage Polyglott Testament . . . With Notes, Original and Selected; Likewise Introductory and Concluding Remarks to Each Book, Polyglott References and Marginal Readings, Chronological Table, Geographical Index, and Maps. . . . By W. Patton: A. C. Goodman & Co.: Hartford   **1511**

718 p   19 cm   NNAB

Added engraved title has imprint *Sumner & Goodman.* Maps.

1852   The New Testament . . . Published by J. M. Alden: Auburn   *1512*

"12mo"   Not Located
O'Callaghan, p 326.

1852   The New Testament . . . Translated from the Latin Vulgate: With Annota-
         tions . . . Edward Dunigan & Brother: New York   *1513*

356 p   15 cm   NN
Rheims Version. See 1845 NT, No 1282.

1852   The New Testament . . . Leavitt & Allen: New York   *1514*

191 p   "18mo"   Not Located
O'Callaghan, p 327.

1852   An Exposition of the New Testament, or The New Covenant of Our Sover-
         eign Saviour. The Anointed. [Version in idiomatic English] By Hezekiah
         Woodruff . . . Henry Oliphant, Printer: Auburn   *1515*

"16mo"   DLC, MH–AH
Of the Gospels, only Matthew is included. Divisions are entitled as follows. The Gospel of
Matthew — "The Good News of Salvation According to Matthew"; The Acts — "The Doings
of the Commissioners"; the Epistles — "The Letter of Paul to the Romans," etc. The object
of the author of this edition was "to benefit the rising generation by presenting to them the Holy
Scriptures . . . in an idiom with which they are familiar. . . ." (From Introduction, as quoted
in Cheek, p 33.) Cheek (p 71) goes on to say that "if the KJ itself was not used as a basis,
Woodruff had a text very close to it."

1853   The Holy Bible . . . With Canne's Notes . . . Stereotyped by James Conner,
         New York . . . Silas Andrus & Son: Hartford   *1516*

"folio"   Not Located
O'Callaghan, p 328. Reprint of 1829 edition (No 666). With Apocrypha, Index, and Tables.

1853   The Holy Bible . . . Translated from the Latin Vulgat: With Useful Notes.
         . . . By the Rev. Geo. Leo Haydock . . . Edward Dunigan and Brother: New
         York   *1517*

1671 p   36 cm   Not Located
O'Callaghan, p 330. Rheims-Douay Version. See 1852, No 1485.

1853? The Holy Bible . . . Translated from the Latin Vulgate . . . With Useful
         Notes, Critical, Historical . . . and Explanatory . . . By the Late Rev. G. L.
         Haydock, and Other Divines . . . The Text Carefully Collated with that of
         the Original Edition, and the Annotations Abridged, by the very Rev. F. C.
         Husenbeth . . . G. Virtue, 26 John Street: New York   *1518*

1 vol: (viii) (691) [1] (385) (2) (4) (x) (355) (3)   32 cm   DGU, NNAB
Rheims-Douay Version. Haydock text edited by Husenbeth. Has colored title page and
added engraved title pages. Family Record follows OT. Verso of Dedication has Certificate of
Accuracy signed by F. C. Husenbeth, Vicar General in the Eastern District of England and
Canon of the English Chapter, dated 1850. All the Approbations on the following two leaves
are by clergymen of the British Isles. NT imprinted *Virtue, Emmins and Roberts, 26 John Street*.
Illustrated with 43 plates.
O'Callaghan (p 329) says this work was originally printed at Bungay in Suffolk, England,
and published in London, 1853, in two volumes with 51 engravings. The plates were later im-
ported into this country and the work issued in New York in 36 numbers. The copy he describes

adds London to the NT imprint, has two pages with the Approbations of three American Archbishops and seven Bishops, and includes one engraving not in the NNAB copy. Father Parsons says it contains many errors.

1853 The Holy Bible ... With Canne's Marginal Notes and References ... Jesper Harding: Philadelphia   **1519**

    1 vol: (5) (6) (570) (112) 573–770   30 cm   NN
    With Apocrypha. *Harding's Fine Edition* at head of title. Has colored frontispieces and added engraved title. Index, Tables, Concordance, and Metrical Psalms at end. Illustrated with numerous woodcuts.

1853 The Comprehensive Bible ... With the Various Readings and Marginal Notes Usually Printed Therewith. A General Introduction ... Introductions and Concluding Remarks to Each Book: The Parallel Passages Contained in Canne's Bible; Dr. Adam Clarke's Commentary ... Rev. J. Brown's Self-Interpreting Bible ... Dr. Blayney's Bible; Bishop Wilson's Bible, edited by Crutwell; Rev. T. Scott's Commentary ... and the English Version of Bagster's Polyglott Bible, Systematically Arranged: Philological and Explanatory Notes: ... Lippincott, Grambo & Co., Successors to Grigg, Elliot & Co.: Philadelphia   **1520**

    1 vol: (6) (92) 93–1090 1091–1094 1097–1430 1431–1460   30 cm   NNAB
    Has illuminated frontispiece and added title page. Preliminary matter includes Order of Books followed by Chronological Order, Editor's Preface (London 1826), General Contents, The Translators to the Reader, Contents of the Old and New Testaments, Analysis and Compendium of the Sacred Scriptures, and Introduction. General Outline of the History of the Jews and Family Record follow OT. NT has frontispiece and title. Chronological Index; Index to the Subjects; and Index to Notes, Introductions, and Concluding Remarks at end. Double center reference columns with chronology.
    For first Comprehensive Bible, see 1832 Andrus and Judd edition, No 770. Other Lippincott editions were issued in 1854 (NNAB); 1855, with Apocrypha and Metrical Psalms (NN); 1857, J. B. Lippincott and Co., with Apocrypha and Metrical Psalms (NNAB, NcD); and 1859, with text in rules and printed on larger fine paper (NNAB).

1853 The Holy Bible ... With Canne's Marginal Notes and References ... Published by Hall, Mills & Co.: Syracuse   **1521**

    1 vol: (744) (138) 747–974 975–1010 (56) (22)   30 cm   NNAB
    With Apocrypha. Frontispiece to each Testament. Preliminary matter includes Advertisement to the Stereotype Edition (New York 1819), To the Reader, Order of Books, and Dates of Writing NT. Index, Tables, etc., Brown's Concordance (stereotyped by B. & J. Collins), and Metrical Psalms at end.

1853 The Holy Bible ... With Canne's Marginal Notes and References ... Phinney & Co.: Buffalo   **1522**

    Reported as (576) (96) 577–768   29 cm   N
    With Apocrypha. Index and Tables at end. Illustrated.

1853 The Holy Bible ... Translated from the Latin Vulgate: The Old Testament was First Published at Doway ... 1609 and the New Testament ... at Rheims ... 1592. With Annotations by Dr. Challoner ... Published by D. & J. Sadlier & Co.: New York   **1523**

    28 cm   DLC
    Rheims-Douay Version. Includes Ward's Errata. See 1845?, No 1249.
    O'Callaghan (p 330) describes a copy with NT dated 1857.

1853   The Holy Bible . . . With References and Various Readings . . . E. H. Butler
         & Co.: Philadelphia   *1524*

28 cm   NN
Butler's Edition appears at head of title; see 1847, No 1328. Has frontispiece and other
plates.

1853   The Cottage Bible, and Family Expositor . . . With Practical Expositions and
         Explanatory Notes. By Thomas Williams . . . To Which are Added the Ref-
         erences and Marginal Readings of the Polyglott Bible, Together with Orig-
         inal Notes, and Selections from Bagster's Comprehensive Bible . . . The
         Whole Carefully Revised . . . Edited by Rev. William Patton . . . Complete in
         Two Volumes . . . Printed and Published by Case, Tiffany and Company:
         Hartford   *1525*

2 vols   28 cm   NNAB
Printed from Conner and Cooke plates of 1833–34 Bible (No 818) which were purchased
by Case, Lockwood & Co. Stereotyped by Conner & Cooke.

1853   The Holy Bible, Translated from the Latin Vulgate . . . The Old Testament,
         first Published . . . at Douay, A.D. 1609; and the New Testament, First Pub-
         lished . . . at Rheims, A.D. 1582. With Annotations, References and . . . In-
         dex. From the Last London and Dublin Editions . . . E. Dunigan & Brother:
         New York   *1526*

968 p   26 cm   Not Located
Listed by DLC Union Catalog. Rheims-Douay Version. Illustrated. See 1844, No 1199.

1853   The Annotated Paragraph Bible . . . Arranged in Paragraphs; with Explana-
         tory Notes, Prefaces to the Several Books, and an Entirely New Selection of
         References to Parallel and Illustrative Passages . . . C. B. Norton: New York
                                                                               1527

25 cm   NNAB
Probably 2 vols, but NNAB has Vol i only, Genesis-Solomon's Song, 720 p. Has Table of
Contents and Index (2 p) and Preface (6 p). Introductions to each book, copious notes below
text, and references in left margin. The editor's name does not appear in this volume. Illustrated.

1853   The Self-Explanatory Reference Bible . . . With Marginal Readings, and
         Original and Selected Parallel References, Printed at Length . . . R. Carter
         and Brothers: New York   *1528*

1 vol: (734) (227) (10) (58)   25 cm   NNAB
The British royal arms appears on the title page; on the verso is Collins' license to print
dated 1852. Preface is unsigned. Tables (10 p) and Metrical Psalms and Paraphrases (58 p)
at end. Map. The actual text of related passages is printed in two central columns in smaller
type. William Collins and Co., Glasgow, Printers appears at end of Metrical Psalms; probably
imported in sheets.

1853-57   A Commentary on the Holy Bible; Containing the Old and New Testa-
         ments . . . With . . . Notes . . . Observations . . . and References . . . by Thomas
         Scott. In Five Volumes, from the Last London Edition . . . W. S. & A. Mar-
         tien: Philadelphia   *1529*

5 vols   "4to"   NN

Scott's Annotated Bible; see 1804–09, No 113. Contains Family Record, Tables, Brown's Concordance, and Metrical Psalms.

Also found with all vols dated 1857. DLC has 1858 edition and OrPR has 1861 set.

[*1853–56*] The Family Bible . . . With brief notes and instructions by Rev. Justin Edwards . . . Including the references and marginal readings of the Polyglot Bible . . . published by the American Tract Society: New York . . . and Boston
1530

3 vols: Vol I, (664); Vol II, 665–1166; Vol III, (441) 665–766   24 cm   NNAB

All volumes are undated. Vol I (copyright 1853) Genesis-Job. Vol II (copyright 1856) Psalms-Malachi, followed by Family Record. Vol III, the matching NT, seems to be a reprint of the 1851 edition (No 1476) with the addition of Tables (p 426–441) and Psalms (AV, p 665–766). The NT title does not mention Justin Edwards.

The object as stated on the verso of title "is to assist common readers to understand the meaning of the Holy Spirit in the Bible. . . ." It also announces the second volume of the OT in preparation, the NT having already been published.

1853 The Holy Bible . . . Lippincott, Grambo & Co., Successors to Grigg, Elliot & Co.: Philadelphia   **1531**

"8vo"   Not Located

O'Callaghan, p 331. Has text inside double rules.

1853 The Holy Bible . . . Lippincott, Grambo, & Co.: Philadelphia   **1532**

1044 p   20 cm   NN

1853 The Holy Bible . . . American Bible Society . . . : New York   **1533**

767 p   19 cm   NNAB

Nonpareil Duodecimo prepared for Sunday Schools, with new ABS standard text and shorter chapter summaries. See 1850 NT, No 1443.

This must have been one of the first Bibles prepared in the new Bible House at Astor Place, opposite Cooper Union, to which the Society moved in 1853. The ABS's earliest depositories from 1816 to 1823 were in various locations on Nassau and Cedar Streets, Cliff near Fulton, and Sloat Lane (Hanover Street) near Exchange; in 1823 it built a new home on Nassau Street which, with various additions, was occupied until 1853. In this fine six-story building all printing and distributing operations could be carried on and the income derived from rented space used to cover maintenance costs. For an interesting description of the publishing processes in the 1860s, see the chapter entitled "For Christians to Read," in *Mark Twain's Travels with Mr. Brown* (Knopf 1940, p 202–209), in which Twain describes his visit to the building in 1867. The ABS moved most of its activities from the Astor Place building in 1936 and in 1953 the building was sold. It was demolished in 1956 to make way for new buildings for Cooper Union.

1853 The English Version of the Polyglott Bible . . . With Marginal Readings . . . Lippincott, Grambo & Co.: Philadelphia   **1534**

1 vol: (824) (256)   15 cm   IU, NN

Illustrated.

NN copy has Metrical Psalms (77 p) and colored frontispiece.

1853 The English Version of the Polyglott Bible . . . The Marginal Readings: Together with a Copious and Original Selection of References to Parallel and Illustrative Passages . . . Stereotyped by L. Johnson . . . Thomas, Cowperthwait & Co.: Philadelphia   **1535**

15 cm   NNAB

Reprint of the 1839 Cowperthwait edition (No 1049) with the addition of the Metrical Psalms at end (62 p).

1853   The Holy Bible . . . American Bible Society . . . : New York   *1536*

965 p   15 cm   NNAB

Agate 24mo possibly first printed in 1852, with new ABS standard text. See 1850 NT,
No 1443. Replaced by the Agate 18mo Bible in 1867 (No 1818).

1853   The Holy Bible . . . C. Sherman, Printer. Miller & Burlock: Philadelphia *1537*

12 cm   NNAB

Reprint of Miller & Burlock 1849 edition (No 1403).

1853/58   The Holy Bible . . . [Printed by Smith and Peters . . . Philadelphia]. Hop-
     kins, Bridgman & Co.: Northampton, Mass.   *1538*

1 vol: (852) (259) (3) (81)   12 cm   NNAB

Each Testament has added engraved title and frontispiece. Metrical Psalms at end. NT
dated 1858.

1853/51   The Holy Bible . . . Sanborn & Carter: Portland   *1539*

"32mo"   Not Located

O'Callaghan, p 332. Has frontispiece. Metrical Psalms. NT dated 1851.

[*5614*] *1853*   תורה נביאים וכתובים [The Old Testament] The Twenty-Four Books
     of the Holy Scriptures: Carefully Translated According to the Massoretic
     Text, on the Basis of the English Version, after the Best Jewish Authorities;
     and Supplied with Short Explanatory Notes. By Isaac Leeser . . . [Stereo-
     typed by L. Johnson & Co., Philadelphia] . . . Published at 371 Walnut Street:
     Philadelphia   *1540*

1 vol: (iv) (1011)   29 cm   NNAB

Leeser Version; see 1845–46, No 1273. Preface (dated 5613, Sept 20th, 1853) and added
title with *Pentateuch* in Hebrew and English precede text. Variant renderings and added words
are placed between parentheses. Text is printed in double columns with notes at foot of page,
always in verse paragraph form. Copyright 1853, by Isaac Leeser.

1853   The New Testament . . . Translated from the Latin Vulgate: With Annota-
     tions by the Right Rev. R. Challoner . . . Together with References . . . Re-
     vised and Corrected According to the Clementine Edition of the Scriptures
     . . . Published by D. & J. Sadlier & Co.: New York . . . Boston . . . Montreal
                                                                                  1541

"4to"   Not Located

O'Callaghan, p 333. Rheims Version. Reprinted separately from Sadlier's 1845? Bible
(No 1249). With engravings.

1853   Explanatory Notes Upon the New Testament. By John Wesley . . . Carlton &
     Phillips: New York   *1542*

734 p   24 cm   ICU

Wesley Version; see 1791 NT, No 35.

1853   The New Testament . . . Designed for the Study of Youth . . . by Ingram Cob-
     bin . . . Edited by D. Mead . . . G. Pratt: New York   *1543*

1 vol: (iv) (426)   20 cm   NN

Illustrated.

1853 The Pronouncing Testament . . . to which is applied . . . the ortheopy . . . by
John Walker . . . by Israel Alger, Jun. A.M. . . . Published by Crocker and
Brewster: Boston   **1544**

Reported as 292 p   20 cm   NjMD

1853 The New Testament . . . Translated from the Latin Vulgate . . . First Published by the English College, at Rheims . . . 1582 . . . Approved by the Most
Rev. John Hughes . . . E. Dunigan & Brother: New York   **1545**

Reported as 356 p   16 cm   NjMD
Rheims Version. See 1845 NT, No 1282.

1853 Polymicrian New Testament . . . Clark & Hesser: Philadelphia   **1546**

"32mo"   Not Located
Wright, p 404. See 1832 Polymicrian NT, No 811.

1854? The Holy Bible, Translated from the Latin Vulgate . . . The Old Testament,
First published . . . at Douay . . . 1609. And the New Testament . . . at Rheims
. . . 1582. With Useful Notes, Critical, Historical, Controversial, and Explana-
tory . . . by G. L. Haydock . . . The Text Carefully Collated with that of the
Original Edition, and the Annotations Abridged by F. C. Husenbeth . . . G.
Virtue: New York   **1547**

1 vol: (691) (385) (x) (356)   32 cm   NN
Rheims-Douay Version. NT imprinted *London and New York, Virtue, Emmins and Roberts.*
See 1853, No 1518.

1854 The Holy Bible . . . With References and Various Readings . . . Jesper Harding: Philadelphia   **1548**

1431 p   30 cm   NNAB
Hogan & Thompson's Edition appears at head of title. With Apocrypha. Has colored frontispiece and title.

1854 The Holy Bible . . . With Canne's Marginal Notes and References . . . Jesper
Harding: Philadelphia   **1549**

1 vol: (4) (6) (570) (112) 573–770   29 cm   NN
Harding's Fine Edition at head of title. With Apocrypha. Colored frontispiece to each
Testament. Family Record precedes NT. Index, Tables, Concordance, and Metrical Psalms at
end. Illustrated with 22 plates.

1854 The Holy Bible . . . With Canne's Marginal Notes and References . . . Published by Phinney & Co.: Buffalo; Ivison & Phinney: New York   **1550**

1 vol: (574) 575–576 (96) 579–768 (32) (28) (6)   29 cm   NNAB
Similar to 1824 Phinney edition (No 485) but Apocrypha has been reset and woodcuts
are different.

1854–56 The Holy Bible . . . With Critical, Explanatory, and Practical Notes . . .
A Copious Collection of Parallel Texts; Summaries to Each Book and Chapter . . . by the Rev. Joseph Benson . . . Carlton & Phillips: New York   **1551**

5 vols   27 cm   MiU, PP
PP has Vols i–iii only, Genesis–Malachi. MiU has Vols iv–v only, NT text. Reprint of
1822–24 edition (No 435). See also 1839, No 1038, for pagination.

1854 A Complete Analysis of the Holy Bible . . . Containing the Whole of the Old and New Testaments Collected and Arranged Systematically, in Thirty Books . . . [based on the work of the learned Talbot] . . . With an Introduction . . . by Nathaniel West . . . Sixth Edition . . . Charles Scribner: New York   *1552*

Reported as (lxiv) (958)   "4to"   KyLo, ViLxW

1854 The Holy Bible . . . Stereotype Edition . . . Printed for the American and Foreign Bible Society, By the Bible Association of Friends in America: Philadelphia   *1553*

26 cm   NNAB
Reprint of the 1831 octavo (No 737).

1854 The Holy Bible . . . Moore, Anderson & Co.: Cincinnati   *1554*

Reported as (576) (86) 577–768 (41) (22)   "4to"   MiAlbC
With Apocrypha. Index, Tables, Concordance, and Metrical Psalms at end. Illustrated.

1854 The Holy Bible . . . Mills, Hopkins & Co.: Syracuse   *1555*

1148 p   "4to"   Not Located
O'Callaghan, p 336. Illustrated.

1854 The Holy Bible, Translated from the Latin Vulgate . . . The Old Testament, First Published . . . at Douay . . . 1609; and the New Testament . . . at Rheims . . . 1582. With Annotations, References, and an . . . Index. Published with the Approbation of J. Hughes, Archbishop of New York. Edward Dunigan & Brother: New York   *1556*

968 p   24 cm   NN
Rheims-Douay Version. See 1844, No 1199.

1854 The Holy Bible . . . With References and Various Readings . . . Published by E. H. Butler & Co.: Philadelphia   *1557*

1 vol: (1214) (336)   24 cm   MB, NN
Butler's Edition appears at head of title. Each Testament has added engraved title page. Family Record follows OT.
Also issued printed on tinted paper; with colored plates and illuminated title pages; and with Apocrypha.

1854? The Holy Bible . . . Barrington & Haswell: Philadelphia   *1558*
"8vo"   MB
With Apocrypha.

1854 [Specimen Number] English Series. The Divine Library; or Cyclopedia of Inspiration. The Holy Bible: . . . According to the Authorized Version; The Sixty-Six Books in Separate Volumes, or Convenient Combination of Volumes, with or without Appendices . . . and a Prepared Student's Memorandum . . . Second Thousand . . . T. H. Stockton: Baltimore   *1559*

(iv) 3–12 13–18 (8)   19 cm   NNAB
The above title is taken from a specimen number containing the First Epistle of John only. It was issued to illustrate a "New, Copyright Plan for the Publication of the Bible," by T. H.

Stockton. Copyright Maryland, 1854. This specimen number contains the following publication notices: (1) The text in this edition is conformed to the recently revised and standard copy of the American Bible Society. (2) The marginal renderings are retained. (3) The paragraphs correspond with those in Bagster's Critical New Testament — Greek and English. (4) Verse numbers in margin. The text is followed by a 14-page Prospectus. See 1858, No 1690.

1854   The Holy Bible . . . New-York Bible and Common Prayer Book Society: New
       York   1560

   1044 p   19 cm   NNAB

1854   The English Version of the Polyglott Bible . . . Lippincott, Grambo & Co.:
       Philadelphia   1561

   Reported as (824) (256) (77)   15 cm   MiU
   With Metrical Psalms.

1854   The Holy Bible . . . [Printed by C. Sherman]. Lippincott, Grambo & Co.:
       Philadelphia   1562

   1 vol: (725) (221) (81)   "32mo"   Not Located
   O'Callaghan, p 337. With Metrical Psalms.

1854/51   The Holy Bible . . . Blake and Carter: Portland   1563
   11 cm   ViU
   Has frontispiece. NT dated 1851.

1854   The New Testament . . . With References and Various Readings . . . Pub-
       lished by E. H. Butler & Co.: Philadelphia   1564

   "4to"   Not Located
   O'Callaghan, p 338. *Butler's Edition* at head of title. Pica type.

[1854]   The New Testament . . . [Stereotyped by John Howe]. Thomas Davis's
         Edition: Philadelphia   1565

   240 p   20 cm   NN

1854   Explanatory Notes Upon the New Testament. By John Wesley . . . New Edi-
       tion. With the Manuscript Corrections of the Author. George Peck, Editor
       . . . Carlton & Phillips: New York   1566

   Reported as 446 p   18cm   ICU
   Wesley Version; see 1791 NT, No 35.
   ICU also has 1846 edition, 16 cm.

1854   The New Testament . . . Smith & English: Philadelphia   1567
   288 p   16 cm   NN

1854   The New Testament . . . Translated from the Latin Vulgate . . . Edward
       Dunigan & Brother: New York   1568

   356 p   15 cm   Not Located
   O'Callaghan, p 338. Rheims Version. See 1845 NT, No 1282.

1854   The Polymicrian Testament . . . Clark & Hesser: Philadelphia   *1569*

"32mo"   Not Located

Wright, p 405. See 1832 NT, No 811.

1855   The Holy Bible . . . Electro-Stereotyped by L. Johnson & Co., Philadelphia.
         Printed by C. Sherman & Co.   H. C. Peck and Theo. Bliss: Philadelphia *1570*

1 vol: (1130) (382)   36 cm   NNAB

Standard Imperial Quarto Bible. Printed from Stereo-Copper Plates appears at head of
title. Has Family Record. Index of Subjects, Harmony of the Four Gospels, and Tables of Scripture Weights, etc., at end. References in center column.

1855   The Holy Bible . . . Translated from the Latin Vulgate: With . . . Notes . . .
         By the Rev. George Leo Haydock . . . Edward Dunigan and Brother: New
         York   *1571*

34 cm   NN

Rheims-Douay Version. Reprint of 1852 Dunigan Bible (No 1485). IaDaM has copy with
NT dated 1854.

1855   The Holy Bible . . . The Text Conformable to the Standard of the American
         Bible Society. John B. Perry . . . Leary & Getz: Philadelphia; Walker &
         Medairy, John Cushing & Co., and Cushing and Bailey: Baltimore   *1572*

30 cm   NNAB

Reprint of Perry's 1852 Bible (No 1487) but without Metrical Psalms at end. Has colored
frontispiece and illuminated titles to both Testaments. Colored illustrations throughout.
Also issued without Apocrypha, and with Metrical Psalms.

1855   The Holy Bible . . . With Canne's Marginal Notes and References . . . Jesper
         Harding: Philadelphia   *1573*

1 vol: (570) (112) 573–770 (35) (18)   29 cm   NNAB

With Apocrypha. Index, Tables, etc., Concordance, and Metrical Psalms at end.

1855   The Holy Bible . . . With Canne's Marginal References . . . To Which are
         Added an Index, References, and a Key Sheet of Questions . . . Harmonies
         of Both Testaments . . . Useful Tables . . . The Text Corrected According to
         the Standard of the American Bible Society . . . Merriam, Moore & Co.: Troy,
         New York   *1574*

29 cm   NN

Reprint of Merriam 1846 edition (No 1289) which was also published in 1850 (No 1419).

1855   The Holy Bible . . . The Text Conformable to the Standard of the American
         Bible Society . . . J. B. Perry: Philadelphia   *1575*

768 p   29 cm   NN

Each Testament has frontispiece. Family Record. Index, Tables, and Metrical Psalms follow NT. References in double center column.
Also issued without date or with Brown's Concordance (87 p).

1855?   The Holy Bible . . . With Canne's Marginal Notes and References . . . Alden
          and Beardsley: Auburn and Rochester   *1576*

29 cm   NN, NNAB

Reprint of Alden, Beardsley & Co., etc. 1852 Bible (No 1488) but with Concordance (31 p) added.

CaOH has a similar edition imprinted *Campbell, Sherrill and Co.; Hamilton, C. W., 1855.* The title page matches line for line but is printed with different type from No 1576. This firm appears in the 1856 Hamilton Directory but not in 1853 or 1858. This Bible was probably imported in sheets with Hamilton title locally printed.

1855 The Holy Bible . . . with references and various readings . . . Apocrypha. In two volumes . . . E. H. Butler & Co.: Philadelphia   **1577**

2 vols in 1: (4) (1787) [1] (2) 3–277 (3) (139) [1] (4) (2) 281–600   29 cm
                                                                         NNAB

Each Testament has engraved frontispiece and lithographed special title. References at foot of page. Chronology after chapter summaries.

1855 The Holy Bible . . . With Canne's Marginal Notes and References . . . Sheldon, Lamport & Blakeman: New York   **1578**

29 cm   NN

Similar to old Phinney editions; see 1824, No 485. Lacks Apocrypha, although it is included in List of Books. Has frontispieces to both Testaments. Tables at end of OT, and Index and further Tables at end. References in outer margins, no rules.

1855 The Holy Bible, Translated from the Latin Vulgate . . . With Annotations, by the Rev. Dr. Challoner; Together with References, and an Historical and Chronological Index. Revised and Corrected According to the Clementine Edition of the Scriptures . . . With the Approbation of J. Hughes . . . D. & J. Sadlier & Co.: New York   **1579**

1 vol: (793) (228)   27 cm   M, NNAB
Rheims-Douay Version. See 1845?, No 1249. Does not have Ward's Errata.

1855 The Holy Bible, Translated from the Latin Vulgate: With Annotations . . . Published with the Approbation of the Most Reverend John Hughes . . . Published by Edward Dunigan & Brother: New York   **1580**

968 p   26 cm   NN
Rheims-Douay Version. See 1844, No 1199.

1855 A Comprehensive Commentary on the Holy Bible; Containing the Text According to the Authorized Version, with Marginal References; Matthew Henry's Commentary; the Practical Observations of the Rev. Thomas Scott; with Extensive Explanatory, Critical, and Philological Notes, Selected from Scott, Doddridge, Clarke, Gill, Patrick, Lowth, Calmet, Stuart, Bush . . . the Whole Designed to be a Digest of the Best Bible Commentaries . . . Edited by the Rev. William Jenks . . . 5 Volumes. Including Supplement, Containing a Concordance, Biographical Notices, an Index to the Bible . . . Tables . . . and an Index to the Commentary . . . Lippincott: Philadelphia   **1581**

5 vols   26 cm   PP
See 1835–38, No 894.

1855 The Holy Bible . . . The References and Marginal Readings of the Polyglott Bible, with Numerous Additions from Bagster's Comprehensive Bible . . . Robinson, Pratt & Co.: New York   **1582**

Reported as (40) (770)   25 cm   MB
Illustrated.

1855   The Holy Bible . . . The Text Conformable to the Standard of the American
Bible Society: Moore, Wilstach, Keys & Overend: Cincinnati   *1583*

1 vol: (576) (88) (192) (41) (22)   31 cm   IaDaM
O'Callaghan, p 341. With Apocrypha, Concordance, and Metrical Psalms.

1855   The Holy Bible . . . Lippincott, Grambo & Co.: Philadelphia   *1584*

"4to"   Not Located
O'Callaghan, p 340. Reprint of Phinney's 1844 Bible (No 1195). Has chromo-lithographed
OT frontispiece and one engraving in each Testament.

1855   The Holy Bible . . . With Marginal Readings, References and Chronological
Dates . . . William J. Moses, and Miller, Orton and Mulligan: Auburn; Miller, Orton & Mulligan: New York   *1585*

1 vol: (xii) (797) (120) (253) 254–256 (23) (39)   "4to"   Not Located
O'Callaghan, p 339. With Apocrypha, Metrical Psalms, and Concordance. Illustrated.

1855? The Holy Bible . . . M. Carey: Philadelphia   *1586*

"4to"   Not Located
Listed in Wright (p 405) under this date, but it is much too late for a Carey imprint.

1855   The Holy Bible . . . American Bible Society . . . : New York   *1587*

1 vol: (1009) (316)   24 cm   NNAB
Small Pica Octavo with new ABS standard text. See 1850 NT, No 1443. Between 1860
and 1872 corrections were made in conformity with the revised standard text. In 1893 this
was reset in slightly larger type but almost line for line. Last printing 1931, 315,000 copies
having been printed.
NNAB also has 1901 edition with Tables (1 p) following NT.

1855   The Holy Bible, Translated from the Latin Vulgate: . . . The Old Testament,
First Published at the English College at Douay . . . 1609, and the New Test-
ament . . . at Rheims . . . 1582. With Annotations . . . References, and . . . Index
. . . Patrick Donahoe: Boston   *1588*

Reported as (691) (191)   22 cm   PLatS
Rheims-Douay Version. See Donahoe's 1852 Bible, No 1499.

1855   The Holy Bible . . . Lippincott, Grambo & Co.: Philadelphia   *1589*

Reported as (824) (258) (77)   18 cm   CS, CSfT
With Metrical Psalms.
Probably same as O'Callaghan entry (p 343).

1855   The Pronouncing Bible . . . By Israel Alger Junr . . . W. S. Young: Philadelphia   *1590*

"12mo"   Not Located
O'Callaghan, p 343. See 1822 NT, No 452.

1855   The Holy Bible . . . Wm. S. & Alfred Martien: Philadelphia   *1591*

1 vol: (1098)(342) (93)   16 cm   NN, NNAB
Metrical Psalms and Index at end.

1855   The Holy Bible . . . Lippincott, Grambo & Co.: Philadelphia   *1592*

1 vol: (824) (251) (77)   "24mo"   Not Located
O'Callaghan, p 343. With Metrical Psalms.

1855   [Polyglott Bible] The Holy Bible . . . [Stereotype Edition]. Published by
John F. Trow: New York   *1593*

1 vol: (856) (259)   15 cm   NN

1855   The Holy Bible . . . Alden and Beardsley: Auburn [New York]   *1594*

1 vol: (824) (251)   14 cm   NN
Stereotype edition. Has added engraved title.

1855   The New Testament . . . Robert R. Collins: New York   *1595*

"8vo"   Not Located
O'Callaghan, p 344.

1855   [The New Testament] de Nu Testament ov or Lord and Savyor Jezus Krist.
Akordin tw de otorizd verfon. In Fonetik Spelin . . . Lonli Bruderz: Sinsinati
1596

1 vol: (xx) 21–343   19 cm   NN

1855   The New Testament . . . Collins: New York   *1597*

Reported as 386 p   "12mo"   **MB**

1855   The New Testament . . . Translated from the Latin Vulgate . . . First Published by the English College, at Rheims . . . 1582. With Annotations . . . Index . . . References . . . Approved by the Most Rev. John Hughes . . . Edward
Dunigan & Brother: New York   *1598*

356 p   16 cm   NNAB
Rheims Version. See 1845 NT, No 1282.

1855   The New Testament . . . Sanborn, Carter & Bazin: Boston; Blake & Carter:
Portland   *1599*

259 p   12 cm   NNAB

1855   Polymicrian New Testament . . . H. C. Peck & Theodore Bliss: Philadelphia
1600

"32mo"   Not Located
Wright, p 407.

1855   A Translation of the Gospels. With Notes. By Andrews Norton . . . Little,
Brown, and Company: Boston   *1601*

2 vols: Vol i, (vii) (443); Vol ii, (iv) (565)   23 cm   NNAB
Vol i contains text; Vol ii, notes. Published posthumously under the editorship of Charles
Eliot Norton and Ezra Abbot.
Andrews Norton (1786–1853), a Unitarian theologian, became professor of Biblical litera-
ture at Harvard Divinity School when it was founded in 1819. He resigned the professorship
in 1830 to carry on his literary and theological work. Among his writings are *The Evidences*

ᴙꙄ

NU TESTAMENT

ov

ꙄR LӨRD AND SꙄVYOR JꞒZUS KRꞫST.

AKӨRDIꞝ TU ᴙꞒ ӨꞪORꞫZD VERꞓON.

IN FꙎNETIK SPELIꞝ.

SꞪNSꞪNꙆTI:
LOꙎLI BRUꝺERZ, FꙎNETIK PUBLIꞓERZ;
FӨR SꙆL BꞫ BUKSELERZ JENERALI.

1855.

of the Genuineness of the Gospels (3 vols, 1837–44) and the unfinished *Internal Evidences of the Genuineness of the Gospels*, published in the same year as his translation. His Greek text seems to be a composite following Griesbach, Lachmann, and Tischendorf (1849). (Cheek, p 82.)

Reprinted several times. NNAB has sixth edition of 1883 (John Wilson and Son, University Press: Cambridge, 20 cm).

1856   The Holy Bible . . . American Bible Society . . . : New York   *1602*

1163 p   40 cm   NNAB

Imperial Quarto, the first ABS pulpit Bible. Has references and chronology. The text, based on the new standard text (see 1852, No 1504), was carefully prepared by a collator and compared with Oxford, Cambridge, and Queen's printers' editions. The *ABS Report* for 1856 (p 37) proclaimed it the best edition since 1611. The Board was so proud of this standard edition that it voted to grant a copy "to each theological seminary, or college having a theological or Biblical department." Originally priced at $10 or $12, depending on the binding.

NNAB also has an 1868 corrected copy.

1856   The Holy Bible . . . [Electro-stereotyped by L. Johnson & Co. Printed by C. Sherman & Son, 1856]. [Standard Imperial Quarto Edition] Published by H. C. Peck & T. Bliss: Philadelphia   *1603*

1 vol: (1130) (382)   37 cm   NN

Text amended according to that of the ABS. Has frontispiece, Family Record following OT, Index, Harmony of the Four Evangelists, and Tables. Printed in Great Primer type. Illustrated.

1856   The Holy Bible, Translated from the Latin Vulgate . . . The Old Testament, First Published . . . at Douay . . . 1609. And the New Testament . . . at Rheims . . . 1582. With Useful Notes, Critical, Historical, Controversial, and Explanatory . . . From the Most Eminent Commentators . . . by the Rev. Geo. Leo Haydock . . . Edward Dunigan and Brother: New York   *1604*

35 cm   DGU-Riggs, NN, PLatS

Rheims-Douay Version. Pagination same as 1852 Bible (No 1485). Has engraved title page and illustrations. Issued in parts.

NN copy is incomplete and has J. B. Kirker, New York, as publisher.

1856   The Holy Bible . . . The Text Conformable to the Standard of the American Bible Society . . . J. Harding: Philadelphia   *1605*

1 vol: (774) (116) 777–1032   30 cm   NNAB

Harding's Royal Quarto Edition appears at head of title. With Apocrypha followed by Family Record. Has colored title pages and references in double center columns. Tables follow OT. Index of Bible at end. Illustrated. See Harding's Royal Quarto of 1857, No 1650.

Also issued with Metrical Psalms and Concordance.

1856   The Holy Bible . . . With Canne's Marginal References . . . To Which are Added, an Index, and References, and A Key Sheet of Questions . . . and Highly Useful Tables . . . The Text Corrected According to the Standard of the American Bible Society . . . E. A. & T. T. More: Dayton, Ohio   *1606*

30 cm   DLC, MnU, NN

Reprint of 1846 Merriam Bible (No 1289). Has frontispiece and other plates.

O'Callaghan (p 357) lists an edition dated 1857.

1856   The Holy Bible . . . The Text Conformable to the Standard of the American Bible Society . . . [Stereotyped by L. Johnson & Co. Printed by T. K. & P. G. Collins]. T. K. Collins, jr.: Philadelphia   *1607*

768 p   30 cm   NN

Agrees with Lippincott, Grambo & Co. edition of 1851 (No 1450) but without Apocrypha, Concordance, or Metrical Psalms. NT has imprint of *J. B. Lippincott & Co., 1856.*

1856 The Holy Bible . . . Apocrypha . . . The Text Conformable to the Standard of the American Bible Society . . . Published by John B. Perry . . . Leary & Getz: Philadelphia; Walker & Medairy, John Cushing & Co., and Cushing & Bailey: Baltimore   *1608*

29 cm   NNAB

Reprint of Perry's 1852 edition (No 1487). Has frontispiece to each Testament. NT title imprinted *John B. Perry; Stereotyped by L. Johnson.*

1856 The Holy Bible . . . Translated from the Latin Vulgat: With Annotations, by the Rev. Dr. Challoner; Together with References . . . Revised and Corrected According to the Clementine Edition of the Scriptures. With the Approbation of the Most Rev. John Hughes, Archbishop of New York . . . Published by D. & J. Sadlier & Co.: New York   *1609*

29 cm   DGU, NN

Rheims-Douay Version. Pagination same as Sadlier 1845? Bible (No 1249).

1856 The Holy Bible . . . With Canne's Marginal Notes and References . . . Jesper Harding: Philadelphia   *1610*

1 vol: (6) (570) 573–748 749–770   29 cm   NN

Family Record follows OT. Index and Tables at end. With Metrical Psalms. Illustrated.

1856 The Holy Bible . . . The Text Conformable to the Standard of the American Bible Society: J. B. Perry: Philadelphia   *1611*

1 vol: (576) (87) 579–768   29 cm   NN

With Apocrypha followed by Family Record. Each Testament has frontispiece (OT in color). Tables follow OT. Index and further Tables at end. Has Brown's Concordance and Metrical Psalms. Illustrated with 20 plates.

1856 The Holy Bible . . . With References and Various Readings . . . Whilt & Yost: Philadelphia   *1612*

1 vol: (787) (277) (599) (41)   29 cm   NN

This is not the same as other Whilt and Yost editions; see 1850, No 1416. With Apocrypha. Has illuminated title to each Testament. Notes and references in the form of footnotes. Brown's Concordance at end. Illustrated with plates.

1856 [The Illustrated Domestic Bible] The Holy Bible . . . With Marginal References, and the Usual Various Readings. Also, Notes; Reflections; Questions; Improved Readings; Improved Divisions of Chapters; The Chronological Order; Metrical Portions Distinguished; and Various Other Advantages, Without Disturbing the Usual Order . . . By the Rev. Ingram Cobbin . . . Published by John W. Fuller & Co.: Utica   *1613*

1 vol: (16) (1000) (375) (xii) (6)   27 cm   NNAB

The Illustrated Domestic Bible appears on added engraved title page. Has fly title with facing map, Preface (Camberwell, Aug. 15, 1847), Key to the Work, and half title: *The Pentateuch* . . . . Family Record follows Isaiah. Historical Connexion of the Old and New Testaments follows OT. NT has map frontispiece and half title: *The Gospels and Acts....* At end are supplementary illustrations and reading guide; also indexes to the engravings, to subjects in the notes, and to the notes and reflections. References and variant readings and renderings are in center column; interpretational notes, etc. at bottom of page. Text and entire printed page are boxed. Has numerous small descriptive illustrations throughout text. See Hueston's 1851 Illustrated Domestic Bible, No 1463.

1856 The Comprehensive Commentary of the Bible . . . Scott's Marginal References, Matthew Henry's Commentary . . . Edited by William Jenks . . . Re-edited and adapted to the views of the Baptist Denomination of Christians by Rev. Joseph A. Warne. J. B. Lippincott & Co.: Philadelphia   *1614*

6 vols   27 cm   NjMD
Baptist Edition appears at head of title. See 1834–38, No 860.

1856 The Holy Bible . . . Stereotype Edition . . . Printed for the American and Foreign Bible Society, by the Bible Association of Friends in America: Philadelphia   *1615*

1061 p   26 cm   NN
Has Brown's Concordance but no Apocrypha.

1856 The Holy Bible . . . With Canne's Marginal Notes and References . . . A. S. Barnes & Co.: New York   *1616*

"4to"   Not Located
O'Callaghan, p 345. *Cambridge Edition* appears at head of title. With Apocrypha. Index, Tables, and Metrical Psalms (22 p) at end. Engravings.

O'Callaghan says the stereotype plates from which the above volume was printed were very badly worn; they seem to have been originally cast for the Collins quarto of 1821 (No 414) with which this edition agrees in every respect, with the Metrical Psalms added.

1856 The Holy Bible . . . Charles Desilver: Philadelphia   *1617*

"4to"   Not Located
O'Callaghan, p 347. Has two colored illustrations and numerous engravings.

1856 The Holy Bible . . . With Marginal Readings, References, and Chronological Dates . . . William J. Moses: Auburn   *1618*

"4to"   Not Located
O'Callaghan (p 348) says this Bible was published in two forms: one with Psalms, Concordance, and Family Record, 1130 p; the other with Apocrypha added, 1250 p. Number of engravings varies. It sold at prices from $4 to $12. Has center references.

1856/55 The Holy Bible, Translated from the Latin Vulgate . . . The Old Testament First Published at Douay . . . 1609; and the New Testament . . . at Rheims . . . 1582. With Annotations, References, and . . . Index. From the Last London and Dublin Editions . . . Published with the Approbation of J. Hughes, Archbishop of New York . . . Edward Dunigan and Brother: New York   *1619*

968 p   24 cm   NN
Rheims-Douay Version. See 1844, No 1199. Has frontispiece, Family Record after OT, Tables at end. NT dated 1855.

1856   The Holy Bible . . . Lindsay and Blakiston: Philadelphia   *1620*

1282 p   "8vo"   Not Located
O'Callaghan, p 348. *Crown Octavo Oxford Edition* appears at head of title. It is questionable
whether this was printed in the United States, or perhaps the printer used the Oxford reference
for text identification.

1856   The English Version of the Polyglott Bible . . . With the Marginal Readings,
        Together with Copious and Original Selection of References to Parallel and
        Illustrative Passages . . . Stereotyped by L. Johnson . . . Charles Desilver:
        Philadelphia   *1621*

16 cm   NNAB
Reprint of Meilke edition of 1832 (No 790) with the Metrical Psalms (64 p).

1856   The English Version of the Polyglott Bible . . . with the Marginal Readings.
        Together with . . . References . . . Exhibited in a Manner Hitherto Un-
        attempted . . . Illustrated with maps and engravings . . . J. B. Lippincott &
        Co.: Philadelphia   *1622*

1 vol: (824) (256) (77)   15 cm   NNAB
      Map, Preface signed T.C., and Tables precede text. Metrical Psalms at end. Although title
page calls for illustrations, there are none in this copy.

1856   The Holy Bible . . . J. B. Lippincott & Co.: Philadelphia   *1623*

1 vol: (824) (251) (77)   15 cm   NNAB
Has frontispiece. Metrical Psalms at end. No references.

1856   The Holy Bible . . . With Marginal Readings and References . . . Published
        by Carlton & Porter: New York   *1624*

Reported as (804) (249)   15 cm   DLC, TNMB

1856   The Holy Bible . . . J. B. Lippincott & Co.: Philadelphia   *1625*

1 vol: (725) (221)   12 cm   NN
Metrical Psalms at end.

1856   The Holy Bible . . . Alden and Beardsley: Auburn and Rochester   *1626*
                                                                                   C

No further information given.

1856   The Holy Bible . . . With Explanatory Notes and Remarks by the Rev. J. B.
        Paterson and the Rev. A. S. Paterson . . . Chas. H. Davis & Co.: Philadelphia
                                                                            1627
                                                                      Privately Owned
Reported to NNAB in 1936 but not examined.

1856   The New Testament . . . American Bible Society . . . : New York   *1628*

844 p   26 cm   NNAB
      Great Primer Octavo, first edition. A similar edition of the Psalms had been printed in
1855 (202 p) and was often bound with this NT. The NT was sometimes bound in four parts
for easier handling by older people. The running heads, chapter summaries, etc. have been
made to conform to the revised standard text. This large type NT has been in print for over
a century.

1856   The New Testament . . . with marginal references, both parallel and explanatory, accurately revised according to the latest standard edition of the English text . . . The book of Psalms in metre . . . Published by Jacob Ernst: Cincinnati   **1629**

Reported as (367) 3–82   25 cm   OC

1856   Explanatory Notes upon the New Testament by John Wesley. 10th Edition. Carlton & Porter: New York   **1630**

Reported as 734 p   24 cm   ICU, N
Wesley Version; see 1791 NT, No 35.
NjMD, NN, and ViU have eleventh edition (dated 1856?). NN also has fifteenth edition (dated 1860?).

1856   Expository Notes, with Practical Observations, on the New Testament . . . Wherein the Sacred Text is at Large Recited, the Sense Explained . . . By William Burkitt . . . Seventh Edition . . . Clark, Austin & Smith: New York
1631

2 vols   24 cm   ICU
See 1794, No 47.

1856   The New Testament . . . Published by Z. Baker & Co.: Worcester   **1632**
288 p   16 cm   NNAB

1856   The New Testament . . . American Bible Society . . . .: New York   **1633**
1 vol: (303) 305–307   12 cm   NNAB
Agate 32mo, possibly first printed in 1855, with new ABS standard text (see 1850 NT, No 1443). The page headings are shorter but not as short as those in the 1853 Nonpareil Duodecimo Bible (No 1533). Contents on p 305–307, but in later printings Contents begin on p 304 and end on p 306.

1856   The New Testament . . . Phinney & Co.: Buffalo   **1634**
344 p   "32mo"   Not Located
"First published by H. & E. Phinney, Cooperstown in 1832, between which time and 1848, they sold rising 200,000 copies for Sunday Schools. E.P." (O'Callaghan, p 351.)

1856   The Polymicrian Testament . . . H. C. Peck & Theodore Bliss: Philadelphia
1635
"32mo"   Not Located
Wright, p 406. See 1832, No 811.

1856   The New Testament . . . Smith and English: Philadelphia   **1636**
Not Located
The two libraries listed in the Union Catalog no longer have this book.

1857   The Holy Bible . . . Translated from the Latin Vulgate . . . [With Haydock's Notes, &c]. Published by Edw. Dunigan and Brother: New York   **1637**
36 cm   DGU
Rheims-Douay Version. Pagination same as 1852 edition (No 1485).
O'Callaghan (p 353) says many corrections were made in the stereotype plates previous to printing this edition.

1857   The Holy Bible . . . With References and Various Readings . . . E. H. Butler:
Philadelphia   *1638*

 2 vols in 1: (787) (277) (139) 281–600 30 cm   NN
With Apocrypha. Has colored frontispieces and titles to both Testaments and separate
printed title page before Isaiah. Family Record precedes NT. References at foot of page.
Illustrated.

1857   The Holy Bible . . . The Text Conformable to the Oxford Edition of the Year
of Our Lord 1610, and the American Bible Society's Original Standard Edition of 1816 . . . [Stereotyped by Jesper Harding & Son]. Jesper Harding &
Son: Philadelphia   *1639*

 1 vol: (576) (116) 579–768 (41) (22) 30 cm   NNAB
 Similar to Harding's 1842 and 1845 editions (No 1129 and No 1253) but reset with two
center reference columns. See also Perry's 1852 Bible, No 1487. *Harding's Fine Edition* appears
at head of title. With Apocrypha. Has frontispiece, illuminated title page, Order of Books, To
the Reader, and Contents. Tables follow OT. NT has Dates of Writing NT Books, frontispiece,
and illuminated title page. Index, Tables, etc. at end. Brown's Concordance and Metrical Psalms.
Illustrated.
 Also published without Apocrypha, Concordance, and Metrical Psalms, or with any one of
these. Number of plates varies.
 The three Oxford-American Bible Society quarto editions issued by Harding in 1857 — including the above — were put out annually, with new title pages and altered dates. Some of
the added material differs. They were later published by William W. Harding, the "fine" and
"superfine" editions by A. J. Holman.

1857–58   The Holy Bible . . . The Text Conformable to the Oxford Edition of the
Year of Our Lord 1610, and the American Bible Society's Original Standard
Edition of 1816 . . . Jesper Harding & Son: Philadelphia   *1640*

 2 vols: Vol ɪ, (787); Vol ɪɪ, (277) (116) 281–600 (41) (22) 30 cm NNAB
 Harding's Superfine Edition appears at head of title. Vol ɪ (1857) has frontispiece, illuminated title page, and Order of Books; text: Genesis-Song of Solomon. Vol ɪɪ (1858) has title
page; text: Isaiah-Malachi, Apocrypha, and NT (with own title page and frontispiece); Concordance and Metrical Psalms at end. See preceding Harding quarto, No 1639; also Butler's
1847 Bible, No 1328.
 Printed in English type, in 50 numbers. Issued without plates or with illuminated titles
and from 8 to 16 engravings. (O'Callaghan, p 355.)

1857   The Holy Bible . . . with Canne's Marginal References . . . Apocrypha and
Concordance . . . an Index and References and a key sheet of questions . . .
The text corrected according to the Standard of the American Bible Society.
Published at the Printing Establishment of the United Brethren in Christ:
Dayton, Ohio   *1641*

 Various paging 30 cm Hist. Soc. of The Evangelical United Brethren Church,
Dayton
 A new edition of Wilbur's Reference Bible; see 1826, No 559. In the preface, the editor
states: "In presenting to the public this copy of a stereotype edition of Wilbur's Reference Bible,
in quarto, the Publishers feel themselves warranted in saying, that it possesses many advantages
over any other quarto Bible now in the market. The Text has been carefully compared with
the standard edition of the American Bible Society, which (from its frequent critical readings)
is believed to be the most correct copy now in circulation. Canne's References and Readings
will be found to be uncommonly correct, and are placed in a centre column, on the plan of
the Polyglot Bible, by which arrangement they are not so liable to injury, or to be rendered
illegible by becoming filled with ink, as when placed in the margin of the page."

"The duodecimo copy of this work having passed through six editions in a very short time, and public feeling appearing to demand a larger size of it for Family use, the Editor feels it due himself and others, to enter into some details of illustration, respecting the manner in which this work was intended to aid in the acquisition of scripture knowledge. . . . Renewed acknowledgments are here tendered to Rev. Dr. Miller of Princeton, Rev. Professor Goodrich of New-Haven, Rev. Justin Edwards, D.D. of Boston, and Messrs. J. E. Worcester and J. W. Gibbs for the assistance received from them in preparing the Tables. By the politeness of Professor G. access has been had to a new work from Edinburgh, from which important aid has been obtained in the application of Walker's general principles of pronunciation. Dr. Miller has revised the pronouncing vocabulary. . . ."

1857?   The Holy Bible . . . Apocrypha . . . With Canne's Marginal Notes and References . . . John Beardsley: Auburn & Buffalo   *1642*

1 vol: (744) (138) 747–1008   29 cm   NN

Each Testament has engraved half title. Index, Tables, Brown's Concordance, and Metrical Psalms at end. Illustrated.

1857   The Holy Bible . . . American Bible Society . . . : New York   *1643*

1588 p   29 cm   NNAB

Pica Reference Octavo, the first printing of the new ABS standard text in this size. This edition was planned for family reading and for use in the conference or lecture room (*ABS Report* 1857, p 33). Its text conformed strictly to that of the 1856 Imperial Quarto (No 1602).

The ABS was proud of its new standard text (1852, No 1504) and had in fact sent copies to eminent citizens and to sovereigns all over the world. No word of criticism of this careful collation had been raised until an Episcopalian minister in Baltimore, the Rev. A. C. Coxe, published in January 1857 a pamphlet accusing the Society of violating its constitutional limitation to distributing the Scriptures "without note or comment," particularly by changing chapter summaries and running heads. The Society's defenders pointed out that the 1611 edition chapter summaries and page headings contained a good deal of interpretation which the editors had attempted to eliminate. The ABS reprinted from its 1851 Report the full report of the Committee that had supervised and recommended the standard text. (See 1850 NT, No 1443.) There was a good deal of comment in the newspapers and religious periodicals, largely reflecting a general lack of information on the history of the English Bible and problems of publication. A long unsigned article in the *Biblical Repository and Princeton Review* of July 1857 (p 507–542) summarized many objections of which the chief was to the changes in chapter summaries, although the writer admitted that the greater number of editions distributed by the ABS did not contain references and that many of the non-reference editions carried shortened summaries. The Committee on Versions issued a report in 1858 defending its work and pointing out the variations in such material in all American editions, as well as the fact that these accessories were not part of the Hebrew and Greek texts. Feeling within the Board of Managers ran high, most of the Committee on Versions resigned, and a new committee was formed to prepare a new standard text.

The above Pica Reference Octavo was the text in which the changes were to be made. All changes were printed in two pamphlets and first appeared in the NTs of 1860 (No 1736 and No 1739) and the Bibles of 1861 (No 1747 and No 1748). This remained the standard of the ABS until 1932 (see No 2328). The plates for existing editions of the new standard of 1852 were changed to contain the corrections. For further information, see *ABS Report* 1852 (p 28–37) and *ABS Report* 1858 (p 31–41); also *Statements and Documents concerning the recent action of The Board of Managers of the American Bible Society, touching the Standard Edition of the English Scriptures, as circulated by that Society,* published by Members of the Late Committee on Versions (pamphlet printed by John F. Trow: New York 1858; 112 p, 22 cm — bound with *ABS Reports* 1861–63).

1857   The Cottage Bible, and Family Expositor . . . With Practical Expositions and Explanatory Notes. By Thomas Williams . . . To Which are Added, the References and Marginal Readings of the Polyglott Bible, Together with Original Notes and Selections from Bagster's Comprehensive Bible . . . The

1857, continued

> Whole Carefully Revised . . . Edited by Rev. William Patton . . . Complete
> in Two Volumes . . . Case, Lockwood and Co.: Hartford   **1644**

2 vols   28 cm   NN

Pagination continuous as in Conner & Cooke Cottage Bible of 1833–34 (No 818). Each volume has frontispiece. Contains Tables, Prefaces to the London and American Editions, List of Authors Consulted, and Introduction. The Expositions precede and the Concluding Remarks follow each Book. Center references, notes at foot of page. Essay on the Historical Connexion Between the Old and New Testaments appears on p 991–994. Maps and plates.

1857   The Comprehensive Commentary of the Bible: Containing the Text Accord-
          ing to the Authorized Version; Scott's Marginal References . . . Edited by
          Rev. William Jenks . . . Joseph Warne . . . Published by Fessenden and Co.:
          Brattleboro   **1645**

28 cm   OrPW

Baptist Edition appears at head of title. See 1834–38, No 860.

1857   The Pictorial Bible . . . Illustrated with More than One Thousand Engrav-
          ings, Representing the Historical Events, After Celebrated Pictures; the
          Landscape Scenes, from Original Drawings, or from Authentic Engravings;
          and the Subjects of Natural History, Costume and Antiquities, from the
          Best Sources . . . C. A. Alvord, Printer. Published by Robert Sears: New
          York   **1646**

Reported as (vi) (1102) 1103–1124 (348) (ii)   27 cm   PSt
Frontispieces to Testaments and added title pages are colored. Has Tables and maps. Wood engravings printed with text. See 1843/44 Redfield Pictorial Bible, No 1168.

1857   The Cottage Bible, and Family Expositor, with Practical Expositions and
          Explanatory Notes. By T. Williams . . . To Which are Added the References
          and Marginal Readings of the Polyglott Bible . . . Edited by W. Patton . . .
          Case, Tiffany, and Co.: Hartford   **1647**

27 cm   NN
Similar to 1833–34 Bible (No 818) and 1857 Bible (No 1644).

1857   The Holy Bible, Translated from the Latin Vulgate . . . The Old Testament
          was First Published . . . at Doway . . . 1609, and the New Testament . . . at
          Rheims . . . 1582. With Annotations by the Rev. Dr. Challoner . . . Revised
          and Corrected According to the Clementine Edition of the Scriptures, with
          the Approbation of the Most Rev. John Hughes, Archbishop of New York
          . . . D. & J. Sadlier: New York   **1648**

26 cm   DGU, NN
Rheims-Douay Version. Reprint of Sadlier's 1845? Bible (No 1249).

1857?   The Holy Bible . . . With Canne's Marginal Notes and References . . . John
          E. Beardsley: Auburn and Buffalo   **1649**

"4to"   Not Located

O'Callaghan, p 356. Text corresponds to that of Collins and Co. 1821 quarto (No 414). With Brown's Concordance, stereotyped by J. Howe (54 p) and the Metrical Psalms and paraphrases (18 p) at end. Illustrated.

1857   The Holy Bible . . . The Text Conformable to the Oxford Edition of the Year of Our Lord 1610, and the American Bible Society's Original Standard Edition of 1816 . . . [Stereotyped by Jesper Harding & Son]. Jesper Harding & Son: Philadelphia   **1650**

1 vol: (774) (116) 777–1032 (41) (22)   "4to"   Not Located

O'Callaghan, p 356. *Harding's Royal Quarto Edition* appears at head of title. With Apocrypha. To the Reader and Contents precede text. Tables follow OT. Illuminated Family Record pages. Verso of NT title has Account of Dates. Index, Tables, Concordance, and Metrical Psalms at end. Illustrated. See Harding's 1856 Royal Quarto Edition, No 1605; also with his 1857 Fine Edition, No 1639.

1857   The Holy Bible . . . Text Conformable to the Standard of the American Bible Society . . . J. B. Lippincott: Philadelphia   **1651**

768 p   "4to"   Not Located

O'Callaghan, p 353. With Apocrypha. Has frontispiece to each Testament. Index, Tables, Concordance, Metrical Psalms, etc. See 1851, No 1450.

1857   The Holy Bible . . . Peck & Bliss: Philadelphia   **1652**

"4to"   Not Located

Wright, p 407.

1857   The Holy Bible . . . The Text Conformable to the Standard of the American Bible Society . . . Published by John B. Perry: Philadelphia. Medairy & Musselman; and Whiting, Cushing and Comstock: Baltimore   **1653**

1 vol: (8) (574) 575–576 (88) 579–768 (41) (22)   "4to"   Not Located

O'Callaghan, p 353. With Apocrypha, Concordance, and Metrical Psalms. NT has *Stereotyped by L. Johnson.*

1857   The Holy Bible . . . With Canne's Marginal Notes and References . . . Published by Phinney & Co.: Buffalo; Ivison & Phinney: New York   **1654**

1 vol: (576) (99) (192) (26) (6)   "4to"   Not Located

O'Callaghan, p 357. With Apocrypha, Metrical Psalms, and Paraphrases.

1857   The Holy Bible . . . The Text Conformable to the Standard of the American Bible Society . . . Whilt & Yost: Philadelphia   **1655**

768 p   "4to"   Not Located

O'Callaghan, p 354. Has colored illustrations.

1857   The Family Bible . . . With Brief Notes and Instructions, Designed to Give the Results of Critical Investigation, and to Assist Common Readers to Understand the Meaning of the Holy Spirit in the Inspired Word. Including the References and Marginal Readings of the Polyglot Bible . . . American Tract Society: New York   **1656**

1 vol: (12) (1166) (6) 3–441   24 cm   CtW, NN, NNAB

Has Prefaces: The Bible, God's Gift for Men, signed J. E. (Justin Edwards); and The Harmony and Perfection of the Holy Scriptures, signed T. C. (Thomas Chevalier). The references, notes, etc. are placed below the text on each page. Family Record follows OT. A Synopsis of Robinson's Harmony of the Gospels, Index, and Tables at end. Illustrated with maps. See 1851 NT, No 1476; also 1853–56 Bible, No 1530.

1857   The Holy Bible, Translated from the Latin Vulgate . . . The Old Testament, First Published . . . at Douay . . . 1609; and the New Testament . . . at Rheims . . . 1582. With Annotations, References, and . . . Index, from the Last London and Dublin Editions . . . E. Dunigan and Brother: New York   *1657*

968 p   24 cm   NN
Rheims-Douay Version. See 1844, No 1199.
O'Callaghan (p 358) says this was printed by James B. Kirker.

1857   The English Version of the Polyglott Bible . . . With Marginal Readings and References . . . J. B. Lippincott & Co.: Philadelphia   *1658*

15 cm   Not Located
O'Callaghan, p 359. Reprint of 1853 Bible (No 1534).

1857   The Holy Bible . . . John E. Beardsley: Auburn and Buffalo   *1659*

1 vol: (824) (251)   "24mo"   Not Located
O'Callaghan, p 359. Stereotype edition.

1857   The Holy Bible . . . American Bible Society . . . : New York   *1660*

1 vol: (609) (194)   14 cm   NNAB
Diamond Reference 16mo printed on fine paper, nicely bound. The first printing in this format of the ABS standard text of 1852; see 1850 NT, No 1443.
Replaced in 1863 by No 1770.

1857   The Holy Bible . . . American Bible Society . . . : New York   *1661*

1 vol: (673) (211)   13 cm   NNAB
Diamond 32mo. The first printing in this format of the ABS standard text of 1852; see 1850 NT, No 1443.

1857   The Holy Bible . . . Stereotype Edition — Polyglot. John F. Trow: New York   *1662*

1 vol: (856) (259)   12 cm   NNAB

1857   The Holy Bible . . . J. B. Lippincott & Co.: Philadelphia   *1663*

"32mo"   Not Located
O'Callaghan, p 359. Reprinted from 1851 Bible (No 1474). With Metrical Psalms.

[*5617*] *1857*   [Old Testament] The Twenty-four Books of the Holy Scriptures carefully translated according to the Massoretic Text, after the best Jewish Authorities, by Isaac Leeser . . . [Stereotyped by L. Johnson & Co., Philadelphia. C. Sherman & Son, Printers]. Published at 1227 Walnut Street: Philadelphia   *1664*

1 vol: (xii) (1243)   16 cm   NNAB
Leeser Version; see 1845–46, No 1273. The text is reset from the 1853 edition (No 1540) with running notes omitted and comments on key passages provided on p 1237–1243. The Preface (signed Tebeth 29, 5616/January 7, 1856) repeats the information of the 1853 edition, with some additional material. Some General Remarks on dates, the canon, and the divisions of the Law follow. The copyright date, appearing on this and on all later printings until 1911, is 1853.
Reprinted as late as 1878 by Sherman & Co. (DW). By 1884, the plates had passed to the Bloch Publishing and Printing Company, Cincinnati. The work was reissued under the

Bloch imprint until 1914. NNAB has 1884 and 1901 copies; MH-AH has 1914 copy. In 1911, the Hebrew Publishing Company, New York, assumed publication from new plates. The prefaces and notes were omitted, and up to 1926 some portions, especially in the Writings, were reset in finer type. NNAB has 1926 copy, 1384 p, 18 cm. In 1912, the Hebrew text and the Lesser translation were printed on facing pages. This last has been reissued as recently as 1958. See 1912, No 2211.

1857? The Psalms, Books of Wisdom, and Canticle of Canticles. Translated from the Latin Vulgate; diligently compared with the Hebrew and Greek, being a Revised and Corrected Edition of the Douay Version, with Notes Critical and Explanatory, by Francis Patrick Kenrick, Archbishop of Baltimore . . . Lucas Brothers, Publishers: Baltimore   **1665**

Reported as 584 p   24 cm   DGU, MB, NN
Bishop Kenrick Version; see 1849, No 1414.
This volume includes Psalms, Proverbs, Ecclesiastes, Canticle of Canticles, Wisdom and Ecclesiasticus.

1857 The New Testament . . . American Bible Society . . . : New York   **1666**
403 p   19 cm   NNAB
Bourgeois Duodecimo School Testament with ABS standard text. See 1850 NT, No 1443.

1857 The New Testament . . . The New-York Bible and Common Prayer Book Society: New York   **1667**
324 p   16 cm   NN

1857 The New Testament . . . Translated from the Latin Vulgate . . . [James B. Kirker, printer]. Edward Dunigan & Bro.: New York   **1668**
"18mo"   Not Located
O'Callaghan, p 362. Rheims Version.

1858 The Holy Bible . . . Translated from the Latin Vulgate. With Useful Notes . . . By the Rev. George Leo Haydock . . . [James B. Kirker, printer]. Edward Dunigan & Brother: New York   **1669**
36 cm   DGU
Rheims-Douay Version. Pagination same as 1852 Dunigan edition (No 1485).
O'Callaghan (p 365) says some errors were corrected and the Approbation page is replaced by an 8-page insert of facsimiles of the Approbation of Archbishop Hughes, a letter of Pope Pius IX, and letters of commendation from a large number of Church dignitaries. Engravings.

1858 The Holy Bible . . . With a Perpetual Genealogical Family Register Entirely New and Original . . . Richard Abbey: New York and Nashville; Published by R. C. Root, Anthony & Co.: New York; Sold by the Methodist Publishing House: Nashville   **1670**
Text ends 7Z2   36 cm   NN
Has presentation leaf engraved in colors, Prefatory Note (signed The Editor and dated Nashville, August 1858), and Order of Books. 50 leaves of Family Record at end, each page containing blank Certificates of Marriage, Births, and Deaths, within colored ornamental border. Copyright 1858.

1858   The Holy Bible . . . The Text Conformable to the Oxford Edition of the
Year of Our Lord 1610, and the American Bible Society's Original Standard
Edition of 1816 . . . Jesper Harding & Son: Philadelphia   **1671**

30 cm   NN, NNAB
Reprint of Harding's Fine Edition of 1857 (No 1639) but with different illustrations.

1858   The Holy Bible . . . The Text Conformable to the Standard of the American
Bible Society . . . Whilt & Yost: Philadelphia   **1672**

768 p   30 cm   Not Located
O'Callaghan, p 364. Similar to 1850 Bible (No 1416) and other reprints of the old Phinney
quarto.

1858/57   The Holy Bible . . . Translated from the Latin Vulgate: With Annota-
tions by the Rev. Dr. Challoner . . . Revised and Corrected According to the
Clementine Edition . . . Published by D. & J. Sadlier & Co.: New York . . .
Boston . . . Montreal   **1673**

29 cm   DGU
Rheims-Douay Version. Similar to 1845? edition (No 1249). NT dated 1857.
O'Callaghan (p 365) describes the engravings, some of which are new. In No 3 of the
NT, *Redeemer of the World*, an African slave in chains is introduced.

1858   The Pictorial Bible . . . Published by Robert Sears: New York   **1674**

29 cm   NN
Reprint of 1857 edition (No 1646).

1858?   The Holy Bible . . . With Canne's Marginal Notes and References . . . Alden
& Beardsley: Auburn and Rochester [New York]   **1675**

1 vol: (744) (138) 747–1003   28 cm   NN
With Apocrypha. Has colored frontispiece and illuminated Family Record pages. Index,
Tables, and Brown's Concordance at end. Illustrations, some in color.

1858   The Holy Bible . . . Translated from the Latin Vulgate: With Annotations
. . . [James B. Kirker, printer]. Edward Dunigan & Brother: New York **1676**

968 p   26 cm   Not Located
O'Callaghan, p 366. Rheims-Douay Version. See 1844, No 1199.

1858   The Holy Bible . . . Apocrypha . . . With Canne's Marginal Notes and References . . . Published by Phinney & Co.: Buffalo; Ivison & Phinney: New
York   **1677**

"4to"   Not Located
O'Callaghan, p 366.

1858   The Holy Bible . . . The Text Conformable to the Standard of the American
Bible Society . . . Published by John B. Perry: Philadelphia; Medairy & Musselman, and Whiting, Cushing and Comstock: Baltimore   **1678**

"4to"   Not Located
O'Callaghan, p 364. Reprint of 1857 Bible (No 1653).

1858 The Holy Bible . . . The Text Conformable to the Standard of the American
Bible Society . . . J. B. Lippincott & Co.: Philadelphia   **1679**

"4to"   Not Located

O'Callaghan, p 364. Reprint of 1851 Bible (No 1450).

1858 The Holy Bible . . . With Marginal Readings, References, and Chronological
Dates . . . William J. Moses: Auburn   **1680**

"4to"   Not Located

O'Callaghan, p 364. See 1856, No 1618.

1858/57 The Holy Bible, Translated from the Latin Vulgate . . . The Old Testa-
ment, First Published at Douay . . . 1609, and the New Testament . . . at
Rheims . . . 1582. With Annotations and References, and . . . Index . . . Patrick
Donahoe: Boston   **1681**

1 vol: (691) (191)   22 cm   DCU–H, NNAB

Rheims-Douay Version. See 1852 Donahoe Bible, No 1499. Family Record precedes NT.
Tables at end. NT dated 1857.

1858 The Holy Bible . . . American & Foreign Bible Society: New York   **1682**

1 vol: (510) (161)   19 cm   NN

Has Tables between Testaments.

1858 The English Version of the Polyglott Bible . . . With Marginal Readings and
References . . . Illustrated with Maps and Engravings . . . J. B. Lippincott
& Co.: Philadelphia   **1683**

1 vol: (824) (256) (77)   "12mo"   Not Located

O'Callaghan, p 367. With Metrical Psalms.

1858 [The Holy Bible] . . . With Marginal Readings . . . Brown: Boston   **1684**

Reported as (856) (259) (76)   11 cm   Mi

General title page missing from cited copy; above taken from NT title. Has colored frontispiece and illustrations. Metrical Psalms at end.

1858? The New Testament . . . [Stereotyped by T. B. Smith & Son. Printed by C.
A. Alvord]. Collins & Brother, Publishers: New York   **1685**

1 vol: (4) (511) 513–548   22 cm   NNAB

Paragraph NT, printed without chapter and verse indication except that chapter and verse
numbers for beginning of text on each page are given at head of page. It follows the editions
of Bagster and of Eyre and Spottiswood for punctuation and orthography, but has quotation
marks for speeches, conversation, and quotations from other parts of the Bible. Contains To the
Reader, Contents, and at the end, Index of Subjects.

1858 The New Testament . . . Translated from the Latin Vulgate . . . Published
by E. Cummiskey: Philadelphia   **1686**

"8vo"   Not Located

O'Callaghan, p 367. Rheims Version.

1858   The New Testament, Translated from the Original Greek, with Chronological Arrangement of the Sacred Books, and Improved Divisions of Chapters and Verses by Leicester Ambrose Sawyer . . . [Lithotyped by Cowles
and Company, Boston. Press of Allen and Farnham]. John P. Jewett and
Company: Boston; Henry P. B. Jewett: Cleveland; Sampson Low, Son and
Company: London   *1687*

1 vol: (xi) 13–423   20 cm   GEU, ICU, MBU–T, MiU, NcAS, NjN, NN, NNAB, NRU

Preface (dated 1858) and Order of Books precede text. Text printed in paragraph form,
divided into sections, with section numbers indented in matching type. Verse numbers omitted.
The Epistles are arranged in chronological order and Hebrews comes just before Revelation.
Copyright 1858.

MB has second edition 1860, Walker, Wise & Co.: Boston. The text was revised to conform
with the 1858 printing of Tischendorf's text. NNAB has third edition 1861 (twelfth thousand),
with additional improvements. A new translation of Sawyer's NT was issued in 1891 (No 2048).

The Rev. Leicester Ambrose Sawyer (1807–1898) was ordained a Presbyterian minister in
1832, but later joined the Congregational Church and then the Unitarian. In 1864 he became
pastor of the First Catholic Congregational Church (Independent) of Boston and called himself
a Christian Rationalist. His translation is based on the Tischendorf Greek text of Leipzig, 1850.
The Preface states that the translation is "a strict literal rendering," aiming "to express the
original with the utmost clearness, force and precision. It adopts a thoroughly modern style,
except for the prayers, and makes freely whatever changes are necessary for this purpose." He
also published an *Introduction to the New Testament* (1883) and *Final Theology* (1891).

In the Preface (p vi–vii) Sawyer praised individual work in Bible translation, saying:
"It is an unfortunate result of King James's translation of the Bible by an imposing council of
learned men, that it has tended to discourage individual effort in respect to a labor of this
kind, and to create a prejudice against it as necessarily incompetent and untrustworthy. . . . But
there are great works which individuals can perform better than multitudes or councils. Councils
did not make the Bible at first. It was made by individuals, each man acting for himself, and
giving utterance to the mighty thoughts that God had given him. A council did not make Para-
dise Lost, and could not; nor has a council ever produced any immortal work of genius or
learning, unless it is the English Bible of King James. . . . As individuals, therefore, have generally been the prosecutors of literary enterprises, in the department of Bible translation no less
than in other departments, and as individuals have been eminently successful and useful in
this department of labor heretofore, both in England and other countries, let it be hoped that
they may be again."

For Sawyer's version of the OT parts, see 1861, No 1745; also 1864, No 1781, and 1883,
No 2001.

1858   The New Testament . . . Translated from the Latin Vulgate . . . [James B.
Kirker, printer]. Edward Dunigan & Bro.: New York   *1688*

"12mo"   Not Located

O'Callaghan, p 368. Rheims Version.

1858   The New Testament . . . American Bible Society . . . : New York   *1689*

380 p.   16 cm   NNAB

Brevier 18mo, second printing (first issued 1857) with ABS standard text. See 1850 NT,
No 1443.

Also printed with Psalms (p 383–478).

1858   The Divine Library; or Cyclopedia of Inspiration. The New Testament . . .
Received Version in Paragraph Form. In Two Volumes. [Stereotyped by
L. Johnson & Co., Philadelphia] T. H. Stockton: Philadelphia   *1690*

2 vols   16 cm   NN

In paragraph form, single column, with verse numbers in left margin and variant renderings at foot of page. The Books in each volume are separately paged. There is no Preface.

Vol ɪ, Matthew-Acts; Index at end (2, 123, 80, 134, 99, 130, 31 p). Vol ɪɪ, Romans-Revelation; Index at end (2, 55, 53, 35, 19, 19, 14, 14, 13, 8, 16, 13, 8, 5, 42, 16, 16, 12, 16, 4, 4, 6, 64, 122 p).

O'Callaghan (p 368) lists a copy in 4 vols with Horne's Introduction (revised by Samuel Prideux Tregelles) and Student's Memorandum Book. NNAB has 1856 volume (108 p, 15 cm) containing Matthew, with Stockton's Baltimore imprint, stereotyped by L. Johnson & Co., Philadelphia, and printed by T. K. & P. G. Collins. O'Callaghan (p 352) lists a similar edition of Matthew, but with 123 p of text, p 124 blank, Index on p 125–130, and 1 leaf and an Appendix containing Horne's Introduction to St. Matthew.

The Divine Library was evidently the project of the Rev. Thomas H. Stockton who lived in Baltimore in 1853–57 and whose dates, according to the Enoch Pratt Free Library in Baltimore, are 1808–1868. For specimen number, see 1854, No 1559.

1859? The Self Interpreting Bible . . . With an Introduction . . . References . . . Summary of . . . Books . . . Analysis of Each Chapter . . . Reflections . . . and . . . Notes; by the Rev. John Brown . . . A New Edition in Which the Text is More Fully Elucidated by Upwards of Eight Thousand Explanatory and Critical Notes and Concluding Observations on Each Book. By the Rev. Henry Cooke . . . [Billin and Brother, New York, Printers and Stereotypers]. Johnson, Fry and Co.: New York   *1691*

1 vol: (xvii) (741) 743–744 (122) 747–1030   43 cm   NN, NNAB, OC

Preliminary matter includes frontispiece, added engraved title, Preface, Order of Books, Tables, Introduction, and Appendix. An Outline of the Principal Prophetic Kingdoms of the Earth follows the OT. With Apocrypha, which has Preface to the Apocryphal Books. Family Record. NT has own title page. Illustrated with 73 plates. "Colophon" with printer's name appears on p 122.

Date supplied by O'Callaghan (p 371) who says "just published."

This very elaborate edition of the latest form of John Brown's Self-Interpreting Bible (see 1792, No 37) was issued in parts and subsequently reissued a number of times; copies are fairly common. ViU has 1870? copy and NBuG has 1890 copy. CtY has 1860? copy and PLatS has 1875? copy, both published by Martin, Johnson and Company.

[*1859*] Illuminated Bible . . . Harper & Brothers: New York   *1692*

35 cm   NN

Reprint of the first edition, 1843–46 (No 1161).

O'Callaghan (p 372) gives the date as 1859 but NN copy has no date.

1859 The Holy Bible According to the Authorized Version, with a Perpetual Genealogical Family Register, Entirely New and Original . . . Southern Methodist Publishing House: Nashville   *1693*

2 vols in 1: 1086 p   35 cm   GEU

Includes 98 p for Family Register. Explanatory Note follows NT. See 1858, No 1670.

1859/62 The Holy Bible, Translated from the Latin Vulgate . . . With Useful Notes . . . Selected from the Most Eminent Commentators . . . By the Rev. Geo. Leo Haydock . . . [James B. Kirker, printer]. Edw. Dunigan & Brother: New York   *1694*

34 cm   NNAB

Rheims-Douay Version. Pagination same as 1852 Bible (No 1485). Preliminary matter includes frontispiece, added engraved title, Order of Books, Advertisement, and Approbations. Index and Family Record follow OT. General Preface and Dr. Witham's Remarks on Reading the Bible precede NT. Index, Tables, List of Readings, and Theological History in Miniature at end. Illustrated. NT dated 1862.

1859?   The Holy Bible . . . Published by Leavitt & Allen: New York   **1695**

    1 vol: (1004) 1005–1120 1123–1431   33 cm   NN, NNAB

With Apocrypha. Has frontispieces and illustrations. Family Record. Reprint of 1854 (No 1548).

Also published with imprint of G. A. Leavitt and varying plates.

"This edition was stereotyped for Hogan & Thompson who printed 500 copies, and sold the plates to Brown of Boston. They without printing any, sold the plates to Leavitt and Allen, who printed the above edition from them in the summer of 1859." (O'Callaghan, p 372.)

1859   The Holy Bible . . . Apocrypha . . . Concordance, the Psalms of David in
      Meter . . . the text conformable to the Standard of the American Bible So-
      ciety. Moore, Wilstach, Keys & Company: Cincinnati   **1695A**

    1 vol: (8) 9–576 (2) 579–768 (42) (22)   30 cm   NNAB

Preliminary matter includes frontispiece and two woodcuts. Apocrypha in smaller type (88 p).

1859   The Holy Bible . . . Leavitt & Allen: New York   **1696**

    1 vol: (574) (96) 579–754 755–768 (36) (28)   29 cm   NNAB

With Apocrypha and Family Record. Tables precede OT. NT has own title. Index, Tables, Concordance, and Metrical Psalms at end. Text boxed in double rules; also double rules between columns of text. No marginal materials.

1859   The Holy Bible . . . With Canne's Marginal Notes and References . . . Corn-
      ish, Lamport & Co.: New York   **1697**

    1 vol: (8) (632) 634–829   29 cm   NN

Has frontispieces to both Testaments. Contains To the Reader, Order of Books, Contents, and Family Record. Verso of NT title has Account of Dates. Lacks Apocrypha, Index, and Tables.

MB has undated copy received in 1891 that has been entered under 1830? because of the inclusion of Canne's Marginal Notes. (However, for Canne's references, see 1807 B, No 143.)

1859   Comprehensive Commentary on the Holy Bible; Containing the Text Ac-
      cording to the Authorized Version; Scott's Marginal References: Matthew
      Henry's Commentary . . . Edited by William Jenks . . . J. B. Lippincott & Co.:
      Philadelphia   **1698**

    6 vols   26 cm   DLC, PSt

Text and commentary in 5 vols; additional volume contains Supplement to the Comprehensive Bible. See 1835–38, No 894.

1859   The Holy Bible . . . with the Apocrypha, . . . Concordance and Psalms in
      Metre. . . . Jesper Harding and Son: Philadelphia   **1699**

    768 p   "4to"   Not Located

O'Callaghan, p 373. Reprint of Harding's Fine Edition of 1857 (No 1639) with Apocrypha in smaller type (116 p). Has colored titles, engravings, and some "Chromo. Lithographs."

1859   The Collateral Bible . . . John Laval and S. F. Bradford: Philadelphia   **1700**

    3 vols   "4to"   Not Located

O'Callaghan, p 373. See 1826–28 Collateral Bible, No 551.

1859 The Holy Bible . . . J. B. Lippincott & Company: Philadelphia   **1701**
  "4to"   Not Located
  O'Callaghan, p 373. Reprint of 1851 Bible (No 1450) with illustrations.

1859 The Holy Bible . . . Phinney & Co.: Buffalo; Ivison & Phinney: New York
                                                                         1702
  Reported as (768) (28) (5) "4to"   MiU
  Reprint of Phinney's quarto of 1824 (No 485) with Apocrypha, Metrical Psalms, and
Paraphrases.

1859 The Cottage Bible, and Family Expositor . . . By Thomas Williams . . . Edited by Rev. William Patton. Case, Lockwood and Company: Hartford **1703**
  2 vols   "8vo"   MiU
  See 1833–34 Conner & Cooke Cottage Bible, No 818.

1859 The Holy Bible . . . Jesper Harding & Son: Philadelphia   **1704**
  1 vol: (499) (156)   "12mo"   Not Located
  O'Callaghan, p 373.

1859 The Holy Bible . . . Delisser & Proctor . . . [Successors to Stanford & Swords]:
  New York   **1705**
  1 vol: (932) (292)   13 cm   NN
  O'Callaghan (p 377) lists a separate NT.

1859 The Holy Bible . . . Jesper Harding & Son: Philadelphia   **1706**
  "32mo"   Not Located
  O'Callaghan, p 373.

1859 The Holy Bible . . . J. B. Lippincott & Co.: Philadelphia   **1707**
  "32mo"   Not Located
  O'Callaghan, p 374. With Metrical Psalms.

1859 The Book of Job, and the Prophets. Translated from the Vulgate, and dili-
  gently compared with the Original Text, being a Revised Edition of the
  Douay Version, with Notes, Critical and Explanatory, by Francis Patrick
  Kenrick, Archbishop of Baltimore . . . Kelly, Hedian & Piet: Baltimore **1708**
  Reported as 737 p   22 cm   DGU, MB, NN
  Bishop Kenrick's Version; see 1849, No 1414.
  This volume includes Job, Jeremiah, Lamentations, Baruch, Ezekiel, Daniel, and the
twelve Minor Prophets.

1859? The New Testament . . . [Paragraph Edition]. Collins and Brother: New
  York   **1709**
  21 cm   NN
  Pagination same as 1858? NT (No 1685). Has two plates.

1859 The New Testament . . . Jesper Harding & Son: Philadelphia   **1710**
  1 vol: (156) (66)   "12mo"   Not Located
  O'Callaghan, p 377. NT from Harding's duodecimo of this year (No 1704). Has Contents
and Metrical Psalms.

1859   The New Testament . . . Published by James B. Smith & Co.: Philadelphia
                                                                          1711
"12mo"   Not Located
O'Callaghan, p 377.

1859   The Cottage Polyglott Testament . . . With Notes, Original and Selected;
         Likewise Introductory and Concluding Remarks to Each Book, Polyglott
         References and Marginal Readings . . . By W. Patton . . . J. S. Gilman: New
         York   *1712*
         1 vol: (12) (711) 712–718   16 cm   NN, NNAB
         Contains Order of Books, Preface signed W. P., Introduction, Table, and Indexes. Illustrated
with maps. Copyright 1859 by A. C. Goodman. See 1833 Village Testament, No 848.

1859   The New Testament . . . James B. Smith & Co.: Philadelphia   *1713*
"18mo"   Not Located
O'Callaghan, p 377.

1859   The New Testament . . . James B. Smith & Co.: Philadelphia   *1714*
"32mo"   Not Located
O'Callaghan, p 377.

1860? The Holy Bible . . . Translated from the Latin Vulgate . . . With Annota-
         tions, by the Rev. Dr. Challoner; Together with References and an Historical
         and Chronological Index. Revised and Corrected According to the Clemen-
         tine Edition . . . [Printed from Stereotype plates, of Fielding Lucas, jr. Balti-
         more, Md.]. John Kelly: Philadelphia   *1715*
         1 vol: (789) (235)   31 cm   NNAB
         Rheims-Douay Version. See 1825 Cummiskey Bible, No 527; also 1832 Lucas Bible,
No 771. Has engravings and portrait album.
         Approbation signed by James A. Wood, Bishop of Philadelphia, without date. As Bishop
Wood was installed in 1860 and died in 1883, this Bible could not have been issued earlier.
The Philadelphia directories have entries for John Kelly as book agent, bookseller, publisher or
printer from 1861 to 1883, but all at different addresses from that given in this imprint: 614
& 617 Samson Street. After 1873 John Kelly & Sons appears.

1860   The Holy Bible . . . The Text Conformable to the Oxford Edition of the Year
         of Our Lord 1610, and the American Bible Society's Original Standard Edi-
         tion of 1816 . . . William W. Harding: Philadelphia   *1716*
         2 vols   30 cm   NNAB
         Reprint of 1857–58 Bible (No 1640). *Harding's Superfine Edition* appears at head of title.

1860   The Holy Bible . . . Text Conformable to the Original Edition of the Year of
         Our Lord 1610, and the American Bible Society's Original Standard Edition
         of 1816 . . . William W. Harding: Philadelphia   *1717*
         29 cm   NN
         Reprint of 1857 Bible (No 1639) except Index, Tables, etc. have different pagination.
Harding's Fine Edition appears at head of title.

1860 The Cottage Bible, and Family Expositor . . . with Practical Expositions and Explanatory Notes. By Thomas Williams. To which are Added the References and Marginal Readings of the Polyglott Bible . . . The Whole Carefully Revised . . . Edited by Rev. William Patton . . . Complete in Two Volumes . . . Printed and Published by Case, Lockwood and Company: Hartford

1718

2 vols   28 cm   NNAB

Continuously paged, as in 1833–34 Conner & Cooke Cottage Bible (No 818). Vol I preliminary matter includes Order of Books, Prefaces to the London and the American editions, and Introduction; Genesis-Solomon's Song. Vol II, Isaiah-Malachi, Matthew-Revelation; appended material to p 1440. Illustrated.

1860/57 The Holy Bible . . . [Stereotyped by J. Fagan]. J. B. Lippincott & Co.: Philadelphia *1719*

28 cm   NNAB

Reprint of 1848 edition (No 1363) except NT has frontispiece and engraved title and is dated 1857. Family Record follows OT. Illustrations not colored.

1860 The Holy Bible . . . In Which All the Proper Names are Divided and Accented as They Should be Pronounced, and a Copious and Original Selection of References and Numerous Marginal Readings are Given: Together with Introductions to Each Book, and Numerous Tables and Maps . . . Carlton & Porter: New York *1720*

1 vol: (xxiii) [1] (771) (x) (246)   26 cm   NBuG, NjMD, NNAB, TNMPH

Biblical Notes and Tables precede each Testament. Family Record follows OT. Has references in double central column. Illustrated.

NBuG copy in 3 vols.

1860 The Comprehensive Commentary on the Holy Bible; Containing the Text According to the Authorised Version . . . Edited by Rev. William Jenks . . . Reedited and Adapted to the Views of the Baptist Denomination of Christians, by Rev. Joseph A. Warne . . . J. B. Lippincott & Co.: Philadelphia *1721*

26 cm   DLC

DLC has Vol III only, Psalm 64–Malachi. *Baptist Edition* appears at head of title; see 1834–38, No 860. Has frontispiece and other illustrations.

1860 The Holy Bible . . . the Proper Names of Which, and Numerous Other Words Being Accurately Accented in the Text, and Divided into Syllables, as they Ought to be Pronounced According to the Orthoepy of John Walker by Israel Alger, jun. . . . Wm. S. Young: Philadelphia *1722*

Reported as (714) (218)   24 cm   GEU, ViU

Includes Tables of Measures and Offices and Conditions of Men. See 1825, No 531. PSt has copy with NT dated 1861.

1860 The Holy Bible . . . E. H. Butler & Co.: Philadelphia *1723*

Reported as (1214) (336)   24 cm   MiU

Butler's Edition appears at head of title. With Apocryha. Has frontispiece and illustrations. Family Record.

1860   The Holy Bible ... American Bible Society ... : New York   *1724*

    1 vol: (758) 759–765   18 cm   NNAB

Nonpareil Duodecimo, 53rd edition. Has Contents on p 759–765. NNAB has no earlier
copies of this format, but it seems in most respects to be the ABS standard text; see 1850 NT,
No 1443. This is probably the book described in the *ABS Report* 1858 (p 30) as a School Bible
set from new Scotch type. See also 1861 Bible, No 1748.

1860   The Holy Bible ... J. B. Lippincott & Co.: Philadelphia   *1725*

    1 vol: (1044) 1045–1117   17 cm   NN
With Metrical Psalms at end.

1860   The English Version of the Polyglott Bible ... J. B. Lippincott: Philadelphia
1726

    15 cm   NNAB

Reprint of Lippincott edition of 1850 (No 1435) with the addition of Metrical Psalms at
end (77 p).

1860   The Holy Bible ... J. B. Lippincott & Co.: Philadelphia   *1727*

    1 vol: (856) (259) (77)   13 cm   NN
Metrical Psalms at end.

1860   The Holy Bible ... Corrected and Revised from the Standard Oxford Edition ... William W. Harding: Philadelphia   *1728*

    1 vol: (819) (256) (87)   12 cm   NNAB
With Metrical Psalms.

1860   The Pentateuch. Translated from the Vulgate, and Diligently Compared
with the Original Text, Being a Revised Edition of the Douay Version. With
Notes, Critical and Explanatory. By Francis Patrick Kenrick, Archbishop
of Baltimore ... Kelly, Hedian & Piet: Baltimore   *1729*

    1 vol: (6) vii–x (8) 17–559   24 cm   DGU, MB, NNAB
Bishop Kenrick Version; see 1849, No 1414.

1860   The Historical Books of the Old Testament. Translated from the Latin Vulgate, diligently Compared with the Original Text, being a revised Edition
of the Douay Version. With Notes, Critical and Explanatory, by Francis
Patrick Kenrick, Archbishop of Baltimore ... Kelly, Hedian & Piet: Baltimore
1730

    1 vol: (6) vii–xiv (4) 19–897   24 cm   DGU, MB, NN, NNAB
Bishop Kenrick Version; see 1849, No 1414.

This volume includes Joshua, Judges, Ruth, 1, 2, 3 and 4 Kings, 1 and 2 Paralipomenon,
Esdras, Nehemiah, Tobias, Judith, Esther and 1 and 2 Maccabees, thus completing the OT.

1860?   The New Testament ... [and Psalms] According to the Commonly Received Version ... Clark, Austin, Maynard & Co.: New York   *1731*

    1 vol: (406) (2) (107) [1]   23 cm   NNAB
Tables follow NT (1 p, verso blank). AV Psalms.
Date assigned by NNAB. Clark, Austin and Smith were publishing in New York in 1856.

1860–80   Commentary on the New Testament. Intended for Popular Use. By D. D. Whedon . . . Carlton & Porter: New York   *1732*

5 vols   20 cm   DLC

Vol ɪ, Matthew-Mark. Vol ɪɪ, Luke-John. Vol ɪɪɪ (New York, Carlton & Lanahan; Cincinnati, Hitchcock & Walden; etc.) Acts-Romans. Vol ɪv (New York, Nelson and Phillips; etc.) Corinthians–ɪɪ Timothy. Vol v (New York, Phillips & Hunt; etc.) Titus-Revelation. AV text with commentary. Illustrated.

NcD also has 1860–80 copy but with imprint of Cranston & Snow, Cincinnati; MiU's copy of this date published by Nelson and Phillips, New York (Vol ɪ marked 21st edition; Vol ɪɪ, 16th edition). Reprinted many times with varying imprints: NcD has 1871 copy (Carlton, New York); ViU has 188– copy (Hunt and Eaton, New York); NBuG has 1888–89 copy (Hunt, New York); DLC and ViU have 1881–1908 copies (Eaton and Mains, New York; Jennings and Pye, Cincinnati; etc.).

1860   The New Testament . . . New York Bible and Common Prayer Book Society: New York   *1733*

1 vol: 801–1044 p   19 cm   NNAB

186–?   The New Testament . . . Translated Out of the Latin Vulgate . . . and First Published . . . Rhemes . . . 1582. Newly Revised . . . According to the Clementine Edition of the Scriptures; with Annotations . . . As Approved by J. Hughes, Archbishop of New York. D. and J. Sadlier and Company: New York   *1734*

18 cm   NNAB

Rheims Version. Pagination same as 1829 Williams NT (No 686).

1860   The Cottage Polyglott Testament: According to the Authorized Version with Notes, Original and Selected; Likewise Introductory and Concluding Remarks to Each Book, Polyglott References and Marginal Readings, Chronological Table, Geographical Index and Maps . . . by William Patton . . . J. S. Gilman: New York   *1735*

15 cm   DLC

Pagination same as 1833 Village Testament (No 848). Illustrated.

1860   The New Testament . . . American Bible Society . . . : New York   *1736*

1 vol: (479) (120)   12 cm   NNAB

Nonpareil 32mo with Psalms, the first of the revised ABS standard texts; see 1857, No 1643.

NNAB has another copy without Psalms, with a label pasted inside the front cover: "To the Defenders of their Country!," issued by the New York Bible Society, May 16, 1861. During the Civil War the ABS supplied more than 3,000,000 Bibles and Testaments to soldiers and sailors on both sides. This NT and the 1861 one (No 1754) made up a large part of that figure.

1860   The Sacred Writings of the Apostles and Evangelists of Jesus Christ, Commonly Styled the New Testament. Translated from the Original Greek, by Doctors George Campbell, James Macknight and Philip Doddridge, with Prefaces, Various Emendations, and an Appendix by Alexander Campbell: Stereotyped from the Third Edition Revised . . . [by J. A. James, Cincinnati]. Printed and Published by H. S. Bosworth: Cincinnati   *1737*

12 cm   KyWAT, MiU, NNAB, OC

Alexander Campbell Version; see 1826 NT, No 567. Reprinted from the 1833 Pocket Edition (No 854). Has General Preface (dated Jan 29, 1826), Preface to the Gospels, Hints to the Reader, and Prefaces and Introductions to Acts-Revelation and to the 3rd and 4th editions. Copyright 6 Aug 1832.

186–? The New Testament of Our Lord and Saviour Jesus Christ, Translated from the Latin Vulgate with Annotations and References . . . F. Lucas, Jr.: Baltimore   *1738*

Reported as 412 p   12 cm   DLC
Rheims Version. See 1831? Lucas NT, No 766.

1860 The New Testament . . . American Bible Society . . . : New York   *1739*

1 vol: (368) (96)   10 cm   NNAB
Diamond 64mo with Psalms, revised ABS standard text; see 1857, No 1643. No printing after 1922; plates scrapped in 1942.

1861? The Holy Bible, Translated from the Latin Vulgate . . . With Annotations, References, and . . . Index. From the Last London and Dublin Editions . . . Revised and . . . Compared with the Latin Vulgate. Carefully Printed from the Edition of 1844 . . . with Approbation of The Most Rev. John Hughes . . . [Stereotyped by Messrs. Rennie, Shea & Lindsay]. Johnson, Fry and Company: New York   *1740*

1 vol: (1020) 1021–1024 (2)   33 cm   NNAB
Rheims-Douay Version. Reprint of 1844 Dunigan Bible (No 1199). See also Johnson and Fry's 1859 Self Interpreting Bible, No 1691. Added engraved title, engraving of Pope Pius ix, Order of Books, Historical Sketch, Admonition, Letter of Pope Pius vi, Prayer, Decree of the Council of Trent, Catalogue of the Sacred Books, and Tables precede text. Family Record and Index at end. Illustrated. Copyright 1861.
Pope (p 732) gives the date as 1863/65, adding that it was issued in 42 parts.

1861 The Holy Bible . . . The Text Conformable to the Oxford Edition of the Year 1610, and the American Bible Society's Original Standard Edition of 1816 . . . W. W. Harding: Philadelphia   *1741*

1 vol: (787) (600) (41) (22)   30 cm   NN
Harding's Superfine Edition appears at head of title. Has added colored title page; frontispiece; other illustrations.

1861 The Family Bible . . . With Brief Notes and Instructions, Designed to Give the Results of Critical Investigation . . . The References and Marginal Readings of the Polyglot Bible . . . Published by the American Tract Society: New York   *1742*

3 vols: Vol i, (16) (576); Vol ii, 577–1061 [1]; Vol iii, (5) 1065–1491 1493–1504   28cm
                                                                                                                              NNAB
Vol i preliminary matter includes Order of Books and Chronological Order; The Bible, God's Gift for Men (signed J. E.); The Harmony and Perfection of the Holy Scriptures (from Preface to the Polyglott Bible — signed T.C.); text: Genesis-Esther. Vol ii, text: Job-Malachi; Family Record pages at end. Vol iii has NT title, Order of Books, and General Introduction to Gospels; NT text; Synopsis of Robinson's Harmony of the Gospels, Indexes, Tables, etc. at end. Each Book has an Introduction. Illustrated with maps in color. Copyright 1861, by the American Tract Society. See 1853–56 octavo, No 1530.
NN has 186– NT with Psalms (p 617–711) and the Synopsis of Robinson's Harmony (p 1493–1496).

1861 The Annotated Paragraph Bible . . . According to the Authorized Version, Arranged in Paragraphs and Parallelisms; with Explanatory Notes, Prefaces to the Several Books, and an Entirely New Selection of References to Parallel and Illustrative Passages . . . The Religious Tract Society: London. Published for the Spingler Institute, Union Square, by Sheldon & Co.: New York **1743**

Reported as (viii) (1471)   27 cm   NRU, ScGrvF
Has frontispiece and other illustrations.

1861 The Holy Bible . . . [with] Proper Names . . . [etc.]. Accurately Accented . . . & Divided into Syllables . . . by Israel Alger, jr. W. S. Young: Philadelphia **1744**

Reported as (714) (218)   24 cm   PSt
See 1825, No 531.

1861 The Holy Bible, Containing the Old and New Testaments. Translated and Arranged, with Notes; By Leicester Ambrose Sawyer. Vol. ii. The Later Prophets. Walker, Wise and Company: Boston **1745**

Vol ii: 384 p   20 cm   INapN, MB, NN, NNAB
Sawyer Version; see 1858 NT, No 1687; also 1883 Job, No 2000. Vol ii includes the Twelve Minor Prophets, Isaiah, Jeremiah, and Ezekial.
NN also has Vol iii, 1862 (6, 7–287, 289–348 p, 19 cm) containing Psalms, Proverbs, Job, Canticles, Lamentations, and Ecclesiastes. The term "Jehovah" is used for "Lord" in Psalm 23 and elsewhere.

1861 The Holy Bible . . . According to the Commonly Received Version . . . American and Foreign Bible Society: New York **1746**

1 vol: (510) (161)   19 cm   NNAB
With Tables and Family Record pages.

1861 The Holy Bible . . . American Bible Society . . . : New York **1747**

1 vol: (958) (296)   19 cm   NNAB
Minion Reference 16mo, with revised ABS standard text; see 1857, No 1643.

1861 The Holy Bible . . . American Bible Society . . . : New York **1748**

765 p   18 cm   NNAB
Nonpareil Duodecimo with revised ABS standard text but short page headings; see 1857, No 1643. Has Contents on p 759–765. This is probably from the type of the 1860 Bible (No 1724) with additional corrections, particularly as to page headings, chapter summaries, and contents.

1861 The English Version of the Polyglott Bible . . . J. B. Lippincott: Philadelphia **1749**

14 cm   NNAB
Reprint of Lippincott 1850 Bible (No 1435) with Metrical Psalms added at end (77 p).

1861? The New Testament . . . As Revised and Corrected by the Spirits. Entered . . . in the year 1861, by Leonard Thorn . . . Published by the Proprietors: New York City **1749A**

1 vol: (157) (10) 158–320   22 cm   NNAB

Order of Books and Introductory Remarks and Explanations by the Spirit of Jesus Christ precede text. Text is printed in verse form, double column. Has Family Record and article, New Dispensation by the Spirit of Christ. Two colored plates, one of which shows the "King of Kings" on a white horse, much in the style of George III. Copyright 1861, by Leonard Thorn.

This translation is based on the AV. The Introduction informs us that Jesus and the Apostles came in spirit and revised and corrected the Books of the NT. In accordance with these corrections, the above Testament was accomplished by mediums through a superior medium. Several Books are shortened. Romans contains only seven chapters, Revelation only three, and Hebrews is entirely omitted. The text is changed throughout. Several pages containing a New Dispensation by the Spirit of Christ, which is intended for spiritualists, are added. See Simms, p 239.

The following appears in the Introductory Remarks and Explanations by the Spirit of Jesus Christ (p 3): "I was born about 1861 years since, in the town of Bethlehem, in Judea. . . . I was about thirty years and four months old when I began to preach. . . . I, Jesus, came in spirit bodily, and revised and corrected the first four books of the new testament, namely, Matthew, Mark, Luke, John, and also the Revelations. . . ."

1861 The New Testament . . . [C. E. P. Brinckloe & Co., printers]. Published by
C. H. Marot: Philadelphia   **1750**

601 p   18 cm   NNAB
Has 1 map.

1861 The New Testament . . . Graves, Marks & Co.: Nashville, Tenn.   **1751**

225 p   13 cm   NN
NN has another copy with "I am a Soldier" and "Hymns" at end (14 p).

1861 The New Testament . . . Tennessee Bible Society, Instituted in the Year
1861: Nashville   **1752**

1 vol: (303) (80)   13 cm   NNAB
Order of Books precedes text. Book of Psalms, with separate title page, at end.
Also published without Book of Psalms.
This NT and the following Nashville edition (No 1753) were among those printed within the Confederacy. See also 1862 NT, No 1763.

1861 The New Testament . . . Bible Board of the Southern Baptist Convention:
Nashville, Tenn.   **1753**

303 p   13 cm   CSmH, NNAB

1861 The New Testament . . . American Bible Society . . . : New York   **1754**

316 p   12 cm   NNAB
Pearl 32mo with revised ABS standard text; see 1857, No 1643. See also 1860 NT, No 1736.

1861 The New Testament . . . According to the Commonly Received Version . . .
American and Foreign Bible Society: New York   **1755**

346 p   12 cm   NNAB
Has Order of Books and Chronological Order.

1861 The New Testament . . . E. Darrow & Bro.: Rochester, N. Y.   **1756**

454 p   10 cm   NN, NNAB
Copy presented to NNAB in 1865 by S. Ide of Claremont, N. H., with note across title that he had printed thousands of these.

1862   The Holy Bible, Translated from the Latin Vulgate . . . First Published by the English College at Douay . . . 1609, and the New Testament . . . at Rheims . . . 1582. With Notes, Selected by Geo. Leo Haydock. E. Dunigan & Brother: New York   *1757*

Reported as 1667 p   34 cm   CtY
Rheims-Douay Version. Probably same as Dunigan's 1852 edition (No 1485) in spite of difference in pagination. Has added engraved title pages to both Testaments. Illustrated.

1862   The Holy Bible . . . American Bible Society . . . : New York   *1758*

1 vol: (855) (262)   19 cm   NNAB
Minion Duodecimo with revised ABS standard text. No chapter summaries or page headings; rules around text. As there had been no printing since 1922, the plates were scrapped in 1942.
The OT was published separately in 1863, particularly for Jews. (*ABS Reports,* 1860, p 29; 1861, p 27; 1863, p 26.) NNAB also has separate NT.

1862   The Holy Bible . . . American Bible Society . . . : New York   *1759*

1 vol: (879) (272)   19 cm   NNAB
Minion 16mo. A squarish book, evidently printed from the same type as previous item (No 1758) but with chapter summaries and page headings.

1862   The Holy Bible . . . American Bible Society . . . : New York   *1760*

1 vol: (771) (243)   15 cm   NNAB
Pearl Reference 18mo with revised ABS standard text.

1862   The New Testament. Translated from the Latin Vulgate, and Diligently Compared with the Original Greek Text. With Notes, Critical and Explanatory, by Francis Patrick Kenrick . . . Second Edition, Revised and Corrected . . . Kelly, Hedian & Piet: Baltimore   *1761*

1 vol: (xv) 17–861   24 cm   DCU, MB, NN, NNAB
Bishop Kenrick's Version; see 1849, No 1414. Introduction (dated May 1862), Explanations, Index, Tables of Epistles and Gospels to be Read on Sundays and Holy Days, and Preface to St. Matthew precede text. Copyright 1862 by Francis Patrick Kenrick.

1862   The New Testament, From the Family Bible: With Brief Notes and Instructions Designed to Give the Results of Critical Investigation . . . The References and Marginal Readings of the Polyglott Bible . . . Published by the American Tract Society: New York   *1762*

1 vol: (781) 782–800   17 cm   NN, NNAB, OCU
Two maps in color and General Introduction to the Gospels precede text. Synopsis of Robinson's Harmony of the Gospels and Chronological Index at end. Copyright 1862.
Also issued with The Bible, God's Gift for Men, signed by J. E.; The Harmony and Perfection of the Holy Scriptures, signed by T.C.; and the Synopsis of Robinson's Harmony before text.

1862   The New Testament . . . [Printed by Wood, Hanleiter Rice & Co., Atlanta, Ga.]. Confederate States Bible Society, Instituted in the Year 1862: Augusta   *1763*

13 cm   CSmH, MBAt, MiU, NcD, NjP, NNAB, PPL–R

Appears to be from identical plates as the Tennessee Bible Society NT of 1861 (No 1752) but with new title pages. Order of Books precedes text. Contains the Book of Psalms with separate title page.

Also published without the Psalms.

The Confederate States Bible Society was organized in 1862. In an effort to secure Testaments, the Society tried to import Bibles and Testaments from the British and Foreign Bible Society. NNAB has a Gospel of Luke published by the BFBS that was one of those that ran the blockade. For details see Harold R. Willoughby, *Soldiers' Bibles through Three Centuries*, University of Chicago Press 1944, p 27–30.

1862–63   The New Testament . . . The Common English Version, Corrected by the Final Committee of the American Bible Union . . . American Bible Union: New York   *1764*

2 vols: Part I, (iv) (326); Part II, (iv) 327–540   15 cm   MiU, MWA, NN

Part I (1862) the Gospels. Part II (1863) Acts–II Corinthians. No separate copy of Part III (Galatians-Revelation) has been located nor does an examination of *The Bible Union Quarterly* for the period indicate such publication. For 1-vol edition with complete NT text, see 1864, No 1787.

This is the first appearance of the American Bible Union Version. The ABU was formed in 1850 by Baptists who were not satisfied with the conservative attitude of the American and Foreign Bible Society (see 1838, No 1007) and were eager for an English "immerse" version. The revision was well underway by 1855, several tentative editions having been published for circulation and comment, particularly the work of Orrin B. Judd and John Lillie. Plans for lithographing the manuscripts were considered but abandoned. In 1857 Dr. Thomas J. Conant and Horatio B. Hackett were secured for the Final Committee. They were later joined by E. Rödiger and G. R. Bliss, and in 1862 by Dr. A. C. Kendrick (see 1842 Bernard Bible, No 1134), but other translators were responsible for the early work. The "Second Revision" was issued in 1866 (No 1804). These revisions appear, through comparison of the texts, to be of a progressive nature. Some of the more radical renderings of the provisional issues were softened in the 1863–64 text (No 1773) but the total effect was to produce a version which became, with each revision, increasingly independent of its basis, the "common" or Authorized Version. Outstanding was the prominence given to the rendering of *baptizo*. See the detailed study by Conant, published as an appendix to Matthew, 1860 and then to the Four Gospels, 1861.

The standard form for the "Revised English Scriptures with Notes" (the legend on the front cover of the quarto parts listed below) consisted of (1) an introduction; (2) the text pages carrying the King James Version, the Greek or Hebrew text, and the Revised text in three parallel columns, verse by verse, with notes to the text in double columns; and (3) the Revised text printed separately in paragraph form. The Greek text was printed from Bagster's edition of Mill's edition of Stephanus' third edition (1550). Of the several OT parts published, only Job (1857) and provisional issues from 1858 to 1864 carry the subsidiary imprint of the Bible Revision Association, Louisville. Ephesians and the 1864 reprint of John also have added imprint of the American Christian Bible Society, Cincinnati. The London agents were Trübner and Co. Many of the parts were also published serially in the monthly *Bible Union Reporter* before bound publication.

1852   The Second Epistle of Peter, the Epistles of John and Jude (by John Lillie).
          iv, 52 p   27 cm   NNAB, NNUT

1854   The above with Revelation (reset).
          xi, 253 p   NNAB

1854   Matthew, chapters 1, 2 (by Orrin B. Judd).
          "8vo"   Not Located

1855   Matthew, chapters 1–3 (by Orrin B. Judd).
          109 leaves   NRCR–S
              NRCR–S copy is undated. PP has 1858 reprint (52 p).

1856   The Gospel of John.
          xvi, 178 p   NRCR–S

1856   The Epistles of Paul to the Thessalonians . . . by the Translator of II Peter-Revelation (by John Lillie).
          viii, 73 p   NNAB

1856   The Epistle to the Ephesians . . . (by N. N. Whiting).

Not Located

1856   Job by Thomas J. Conant.
xix, 85 p   NNAB
  NNUT has octavo.

1857   The Book of Job . . . By Thomas J. Conant.
xxx, 165 p   NNAB

1857   The Epistle to the Ephesians . . . (by N. N. Whiting).
vi, 39 p   NNAB, NRCR–S

1857   The Epistle to the Hebrews (by N. N. Whiting).
vi, 90 p   NNAB

1858   The Acts of the Apostles (by Alexander Campbell).
vi, 224 p   NNAB

1858   The Gospel according to Mark . . . (by N. N. Whiting).
vi, 134 p   NNAB

1859   The Gospel of John . . . (by J. W. Morton).
xvi, 171 p   NNAB, NRCR–S
  NNAB and NRCR–S also have 1864 reprint.

1860   The Gospel according to Matthew.
xxx, 171, 107 p   NNAB

1860   Epistle to Philemon . . . (by H. B. Hackett).
94 p   NNAB

1860   The Gospel according to Luke (by N. N. Whiting).
viii, 273 p   NNAB, NRCR–S
  NNAB and NRCR–S also have 1864 reprint.

1860   The Epistles of Timothy and Titus (by N. N. Whiting).

Not Located

1861   The Sacred Scriptures . . . (all quarto parts issued to date in one "immerse" volume).

NNAB

1868   The Book of Genesis, by Thomas J. Conant.
xxi, 209 p   NNAB

1871   The Psalms . . . by Thomas J. Conant.
xxi, 210 p   24 cm   NNAB
  Copyright 1869; Introduction dated 1870. NNAB also has 1885 reprint by American Baptist Publication Society.

1872   The Book of Proverbs . . . by Thomas J. Conant.
xxxiv, 151, xiii, 88 p   NNAB

1874   Isaiah 1–13:22, by T. J. Conant.

Not Located

  Encyclopedia Britannica 11th ed, vi, p 823a.

1878   Joshua, Judges, Ruth, by T. J. Conant.

Not Located

  Simms, p 183.

1884   Joshua, Judges, Ruth, 1 and 2 Samuel, 1 and 2 Kings . . . by Thomas J. Conant (Am. Bapt. Pub. Soc.).
xxv, 385 p   23 cm   NNAB

During the Civil War, thousands of Gospels in the ABU Version were distributed to the soldiers, in "convenient size and shape for a side-pocket." In 1864 the ABU was suggesting these for distribution to immigrants and in 1865, to freed slaves. NNAB has none of these Gospels.

NRCR–S has considerable manuscript material relating to the ABU Version. For further information, see *Documentary History: consisting of a reprint of its constitution, annual reports, quarterly papers . . . etc., in the form of the Bible Union Quarterly*, edited by W. H. Wyckoff and C. A. Buckbee, 4 vols.

In 1882 and 1883, the American Bible Union passed over its work to the American Baptist Publication Society. See 1891 Improved Edition, No 2048.

1863   The Holy Bible . . . Apocrypha . . . Concordance, The Psalms . . . in metre
. . . The Text conformable to the standard of the American Bible Society . . .
J. B. Lippincott & Company: Philadelphia   *1765*

Reported as (576) (88) 577–768 (22) (41)   29 cm   VtHi

1863   The Holy Bible . . . Apocrypha . . . Canne's Marginal Notes . . . Index . . .
Table . . . Blakeman & Mason: New York; Breed, Butler & Co.: Buffalo   *1766*

Reported as (576) (96) 577–768 (28) (6)   29 cm   VtHi

1863   The Holy Bible . . . The Text Conformable to the Original Edition of the
Year of Our Lord 1610, and the American Bible Society's Original Standard
Edition of 1816 . . . [Stereotyped by Jesper Harding & Son]. William W.
Harding: Philadelphia   *1767*

1 vol: (768) (41) (22)   29 cm   NNAB
With Apocrypha. *Harding's Fine Edition* appears at head of title. See 1857, No 1639.

1863   The Comprehensive Commentary on the Holy Bible . . . Edited by Rev. William Jenks . . . J. B. Lippincott: Philadelphia   *1768*

5 vols   26 cm   MiU
MiU lacks Vols II–IV. See 1835–38, No 894.

1863   The Holy Bible . . . American Bible Society . . . : New York   *1769*

1 vol: (747) (235)   15 cm   NNAB
Pearl 18mo with revised ABS standard text. Bound in leather with envelope flap.

1863   The Holy Bible . . . American Bible Society . . . : New York   *1770*

1 vol: (609) (194)   15 cm   NNAB
Diamond Reference 16mo with revised ABS standard text. Similar to 1857 Bible (No 1660)
but with new page and chapter headings and other changes to make it conform to the new
standard. Bound in leather with envelope flap.

1863   The Holy Bible . . . William H. Hill, Jr.: Boston   *1771*

1 vol: (852) (259)   11 cm   NNAB
Civil War Pocket Bible bound in red leather with envelope flap.

1863   The New Testament, with Brief Explanatory Notes or Scholia. By Howard
Crosby . . . [John F. Trow, Printer, Stereotyper, and Electrotyper]. Charles
Scribner: New York   *1772*

543 p   20 cm   NNAB
Has footnotes below rule. Copyright by Howard Crosby, 1863.
The author states in his Dedication to Prof. Tayler Lewis, LL.D.: "I have not attempted
to write a commentary. No doctrinal dissertation or practical remarks will be found in this book.
I have put the word 'scholia' on the title-page as designating to a scholar's mind the true char-
acter of the Notes, which are intended simply to remove the surface-difficulties of the text. . . ."

1863–64   The New Testament . . . The Common English Version, Corrected by
the Final Committee of the American Bible Union. Fifteenth Thousand . . .
American Bible Union: New York   *1773*

2 vols: Vol I, 326 p; Vol II, (iv) 327–540   15 cm   KyLo

ABU Version; see 1862–63 NT, No 1764. Vol ɪ dated 1863; Vol ɪɪ, 1864. Text ends with ɪɪ Corinthians.

KyLo has another copy of Vol ɪ with *Eleventh Thousand* on title page, and another set with *Second Thousand*. MH–AH has Vol ɪ only with *Eleventh Thousand*.

1863   The New Testament ... In Which All the Proper Names and Words of Two Syllables and More are Divided and Accented as They Should be Pronounced ... Carlton & Porter: New York   *1774*

Reported as 372 p   "16mo"   BM

1863   The New Testament ... [Printed by Franklin Steam Printing House, Atlanta, Ga.]. Bible Society of the Confederate States, Instituted in the Year 1862: Augusta, Ga.   *1775*

13 cm   DLC, NN, NNAB

Reprint of 1862 Confederate Bible Society edition (No 1763) with Psalms.

1863   The New Testament ... American Bible Society ... : New York   *1776*

316 p   12 cm   NNAB

Pearl 32mo with revised ABS standard text. Similar to 1861 NT (No 1754) except that chapter summaries are in smaller type and some text has been reset to fill the extra space.

1864?   The Devotional Family Bible ... With Practical Experimental Reflections on Each Verse and Rich Marginal References and Readings. By Rev. Alexander Fletcher ... Virtue and Yorston: New York   *1777*

2 vols: (1621) (64)   36 cm   DLC, MB, NN

Continuously paged. Has frontispieces to both Testaments. Footnotes, with center references. Contains Family Record. Originally published in 42 parts. See 1835?, No 891.

1864   The Holy Bible ... The Text Conformable to the Oxford Edition of the Year of Our Lord 1610, and the American Bible Society's Original Standard Edition of 1816 ... William Harding: Philadelphia   *1778*

2 vols   30 cm   NNAB

Reprint of Jesper Harding's 1857–58 Superfine Edition (No 1640). Has engraved frontispieces, illuminated titles, and engravings, which are different from those in the 1857–58 and 1860 (No 1716) editions.

1864   [The Illustrated Domestic Bible] The Holy Bible ... With Marginal References, and the Usual Various Readings ... Notes; Reflections; Questions ... and Various Other Advantages, Without Disturbing the Uusual Order ... By the Rev. Ingram Cobbin ... Printed and Published by Case, Lockwood and Company: Hartford   *1779*

27 cm   NNAB

Similar to 1851 Hueston edition (No 1463) but with Brown's Concordance at end (48 p).

1864   The English Version of the Polyglott Bible ... J. B. Lippincott: Philadelphia
                                                                        1780

15 cm   NNAB

Reprint of 1850 Lippincott edition (No 1435) but with Metrical Psalms at end (77 p).

1864   Daniel, with Apocryphal Additions, by Leicester A. Sawyer . . . Walker, Wise
and Company: Boston   *1781*

Reported as 144 p   20 cm   DLC
Sawyer Version; see 1858 NT, No 1687; also 1883 Job, No 2000. Notice by the Publishers
concerning the series appears on p 142–144.

1864   The New Testament . . . According to the Commonly Received Version . . .
American and Foreign Bible Society: New York   *1782*

Reported as 288 p   24 cm   DLC
With Book of Psalms.

1864   The New Testament . . . American Bible Society, Instituted . . . : New York
1783

24 cm   NNAB
A new issue of the 1850 Pica Octavo NT (No 1443), now conforming to the revised ABS
standard text.

1864   The New Testament . . . With Explanatory Notes and Practical Observations. By Rev. Sylvanus Cobb, D.D. Published by the Commentator: Boston
1784

Reported as (xx) (687)   23 cm   DLC

1864   The New Testament. Translated from the Original Greek, by H. T. Anderson . . . [Stereotyped by the Franklin Type Foundry, Cincinnati, Ohio].
Published for the Author: Cincinnati   *1785*

569 p   21 cm   DLC, IU, NcAS, NN, NNAB, OC
Dedication and Preface, signed H. T. Anderson, Harrodsburg, Ky., 1864, precede text.
Copyright 1864, by H. T. Anderson.
    The Rev. Henry Tompkins Anderson (1812–1872), a minister of the Disciples of Christ and
at one time a pastor in Louisville, Kentucky, was the translator of this NT. It does not seem to
follow any particular text but is an "immersion" version. His aim was "to express the Truth
of God as it is contained in the original . . . in the English language as now spoken." The
language is for the most part that of the AV, and the translator says that whenever the AV
expressed the sense of the original "in good English" he has adopted it.
    A revised edition was issued in 1866 (No 1805) and an edition was printed in England in
1867. After publication of Tischendorf's Greek NT, showing readings of the Codex Sinaiticus,
Anderson began a new translation. It was completed shortly before his death but not published
until 1918? (No 2243).

1864   [All in special letters: The New Testament . . . in fonetik spelling . . . Elias
Longley: Cincinnati]   *1786*

19 cm   OC
Reprint of 1855 Longley Brothers phonetic NT (No 1596).

1864   The New Testament . . . The Common English Version, Corrected by the
Final Committee of the American Bible Union. Thirtieth Thousand . . . [Hol-
man, Printer]. American Bible Union: New York   *1787*

766 p   15 cm   ICU, NN, NNAB
ABU Version; see 1862–63 NT, No 1764. Seems to be reprint of the 1862–63 edition with
the rest of the NT added. Has text in single column, paragraph form, with verse numbers in
margin. Alternative readings and renderings at foot of page. Copyright 1862, by The American
Bible Union.

1864   The New Testament . . . [Printed by Evans & Cogswell: Columbia, S. C.].
Confederate States Bible Society, Instituted in the Year 1862: Augusta, Ga.
1788

13 cm   NcD
Reprint of 1862 NT (No 1763).

1865   The Holy Bible . . . The Text Conformable to the Standard of the American
Bible Society . . . Published by John Edwin Potter: Philadelphia   **1789**

30 cm   NNAB
Pagination same as Perry edition of 1852 (No 1487). Printed by Collins. Frontispieces,
added engraved title pages, Order of Books, To the Reader, and Contents precede text. Tables
follow OT. With Apocrypha, followed by Family Record and Portrait Album pages. NT title
has Account of Dates on verso. Index, Tables, etc., Metrical Psalms, and Concordance at end.
Illustrated.

1865–66   The Comprehensive Commentary on the Holy Bible, . . . the Authorised
Version, Scott's Marginal References, Matthew Henry's Commentary . . .
Observations of Rev. Thomas Scott, with . . . Notes . . . Edited by Rev. Wil-
liam Jenks . . . J. B. Lippincott & Co.: Philadelphia   **1790**

6 vols   26 cm   MiU
Has frontispiece. Vol vi, the supplementary volume, contains a new Concordance (1865).
See 1835–38, No 894.

1865?   The New Testament . . . the Common English Version Corrected by the
Final Committee of the American Bible Union; Second Revision. American
Bible Union: New York   **1791**

Reported as 488 p   23 cm   KyLo
ABU Version; see 1862–63 NT, No 1764. This seems to be the first edition of the second
revision; see 1866 NT, No 1804, for further description.

1865   The Emphatic Diaglott: Containing the Original Greek text of what is
commonly styled the New Testament, according to the recension of Dr. J.
J. Griesbach, with an Interlineary word for word English Translation; a new
Emphatic Version, based on the Interlineary Translation, on the renderings
of eminent critics, and on the various readings of the Vatican Manuscript
together with illustrative and explanatory footnotes, and a copious set of
references to the whole of which is added a valuable alphabetical appendix.
By Benjamin Wilson . . . Published by the Author: Geneva, Illinois   **1792**

Reported as (iv) 419 leaves; 44 p   17 cm   DLC, ICU
The interlinear English translation is printed in small type below the Greek, with the Emphatic Version in a narrower column at the right. Notes, references, etc. below text. Words
rendered emphatic by the Greek article are printed in small capitals; Greek emphatic substan-
tive pronouns are translated in black letters. Adjectives and pronouns only comparatively emphatic are translated with the initial letter in capitals and so are the translations of all Greek
substantives. According to the Preface (dated Aug 1864) the work was first issued in parts to
subscribers. Copyright 1864, by B. Wilson (b. 1817).
DLC has card listing first edition, New York 1864, but no copy has been located. Later
editions were issued by Fowler and Wells, New York in 1865 (MH-AH); by Samuel R. Wells,
New York in 1870 (NNAB, NNUT); and again by Fowler and Wells in 1883 and 1902 (both
NNAB). In 1902 the text was endorsed by the Watch Tower Bible and Tract Society and
offered at reduced price with a year's subscription to *Zion's Watch Tower.* See 1927 NT,
No 2291; also 1942 NT, No 2402.

Wells also printed in 1878 Wilson's *Accompaniment to International S. S. Lessons Third and Fourth Quarters, 1878. Studies in Luke ... With Alphabetical Appendix of Names, Weights, Coins, Words and Phrases,* which included the front matter, text, and appendix as in the above NT (unpaged, 20 cm, NNAB, NjNbS).

1865 The New Testament. The Common English Version, Corrected by the Final
         Committee of the American Bible Union. Fifty-Fifth Thousand ... Amer-
         ican Bible Union: New York   *1793*

16 cm   ICU, NN, NNAB

ABU Version; see 1862–63 NT, No 1764. Reprint of 1864 edition (No 1787). At end are 2 p of advertising: one relating to the availability of ten separate portions, at 20 copies for $1, particularly suitable for "the soldier, the sailor, the immigrant and the freedman"; the other covering the NT which was available at $1 to $5. There was also a "cheap" edition in cloth, without rules, at 75¢.

1865 The New Testament ... The Common English Version. Corrected by the
         Final Committee of the American Bible Union. Third Revision. American
         Baptist Publication Society: Philadelphia   *1794*

488 p   16 cm   NjMD, NN

ABU Version; see 1862–63 NT, No 1764. Brevier 18mo, with text inside rules. *40th Thousand* appears at bottom of title. Copyright 1865.

Although this edition is marked third revision, it seems to be exactly like the second revision (see 1865? NT, No 1791; also 1866 NT, No 1804). A note on the verso of the title page explains the purpose of the translation and a one-page Preface explains the processes.

1866 The Holy Bible ... [Harper and Bros.]: New York   *1795*

5 vols   34 cm   NN

Has title page in red and black and added illustrated titles in color to each volume. Vol ɪ has presentation page. Vol ɪɪ title reads *The Illuminated Bible ... With 1600 Engravings.* With Apocrypha. Family Record at end of Vol ɪɪɪ. Index, Tables, and Concordance. See 1843–46 B, No 1161.

1866 The Holy Bible ... The Text Conformable to the Standard of the American
         Bible Society ... J. E. Potter and Co.: Philadelphia   *1796*

1 vol: (767) (22) (41)   30 cm   NN

With Apocrypha. Has frontispiece. Index, Tables, etc., Concordance, and Metrical Psalms at end. Illustrated, some plates colored.

1866 The Comprehensive Bible ... The Various Readings and Marginal Notes ...
         A General Introduction ... Introductions and Concluding Remarks to Each
         Book ... Parallel Passages ... Philological and Explanatory Notes ... J. B.
         Lippincott & Co.: Philadelphia   *1797*

29 cm   NNAB

Reprint of 1853 Lippincott, Grambo & Co. edition (No 1520) but with Apocrypha (101 p), and Metrical Psalms at end (24 p). Frontispiece is black and white; NT does not have frontispiece. Family Record follows Apocrypha.

1866 The Holy Bible ... The Text Conformable to the Original Edition of the
         Year of Our Lord 1610, and the American Bible Society's Original Standard
         Edition of 1816 ... William W. Harding: Philadelphia   *1798*

2 vols   29 cm   NNAB

Reprint of Jesper Harding's 1857–58 Superfine Edition (No 1640) but with different illustrations, in addition to illuminated Family Record pages and Portrait Album. *Arranged for Photographic Portraits of Families* appears at head of title.

1866 Comprehensive Commentary on the Holy Bible. . . . Authorized Version, with Marginal References, Matthew Henry's Commentary Condensed . . . Edited by William Jenks . . . Lippincott & Co.: Philadelphia **1799**

6 vols 26 cm NB

NB lacks Vols ɪv and vɪ. See 1835–38, No 894.

1866 The Holy Bible . . . With the Marginal References, and the Various Readings. Also, Notes; Reflections; Questions; Improved Readings; Improved Divisions of Chapters; the Chronological Order; Metrical Portions Distinguished; and Various Other Advantages, Without Disturbing the Usual Order of the Books, Verses, and Chapters, by the Rev. Ingram Cobbin . . . Case, Lockwood and Company: Hartford **1800**

"4to" DLC

Has frontispiece and half-title with *The Illustrated Domestic Bible*. Brown's Concordance at end. Contains Photo Album and Family Record pages. Illustrated. See 1851, No 1463.

1866 The Holy Bible . . . American Bible Society, Instituted . . . : New York **1801**

20 cm NNAB

A new edition of the 1852 Brevier Duodecimo (No 1505), now conforming to the revised ABS standard.

1866 The English Version of the Polyglott Bible . . . J. B. Lippincott & Co.: Philadelphia **1802**

15 cm NNAB

Reprint of 1850 Lippincott edition (No 1435) with addition of Metrical Psalms at end (77 p).

NNAB also has a similar undated edition with the imprint of *Claxton, Remsen & Haffelfinger, Philadelphia*, stereotyped by *J. Fagan & Son, Phila.* For this publisher, see 1869, No 1842.

1866 A New Translation of the Hebrew Prophets, with an Introduction and Notes. By George R. Noyes . . . Third edition. With new introduction and Notes. American Unitarian Association: Boston **1803**

2 vols: Vol ɪ, (xci) (271); Vol ɪɪ, (iii) (413) 20 cm NN

Noyes Version; see 1827, No 592. Vol ɪ contains Joel, Amos, Hosea, Isaiah, Micah, Nahum, Zephaniah, Habbakkuk, and Obadiah. Vol ɪɪ contains Jeremiah, Lamentations, Ezekiel, Haggai, Zechariah, Malachi, Jonah, and Daniel.

NNAB has Vol ɪ, fifth edition, 1880, and Vol ɪɪ, sixth edition, 1880.

1866 The New Testament . . . The Common English Version, Corrected by the Final Committee of the American Bible Union. Second Revision . . . 6th Thousand. Pica 8vo Edition. [Thomas Holman, Printer.] American Bible Union: New York; Trübner & Co.: London **1804**

1 vol: (2) 5–488 23 cm ICU, NN, NNAB

ABU Version; see 1862–63 NT, No 1764. First printed in this size in 1865? (see No 1791). Called the "Pulpit and Family Testament" (*Documentary History* ɪv, p 349; specimen pages, p 350–351). Text printed in single column, paragraph form, with verse numbers raised in text in smaller type. Alternative readings and renderings below text, separated by single rule. Note on verso of title page: "This Revised Testament has been prepared under the auspices of the American Bible Union, by the most competent scholars of the day. . . ." Copyright by the American Bible Union, 1865.

Other editions in this size were issued in 1867: 12th Thousand (NNAB) and 14th Thousand (KyLo); in 1869: 20th Thousand (NN); and in 1871 (NN).

1866   The New Testament. Translated from the Original Greek, by H. T. Anderson. Revised Edition . . . [Stereotyped at the Franklin Type Foundry, Cincinnati]. John P. Morton & Company: Louisville, Kentucky   *1805*

Reported as 568 p   21cm   ICU, TNDC

Anderson Version; see 1864 NT, No 1785. Although the title page calls this a revised edition, it seems to be revised only in terms of type and format.

1866   The New Testament . . . The Common English Version. Corrected by the Final Committee of the American Bible Union. Second Revision, Willingham Memorial. [Thomas Holman, New York, printer and Electroplates, Smith and McDougal, New York.] American Bible Union: New York   *1806*

488 p   16 cm   KyLo, NN

ABU Version; see 1862–63 NT, No 1764. *2d Thousand, Brevier 18mo* appears at bottom of title page. Copyright 1865.

IU and ViLxW have second revision for this year but with Amory Memorial in title. NjMD has second revision of this date with Trübner, London, in imprint and marked 30th Thousand.

1866   The New Testament. Translated from the Original Greek, by H. T. Anderson . . . Stereotyped and Printed for the Author by J. P. Morton & Co.: Louisville, Kentucky   *1807*

408 p   13 cm   ICU, NN, TNDC

Anderson Version; see 1864 NT, No 1785.

1866   The New Testament . . . The Common English Version, Corrected by the Final Committee of the American Bible Union. Second Revision, Merrill Memorial. 10th Thousand. Agate, 32mo Edition. [Composed and Electrotyped by Lange & Bro., Printers. Thomas Holman, Printer.] American Bible Union: New York; Trübner & Co.: London   *1808*

488 p   10 cm   NjMD, NNAB

ABU Version; see 1862–63 NT, No 1764. Note on translation precedes text. Text in single column, paragraph form, with verse numbers raised in text in smaller type. Alternative readings and renderings at foot of page. Copyright 1866.

Other printings in this size were issued in 1866: Amory Memorial (ViLxW); in 1871: Merrill Memorial (NN); and in 1888 by the American and Foreign Bible Society (NN).

1867   The Holy Bible . . . The Text Conformable to the Oxford Edition, and the American Bible Society's Standard of 1816 . . . William W. Harding: Philadelphia   *1809*

1 vol: (915) (116) (277) 1019–1032 (41) [1] (22) (4)   32 cm   NNAB

Harding's Superfine Edition appears at head of title, but this does not correspond to Jesper Harding's Superfine Edition of 1857–58 (No 1640) or to any of the 1857 Harding editions. The Apocrypha and Index pages are from the 1857 Royal Quarto Edition (No 1650). Frontispiece, To the Reader, Order of Books, and Contents precede text. Tables follow OT. Portrait

Album and frontispiece precede NT. Index, Tables, etc., Concordance, and Metrical Psalms at end. Center references. Entire printed page enclosed in single rule border. Illustrated.

1867   The Holy Bible . . . American Bible Society, Instituted . . . : New York   *1810*

29 cm   NNAB

A new issue of the 1857 Pica Reference Octavo (No 1643), now conforming to the revised ABS standard text. Although other Bibles had been published earlier with the corrections, this is the one ordered to be prepared in 1858.

1867   The Cottage Bible, and Family Expositor . . . With Practical Expositions and Explanatory Notes. By Thomas Williams . . . To Which are Added, the References and Marginal Readings of the Polyglott Bible . . . The Whole Carefully Revised . . . Edited by Rev. William Patton . . . Complete in Two Volumes . . . Published by Brainard & Sampson: Hartford   *1811*

2 vols: (ii) (736) 737–1440 (25)   27 cm   NNAB

Contains Prefaces to London and American editions and an Introduction. Has two sections of comment at foot of page in double columns, those in lower group coming from many commentators. Indexes, Dictionary, and 3 maps at end of Vol II. Many engravings. Copyright 1861. See 1833–34, No 818.

1867   The Holy Bible . . . American Bible Society, Instituted . . . : New York   *1812*

26 cm   NNAB

This fourth printing of a new form of the 1851 Pica Royal Octavo (No 1467) was first published in 1862 with corrections according to the revised ABS standard text. Last printing, 1929, a total of 96,000 copies having been run off from these plates.

1867   The Annotated Paragraph Bible: . . . According to the Authorized Version, Arranged in Paragraphs and Parallelisms; with Explanatory Notes, Prefaces to the Several Books, and . . . References to Parallel and Illustrative Passages . . . Sheldon & Company: New York and Boston   *1813*

3 vols   24 cm   ICU

Similar to 1861 one-volume edition (No 1743). Continuously paged.

1867   The Holy Bible . . . American Bible Society, Instituted . . . : New York   *1814*

1 vol: (770) (241)   23 cm   NNAB

Bourgeois Octavo, with revised ABS standard text.

1867   The Holy Bible, Translated from the Latin Vulgate . . . First Published by the English College at Douay . . . 1610; and the New Testament . . . at Rheims . . . 1582 . . . P. O'Shea: New York   *1815*

Reported as (736) (216)   19 cm   PLatS

Rheims-Douay Version.

1867   The Holy Bible . . . With Brief Notes and Instructions . . . Including the References and Marginal Readings of the Polyglot Bible . . . American Tract Society: New York   *1816*

3 vols   17 cm   ViU

Vol I, Genesis-Esther. Vol II, Job-Malachi. Vol III, Matthew-Revelation. See 1853–56 Family Bible, No 1530.

1867   The Holy Scriptures, Translated and corrected by the Spirit of Revelation, by Joseph Smith, Jr., the Seer . . . [Westcott & Thomson, Stereotypers, Philada.]. Published by the Church of Jesus Christ of Latter-Day Saints. Joseph Smith, I. L. Rogers, E. Robinson, Publishing Committee: Plano, Illinois   *1817*

1 vol: (917) (286)   18 cm   NN

Later editions have varying imprints. From 1881, when the headquarters were moved from Plano, Illinois, *Lamoni, Iowa* appears on title page but copyright date is 1867. From 1892, *Published by the Reorganized Church of Jesus Christ of Latter Day Saints: Lamoni, Iowa* appears in imprint (CtY has 1909 copy; ICMcC has 1920 one). From 1921, place of publication is altered to *Independence, Missouri* (NN has 1925 copy). From 1936, title page reads *Inspired Version. The Holy Scriptures . . . Reorganized Church of Jesus Christ of Latter Day Saints. Herald Publishing House: Independence, Missouri*; no copyright. For this edition new plates were made from the old by photographic process, the page being enlarged from 4½ × 6¾ inches to 5 × 8¼ inches. (NNAB has 1936 copy with Concordance and maps; for corrected and reset edition, see 1944, No 2425.)

Joseph Smith (1805–1844), founder of the Church of Jesus Christ of Latter Day Saints (Mormon), based his version of the Bible on a "direct revelation" which he first received in June 1830. The following extracts concerning his work are quoted from the Preface of the above edition:

As concerning the manner of translation and correction, it is evident, from the MSS. and the testimony of those who were conversant with the facts, that it was done by direct revelation from God.

It was begun in June, 1830, and was finished July 2, 1833. . . . The MSS., at his death, in 1844, were left in the hands of his widow, where they remained until the spring of 1866, when they were delivered to Wm. Marks, I. L. Rogers, and Wm. W. Blair, a Committee . . . to procure them for publication; and were by them delivered to the Committee of Publication, consisting of Joseph Smith [Jr.], Israel L. Rogers, and Ebenezer Robinson, and are now presented as they came into our hands.

On Smith's death the church split and this text is that of the Reorganized Church of Jesus Christ of Latter Day Saints (Independence, Missouri). The Utah group continued to use the King James Version.

1867   The Holy Bible . . . American Bible Society, Instituted . . . : New York *1818*

965 p   15 cm   NNAB

Agate 18mo, which replaces 1853 Agate 24mo (No 1536). Has revised ABS standard text with new page headings and chapter summaries, more like those in the 1862 Pearl Reference 18mo (No 1760) than in the 1861 Nonpareil Duodecimo (No 1748).

1867   A New Translation of the Book of Psalms and of the Proverbs, with Introductions, and Notes, chiefly Explanatory. By George R. Noyes . . . Third edition. American Unitarian Association: Boston   *1819*

421 p   20 cm   NNAB

Noyes Version; see 1827, No 592. Third edition apparently signifies the third edition of the Psalms only.

A fourth edition was issued in 18??; a fifth in 1874; sixth, 1880; seventh, 18??; eighth, 1890. NNAB has fifth, sixth, and eighth editions.

1867   The New Testament . . . The Common English Version, Corrected by the Final Committee of the American Bible Union. Second Revision, Willingham Memorial. American Bible Union: New York; Trübner & Co.: London   *1820*

Reported as 488 p   24 cm   KyLo, MiU
ABU Version; see 1862–63 NT, No 1764.

1867 [The New Testament] Expository Notes with Practical Observations . . . Wherein the Sacred Text is at Large Recited, The Sense Explained . . . By William Burkitt . . . Ninth Edition . . . Clark & Maynard, Publishers: New York   *1821*

2 vols: Vol I, (6) (725) 726–764 (2)   24 cm   NNAB
NNAB has Vol I only; Vol II not located. Contains Dedication to the Bishop of London, to Lord Fitzwalter, to Family Governors, and Prayer by W. Burkitt. Index of Subjects at end. Interpretational notes printed in small type between sections of text. For William Burkitt, see 1794, No 47.

1867 The New Testament . . . J. B. Lippincott & Co.: Philadelphia   *1822*

Reported as 240 p   24 cm   ICU

1867 The New Testament . . . With Explanatory Notes and Practical Observations by The Rev. Sylvanus Cobb, D.D. 5th Edition. G. W. Quinby: Boston, Mass. and Augusta, Maine   *1823*

24 cm   MH–AH
Similar to Cobb's 1864 NT (No 1784).

1867 The New Testament . . . American Bible Society . . . : New York   *1824*

427 p   22 cm   NNAB
Small Pica Octavo with revised ABS standard text. According to the *ABS Report* 1864 (p 27), this was first issued in 1864 or 1863 in 9 separate parts. NNAB has some parts, 1864. Also issued with Psalms (109 p). New plates were made in 1889 when 612,000 copies had been printed. No printing after 1922; plates scrapped.

1867 [The New Testament] The Descriptive Testament . . . With Notes, Explanatory of the Rites, Customs, Sects, Phraseology, Topography, and Geography, Referred to in this Portion of the Sacred Pages . . . By I. Cobbin. Edited by D. Mead . . . Clark & Mead: New York   *1825*

1 vol: (iv) (426)   19 cm   NNAB
Illustrated. For Cobbin's Illustrated Domestic Bible see 1851, No 1463.

1867 The New Testament . . . According to the Commonly Received Version . . . American and Foreign Bible Society: New York   *1826*

346 p   11 cm   NN

1868? Holland's Illustrated Bible Containing references . . . critical and explanatory notes, condensed concordance, illustrated with 900 highly finished engravings. W. J. Holland and Co.: Springfield, Mass. and Chicago, Ill. *1826A*

Reported as viii–xviii (1052) (391) 392–424   36 cm   Congregational Church, Castleton, Vermont

List of illustrations — engravings but not halftones — precedes text. Illustrations are set in the body of the text. NT has commentary at foot of page. Center references. Concordance at end. Except for the style of illustration, this is similar to the Illuminated Bibles of the late 1890s (see 1897, No 2075; also 1898, No 2093).

W. J. Holland is listed as a publisher in Springfield city directories from 1864 to 1868. W. J. Holland and Company appears from 1868 to 1883.

1868   The Holy Bible . . . The Text Conformable to the Original Edition of the
Year of Our Lord 1610, and the American Bible Society's Original Standard
Edition of 1816 . . . William W. Harding: Philadelphia   *1827*

30 cm   NNAB
Reprint of Jesper Harding's Fine Edition of 1857 (No 1639) but with different illustrations and Portrait Album pages added. *Arranged for Photographic Portraits of Families* appears
at head of title. Has colored illuminated added titles to both Testaments dated 1867.

1868   The Complete Analysis of the Holy Bible . . . Containing the Whole of the
Old and New Testaments, Collected and Systematically Arranged in Thirty
Books . . . By Rev. Nathaniel West . . . Diligently revised and enlarged . . .
A. J. Johnson: New York [and others]   *1828*

1 vol: (lxiv) (925) 926–1097   28 cm   DLC, KWi, NNAB
Contains frontispiece, Dedication, Introduction, Tables, Indexes, Family Record, Diction-
aries of Proper Names, Statistics of the Existing Religious Denominations of the World, History
of the Bible, and map of Palestine. Text arranged according to subject into Books, Chapters,
and Sections: e.g. Book I, Arts and Sciences; Chapt. I, Agriculture; Sect. I, Land; Bad, etc.
Has Indexes on p 926–1097, with Testamonials (6 p) at end. Copyright 1867, A. J. Johnson.
See 1854, No 1552 for earlier edition; also 1871, No 1868 for Hitchcock's revision.
DLC copy is paginated lxiv, 1935 p. Number of publishers given in imprint varies with
copies.

1868   The Holy Bible . . . According to the Authorized Version; with Marginal
References, and the Usual Various Readings . . . By the Rev. Ingram Cobbin
. . . W. A. Burnham: Syracuse, New York   *1829*

28 cm   ICU
Has illustrated half-titles and maps. Binder's title: *Domestic Bible;* see 1851 Illustrated
Domestic Bible, No 1463.

1868   The Holy Bible . . . American Bible Society, Instituted . . . : New York *1830*

1 vol: (1008) (312)   26 cm   NNAB
Small Pica Royal Octavo with references. Revised ABS standard text.

1868   The Comprehensive Commentary on the Holy Bible . . . Scott's Marginal
References: Matthew Henry's Commentary . . . edited by William Jenks . . .
reedited . . . by Joseph A. Warne . . . J. B. Lippincott & Co.: Philadelphia
                                                                           1831

6 vols   26 cm   KyLoS
Baptist Edition appears at head of title. See 1834–38, No 860.

1868   The Holy Bible . . . [Stereotyped by J. Fagan, Printed by T. K. & P. G. Col-
lins]. J. B. Lippincott & Co.: Philadelphia   *1832*

Reported as 1440 p   21 cm   Privately Owned

1868   The Holy Bible . . . American Bible Society . . . : New York   *1832A*

1 vol: (673) (211)   13 cm   NNAB
Diamond 32mo. A reprint of 1857 (No 1661) but with revised page headings and chapter
summaries.

1868   A New Translation of Job, Ecclesiastes, and the Canticles, with Introductions, and Notes, chiefly Explanatory. By George R. Noyes . . . Fourth Edition, carefully revised, with additional notes. American Unitarian Association: Boston   *1833*

1 vol: (iii) (351)   20 cm   NNAB
Noyes Versions; see 1827, No 592. The first three editions were of Job only. A fifth edition was issued in 18??. NNAB has sixth edition, 1880.

1868   The New Testament . . . [and Psalms] . . . American Bible Society, Instituted . . . : New York   *1834*

485 p   16 cm   NNAB
Brevier 18mo with revised ABS standard text. NT text ends on p 386 and was often printed alone.

1868   The New Testament . . . The Common English Version, Corrected by the Final Committee of the American Bible Union. Second Revision, Amory Memorial. 30th Thousand. Brevier 18mo Edition. American Bible Union: New York; Trübner & Co.: London   *1835*

16 cm   DLC, NNAB
ABU Version; see 1862–63 NT, No 1764. Reprint of 1866 edition (No 1806). DLC also has 1870 reprint in this size.

1868   The New Testament . . . American Bible Society, Instituted . . . : New York
                                                                 1836
405 p   13 cm   NNAB
Agate 32mo.

1869   The Holy Bible . . . American Bible Society, Instituted . . . : New York *1837*

1 vol: (936) (294)   40 cm   NNAB
Great Primer Imperial Quarto with revised ABS standard text. The price for this Bible in 1869 was $20 in morocco. In 1959 it sold for $70 in red morocco.

1869   The Illustrated Polyglot Family Bible . . . Together with the Apocrypha, Concordance and Psalms in Metre . . . Also, a History of the Translation of the Bible, and Religious Denominations; Over One Hundred Scripture Illustrations . . . Together with Tables of Scriptural Coins and Money Terms, with Their Value Expressed in the Money of the United States. By James Ross Snowden . . . W. Flint: Philadelphia   *1838*

1 vol: (576) (116) 579–768 (41) (22) (4)   31 cm   NN
Similar to Perry Bible of 1852 (No 1487). Has frontispiece and other plates. Additional preliminary matter separately numbered. Family Record pages, including wedding certificate, in purple and gold. Portrait Album at end. Copyright 1869, by W. Flint.
NNAB has copy imprinted *J. S. Goodman & Company, Chicago*, but with copyright as above. It seems to be the same book.

1869   The Holy Bible . . . Zeigler, M'Curdy & Co.: Philadelphia and Cincinnati
                                                                 1839

Reported as iii–vi, v–vii [9] (1093) (6) (46) (63) (83) [1]   28 cm   ViU
Contains frontispiece, Tables, A New Geographical and Historical Index, A New and Complete General Index and Concise Dictionary of the Bible, and A Concordance to the Holy Scriptures by John Brown. Has Family Record and Family Album pages. Illustrated.

1869   The Complete Analysis of the Holy Bible . . . Containing the Whole of the
Old and New Testaments, Collected and Systematically Arranged in Thirty
Books . . . By Rev. Nathaniel West . . . A. J. Johnson: New York   *1840*

28 cm   MBU–T, PChW
Reprint of 1868 edition (No 1828).

1869   The Devotional and Practical Polyglott Family Bible . . . with the Marginal
Readings and a Full and Original Selection of References to Parallel and
Illustrative Passages . . . National Publishing Company: Cincinnati   *1841*

27 cm   PSt
Has frontispiece and added engraved title. Concordance and Index. Illustrated.

1869   The Comprehensive Commentary on the Holy Bible . . . According to the
Authorized Version; Scott's Marginal References; Matthew Henry's Commentary, Condensed . . . the Practical Observations of Rev. Thomas Scott
. . . with . . . Notes, Selected from Scott, Doddridge . . . Edited by Rev. William Jenks . . . Claxton, Remsen & Haffelfinger: Philadelphia   *1842*

5 vols   26 cm   DLC
Has frontispiece. Vol I, Genesis-Judges. Vol II, Ruth-Psalm LXIII. Vol III, Psalm LXIV-Mala-
chi. Vol IV, Matthew-John. Vol V, Acts-Revelation. See 1835–38, No 894.
Usually printed at this period by J. B. Lippincott and Co. Because of the destruction of
their records by fire, Lippincott is now unable to give any information about the length of time
they published this work.

1869   The Annotated Paragraph Bible . . . arranged in paragraphs and parallelisms;
with explanatory notes . . . Sheldon & Company: New York; Gould & Lincoln: Boston   *1843*

3 vols: 1471 p   25 cm   ICU
See 1861, No 1743.
ICU has another set in 2 vols, with London imprint added. NB has NT only for this year.

1869   The Holy Bible . . . from the Latin Vulgate . . . with annotations by the Rev.
Dr. Challoner . . . references . . . index. With the approbation of the Provincial Council . . . The Catholic Publication Society . . . : New York   *1844*

20 cm   OGK
Rheims-Douay Version. Pagination same as 1837 Fielding Lucas edition (No 978).

1869   The New Testament: Translated from the Greek Text of Tischendorf, by
George R. Noyes, D.D., Hancock Professor of Hebrew and Other Oriental
Languages, and Dexter Lecturer on Biblical Literature . . . [Printed by John
Wilson and Son: Cambridge, Mass.]. American Unitarian Association:
Boston   *1845*

1 vol: (vi) (570)   20 cm   ICU, MdBP, MiU, MWA, NB, NN, NNAB
Noyes Version; see 1827, No 592. Preface, Editorial Note, and Table of Books precede text.
Text printed in single column, paragraph form, with verse numbers in left margin. Copyright
1868.
It was Noyes's aim "to make a version more free from wholly or nearly obsolete words and
phrases," and at the same time "to retain . . . the savor and spirit of our familiar version." This
NT was translated from the text of Tischendorf, using the eighth critical edition up to Luke 18:9,
the second edition of his Synopsis Evangelica to the end of the Gospel of John, and the seventh

edition of 1859 for the remainder. In the Preface, Dr. Noyes asks the reader "to bear in mind the Greek text which I have followed; otherwise some of my departures from the Common Version might seem to be unnecessary or arbitrary." The NT was published posthumously, although the translator had given the complete MS to the printer and had revised the proof sheets to the end of Philippians. Ezra Abbot completed this work, added a few notes, and appended a list of readings from Tischendorf's eighth edition through the sixth chapter of John.

Reprints were issued in 1870, 1873, 1878, and 1880. NNAB has 1870 and 1878 editions.

1869   The Four Gospels translated from the Greek Text of Tischendorf, with the Various Readings of Griesbach, Lachmann, Tischendorf, Tregelles, Meyer, Alford, and others; and with Critical and Expository Notes. By Nathaniel S. Folsom. A. Williams and Company: Boston   *1846*

1 vol: (xv) (293) 295–476   21 cm   NNAB

Second edition issued in 1871; third edition (Cupples, Upham, and Company: Boston), 1885.

Nathaniel Smith Folsom (1806–90) was a Biblical scholar serving as professor of Biblical literature at Western Reserve College, Hudson, Ohio, 1834–36, as a Congregational minister in New England, 1840–47, and becoming a Unitarian minister at Haverhill, Mass. in 1848. He served for two years as editor of *The Christian Register*, a Unitarian weekly magazine, and in 1849–61, as professor at the Unitarian Theological Seminary at Meadville, Pa. His later years were spent in teaching and writing at Lawrence, Mass. He also published a commentary on Daniel. (See Cheek, p 49 and 140.)

187–   The Devotional Family Bible: with Practical and Experimental Reflections on Each Verse . . . and Rich Marginal References . . . By the Rev. Alexander Fletcher . . . Virtue & Co.: New York   *1847*

37 cm   NN

Reprint of 1835 edition (No 891). Has added engraved title page and illustrations.

187–   The Holy Bible, Translated from the Latin Vulgate . . . With Annotations by the Rev. Dr. Challoner. With the Approbation of the Most Rev. John McCloskey, Archbishop of New York. Part 19–20 . . . D. & J. Sadlier & Co.: New York   *1848*

34 cm   NN

Rheims-Douay Version, edited by Dr. Challoner. NN copy incomplete; above taken from cover. Published in parts. In original covers.

1870?   New Devotional and Practical Pictorial Family Bible . . . Together with a Carefully Abridged Edition of Dr. Wm. Smith's Complete Dictionary of the Bible . . . Embellished with over 1000 Fine Scripture Illustrations . . . Nelson & Phillips: New York   *1849*

Reported as (11) iv-viii (136) (640) (104) 641–843 (128) (44) (36)   33 cm   NBuG

Nelson and Phillips Superfine Edition appears at head of title. Has frontispiece and some colored illustrations. With Apocrypha, Concordance, and Metrical Psalms.

187–   The Holy Bible; the Illustrated Explanatory Family Bible. With the Apocrypha, Psalms in Metre, and Marginal References and Readings, and Brown's Complete Concordance . . . A Pictorial History of the Books of the Bible, by Washington B. Erben, the Improved Pictorial Dictionary of the Bible, by Alfred Nevin, and the Illustrated Christian Denominations of the World, Their Doctrines, Government, and History, by Clement M. Butler.

187–, continued

> Together with Blackwood's Concise Treatise on the Genuineness, Authenticity, Inspiration, Preservation, and Value of the Word of God, and Other Historical and Explanatory Matter . . . J. B. Burr Publishing Co.: Hartford
> *1850*

32 cm   DLC
Illustrated.

1870 The Holy Bible . . . The Text Conformable to the Oxford Edition, and the American Bible Society's Standard of 1816 . . . William W. Harding: Philadelphia   *1851*

32 cm   NNAB
Reprint of Harding's 1867 Superfine Edition (No 1809).

187–? The Holy Bible . . . The Text Conformable to the Standard of the American Bible Society . . . [Stereotyped by J. Fagan & Son, Philadelphia]. New-World Publishing Co.: Philadelphia   *1852*

1 vol: (viii) 9–576 (104) 578–768 (41) (22)   31 cm   NN
  May be related to Harding's 1857 Fine Edition (No 1639). Has frontispiece engraved by John C. McRae, New York (active 1855–80). Index, Tables and other Useful Matters, Brown's Concordance, and Metrical Psalms at end. Family Record, marriage certificate, pages for photographs. Illustrated.
  NN date 185–?.

1870 New Illustrated Devotional and Practical Polyglot Family Bible . . . The Text Conformable to the Standard of the American Bible Society . . . Embellished with Over 200 Fine Scripture Illustrations . . . National Publishing Company: [Cincinnati?]   *1853*

Reported as (768) (104) (41) (22)   31 cm   FU
  Contains A History of the Religious Denominations of the World, Harmony of the Four Gospels, Valuable Treatises, History of the Translation of the Bible, and Chronological and Other Useful Tables. With Apocrypha. Index, Concordance, and Metrical Psalms. Illustrated. See 1869, No 1841.

1870/69 The Holy Bible . . . The Text Conformable to the Original Edition of the Year of Our Lord 1610, and the American Bible Society's Original Standard Edition of 1816 . . . W. W. Harding: Philadelphia   *1854*

Reported as (576) (116) 579–754 1019–1032 (22)   30 cm   NcD
  Has frontispiece and title page in red and black. With Apocrypha. Contains Family Record and Album pages. Illustrated. NT dated 1869. See Jesper Harding's 1857 Fine Edition, No 1639.

1870 The Holy Bible, Translated from the Latin Vulgate . . . First Published by the English College, at Douay . . . 1609; and the New Testament . . . at Rheims . . . 1582. With Annotations. From the Last London and Dublin Editions: T. W. Strong: New York   *1855*

Reported as 968 p   26 cm   PLatS
  Rheims-Douay Version. See Dunigan's 1844 Bible, No 1199. Has frontispiece and other illustrations. Family Record pages.

1870? The Holy Bible . . . Commentary and Critical notes . . . Adam Clarke . . .
A new Edition with the Author's final corrections . . . Phillips & Hunt: New
York; Walden & Stowe: Cincinnati   *1856*

25 cm   OC
Adam Clarke's Commentary; see 1811–25, No 188; also (for the revised edition) 1837,
No 974.
Walden and Stowe were publishing in Cincinnati in the 1870s and 1880s. TNMPH says
this work was first listed by the Methodist Book Concern in 1884 and continued to appear
into the 1940s, all with the NT in 2 vols, edited by Daniel Curry, D.D. NcD and OClW have
copies dated 1883?, published by Hunt only.

1870/69 Annotated Paragraph Bible; Containing the Old and New Testaments,
According to the Authorized Version . . . With Explanatory Notes . . . Sheldon: New York   *1857*

2 vols in 1: 1471 p   24 cm   KyLo
Illustrated with maps. See 1861, No 1743.
KyLo also has copy in 2 vols dated 1871/72.

1870? The Holy Bible . . . J. E. Potter: Philadelphia   *1858*

1 vol: (vii) (576) (104) 578–768 (22) (41)   "4to"   Not Located
Potter's Standard Edition appears at head of title. With Apocrypha. Index, Tables, Con-
cordance, and Metrical Psalms. Illustrated. Similar to old Phinney editions; see 1824, No 485.
Copy attributed to NN, but not found 1959.

1870 The Comprehensive and Self-Interpreting Family Bible . . . Marginal Readings and References . . . Introduction . . . Edited by Calvin E. Stowe . . .
Worthington, Dustin & Co.: Hartford   *1859*

Reported as (viii) (96) (576) (104) 579–768 (22) (41)   "4to"   MB
With Apocrypha, Illustrated Bible Dictionary, Concordance, and Metrical Psalms. Illus-
trated. Pagination would indicate this is related more to the old Phinney editions (see 1824,
No 485) than to any of the annotated editions.

1870 The Holy Bible, Translated from the Latin Vulgate . . . Being the Edition
Published . . . at Rheims . . . 1582, and at Douay, 1609, as Revised and Corrected, in 1750, According to the Clementine Edition of the Scriptures, by
. . . Challoner . . . With His Annotations . . . D. & J. Sadlier & Co.: New York
[etc.]   *1860*

Reported as 5–1531 p   19 cm   DLC
Rheims-Douay Version, edited by Dr. Challoner. Has colored frontispiece and other plates,
and added engraved title pages. Illustrated.

1870 The Holy Bible . . . American Bible Society, Instituted . . . : New York *1861*
1 vol: (804) 805–812   19 cm   NNAB
Nonpareil Duodecimo second edition. Has Contents on p 805–812.

1870 The Sacred Writings of the Apostles and Evangelists of Jesus Christ, com-
monly styled the New Testament. Translated from the original Greek by
Doctors George Campbell, James MacKnight and Philip Doddridge . . . by
Alexander Campbell. First Stereotyped edition. [Printed and bound by Elm
Street Printing Company.] Franklin & Rice: Cincinnati   *1862*

Reported as (452) (86)   26 cm   TNDC

Alexander Campbell Version; see 1826 NT, No 567. Reprint of the 1839 edition (No 1058). Has title page in red and black.

TNDC also has third, fifth, and sixth stereotype editions dated 1871, 1873, and 1874 respectively. MoU has fourteenth edition published by G. W. Rice, 1882.

1870 The New Testament . . . The Common English Version, Corrected by the Final Committee of the American Bible Union. Second Revision, Amory Memorial. American Bible Union: New York; Trübner & Co.: London *1863*

16 cm   DLC

ABU Version; see 1862–63 NT, No 1764. Reprint of 1866 edition (No 1806).

1871 The Holy Bible, Translated from the Latin Vulgate: With Annotations by Dr. Challoner, Together with References and an Historical and Chronological Index. Revised and Corrected According to the Clementine Edition of the Scriptures . . . J. Kelly: Philadelphia   *1864*

32 cm   DLC

Rheims-Douay Version, corrected by Dr. Challoner. Illustrated.

1871 The Holy Bible . . . The text Conformable to the Oxford Edition and the American Bible Society's standard of 1816 . . . William W. Harding: Philadelphia   *1865*

32 cm   NNAB

Reprint of Jesper Harding's 1857 Royal Quarto Edition (No 1650). *Harding's Royal Edition* appears at head of title page. With Apocrypha in smaller type, double center reference columns, engravings, and plates.

1871 The Latest Illustrated Polyglot Family Bible . . . [Stereotyped by J. Fagan & Son]. C. F. Vent: New York and Cincinnati; A. H. Hubbard: Philadelphia; E. Hannaford & Co.: Cincinnati and Chicago; J. S. Goodman & Co.: Chicago; F. A. Hutchinson & Co.: St. Louis   *1866*

31 cm   NNAB

Similar in many respects to Perry Bible of 1852 (No 1487) and Flint Bible of 1869 (No 1838) but Apocrypha has 104 p. Frontispieces, To the Reader, and Contents precede text. Tables follow OT. With Apocrypha, followed by Family Record. NT has frontispiece and Account of Dates on verso of title. Index, Tables, etc., Concordance, Metrical Psalms, Bible Lyrics, Bible Aids for Prayer, Tables, History of Religions, Index, and Gospel Harmony at end. Illustrated. Copyright 1871, by J. Fagan & Son, Stereotypers, Philadelphia.

1871 The Holy Bible . . . The Text Conformable to the Original Edition of the Year of Our Lord 1610, and the American Bible Society's Original Standard Edition of 1816 . . . William W. Harding: Philadelphia   *1867*

30 cm   NNAB

Reprint of Jesper Harding's Fine Edition of 1857 (No 1639). Index and Tables at end are from different set of plates. Illustrated.

1871 The Holy Bible . . . Apocrypha . . . Canne's Marginal notes . . . Oakley, Mason & Co.: New York   *1867A*

1 vol: (2) (576) (96) (2) 579–768 (32) (28) (6)   30 cm   NNAB

Contains To the Reader (from Collins' Bible), Order of Books, and Contents. Engraved frontispiece precedes each Testament. Tables follow OT. Apocrypha in smaller type. Family Record, 4 p. Index, etc. (p 755–768), Concordance, and Metrical Psalms at end. Four engravings.

1871 [The Holy Bible] Hitchcock's New and Complete Analysis of the Holy
Bible: or the Whole of the Old and New Testaments Arranged According to
Subjects in Twenty-Seven Books on the Basis of Matthew Talbot, as Improved with Indexes, Tables, etc. by Nathaniel West . . . Revised and Edited
by Rev. Roswell D. Hitchcock . . . A. J. Johnson: New York   *1868*

1 vol: v-xlvii [1] (685) [1] 687–1159 [1] (8) (19) [1]   28 cm   NNAB

Frontispiece, Dedication, Preface signed by Hitchcock, Publisher's Announcement (including letter from Fred B. Perkins) are all dated 1869. The frontispiece, *The Entrance of Thy
Words Giveth Light*, drawn by Thomas Nast and engraved by R. Kupfer, symbolically shows
man's progress with a missionary leading a heathen from his idols. Nast's name appears also
on three other less original engravings. Explanation and Contents precede text, which is arranged according to subject. Full Bible texts are printed under each subject. Cruden's Concordance, Dictionaries, Tables, etc., History of Bible, Family Record, and Recommendations at end.
Copyright by A. J. Johnson, 1869. Printer's notice (Wynkoop & Hallenbeck).
   1870 copy ascribed to NN could not be located in 1959.
   This analysis was first prepared by "a wealthy currier of England," Matthew Talbot, and
published about 1800. The material was arranged by subject in thirty Books divided into chapters and sections, giving every verse in the Bible but once. The two indexes (one really a table
of contents, the other alphabetical) were inadequate. A plagiarized edition was published in
1848 by an Englishman named Whowell as *Analogy of the Old and New Testament Systematically Classified*. In 1853 came Nathaniel West's revision of Talbot's work, in which there was
little change except that West included twelve verses that Talbot had inadvertently omitted
(making a total of 31,173) and added a Consulting Apparatus of nine tables and indexes — a
great labor but of considerable practical value.
   A. J. Johnson bought the plates of the 1853 West edition from Scribner & Co. and asked
Fred B. Perkins to see what they needed for improvement. He found many typographical errors,
and recommended a revision in view of more recent scholarship. The old plates were then
scrapped and the Rev. Roswell D. Hitchcock of Union Theological Seminary, New York, was
employed to undertake a thorough revision. The work was completely recast, the Books reduced from thirty to twenty-seven, new indexes were provided, and Cruden's Concordance,
newly set, was added. Mr. Perkins and the Rev. George W. Sheldon, of Union Theological, also
aided in the work. As copy they used the recent text of the American Bible Society. In regard
to the accuracy of that text, Mr. Perkins stated that he could find but one typographical error
and that was a "somewhat doubtful case of 'wrong font.'" More "historical methods" were
employed in this analysis, the division into chapters was by "thoughts" rather than by verses,
and cross references were used. The indexes and tables were reduced to four.

1871 Critical and Explanatory Pocket Bible; the Holy Bible According to the
Authorised Version, with Original and Selected Parallel References and
Marginal Readings . . . Gould: Boston   *1869*

4 vols   "16mo"   CoD

Vol ɪ edited by Robert Jamieson, Vol ɪɪ by A. R. Fausset & B. M. Smith, Vol ɪɪɪ by David
Brown, and Vol ɪᴠ by A. R. Fausset.

1871 The Holy Bible . . . Samuel D. Burlock & Co. . . . : Philadelphia   *1870*

1 vol: (714) 3–79   14 cm   NNAB

Includes Metrical Psalms, Scripture Paraphrases, and Hymns. Printed from worn plates.
NT title has no imprint but J. Fagan & Son, Electrotypers, Philad'a. Sherman & Co., Printers
appears on verso.

1871 The Holy Bible . . . United Presbyterian Board of Publication: Pittsburgh
                                                                          1871

1 vol: (870) (265) (82)   13 cm   NNAB

J. Fagan & Son, Electrotypers, Philad'a. Sherman & Co., Printers appears on verso of NT
title. Metrical Psalms at end.

1871   The English Version of the Polyglott Bible . . . Thompson, Bigelow & Brown:
        Boston   *1872*

Reported as (856) (259)   12 cm   OC
Each Testament has extra colored title page.

1871   The Pictorial Home Bible, Devotional and Explanatory: Containing the
        Old and New Testaments, With the Apocrypha . . . By M. Laird Simons . . .
        Philadelphia   *1873*
                                                                            DLC
No further information given. See 1875, No 1912.

1872   The Holy Bible . . . With References and Various Readings . . . Pica Marg.
        Ref. Crown 4to. A. J. Holman & Co.: Philadelphia   *1874*

1 vol: (2) (38) 9–857 (139) 3–264 (60) (24)   31 cm   NNAB
Holman's Edition appears at head of title, which is printed in red and black with seal:
Let there be light. Frontispiece, Order of Books, and Improved Comprehensive Helps to the
Study of the Bible (by Nevin, Rawson, & Horne) precede text. With Apocrypha, followed by
Family Record. Maps of Jerusalem, Concordance, and Metrical Psalms at end. Illustrated.
     This is the first edition published by A. J. Holman and Company, still active. The history
of this firm goes back to the beginning of the century. Solomon Conrad went into business
about 1801 and was joined by Benjamin and Jacob Johnson (see 1792 NT, No 41; also 1804,
No 114). Other combinations followed: Kimber, Conrad and Co. with Jacob Johnson (see 1807,
No 143), Kimber and Sharpless (see 1823, No 460), Jesper Harding (see 1826–28, No 551),
Jesper Harding and Son (see 1857, No 1639), William W. Harding (see 1860, No 1728). Mr.
Holman had been with the Harding firm from 1839 and gained control about 1864. The president
of the firm in 1958 was Scott Lamb, Sr.; his son, Scott Lamb, Jr., was also a member of the firm.
     The seal with the legend *Let there be light* appears on many books with other imprints and
occasionally with no imprint. It would appear that these books were supplied by the firm to
local distributors who issued them with their own imprints. An effort has been made to try to
tie these editions up with Holman imprinted editions but, as many of them have a great deal
of separately numbered and varying additional material, it has been impossible to do this without asking many libraries for data they have neither the time nor staff to supply.

Holman device, No 1874

TRADE-MARK.
National Publishing Company
device, No 2024

1872   The Holy Bible . . . The Text Conformable to the Oxford and the American
        Bible Society's Standard Editions . . . A. J. Holman & Co.: Philadelphia *1875*

31 cm   NNAB
     Similar to 1852 Perry Bible (No 1487) but Apocrypha has 104 p. *Holman's Edition* ap-
pears at head of title page; *Pica 4to Marg. Ref.* appears at bottom. Preliminary matter includes

frontispiece, Order of Books, Chronological Order, Introductory History of the Bible, History of the Books, Science, Literature, Testimony, Scripture Difficulties, Tables, etc., Bible Dictionary (104 p), and Table of Events in the Life of Paul. Tables follow OT. With Apocrypha followed by Family Record. Account of the Dates of Writing NT appears on verso of NT title. Index, Tables, etc., Brown's Concordance, and Metrical Psalms at end. In spite of title page identification, references are in double center columns. Illustrated.

This Bible was printed from Harding plates passed on to Holman. It was discontinued about 1880.

1872   The Holy Bible . . . Together with Marginal References, Apocrypha, Concordance and Psalms. The Text Conformable to the Oxford Edition, and the American Bible Society's Edition of 1816. W. W. Harding: Philadelphia
1876

31 cm   CtY

Harding's Royal Edition appears at head of title. Reprint of Jesper Harding's 1857 Royal Quarto Edition (No 1650). Illustrated.

1872   The Latest Illustrated Polyglot Family Bible Containing the Old and New Testaments, Together with the Apocrypha . . . To Which are Appended a Concordance, the Psalms of David in Metre, Selections from Bible Lyrics, and Also an Illustrated Bible Dictionary . . . C. F. Vent: New York and Cincinnati; Hubbard Bros.: Philadelphia [etc.]   *1877*

31 cm   MiU

Reprint of 1871 edition (No 1866).

1872   The People's Standard Edition of the Holy Bible, Containing the Old and New Testaments, and the Apocryphal Writings . . . : Philadelphia [etc.]
1878

Reported as (576) (104) 579–768 (41) (22)   DLC

No further information given. May be related to Jesper Harding's Fine Edition of 1857 (No 1639).

1872   Hitchcock's New and Complete Analysis of the Holy Bible: or, the Whole of the Old and New Testaments Arranged According to Subjects in Twenty-Seven Books on the Basis of Matthew Talbot, as Improved . . . by Nathaniel West . . . Revised and Edited by Rev. Roswell D. Hitchcock . . . [Stereotyped by Wynkoop & Hallenbeck]. A. J. Johnson: New York   *1879*

28 cm   NNAB

Reprint of 1871 edition (No 1868). Copyright by A. J. Johnson, 1869.

1872   The Holy Bible, Translated from the Latin Vulgate . . . T. W. Strong: New York   *1880*

968 p   25 cm   Not Located

Rheims-Douay Version. See 1844 Dunigan Bible, No 1199.
Copy ascribed to NN, but not found 1959.

1872   The Holy Bible . . . American Bible Society, Instituted . . . : New York   *1881*

1159 p   19 cm   NNAB

Brevier Duodecimo first edition. A note points out an error in Neh 13:21 (*thine,* for *time*) reported in Feb 1879 "after 500,000 copies had been issued." Also marked is Mt 15:3, *who,* for *why.* New plates were made in 1889. Last printing 1931, 2,073,000 copies having been printed.
NNAB also has 1927 copy with Concordance (211 p).

1872?   The Holy Bible . . . United Presbyterian Board of Publication: Pittsburgh
                                                                                1882

Reported as 804 p   MiU
Contains Metrical Psalms (1872) and Paraphrases.

1872   The New Testament . . . Translated Out of the Latin Vulgate . . . First Pub-
         lished . . . Rheims . . . 1582. Newly Revised and Corrected According to the
         Clementine Edition of the Scriptures; with Annotations . . . As Approved
         by the Right Reverend John Hughes, Archbishop of New York . . . D. & J.
         Sadlier & Co.: New York   *1883*

17 cm   PLatS
Rheims Version. Pagination same as 1842 Devereaux NT (No 1151).

1873   The Holy Bible . . . Conformable to the Standard of the American Bible
         Society. Also, with A Cyclopedia . . . By Albert Leighton Rawson . . . Amer-
         ican Publishing Company: Philadelphia   *1884*

32 cm   NNAB
Similar to Harding's Fine Edition of 1857 (No 1639). Frontispieces, Order of Books, To
the Reader, Contents, Dictionary of the Holy Bible by Albert Leighton Rawson, Passages from
the OT in the NT, Tables, Names and Titles of Jesus, Analysis of the Bible, etc., maps, and
Introduction precede text. With Apocrypha. Frontispiece and Account of Dates precede NT.
Index, Tables, etc., Brown's Concordance, Metrical Psalms, and Portrait Album pages at end.
Illustrated.

1873   The Holy Bible . . . Translated from the Latin Vulgate . . . Annotations by
         . . . Challoner . . . Corrected According to the Clementine . . . Scriptures:
         J. Kelly & Sons: Philadelphia   *1885*

1 vol: (90) (909) (258)   32 cm   NN
Rheims-Douay Version, edited by Dr. Challoner. A Catholic Dictionary of the Bible precedes text.

1873   The Holy Bible . . . With References and Various Readings . . . A. J. Holman
         & Co.: Philadelphia   *1886*

1 vol: (6) (48) (104) [1] iv-viii 9–857 (139) 3–264 755–760 (60) (24)   31 cm
                                                                                NNAB
Reprint of Holman's 1872 edition (No 1874) but with different supplementary matter.
Frontispiece, illuminated page with Commandments, Comprehensive Helps to the Study of
the Bible, History of the Books, Pronouncing Bible Dictionary (by Smith, Kitto and Fairbairn),
Order of Books, Chronological Order, and Contents precede text. With Apocrypha, followed by
Family Record. Map, frontispiece, and illuminated Lord's Prayer precede NT. Indexes, Tables,
etc., Concordance, Metrical Psalms, and Family Portrait pages at end. Illustrated.

1873?   The Complete Domestic Bible . . . to which is added . . . Pronouncing Dic-
          tionary . . . J. W. Lyon: Guelph, Ontario   *1887*

1 vol: (10) (24) (112) (74) (22) (16) (6) 9–640 (104) (4) (32) 17–24 (2) 643–848
(44) (36) (12) (12) (16) (16) (2) (4)   31 cm   NNAB
Contains History of the Books of the Bible by the Rev. W. B. Erben (c. 1873), William
Smith's Pronouncing Dictionary (c. 1873), and Dobbin's False Gods. With Apocrypha, Con-
cordance, Metrical Psalms, illuminated Family Record pages and marriage certificate, and
Portrait Album. Engravings. Copyright 1873, by Hubbard Bros.
DLC and MdBJ have copies imprinted Philadelphia instead of Guelph.

1873/74   The Holy Bible . . . The Text Conformable to the Oxford Edition, and the American Bible Society's Edition of 1816 . . . William W. Harding: Philadelphia
1888

31 cm   NNAB

Reprint of Harding's 1857 Fine Edition (No 1639) but with new illustrations and some other supplementary matter. Frontispiece, Illustrated History of the Bible, Miracles and Parables of the Testaments, Prophecies, Chronologies, Bible Dictionary, To the Reader, Order of Books, and Contents precede text. Tables follow OT. With Apocrypha, followed by Family Record. Index, Tables, etc., Brown's Concordance, and Metrical Psalms at end. Illustrated. NT, dated 1874, has frontispiece, illustrated title page, and Account of Dates.

1873   The Self-Interpreting Holy Bible . . . With an Introduction; Illustrations; A Summary of the Several Books . . . and Numerous Explanatory Notes by the Rev. John Brown. Explanatory and Critical Notes . . . by The Rev. Henry Cooke . . . American Publishing Co.: New York   *1889*

1 vol: (166) (1380) (83)   30 cm   NN

Added engraved title reads *Brown's Self-Interpreting Bible . . . Notes by Rev. Cooke . . . Re-edited with Additions by Rev J. L. Porter*; for Brown's Bible, see 1792, No 37. With Apocrypha. Also Concordance and Dictionary of the Bible. Illustrated. See also 1878 B, No 1928.

1873   Hitchcock's New and Complete Analysis of the Holy Bible: or, the Whole of the Old and New Testaments Arranged According to Subjects in Twenty-Seven Books. On the Basis of Matthew Talbot, as improved with Indexes, Tables, and Other Valuable Matter by Nathaniel West . . . Together with Cruden's Concordance . . . Revised by John Eadie . . . Revised and Edited by Rev. Roswell Hitchcock . . . A. J. Johnson: New York   *1890*

28 cm   NN

Reprint of 1871 edition (No 1868).

1873   The Holy Bible . . . With Apocrypha, Concordance, and Psalms . . . Appended a . . . Bible Dictionary . . . A Concise History of all Religious Denominations, and Many Other . . . Aids to the Study of the Holy Scriptures . . . by . . . Alfred Nevin, Thomas H. Horne . . . Richardson & Co.: Boston *1891*

Various paging   "4to"   MB

Illustrated, two plates colored. Possibly a Holman edition?

1873   The Holy Bible . . . With Critical and Explanatory and Practical Notes . . . Rev. Joseph Benson . . . Phillips and Hunt: New York; Hitchcock & Walden: Cincinnati   *1892*

5 vols   "4to"   NcD

Vol ii is dated 1873, other volumes undated. Imprints vary with volumes: Nelson and Phillips, New York, and Walden & Stowe, Cincinnati also used. See 1822–24 edition, No 435.

1873-81   The Holy Bible, According to the Authorized Version A.D. 1611, With an Explanatory and Critical Commentary and a Revision of the Translation, by Bishops and Other Clergy of the Anglican Church. Edited by F. C. Cook . . . Scribner, Armstrong & Co.: New York   *1893*

10 vols   25 cm   ViU

OT in six vols numbered i-vi; NT in four vols numbered i-iv. Binder's title: *The Bible Commentary*. NT Vols i-iv imprinted *New York, C. Scribner's Sons*. Vol i dated 1875; 1873 date taken from Vol iii.

This is known as "The Speaker's Commentary" and was prepared in England at the suggestion of the Right Honorable J. Evelyn Denison, Speaker of the House of Commons. The editor, F. C. Cook, began work in 1864, and the commentary was published in 10 vols from 1871 to 1881 by the University Press, Cambridge. The text is the AV with a great deal of comment in which variant renderings are given. The editors were outstanding clergymen of the period.

American editions bear the imprint of Scribner, Armstrong and Co., New York, and of Charles Scribner's Sons. NT Vols II-IV (1880, 1881, and 1882) examined at NN give no indication as to place of printing and Charles Scribner's Sons in 1959 could give no information as to whether the books were ever printed here. The set was not included in a 1912 list of imported items. It was many times reprinted. OC has a set in 12 vols, including the Apocrypha, dated 1874–81.

1873 The Holy Bible . . . American Bible Society, Instituted . . . : New York *1894*

 1285 p   19 cm   NNAB

Bourgeois Duodecimo first edition. Last printing 1928, making a total of 308,000 copies in this format.

1873 The Holy Bible . . . Translated from the Latin Vulgate . . . Being the Edition
        Published at Rheims . . . 1582, and at Douay, 1609, as Revised and Corrected,
        in 1750, According to the Clementine Edition of the Scriptures, by . . . Chal-
        loner. D. & J. Sadlier: New York   *1895*

 15 cm   PLatS

Rheims-Douay Version. Reprint of 1870 Sadlier edition (No 1860). Has colored illustrations.

1873 The Holy Bible . . . S. D. Burlock & Co.: Philadelphia   *1896*

 1 vol: (678) (210)   14 cm   NNAB
 Metrical Psalms at end.

1874 Brown's Self-Interpreting Bible . . . Containing the Old and New Testa-
        ments, with Marginal References and Readings . . . With Critical and Ex-
        planatory Notes and Practical Reflections, by Rev. John Brown . . . with
        Several Thousand Additional Notes by Rev. Henry Cooke . . . New Edition,
        with Important Additions, by Rev. J. L. Porter . . . American Edition, Edited
        by Rev. William Blackwood . . . John E. Potter and Company: Philadelphia
                                                                               1897

 1 vol: (6) (lxxi) (32) (64) (80) (988) (104) (12) 989–1446 (64) (4)   33 cm
                                                                             NNAB

Brown's Self-Interpreting Bible; see 1792, No 37. Frontispieces, Editor's Preface (signed J.L.P., Belfast, 1873), Preface to Original Edition (signed J. Brown), Order of Books, Chronological Order of Books, Historical Sketch of English Translations, Memoir of the Rev. John Brown by his grandson, Memoirs of the Rev. Drs. Cooke and Porter by the American Editor, An Introduction to the Right Understanding of the Oracles of God, Christ and His Kingdom in Shadows by the Rev. C. P. Krauth, Christian Denominations by Rev. C. M. Butler, and New and Improved Dictionary of the Bible by Rev. Alfred Nevin precede text. Brief Outline of History . . . Prophetic Kingdoms of the East follows OT. With Apocrypha, followed by Family Record. Names and Titles Given to Jesus and to the Church, Similies, Synonymous Terms, Gospel Harmonies, Tables, Index and Dictionary, Metrical Psalms, Paraphrases, Hymns, and Family Album at end. Illustrated. Copyright 1873, Press of John E. Potter & Co.

1874   The Holy Bible . . . The Text Conformable to the Oxford Edition, and the
American Bible Society's Edition of 1816 . . . W. W. Harding: Philadelphia
1898

33 cm   NcAS

Reprint of Jesper Harding's Royal Quarto Edition of 1857 (No 1650). Has frontispiece.
With Apocrypha, Concordance, and Metrical Psalms. Illustrated.

1874   The Holy Bible, Translated from the Latin Vulgate . . . Revised with Anno-
tations by the Right Rev. R. Challoner . . . Together with References, and
. . . Index. Now Carefully Corrected According to the Clementine Edition
. . . Thomas Kelly, Publishers: New York   *1899*

33 cm   NNAB

Rheims-Douay Version. Reprint of 1873 J. Kelly & Sons edition (No 1885). Preliminary
matter includes engraving of Pope Pius ix, Approbations, Letter from Pope Pius vi, illuminated
text of Ten Commandments, Catholic Dictionary, Dedication to American Catholics, Historical
Sketch, List of Commentators, Approbations, Prayers, and Order of Books. Index and Family
Record follow OT. Preceding NT are illuminated text of Lord's Prayer, Preface, Admonition,
etc. At end are Tables, Index, and Family Portrait pages. Illustrated.

1874   The Holy Bible . . . The Text Conformable to the Oxford and the American
Bible Society's Standard Editions . . . A. J. Holman & Co.: Philadelphia *1900*

32 cm   CtY

Has frontispiece and other illustrations.

1874   The Holy Bible . . . with the Apocrypha, Concordance and Psalms. The
text conformable to the Oxford and the American Bible Society's standard
editions. Published by A. H. Redford, agent, for the M. E. Church, South:
Nashville   *1901*

Various paging   32 cm   TNMB

1874   The Holy Bible . . . Over One Hundred Thousand Marginal References . . .
The Whole Embellished with Twelve Hundred Illustrations . . . A. J. Holman
& Co.: Philadelphia   *1902*

1 vol: (6) (vii) 9–16 (104) (8) (96) (40) 9–857 (139) (11) (6) (18) 3–264 837–848
(60) (24) (4)   31 cm   NNAB

Reprint of Holman's 1872 edition (No 1874) with additional supplementary matter;
p 837–848 from "Antique Letter" edition. Frontispiece and illuminated title, Introduction, Contents, Order of Books, Chronological Order, Pronouncing Dictionary (Smith, Kitto & Fairbairn), Religious Denominations by Rev. Wm. H. Munroe, Cities in the Bible by Rev. Wm. F. B.
Jackson, and History of the Books precede text. With Apocrypha, followed by Family Record.
Map, frontispiece, illuminated Lord's Prayer, and History of the Bible precede NT. Indexes,
Concordance, Metrical Psalms, and Family Portraits at end. Illustrated.

1874   The Illustrated Polyglott Family Bible . . . with the Apocrypha . . . Concordance, the Psalms of David in Metre . . . and a Comprehensive Dictionary . . . Quaker City Publishing Co.: Philadelphia   *1903*

1 vol: (576) (104) 579–754 755–768 (41) (36) (136) (24)   31 cm   NNAB

Frontispiece, To the Reader, Order of Books, Contents, and illuminated page with Ten
Commandments precede text. Also has Tables and Erben's Introduction to the Holy Scriptures.
Illustrated.

1874 The Comprehensive Commentary on the Holy Bible; Containing the Text
According to the Authorized Version; Scott's Marginal References; Matthew
Henry's Commentary, Condensed, but Retaining Every Useful Thought; the
Practical Observations of Rev. Thomas Scott . . . with Extensive Explanatory,
Critical, Philological Notes . . . Ed. by Rev. William Jenks . . . : Philadelphia
1904

IU, PP–W
   Baptist Edition appears at head of title. See 1834–38, No 860; also 1869, No 1842. Has
frontispiece and other illustrations and maps. No further information given. Possibly published
by Lippincott; size 28 cm?

1874 New Illustrated Bible for the Young with a Brief History of Each Book
Prefixed to the Same, the Four Gospels Arranged as a Harmony, and the
Original Metrical Form of the Poetical Books Retained. And Containing
Short Biographies of the Evangelists and Apostles, Descriptive and His-
torical Notes, Etc. . . . Oldach & Mergenthaler: Philadelphia   *1905*

   1 vol: (20) 15–500   27 cm   NNAB
   Frontispiece, illuminated title (copyright 1872), Introduction, Contents, List of Illustrations, "The Bible," and illuminated text of Ten Commandments precede text, which is somewhat condensed and adapted. A Short History of the Jews, half title with *The Gospel Harmony*,
and illuminated text of The Lord's Prayer at end of OT. Text of NT is in harmonized form
with references for each Gospel given under the sub-titles. At end are Account of the Final
Destruction of Jerusalem and Biographical Sketches of the Apostles. Illustrated.

1874 The New Testament [and Psalms] . . . American Bible Society, Instituted
. . . : New York   *1906*

   1 vol: (424) (109)   24 cm   NNAB
   Pica Octavo first edition.

1874 The New Testament . . . The Common English Version, Corrected by the
Final Committee of the American Bible Union. Second Revision. American
Bible Union: New York   *1907*

   Reported as 488 p   IU
   ABU Version; see 1862–63 NT, No 1764.

1874 The Gospels . . . and the Acts . . . American Bible Society, Instituted . . . :
New York   *1908*

   253 p   21 cm   NNAB
   Small Pica Octavo, with *The Gospels and Acts of the Apostles. Presented by the American
Bible Society to the Ohio and Mississippi R. R. Co.* stamped in gold on cover. Printed label
inside front cover says this is not to be removed from the car. It is one of many large type volumes placed by the ABS in special racks in railroad cars at this period "by the consent of the
President and Directors . . . entrusted to the Employes of the company, who will see that it is
always accessible to the Passengers, and kept in the rack when not in use."

1875? The Holy Bible, Translated from the Latin Vulgate . . . The Old Testament
was First Published . . . at Doway . . . 1609: and the New Testament at
Rheims . . . 1582. With Annotations by the Rev. Dr. Challoner . . . Revised
and Corrected According to the Clementine Edition . . . D. & J. Sadlier &
Co.: New York   *1909*

   34 cm   NBuG

Rheims-Douay Version. Similar to 1845? edition (No 1249). Has frontispiece and added title page in color. Text within ornamental border. Errata of the Protestant Bible by Thomas Ward included.

1875?   The Holy Bible: Containing the Entire Canonical Scriptures, According to the Decree of the Council of Trent . . . The Old Testament First Published at Douay . . . 1609. The New Testament . . . at Rheims . . . 1582. Revised and Corrected According to the Clementine Edition of the Scriptures, With Annotations by the Rev. Dr. Challoner . . . John E. Potter and Co.: Philadelphia **1910**

Reported as (128) (789) (235)   33 cm   C
Rheims-Douay Version. There are other unnumbered pages at various points in the book and 5 leaves at end for Family Record and Portraits. The text is preceded by A History of the Holy Catholic Bible, which has copyright entry dated 1875. Contains Approbations of 51 American bishops and archbishops. Pope (p 476) says this was printed from the stereotype plates of Fielding Lucas, Jr., of Baltimore; see also Pope, p 677.

1875   The Holy Bible . . . Apocrypha, Concordance and Psalms. The Text Conformable to the Oxford and the American Bible Society's Standard Editions. A. J. Holman & Co.: Philadelphia **1910A**

1 vol: (7) iv-viii (2) 9–32 (104) (32) (32) 9–636 (4) (4) 33–48 643–848 (44) (86) (4)   32 cm   NNAB
Holman's Edition appears at head of title. Preliminary matter includes frontispiece and illuminated Lord's Prayer, Contents, Order of Books, maps, Bible Helps, Dictionary, Bible Scenery, and Biographical and Historical Accounts. Family Record and further Biographical and Historical Accounts precede NT. Chronological Index, List of Names, Concordance, and Metrical Psalms at end.
NNAB also has copy of similar edition imprinted *Cooperative Bible and Publishing Co., Muscatine, Iowa,* which has Apocrypha (104 p) and a somewhat different collection of supplementary matter.

1875   The Holy Bible . . . American Bible Society, Instituted . . . : New York **1911**

876 p   22 cm   NNAB
Minion Reference Octavo first edition, with center reference column.

1875   The Pictorial Home Bible . . . conformable to the standard of the American Bible Society . . . Cyclopedia and Guide by J. Samuel Vandersloot, and through various contributions by M. Laird Simons . . . Sold by Subscription only. Published by F. Scofield and Company: Philadelphia **1912**

1 vol: (640) (104) 643–848, other matter var. paged   31 cm   DLC, PP
Added matter includes colored printings of the Ten Commandments, and wedding certificate, several sections prepared by Vandersloot, Apocrypha, metrical Psalms, etc.

1875–88   An Illustrated Commentary on the New Testament, for Family use and reference, and for the great body of Christian workers of all denominations. By Rev. Lyman Abbott . . . A. S. Barnes & Company: New York, Chicago, New Orleans **1913**

5 vols: Vol i, (333); Vol ii, (65) (148); Vol iii, (245); Vol iv, (262); Vol v, (230) 23 cm   MB, MH–AH
AV text with commentary. Has frontispiece and other illustrations and maps.
These volumes were all listed in the *Publisher's Trade List Annual* for the years in which they appeared. They remained in print and were later listed in the 1912 *U. S. Catalogue of*

Books in Print. Matthew and Mark were published in 1875, Acts in 1876, Luke in 1878, John in 1879, and Romans in 1888. No more were published. Issued in two series, one sometimes referred to as the Subscription Edition. Mark is sometimes bound up with Matthew, but is more often found with Luke.

The following incomplete holdings have also been reported: NPV has Vols I-IV dated 1878-79. DLC has two copies of Vol I: one containing Matthew and Mark and dated 1875. (399 p) and another from the Subscription Edition dated 1876. OO has Matthew dated 1878, copyright 1875 (333 p). CtY, NcD, and NN have Acts dated 1876; ICN has Acts dated 1878. OClW has Romans. NN has the following part dated 1873: New Testament with Notes and Comments. Vol I, No 1: Matthew Ch. 1 (21 cm).

1876   The Holy Bible . . . The Text Conformable to the Oxford Edition, and the American Bible Society's Edition of 1816 . . . William W. Harding: Philadelphia   *1914*

32 cm   NNAB

Reprint of Jesper Harding's 1857 Fine Edition (No 1639) but with preliminary matter as in 1873/74 edition (No 1888).

1876   The Holy Bible . . . With Marginal References . . . The Text Conformable to the Oxford Edition, and the American Bible Society's Edition of 1816 . . . L. U. Snead and Company: Mount Union, Ohio   *1915*

31 cm   NN

Pagination similar to Harding's 1857 Royal Quarto Edition (No 1650). Has Tables and illustrations — some colored.

1876?   The Holy Bible, Translated from the Latin Vulgate . . . 1609 . . . 1582. With Annotations by . . . Challoner . . . Revised and Corrected According to the Clementine Edition of the Scriptures . . . D. & J. Sadlier: New York   *1916*

Reported as (93) (16) (793) (228)   31 cm   .   PLatS

Rheims-Douay Version. See 1845?, No 1249. Illustrated.

1876?   The Annotated Paragraph Bible . . . According to the Authorized Version, Arranged in Paragraphs and Parallelisms; With Explanatory Notes, Prefaces to the Several Books, and an Entirely New Selection of References to Parallel and Illustrative Passages . . . Sheldon & Company: New York   *1917*

26 cm   ViU

Reprint of 1861 edition (No 1743). Has frontispiece. Paged continuously.

1876   The Holy Bible . . . Translated Literally from the Original Tongues . . . American Publishing Company: Hartford   *1918*

1 vol: (892) (276)   26 cm   ICN, MnM, NcAS, NNAB

Preface signed Julia E. Smith, Glastonbury, March 23rd, 1876. The Books of the OT are arranged in the Jewish order, with Chronicles at the end.

Julia Evelina Smith (1793-1886) was the first woman to translate the whole Bible. Her parents belonged to the small Sandemanian sect founded in Scotland about 1730, which had as an ideal the restoration of the apostolic church. A member of a picturesque family, she was an outspoken worker for women's suffrage, refusing to pay taxes — particularly on a fine herd of Jersey cattle. In her 87th year, to the consternation of many of her former supporters, she married the Hon. Amos Parker of New Hampshire. Her portrait is to be found in Simms, facing p 156.

The following is taken from the Preface to the above work:

> Over twenty years ago, when I had four sisters, a friend met with us weekly to search the Scriptures, we being desirous to learn the exact meaning of every Greek and Hebrew word, from which King James's forty-seven translators had taken their

version of the Bible. We saw by the margin that the text had not been given literally, and it was the literal meaning we were seeking. . . . I soon gave my attention to the Hebrew, and studied it thoroughly, and wrote it out word for word, giving no ideas of my own, but endeavoring to put the same English word for the same Hebrew or Greek word, everywhere, while King James's translators have wholly differed from this rule; but it appeared to us to give a much clearer understanding of the text.

It had never at that time entered my mind that I should ever publish the work, but I was so much interested and entertained to see the connection from Genesis to Revelation, that I continued my labors and wrote out the Bible five times, twice from the Greek, twice from the Hebrew, and once from the Latin — the Vulgate. These three languages were written over the head of our Saviour. They are now dead languages and cannot be altered. . . . It may be thought by the public in general, that I have great confidence in myself, in not conferring with the learned in so great a work, but as there is but one book in the Hebrew tongue, and I have defined it word for word, I do not see how anybody can know more about it than I do. . . .

As a result of the use of the same English word for the same Hebrew or Greek word, the English of this translation is quite unnatural. The work was published at Miss Smith's own expense. Apparently the above edition was the only one published.

1876   The Holy Bible . . . American Bible Society, Instituted . . . : New York   *1919*

1 vol: (809) (252)   17 cm   NNAB
    Agate Reference 16mo Centennial Edition (first edition). Chronology removed 1900; plates scrapped 1942.

1876   The Holy Bible . . . Latin Vulgate . . . Rheims . . . Douay . . . Revised . . . by the Ven. Richard Challoner . . . with his annotations for clearing up the principal difficulties of Holy Writ . . . Published by D. & J. Sadlier & Co.: New York and Montreal   *1920*

15 cm   NjMD
    Rheims-Douay Version. Reprint of 1870 edition (No 1860).

1876   The New Testament . . . Latin Vulgate . . . Rheims . . . with annotations, references, and an historical and chronological index. With full-page engravings. The Catholic Publication Society: New York   *1921*

Reported as 183 p   32 cm   NjMD
    Rheims Version.

1876   The New Testament . . . the standard of the American Bible Society . . . Published by authority of the General Eldership of the Church of God: Harrisburg, Pa.   *1921A*

1 vol: (416) (47)   17 cm   NNAB
    At head of title *Reference and Pronouncing Testament.* On p 3 a Key to the principles of pronunciation. References follow verses, keyed to the word within the verse by asterisk. Copyright 1836 by John Winebrenner, V. D. M. A reprint of 1836 NT, No 964.

1877?   The Holy Bible . . . With . . . A Concise History of All Religious Denominations . . . By the Following . . . Authors, Rev. Alfred Nevin . . . Thomas H. Horne . . . Wm H. Munroe . . . [and others]. With Over Two Thousand . . . Engravings . . . Western Publishing House: Chicago   *1922*

33 cm   ICU
    Has colored frontispiece and added title page with *Latest Illustrated Reference Family Bible.* With Apocrypha. Contains Cruden's Complete Concordance, Bible, Dictionary, Complete

History of Each Book of the Bible, Metrical Psalms, and Family Record and Album pages.
See Richardson editions of 1873 and 1877, No 1891 and No 1924.

1877?   The Holy Bible . . . The Text Conformable to the Oxford and the American
Bible Society's Standard Editions . . . S. R. Gray: Albany   *1923*

1 vol: (14) (xvi) (16) (104) (2) (48) (viii) 9–640 (104) (4) (6) 643–847 (3) (32)
(44) (36)   33 cm   NNAB

Holman device on title page; "Antique" type. Frontispiece, Preface, Introductory History,
Revelation, etc. (F. W. Farrar), Chronologies, etc., Comprehensive Dictionary of the Bible
(William Smith), History of the Books of the Bible (Alfred Nevin), History of Herod, Order
of Books, and maps precede text. Tables, Indexs, etc. follow OT. With Apocrypha and Family
Record. Engraved frontispiece and maps precede NT. At end are Indexes, etc., Lists of Texts,
Concordances, and Metrical Psalms. Illustrated. Copyright 1872, 1873, 1875, and 1877.

1877   The Holy Bible . . . With . . . Important and Useful Aids to the Study of the
Holy Scriptures . . . By Rev. Alfred Nevin . . . Rev. Thomas H. Horne, [etc.].
W. L. Richardson & Co.: Boston   *1924*

32 cm   NN

Has frontispiece and half title with *Latest Illustrated Reference Family Bible*. With Apocrypha. Cruden's Concordance, Dictionary, and Metrical Psalms. Possibly a Holman edition?

1877   Hitchcock's . . . Analysis of the Bible . . . : New York   *1925*
NjP

Reprint of 1871 Bible (No 1868) with Cruden's Concordance. No further information
given.

1877   The Holy Bible . . . American Bible Society, Instituted . . . : New York *1926*

1 vol: (726) (226)   15 cm   NNAB

Agate 24mo first edition which replaces the 1853 edition (No 1536) and the corrected
edition of 1867 (No 1818). Last printing 1929, 3,783,940 copies having been printed.

1877   The Holy Bible . . . United Presbyterian Board of Publication: Pittsburgh
1927

13 cm   NNAB

Similar to 1871 edition (No 1872) but the Metrical Psalms are from different plates and
have index (166 p). Copyright 1871.

1878   The Self-Interpreting Holy Bible . . . Conformable to the Standard of the
American Bible Society, with an Introduction; Illustrations; A Summary of
the Several Books; An Analysis of Each Chapter; A Paraphrase and Evangelical Passages; and Numerous Explanatory Notes; By the Rev. John Brown
. . . and the Text More Fully Elucidated by Many Thousand Explanatory
Notes, and Introductory Observations on Each Book; by the Rev. Henry
Cooke . . . American Publishing Company: New York   *1928*

1 vol: (9) iv-viii (8) (26) (24) (24) (20) (16) (12) (134) (1380) (18) (60) (2)
(23) (14)   33 cm   NNAB

Brown's Bible; see 1792, No 37. Preliminary matter includes illuminated page, added en-
graved title page (*Re-edited with additions by the Rev. J. L. Porter*), Contents, Order of
Books, etc., To the Reader, Contents, Rules for Understanding the Scriptures, History of the
Books of the OT, Concise Account of the Cities of the Bible, Scenes in Bible Lands, etc. (A. L.
Rawson), and Dictionary of the Bible (A. L. Rawson). With Apocrypha, followed by Family

Record. NT has Order of Books, illuminated Lord's Prayer, frontispiece, and History of the Books of the NT. Index, Tables, etc., Metrical Psalms, and Portrait Album at end. Illustrated.

1878?   The Holy Bible . . . Together with Apocrypha . . . Concordance . . . The Psalms of David in Metre . . . Index, Tables, and Other Useful Matters. The Text Conformable to the Standard of the American Bible Society . . . [Stereotyped by J. Fagan & Son]. Charles H. Yost [Successor to Whilt & Yost]: Philadelphia   *1929*

1 vol: (574) (104) 579–754   32 cm   NNAB
Illuminated frontispiece has copyright 1878. Contains Dictionary of the Bible, History of the Books, History of all Religions, etc. Illustrated.

1878   The New Testament: Newly Translated [from the Greek Text of Tregelles] and Critically Emphasised with an Introduction and Occasional Notes. By Joseph B. Rotherham. Second Edition . . . Samuel Bagster and Sons: London; John Wiley and Sons: New York   *1930*

1 vol: (xvi) (492) (4)   25 cm   NNAB
Preface to Second Edition (dated London, 1878) and an Introduction precede text, which is printed in single column, paragraph form, with verse numbers raised in text in smaller type. At end are Index to Principal Notes and Bagster's List of Publications.
DLC and MiU have copies dated 1890.
The Rev. Joseph Bryant Rotherham (1828–1909) was first a Wesleyan minister, then a Baptist, and later a minister of the Disciples of Christ. His NT was first printed in London in 1872 and was followed by a second edition in 1878. It uses an elaborate system of symbols and type to show various classes and relationships of textual material. The NT was based on Tregelles' Greek text, but in 1897 was conformed to the Westcott and Hort text. A third edition was published in 1897 and the OT, based on Ginsberg's Hebrew text, was published in London in 1901–02. This is an "immersion" version. It is uncertain when this NT was first printed in America. It is possible that the above edition may have been printed in England. For the twelfth edition, revised, see 1896 NT, No 2073.

1878   The New Testament . . . The Text Conformable to the Oxford and American Bible Society's Editions . . . A. J. Holman: Philadelphia   *1931*

Reported as 398 p   24 cm   ViU

1878   New Testament . . . American Bible Society, Instituted . . . : New York *1932*

288 p   12 cm   NNAB
Pearl Agate 32mo first edition. New electrotype plates were made in 1883.

1878   The New Testament . . . With Explanatory Notes, by John S. C. Abbott and Jacob Abbott. Embracing Also a Brief Biography of Our Saviour the Christ; Biographies of the Writers . . . H. S. Goodspeed: New York   *1933*

ViU
No further information given. Illustrated.
Jacob Abbott (1803–79) was a well-known Congregationalist minister and writer. He was the author of the Rollo books and other books for children.

1879?   The Holy Bible . . . with the Apocrypha . . . A concordance, the Psalms in metre, an index, tables . . . The Text conformable to the Standard of the American Bible Society. T. Buckley: Cincinnati   *1934*

Reported as (576) (88) 577–768 (41) (22)   35 cm   OC
Contains Apocrypha, Concordance, and Metrical Psalms. Illustrated.
T. Buckley is listed in the Cincinnati directory only in 1879, as a book dealer specializing in Bibles and pictures.

1879/74   The Holy Bible . . . American Bible Society, Instituted . . . : New York
                                                                          1935

    1 vol: (804) (247)   33 cm   NNAB
Pica Reference Quarto, first printed 1873/74. NT dated 1874 and marked fourth edition.
Chronology removed 1900. Known as the Lectern Bible in 1959 and priced at $14 to $28 (1874,
from $3 to $9) depending on binding.

1879   The Holy Bible . . . With Complete Concordance . . . A. J. Holman: Phila-
    delphia   *1936*
    32 cm   ViU
With Apocrypha. Illustrated.

1879   The Holy Bible, Translated from the Latin Vulgate . . . The Old Testament
    was First Published . . . at Douay . . . 1609, and the New Testament . . . at
    Rheims . . . 1582. Revised with Annotations by . . . Challoner . . . Now Care-
    fully Corrected According to the Clementine Edition of the Scriptures . . .
    T. Kelly: New York   *1937*
    31 cm   NNU–W
Rheims-Douay Version. Pagination same as 1873 J. Kelly & Sons edition (No 1885). Has
frontispiece. Added engraved title to each Testament. With references, Index, and Dictionary.

1879   The Holy Bible . . . With Cruden's Complete Concordance, Embracing
    Every Passage of the Scripture in the Largest Editions. Comprehensive Bible
    Dictionary, in Which Every Important Scriptural Word is Fully Explained
    . . . Apocrypha and Psalms . . . [A. J. Holman and Company?]: Philadelphia
                                                                          1938
                                                                           IU
No further information given. Has colored frontispiece and other illustrations.

1879   The Book of Job, translated from the Hebrew text with an introduction, a
    summary of each chapter and brief notes in explanation of obscure passages,
    by John, Bishop of Frederiction and Metropolitan of Canada. J. & A. Mc-
    Millan, printers: Saint John, New Brunswick   *1939*
    Reported as (xxxiv) 35–149   19 cm   CaOTP
This is a translation by a Canadian printed in Canada. The translator was John Medley, first
Bishop of Fredericton and third Metropolitan of the ecclesiastical province of Canada — a
province made up of the dioceses of Newfoundland, Nova Scotia, Fredericton (province of New
Brunswick), Quebec, and Montreal.

1879–83   A Popular Commentary on the New Testament. By English and Amer-
    ican Scholars of Various Evangelical Denominations . . . Edited by Philip
    Schaff . . . C. Scribner's Sons: New York   *1940*
    4 vols   25 cm   ICU, NNUT
Illustrated.
Also found with *T. and T. Clark, Edinburgh* in imprint. Possibly printed in Scotland?

188–   The Holy Bible Translated from the Latin Vulgate . . . The Old Testament,
    First Published . . . at Douay . . . 1609, and the New Testament . . . at Rheims
    . . . 1582. With . . . Notes . . . from the Most Eminent Commentators . . . by
    the Rev. Geo. Leo Haydock . . : Machell & Smith: New York   *1941*
    1 vol: (16) (48) (1667)   32 cm   NN

Rheims-Douay Version. Has frontispiece. Added engraved title to each Testament. Contains Dedication, Admonition, Advertisement, Preface, Index, Etc. Illustrated with plates, maps, and portraits. See 1852 Dunigan edition, No 1485.

1880 The Holy Bible . . . With Cruden's Complete Concordance, Embracing Every Passage of Scripture in the Largest Editions . . . A. J. Holman & Co.: Philadelphia **1942**

2 vols in 1   32 cm   NBuG
Has frontispiece and illustrations. Copyright 1877.

1880? The Holy Bible . . . 100,000 Marginal References and Readings . . . Embellished with Nearly Two Thousand Illustrative Engravings . . . M. R. Gately & Co.: New York **1943**

1 vol: (11) (viii) (16) (48) (128) 9–640 (104) 643–848 (44) (36)   31 cm   NNAB
Preliminary matter includes presentation page (with date 188–, to be filled in), frontispiece, added engraved title, Order of Books, History of the Translation of the English Bible, Contents, map, Description of Israelite Tabernacle (copyright 1879, by J. R. Jones), History of Books of the Bible, Map of the Holy Land (copyright 1876), Household Dictionary of the Bible, and maps of Jerusalem. Text has center references. Tables follow OT. With Apocrypha, followed by Family Record. Index, Concordance, Metrical Psalms, and Portrait Album at end. Illustrated. Copyright 1879, by J. R. Jones.
J. R. Jones founded the National Publishing Company, also known as National Bible Press, in 1863. Many editions bearing his name as copyright holder have other imprints.

188– The Polyglot Family Bible . . . Hitchcock & Walden: Cincinnati **1944**

1 vol: (576) (104) 578–786   30 cm   NN
With Apocrypha. Has frontispiece. Concordance and Metrical Psalms. Illustrated.

188– The Holy Bible, Translated from the Latin Vulgate . . . The Old Testament was First Published . . . at Doway . . . 1609; and the New Testament . . . at Rheims . . . 1582. With Annotations by . . . Challoner . . . Revised and Corrected According to the Clementine Edition . . . D. & J. Sadlier & Co.: New York **1945**

"4to"   NN
Rheims-Douay Version. Pagination same as 1845? edition (No 1249), without Ward's Errata. Has frontispiece to each Testament. With references, Index, Tables, and Family Record. Illustrated.

188–? The New Testament . . . Together with the Book of Psalms . . . The Whole edited by Rev. Samuel P. Linn . . . J. E. Potter & Co.: Philadelphia **1946**

Reported as 571 p   25 cm   MiU
This is one of Potter's Standard Editions.

188–? The New Testament . . . J. E. Potter: Philadelphia **1947**

Reported as 453 p   MiU
No further information given. This is one of Potter's Standard Editions.

1881? The Holy Bible . . . Commentary by . . . Jamieson . . . and Bickersteth . . . Supplement by A. L. Rawson . . . Virtue and Co.: New York **1948**

1 vol: (730) (459) (423); other matter var. paged   36 cm   NNAB
Has ERV NT (76 p) added after AV text; for ERV, see 1881 NT, No 1953.

This may be an English publication. Title pages to OT and NT commentary supplement have imprint of *James S. Virtue, City Road and Ivy Lane*; NT title adds *London*. ERV NT has no imprint. The Virtue firm published a similar 3-vol illustrated edition in London in 1861–65.

James Sprent Virtue (1829–92) took over his father's business in 1855. He was joined in 1871 by S. Spaulding and later by F. R. Daldy.

1881   The Family Bible . . . Apocrypha, Concordance, Psalms in metre, Chronological Index, etc., Marginal References and Readings . . . fine . . . engravings . . . Baird & Dillon: Chicago and New York   **1949**

1 vol: (6) iii-viii (64) (104) (20) (61) 9–636 637–640 (104) (10) 643–836 (2) iii-viii
649–820 837–848 (44) (36) (4)   33 cm   NNAB

Amies' New and Improved Edition appears at head of title. ERV NT follows AV text; for ERV, see 1881 NT, No 1953. Has variety of supplementary matter, some copyright by A. J. Holman, 1872 (see No 1874 — probably a Holman edition). With Apocrypha in smaller type, and Brown's Concordance. NT imprinted *Philadelphia and New York, William T. Amies, 1881*. ERV NT has no imprint, but has usual Introduction and is followed by List of American Preferred Readings and Renderings (double paged, 1–172).

1881   The Holy Bible . . . with a Comprehensive Bible Dictionary . . . A Complete
History of the Books of the Bible . . . Apocrypha and Psalms, Brown's Com-
plete Concordance . . . and Many Other . . . Helps to the Study of the Holy
Scriptures . . . with Numerous Engravings on Steel and Wood . . . American
Bible Publishing Co.: New York   **1950**

1 vol: (636) (104) (392); other matter var. paged   33 cm   NNAB

While the OT and Apocrypha sections are similar to those in Holman and National Publishing Co. editions, the NT has been reset with the ERV in inner column; for ERV, see 1881 NT, No 1953. The AV NT was set from an ABS octavo edition, and the ERV one from the Oxford Large Pica edition; there is no imprint on either NT title. The Preferences of the American Committee follow text directly on same page. Most of supplementary matter is illustrated, some in color. Various copyrights by the publisher.

NNAB also has a similar edition imprinted *Hubbard Brothers, Philadelphia,* with Brown's Concordance and a section on The Jewish Tabernacle (copyright 1883, by the Rev. G. C. Needham, 12 p).

1881   The Holy Bible . . . Revised . . . Notes and Reflections by Rev. John Brown
. . . Marginal References and Readings . . . Notes, etc., by Rev. Henry Cooke
. . . Hubbard Brothers: Philadelphia   **1951**

1 vol: (574) (104) 579–754 649–815; other matter var. paged   31 cm   NNAB

Has AV and ERV NTs, as in Baird and Dillon 1881 edition (No 1949) which this Bible resembles in many ways. Includes Brown's Concordance, but John Brown's Notes and Reflections seem to be omitted. With Apocrypha in smaller type. Elaborate wedding certificate and Family Record in black and white. Many Doré illustrations.

1881?   The Holy Bible . . . Concordance . . . Bible Dictionary . . . Apocrypha and
Psalms . . . [and many other features] . . . L. W. Jewell & Co.: Washington,
D. C.   **1952**

31 cm   NNAB

Cited copy consists only of title pages and a few pages of text from a mutilated book. AV text with ERV NT printed separately (147 p). All titles have the Holman device but both NTs lack imprint.

1881   The New Testament . . . Revised Version . . . A.D. 1881 and the Authorized
English Version of the New Testament, with Introduction, and Various

Readings from the Three Most Celebrated Manuscripts of the Original Greek
Text. By Constantine Tischendorf. In Parallel Columns on Same Pages . . .
George Munro, Publisher: New York   *1953*

1 vol: (105) (122)   32 cm   MH–AH, NN, NNAB

Seaside Library . . . Vol XLIX appears at head of title page. Has ERV and AV texts in
parallel columns. AV is printed in traditional verse paragraph form; the ERV is in paragraph
form with verse numbers in matching type, chapter numbers in bold face in margins, and alternative readings and renderings at foot of page. Poetical matter usually appears printed in separate lines. An Introduction dated Nov. 11, 1880 gives the history of the revision. Tischendorf's
Introduction and the Committee's Preface follow John, part 1. Printed in an Appendix at the
end are preferred renderings of the American Committee which were not accepted by their
British colleagues. Published as a double number, copyright 1881 by Munro, entered at second
class rates, May 21st and May 23rd, 1881.

Because of advances in archaeological and Biblical scholarship during the nineteenth century, the need for a revision of the AV constantly became more apparent. Numerous American
efforts to supply a satisfactory revision have already been listed. The Revised Version (ERV)
was begun at the suggestion of the Bishop of Winchester, who submitted in 1870 to the Convo-
cation of the Province of Canterbury (Church of England) a proposal for a revision to correct
places were the Hebrew and Greek texts underlying the AV had been at fault or wrongly
translated. On its adoption a committee was appointed to set up rules and committees of revisers, which included the outstanding Biblical scholars of the day, who represented various
denominations. The revisers began work in England in 1871; in 1872 two American committees
began joint work, meeting regularly every month for eight years in the old Bible House at Astor
Place (but they were not associated in any way with the ABS). The costs of the English group
were met by the Oxford and Cambridge University presses in return for exclusive copyright
privileges, no changes to be made for fourteen years after publication of the whole Bible. The
expenses of the American group — working without compensation — were met by private
subscription, donors to receive handsomely bound memorial copies when the work was com-
pleted. (These memorial copies are not included in this list as they were printed in England.)
The members of the American Committee were: for the OT: C. A. Aiken (Princeton), T. W.
Chambers (New Brunswick), T. J. Conant (Rochester), G. E. Day (Yale), J. DeWitt (New
Brunswick), W. H. Green (Princeton), G. E. Hare (Philadelphia), C. P. Krauth (Lutheran,
Philadelphia), T. Lewis (Union), C. M. Mead (Andover), H. Osgood (Rochester), J. Packard
(Alexandria), C. E. Stowe (Andover), J. Strong (Drew), C. V. A. VanDyck (Beirut, translator
of the Arabic B); for the NT: E. Abbot (Harvard), J. K. Burr (Drew), T. Chase (Haverford),
G. R. Crooks (Drew), H. Crosby (NYU), T. Dwight (Yale), H. B. Hackett (Rochester),
J. Hadley (Yale), C. Hodge (Princeton), A. C. Kendrick (Rochester), A. Lee (Bishop of
Delaware), M. B. Riddle (Hartford and Western), P. Schaff (Union), C. Short (Columbia),
J. H. Thayer (Andover, Harvard), E. A. Washburn (Calvary Church, N. Y.), and T. D.
Woolsey (Yale). For further details as to personnel, methods, etc., one may consult the many
good books on the history of the English Bible, or the pamphlet issued by the ABS, *A Ready-
Reference History of the English Bible* (40 p).

The ERV New Testament was published in England, May 17, 1881, and in the United
States on May 20. Advance interest in the NT was so high that a million orders were received
before publication and the New York representative of the Oxford University Press sold more
than 365,000 copies in the first year, most of them within the first few days of publication. It
is said that more than 3,000,000 copies were issued during the first year. The Chicago *Tribune*
and the Chicago *Times* published the entire NT in their issues of May 22, Matthew-Romans
having been telegraphed from New York and the rest set from a copy rushed to Chicago. Some
periodicals issued special editions containing the complete ERV NT (see No 1954). The Introduction to one of the many editions that followed says that the revisers gave their work "to the
people free of copyright," probably because the expenses of the American committee were covered by donations. There seemed to be no restrictions on the use of the text or the form in
which it should appear, as the following entries for this period indicate.

The new text actually followed the language and style of the AV, the changes consisting
mainly in the correction of erroneous Greek readings or renderings, inconsistences in translation and vocabulary, and the clarification of obscure renderings. In spite of its large initial sale,
however, the ERV never became generally popular. Although it represents very accurately the

best Greek text of its day and although the rendering in the Epistles is clearer than in the AV, the public was disappointed by changes in familiar passages and in its rather stiff style.

The Old Testament was published in 1885 (see No 2019). For the American Standard Edition of the Revised Version (ASV), see 1901, No 2124. For the Revised Standard Version (RSV), see 1946 NT, No 2453.

1881   The Revised Version of the New Testament. Harper's American Edition . . . Franklin Square Library. [Published by Harper and Brothers: New York]
1954

121 p   28 cm   MH, NN, NNAB
ERV; see 1881 NT, No 1953. Special issue of the *Franklin Square Library* (No 188, May 27, 1881) containing complete ERV NT, with the Committee's Preface and a collection of the preferred readings of the American Committee. Price, 20¢.

1881   The New Testament . . . Containing the Old [King James] Version and the New Revised Version, in Parallel Columns . . . with a Concise History of Revision. By Rev. Moseley H. Williams . . . The National Publishing Co.: Philadelphia
1955

1 vol: (xxiii) 31–971 973–992   25 cm   GEU, MH–AH, NcD, NNAB
Contrasted Editions appears at head of title. AV and ERV printed in parallel columns; for ERV, see 1881 NT, No 1953. Has History by Williams (50 p).

The Historical Society of The Evangelical United Brethren Church, Dayton, has a similar edition "embellished with over 100 fine engravings on steel and wood," imprinted *United Brethren Publishing House, Rev. W. J. Shuey, Agent, Dayton, Ohio.*

1881   The New Testament . . . revised A.D. 1881. Western Methodist Book Concern Press: Cincinnati
1956

Reported as 447 p   24 cm   TNMB
ERV; see 1881 NT, No 1953.
NjMD has copy paged 3–460.

1881   The Revised New Testament. Embracing the Complete Text of the Revised Version: Also a Concise History of the Revision and of Previous Versions and Translations . . . by Francis S. Hoyt, D.D. . . . Illustrated with More than One Hundred Fine Engravings . . . Including Map . . . Phillips and Hunt: New York
1957

1 vol: (16) 21–575 576–587 591–640   24 cm   NN, NNAB
ERV; see 1881 NT, No 1953. *People's Edition* appears at head of title page.
NN and KyU have copies of similar edition imprinted *Jones Brothers and Co., Cincinnati.*

1881–90   An American Commentary on the New Testament, edited by Alvah Hovey, D.D. The American Baptist Publication Society: Philadelphia **1958**

Variously paged   23 cm   PPABP
This commentary consists of books published separately and bound in various combinations. The text is that of the AV. Name of editor, copyright date, and pagination follow title below:

Matthew.   John A. Broadus, c 1886, 610 p
Mark.   W. N. Clarke, c 1881, 261 p
Luke.   George R. Bliss, c 1884, 355 p
John.   Alvah Hovey, c 1885, 423 p
Acts.   (A new edition, revised and greatly enlarged by the author. Edited by
   Alvah Hovey in consultation with Ezra Abbot.) Horatio B. Hackett, c 1882,
   345 p

Romans. Albert N. Arnold and D. B. Ford, c 1889, 328 p
Corinthians. E. P. Gould, c 1887, 226 p
Galatians. Alvah Hovey, c 1890, 78 p
Ephesians. Justin A. Smith, c 1890, 101 p
Philippians. J. B. Gough Pidge, c 1890, 62 p
Colossians. Edwin C. Dargan, c 1890, 57 p
Thessalonians. William Arnold Stevens, c 1890, 103 p
Pastoral Epistles. H. Harvey, c 1890, 164 p
Hebrews. A. C. Kendrick, c 1889, 207 p
James. Edwin T. Winkler, c 1888, 74 p
Peter. Nathaniel Marshman Williams, c 1888, 112 p
Epistles of John. Henry A. Sawtelle, c 1888, 85 p
Jude. N. M. Williams, c 1888, 23 p
Revelation. Justin A. Smith in consultation with James Robinson Boise, c 1884, 317 p

For similar edition of the OT parts, see 1904–39, No 2159.

1881 The Revised New Testament . . from the Authorized English Edition, with All the Marginal References and Readings, Together with Preface Embracing a History of the Revision and Readings Preferred by the American Committee . . . William T. Amies: Philadelphia   **1959**

Reported as (xiv) (580)   23 cm   MH–AH, PP
ERV; see 1881 NT, No 1953. May be similar to Ziegler edition of this year (No 1963).
NN has copy published by C. H. Yost, Philadelphia that seems to resemble this NT although the title page is not the same.

1881 The New Testament . . . Revised A.D. 1881 . . . Exact Reprint of the Text and Footnotes of the Authorized Oxford and Cambridge Editions of the British and American Revision Committees . . . Introduced into the Margins. Parallel Passages Printed at Length with an Appendix of Helps to the Study of the New Testament, Containing Condensed Concordance . . . to the Revised New Testament . . . I. K. Funk & Co., Publishers: New York   **1960**

1 vol: (xiv) (275) 278–281 (68)   23 cm   MB, MH–AH, NNAB
ERV; see 1881 NT, No 1953. *Teachers' Edition* appears at head of title. Contains Certificate of Accuracy (signed by J. Sanderson, D.D., J. Dixon, D.D., and the Rev. Wm. Hall; copyright by Funk, 1881), Introduction (2 p), and Helps to the Study of the ERV NT by the Rev. W. F. Crafts (68 p). Text is printed in small type in two narrow columns, with two narrower columns in smaller type between, giving the text of related passages taken from Bagster's Reference Bible, Bagster's Scripture Treasury, and other works. ERV marginal matter at foot of page.

1881 The New Testament . . . Revised 1881. Text Conformable to that of the Universities of Oxford and Cambridge. Containing a History of the Books of the New Testament . . . A. J. Holman & Co.: Philadelphia   **1961**

1 vol: (xxxi) (454) 455–465   23 cm   MH–AH, NN, NNAB
ERV; see 1881 NT, No 1953. *Authorized Revised Version* appears at head of title page. Fly title carries statement that the proofsheets were read and corrected by the Rev. J. B. Falkner, D.D., of Philadelphia and the accuracy of the text is guaranteed by Westcott and Thomson, Electrotypers, Philadelphia. Preliminary matter includes A Summary of the Books of the NT (13 p).
MH–AH, NjMD, NN, and NNAB have another edition with A Gospel Harmony and Chronological Table of the Apostolic Age by Dr. Falkner (46 p, illustrated).

1881   The New Testament . . . Revised A.D. 1881 . . . Harper & Brothers: New
York   *1962*

1 vol: (xxvi) (652)   22 cm   NN, NNAB
ERV; see 1881 NT, No 1953. The Preferences of the American Committee are printed at
foot of page instead of at end, but a 1-page list before text gives certain generally preferred
readings and renderings.

1881   The Revised Version of the New Testament, with a History of the Present
and Former Revisions, Being a Literal Reprint of the English Edition from
the University Presses. With an Account of the New Testament Writers,
[etc.]. [Ferguson Bros. and Co., printers.] P. W. Ziegler & Co.: Philadelphia
1963

1 vol: (20) (20) (xiv) (568) 569–580   22 cm   NN, NNAB
ERV; see 1881 NT, No 1953. Contains History of Present and Former Revisions by J.
Thomas Ziegler, and Christ's Testimony to Christianity by P. Schaff, D.D., LL.D. Illustrated.
Copyright by Ziegler and Co., 1881.

1881   The Pictorial New Testament with Notes by the Abbotts . . . Revised and
Adapted to the New Version by Rev. Lyman Abbott . . . Embracing Also a
History of the Revision . . . Aids to the Bible Student . . . with Fifty-Four
Full Page Maps and Engravings. H. S. Goodspeed & Co.: New York   *1964*

1 vol: (xxix) 33–905 907–969   21 cm   NNAB, NNU–W
ERV; see 1881 NT, No 1953. Lyman Abbott's Preface (2 p) dated 1881. Marginal material
printed below text with notes below that. Introductions to each Book. At end, after Preferences
of the American Committee, are A History of the Revision by Dr. Abbott, May 1881; Tables;
Biographies of the Writers; and Publisher's List, showing the book sold for $2. Illustrated with
engravings. Copyright 1881, by Goodspeed.

1881   The Revised Version of the New Testament . . . Revised A.D. 1881. To
Which is Added a History of the English Versions of the Bible, with Their
Several Revisions. From the Oxford and Cambridge Print . . . John E. Potter
& Company: Philadelphia   *1965*

1 vol: (xxiii) (36) 25–563 564–576   21 cm   NNAB
ERV; see 1881 NT, No 1953. Contains an illustrated History of English Versions.

1881   The New Testament . . . Revised A.D. 1881. [Rand, Avery and Co., Printers,
Boston.] The Henry Bill Publishing Company: Norwich, Conn. [etc.]   *1966*

1 vol: (xxii) (535) 537–552   20 cm   MH–AH, NN, NNAB, ViU
ERV; see 1881 NT, No 1953. Certificate of Accuracy by L. T. Chamberlain, May 24, 1881
appears on verso of title page.
NN and NNAB also have copies with AV text printed on facing pages (double pagination).

1881   The New Testament . . . Containing the New Revised Version of 1881. Americanized: Having the American Committee's Preferences Incorporated into
the Text, and the English Placed in the Appendix. Text of New Version,
Oxford. Large Pica Edition. Hubbard Bros., Publishers: Philadelphia [etc.]
1967

1 vol: (xxii) (451) 453–461   20 cm   NNAB
ERV; see 1881 NT, No 1953. *Americanized Edition* appears at head of title page. Reprinted
from the Oxford Large Pica edition but with the American preferred readings in the text. Intro-

duction (2 p) signed by H. G. Weston and Wm. R. Nicholson. Preferences of the English Committee at end. Copyright 1881.

NN and NNAB have undated copies of a similar edition with AV on facing pages.

1881   The New Testament . . . [Comparative Edition]. Containing . . . the King James Version, and the New Revised Version, Arranged in Parallel Columns for Comparison and Reference . . . Porter & Coates: Philadelphia   ***1968***

1 vol: (19) 23–680 681–690   20 cm   MB, MH–AH, MiU, NcD, NN, NNAB, ViU
AV and ERV printed in parallel columns; for ERV, see 1881 NT, No 1953.

1881   The New Testament . . . the King James . . . Version . . . [and] Revised Version 1881 . . . Scammell & Company, Publishers: St. Louis [and others] *1969*

1 vol: (xviii) (658)   20 cm   NN, NNAB
Parallel Edition appears at head of title page. AV and ERV printed in parallel columns; for ERV, see 1881 NT, No 1953. Copyright 1881, by Scammell.

1881   The Revised Version of the New Testament, with a History of Revision, Embracing the Authorized Version of the Anglo-American Revision . . . Together with . . . Account of the Origin of the New Testament . . . Illustrated with Fac-similes of Original Manuscripts . . . Scammell & Company, Publishers: St. Louis [and others]   ***1970***

1 vol: (76) (xviii) (483) 485–496   20 cm   NN, NNAB
ERV; see 1881 NTs, No 1953 and No 1972. History of the Revision precedes the second NT title page which has no imprint; but, in box, *This Edition is the Official Text, authorized by the American Committee of Revision. Officers: Philip Schaff, President. George E. Day, Secretary. New York, May 20, 1881.* A statement signed by G. I. Jones and Co., Publishers and Book Printers, and by the manager and three proofreaders, dated 1881, assures that this has been carefully read and twice compared with official copies from England and most carefully proofread (p 496). Copyright 1881 by Scammell and Co. must apply to the History of the Revision, for the Preface (1 p) states that the American Committee has declared that the "work shall be given to the people free of copyright."

1881   The Sinai and Comparative New Testament. The Authorized English Version; with Introduction, and various Readings from the three most celebrated Manuscripts of the original Greek Text, by Constantine Tischendorf; Tauchnitz Edition, Vol. 1000. With the various readings so inserted in the text, that the whole Scripture according to either the Sinai, Vatican, Alexandrian, or the Received Greek, can be read by itself, while the variations are all compared with facility. By Edwin Leigh. Ivison, Blakeman, Taylor, and Company: New York   ***1971***

1 vol: (xix) (153)   19 cm   NNAB
Vol. i — The Gospels appears on cover, with sub-title: *Four in One; Sinai, Vatican, Alexandrian: the three oldest and best Copies. The New Testament as the early Christians had it in the Fourth Century . . . compared with the Modern Received Greek of the Sixteenth Century.* There is no record that further volumes were published with the remainder of the NT. Frontispiece shows facsimiles from four MSS.

In the Tauchnitz edition (Vol 1000 of the Collection of British Authors, 1869) the text is straight AV, with the readings indicated in footnotes. Mr. Leigh, by using different type faces and a system of bracketing, here exhibits the different readings in a continuous text.

1881   The New Testament . . . Revised 1881 . . . American Tract Society: New
York   *1972*

    1 vol: (xxii) (483) 485–496   19 cm   MiU, NNAB
ERV; see 1881 NT, No 1953. Has Preface. Preferences of American Committee at end.

    Numerous editions of the ERV NT similar in pagination and format, copies of most of which
are held by NN and NNAB, were issued during 1881 by the following publishers: in New York
by Baker, Pratt and Co., by Dodd, Mead and Co., and by Charles T. Dillingham; in Boston by
Estes and Lauriat, and by Lee and Shepard; in Chicago by J. S. Goodman and Co.; and in
Philadelphia an Anglo-American Edition, Facsimile of the Cambridge Edition, was issued by
Hubbard Bros.

    Other editions appeared this year containing a variety of added matter: J. S. Goodman and
Co., Chicago, and Scammell and Co., St. Louis, issued editions with A History of the Revision
added (the Scammell NT is illustrated). Hubbard Bros., Philadelphia, and the Goodman firm
issued editions with A History of the Revision, Anglo-American Edition, prepared by Isaac H.
Hall (119 p). The American Tract Society, American Book Exchange, Dodd, Mead and Co.,
and James Pott and Co., all of New York, issued editions printed with the AV on facing pages,
text has double pagination.

    In 1882 the American Baptist Publication Society of Philadelphia published an edition
with the preferred readings of the American Committee printed in the text and the English ones
in a supplement.

1881   The New Testament . . . Revised A.D. 1881 . . . R. Worthington: New York
1973

    1 vol: (xxiv) (594) (13)   19 cm   MH–AH, NN, NNAB
ERV; see 1881 NT, No 1953. Has Preface of the Committee, 1880. Text followed by the
Preferences of the American Committee. Pagination is the same as that of the Oxford and Cam-
bridge editions and the text is set line for line but in smaller type.

1881   The New Testament . . . The Old and New Compared. The New Revision
of the Bible, by the Oxford Press, England, Compared with the King James,
and the Changes Indicated. Edited by S. L. Marrow. S. L. Marrow & Co.:
Indianapolis   *1974*

    1 vol: (xv) (450)   18 cm   InUpT, NBuG, NN
AV and ERV printed in parallel columns; for ERV, see 1881 NT, No 1953.

1881   The New Testament . . . Revised A.D. 1881 . . . Fords, Howard & Hulbert:
New York   *1975*

    1 vol: (xxx) (483) 485–495   18 cm   DLC, MA, MH–AH, MiU, NN, NNAB
ERV; see 1881 NT, No 1953. *American Edition* appears at head of title page. Contains
American Preface by Roswell D. Hitchcock, dated June 28, 1881. The readings of the American
Committee have been incorporated in the text and the Preferences of the English Revisers are
in the supplement.

    NNAB has another copy marked second impression with errors corrected, Aug 1881. PPi
has copy imprinted *Published for Samuel Williams, formerly Pastor First Baptist Church, Pittsburgh, Pa., by Fords, Howard, & Hulbert, New York*; bound with this are *Samuel Williams'
Reply to Lectures on the Nature, Subjects, and Mode of Christian Baptism*, by John T. Pressley
(2nd edition, Published by Moore, Anderson and Co., Cincinnati, 1853, 96 p) and two other
pamphlets. Andover Newton Theological School has copy without the extra pamphlets.

    "Various works sought to capitalize on the RV shortly after it came out, but the only one
which claimed fresh revision for itself was the New Testament of Samuel Williams (New York,
1881). This not only incorporated the American preferred readings, but was still further
'amended.' Among his own readings was the one 'immerse.'" (Cheek, p 43–44 and 149; cf.
Simms, p 252 ff.)

1881 The New Testament . . . Revised A.D. 1881 . . . American Book Exchange: New York   **1976**

1 vol: (19) 23–424 425–434   17 cm   Co, CU, MH–AH, Mi, NcD, NN, NNAB
ERV; see 1881 NT, No 1953. Has Preface. Preferences of the American Committee at end.
No alternative readings and renderings.

1881 The New Testament . . . Revised A.D. 1881 . . . Baker, Pratt & Co.: New York   **1977**

1 vol: (xxv) (442)   17 cm   NNAB
ERV; see 1881 NT, No 1953. Has List of Preferences of the American Committee at end,
but they are also printed at foot of page below rule.
Similar editions were published this year by Robert Clarke and Co., Cincinnati (OC);
Harper and Bros., New York (NNAB); and Leggat Bros., New York (MH–AH).

1881 The New Testament . . . American Book Exchange: New York   **1978**

496 p   17 cm   MiU, NNAB

1881 The New Testament . . . Revised A.D. 1881. Text Conformable to that of the Universities of Oxford and Cambridge. Containing a History of the Books of the New Testament . . . A. J. Holman & Co.: Philadelphia   **1979**

1 vol: (xxxiv) (405) 407–419   17 cm   MH–AH, NNAB
ERV; see 1881 NT, No 1953. Publisher's statement on the accuracy of the text appears
on verso of title page (see No 1961). Includes Summary of the Books of the NT, by the Rev.
Stanley Leathes, M.A. (12 p).

1881? The New Testament . . . Revised 1881. The American Oxford Edition . . . J. S. Ogilvie: New York   **1980**

1 vol: (xviii) (341)   17 cm   MH–AH, NNAB
ERV; see 1881 NT, No 1953.

1881 The New Testament [and Psalms] . . . American Bible Society, Instituted . . . : New York   **1981**

1 vol: (490) 493–614   14 cm   NNAB
Brevier 24mo eighth edition; first printed in 1875. The Psalms are dated 1880.

1881 The Sacred Writings of the Apostles and Evangelists . . . New Testament . . . George Campbell, James MacKnight and Philip Doddridge . . . Alexander Campbell. [Stereotyped from the third edition revised, by J. A. James, Cincinnati.] Central Book Concern: Cincinnati and Chicago   **1982**

Reported as 336 p   13 cm   TNDC
Alexander Campbell Version; see 1826 NT, No 567.

1881 The New Testament . . . Being the Version Set Forth A.D. 1611 Compared with the Most Ancient Authorities and Revised A.D. 1881. Leggo Bros. & Co., Publishers: New York   **1983**

1 vol: (xxi) (2) (405) 407–419   6 cm   MH–AH, NNAB
ERV; see 1881 NT, No 1953. This is a miniature edition, not very well reproduced, with
Preface before title page. Dated 1881 on cover.

1882   The Holy Bible . . . [with Revised New Testament, 1881]. Concordance . . .
         Dictionary . . . History of Each Book . . . Apocrypha and Psalms, [etc]. By
         . . . Eminent Biblical Writers and Authors . . . Bradley, Garretson & Co.:
         Philadelphia and Brantford, Ont.; Wm. Garretson & Co.: Columbus, Chi-
         cago, Nashville, St. Louis, San Francisco   *1984*

    1 vol: 9–574 (104) 579–754 (147); other matter var. paged   33cm   NNAB
    Holman shield appears on title page. Format of OT and Apocrypha follows that of A. J.
Holman edition of 1872 (No 1874). ERV NT follows AV text; for ERV, see 1881 NT, No 1953.
Has 2000 illustrations.

1882? The Holy Bible . . . With Cruden's Complete Concordance . . . Compre-
         hensive Bible Dictionary. Apocrypha and Psalms, a Concise History of All
         Religious Denominations, and Many Other Important and Useful Aids to
         the Study of the Holy Scriptures . . . H. S. Goodspeed & Co.: New York *1985*

    Reported as 1624 p   33 cm   MnU
    Has engraved half-titles. ERV NT follows AV text; for ERV, see 1881 NT, No 1953. Metri-
cal Psalms at end (36 p).
    MnU gives date as 1877 but ERV NT did not appear until 1881.

1882? The Holy Bible . . . Concordance . . . 100,000 Marginal References and
         Readings. Apocrypha and Psalms in Metre . . . Dictionary . . . Dr. William
         Smith, Dean Milman, Rev. John Kitto, D.D., Drs. von Ewald and Michelson
         and other eminent authorities . . . two thousand . . . engravings, on steel,
         wood and in colors. Cannon Bros. and Co.: Elmira, New York   *1985A*

    1 vol: 9–636 (104) 643–1029; other matter var. paged   32 cm   NNAB
    Contrasted Editions appears at head of NT title page. ERV and AV NTs are printed in
parallel columns; for ERV, see 1881 NT, No 1953. Has variety of supplementary matter before
OT. At end are List of Preferences of the American Committee, Chronological Index, List of
Names, Concordance, Metrical Psalms, and Portrait Album. Illustrations and illuminated Lord's
Prayer, etc. Copyright 187?, 1881, and 1882, by J. R. Jones; probably printed by the National
Publishing Co.

1882   The Comprehensive Commentary on the Holy Bible . . . Authorized Ver-
         sion; Scott's Marginal References. Matthew Henry's Commentary, Con-
         densed . . . The . . . Observations of Rev. Thomas Scott, with . . . Notes,
         Selected from Scott, Doddridge . . . Edited by Rev. William Jenks . . . E.
         Claxton & Co.: Philadelphia   *1986*

    6 vols   26 cm   Not Located
    Reprint of 1835–38 edition (No 894). Has a new Concordance and illustrations. See also
note under 1869, No 1842.
    Union Catalog locates copy at NN, but not found 1959.

1882? The Holy Bible: Containing the Entire Canonical Scriptures, According
         to the Decree of the Council of Trent; Translated from the Latin Vulgate
         . . . The Old Testament, First Published . . . at Douay . . . 1609. The New
         Testament . . . at Rheims . . . 1582. With Notes . . . by Geo. Leo Haydock . . .
         Annotations Abridged by F. C. Husenbeth. To which is added a Compre-
         hensive History of the Books of the Holy Catholic Bible, by Bernard O'Reilly.
         National Publishing Co.: Philadelphia   *1987*

    Reported as (693) (387) (356); other matter var. paged   "4to"   IU

Rheims-Douay Version. See 1853 Virtue edition, No 1518.

CaOOSJ has a copy similar to this imprinted *William Briggs, Publisher, Toronto, Canada* but with United States copyrights dated 1883 and 1884. While the pagination varies slightly from No 1518, the librarian says the book closely resembles a two-volume edition of Virtue, Emmins & Roberts, tentatively dated 1850. The CaOOSJ copy contains in the added matter a Preface to the Reader, A Comprehensive History of the Books of the Holy Catholic Bible, Written expressly for this Edition (56 p) and the Life of the Blessed Virgin Mary ... (12 p) all written by Bernard O'Reilly, D.D., L.D. (graduate of Laval University, Quebec).

1882? The Holy Bible ... With Cruden's Complete Concordance ... A Complete History of Each Book of the Bible ... A Concise History of All Religious Denominations ... By the Following Eminent Biblical Writers and Authors: Rev. Alfred Nevin ... Rev. Thomas H. Horne ... Rev. Wm. H. Munroe [and others] ... N. D. Thompson & Co.: St. Louis   **1988**

Reported as 1727 p   IU

Has colored frontispiece and other illustrations. Contains Family Record and Family Album pages. NT title has added: *The Revised Version of the New Testament; Being the Version Set Forth ... 1611. Compared with the Most Ancient Authorities and Revised ... 1881.* Possibly a Holman edition; quarto size?

Although this Bible has copyright date of 1877, it cannot have been published before 1881 since it contains the ERV NT; for ERV, see No 1953.

1882 The Illustrated New Testament ... Comprising Both the Present Version ... and the Revised Version, 1881. Elucidated with ... Notes ... Historical and Biographical Dictionary ... History of the Various Translations and Versions ... Tables ... Commentary ... with over Three Hundred Engravings and Maps ... O. A. Browning & Co.: Toledo, Ohio   **1989**

1 vol: (875) (39)   26 cm   NNAB

The Standard Comparative Edition appears at head of title page. History of the Versions, Family Record, maps, and Introduction precede text. AV text is printed in large type with the ERV following in smaller type, verse by verse, in double columns; for ERV, see 1881 NT, No 1953. There are full notes at foot of page, often giving additional renderings, etc. Bible Dictionary at end. Illustrations in text or full page. Copyright 1882, by Browning and Co.

1882 The New Testament ... Being the Version Set Forth A.D. 1611 ... Revised A.D. 1881. The Revision of 1881 Compared with the Version of 1611: Showing, at a Glance, What is Common to Both, and, by Diacritical Marks and Footnotes, What is Peculiar to Each. By Rufus Wendell ... [printed by D. G. F. Class, composition by Payne Brothers, and electros by Joseph P. Felt, New York]. Rufus Wendell, Publishers: Albany   **1990**

1 vol: (28) (601) 602–616   25 cm   ICN, MB, MH–AH, NjMD, NN, NNAB

ERV; see 1881 NT, No 1953. *Student's Edition* appears at head of title page. Contains Editor's Preface and the Revisers' Preface. Underscores indicate the differences from the AV, and AV readings are printed at foot of page. Copyright by Wendell, 1882.

1882 The New Testament ... The Text conformable to the Oxford and American Bible Societies' Editions. A. J. Holman & Co.: Philadelphia   **1990A**

1 vol: (399) (3) 3–96 (6)   23 cm   NNAB

A decorative initial is used at the beginning of each chapter. Has Table of Scripture Measures, etc., and Psalms at end.

1882   The New Testament . . . Containing the Old and New Versions . . . Readings
. . . Notes . . . History of the Revision . . . by Daniel Curry . . . N. Tibballs &
Sons: New York   **1991**

1 vol: (xviii) (660)   20 cm   MH–AH, NN

Columbian Oxford Double Testament appears at head of title page. Contains AV and ERV
texts and History of the Revision; for ERV, see 1881 NT, No 1953.

NN copy has inscription that the editorial work was done by Wilberforce Eames.

1882?   The New Testament . . . [Self-Pronouncing Edition]. American Baptist Publication Society: Philadelphia, Boston, New York, [etc.]   **1992**

Reported as 313 p   16 cm   ViU

1883?   The Holy Bible . . . with Complete Concordance . . . 100,000 Marginal
References and Readings, and . . . Smith's Standard Bible Dictionary, A
Complete History of the Books of the Bible . . . A History of all Religious
Denominations. Apocrypha and Psalms in Metre . . . With Revised New
Testament . . . Over 2500 Scripture Illustrations on Steel, Wood, and in
Colors . . . Baird and Dillon: New York   **1993**

1 vol: 9–636 (104) 643–1029; other matter var. paged   32 cm   NNAB

Has AV and ERV NTs printed in parallel columns with AV references, etc., in center col-
umn and ERV marginal readings and renderings in lower part of column; for ERV, see 1881
NT, No 1953. Supplementary matter includes a Commendation awarded at the International
Cotton Exposition, Atlanta, Ga., 1881; Valuable Table . . . Principal Events of the History of
the World from A.D. 98 to 1882, by the Rev. William Brown, D.D. (copyright 1882, 2 p);
A Comprehensive Description of the Israelitish Tabernacle (copyright 1879, 18 p); William
Smith's Dictionary of the Bible (copyright 1883, 128 p); Smith's Comprehensive History of
the Books of the Bible (48 p); Philip Smith's The Patriarchs (copyright 1883, 48 p); and many
other sections, all illustrated. Has engravings and many colored plates, including elaborate wedding certificate. Probably printed by the National Publishing Co. since the copyrights are all
in the name of J. R. Jones, founder of the firm.

NNAB has another similar edition imprinted *Charles H. Whiting: Boston,* which also has
a quantity of supplementary matter, separately paged. DLC has similar edition dated 1881?,
published by M. R. Gateley, Boston, M. R. Gateley and Company, New York, etc.

1883?   The Holy Bible . . . to which are added special explanatory features, designed to aid the reader . . . Hubbard Brothers: Philadelphia   **1994**

1 vol: 9–636 637–640 (104) (392); other matter var. paged   32 cm   NNAB

AV and ERV NTs printed in parallel columns, followed by Preferences of the American
Committee; for ERV, see 1881 NT, No 1953. Preliminary matter includes History of the
Books of the Bible (28 p), Smith's Comprehensive Pronouncing Dictionary (112 p), and
Jewish Tabernacle and Priesthood (copyright 1883 by G. C. Needham; the only dated copy-
right in this book). Text followed by A Chronological Index and Concordance.

1883?   The Holy Bible: Containing the Authorized Edition of the New Testament
and the Revised Version of A.D. 1881, Arranged in Parallel Columns; with
Cruden's Complete Concordance . . . Dictionary; etc. . . . . H. J. Richards &
Co.: Kansas City, Missouri   **1995**

1 vol: (636) (104) (396) 397–400; other matter var. paged   32 cm   NNAB

Has Holman trademark on title page and resembles Holman editions. With Apocrypha.
AV and ERV NTs in parallel columns; for ERV, see 1881 NT, No 1953. See also 1883?, Hoye
edition, No 1997.

1883 The Family Bible . . . Apocrypha, Concordance, Psalms in Metre, Chronological Index, etc. . . . Marginal References and Readings . . . Fine . . . engravings. William T. Amies: Philadelphia   **1996**

32 cm   NNAB
Similar to 1881 Family Bible (No 1949) except for some difference in supplementary
matter. *Amies' New and Improved Edition* appears at head of title page. ERV NT, without
imprint, follows AV text; for ERV, see 1881 NT, No 1953.

1883? The Holy Bible: . . . Authorized . . . New Testament and the Revised Version of A.D. 1881 Arranged in Parallel Columns: With . . . Concordance . . .
History of Each Book . . . Illustrated. Cities of the Bible . . . Biblical Antiquities; Scenes and Events in the Life of Christ; Historical Illustrations . . .
Biographical Sketches of the Translators and Reformers; Gallery of Scripture Illustrations; Bible Aids; Apocrypha and Psalms . . . By . . . Eminent
Biblical Writers and Authors . . . James A. Hoye & Co.: Boston   **1997**

1 vol: (636) (104) (396) 397–400; other matter var. paged   32 cm   NNAB
Holman's "Antique type" edition; probably published by Holman. Temperance Pledge
has copyright of 1883. For ERV, see 1881 NT, No 1953.

1883 Holy Bible . . . With Complete Concordance . . . Psalms . . . A. J. Holman &
Co.: Philadelphia   **1998**

1 vol: (574) 579–768; other matter var. paged   32 cm   NNAB
Holman's Edition appears at head of title. See 1872, No 1875. Preliminary matter includes
frontispiece; added engraved title with *Illustrated Family Bible* (copyright 1882); List of
Copyrights and Awards; Preface; Introductory History of the Bible; Earliest Editions of the
Bible Published in America; map; Historical Illustrations of Ancient Coins and Gems; Coins,
Money and Weights of the Bible, by F. W. Madden; Comprehensive Dictionary of the Bible
with Nearly Five Hundred Illustrations, Compiled from the Latest Editions of William Smith
(copyright 1872); Biblical Illustrations Showing Manners and Customs of the Ancients, etc.;
History of Herod, King of Jews; Order of Books; and Contents. Tables and Family Record
follow OT. NT has frontispiece. Index, Tables, etc., Brown's Concordance, Metrical Psalms,
and Photo Album at end. Illustrated.

1883 The Holy Bible . . . American Bible Society, Instituted . . . : New York *1999*

1 vol: (910) (281)   16 cm   NNAB
Minion 18mo first edition, from new plates. Last printing 1931, 3,221,000 copies having
been printed.
NNAB also has 1920 edition in which pagination has been made continuous (1191 p),
with one page of Tables at end.

1883 Job: Analyzed, translated and accompanied with critical studies, by Rev.
Leicester A. Sawyer, translator of the Scriptures, etc. Published by the
author: Whitesboro, New York   **2000**

102 p   19 cm   CtY, NNAB
Sawyer Version; see 1858 NT, No 1687. The following parts were also published at the
translator's expense at Whitesboro (all printed by T. J. Griffiths, Utica):

    188– Early Generations. Gen 1–11

                                      CtY

    1883 Daniel.
        Copyright 1882, 87 p, 19 cm   CtY, NNAB

    1883 Revelation of John.
        Copyright 1883, 70 p, 20 cm   CtY, NNAB

1884   The Bible, Analysed ... published in parts of books, single books, and
       collections of books ... Abraham. Gen 12:1–25:11.
       Copyright 1884, 83 p, 19 cm   CtY, NNAB

  1885   Gospel according to John
         Copyright 1884, 124 p, 19 cm   CtY, NNAB

  1887   Isaiah.
         Copyright 1884, 182 p, 19 cm   CtY, NNAB

  1888   Esther and the Song of Songs
         Copyright 1884, 67 p, 19 cm   CtY, NNAB

  1889   Introduction.
         Copyright 1883, 56 p   NNAB

For Sawyer's new translation of the NT, see 1891, No 2047.

1883   The New Testament. In Two Volumes ... Prepared by J. Glentworth Butler
         ... Funk and Wagnalls: New York   **2001**

       2 vols: Vol I, 685 p; Vol II, 831 p   26 cm   NNAB
       The Bible-Work, or, Bible Readers' Commentary appears at head of title page. Vol I is
"a Life of Christ, wherein the words of the inspired Biographers are woven into a consecutive,
complete story, and accompanied with select thoughts from garnered studies of the wise and
devout that have sought to interpret that story." Vol II contains Acts, Epistles, and Revelation.
The text is interspersed with a great deal of comment and is indexed and illustrated. First published, 1879.
       This was enlarged to include the OT in 11 vols. GEU has an edition of 1887; CoD, 1889
(9 vols only), and DWP, 1892.
       James Glentworth Butler (1821–1916) was graduated from Yale Divinity School in 1849,
was ordained to the Presbyterian ministry in 1852, and served as pastor of the Walnut Street
Presbyterian Church, Philadelphia until 1868. From 1868 to 1871 he served as corresponding
secretary of the American and Foreign Christian Union. He devoted his remaining years to
scholarly work.

1883   The New Testament ... translated out of the original Greek ... with apos-
         tolic references by Cortes Jackson. Collier and Cleaveland, printers: Den-
         ver, Colorado   **2002**

       Reported as 388 p   25 cm   CoD
       Has Preface and Tables. Copyright 1881.
       Mr. Jackson was a member of the Disciples of Christ.

1884   The Holy Bible, Translated from the Latin Vulgate ... With Notes ...
         Selected ... by the Rev. George Haydock. Revised and Corrected Under
         the Superintendence of the Very Rev. Frederick Canon Oakeley ... With
         the Approbation of his Eminence the Cardinal Archbishop of Westminster.
         And Imprimatur John Cardinal M'Closkey, Archbishop of New York ...
         P. F. Collier, Publisher: New York   **2003**

       2 vols in 1: (792) (755) 756–781; other matter var. paged   36 cm   NNAB
       Rheims-Douay Version, Haydock's text edited by Oakeley and Law. Preliminary matter
includes engraved title page and engraving, Relation of Church to Holy Scriptures, On the
Latin Vulgate .... Engravings by Doré, Preface to the American Reader — Bernard O'Reilly
(1884), and The Bible: What It Is, etc. Index follows OT. Preface precedes NT. Indexes, Tables,
Addenda from the Writings of St. Jerome, and Order of Books at end. Illustrated.

1884   The Holy Bible ... With Cruden's Complete Concordance, Embracing
         Every Passage of Scripture in the Largest Editions ... A. J. Holman: Phila-
         delphia   **2004**

       1388 p   32 cm   DLC, NN

Holman's Edition appears at head of title. OT marked "Crown 4to"; NT, "pica quarto." AV and ERV NTs printed in parallel columns; for ERV, see 1881 NT, No 1953. With Apocrypha, Family Record, The Parables of Jesus Christ, and Metrical Psalms. Illustrated.

1884   The Holy Bible . . . 100,000 Marginal References and Readings . . . Over 2500 Scripture Illustrations . . . H. L. Warren & Co.: Philadelphia   **2005**

30 cm   NN

Similar to Baird & Dillon's 1883? edition (No 1993). Each Testament has engraved frontispiece and title page in red and black. Contains Bible Dictionary, History of Religious Denominations, Description of the Tabernacle of the Israelites, Index, Family Record, etc. With Apocrypha, Concordance, and Metrical Psalms. AV and ERV NTs printed in parallel columns. Illustrated. Copyright 1881.

NN has another copy with copyright 1884 without device on title page (28 cm).

1884   William Tyndale's Five Books of Moses, called the Pentateuch, being a verbatim reprint of the edition of M.CCCCC.XXX. Compared with Tyndale's Genesis of 1534, and the Pentateuch in the Vulgate, Luther, and Matthew's Bible, with Various Collations and Prolegomena. By the Rev. J. I. Mombert, D.D.   Anson D. F. Randolph & Co.: New York   **2006**

1 vol: (cxlviii) (635)   27 cm   NNAB

Tyndale Version; see 1837 NT, No 990. Frontispiece is double-folded plate showing William Tyndale's autograph letter, from a photograph of the original in the Archives du Royaume Belgique. Cited copy is No 252 of 500 copies.

1884?   The New Testament in Both Authorized and Revised Versions Carefully Annotated by Howard Crosby . . . Charles F. Alden & Company: Boston   **2007**

1 vol: (iv) (597) [1] (6)   26 cm   MH–AH, NN, NNAB, ViU

Printed with AV and ERV in parallel columns; for ERV, see 1881 NT, No 1953. Interleaved with blank pages; also blank pages at end for notes. Colored maps. Copyright 1884.

1884–85   The New Covenant: Containing I. An Accurate Translation of the New Testament. II. Harmony of the Four Gospels. III. A Chronological Arrangement of the Text. IV. A Brief and Handy Commentary . . . By J. W. Hanson . . . The Universalist Publishing House: Boston and Chicago   **2008**

2 vols: Vol I, (xii) (354) 355–358; Vol II, (xv) [1] (416)   20 cm   MMeT–Hi

Vol I (1884) contains The Four Gospels printed as a Harmony. Vol II (1885) contains the remainder of the NT in chronological arrangement modeled after that of Conybeare and Howson. This is an "immersion" version, with notes. Has Introduction, Chronology of Jesus Christ's Ministry, and an Index. Vol I copyright 1883, by J. W. Hanson; Vol II, 1885.

NNAB has Vol I only.

Rev. John Wesley Hanson was a Universalist minister who was pastor of the New Covenant Church of Chicago from 1869 to 1884. His translation is a modern speech version (except in prayer), and is the first American translation to be based on the Greek text of Westcott and Hort (Cheek, p 44). The notes give a Universalistic interpretation. See Simms, p 253.

1884   Brief Notes on the New Testament. The Gospels, by Geo. W. Clark . . . The Acts, Epistles, and Revelation, by J. M. Pendleton . . . American Baptist Publication Society: Philadelphia   **2009**

748 p   18 cm   NjPT, NN

1885   The Holy Bible . . . Concordance . . . Apocrypha and Psalms . . . A. J. Holman & Co.: Philadelphia   **2010**

1 vol: (49) (857) (104) (28) (7) (396) (184)   33 cm   NNAB

Holman's Edition appears at head of title page. OT is reprinted from Holman's 1872 Crown Quarto Bible (No 1874). NT is titled *Parallel Edition* and has AV text in left column and ERV text in right, with AV and ERV alternative readings and renderings separated by a double rule in center column; for ERV, see 1881 NT, No 1953. The Concordance is Cruden's, not the one by Brown which had been used for so long.

1885   The Holy Bible, Translated from the Latin Vulgate . . . The Old Testament, First Published . . . at Douay . . . 1609, and the New Testament . . . at Rheims . . . 1582. With Useful Notes . . . By the Rev. Geo. Leo Haydock. Only Correct and Unabridged Edition Now Issued . . . T. Kelly: New York   **2011**

Reported as 1916 p   33 cm   DLC

Rheims-Douay Version. May be similar to 1852 Dunigan edition (No 1485).

1885   The Holy Bible . . . The Authorized and Revised Versions of the Old and New Testaments Arranged in Parallel Columns . . . Concordance . . . Dictionary . . . History of each Book . . . and other Bible aids. By . . . Eminent Biblical Writers and Authors . . . Hill & Harvey: Baltimore   **2012**

1 vol: (1070) 1071–1076 (5) (396) 397–400; other matter var. paged   32 cm   NNAB

The Parallel Bible appears at head of title page; presentation page has *Pictorial Family Bible. A. J. Holman Company, Philadelphia, Printers.* AV and ERV texts printed in parallel columns with ERV marginal material in center column; for ERV, see 1885 OT, No 2019, and 1881 NT, No 1953. Preferences of the American Committee are given at end of each Testament. Illustrated.

NNAB also has similar edition with Holman imprint dated 1888. KyLo has similar edition imprinted *Gately and Co., Cincinnati.*

1885?   Pictorial Family Bible . . . Authorized and Revised Versions, in Parallel Columns . . . Cranston and Stowe: Cincinnati [etc.]   **2013**

Reported as (1018) 1025–1338; other matter var. paged   32 cm   IU

Seems to be smilar to 1891 Holman edition (No 2040). *Parallel Edition* appears at head of title page. ERV and AV texts printed in parallel columns. Has colored presentation page, frontispiece, and title in red and black. Contains Aids for Readers and Students, Family Record, and Album. Illustrated.

Similar editions with different supplementary matter were published by Lakeside Installment Co., Chicago, 1886? (NBuG) and Gay Bros. and Co., New York, 1886 (no device on title page; NN).

1885?   The Approved Holy Catholic Bible . . . Containing the Entire Canonical Scriptures, According to the Decree of the Council of Trent; Translated from the Latin Vulgate: The Old Testament . . . 1609; the New Testament . . . 1582 . . . with Annotations by . . . Challoner; to Which is Added The History of the Holy Catholic Bible, and Calmet's Catholic Dictionary of the Bible; Each Edited by the Rev. I. F. Horstmann. Prepared under . . . the Most Rev. James F. Wood, D.D. Archbishop. . . . John E. Potter: Philadelphia   **2014**

Reported as (789) (222); other matter var. paged   31 cm   OC

Rheims-Douay Version, edited by Dr. Challoner. See 1875?, No 1910. Contains Orsini's Life of the Blessed Virgin (copyright 1883, 86 p), Horstmann's History of the Bible (128 p),

Calmet's Catholic Dictionary of the Bible (copyright 1879, 89 p), Parables or Our Lord (copyright 1885, 24 p), and various illustrations, certificates, portrait gallery, etc.

PLatS has similar edition imprinted *George V. Jones, Boston, Mass.,* and another with Potter imprint but dated 1886.

1885 The Holy Bible . . . Being the Version Set Forth A.D. 1611 . . . Revised . . .
Harper & Brothers: New York   **2015**

1 vol: (vii) (393) [1] (10) (121)   29 cm   CSmH, MH–AH, NN, NNAB, ViU

ERV; see 1881 NT, No 1953; also 1885 OT, No 2019. Has Preferences of the American Committee printed at foot of page and ERV marginal notes in two center columns. ViU and NNAB also have later similar editions, dated 1889 and 1890 respectively.

1885 Riverside Parallel Bible . . . Being the . . . King James's Version; Arranged
in Parallel Columns with the Revised Versions of 1881 and 1885 . . . Houghton, Mifflin and Co.: Boston   **2016**

1 vol: (xv) (1304) (x) (408)   26 cm   IU, KyLo, MB, NNAB

AV and ERV texts printed in parallel columns, with references below AV and variant readings and renderings below ERV; for ERV, see 1885 OT, 2019, and 1881 NT, No 1953. Rules around page.

NNAB also has similar edition with signatures instead of page numbers, no rules, and imprint of *B. B. Russell, Boston.*

1885? The Parallel Bible — Authorized Edition . . . in Parallel Columns with the
Revised Version . . . H. Hallett: Portland, Maine   **2017**

Unpaged   25 cm   NNAB

AV and ERV printed in parallel columns; for ERV, see 1881 NT, No 1953, and 1885 OT, No 2019. Printed on poor paper, with imprint in rubber stamp below a simple device. AV text has references at foot of page. Includes Epistle Dedicatory of AV, and Revisers' Prefaces and list of ERV Committee members.

1885? The Holy Bible, Translated from the Latin Vulgate . . . at Rheims . . . 1582
and at Douay . . . 1609, as Revised and Corrected in 1750 according to the
Clementine Edition . . . Richard Challoner . . . D. & J. Sadlier: New York
                                                                        2018

15 cm   IaCfT, IMunS

Rheims-Douay Version, edited by Dr. Challoner. Pagination same as 1870 Sadlier edition (No 1860).

MiU has separate NT (1199–1531 p).

1885 The Revised Version of the Old Testament with marginal notes and the
readings and renderings preferred by the American revisers printed as footnotes. In four parts . . . Harper's American Edition. Harper's Franklin Square Library, Harper and Brothers: New York   **2019**

29 cm   NNAB

Issued in four parts (No 472, No 474, No 476, and No 478) on June 5, 12, 19, and 26, 1885, at 20¢ each. Paged continuously. NNAB has Part i and ii only, 200 p. Copyright 1885, by Harper and Brothers.

This is possibly the first American printing of the ERV OT. The ERV OT was published by the University Presses in England on May 19, 1885, with a Preface dated 1884, in format similar to the NT (see 1881, No 1953). The Apocrypha, the work of the NT Company on Ecclesiasticus, Tobit, Judith, Wisdom, and 1 and 2 Maccabees (completed later by the OT Company) was published in England in 1895. For an official edition of the Bible with revised references, see 1898, No 2091. An edition of the NT with still fuller references by W. F. Moulton and F. H. A. Scrivener, edited by A. W. Greenup and J. H. Moulton, was published at Oxford in 1910.

1885   The Old Testament . . . Revised 1885. [Printed by Rand, Avery and Company, Boston.] The Henry Bill Publishing Company; Norwich, Connecticut
                                                                        2020

   1 vol: (xi) (1019) 1021–1035   25 cm   NNAB
   ERV; see 1885 OT, No 2019. Verso of title page has certificate by L. T. Chamberlain, Brooklyn, June 1, 1885, that this is printed word for word from the edition of the English University Presses. The verse numbers are placed in the text instead of in the margin as in the English editions and the marginal material is at the bottom of the page. The Preferences of the American Committee appear at the end.
   NN and NNC have copies bound with the NT (xvi, 313 p). NNAB and OrP have undated copies of the complete Bible imprinted *Thomas Y. Crowell and Co., New York.*

1885?   The Illustrated New Testament . . . Version Set Forth 1611, and the Revised Version of 1881 . . . Notes . . . Historical and Biographical Dictionary . . . By Rev. John Brown . . . O. A. Browning & Co.: Toledo, Ohio   *2021*

   26 cm   MiU
   Reprint of 1882 ERV NT (No 1989). *The Standard Comparative Edition* appears at head of title page. Copyright 1885.

1885   [The New Testament] Cranston & Stowe: Cincinnati   *2022*

   20 cm   NNAB
   A reprint of 1855 Phonetic NT, No 1596. Preliminary matter includes alphabet, explanation, introductory remarks and contents. The system omits c, q and x but adds 20 symbols. No editor indicated.

1885   [The New Testament] The Teaching and Acts of Jesus of Nazareth and His Apostles. Literally Translated Out of the Greek. [Privately printed]: Chicago   *2023*

   Reported as (xx) (389)   17 cm   DLC, ICU, MH–AH
   The translator was W. D. Dillard. Copyright 1885.
   The following is from the Preface to this work (p v) as quoted in Cheek (p 45): "Now, there ought to be a uniform standard of translation. Words of the same meaning, whether they be Chaldee, Hebrew, or Greek, should be translated into vernacular English words, having the same meaning. . . . Now we propose to render every word in the New Testament Greek into plain vernacular English words; just as they would now be written, if the facts they relate had occurred in our day and in our country. . . ." In spite of Dillard's intentions, the text is mainly a rewording of the AV.

1886   The Holy Bible . . . The Authorized and Revised Versions . . . Concordance . . . Psalms . . . in metre. U. S. Publishing House: Chicago   *2023A*

   1 vol: 9–1018 1033–1334; other matter var. paged   32 cm   NNAB
   AV and ERV printed in parallel columns; for ERV, see 1881 NT, No 1953, and 1885 OT, No 2019. *Parallel-Column Edition* appears at head of title page, which has device of National Publishing Co. Variously paged extra matter precedes text. Between OT and NT are Family Record pages, Life of Christ, Life of Paul, and illustrated Parables, Chronology, Teacher's Text Book, Cruden's Concordance, Metrical Psalms, and Photograph Album at end. Engravings and illuminated plates. Entered at Washington, 1886.

1886   The Holy Bible . . . The Text Conformable to the Oxford and American Bible Society's Standard Editions . . . John E. Potter & Co.: Philadelphia   *2024*

   1 vol: (2) 9–16 9–626 (12) 643–836 (12)   31 cm   NNAB
   Title page has *Light of the World* device of the National Publishing Company; NT does not have imprint. Frontispiece, History of the Translation of the English Bible, and Contents

precede text. Tables, Family Record, etc. follow OT. NT has frontispiece. Index and Tables at end. Illustrated. (See illus, No 1874, p 280 above.)

1886   The Holy Bible . . . [Wendell's Diacritical Edition]. The Revision of 1881 and 1885 Compared with the Version of 1611: Showing at a Glance What Words are Common to Both, and by Diacritical Marks and Foot-Notes What are Peculiar to Each. By Rufus Wendell, Editor of the "Student's Revised New Testament." [Electrotyped and printed by John Wilson and Co., University Press, Cambridge, Mass.] Revised Bible Publishing Company: Albany   **2025**

1 vol: (xviii) (872) 873–886 (8) v–xiv (268) 269–276   25 cm   ICU, MB, MH, NNAB
ERV; see 1881 NT, No 1953, and 1885 OT, No 2019. AV variations from the ERV are shown in footnotes and by various signs. Copyright 1886.
OC has similar edition dated 1889 by Bradley of Boston.

1886?   Holy Bible; Containing the King James and the Revised Versions, Arranged in Parallel Columns, a Complete Concordance, the Psalms of David in Metre, W. S. Smith's Standard Bible Dictionary, a Concise History of All Religious Denominations . . . P. W. Ziegler: Philadelphia   **2026**

"4to"   IdIf
AV and ERV in parallel columns; for ERV, see 1881 NT, No 1953, and 1885 OT, No 2019. Illustrated. Copyright 1886.
ViW has similar copy dated 1885.

1886–93   Scriptures, Hebrew and Christian, arranged and edited as an Introduction to the Study of the Bible by Edward T. Bartlett . . . and John P. Peters . . . G. P. Putnam's Sons, The Knickerbocker Press: New York and London
2027

3 vols: Vol I, (xii) (545); Vol II, (xi) (569); Vol III, (xii) (601)   21 cm   MA
Vol I (1886) contains Hebrew Story from Creation to the Exile; "the story is told in the words of the Bible, but with considerable condensation and rearrangement." Vol II (1889), Hebrew Literature; Indexed contents on p 561–569. Vol III (1893), Christian Scriptures; Quotations from the OT on p 591–601. The text in the main follows the AV or ERV but has been changed in places in the interests of simplifying passages or idioms, and has been condensed and rearranged with glosses added, usually in parentheses. The Divine Name is rendered "Jehovah."
NNAB has Vol I only.
Both editors were on the faculty of the Protestant Episcopal Divinity School in Philadelphia when the above work was prepared. John Punnett Peters (1852–1921) was an Episcopalian clergyman and Hebrew scholar who described himself as a "conservative-radical Churchman." His translation of the Psalms appeared in *The Psalms as Liturgies* (192?).

1887   The New Testament . . . Translated from the Latin Vulgate . . . First Published by the English College at Rheims . . . 1582. With Annotations, References, and . . . Index. Published with the Approbation of His Eminence Cardinal John McCloskey . . . Robert Coddington: New York   **2028**
1 vol: (429) (3)   20 cm   NNAB
Rheims Version. Imprimatur signed by Bishop McCloskey, 1882. Tables and Index at end. See 1840 Cummiskey NT, No 1087.

1887   The New Testament . . . American Bible Society, Instituted . . . : New York
2029
452 p   13 cm   NNAB
Nonpareil 32mo eighth edition, possibly first printed in 1885.
Also issued with Psalms (114 p).

1888?   The Holy Bible, Translated from the Latin Vulgate . . . With Annotations,
by the Rev. Dr. Challoner . . . John E. Potter & Co.: Philadelphia   **2030**

Reported as (86) (10) (128) (789) (221)   MiU
Rheims-Douay Version. See 1875, No 1910. Size not given; possibly 31 cm?

1889   The New Testament . . . translated out of the original Greek . . . with apostolic references by Cortes Jackson. Standard Publishing Company: Cincinnati   **2031**

Reported as 510 p   24 cm   TNDC
Copyright 1881. See 1883 NT, No 2002.

1889–91   The People's New Testament. The common and revised versions, with
references and colored maps. With explanatory notes by B. W. Johnson . . .
Christian Publishing Company: St. Louis   **2032**

2 vols: Vol I, 542 p; Vol II, 512 p   23 cm   TNDC
ERV; see 1881 NT, No 1953. Vol I dated 1889; Vol II, 1891.
TNDC also has reprint of Vol II dated 1896; two other copies of Vol I with imprint of
J. H. Smart & Co., Kansas City, one dated 1889 and the other 1890 and marked sixth edition; and
an undated set of Vols I and II probably published between 1910 and 1920.
DLC has a *Commentary for the People* by B. W. Johnson, St. Louis, 1886. Mr. Johnson
was associated with the Disciples of Christ.

1889   The New Testament . . . American Bible Society, Instituted . . . : New York
                                                                   2033

262 p   19 cm   NNAB
Minion Duodecimo, without chapter summaries or page headings.

189–   The Holy Bible, Translated from the Latin Vulgate . . . The Old Testament
First Published . . . at Douay . . . 1609, and the New Testament . . . at Rheims
. . . 1582 . . . Published with the Approbation of His Eminence James Cardinal Gibbons, Archbishop of Baltimore . . . Catholic Bible House: Philadelphia   **2034**

Reported as (1086) (306)   21 cm   KAS
Rheims-Douay Version. Illustrated.

189–?   The Holy Bible . . . Oxford Bible Reprint . . . S. H. Kerins & Co.: Columbus,
Ohio   **2035**

Reported as (1000) (332) (16)   21 cm   ICU
The Oxford Bible. The S. S. Teacher's Edition appears at head of title. Appended are Helps
to the Study of the Bible, Index, and maps.

1890?   The Holy Bible . . . Special explanatory features, designed to aid the reader
to a fuller, clearer, and easier understanding of the inspired text. Edgewood
Publishing Company. [n. p.]   **2036**

Reported as (640) (104) (389) 389–392 837–848   32 cm   OC
AV text with ERV and AV NTs in parallel columns. May be similar to 1881? American
Bible Publishing Company edition (No 1950).
OC says this Bible has no indication of place or date. The Family Record seems to have
been filled out in the 1920s.

1890 The Holy Bible . . . [Authorized Version with ERV New Testament at end] . . . Concordance . . . Apocrypha and Psalms . . . Henry Altemus: Philadelphia   **2037**

1 vol: (574) (104) 579–768 (176); other matter var. paged   32 cm   NNAB

Altemus' Edition appears at head of title page, which has device, *And there was Light,* on an open book. Although the device is not Holman's, this Bible is very like his 1872 edition (No 1875). Has Tables, Historical Data, etc. ERV NT (see 1881, No 1953) follows Brown's Concordance. With Metrical Psalms. Illustrated.

1890 The Holy Bible . . . Embracing Every Passage of Scripture in the Largest Editions . . . A. J. Holman & Co.: Philadelphia   **2038**

Various paging   32 cm   NcD

Title page printed in red and black. With Apocrypha, Concordance, and Psalms. Illustrated.

1890? The New Testament . . . Translated from the Latin Vulgate . . . 1582. With Annotations, References, and Historical and Chronological Index . . . P. J. Kenedy & Sons: New York   **2039**

19 cm   NN

Rheims Version. Pagination same as 1840 Cummiskey NT (No 1087).

KAS has similar edition imprinted *Baltimore Publishing Company, Baltimore* (21 cm).

1891 The Pronouncing Edition of the Holy Bible. Containing the Authorized and Revised Versions . . . Arranged in Parallel Columns . . . Concordance . . . References . . . Tables; A History of Ancient Biblical Manuscripts, with Facsimiles . . . The Earliest Printed Editions of the Bible; A History of the Revision . . . Etc. . . . A. J. Holman & Co.: Philadelphia   **2040**

1 vol: 9–1018 1019–1026 1037–1338 1339–1342; other matter var. paged   32 cm   NNAB

ERV and AV printed in parallel columns; for ERV, see 1881 NT, No 1953, and 1885 OT, No 2019. Judges' Report, U. S. Centennial Commission, awarding prizes to Holman, appears on verso of title page. Appendixes with Preferences of American Revisers follow OT and NT. Illustrated.

[1891] The Holy Bible . . . With Marginal References. The Text Conformable to the Oxford and American Bible Society's Standard Editions. B. F. Johnson & Co.: Richmond, Virginia.   **2041**

1 vol: (16) (16) 9–790 9–12 (8) (48)   31 cm   NNAB

Self-Pronouncing Edition appears at head of title page, which has device of globe and *Light of the World.* Order of Books, History of the Translation of the English Bible, Contents, Explanatory Key to the Vowel and Consonant Sounds in the Perfect Self-Pronouncing Bible, and Self-Pronouncing Dictionary of the Proper Names precede text. Text has center column of references. Table of Passages, Characteristics of the Prophetical Books, and Family Record follow OT. Account of Dates of Writing appears on verso of NT title. Index, Tables, and Brown's Concordance at end. Copyright 1891.

1891 The Holy Bible . . . interleaved . . . being the Version set forth A.D. 1611 compared with the most ancient Authorities and Revised. The Interleaving of this book is protected by Copyright, 1891, by C. E. Arbogust, Xenia, O. All Rights Reserved. C. E. Arbogust & Co.: Xenia, Ohio   **2042**

1 vol: v–viii (2) (393) (2) (vi) (121)   30 cm   Not Located

ERV text, printed in double columns with interleaved blank pages. NT title adds *A.D. 1881* after *and Revised.* See 1885, No 2015.

1891   Wilmore's New Analytical Reference Bible Containing the Following Inval-
uable Aids to the Proper Study of the Word of God: The Holy Bible, with
Marginal Notes and Analytical References. Comprehensive Bible Helps . . .
Revised and Edited by Philip Schaff . . . A Complete Analysis of the Holy
Bible Arranged in Subjects. Edited by Roswell D. Hitchcock. Cruden's Con-
cordance . . . Revised by John Eadie . . . J. A. Wilmore & Co.: New York   **2043**

    1 vol: (1127) (15) (1062)   29 cm   MH–AH, NNAB

Preliminary matter includes List of Contents, Preface signed by Philip Schaff, Publishers'
Announcement, How to Use the Bible, Order of Books, and Alphabetical Order. Comprehensive
Bible Helps, maps, Family Record, Complete Analysis of the Holy Bible, and Cruden's Con-
cordance follow Part 1. The Biblical text (Part 1) has center references to the sections of the
Analysis. The Analysis (Part 11) is reset page for page from the 1871 edition (No 1868), except
that the Contents of Sections, Scripture Index of Verses, and the material following Cruden's
Concordance are omitted in this edition. Copyright 1891.

[1891–1931]   The Numerical Bible. Being a Revised Translation of the Holy
Scriptures with Expository Notes: Arranged, Divided, and Briefly Charac-
terized according to the Principles of their Numerical Structure . . . Loizeaux
Brothers: New York   **2044**

    7 vols   23 cm   Not Located

The volumes are unnumbered and cover Genesis to 11 Samuel, the Psalms, Ezekiel, and
the NT. The copyright date sometimes appears on verso of title.

        1891   The Pentateuch. 623 p
              NNAB has fifth edition, [1931].

        1894   The Covenant History — Joshua to 2 Samuel. vi, 3–489 p
              NNAB has third edition, [1918].

        1896   The Psalms. 6, 3–486, 60 p
              Includes Appendix: The Witness of Arithmetic to Christ, etc. NNAB has fourth
              edition, [1924].

        1897   The Gospels. 626 p
              NNAB has fourth edition, [1932].

        1901   Acts to 2 Corinthians. 576 p
              NNAB has fourth edition, [1924].

        1903   Hebrews to Revelation. 509 p
              NNAB has third edition, [1922].

        1931   Ezekiel. The Text of the whole book and the Notes on Chaps. 1 to 37 by
              the late F. W. Grant. Notes on Chaps. 38 to 48, with a Historical Chart
              of the Prophets, Plans illustrating the Temple, and the Future Division of
              the Land, by J. Bloore. 399 p
              NNAB Preface signed "E.F."

Frederick W. Grant (1834–1902) was a leader among the Plymouth Brethren. Born in
the Putney district of London, he emigrated to Toronto at the age of 21. Later he moved to
Brooklyn, and then to Plainfield, New Jersey. After his attention had been drawn to the "Pentateuch" of the five books in the Psalter and to the acrostic Psalms, he began to look for evidences
for a law of numbers as a key to the interpretation of the Scriptures as a whole. He published
the basis of his numerical system in 1876. In 1891, he began the publication of the above
revision of the King James Bible. He finished the NT, but his death occurred before the OT
could be completed. Certain parts of the Numerical Bible have been reprinted several times.

1891   The Holy Bible, Translated from the Latin Vulgate . . . Douay . . . 1609; . . .
Rheims . . . 1582, With Annotations, References, and Index . . . John Murphy
& Co.: Baltimore   **2045**

    Reported as 968 p   23 cm   KAS
    Rheims-Douay Version.

1891   The Holy Bible Translated from the Latin Vulgate . . . Douay . . . 1609,
. . . at Rheims . . . 1582. With Annotations, References, and an Historical
and Chronological Index . . . Approbation of the Most Rev. Dr. Denvir, late
Bishop of Down and Connor . . . Benziger: New York   **2046**

Reported as (752) (216)   19 cm   OT
Rheims-Douay Version.

1891   [The New Testament] The Bible: Analyzed, Translated and Accompanied
with Critical Studies, Published in Parts of Books, Single Books and Collections of Books, by Rev. Leicester A. Sawyer . . . [T. J. Griffiths, Printer,
Utica]. L. A. Sawyer: Whitesboro, New York   **2047**

1 vol: (viii) 9–622   20 cm   DLC, NN, NNAB
Sawyer Version; see 1858 NT, No 1687. This contains a new translation with improved
renderings and a different arrangement of the order of books. The normal chapter and verse
arrangement has been used, with verse numbers in text. The Preface states that critical studies
designed to accompany the text "are unavoidably reserved for a separate publication." Copyright
1883, by Rev. L. A. Sawyer.

1891?   The New Testament . . . American Bible Union Version. Improved Edition
. . . [Edition with Immerse]. American Baptist Publication Society: Philadelphia   **2048**

590 p   16 cm   ICU, MH, NNAB
Prefatory Note precedes text, which is in single column, paragraph form, with verse numbers
raised in smaller type. Has alternative readings and renderings at foot of page.
The American Baptist Publication Society took over the work of the American and Foreign
Bible Society and the American Bible Union, and a new committee was formed in 1883 to
"improve" the ABU Version (see 1862–63 NT, No 1764). This committee consisted of Alvah
Hovey, D.D., President of Newton Theological Seminary; John A. Broadus, D.D., President
of Louisville Theological Seminary; and Henry G. Weston, D.D., President of Crozer Theological
Seminary. The NT was issued first and appeared in two forms, one rendering the Greek word
baptizo as "baptize," the other as "immerse." It was further revised for publication with the
OT in 1912 by the Rev. J. W. Willmarth, D.D. The ascribed date of 1891 is taken from the
Introduction to the NT in the 1912 Bible (No 2209).
The work on the OT was assigned in 1889 to Professor Bernard C. Taylor, Crozer Theolog-
ical Seminary (the parts previously translated by Dr. Conant — see No 1764 — and the rest
of the Pentateuch); Professor J. R. Sampey, D.D., Southern Baptist Theological Seminary
(Chronicles, Ezra, Nehemiah, Esther, Ecclesiastes, Song of Solomon, and Lamentations); Prof.
William R. Harper, University of Chicago (Isaiah and the minor prophets); and Prof. Ira M.
Price, Ph.D., University of Chicago (Jeremiah, Daniel, and Ezekiel). Dr. J. M. P. Smith, also
of the University of Chicago, read proof of Dr. Harper's section. The OT was not published
separately and first appeared in the 1912 Bible mentioned above.

1892?   Holy Bible . . . The King James and the Revised Versions . . . Parallel Columns. The text conformable to that of the Universities of Oxford and Cambridge . . . Concordance . . . Psalms . . . in Metre . . . Henry Sphar: Cincinnati   **2049**

Reported as 9–1018 (viii) 1033–1338; other matter var. paged   32 cm   OC
Self-Pronouncing Edition appears at head of title page, which is in red and black with
device of open Bible on closed Bible and *Light of the World* (trademark of the National Publishing Company). ERV and AV texts printed in parallel columns; for ERV, see 1881 NT,
No 1953, and 1885 OT, No 2019. Among the supplementary matter is the Hoffman Gallery of
NT illustrations. Preferred Readings of American Revisers follow OT and NT. Many colored
plates. Copyright 1892; some material copyright by J. R. Jones, 1891.

Similar editions with slightly varying extra matter were published by J. H. Buckmaster, Toledo, Ohio (OC); Gately and Fitzgerald, Philadelphia (with AV Apocrypha — NNAB); Langan and Bro., New York and Providence (with AV Apocrypha — NNAB); and Great Eastern Publishing Co., Philadelphia (PHi). NNAB has another similar edition with no imprint information.

1892   The Holy Bible . . . With Marginal References . . . Self-Pronouncing Edition in which all the Proper Names are Divided, Accented, and Marked with the Vowel Sounds, Showing How They Should be Pronounced. The Southwestern Co., Publishers and Booksellers: Nashville   **2050**

1 vol: (605) 606–608 33–310; other matter var. paged   32 cm   NNAB

The title page device of the world with an open Bible on a closed one is that of the National Publishing Co. Preliminary matter includes presentation page, illuminated title page (with *Pictorial Family Bible*), History of the Translation of the English Bible, Contents, map and plans, Bible Stories for the Young Illustrated by Well-known Artists, Key to Pronunciation, and dictionary of Proper Names. Old Testament Passages Quoted by Christ and Apostles . . . , Characteristics of the Prophetical Books, Family Record, and Photographic Illustrations of the Holy Land follow OT. *Combination Self-Pronouncing Edition* (AV–ERV) appears at head of NT title page, which has Order of Books on verso. Preface to ERV, How to Read the Combination New Testament, and Key to Pronunciation precede NT. Changes of ERV are at foot of page with references and alternative readings and renderings in center column; for ERV, see 1881 NT, No 1953. Chronological Index, Preferences of the American Committee, and Concordance at end. Many illustrations.

1892   The Holy Bible . . . Cruden's Concordance, Embracing Every Passage of Scripture in the Largest Editions . . . A. J. Holman & Co.: Philadelphia   **2051**

32 cm   NN

With Apocrypha, Concordance, and Metrical Psalms. Illustrated.

1892   The Holy Bible . . . National Publishing Company: Philadelphia   **2052**

Reported as 782 p   30 cm   Nat'l. Pub. Co.

Frontispiece shows Moses and the tablets of the law. History of English translations (8 p) and 60 p of other matter follow text. This is not the same as the 1870 edition (No 1853).

1892?   The Holy Bible . . . [International Series, Divided Verses, Revised Version, 1881–1885]. Being the Version Set Forth in 1611 . . . and Revised. Self-Pronouncing. With References . . . International Bible Agency: New-York   **2053**

1 vol: (vi) (947) [1] (2) (291) [1] (66) (268)   21 cm   NNAB

ERV; see 1881 NT, No 1953, and 1855 OT, No 2019. Long Primer Octavo, Clear Type Edition. Has Introduction, American Committee Preferences, Bible Readers' Aids by Rev. Charles H. H. Wright, and Word Book. Text printed in verse instead of paragraph form. To the marginal material of the ERV the editors have added more references showing in the Gospels parallel passages, and page headings with a new system of chapter and verse indication at the upper corners of the page. Maps.

The International Bible Agency was formed in 1892 by the Methodist Book Concerns of New York and Cincinnati and the United Brethren Concern of Dayton, each one being an equal partner. The Agency originally purchased minion, bourgeois and small pica Bibles from William Collins and Son of Glasgow, but gradually new editions were set, plated, and sold by them. These were printed by the Methodist Book Concern but published under the imprint of the International Bible Agency. The Agency was purchased in 1902 by the John C. Winston Company (see 1902 NT, No 2145).

1892   The Holy Bible . . . Geo. W. Ogilvie & Co.: Chicago   **2054**

20 cm   NNAB

All text in cited copy lacking after Zech 8:23 (p 758). Has Table of added matter and Epistle Dedicatory; references in outer columns. Extra material includes illustrations "arranged for the Olivet Series of Oxford Teacher's Bibles" (copyright 1896 by Wilmore-Andrews Publishing Co.) and Bible Study Helps, Subject Index, and Concordance prepared for the Clarendon Press (336 p). Colored maps are marked *E. F. Fisk, N. Y.* Copyright 1892 by Van Cleve-Andrews Publishing Company. Seems to be closely related to Oxford editions but printed in U. S. See note with 1896?, No 2072.

DLC has similar edition (1096 p, 18 cm).

1892 The Holy Scriptures of the New Testament Translated and Corrected by the Spirit of Revelation, by Joseph Smith, Jr., Reorganized Church of Jesus Christ of the Latter Day Saints: Lamoni, Iowa **2055**

Reported as 374 p   26 cm   MH

Joseph Smith Version; see 1867, No 1817. Cited copy is bound up with *The Book of Mormon*, by Joseph Smith, Jun., Published by the Reorganized Church of Jesus Christ of Latter Day Saints, Lamoni, Iowa, 1892.

The Church headquarters at Independence also has a copy like the above.

1893 The Holy Bible . . . Published by the Publishing House of the Methodist Episcopal Church, South: Nashville **2056**

Reported as 836 p   59 cm   TNMB

Only one copy of this "Exhibition Bible" was produced. It was manufactured by the Methodist Publishing House, Barbee & Smith, Agents, expressly for exhibition at the World's Columbian Exposition at Chicago in 1893, to show the mechanical attainments in bookmaking in the southern states at the time. It received a Certificate of Award, accompanied by a "Medal for Specific Merit," and was later exhibited at the Tennessee Centennial Exposition, Nashville, 1897. It is printed in letters of pure gold on sheets of sheepskin, each page having a border about three inches wide illuminated in color. The materials used in its manufacture cost $1700 and the work took many months. The text is set in 12-point Modern Roman in parallel columns, double leaded. The borders were printed first, then the gold leaf laid on the plate and pressed into the vellum by a revolution of the press cylinder. Although it was first planned to print fine pulpit Bibles from this type, there seem to have been no such editions published. The above copy is on permanent exhibition at the Methodist Publishing House, Nashville, Tenn.

1893 The Holy Bible . . . Embracing Every Passage of Scripture in the Largest Editions . . . Henry Altemus: Philadelphia **2057**

1 vol: (6) vii–xii (8) 9–576 (8) 579–768   32 cm   NNAB

Reprint of Holman's 1872 edition (No 1875) and similar to the 1890 Altemus Bible (No 2037). *Altemus' Edition* appears at head of title page, which has device, *And there was Light,* on an open book (not quite like the Holman or National Publishing Company device). Lacks Apocrypha. Frontispiece, Introduction, Order of Books, Contents, maps, and Life of Our Lord precede text. Tables and Family Record follow OT. NT has frontispiece. Index, Tables, etc. at end. Illustrated.

The phrase on the title page, *Embracing Every Passage of Scripture in the Largest Editions,* is usually used for editions with a Concordance; however, this copy has no Concordance nor does the word appear in the title. See 1884 Holman edition, No 2004.

1894 The Holy Bible . . . American Bible Society, Instituted . . . : New York **2058**

1 vol: (724) (227)   16 cm   NNAB

Pearl Reference 24mo. 12,000 copies were printed from new electroplates. Chronology removed from reference columns in 1900.

1894? The Holman New Self-Pronouncing Sunday School Bible . . . Holman: Philadelphia **2059**

"16mo"   FT

Contains Sunday School Teachers' Ready Reference Handbook, Tabular Chronologies, and Specially Arranged Subjects, together with Concordance, Dictionary, and Four Thousand Questions and Answers.

Trade

1895?   Combination Holy Bible showing in simple form all changes, additions and
Mark
omissions that appear in the Revised Version. National Bible Press: Philadelphia   **2060**

Reported as 17–864 33–310; other matter var. paged   33 cm   Nat'l Bible Press
Self-Pronouncing Edition appears at head of title page. Copyright 1895. For ERV, see 1881 NT, No 1953 and 1885 OT, No 2019.

1895   The Holy Bible . . . With complete concordance, Embracing Every Passage
of Scripture in the Largest Editions . . . A. J. Holman & Co.: Philadelphia
2061

1 vol: (772) (104) 777–1017; other matter var. paged   32 cm   NNAB
Similar to Harding's 1856 Royal Quarto (No 1605). Contains Preface, Introduction, Historical Accounts, Dictionary of the Bible, Index, Tables, Concordance, etc. With Apocrypha and Metrical Psalms. Illustrated.

1895   The Holy Bible . . . American Bible Society, Instituted . . . : New York   **2062**

27 cm   NNAB
Pagination same as 1868 Small Pica Reference Royal Octavo (No 1830). Has Family Record after OT; Tables (1 p) and 8 colored maps after NT.

1895   The Self-Pronouncing S. S. Teacher's Combination Bible Showing in Simple
Form all Changes, Additions and Omissions Made by the Revisers in the
King James Version. Enabling Bible Readers to See at a Glance Wherein
the Two Versions Differ . . . The Text is Conformable to that of the Oxford
Bible . . . [No publisher or place]   **2063**

1 vol: 17–1056 3–342; other matter var. paged   21 cm   NNAB
Fine Art Edition appears at head of title page. Frontispiece, Preface, Key to Pronunciation, Order of Books, Synopsis of the Books, and How to Read the Combination Bible precede text, which has ERV readings at foot of page. Family Record follows OT. At end are plates, Helps to the Study of the Bible, Notes, Summaries, Tables, etc., Index, Concordance, Dictionary of Names, Indexed Atlas, and additional plates. Copyright 1895, by J. R. Jones, which would indicate that this is a National Publishing Company edition even though the trademark on title page is somewhat similar to Holman's.
MiU has similar edition of 1902? published by the Southwestern Company, Nashville, Tenn.

1895?   The Self-Pronouncing Sunday-School Teachers' Bible . . . Conformable to
the Edition of 1611 . . . National Bible Press: Philadelphia   **2064**

1 vol: (vii) (2) 17–976 (296) (144)   21 cm   NNAB
Title page has device, *The Light of the World,* on open Bible on shield. Frontispiece, Order of Books, Key to Pronunciation, and Epistle Dedicatory precede text. Concordance at end. Copyright 1895, by J. R. Jones.

1895   The Self Pronouncing Holy Bible . . . The Text Conformable to that of the
Edition of 1611 . . . [Composition by the Riverside Press, Cambridge, Mass.].
A. J. Holman Co.: Philadelphia   **2065**

1 vol: (8) 7–947 (289) (2) (12)   15 cm   NNAB

Holman Edition appears at head of title. Known as the "Minion 24mo" edition. Frontispieces, Preface, Key to the Pronunciation, and Order of Books precede text. Maps at end. Illustrated with sepia half-tones of photographs of the Holy Land. Copyright 1895, by A. J. Holman & Co.

Also published by the American Baptist Publication Society, with offices in Philadelphia, Boston, Chicago, Dallas, New York, St. Louis, and Atlanta. For later edition with some changes in marginal format, see 1921?, No 2252.

1895–1906 The Modern Reader's Bible: A Series of Works from the Sacred Scriptures Presented in Modern Literary Form . . . Edited with an Introduction and Notes by Richard G. Moulton . . . [Printed at the Norwood Press, Norwood, Mass.]. The Macmillan Co.: New York **2066**

22 vols 14 cm NN, NNAB

Several volumes are dated 1895; Vol i is dated 1896. Text is printed in paragraph form with verse numbers in margin. Subject headings replace chapter headings. Poetic passages are presented in poetry form. Bible Aids, etc. are sometimes appended to text.

Number of volumes in sets of this Bible varies. It has been published in many editions, with title changed slightly in some. A 1-vol edition was issued in 1907 (see No 2178).

Richard Green Moulton (1849–1924) was a British-born American educator and critic who taught at the University of Chicago, 1892–1919. Although Shakespeare was his special field, he is best known for the above work. It is not a new version, but a new arrangement of the ERV (see 1881 NT, No 1953; also 1885 OT, No 2019). 1895 appears to be the first date of publication of any part of the Modern Reader's Bible. In the Editor's Note, Dr. Moulton states that "the text . . . is one constructed specially for this work for which the Editor is solely responsible. It is based upon the English Revised Version, with choice between the readings of the text and margin, and such slight changes of wording as are involved in the adaptation to modern literary structure."

1895–98 The Woman's Bible . . . European Publishing Company: New York **2067**

2 vols: Part i, 152 p; Part ii, 217 p 23 and 25 cm KU, NNAB

NNAB has Part i only (1895): Comments on Genesis, Exodus, Leviticus, Numbers, and Deuteronomy. KU has Part ii only (1898): Comments on the Old and New Testaments from Joshua to Revelation; also contains an Appendix of Letters and Comments, a Resolution of National-American Woman Suffrage Association repudiating *The Woman's Bible*, and Speech of Susan B. Anthony.

KU also has third edition of Part i, 1898.

This Bible does not contain the complete text. It was prepared by a Revising Committee, chaired by Elizabeth Cady Stanton. The following members, in addition to Mrs. Stanton, made comments: Lillie D. Blake, Frances E. Burr, Lucinda B. Chandler, Clara B. Colby, Ellen B. Dietrick, Matilda J. Gage, Ursula N. Gestefeld, Rev. Phebe Hanaford, Clara B. Neyman, Louisa Southworth, and an anonymous contributor. The original plan was to produce a complete edition of the Bible, in which only those passages "directly referring to women, and those also in which women are made prominent by exclusion" would be subject to revision. Since the published material was of a provisional nature, selected texts were lifted out and presented with comments. ". . . the Revising Committee refer to a woman's translation of the Bible [see Julia E. Smith's 1876 edition, No 1918] as their ultimate authority for the Greek, Latin and Hebrew text . . ." (Part i, p 149). However, the quoted texts conform closely to the King James Version.

1895? The New Testament with commentaries, references, harmony of the Gospels . . . illustrated and explained by over one hundred photographs . . . notes . . . by John Brown . . . assisted by Josiah L. Porter . . . descriptions . . . of photographs by Rev. James W. Lee . . . Photographic artist Prof. Robert E. M. Bain . . . N. D. Thompson Publishing Co.: New York and St. Louis **2068**

1 vol: (xlvi) (539) 30 cm NNAB

Text printed in double columns with Brown's notes and references in two center columns and further "reflections," etc. at foot of page. Preceded by various tables and Harmony. Illustrated with half-tones of photographs of Bible Lands. For John Brown, see 1792, No 37. For Thompson's new illustrated edition of Brown's Bible, see also 1896?, No 2070.

1895?   The Self-Pronouncing New Testament . . . with Psalms. National Bible
    Press: Philadelphia   **2069**

1 vol: 17–482 485–600   22 cm   NNAB

Has illuminated Lord's Prayer; half-tone illustrations; History of the Psalms before Psalms text. Set in Pica type.

NNAB also has Red Letter edition with 6-page Preface.

1896?   The Self-Interpreting Bible . . . With Commentaries, References, Harmony
    of the Gospels and Helps Needed to Understand and Teach the Text, Illus-
    trated and Explained by Over Four Hundred Photographs Showing the
    Places of Bible Events as they Appear Today . . . References, Explanatory
    Notes, and Tabulated Statistics by John Brown . . . Revised and Enlarged
    by Henry Cooke . . . and Josiah I. Porter . . . N. D. Thompson Publishing
    Company: New York and St. Louis   **2070**

4 vols   30 cm   DLC, OC

This is a new illustrated edition of Brown's Bible; see 1792, No 37.

CaBVi and CaNSHK have copies copyright 1896 imprinted *World Publishing Company, Guelph, Ontario.*

DLC also has 1901? and 1905? editions, the first titled *The Bible Cyclopedia . . . Five Hundred Photographs . . . by Robert E. Bain . . . edited by . . . James W. Lee.* Other editions were published during this period by Whitaker and Ray Co., San Francisco, 1896 (C); The Martin and Hoyt Co., Atlanta, copyright 1905 (NN); and the Bible Educational Society, St. Louis, in 1905? (OCK) and 1908? (NN).

The NT was issued separately by the Thompson firm in 1895–96 (xlv, 539 p; KyLo and NcD); J. Q. Adams and Co., Boston, 1909 (NNAB); and The Bible Educational Society, St. Louis, in 1909 (DLC), 1911 (ViU), 1916 (NN), 1917 (USl), and 1922 (imprinted Chicago instead of St. Louis; NNU–W).

1896   The Holy Bible . . . [Printed by Berwick & Smith, Norwood Press, Norwood,
    Mass.]. Thomas Nelson & Sons: New York   **2070A**

1 vol: (4) (599) (3) (185)   25 cm   NNAB

Epistle Dedicatory and Order of Books precede text, which is printed with center references and Chronology. At end are Illustrated Bible Helps from the Illustrated Bible Treasury (copyright 1896 by Nelson, 64 p) and Combined Concordance (113 p). Colored maps.

NNAB has another copy with Illustrated Bible Treasury (350 p) and Concordance (311 p); no printer given.

1896?   The Holy Bible . . . Samuel Bagster & Sons, Limited: London; James Pott
    and Company: New York   **2071**

1 vol: (6) 5–1309 (27)   24 cm   NNAB

Dedication to King James and Order of Books precede text. Dictionary of Names at end; also colored maps dated 1896, with imprint of New York printer. Illustrated.

1896?   The Holy Bible . . . Wilmore-Andrews Publishing Co.: New York   **2072**

Reported as (1000) (32) (336)   20 cm   DLC

Oxford Bible. The S. S. Teacher's Edition . . . Olivet Series appears at head of title page. Contains Helps to the Study of the Bible, Summaries, etc., Concordance and maps. Appended materials vary with copies. See 1892, No 2054.

Oxford's 1906 Catalog (American Branch) carries an injunction inside the front wrapper against Wilmore-Andrews for using the Oxford name.

1896   The New Testament: Newly Translated [from the Greek Text of Tregelles] and Critically Emphasised, with an Introduction and Occasional Notes. By Joseph B. Rotherham. 12th Edition, Revised. 14th Thousand . . . [Robert Drummond, Electrotyper and Printer, New York]. J. Wiley & Sons: New York   **2073**

Reported as (xvi) (492)   21 cm   ICU, MH–AH
Rotherham Version; see 1878 NT, No 1930. Has Preface to Second Edition.
Also published by F. H. Revell Co., New York, 1896. GEU has copy imprinted *American Baptist Publication Society, Philadelphia.*

1896?   The Interlinear Literal Translation of the Greek New Testament, with the Authorized Version conveniently presented in the Margins for Ready Reference, and with the Various Readings of the Editions of Elzevir 1624, Griesbach, Lachmann, Tischendorf, Tregelles, Alford and Wordsworth. Arthur Hinds and Company . . . : New York   **2074**

1 vol: (viii) (670)   21 cm   NNAB
This work clearly is an edition of *The Englishman's Greek New Testament*, first published in London by Bagster in 1877. The size of the type page has been increased — evidently by photographic process, and then printed from plates. The first indication of a date is found in later printings, which include *Copyright, 1897, by Hinds & Noble* at foot of title page. The body of the page contains the Greek text with sublinear literal renderings. The AV is printed in the outer margin in paragraph form, and the critical readings are at foot of page. For the Interlinear OT, see 1897, No 2082.
NNAB also has *The Greek-English New Testament, being the Original Greek Text with a Literal Interlinear Translation,* an undated text edition without AV or readings, published by the Handy Book Company, Reading, Pennsylvania (xii, 670 p, 20 cm); and three copies of *The Interlinear Literal Translation . . . To which has been added A New Greek-English New Testament Lexicon, supplemented by a Chapter elucidating the Synonyms of the New Testament, with a Complete Index to the Synonyms by George Ricker Berry* (vii, 670, vi, 137 p, 23 cm): one by Hinds, Noble & Eldredge, New York, no date; a second by the Handy Book Company, Reading, Pa., no date; and the third by Wilcox & Follett Company, Chicago, 1946.

1897   The New Illuminated Holy Bible, Self-Pronouncing with Marginal References and Concordance. 800 Original Illustrations . . . The Text Conforms to that of the Oxford Bible Printed at the University Press, Oxford . . . [Printed by The Riverside Press, Cambridge, Mass. and Electrotyped by H. O. Houghton and Company]. American Bible Union: Philadelphia   **2075**

1 vol: (vi) (967) (299) (97)   29 cm   NNAB
Edition De Luxe appears at head of title. Presentation page, Preface, Order of Books, Key to Pronunciation, and frontispiece (*The Creation*) precede text. Has Family Record. Frontispiece to NT. Concordance at end. Illustrated with half-tones, many set in the body of text. Copyright 1897, by Frank E. Wright.
NNAB has another copy published by the American Bible House, Philadelphia and New York, and printed by J. B. Lippincott Co., no date, which was probably printed at a later time (27 cm). DLC has an 1898? edition of *The New Illustrated Holy Bible,* International Bible Agency, New York, which seems to be a reprint. Also published by P. F. Collier, New York.

1897   Nave's Topical Bible. Digest of the Holy Scriptures. More Than Twenty Thousand Topics and Subtopics, and One Hundred Thousand References to the Scriptures . . . by Orville J. Nave . . . Chaplain in the Army of the United States. From the Press of Eaton and Mains, Topical Bible Publishing Company: New York   **2076**

1615 p   25 cm   NNAB

Brings together in cyclopedic form and under familiar headings all the Bible contains on particular subjects, some verses appearing several times. Has Index showing the pages and columns in which each verse of Scripture is found (p 1465–1615). Copyright 1896 and 1897, by Orville J. Nave.

NNAB also has an undated copy imprinted *International Bible Agency, New York.*

Chaplain Nave claimed that the above work was much more satisfactory than the previous classifications of verses (see West's 1854 edition, No 1552; also Hitchcock's 1871 edition, No 1868). It was the work of fourteen years. On subjects relating to law he secured the assistance of the Hon. John Welch, Judge of the Supreme Court of the State of Ohio.

NN has copy of 1901 fifth edition (12,000 copies printed) which has on verso of title page: First edition, 1897, 5,000; Second edition, 1898, 10,000; Third edition, 1899, 10,500. A fourth edition was printed in 1900, 10,500 copies. The Topical Bible Publishing Co. issued a later printing in 1904 from Lincoln, Nebraska, marked "one Hundredth Thousand." In 1952 the Topical Bible was published by Moody Press, Chicago; seven editions in cloth and one in leather were issued by this firm by November 1958.

1897   The Holy Bible . . . Embellished with 852 Illustrations . . . [W. B. Conkey Company, Publishers, Printers and Binders, Chicago]. The Christian Herald: New York   **2077**

1 vol: (viii) (1021) (iv) (313)   23 cm   NN, NNAB

Illustrations are in most cases set in the body of text. Copyright 1897, by Louis Klopsch. See 1898, No 2088; also 1897 ABU edition, No 2075.

1897?   The Emphasised Bible. A New Translation . . . with Expository Introduction . . . References, and Appendices of Notes. This Version has been Adjusted, in the Old Testament, to the Newly Revised "Massoretic-Critical" Text . . . in the New Testament to the Critical Text . . . of Drs. Westcott and Hort. By Joseph Bryant Rotherham. Standard Publishing Co.: [Cincinnati]   **2078**

4 vols in 1: (iv) (920) (272)   23 cm   NN

Rotherham "Emphasised" Bible; see 1878 NT, No 1930. Each vol has separate title page. Copyright 1897, by Joseph Bryant Rotherham.

Although all the parts are copyright 1897, the OT was not published in England until 1901–02 and it seems unlikely that it was printed in this country earlier. This Bible may have been printed in England, but if it was printed in this country it was probably done between 1901 and 1916. See also 1902 OT, No 2139.

1897   The Holy Bible . . . American Bible Society, Instituted . . . : New York   **2079**

1 vol: (876) (271) (5)   22 cm   NNAB

Bourgeois Reference Octavo with Tables after text (1 p), Family Record (4 p), and colored maps (8 leaves). Two thousand copies were printed from new electroplates.

In 1897, at the suggestion of the Massachusetts Bible Society and on the recommendation of the Committee on Versions, the Board of Managers approved the elimination from all reference editions of the dates from Ussher's Chronology, which had previously appeared at the head of reference columns. The decision was made too late to affect the above Bible, but NNAB has an edition of 1898 from which the Chronology has been removed.

1897?   The Holy Bible . . . T. Nelson & Sons: New York   *2080*

1 vol: (956) (290)   21 cm   NN

Has W. Wright's Illustrated Bible Treasury at end.

This was originally an English publication, but had been printed in America for many years.

1897?   The Oxford Self-Pronouncing Bible, S. S. Teacher's Edition . . . Appointed to be read in Churches. [Printed by Manhattan Press, New York, U. S. A., from electrotype plates made at the University Press, Oxford.] Oxford University Press, American Branch: New York; . . . Henry Frowde: London

2081

Reported as (1056) (300)   21 cm   DLC, OT, ViU

Preface dated 1897, but probably printed later. Contains the Oxford Cyclopedia Concordance (copyright 1903, 300 p).

ViU copy has Bible Helps (279 p with Atlas) which may be an older supplement.

1897?   The Interlinear Literal Translation of the Hebrew Old Testament with the King James Version and the Revised Version conveniently printed in the Margins for Ready Reference and with Explanatory Textual Footnotes supplemented by Tables of the Hebrew Verb, and the Hebrew Alphabet, by George Ricker Berry . . . Part I — Genesis and Exodus. Hinds & Noble, Publishers: New York

2082

Part I: (vii) a-i (403)   25 cm   NNAB

No further parts of the OT were published. Verso of title has The Value of Hebrew and Greek to Clergymen. Introduction (p iii–vii) and Hebrew Verbs, Explanatory Statements, Abbreviations, and Hebrew Alphabet (p a-i) precede text. Publisher's Advertisements at end (25 p). Cited copy has the following legend rubber-stamped above publisher's imprint: "Handy Book Company, Reading, Penna. Publishers of all Translations formerly of." The tailpiece bears the Handy Book Company imprint. Copyright 1896, by Arthur Hinds. Copyright 1897, by Hinds & Noble.

Reprinted by Wilcox and Follett in 194–. For the Interlinear NT, see 1896?, No 2074.

1897   The Emphasised New Testament. A New Translation Designed to Set Forth the Exact Meaning, the Proper Terminology, and the Graphic Style of the Sacred Original; Arranged to Show at a Glance, Narrative, Speech, Parallelism, and Logical Analysis; and Emphasised Throughout after the Idioms of the Greek Tongue. With Select References and an Appendix of Notes. This Version has been Adjusted to the Critical Text "formed exclusively on documentary evidence" of Drs. Westcott and Hort. By Joseph Bryant Rotherham . . . [Robert Drummond, Electrotyper and Printer, New York]. J. Wiley & Sons: New York

2083

Reported as 272 p   26 cm   CU, DLC, PP

Rotherham "Emphasised" Testament; see 1878 NT, No 1930. This is the third edition of Rotherham's NT and is a reprint of the 1897 London edition.

Wiley's catalog for 1900 lists the above edition at $2, but the present firm has no record of when it began printing here.

1897   The New Dispensation. The New Testament Translated from the Greek by Robert D. Weekes . . . Funk and Wagnalls Company: New York and London

2084

1 vol: (viii) (525)   21 cm   MA, MB, NCH, NNAB

Preface signed by Robert D. Weekes, East Orange, N. J., 1897. Printed in paragraph form. The order of the Epistles follows that recommended by Conybeare and Howson. Copyright 1897, by Funk & Wagnalls Co.

Robert Dodd Weekes (1819–98) was a Congregational layman who held various positions in teaching and business. His translation is based "in general" on the Greek text of Westcott and Hort. The Preface states that his aim was to "ascertain the thought of the writers, and then to express such thought correctly . . . with as little deviation from a literal rendering as practicable, and at the same time retaining in good measure the familiar style of the older [AV] version."

1897 The New Testament Emphasised. Based upon a Study of the Original Greek Text by Rev. Horace E. Morrow. [Norwood Press. J. S. Cushing & Co. — Berwick & Smith, Norwood, Mass.] Charles Reynolds: Middletown, Connecticut **2085**

1 vol: iii–ix 3–435 (4)   21 cm   NNAB

Preface, Explanations, Key to Pronunciation, and List of Proper Names precede text. Copyright 1897, by H. E. Morrow.

FULL-FACE type is used to denote emphasis; *italic* denotes a lesser degree of emphasis; and the "italic is also used to indicate impressive utterance, as in the impressive phrases in the discourses of our Lord, and in the didactic portions of the Epistles." (Explanations, p iv.)

The Rev. Horace E. Morrow was born in Gloucester, Mass. He attended Gloucester High School and Wesleyan University, and studied at Andover Theological Seminary before being ordained as a minister of the Congregational Church.

1898 The Holy Bible . . . with Marginal References and Readings . . . Elegantly Illustrated . . . John E. Potter & Company, Limited: Chicago **2086**

1 vol: (ix) (744) 748–974   32 cm   NNAB

New Oxford Quarto Edition appears at head of title page. Only illustration in cited copy is poor quality frontispiece. Copyright 1898, by John E. Potter.

1898 The Holman Comparative Self-pronouncing S. S. Teachers' Bible containing, in combined text, the Authorized and Revised versions . . . Sm. Pica 8vo. A. J. Holman and Company: Philadelphia **2087**

1 vol: (12) 13–1156 (12) 13–361 [1] (256) (20)   23 cm   NNAB

Linear Parallel Edition appears at head of title page, which has device of shield with *Let There Be Light*. Preliminary matter includes Publishers' Preface (explaining this edition), Revisers' Preface, Key to Pronunciation, List of British and American OT Revisers, and Table of Books. Preferences of the American Committee follow each Testament. Revisers' Preface and List of NT Revisers precede NT, which has no imprint on title. At end are A New Concordance by James P. Boyd, A.M. (copyright 1897) and new Biblical Atlas with Index (copyright 1898). Text printed in single column, standard verse form (no indication of poetry form), with the different readings and renderings of the AV and ERV in small type; for ERV, see 1881 NT, No 1953, and 1885 OT, No 2019. References and alternative readings and renderings are given in the margin. Copyright 1898.

DLC has separate NT of this date.

1898 The Holy Bible . . . Embellished with 852 Illustrations . . . W. B. Conkey Company: Chicago. New York **2088**

23 cm   NNAB

Similar to 1897 Christian Herald edition (No 2077) but with Analytical and Comparative Concordance Newly and Expressly Prepared for The Holman Art Bible, by James P. Boyd, at end (216 p). Contents and List of Illustrations precede each Testament. Illustrations are mostly in text. Copyright 1897, by Robert O. Law.

1898? The Holy Bible . . . [Nelson's Series]. T. Nelson and Sons: New York **2089**

1 vol: (879) (267) (vi); other matter var. paged   22 cm   NN

Added to text are Illustrated Bible Helps (64 p), A New Concordance to the Authorized and Revised Versions (311 p), Subject Index, and Pronouncing Dictionary.

Issued with or without maps.

Originally published in England but for many years printed in America. The Bible Helps were always printed in this country.

1898   The Comprehensive Teachers' Bible . . . Together with New and Revised
Helps to Bible Study. A New Concordance. Elementary Introductions to
the Hebrew and Greek Languages and an Indexed Bible Atlas . . . [Man-
hattan Press, New York, printer]. S. Bagster and Sons, Limited: London;
James Pott & Co.: New York   **2090**

1 vol: (906) (281); other matter var. paged   22 cm   DLC, NNAB
Illustrations to Bagster's Comprehensive Teachers' Edition (20 leaves) precede title page.
Order of Books, General Contents, Note on the Study of Hebrew, and Key to Pronunciation pre-
cede text. At end are Bible Helps, General Index, Concordance, Index to Maps, Comparative
Chronology, and plates and maps. Copyright 1898, by James Pott & Co.
Also published as *The Bagster Art Bible . . . profusely embellished with full page illustra-
tions . . . [J. Little and Co., Printer]*, with colored title page and same copyright as above.

1898   The Holy Bible . . . Being the Revised Version Set Forth A.D. 1881–1885,
with Revised Marginal References. Printed for the Universities of Oxford
and Cambridge. The Riverside Press: Cambridge, Mass., U. S. A., for the
Oxford University Press, James Pott and Co., Agents: New York   **2091**

1 vol: (xvi) (909) (xiv) (276)   22 cm   DLC, NN, NNAB, ViU
ERV; see 1881 NT, No 1953, and 1885 OT, No 2019. Lacks Apocrypha. Text printed in
double columns, with references in margins and alternative renderings, etc. placed at foot of
page. Preferred Renderings of the American Committee follow each Testament. Index at end.
Maps. Copyright 1898, by Oxford University Press, American Branch; Electrotyped and printed
at the Riverside Press.
In 1898 a new edition of the ERV, including the Apocrypha, was published at Oxford,
which contained a new set of references compiled mainly by Dr. F. H. A. Scrivener and
Dr. W. F. Moulton. This is the first American edition with the new references. See also following entry, No 2092.

1898   The Holy Bible . . . Being the Revised Version Set Forth 1881–1885. With
the Readings and Renderings Preferred by the American Revision Com-
panies Incorporated in the Text, and with Copyright Marginal References.
[Electrotyped and printed at the Riverside Press, Cambridge, Mass.] . . .
for the Universities of Oxford and Cambridge. Oxford University Press,
American Branch, and Cambridge University Press, James Pott & Co.,
Agents: New York   **2092**

1 vol: (xvi) (909) (xiv) (276)   21 cm   NNAB
ERV; see 1881 NT, No 1953, and 1885 OT, No 2019. This is the first edition of the ERV
issued under the authority of the two University Presses in which the American preferences
are incorporated in the text and in the margins, while the corresponding English renderings are
placed in the Appendix. Maps. Copyright 1898. See also preceding entry, No 2091.
Also published with Apocrypha following the NT (182 p); illustrated; NT title dated 1900.

1898   The New Illuminated Holy Bible Self-Pronouncing with Marginal Refer-
ences, Maps and Numerous Helps. Nearly 600 Original Illustrations . . .
Published by American Bible House for the Syndicate Publishing Company:
New York   **2093**

1 vol: (848) (279) (33)   20 cm   MH, NNAB
Announcement, Order of Books, and Key to Pronunciation precede text. Teachers' Helps at
end. Illustrated. Copyright 1898, by Frank E. Wright. See 1897 deluxe edition (No 2075) which
is similar but not identical.
MH copy has a 143-page supplement in place of the 33-page Teachers' Helps at end.

1898? The Holman New Self-Pronouncing Sunday-School Teacher's Bible . . .
Conformable to the Edition of 1611 . . . King James' Version . . . with . . .
Eighty . . . Photographic Views of Scenes in Bible Lands . . . A. J. Holman
& Co.: Philadelphia   **2094**

Reported as (6) (1264) (362) (viii)   20 cm   DLC
Pictorial Edition appears at head of title. Large Bourgeois Octavo with references. Contains Helps to Bible Study and blank pages for "Ms. notes" at end. Illustrated.
NNAB has separate NT (Red Letter Edition) with the sayings of Christ printed in red,
sepia half-tones of scenes in the Holy Land, and Psalms from a matching Bible (971–1264, 603–
677 p; 20 cm).

1898 The Teachers' Bible . . . Together with a Selection of New and Revised
Illustrative Helps To Bible Study and a New Concordance . . . Samuel Bagster and Sons, Limited: London; James Pott & Co.: New York   **2095**

1 vol: (vi) (585) (188) (34) (96) (95) (34)   19 cm   NN, NNAB
Epistle Dedicatory, Order of Books, and Chronological Order precede text. At end are
illustrations, Bible Helps, Concordance, Index to Bible Atlas, Table of Comparative Chronology,
and maps and plans (the latter printed in New York). Copyright 1898, by James Pott & Co.

1898? The Holy Bible . . . [Type set at the University Press, Oxford; printed
by the Manhattan Press, New York]. Oxford University Press, American
Branch: New York . . . London   **2096**

1 vol: (4) (1276)   15 cm   NNAB
Minion 24mo with Oxford device on title page. Has Dedication to King James and Order
of Books (2 p). 6 colored maps at end. The suggested date is based on the printer of No 2090.

1898 The Emphasised New Testament . . . Joseph Bryant Rotherham . . . Fleming H. Revell Company: New York   **2097**

26 cm   PPPD
Rotherham "Emphasised" Testament; see 1878 NT, No 1930. Similar to Wiley's edition
of 1897 (No 2083).

1898 The New Testament . . . Translated from the Latin Vulgate . . . at Rheims
. . . 1582. With Annotations, References, and . . . Index. With the Imprimatur
of the Most Rev. M. A. Corrigan . . . Benziger Brothers, Printers to the Holy
Apostolic See: New York, Cincinnati, and Chicago   **2098**

1 vol: (4) (484) 485–495   20 cm   NNAB
Rheims Version. Imprimatur signed by Michael Augustine, Archbishop of New York, 1897.
Index and Tables at end.
Pope (p 481) says the text of this NT is from Cardinal Vaughan's edition of 1896 "and
represents the English tradition in America before the Baltimore text of 1899. But this type of
text is not common in America."

1898 The Four Gospels. A New Translation from the Greek Text direct, with
Reference to the Vulgate and the Ancient Syriac Version. By Very Rev.
Francis Aloysius Spencer, O.P. Preface by His Eminence James, Cardinal
Gibbons. William H. Young & Company: New York   **2099**

Reported as (xii) (280)   20 cm   DLC
Includes *Approbatio ordinis*, Preface, Introductory Remarks, Table of Gospels for the
Church Year, and five plates.

NcAS has 1900 edition marked *Third Thousand*. NNAB has 1901 edition marked *Fourth Thousand.*

Seymour Hobart Spencer (1845–1913) planned as a youth to follow his father into Episcopal orders. In 1866 he became a Roman Catholic and, upon entering the Paulist novitiate, took the name of Francis Aloysius. After his ordination, he transferred to the Dominican order in 1871, where he was several times Superior and once Provincial. He translated the Four Gospels from the Latin Vulgate (1898) and from the Greek (1901), the latter being published in four editions. (Although all the sources consulted say that Father Spencer's translation from the Vulgate was published in 1898, no copy of a translation based on the Latin text alone has been discovered in this study. The NcAS 1900 and the NNAB 1901 copies of the Gospels are from the Greek and are copyright 1898. Their title pages read exactly like the above DLC copy and there is nothing in the translator's preface to indicate a previous edition.)

Father Spencer undertook a translation of the complete NT from the Greek texts available at the time. He died shortly after completing the manuscript, which remained unpublished for some time. In 1935, when the American hierarchy of the Catholic Church recognized the need for a new translation in English, Father Spencer's translation was brought to light. It was carefully edited and published in 1937 (No 2363) and was revised in 1940.

1899 The Holy Bible, Translated from the Latin Vulgate . . . With Annotations, References, and . . . Index. From the Last London and Dublin Editions. The Whole Revised and . . . Compared with the Latin Vulgate. Published with the Approbation of the Most Reverend John Hughes . . . P. J. Kenedy, Publisher to the Holy See, Excelsior Catholic Publishing House: New York *2100*

968 p   24 cm   NNAB

Rheims-Douay Version. Approbations, Order of Books, Table, Admonition, etc., and Catalogue of the Sacred Books precede text. Has Family Record. Frontispiece (*Crucifixion*) and Order of Books precede NT. Tables and Index at end.

1899 The Holy Bible, Translated from the Latin Vulgate . . . With Annotations, References, and . . . Index. The Whole Revised and . . . Compared with the Latin Vulgate. Published with the Approbation of His Eminence James Cardinal Gibbons, Archbishop of Baltimore . . . Benziger Brothers, Printers to the Holy See: New York, Cincinnati, Chicago   *2101*

1 vol: (1086) (306)   21 cm   NNAB

Rheims-Douay Version. Approbation of Cardinal Gibbons (1899), Preface, and Order of Books precede text. Has Family Record. At end are Index, Tables, Readings, and Order of Books. Maps.

This is a new edition, carefully revised. Some explanatory phrases have been added, not in brackets. (Pope, p 482.)

Union Catalog lists 1899? copies at NN imprinted *P. J. Kenedy and Son, New York* and *John Murphy Company, Baltimore,* but these could not be found, 1959. MiDP has copy with imprint of *H. L. Kilner & Co., Philadelphia.*

1899–1901 [The New Testament] The Modern American Bible . . . The Books of the Bible in Modern American Form and Phrase with Notes and Introduction. By Frank Schell Ballentine . . . Thomas Whittaker: New York   *2102*

5 vols   16 cm   ICU, NNAB

Despite its title, *The Modern American Bible,* only the NT was ever published. The grouping of the Books was designed to give an historical view, and they were published as follows: Part i (1899?, vi, 123 p): S. Mark. Part ii (1899?, 298 p): S. Matthew, S. Peter, S. Jude, and S. James. Part iii (1899?, 331 p): S. Luke (Gospel-Acts). Part iv (1901?, 339 p): S. Paul (Thessalonians, Corinthians, Galatians, Romans, Colossians, Ephesians, Philemon, Phillipians, i Timothy, Titus, ii Timothy, and Hebrews). Part v (1901?, xxiii, 309 p): S. John (Gospel, Letters, Revelation). All parts are undated; dates are taken from Introduction (1899) and copyrights (1899, 1901). Text printed in paragraph form, without verse numbers, in single column. Direct discourse in quotation marks and poetry printed as poetry. Extensive notes follow text.

NN has Part iv only.

The Rev. Frank Schell Ballentine (1859–1936) was affiliated with the Protestant Episcopal Church. Mr. Ballentine, on reading the Four Gospels in modern French as translated by Henri Lasserre, Paris, 1887, determined to "attempt to translate the various Books of the Bible into modern American idiomatic English." He first published the Four Gospels (*Good News — The Four Gospels in a Modern American Dress by Frank Schell Ballentine*. Good News Publishing Co., Scranton, Pennsylvania, 1897) and then turned to the translation of the complete NT. His translation is based on the Textus Receptus and later Greek texts.

1899   The New Testament . . . With all the Words Recorded Therein, as Having Been Spoken by Our Lord, Printed in Color . . . [Printed at] The Christian Herald. Louis Klopsch, Proprietor. Bible House: New York   *2103*

457 p   15 cm   BM, CSmH, NNAB

Copyright 1899 by Louis Klopsch, Entered at Stationer's Hall.

This is the first "Red Letter" NT and was many times reprinted. NNAB has third edition, 1900, and eighth edition, 1903; NN also has copy of eighth edition.

1899?   The New Testament . . . With Notes, Instructions and References . . . [Pocket Edition]. American Tract Society: New York   *2104*

15 cm   DLC

Pagination same as 1862 edition (No 1762).

1899   The New Testament . . . Clear-Type Pocket Edition . . . Fleming H. Revell Company, Publishers of Evangelical Literature: Chicago, New York, Toronto   *2105*

362 p   14 cm   ICN, NNAB, ViU

This is called the Marked NT, and has special passages underscored and marked in the margin in red and black. Copyright 1899, by the Bible Institute Colportage Association. No information has been secured to show if this was acually printed in America.

NN has copy with Oxford imprint only.

1899   The New Testament . . . American Bible Society, Instituted . . . : New York   *2106*

400 p   12 cm   NNAB

Agate 32mo. Three sets of electro plates for this book were made in 1899. Although the figure *13,150,000 Printed* appears at the foot of the Order of Books, this book is not the same as the 1868 Agate 32mo (No 1836); Agate 32mos had been printed as early as 1851 and this may be the total figure. About this time, instead of entering the number of the edition on the contents page (meaning the number of times books had been printed from the same plates), the ABS began entering the number of copies that had been printed.

Also issued with Psalms (p 401–503).

1899?   The New Testament . . . T. Nelson & Sons: New York   *2107*

Reported as 458 p   "16mo"   MiU

Long Primer 16mo Self-pronouncing Testament. Originally published in England but printed in America for some time.

1900?   The Holy Bible . . . Authorized Edition of the New Testament . . . and the Revised Version of A.D. 1881 . . . Apocrypha and Psalms . . . A. J. Holman & Co.: Philadelphia   *2108*

1 vol: (774) (104) (400); other matter var. paged   32 cm   NNAB

Holman's Royal Quarto; AV text with ERV NT (see 1881 NT, No 1953). ERV and AV NTs printed in parallel columns. Contains illuminated Ten Commandments, Temperance Pledge, Lord's Prayer, etc.

1900?   The Holy Bible . . . With Complete Concordance, Embracing Every Passage of Scripture in the Largest Editions . . . Sold by the C. Foster Publishing Co.: Philadelphia   **2109**

Reported as (6) iii–iv (16) (16) (96) (16) 9–754 (8)   32 cm   DLC
Concordance and other materials precede text. Maps at end.

1900?   The Holy Bible . . . Self-Prononuncing Edition . . . [Made specially for the Gideons]. National Bible Press: Philadelphia   **2110**

Reported as 1272 p   25 cm   IaU
The Christian Commercial Men's Association of America (now known as the Gideons, or the Gideons, International) resulted from a meeting in the fall of 1898 of John H. Nicholson of Janesville, Wisconsin, and Samuel E. Hill of Beloit in a hotel in Boscobel, Wisconsin, and was organized, with William J. Knights of Wild Rose, Wisconsin, in July 1899 at Beaver Dam. Their inspiration was the story of Gideon in Judges 6 and 7; their initial concern was the religious life of commercial men who spent long periods away from home, staying in hotels. They began placing Bibles in hotels in 1908. The movement extended to serve other institutions and became widespread here and abroad.

Among later editions issued were the following: Master Guide Red Letter Edition in 1939? (DLC); Minute Reference Red Letter Edition in 1943?, printed and bound especially for Good Will Distributors, Gastonia, N. C., copyright 1943, by National Bible Press; and Gideon Edition in 1944? (MiD).

1900?   The Holy Bible . . . National Bible Press: Philadelphia   **2111**

1 vol: (10) 5–1223 (21)   24 cm   NNAB
Self Pronouncing Edition appears at head of title page, which has National device. Pica Octavo with center references. Preliminary matter includes presentation page, frontispiece, Order of Books, Tables of Pronunciation Marks, and Epistle Dedicatory. Family Record follows OT. Table for Daily Bible Reading and Atlas at end.

IU has 1924 edition.

1900?   The Red-Letter Edition of the Holy Bible . . . Showing the Whole of Our Lord's Words in Red . . . Nelson's Series. [Printed by Berwick and Smith Co., Norwood, Mass.] Thomas Nelson and Sons: New York   **2112**

1 vol: (841) (256); other matter var. paged   21 cm   NNAB
Self-Pronouncing Bourgeois Octavo with center references; no chronology. Contains Epistle Dedicatory, Order of Books, Publisher's Note on Pronunciation System (New York 1900), and Key. List of Alternative Pronunciations, Bible Dictionary (copyright 1900, 118 p), Concordance (243 p), and Atlas follow text.

NN has undated Teacher's Edition (not Red Letter) with same pagination. MiU has copy that seems similar, dated 195–?.

1900?   The Holy Bible . . . [Nelson's Series] . . . [Printed by Berwick & Smith, Norwood Press, Norwood, Mass.] Thomas Nelson & Sons: New York   **2113**

1 vol: (2) (600) (2) (186)   21 cm   NNAB
Minion Octavo, Large Page, Single Column Reference (no chronology) edition. Dedication to King James and order of Books precede text. A Concise Bible Dictionary (copyright 1900, vi, 118 p), Combined Concordance (243 p) and Atlas follow text.

1900?   The Holy Bible . . . The Wm. Hengerer Co.: Buffalo   **2114**

Reported as (812) (32)   19 cm   DLC
Helps to the Study of the Bible follow text.

1900   The Holy Bible . . . Self-Pronouncing Edition . . . National Bible Press:
Philadelphia   **2115**

Reported as (viii) (638) (195) [1]   19 cm   Nat'l. Bible Press
Nonpareil type. A frequently reprinted standard edition for which similar plates were also
owned and used by the Oxford University Press, Nelson, Winston, and possibly by Holman.
There were also similar plates for Red Letter editions.
    NNAB has undated editions published by Nelson (Red Letter) and Winston with no
indication of place of printing. NNAB also has editions (undoubtedly printed in England)
with imprint of Henry Frowde, New York, and Humphrey Milford, New York (both probably
by Oxford), and James Pott and Company (one for the Connecticut Bible Society). These are
all paged (8) (638) 641–835, with several combinations of added matter.

1900?   The Holy Bible . . . A. J. Holman & Co.: Philadelphia   **2116**

1 vol: (804) 11–55   19 cm   NN
Has Helps to Bible Study at end. Plates and colored maps.

1900?   The Self-Interpreting New Testament, compiled and arranged by Ashley
S. Johnson. [Printed by Ogden Brothers & Company, Knoxville, Tenn.]
Published by the author: Kimberlin Heights [Tennessee]   **2117**

Reported as 424 p   25 cm   TNDC
Mr. Johnson was a member of the Disciples of Christ.

1900–01   The Twentieth Century New Testament. A Translation into Modern
English Made from the Original Greek. Westcott & Hort's text — In three
Parts . . . Fleming H. Revell Company . . . : New York   **2118**

3 vols: Part i, (vii) (254); Part ii, (x) (4) 259–380; Part iii, (10) 381–513   19 cm
NNAB, PP
    PP has Part i only: The Five Historical Books (undated, printed by Press of Braunworth &
Co., Brooklyn). NNAB has Parts ii and iii only: Paul's Letters to the Churches (copyright 1900;
printed by Caxton Press, New York); The Pastoral, Personal, and General Letters, and the
Revelation (copyright 1901, printed by Caxton Press, New York). Tentative edition, printed
in single column, paragraph form, with verse numbers in right margin. Has section headings.
OT quotations, etc. appear in italics. Poetry in appropriate form; quotation marks for direct
discourse. References at foot of page.
    NNAB also has two copies of Part i printed in slightly different form from Parts ii and
iii: one with no printer, but probably an American edition; the second an 1899 third edition
by Revell, printed in England.
    This translation, published simultaneously in New York and London, was made "by a com-
pany of about twenty persons, members of various sections of the Christian Church" in England.
In addition to the Westcott and Hort text, the committee used the manuscript of the then unpublished Weymouth translation (see 1943 NT, No 2418). The project grew out of the desire
on the part of a number of people for a modern English version. Among them were Mrs. Mary
Higgs, the first woman to take a science degree at Girton College (Cambridge), a Congregationalist minister's wife, Sunday school teacher, and mother; and Ernest de Merindol Malan,
a railway engineer and Greek student. A group of interested persons — who insisted on ano-
nymity — worked for a number of years at considerable personal sacrifice and without any compensation. Some years ago their records were given to the John Rylands Library at Manchester,
England. The translation was popular in the United States for many years. (See Simms, p 278–
281.)

1900? The New Testament ... The Self-Pronouncing Edition with References ...
Brethren Publishing House: Elgin, Illinois   **2119**

Reported as 490 p   18 cm   IU

Has cover title: *The Pilgrim Bible. Lessons Marked for Christian Youth. The Blue Lines to Heaven.*

1900? The New Testament . . . [Self-Pronouncing Edition]. American Baptist
Publication Society: Philadelphia [etc.]   **2120**

Reported as 313 p   16 cm   ICU

1900 The Self-Pronouncing New Testament . . . Containing the Sayings of Christ
Printed in Red ... A. J. Holman Co.: Philadelphia   **2121**

1 vol: (421) (5)   12 cm   DLC, NNAB

Holman's Edition appears at head of title. Nonpareil 32mo with Key to Pronunciation before text and Publisher's Advertisement at end. Copyright 1900, by A. J. Holman & Co.

1900? The New Testament ... J. H. Sears & Co., Inc. ... : New York   **2122**

515 p   11 cm   IaU, NNAB

1901 The Holy Bible, Translated from the Latin Vulgate . . . With Annotations,
References, and . . . Index . . . With Approbation of the Most Reverend
Archbishop of New York . . . P. J. Kenedy, Publisher to the Holy Apostolic
See, Excelsior Catholic Publishing House: New York   **2123**

24 cm   NNAB

Rheims-Douay Version. Reprint of 1899 edition (No 2100).

1901 The Holy Bible . . . Being the Version set forth A.D. 1611 . . . Revised A.D.
1881–1885. Newly edited by the American Revision Committee A.D. 1901.
Standard Edition. [Printed by Norwood Press, Cushing and Co., Berwick
and Smith.] Thomas Nelson & Sons: New York   **2124**

1 vol: (xiv) (969) (3) (xvi) (295) [1]   23 cm   IU, MH–AH, NN, NNAB

Long Primer Square Octavo. Verso of title has statement from the secretaries of the OT and NT committees as to the authenticity of editions published by Nelson and Sons. Prefaces to the American edition and to the ERV editions of 1885 and 1881 (see OT, No 2019 and NT, No 1953) precede the text of each Testament. The OT and NT are followed by appendices showing differences between ERV and this text. Printed in double columns, paragraph form, with verse numbers in text. Has center references and alternative readings and renderings in outer margins. Page headings are in bold-face type. 12 maps with index at end (10 p). Copyright 1901, "To insure purity of text."

This is the first edition of the ASV — properly known as the American Standard Edition of the Revised Version, or more commonly, as the American Standard Version — which was issued on Aug 26, 1901. Although the British Committee disbanded soon after publication of the ERV, its American counterpart kept at work. Members of the American Committee felt that the lists of their preferences printed in the ERV editions did not adequately represent their wishes, as the lists had been prepared late and had not been fully examined by the British group. They further felt that often the language of the ERV was more British than American. According to agreement, they were unable to sanction editions other than those of the two university presses for fourteen years, but as that period ended they were ready with a revised text. The new version had page headings; altered paragraphing, punctuation, and use of italics; revised marginal readings and renderings and cross-references; and changes in the text which the whole American Committee had approved, including the use of "Jehovah" for the Tetragrammaton. The Committee's reasons for these changes are fully set forth in the prefaces to both Testaments, which appear in most Nelson editions.

This version represented the best scholarship and Biblical learning of its time and was more widely used than the ERV both in this country and in Britain. It was copyrighted by Thomas Nelson and Sons, who had invested considerable sums in the project. In 1929 the copyright was renewed by the International Council of Religious Education, but the text was still printed exclusively by the Nelson firm. These editions all carry on the verso of title page the statement, "This Standard American Edition of the Revised Version of the Bible, and editions in conformity with it published by Messrs. Thomas Nelson & Sons and certified by this endorsement, are the only editions authorized by the American Committee of Revision — George E. Day, Secretary of the Committee and of the Old Testament Committee and by J. Henry Thayer, Secretary of the New Testament Committee." Editions printed before 1910 carry the address of the publisher as 37 East 18th Street. From 1910 to 1930, the firm was on Fourth Avenue, the address appearing variously as Fourth Avenue Building, Fourth Avenue and 27th Street, 381 Fourth Avenue, and 381–385 Fourth Avenue. The Nelson firm then moved to 385 Madison Avenue, and in 1951 to 19 East 47th Street. The address seldom appears in recent years.

NN has the printer's copy for the first edition of the ASV OT (4 vols, 25 cm) placed on indefinite loan in 1924 by Thomas Nelson and Sons: Vol i, Genesis-Ruth, 621 p; Vol ii, i Samuel-Esther, 518 p; Vol iii, Job-Song of Solomon, 355 p; Vol iv, Isaiah-Malachi, 526 p. It is the British first edition of the ERV, 1885, printed in single column, with MS references in the outer margin and text changes in the inner margin. A rubber stamp has been used for "Jehovah." MS note on fly-leaf of each vol reads, "From this copy in four volumes was printed The Standard Edition of the American Revised Version, 1901. Horace Osgood, member of the American Revision Company, 1874–1901. Given to Tileston F. Chambers, January 1905. All the references in this volume were made by H. Osgood."

1901? The Holy Bible . . . Being the Version Set Forth A.D. 1611 . . . Revised A.D. 1881–1885. Newly Edited by the American Revision Committee A.D. 1901. Standard Edition. Thomas Nelson & Sons: New York   **2125**

1 vol: (2) (ix) [1] (922) (2) (vi) (285) [1]   21 cm   NNAB

ASV; see previous entry, No 2124. Bourgeois Octavo (smaller than the first edition) with center references but without the 1881–1885 Prefaces or List of Variants. At end are Index to Maps (8 p) and 12 p of colored maps.

NNAB also has similar edition of the OT (with black and white maps, copyright 1913), a separate NT, and later editions of the complete Bible.

1901 The Holy Bible. Red Letter Edition . . . Many Thousands of Parallel References and Marginal Readings. Old Testament — Passages and Incidents Quoted or Referred to By Our Lord and Saviour Printed in Red . . . New Testament — The Words Recorded as Having Been Spoken by Our Lord and Saviour Printed in Red. Old Testament Passages Generally Regarded as Prophetic of Our Saviour Indicated by * . . . Large Type. Octavo . . . The Christian Herald, Louis Klopsch, Proprietor, Bible House: New York   **2126**

1 vol: (xvi) 17–1272 (48) (268) (32)   21 cm   DLC, NNAB

Self-Pronouncing Helps and References appears at head of title. Preliminary matter includes From the Fly-Leaf of D. L. Moody's Bible, Order of Books, Synopsis of Books of the Bible, Key to Pronunciation, and Explanatory Note. The Bible Readers' Aids edited by C. H. H. Wright (American Edition), A Word Book, and maps at end. Supplementary matter is illustrated. Copyright 1901, by Louis Klopsch; NT copyright 1899, by Louis Klopsch.

This Bible was often reprinted. PPPrHi has 1902 edition. NNAB has editions of 1904 and 1913, one of the latter with added copyrights of 1905 by Klopsch and 1913 by the Christian Herald, and another imprinted *World Syndicate Company, Inc., New York*, with the 1905 and 1913 copyrights.

1901 The Holman New Self-Pronouncing Sunday-School Teacher's Bible . . . Translated out of the Original Tongues . . . Minion 8vo. Refs. [Type com-

posed by the Riverside Press, Cambridge, Mass.] A. J. Holman & Co.:
Philadelphia   *2127*

1 vol: (1034) (109) (128) (94) (8) (12)   20 cm   NNAB

Preface, Order of Books, and Key to Pronunciation precede text. Has Teachers' Reference Hand Book (copyright 1901), Bible Dictionary by James P. Boyd (copyright 1896), Four Thousand Questions and Answers, Bible Atlas Index, and colored maps and plans (copyright 1898) at end. Copyright 1892, by A. J. Holman & Co.

In this edition the chapter headings have been changed and Arabic instead of Roman numerals are used for chapters.

1901?   The Teachers' Bible . . . With . . . New and Revised Helps to Bible Study,
a New Concordance, Elementary Introduction to the Hebrew and Greek
Languages, and an Indexed Bible Atlas . . . [Printed by Braunworth & Co.,
Brooklyn, New York]. Bagster and Sons, Ltd.: London; James Pott & Co.:
New York   *2128*

1 vol: (929); other matter var. paged   20 cm   NNAB

Minion Octavo with references in center column and chronology. Contains Epistle Dedicatory and Order of Books. At end are Illustrations to Bagster's Teachers' Bible (16 plates), Bible Helps (90 p), Symbolical Language of Scripture (4 p), Bagster's Concordance, Atlas, and maps. Copyright 1901, by James Pott & Co.

1901?   The Holman New Self-Pronouncing Sunday-School Teacher's Bible . . . The
Text Conformbale to that of the Edition of 1611 . . . A. J. Holman & Co.:
Philadelphia   *2129*

Reported as (1264) (64) (128) (viii)   20 cm   DLC

Contains A New Gallery of Illustrations Portraying Recent Archaeological Excavations and Discoveries in Babylonia, etc., revised, selected and described by Rev. H. V. Hilprecht (A. J. Holman & Co., Philadelphia, 1897). Illustrated. See 1898?, No 2094.

1901?   The Holy Bible . . . Being the Version Set Forth A.D. 1611 . . . Revised
A.D. 1881–1885. Newly Edited by the American Revision Committee A.D.
1901. Standard Edition . . . Thomas Nelson & Sons: New York   *2130*

1 vol: (viii) (814) (vi) (252)   18 cm   IU, NNAB

ASV; see 1901, No 2124. Minion 16mo Black Faced Pronouncing Reference Bible from plates by J. J. Little & Co., New York, printed by Norwood Press.

NNAB has two copies purchased in 1907, with publisher's address at 37 E. 18th Street: one has Index (8 p) and 12 colored maps. A third copy, with "To insure purity of text" added after copyright and address (381–385 Fourth Avenue), also has Nelson's Concise Bible Dictionary (copyright 1900, 122 p), Concordance (copyright 1903 with 18th Street address, 234 p), and Index with colored maps. NNFM has Masonic Edition with presentation page and plate, *The Light of Masonry.*

1901?   The Holy Bible . . . Being the version set forth A.D. 1611 compared with
the most ancient authorities and revised A.D. 1881–1885. Newly Edited by
the American Revision Committee A.D. 1901. Standard Edition. Thomas
Nelson & Sons: New York   *2131*

1 vol: (xi) [1] (1002) (vii) [1] (300)   16 cm   NNAB

ASV; see 1901, No 2124. Minion 24mo, without references. Includes ASV Prefaces but not the ERV ones nor the variants from the ERV. Cited copy purchased in 1903.

NNAB also has the following editions (all undated) printed from the same plates: Sunday School Scholar's Edition illustrated in color; contains Practical Helps for Sunday-School Scholars, edited by A. F. Schauffler, D.D. (copyright 1905, by Nelson; 64 p and 12 colored maps); purchased in 1907. Boy Scout Edition (purchased 1916) bound in khaki with Scout emblem on cover; publisher's address listed as 381–385 Fourth Avenue; "To insure Purity of Text" appears on verso of title page; contains a 6-page insert with reading suggestions for Scouts, The Scout Oath and The Scout Law, and How to become a Scout; 12 colored maps (NNAB also has separate NT from this edition). An edition with sepia reproductions of paintings and 12 colored maps. An edition bound in 2 vols, boxed, and printed on india paper; publisher's address listed as 381–385 Fourth Avenue; "To insure Purity of Text" added on verso of title page; purchased in 1911.

1901?   The Holy Bible . . . Revised 1881–1885. Newly Edited by the American Revision Committee 1901. Standard Edition. T. Nelson & Sons: New York   *2132*

1 vol: (viii) (822) (vi) (242)   15 cm   IU, NNAB
ASV; see 1901, No 2124.
NNAB copy is a Ruby 32mo Pocket edition purchased in 1909; publisher's address listed as 37 E. 18th Street; no printer. NNFM has Masonic Edition with Masonic presentation pages, Masonic quotation, and special cover.

1901   The Emphasised New Testament; A New Translation Designed to Set Forth the Exact Meaning, the Proper Terminology, and the Graphic Style of the Sacred Original; Arranged to Show at a Glance Narrative, Speech, Parallelism, and Logical Analysis; and Emphasised Throughout After the Idioms of the Greek Tongue. With Select References and an Appendix of Notes. By Joseph Rotherham. John Wiley & Sons: New York   *2133*

Reported as 272 p   26 cm   PLatS
Rotherham's "Emphasised" Version; see 1878 NT, No 1930.

1902?   The Indexed Bible. Alphabetically Indexed with Reference to Biblical Biography, Geography, History and Theology . . . Illustrated with Over Four Thousand Questions and Answers . . . This Work has been Written, Compiled and Printed Under the Special Supervision of the Jno. A. Dickson Publishing Co. . . . The Jno. A. Dickson Publishing Co.: Evansville, Indiana   *2134*

Reported as (874); other matter var. paged   29 cm   DLC
Has illustrations and maps.
DLC also has copy imprinted *The Indexed Bible Publishing Co., Evansville, Indiana*; and two other similar editions with Chicago as place of publication and varying added matter, dated 1905? and 1907?.

1902   The Self-Pronouncing S. S. Teachers' Combination . . . Bible Showing in Simple Form all Changes, Additions and Omissions made by the Revisers in the King James Version . . . Conformable to the Edition of 1611 . . . The Southwestern Company: Nashville   *2135*

1 vol: 17–871 3–288; other matter var. paged   20 cm   NNAB
        Similar to 1895 edition (No 2063) but not identical. *Fine Art Edition* appears at head of title page. Printed in Large Face Minion type with ERV renderings at foot of page in smaller type. Preliminary matter includes frontispiece, Preface, Key to Pronunciation, Order of Books, Synopsis of the Books, and Note on How to Use Combination Bible. At end are Bible Helps (64 p), Concordance (144 p), 5000 Questions and Answers (94 p), MS note pages, Smith's Bible Dictionary (112 p), Indexed Atlas, and maps and plans. Has colored illustrations. NT has no imprint — possibly printed by National Publishing Co. Copyright 1895 and 1902, by J. R. Jones.

1902 The Holy Bible ... A. J. Holman and Company: Philadelphia **2136**

Reported as (610) 611–800 (121)   17 cm   LN

Holman Edition appears at head of general title. NT title reads *The Self-pronouncing New Testament ... Agate 32mo.* At end are Scholars' Ready Reference Handbook of Biblical History, Tabular Chronologies, and Specially Arranged Subjects.

1902 The Holy Bible ... National Bible Press: Philadelphia **2137**

1 vol: (836) (254)   14 cm   NNAB

Self-pronouncing Edition appears at head of title page. Agate 32mo with chapters numbered serially. Contains Helps for Sunday School Scholars (copyright 1902, by J. R. Jones). Sepia illustrations.

1902 The Self-Pronouncing Holy Bible ... A. J. Holman: Philadelphia **2138**

1 vol: (842) (261)   14 cm   NNAB

Holman Edition appears at head of title page. Agate 32mo with Publisher's Preface, Order of Books, and Key to Pronunciation before text, and maps at end. Copyright 1902, by A. J. Holman & Co. This book is not the same as the other Holman Bible for this year (No 2136).

1902 [Old Testament] The Emphasised Bible, a new translation designed to set forth the exact meaning ... Joseph Bryant Rotherham ... Fleming H. Revell Company: New York, Chicago, Toronto **2139**

3 vols: Vol I, (288); Vol II, 289–608; Vol III, 609–920   26 cm   NjMD

Rotherham "Emphasised" Version; see 1878 NT, No 1930. Vol I: Genesis-Ruth. Vol II: 1 Samuel-Psalms. Vol III: Proverbs-Malachi.

In *Reminiscences ... by J. B. Rotherham*, J. George Rotherham says: "In the autumn of 1902 my father visited Glasgow. The printing of the *Emphasised Old Testament* had just been completed" (p 93). There is no indication in this OT as to place of printing or copyright; it may not have been printed in the United States.

1902? The Twentieth Century New Testament ... Complete in one Volume ... Fleming H. Revell Co.: New York **2140**

1 vol: (17) (513)   23 cm   NN

Twentieth Century Version; see 1900–01 NT, No 2118. The three parts of the tentative edition are gathered into one volume and p 501 has been reset.

The Revell Company has a copy of an illustrated subscription edition. DLC, NcD, and ViU have 1903? edition (19 cm).

1902 The Reference Passage Bible New Testament; Comprising All the Books of the New Testament Complete, Arranged in Topics, with the Reference Passages Given in Full Text Upon the Same Page ... The Gospels are Arranged in Parallel Columns, in Chronological Order, Giving Time and Place. The Acts, Epistles and Revelation are Arranged in Consecutive Order with Instructions, Maps and Indices. Compiled by I. N. Johns ... The Alpha Publishing Co.: Sunbury, Pa. **2141**

Reported as (vii) (1438)   21 cm   ViU

Gospels printed in harmony form in four columns on two pages with reference passages in smaller type. Rest of text printed in double columns with all referred passages given in full after each section, usually covering the facing right page. Tables and maps at end. Copyright 1902.

Later printings with this copyright date have varying pagination.

1902?   Translation of the New Testament from the Original Greek. By Rev. W. B.
Godbey ... M. W. Knapp, Office of God's Revivalist: Cincinnati   **2142**

373 p   20 cm   ICU, NNAB

Preliminary matter includes Dedication To the Holiness People in All Lands, Prologue, and Synopsis of the Harmony. Text of Gospels printed as Gospel Harmony (based on Robinson) in parallel columns. Text of Acts-Revelation printed in paragraph form, single column, with verse numbers in text. Apologue at end.

The Rev. W. B. Godbey (1833–1920) was a minister of the Methodist Episcopal Church South, the author of NT commentaries, and a prominent "holiness" preacher. His translation is based on Tischendorf's edition of the Codex Sinaiticus which he regarded as an infallible copy of the original text. He did not follow the Codex Sinaiticus order of books and omitted the Epistle of Barnabas and the Shepherd of Hermas. In the Prologue he states that the Codex Sinaiticus was published in 1859, the year he graduated from college, and shortly thereafter he secured a copy of Tischendorf's edition. When he was assigned to camp-meetings in 1884 he began expounding the Scriptures from the Greek and many people urged him to publish a translation. After 20 years he yielded to this pressure.

1902   [New Testament] The American Bible ... The Books of the Bible in Modern
English for American Readers. Frank Schell Ballentine. Good News Publishing Company: Scranton, Pennsylvania   **2143**

5 vols   15 cm   MB, NN, NNAB

Ballentine Version; see 1899–1901 NT, No 2102. Vol ɪ: Matthew, Peter, Jude, James, Hebrews (345 p). Vol ɪɪ: Mark (123 p). Vol ɪɪɪ: Luke (Gospel-Acts; 331 p). Vol ɪᴠ: John (Gospel, Letters, Revelation; 309 p). Vol ᴠ: Paul (300 p). Each vol has names of Books included on title page. Introduction dated 1901. Copyright 1902.

1902?   The Self-Pronouncing New Testament ... A. J. Holman & Co.: Philadelphia
2144

Reported as 261 p   14 cm   DLC

This is the NT of Holman's Self-Pronouncing Bible of this year (No 2138). *Holman Edition* appears at head of title.

1902?   The "International" Christian Worker's New Testament. Indexed and
Marked by the Best Methods of Bible Marking on all Subjects Connected
with the Theme of Salvation ... Printed and Bound at the International
Press: Philadelphia   **2145**

432 p   13 cm   NNAB

Title in red and black with device, two halves of globe between torches and *International*. Explanations appear on verso of title page; Explanation of Markings (1 p) follows. Has Summary of References by various subjects (7 p) at end. Copyright 1902, by John C. Winston Co. See International Bible Agency Bible 1892?, No 2053.

NNAB has another copy imprinted *Mennonite Publishing House, Scottsdale, Pa.* (425 p). DLC has two copies: one same as above but imprinted *The J. C. Winston Co.;* the other dated 1903.

1902?   The New Testament ... T. Nelson & Sons: New York   **2146**

Reported as 463 p   10 cm   DLC

Ruby 32mo. Nelson was very active in producing new editions in this country during this period; this NT is probably one of those produced here and entered at the copyright office.

1903?   The Holy Bible ... King James' Version. Marginal References. 20th Century Edition ... A. J. Holman & Co.: Philadelphia   **2147**

Reported as 1232 p   33 cm   DLC

Pictorial Family Bible appears on added title page, in color. This is a self-pronouncing edition with illustrations and maps. The 20th Century Edition is first listed in Holman's Catalog of 1904/05.

ViU–L reports copy with 1040 p, which may be same as above.

1903?   The Holy Bible ... Self-Pronouncing Edition ... America Publishing Co.: Chicago   **2148**

Reported as (667) (157) 669–879; other matter var. paged   31 cm   MH–AH

With Apocrypha. Frontispiece and plates, some colored. Added matter includes Introduction, references, maps, History of Denominations, Story of the Books of the Bible, Bible Dictionary, Questions and Answers, Concordance, Metrical Psalms, and Subject Index. The latest copyright date of added material is 1902.

1903   The Pulpit Bible, by Joseph Parker ... Funk & Wagnalls: New York   **2148A**

Reported as 1351 p   30 cm   NcD

Contains complete text with commentary and a Textual Index to Dr. Parker's Works.

This work was first published in England in 1901 by Hodder and Stoughton. There is no indication in the cited copy that it was not printed in this country. Dr. Parker had earlier published a commentary, without text, in several volumes.

1903   The Holy Bible ... With the Marginal Readings Adopted by General Convention. Authorized to be read in Churches ... [Printed by Norwood Press, Norwood, Mass.]. Thomas Nelson & Sons: New York   **2149**

1 vol: (1507) (279)   23 cm   DLC, NNAB, USl, ViU

With Apocrypha. At end are colored maps and an Appendix containing a selection of renderings preferred by the Commission on Marginal Readings to those in the text or margin of the Bible, but not to be used in public reading. The suggested changes appear in the margins with the related word or words in the text underscored. Copyright 1903, by Thomas Nelson and Sons.

In order to provide an English Bible preserving the AV text but reflecting modern scholarship and changes in the English language, the General Convention of the Protestant Episcopal Church in 1895 appointed a Commission of Bishops and Presbyters (reappointed in 1898) to consider marginal readings that could be "authorized for the instruction of our people." To this end they studied the marginal readings of the 1611 edition of the AV and prepared a report listing suggested marginal readings from the AV and ERV and others based on further study of the Hebrew, Greek, Latin, Syriac, and other early versions

NNAB has a *Report of the Joint Committee on Marginal Readings in the Bible to the General Convention of 1901* (249, 82 p, 23 cm), giving the members of the committee, all the suggested changes (except for the Apocrypha), 82 p of specimen pages, and one leaf in lectern size. In the specimen pages the suggested changes are printed in smaller type above the word or words to be replaced, which are underscored. Copyright by Arthur C. A. Hall and Charles W. E. Body, members of the Committee.

The commission consisted of 5 Bishops and 5 clergymen, of whom 2 died and 4 resigned before the work was completed, others being appointed to replace them. A report on the NT issued in 1898 listed more changes than were included in the 1901 report.

1903?   The Holy Bible ... [International Series]. International Bible Agency: New York   **2150**

Reported as (1347) (48)   17 cm   DLC

Contains Practical Aids for Sunday-School Scholars, edited and arranged from the works of Rev. Charles H. Wright, and others. Illustrations and maps. See 1902? International NT, No 2145.

MiU and NNAB have copies imprinted *A. C. McClurg Co., Chicago*, and marked Large Minion 12mo. Clear Type Edition; Practical Aids not included.

[*5664*] *1903* תהלים The Book of Psalms. The Jewish Publication Society of America: Philadelphia   *2151*

311 p   13 cm   NNAB

The facing series title reads: חורה נביאים וכתובים *The Twenty-four Books of the Holy Scriptures. Translated from the Massoretic Text for the Jewish Publication Society of America.* Copyright 1903. For the complete OT in the Jewish Publication Society Version, see 1917, No 2234.

Before the turn of the century initial steps were taken to produce a new English version of the Hebrew Scriptures for Jews. In 1892, the Jewish Publication Society of America selected a committee, headed by Dr. Morris Jastrow and, from 1903, by Dr. Solomon Schechter, to procure scholars to undertake independent translations of the various books. (A list of the translators can be found in the Preface to the 1917 Bible, No 2234.) Because of the complexity of this plan, the project languished from 1901 to 1908, and only the above Book of Psalms, translated by Kaufman Kohler and revised by the committee, was issued in this period.

The Book of Psalms in the 1917 OT is a revision of this text. It was again issued separately in 1925 in a format resembling the 1903 edition, but the text is that of the 1917 version (289 p, 13 cm, NNAB).

1903?   The Self-Pronouncing New Testament . . . With the Words of Jesus Printed in Red . . . [No publisher or place]   *2152*

Reported as 3–255 [1] (67) [1]   19 cm   ViU

Red Letter Art Edition appears at head of title page. Words of Jesus printed in red. Contains The Prayers of Jesus (1 p) and The Book of Psalms (copyright 1903, by J. R. Jones). Illustrated with plates printed on both sides, colored maps, and plan. Possibly published by National Publishing Co., Philadelphia?

1903   The Worker's New Testament. Self-Pronouncing Vest-Pocket Edition . . . with Scripture References to be Used in Meeting All Kinds of Religious Difficulties; Hints and Helps to the Study of the New Testament, by Rev. William Evans . . . J. S. Ziegler & Co.: Chicago   *2153*

Reported as 334 p   15 cm   DLC

1904?   The Holy Bible . . . Being the Version Set Forth A.D. 1611 . . . Revised A.D. 1881–1885. Newly Edited by the American Revision Committee A.D. 1901. Standard Edition. American Bible Society . . . Published by Thomas Nelson & Sons: New York   *2154*

1 vol: (4) (1040) (8) (304)   33 cm   NNAB

ASV; see 1901, No 2124. English Quarto Pulpit Bible printed for the ABS by Nelson. For ABS editions of the ASV, see note under 1905, No 2169. Does not have Prefaces or references. Contains Family Record (4 p).

1904?   The Holy Bible Containing the Old and New Testaments and Apocrypha . . . [Plates designed and electrotyped by D. B. Updike, the Merrymount Press]. R. H. Hinkley Company: Boston   *2155*

14 vols   25 cm   DLC, NN, NNAB

Each volume is separately paged. Dedication to King James precedes text, which is printed in paragraph form without verse numbers but with chapter numbers above, at inner corners. Illustrated with photogravure plates of famous paintings.

An edition of 86 copies was printed on Japan paper. Another edition of 1,000 copies on handmade paper was issued with the imprint of the Grolier Society (BM, 1907). Unbound sheets seem to have been purchased at various times and bound up by other distributors. Neither the R. H. Hinkley Company nor the Grolier Society has been able to supply full data. PMck has 1909 copy; NBuG has one dated 1920?

1904? The Holy Bible . . . [A. J. Holman Co.: Philadelphia]   **2156**

"4to"   MH

Union Catalog card has "Holman Self-Explanatory Edition, with Text Fully Elucidated by Explanatory and Critical Notes and Introductory Observations on Each Book." *Pictorial Family Bible* appears on added illustrated title page. Plates, maps, and other illustrations.

1904? The Holy Bible . . . A. J. Holman: Philadelphia   **2157**

19 cm   DLC

Holman Edition appears at head of title page.

1904–27 The Student's Old Testament Logically and Chronologically Arranged and Translated by Charles Foster Kent . . . Charles Scribner's Sons: New York   **2158**

6 vols   23 cm   NNAB

Vol I: Narratives of the Beginnings of Hebrew History from the Creation to the Establishment of the Hebrew Kingdom .. with Maps and Chronological Chart . . . 1904 (xxxv, 382 p). Vol II: Israel's Historical and Biographical Narratives from the Establishment of the Hebrew Kingdom to the End of the Maccabean Struggle . . . with Maps and Chronological Charts . . . 1905 (xxxi, 506 p). Vol III: The Sermons, Epistles and Apocalypses of Israel's Prophets from the Beginning of the Assyrian Period to the End of the Maccabean Struggle . . . with Maps and Chronological Charts . . . 1910 (xxv, 516 p). Vol IV: Israel's Laws and Legal Precedents from the Days of Moses to the Closing of the Legal Canon . . . with Plans and Diagrams . . . 1907 (xxxv, 301 p). Vol V: The Songs, Hymns, and Prayers of the Old Testament . . . 1914 (xxi, 305 p). Vol VI: Proverbs and Didactic Poems . . . [with the collaboration of C. C. Torrey and F. C. Porter] . . . 1927 (xxvii, 200 p).

In his preface to Vol I, Prof. Kent describes his purpose in the following terms:

> While this work aims to do three things, (1) to rearrange the writings of the Old Testament in a logical order, (2) to indicate their approximate dates and the classes of writers from which they come, and the more important reasons for the critical analysis of the different books, and (3) to introduce the reader by means of a clear translation to the beauty and thought of the original, it also seeks by occasional interpretative notes upon obscure passages, and by titles and brief side-headings, to make clear the thought of each section and the logical relations of the parts to the whole. (p x)
>
> Moreover, the classification must be more fundamental than that of a mere rearrangement of the books, for many of them are composite, containing the most varied material drawn from originally distinct sources. (p vi)

In Vol I the text, which is incomplete, is arranged according to possible sources. Poetry is printed in appropriate form.

Charles Foster Kent, Ph.D. (1867–1925) was a Congregationalist Biblical scholar who became Woolsey Professor of Biblical Literature at Yale in 1901. His aim was to translate the original texts into their modern English equivalents. He sought to conserve all that was good in previous translations, indicating in the margins any fundamentally different reading and preserving the Hebrew idiom where "thoroughly naturalized" into English. He also edited a 6-vol Historical Bible with an annotated text, various books on Biblical history, and served as joint editor with Frank Knight Sanders on *The Messages of the Bible*, a projected 12-vol set of which 11 vols were published. See also Kent's Shorter Bible (1918 NT, No 2242, and 1921 OT, No 2253) in which he was assisted by other scholars. George Dahl in *DAB* says of Kent that he "did more than any other American scholar of his day to make accessible to the public the significant results of modern biblical study."

Professor Kent served as co-editor with Henry A. Sherman, head of the Department of Religious Literature of Charles Scribner's Sons, for the purpose of translating and arranging *The Children's Bible, Selections fom the Old and New Testaments*, Charles Scribner's Sons, New York, 1922 (xviii, 329 p; 24 cm; NNAB). This is Bible text "in the language of the child" — essentially the AV simplified and printed in modern literary style to meet the minds of children.

1904–39   An American Commentary on the Old Testament . . . American Baptist
     Publication Society: Philadelphia   **2159**

Variously paged   23 cm   PPABP

This commentary consists of books published separately and bound in various combinations. The text is that of the AV, except in Ezekiel which has ASV with Matthews' own translation.
Name of editor, copyright date, and pagination follow title below:

> Genesis.   Calvin Goodspeed and D. M. Welton, c. 1908, 253 p.
> Exodus.   Walter R. Betteridge, c. 1914, 405 p.
> Leviticus.   George F. Genung, c. 1905, 108 p.
> Numbers.   George F. Genung, c. 1906, 144 p.
> Deuteronomy.   Walter R. Betteridge, c. 1915, 130 p.
> Joshua.   George F. Genung, c. 1931, 113 p.
> Judges.   Daniel M. Welton, c. 1931, 102 p.
> Ruth.   John B. Gough Pidge, c. 1931, 19 p.
> Samuel.   I. G. Matthews, c. 1931, 182 p.
> Job.   J. T. Marshall, c. 1904, 131 p.
> Psalms.   George R. Berry, c. 1934, 251 p.
> Proverbs.   George R. Berry, c. 1904, 99 p.
> Ecclesiastes.   J. T. Marshall, c. 1904, 40 p.
> Song of Songs.   George E. Merrill, c. 1905, 38 p.
> Jeremiah.   Charles Rufus Brown, c. 1907, 256 p.
> Ezekiel.   I. G. Matthews, c. 1939, 189 p.
> Minor Prophets, Vol I:
>> Hosea, Obadiah, Jonah.   John B. Gough Pidge, c. 1935, (73) (13) (36).
>> Joel.   Philip A. Nordell, c. 1935, 31 p.
>> Amos.   Hugh Ross Hatch, c. 1935, 56 p.
>> Micah.   W. J. McGlothlin, c. 1935, 30 p.
> Minor Prophets, Vol II:
>> Nahum.   W. J. McGlothlin, c. 1935, 20 p.
>> Habakkuk, Zephaniah.   John B. Gough Pidge, c. 1935, (24) (22).
>> Haggai, Malachi.   I. G. Matthews, c. 1935, (18) (38).
>> Zechariah.   Mitchell Bronk, c. 1935, 34 p.

For similar edition of the NT, see 1881–90, No 1958.

1904   The New Testament . . . Translated from the Latin Vulgate . . . With Anno-
     tations from Approved Sources and an Historical and Tabular Index . . . :
     Chicago   **2160**

Reported as (xiii) (288) (8)   28 cm   DLC, ICN

Rheims Version. Illustrated with portrait frontispiece and 164 plates. There is no indication
of publisher in this NT.

1904   The New Testament Revised and Translated by A. S. Worrell, with Notes
     and Instructions designed to aid the earnest Reader in obtaining a clear
     Understanding of the Doctrine, Ordinances, and primitive Assemblies, as
     revealed in these Scriptures . . . Published by A. S. Worrell: Louisville **2161**

1 vol: (3) (iv) (396) (26)   25 cm   InUpT, MBrZ, MH–AH, NN, PPABP

Printed in paragraph form with introductions and appendices. The notes appear between
chapters or at foot of page. Copyright 1904, by A. S. Worrell.

Reprinted from original plates in 1907 by the American Baptist Publication Society, Philadelphia (NNAB).

Adolphus S. Worrell (1831–1908) based his translation of the NT on the Greek text that
parallels the ERV and on the Westcott and Hort text, as modified by Scrivener, and others.
(See Cheek, *Journal of Biblical Literature*, June 1953, p 108.) In the Preface Worrell states
that "the writer, under the guidance of the Holy Spirit (as he believes), undertook the im-
mensely responsible task of furnishing to the public, a correct and literal translation of the
Scriptures, put up in good style, with brief notes. . . ." An "immerse" version.

1904 [New Testament: Gospels, Selections] The Life and Morals of Jesus of Nazareth, Extracted textually from the Gospels in Greek, Latin, French, and English by Thomas Jefferson. With an introduction. Government Printing Office: Washington   **2162**

1 vol: 18 pages; 8, 82, 4 leaves   23 cm   NNAB

This is a facsimile of Jefferson's original book, now at the Smithsonian Institution, made by pasting up in parallel columns, two to a page, extracts from the Greek, Latin, French, and English texts of the Gospels in harmony form (82 numbered leaves). Nine thousand copies were printed by resolution of Congress in 1904. The English text was from a Testament printed in 1804 (see No 116). Dr. Edgar J. Goodspeed has learned that the Latin and Greek were from a London edition of 1794, and the French from a Testament printed in Paris, 1802–1803.

According to the Introduction by Cyrus Adler, Jefferson's original idea had been to prepare a collection of Bible passages for the Indians. He refers to the project in letters to several correspondents in 1803 and 1804, indicating that he had prepared such a collection during "two or three nights" in Washington while he was President and produced a booklet of some 46 pages, using only the English text. In 1816 he wrote to Charles Thomson about his "Philosophy of Jesus; it is a paradigma of his doctrines. . . . A more beautiful or precious morsel of ethics I have never seen; it is a document in proof that I am a *real Christian,* that is to say a disciple of the doctrines of Jesus." His aim was to extract for his own use only what he considered the genuine morals of Jesus, free of later additions, etc. Probably prepared in its present form in 1819, Jefferson's book was known only to his closest correspondents. He was averse to any publicity for it, fearing misrepresentation of his ideas on religion.

Even before the publication cited here, there appeared a collection of the texts in English made up from the MS list of contents, *The Life and Morals of Jesus of Nazareth extracted textually from the Gospels,* N. D. Thompson Publishing Co.: St. Louis, Chicago, and New York (168 p with frontispiece; 19 cm; copyright 1902). The following English editions have also been published: *The Thomas Jefferson Bible,* David McKay: Philadelphia, 1904 (xxiii, 161 p; 14 cm; copyright by George W. Ogilvie). *The Thomas Jefferson Bible* edited by Henry E. Jackson, Boni and Liveright: New York, 1923 (xi, 333 p; 22 cm), Weymouth and AV texts (for the Weymouth Version, see 1943 NT, No 2418). *The Life and Morals of Jesus of Nazareth* edited and with a foreword by Douglas Lurton, Wilfred Funk, Inc.: New York, 1944 (xiii, 132 p; 17 cm). *The Life and Morals of Jesus of Nazareth* with an introduction by Henry Wilder Foote, The Beacon Press: Boston, 1951 (151 p; 18 cm); printed in red and black, with Jefferson's title, p 60 of the text (double), and the first page of his table of texts in facsimile. NNAB has all of the above editions.

1904 The Student's Chronological New Testament . . . with Introductory Historical Notes and Outlines by Archibald T. Robertson . . . Fleming H. Revell Company: New York, etc.   **2163**

Reported as 359 unnumbered p   21 cm   NcWfC

ASV; see 1901, No 2124. The Books are arranged in chronological order with Mark preceding Matthew, James following Acts, and 1 Thessalonians as the first of the Epistles of Paul. Copyright 1904.

1904? The Twentieth Century New Testament. A Translation into Modern English Made from the original Greek — Westcott & Hort's Text — by a company of about twenty scholars representing the various sections of the Christian Church. Revised Edition. Fleming H. Revell Company: New York   **2164**

1 vol: (4) iii–xxxi (5) 5–523 [1]   20 cm   NNAB

Twentieth Century Version; see 1900–01 NT, No 2118. The format is similar to that of the 1-vol 1902? tentative edition (No 2140).

This version was reprinted frequently without date, except in later printings when the printer's code appears at the lower right of p 523. NNAB has a copy of the Boy Scout Edition, 1916?. The Revell Company has a copy of The Gospels and the Book of Acts, 1905? (xx, 2,

5–269 p; 18 cm). The Gospel of St. Matthew was issued separately as a booklet in 1910?
(Revell Company). St. Mark (40 p) and St. John (165–210 p) were issued in 1917? (NNAB).

1904   The Harmonized & Subject Reference New Testament: King James' Version
         Made into a Harmonized Paragraph, Local, Topical, Textual, and Subject
         Reference Edition, in Modern English Print . . . Arranged by James W.
         Shearer . . . Subject Reference Co.: Delaware, New Jersey   **2165**

1 vol: (xii) (649)   18 cm   DLC, NN, NNAB, ViU
         Printed in modern prose and poetry form, single column, but with chapter and verse
indication. Has section and paragraph headings. In the Gospels the paragraphs are numbered
according to the Outline Harmony, with maps (p 613–634), and additional numbers indicate
parallel passages. Acts-Revelation have separate paragraph numbering for each book. Index II
(p 635–649) discusses points at which harmonizing schemes differ. Copyright 1904, by James
William Shearer; also entered at Stationer's Hall, London.
         The Outline Harmony had been published as early as 1901, the maps having been copy-
right in 1892.

1904   The New Testament . . . With All the Words Recorded Therein, as Having
         Been Spoken by Our Lord, Printed in Color. Revised Version . . . The
         Christian Herald: New York   **2166**

Reported as 420 p   16 cm   DLC
         This is not the same as the 1899 edition (No 2103).
         When requested for identification of "Revised Version," DLC reported the book lost since
1932.

1905? The Red Letter Holy Bible. The Prophetic Types and Prophecies in the
         Old Testament Referring to Christ and Also the References to Portions of
         the Old Testament Quoted and Referred to by Jesus are Printed in Red. The
         Words Spoken by Jesus . . . are Printed in Red . . . Containing Sixty Thousand
         Original and Selected Parallel References and Marginal Readings . . . The
         John C. Winston Co.: Philadelphia   **2167**

Reported as (1149) (4) 37–64 (268) (75)   25 cm   DLC, MB
         One of the International Series. Contains The Bible Readers' Aids with an Extended Com-
bination Concordance. Illustrations and maps.

1905? Christian Worker's Holy Bible . . . ["International" Series. Self-Pronouncing
         Edition]. Indexed and Marked in Red by the Best Method of Bible Marking
         on all Subjects Connected with . . . The Theme of Salvation . . . Three Thou-
         sand Selected Texts Arranged in Sequence . . . and . . . Introduction on the
         Many Uses of this Christian Worker's Bible . . . by . . . Jesse Lyman Hurlbut
         . . . Printed and Bound at the International Press . . . The John C. Winston
         Co.: Philadelphia   **2168**

1 vol: (xii) (1149) (3) (ix–xxvi)   21 cm   DLC, NNAB
         Long Primer Octavo Self-Pronouncing Clear Type Edition, with system of marking sim-
ilar to that in the Christian Worker's 1902? NT (No 2145) and same device on title page.
Preliminary matter includes short title, How to Use the Christian Worker's Bible, Index to
References, The Christian Worker's Bible Introduction by Jesse Lyman Hurlbut, Order of
Books, and Key to Pronunciation. Has center references and chronology. NT title has statement,
*Containing About Fifteen Thousand Original and Selected Parallel References and Marginal
Readings.* Summary of References and colored maps at end. Copyright 1905, by the John C.
Winston Co.
         NNAB copy received as gift in 1905.

1905 The Holy Bible . . . Being the Version Set Forth A.D. 1611 . . . and Revised A.D. 1881–1885. Newly Edited by the American Revision Committee A.D. 1901. Standard Edition. American Bible Society . . . Published by Thomas Nelson & Sons: New York   **2169**

1 vol: (4) (1002) (4) (300)   16 cm   NNAB
ASV; see 1901, No 2124. Label inside cover reads "This is No. 1 of the first one hundred copies of the American Revised Version of the Bible, in this size, published by the American Bible Society, March, 1905."

When the ABS was established in 1816, its constitution limited distribution of the Scriptures in English to the "version in common use," which was then the AV. After publication of the ERV and ASV, there were requests that the ABS publish these versions. In 1904, after two years of discussion, the constitution was changed to permit distribution of the two revisions. By agreement with Thomas Nelson and Sons, the distribution of the ASV was limited to inexpensive editions only. During 1904/05, the ABS issued Bibles in Minion type (available in three bindings) and a quarto Bible in English type to be sold only to churches for pulpit use. They also issued Minion type Testaments with and without Psalms. In all of these editions, the ERV and ASV prefaces were omitted.

1905 The Corrected English New Testament. A Revision of the "Authorized" Version [By Nestle's Resultant Text]. Prepared with the Assistance of Eminent Scholars and Issued by Samuel Lloyd . . . with Preface by the Bishop of Durham . . . G. P. Putnam's Sons, The Knickerbocker Press: New York   **2170**

1 vol: (xxviii) (516)   28 cm   DLC, NNAB
Has Preface, Introduction, and other preliminary matter. Printed in paragraph form. Copyright 1905, by Samuel Lloyd.

This NT was first printed in England in 1905, a tentative edition having been circulated privately in 1904 with which the grammarian G. W. Moon had been associated. The above edition closely resembles the smaller English one. The American plates were evidently taken from the English type, but the marginal references have been reset and enlarged and the page headings of the English edition have been omitted.

Mr. Lloyd, a Life Governor of the British and Foreign Bible Society, explains in his Introduction that he acted as general editor, receiving assistance from a large number of scholars, whom he lists. He was a member of the Church of England and lived in Birmingham.

1905? The New Testament, and Familiar Hymns and Tunes, with Selections and Forms . . . American Tract Society: New York, Boston [etc.]   **2171**

Reported as 395 p   19 cm   DLC
DLC card has: 10,000 copies printed October 1905; 50,000 printed July 1907.

1905? The New Covenant Called the New Testament . . . Being the Version Set Forth A.D. 1611 . . . Revised A.D. 1881. Newly Edited by the New Testament Members of the American Revision Committee A.D. 1900. Standard Edition. American Bible Society. Published by Thomas Nelson & Sons: New York   **2172**

1 vol: (4) (516)   12 cm   NNAB
ASV; see 1901, No 2124. Copyright 1901, by Thomas Nelson & Sons.

Cited copy has label with notation: "This is No. 1 of the first one hundred copies of the American Revised Version of the New Testament, in this size, published by the American Bible Society, March, 1905." See note under 1905, No 2169. NNAB also has copies with the Psalms (170 p).

1905 Personal Worker's New Testament; Arranged by 1. J. Wilbur Chapman, 2. William Edward Biederwolf, 3. Robert Augustus Walton, 4. Henry Ostrom . . . The Winona Publishing Company: Chicago   **2173**

Reported as (5) (516)   12 cm   DLC
ASV; see 1901, No 2124.

1906 The Analytical Holy Bible. Self-Pronouncing, Self-Interpreting, Self-Explanatory . . . Edited and arranged by Arthur Roberts. Nearly one hundred pages of halftone illustrations. Egyptian Publishing Company: Carbondale, Illinois
                                                                              2174

1 vol: (6) (788) (6) 789–1066 (379)   28 cm   NNAB
Preliminary matter includes presentation page, Preface, Directions, etc., and Order of Books. Text printed in double columns with a center column of notes keyed to the text by raised numerals. Full text of all references printed below text. Short introductions to each Book. Halftone Family Record pages precede NT title. Subject, Topical and Word Index at end. Copyright 1904, 1904, 1905, and 1906, by Arthur Roberts.

1906? The Holy Bible . . . With Introductions and Notes, and a Harmony of the Gospels and Outline of the Life of Christ . . . American Tract Society: New York   **2175**

Reported as (1491) (12)   26 cm   DLC
Self-Explanatory Edition appears at head of title. NT has references and marginal readings of the Polyglot Bible. Maps.
For revised edition, see 1952 Concordia Bible, No 2507.

1907 Student's Bible; King James Version, with Copious Readings from the American Revised Version, with Marginal Notes . . . by O. J. Nave and A. S. Nave . . . Topical Bible Publishing Co.: Lincoln, Nebraska   **2176**

1 vol: (10) (1716) (81) (3) (24)   24 cm   NNAB
Has marginal references and notes at foot of page. Index and Concordance. Maps with Index.
Reprinted by Moody Press in 1957.

1907? The Holy Bible. Red Letter Edition . . . Many Thousands of Parallel References and Marginal Readings . . . Passages and Incidents Quoted or Referred to by Our Lord and Saviour are Printed in Red . . . The Words Recorded as Having Been Spoken by Our Lord and Saviour are Printed in Red . . . The Christian Herald. Louis Klopsch, Proprietor, Bible House: New York   **2177**

1 vol: (1203) (32) (268) (32)   20 cm   NNAB
This India paper edition is not a reprint of the 1901 Red Letter Edition (No 2126). Explanatory Note (1901) and Order of Books precede text. The Bible Readers' Aid by C. H. H. Wright, Concordance, Word Book, colored maps, and plan at end. Copyright 1907, by Louis Klopsch.

1907 The Modern Reader's Bible. The Books of the Bible with Three Books of the Apocrypha, Presented in Modern Literary Form. Edited with Introductions and Notes, by Richard G. Moulton . . . [Printed at Norwood, Mass.]. Macmillan Co.: New York   **2178**

1 vol: (iv) (1733)   20 cm   DLC, KyLo, MB, NjMD, NNAB
ERV text rearranged by Dr. Moulton; see 1895–1906, No 2066. The usual order of books has been changed to combine books of history, prophecy, poetry, and philosophy for the OT,

and history and literature for the NT. Text printed in normal prose and poetry form with verse numbers in outer margins. Copyright 1895, 1896, 1897, 1898, 1899, and 1907.

NN has 1915 edition. OC has 1921 and 1935 editions.

1907   The Holy Bible . . . Parallel References and Marginal Readings . . . World Syndicate Co., Inc.: New York   **2179**

Reported as (iv) (1203) (31)   18 cm   NRU

Contains Bible Readers' Aids, maps, and plans.

The World Syndicate Company was formed early in the century by former employees of the Syndicate Company (see 1898 Bible, No 2093). They first used a set of plates for a Teachers Bible with center references leased from the Christian Herald (No 2177?). Printed from new plates this book is still in print. (For changes in the corporate name, see 1928? Bible, No 2295.) About 1914 the firm leased from the Christian Herald a set of plates for a Minion Reference Bible, smaller than the above, which World no longer uses. The firm also had made plates for three other often reprinted Bibles: a Junior Bible and a "Chain Store Bible", both still in print, and a Brevier Bible now discontinued. (Information supplied by The World Publishing Company, Aug. 1959.)

1907?   A Comprehensive Commentary . . . The New Testament . . . with an original commentary . . . including the words recorded as having been spoken by our Saviour printed in Bold Face Type . . . National Bible Press: Philadelphia
2180

Reported as 225 p   20 cm   DLC

Square Octavo with commentary at foot of page. Illustrated. Copyright 1907, by J. R. Jones.

1907   The New Testament, and Familiar Hymns and Tunes with Selections and Forms . . . American Tract Society: New York, Boston, [etc.]   **2181**

19 cm   DLC

A reprint of 1905 NT, No 2171.

1908   The Ideal Holy Bible . . . Self-Pronouncing, Self-Interpreting, Self-Explanatory . . . Edited and Arranged by Arthur Roberts . . . One Hundred Pages of Halftone Illustrations . . . Spiegel, May, Stern Company: Chicago   **2182**

30 cm   DLC

Same as 1906 Analytical Holy Bible (No 2174). Illustrated.

1908–10?   The Bible and its Story Taught by Picture Lessons . . . Auxiliary Educational League, Inc.: New York   **2183**

1926 p   26 cm   NNAB

Text is printed in single column with some notes, many of them containing variant readings and renderings of the ERV and ASV. Has introductions to each Book. Revelation is printed in smaller type, double column. The last section contains Self-Help Question Lessons, edited by Charles F. Horne and copyright 1917 by F. R. Niglutsch. This work was published serially in 82 sections (24 p each) with full-page illustrations — usually 8 — and accompanying text and comments on facing thin-paper sheets before continuous text. Separate sections were sold at 25¢, but no subscription was accepted for less than the full set. It was edited by Prof. Charles F. Horne, College of the City of New York, assisted by the Rev. Prof. Julius Bewer, Union Theological Seminary. Copyright 1908, 1909, and 1910, by F. R. Niglutsch, but beginning with Section 61 the publisher and copyright holder is Ira R. Hiller.

Also bound in 10 vols, with illustrations throughout.

1908?   The Marginal Chain-Reference Bible containing Thompson's Original and
Exhaustive System of Topical Chain References in which topics printed on
the margins are . . . connected . . . to enable the reader to trace . . . through
the entire Scriptures any important subject . . . A New and complete subject-
index . . . self-pronouncing text . . . Compiled and edited by Frank Charles
Thompson, D.D., Ph.D. Published by Henry Frowde . . . : London . . . ;
Eaton & Mains: New York; Chain-Reference Bible Publishing Company:
Mt. Morris, N. Y.   *2184*

1 vol: (viii) (876) (271) (3) (58)   23 cm   NNAB
Has Preface by Dr. Thompson (Geneseo, 1908), Explanations, and Tables. Text in standard
double column form, with references in wide outer margins. Subject Index at end, followed by
Atlas and maps (8 p, 12 colored maps). Copyright 1908; Printed in the United States.

1908   Holy Bible . . . with Sixty Thousand Original and Selected Parallel References and Marginal Readings and the "International" Handy Bible Encyclopedia and Concordance. International Press: [Philadelphia]   *2185*

1 vol: (1149) (390)   21 cm   NNAB
Text is similar to 1905? Christian Worker's Bible (No 2168) but does not have system
of marking. *"International" Standard Teachers Bible Series Self-Pronouncing Edition* appears
at head of title. Preliminary matter includes Order of Books and Key to Pronunciation. International Teachers' Handy Bible Encyclopedia and Concordance (edited by Hurlbut and McClure)
and maps at end.

1908–22   The Bible for Home and School . . . edited by Shailer Mathews . . . The
Macmillan Company: New York   *2186*

14 vols   17 cm   DLC
Each volume is separately paged; name of editor, date, and pagination follow title below:

Genesis.   Hinckley G. Mitchell, 1909, viii, 379 p.
Deuteronomy.   W. G. Jordan, 1911, xii, 263 p.
Judges.   E. L. Curtis, 1913, xii, 201 p.
I Samuel.   Loring W. Batten, 1919, viii, 236 p.
Job.   George A. Barton, 1911, xii, 321 p.
Isaiah.   John Edgar McFayden, 1910, xiv, 423 p.
Amos, Hosea, Micah.   John M. Powis Smith, 1914, viii, 216 p.
Matthew.   A. T. Robertson, 1911, xiv, 294 p.
Mark.   Melancthon W. Jacobus, 1915, x, 259 p.
Acts.   George Holley Gilbert, 1908, x, 267 p.
Corinthians.   James S. Riggs and Harry Lathrop Reed, 1922, x, 314 p.
Galatians.   Benjamin W. Bacon, 1909, viii, 135 p.
Colossians and Ephesians.   Gross Alexander, 1910, x, 132 p.
Hebrews.   Edgar J. Goodspeed, 1908, xii, 132 p.

This Bible was planned particularly for the "intelligent Sunday School teacher," clergymen, and lay readers, with the hope of stimulating intelligent use of the Bible in the home and
the school. The text is the ERV and ASV supplemented with "all important renderings from
other versions," and is printed in paragraph form, single column, with verse numbers in inner
margin and references and notes below text. In Genesis the various sources are indicated by
letters in the outer margins. The comments, notes, and introductions were intended to place
at the disposal of the general reader the best results of modern scholarship. Most volumes carry
several pages of publisher's advertisements at the end. John by Shailer Mathews and Romans
by Edward L. Bosworth were advertised but there was no further publication in this series.

1908?   The Holy Bible . . . Being the version set forth A.D. 1611, Compared . . .
1881–1885. Newly Edited by the American Revision Committee, A.D. 1901,

Standard Edition. Made specially for the Standard Publishing Co., Cincinnati, Ohio, by the publishers, Thomas Nelson & Sons: New York   *2187*

16 cm   NNAB

ASV; see 1901, No 2124. Reprint of 1901? edition (No 2131). Minion 24mo. Table of Contents for Training Class Bible prepared by Herbert Moninger (copyright 1908) (1 leaf) inserted after title page. A 24-p insert of the Helps with 12 colored maps follows text.

1908 The Reference Passage Bible New Testament . . . Arranged in Topics, with the Reference Passages Given in Full Text Upon the Same Page . . . The Gospels are Arranged in Parallel Columns, in Chronological Order . . . The Acts, Epistles and Revelation are Arranged in Consecutive Order . . . Compiled by I. N. Johns . . . Sixth Edition . . . The Alpha Publishing Co.: Lincoln, Nebraska   *2188*

1450 p   22 cm   NNAB

For first edition, see 1902, No 2141. Introduction signed I. N. J., General Outline of the Life of Christ, and Table of Contents precede text. Chronological Index, Chapter and Verse Index, Alphabetical Index, Prophecies and Their Fulfillments Relating to Christ, and Life of Christ at end. Copyright 1902, by the Alpha Publishing Co.

Later printings were issued in 1909 (50th Thousand Edition, MBAt), 1911 (75th Thousand Edition, NcD), 1912 (85th Thousand Edition, NNAB), 1913 (95th Thousand Edition, OC), and 1915 (100 Thousand Edition, NNAB).

1909? The New Indexed Bible . . . Alphabetically Indexes and Combines the Studies of Biblical Biography, Geography, History, Theology, the Cardinal Virtues, Moral Philosophy, and Character Building. Illustrated with 160 Photographs of Places of Biblical Events . . . Revised and Enlarged from the Original Edition . . . J. A. Dickson Publishing Co.: Chicago   *2189*

28 cm   DLC

A new edition of the 1902? Indexed Bible (No 2134). Has illustrations and maps.

1909 The Holy Bible . . . Illustrated with Eighty-Four Photogravures by Modern Artists. Current Literature Publishing Co.: New York   *2190*

Reported as (956) (290)   26 cm   CO

Family Record follows OT (2 leaves). Index and colored maps (14 p). Plates are mounted.

1909 The New Indexed Bible . . . Alphabetically Indexes and Combines the Studies of Biblical Biography, Geography, History, Theology, the Cardinal Virtues, Moral Philosophy and Character Building . . . Illustrated with a Large Number of Photographs of Places of Biblical Events . . . Revised and Enlarged from the Original Edition . . . J. A. Dickson Publishing Company: Chicago   *2191*

24 cm   DLC

Similar to 1902? and 1909? Indexed Bibles (No 2134 and No 2189). *Indexed Teachers Bible* appears as cover title. Has frontispiece, illustrations, and maps.

1909 The Scofield Reference Bible . . . Authorized Version with a New System of Connected Topical References . . . with Annotations, Revised Marginal Renderings, Summaries, Definitions, and Index to Which are Added Helps at Hard Places, Explanations of Seeming Discrepancies, and a New System of Paragraphs. Edited by Rev. C. I. Scofield . . . [and Consulting Editors].

1909, continued

[Printed by Eaton & Mains, New York.] Oxford University Press, American
Branch: New York [etc.]   **2192**

1 vol: (8) 3–1362 (8) (12)   21 cm   DLC, NN, NNAB, ViU
    Introduction signed C. I. Scofield, Order of Books, How to Use the Subject References,
and Introduction to the Pentateuch precede text. Introductions to each Book. Introduction to
the Four Gospels and How to Use the Subject References precede NT. Index, Indexed Atlas,
and maps at end. Copyright 1909, by Oxford University Press, American Branch.
    Cyrus Ingerson Scofield (1843–1921), first a lawyer and later a Congregationalist minister
(for many years in Dallas, Texas), was a popular lecturer on Bible study. He began work on
this Bible in 1902. He was assisted by a Board of Editors: Henry G. Weston, LL.D., James M.
Gray, D.D., William J. Erdman, D.D., Prof. W. G. Moorehead, D.D., Elmore Harris, D.D.,
Arthur T. Pierson, D.D., and Arno C. Gaebelein, D.D. The reference system and the introductions to the various books set forth premillennial and dispensational teachings although the text
is the King James Version. This edition proved very popular, many people purchasing it for its
good type, reference system, and special notes. For further details, consult Dr. Arno C. Gaebelein's "The Story of the Scofield Reference Bible," in *Moody Monthly* (Oct 1942, p 65–66, 99;
Nov 1942, p 128–129, 135; Dec 1942, p 202–203, 233; Jan 1943, p 277–279; Feb 1943, p 343–
345; Mar 1943, p 400–401, 419) and John Wick Bowman's "Dispensationalism," in *Interpretation* (Apr 1956, p 170–187).

1909   [The New Testament] The Bible in Modern English. A Rendering from the
        Originals by an American Making Use of the Best Scholarship and Latest
        Researches at Home and Abroad . . . First Edition. Ten Thousand. The
        Perkiomen Press: Perkiomen, Pa.   **2193**

1 vol: (12) (461) (3)   19 cm   DLC, NNAB
    Ballentine Version; see 1899–1901 NT, No 2102. This is a revision of the 1899–1901 edi-
tion, but it was poorly printed and was withdrawn after 3,000 copies were sold. Issued anony-
mously by Mr. Ballentine at Perkiomen, which was the name of his parish and not a town.
Copyright 1910, by "The Perkiomen Press"; copyright 1909 blanked out by printer. See also
1922 NT, No 2258.

1910   Wilmore's New Analytical Reference Bible . . . with Marginal Notes and
        Analytical References. Comprehensive Bible Helps . . . Revised and Edited
        by Philip Schaff . . . The Whole Bible Arranged in Subjects. Edited by
        Roswell D. Hitchcock. Cruden's Concordance . . . Revised by John Eadie.
        H. F. Giere: New York   **2194**

30 cm   NN
Reprint of 1891 edition (No 2043).

1910   The Holy Bible Marked on Temporal Blessings . . . [International Series. Self-
        Pronouncing Edition]. Marked by the Best Methods of Bible Marking on
        all Subjects Connected with the Theme of Temporal Blessings . . . Marked
        by J. G. Lawson . . . The John C. Winston Co.: Philadelphia   **2195**

Reported as (1149) (xiv)   24 cm   DLC
    Clear Type Edition. Text similar to 1905? Christian Worker's Bible (No 2168). Contains
Bible Encyclopedia and Concordance, edited by Hurlbut and McClure.

1910? The Cross-Reference Bible . . . American Standard Edition of the Revised
        Bible . . . with Variorum Readings and Renderings with Topical Analysis
        and Cross References. Harold E. Monser . . . Editor-in-Chief . . . The Cross
        Reference Bible Company: New York, Chicago, Champaign, Ill.   **2196**

1 vol: (xx) (1744) (iv) 1745–2414   24 cm   MB, Mi, NBP, NjMD, NNAB, OrP,
                                                                   PMck

ASV; see 1901, No 2124. ASV Preface, Preface for the Cross-Reference Bible, List of Abbreviations, Order of Books, and Analysis of Pentateuch precede text, printed with references in margins and a large body of variant readings and notes below. Extracts from the 1901 Preface and Lists of OT Incidents and Quotations in the NT precede NT. Index and Nelson's Atlas at end. Other editors include Charles Reign Scoville, Ira M. Price, R. A. Torrey, A. T. Robertson, Andrew C. Zenos, Milton S. Terry, D. R. Dungan, John R. Sampey, J. W. Monser, and F. C. Eiselen. Copyright 1910, by H. E. Monser.

Reprinted in 1959 by Baker Book House.

1910?   The Holy Bible . . . Being the Version set forth A.D. 1611 compared with the most ancient authorities and revised A.D. 1881–1885. Newly Edited by the American Revision Committee A.D. 1901. Standard Edition. Thomas Nelson and Sons: New York   **2197**

1 vol: (x) (996) (vi) (288)   19 cm   DLC, NNAB, ViU

ASV; see 1901, No 2124. Brevier Duodecimo without references. Has Scripture Proper Names Marked for Correct Pronunciation at end (20 p). Copyright 1901.

1910?   The Holy Bible . . . Peerless Bible Company: Chicago   **2198**

1 vol: (6) 5–1347 (19)   17 cm   MiU, NNAB

"International" Series Self-Pronouncing Edition appears at head of title page, which has device of International Press. Large Minion Duodecimo Clear Type Edition. See 1903?, No 2150.

NNAB copy has presentation page for Anointed High Priests of the Indiana Council, Masonic Order, and colored maps. NNAB has another undated copy imprinted *The John C. Winston Co.*, with sepia illustrations, and Practical Aids by Wright, Whitehouse, and Spurrell (Copyright 1903).

1910?   The New Covenant Commonly Called the New Testament . . . Version Set Forth 1611 . . . and Revised 1881; Newly Edited by the New Testament Members of the American Revision Committee 1900. Standard Edition . . . Thomas Nelson & Sons: New York   **2199**

1 vol: (viii) (559) (3) (196)   19 cm   NNAB

ASV; see 1901, No 2124. Pica Duodecimo on India paper, printed in single column with alternative readings and renderings at foot of page. Usual copyright 1901, etc. on verso of title; publisher's address listed as Fourth Avenue Building, Fourth Ave. and 27th St.

1910?   The New Covenant Commonly Called the New Testament . . . Being the Version Set Forth 1611 A.D. . . . Revised A.D. 1881. Newly Edited by the New Testament Members of the American Revision Committee A.D. 1900. Standard Edition . . . Thomas Nelson & Sons: New York   **2200**

1 vol: (xiv) (538)   12 cm   NNAB

ASV; see 1901, No 2124. Nonpareil 32mo Emphasized Edition. The words of Christ appear in black-face type. Printed in double-column form with page headings and alternative readings and renderings at foot of page. Preliminary matter includes ASV Preface, Notes about Pronunciation System (2 p), and Order of Books.

Cited copy purchased by NNAB in 1911. NNAB also has: an edition with Psalms (180 p); an edition with only the Gospels and Acts and 24 p Supplement, purchased in 1911 (issued by the Pocket Testament League; copyright 1911 by Nelson); a Pocket Testament League Edition (without Supplement) purchased in 1914; two later copies, one in limp leather and the second bound in khaki with Service Edition end papers; and two other copies bound in tan cloth, one a Boy Scout Edition purchased in 1916, with same pagination as above but in reduced size (probably photographed down). All NNAB copies have publisher's address as 381–385 Fourth Ave.

1910?   The New Covenant Commonly Called the New Testament . . . American
Revision Committee A.D. 1900. Standard Edition . . . [J. S. Cushing Co. —
Berwick & Smith Co., Norwood Press, Norwood, Mass., Printers]. Thomas
Nelson & Sons: New York   **2201**

1 vol: (x) (516) (170)   12 cm   DLC, NN, NNAB
ASV; see 1901, No 2124. Has Revisers' Preface and Order of Books. Psalms at end. Copy-
right 1901. Publisher's address given as Fourth Avenue Building, 4th Ave. and 27th St.
Also issued without Psalms.

1910?   The New Covenant . . . American Revision Committee, A.D. 1900. Standard
Edition. Thomas Nelson & Sons: New York   **2202**

1 vol: (ix) [1] (483) [1]   12 cm   NNAB
ASV; see 1901, No 2124. Ruby 32mo NT printed in double column form. Has Revisers'
Preface. Usual copyright 1901, etc. appears on verso of title page; publisher's address, 381–385
Fourth Ave.

1911?   The Holy Bible . . . Marginal readings and parallel texts: with commentary
and critical notes . . . by Adam Clarke . . . a new edition with the author's
final corrections . . . Eaton & Mains: New York; Jennings & Graham: Cincinnati   **2203**

6 vols   27 cm   MiU
Clarke's Commentary; see 1811–25, No 188. Has maps and Tables. Illustrated. Vols v and
vi have added title, *A New Edition, condensed and supplemented from the best modern authorities: By Daniel Curry.* Vol vi copyright 1911, by Mrs. James Armstrong.

1911   Marginal Chain-Reference Bible . . . Containing Thompson's Original & Exhaustive System of Topical Chain References; Compiled and Edited by
F. C. Thompson . . . Chain-Reference Bible Co.: Lincoln, Nebraska   **2204**

23 cm   WRac
Reprint of 1908 edition (No 2184). Marked fourth edition.

1911   The 1911 Bible. The Holy Bible . . . 1611, the Text Carefully Corrected and
Amended by American Scholars, 1911. With a New System of References
. . . Oxford University Press, American Branch: New York   **2205**

1152 p   21 cm   IU, NN, NNAB
Contains a new system of references prepared by the Rev. C I. Scofield, D.D. (see 1909,
No 2192), "tracing through the whole Bible the greater themes of the Divine revelation," and
a new "collected-Reference system," grouping at one passage the most important occurrences
of its most characteristic meaning. Although the text is printed in verse form, paragraphing is
indicated by the insertion of blank lines. Copyright 1911, by the Oxford University Press,
American Branch.
The Preface states that the text of this edition, commemorating the first publication of the
AV, has been carefully scrutinized by a "committee of 34 eminent Hebrew and Greek scholars,
representing all of the great evangelical bodies and many foremost Universities and Schools
of Divinity." It claims to be "neither a new translation nor revision, but a scholarly and carefully
Corrected Text." The Preface makes no further remarks on changes, but archaic words such
as "leasing" (Psalm 4:2, 5:6) and "prevent" (Psalm 88:13) have been changed to "lies" and
"come before." In Mt 23:24 the text reads "strain out a gnat."

1911–12   [The Holy Bible] The First Book of Moses, called Genesis . . . American
Bible Society, Instituted . . . : New York   **2206**

31 vols   12 cm   NNAB

Each volume of this Brevier 32mo Pocket Edition is separately paged and bound in flexible red cloth. Above title taken from first volume.

1911–12 [The New Testament] . . . A Comparison of the . . . Text as it is given in the Protestant and Roman Catholic Bible Versions in the English Language in Use in America. With a Brief Account of the Origin of the Several Versions. By Frank J. Firth . . . Fleming H. Revell Company: New York **2207**

2 vols: Vol I, 501 p; Vol II, 585 p   23 cm   NNAB

Vol I (1911) contains the Holy Gospel; Gospel Subject Index at end (p 495–501). Vol II (1912) has the Acts of the Apostles, The Epistles, and the Revelation of St. John the Divine. The four texts (AV, Rheims, ASV, and ERV) are printed in parallel columns across each opening, without notes. The AV (set from an Oxford University Press, American Branch edition) and the Rheims text (from the 1899? H. L. Kilner & Co., Philadelphia edition; see note under No 2101) are in verse form; the ASV (from a Nelson edition) and the ERV (from an Oxford, American Branch and Cambridge-James Pott edition) are in paragraph form.

1912? Campbell Morgan Analyzed Bible; Holy Bible . . . with Topical Headings and References and Twenty-Five New and Instructive Outline Maps . . . Standard Edition. With Analysis and Spiritual Interpretation of Each Book, by the Rev. C. Campbell Morgan . . . Thomas Nelson & Sons: New York **2208**

21 cm   MsLE

ASV; see 1901, No 2124. Reprint of 1901? Bourgeois Octavo (No 2125) with added matter. Copyright 1912.

1912 The Holy Bible . . . An Improved Edition. Based in Part on the Bible Union Version . . . American Baptist Publication Society: Philadelphia   **2209**

1 vol: (6) 7–1086 (8) 9–311 [1]   20 cm   NNAB

Improved Version; see 1891? NT, No 2048. Each Testament has Prefatory Notes, with information on the history of the version. NT marked fourth edition. Words which appear in italics in the AV are here printed in roman type or occasionally in brackets. The poetic form is used for much of the Prophets as well as for Job, Psalms, and Proverbs. Some alternative readings and renderings are given at foot of page. In the NT, "immerse" and related words are given in parentheses after the anglicized form of the Greek word.

In Isaiah 7:14, "young woman" (instead of "virgin" as in the AV) is used with a note: "The Hebrew word means 'a young woman of marriageable age'; it implies nothing one way or the other as to virginity." This translation was also adopted in the Jewish Publication Society (1917), Moffatt (1924), American (1935), and RSV versions. Knox uses "maid." (*The Bible Translator* IX, No 3 [July 1958] p 104.)

NN and NNAB have copies of a 1913 reprint.

1912 The Holy Bible . . . Printed for the New York Bible Society, New York. American Bible Society: New York   **2210**

19 cm   NNAB

Reprint of the 1872 Brevier Duodecimo (No 1881).

1912? תורה נביאים וכתובים Twenty-Four Books of the Holy Scriptures. Carefully translated after the Best Jewish authorities by Isaac Leeser. Hebrew Publishing Company: New York   **2211**

4 vols: 1384 p   19 cm   NNAB

Leeser Version; see 1845–46, No 1273. One line of Hebrew appears at head of title. Hebrew and English texts on facing pages, double numbered. Hebrew text begins on verso of title page.

There are separate title pages for the Second Part, Division 1 (Judges, Joshua, 1 and 2 Samuel, and 1 and 2 Kings); Second Part, Division 2 (the later Prophets); and Third Part (Hagiographa).

The publisher reports that this work first appeared in 1912 in this form. It was reprinted several times.

1912?   Nelson's Explanatory New Testament, with Copious Notes and Comments and an Introduction to Each Book, the Words of Christ . . . in Bold Face Type . . . American Revision Committee A.D. 1900. Standard Edition. Thomas Nelson & Sons: New York   **2212**

1 vol: (xvi) (656)   16 cm   DLC, NNAB, ViU

ASV; see 1901, No 2124. Has various introductions and prefaces; also introductions and outlines to each Book. Marginal readings and renderings are printed below text within rules, with copious notes at foot of page. Copyright 1901–12, by Thomas Nelson & Sons.

1913   The New Indexed Bible. Alphabetically Indexes and Combines the Studies of Biblical Biography . . . Revised and Enlarged from the Original Edition . . . John A. Dickson Publishing Co.: Chicago   **2213**

1 vol: (208) (967) (235)   26 cm   NNAB

In three parts: Part I contains History of the Bible, History of the Books of the Bible, History of the English Translation of the Bible, Note about Indexed Bible, Science of Character Building, Science of Theology, The Laws of the Great Kingdom, Index and Digest, and note on how to read the Bible in a year. Part II contains Key to Pronunciation and Order of Books; OT text followed by Family Record pages, History of Period between the Old and New Testaments, Index to Bible Atlas, maps, List of Illustrations, etc. Part III contains NT text; compilation of the Sayings of Christ, Collation of Scriptures with Index, and Concordance at end. Illustrated. Copyright 1909 and 1913, by John A. Dickson Publishing Co. For earlier editions of the Indexed Bible, see 1902?, No 2134 and 1909?, No 2189.

1913?   The Red Letter Edition of the Holy Bible . . . Showing the Whole of Our Lord's Words in Red . . . T. Nelson & Sons: New York   **2214**

Reported as (viii) (835) (121)   13 cm   MH

Red Letter Holy Bible appears as cover title. Contains 4000 Questions and Answers; Aids to Bible Studies at end. Illustrated.

Date supplied by Nelson firm as probable first printing of this Bible.

1913   The New Testament. Volume III: St. Paul's Epistles to the Churches. Part I: The Epistles to the Thessalonians by the Rev. Cuthbert Lattey, S.J. [Printed at the Plimpton Press, Norwood, Mass.] Longmans, Green, and Co.: New York, etc.   **2215**

1 vol: (xiv) (21)   23 cm   NNAB

This is the first published part of The Westminster Version of the Sacred Scriptures, which was the work of a group of Roman Catholic Scholars under the editorship of the Rev. Cuthbert Lattey, S.J. Subsequent issues were imported from England, where the translating was done. The Minor Prophets have also been printed in England. The NT was completed in parts in 1935; printed in a 1-vol edition, revised, in 1948; and published with the Douay OT in the Heirloom Bible by Hawthorn Books, 1958 (printed in England).

1913?   [New Testament] Precious Promise Testament . . . with all the Promises Printed in Red and a Complete Index to Every Subject and Important Word . . . Edited by J. G. Lawson . . . The John C. Winston Co.: Philadelphia **2216**

1 vol: (313) (82)   16 cm   NNAB

Minion Duodecimo Self-Pronouncing Clear Type Edition. The "most comforting portions" are over-printed in red. Subject Index to the NT, compiled by J. G. Lawson, at end. Copyright 1913, by Winston.

NNAB has another copy, imprinted *Universal Book and Bible House, Philadelphia* and copyright 1942 by Universal, with more expanded preliminary matter and additional material at end (continuously paged). It contains Fausset's History of the Apostles and The Hour of Prayer (32 p). DLC has 1945? copy without The Hour of Prayer.

1914? The Holy Bible, Translated from the Latin Vulgate . . . Published with Approbation of . . . Cardinal Gibbons . . . John Murphy Company, Publishers . . . Printer to the Holy See: Baltimore and New York   **2217**

21 cm   DLC, NcD, NN, NNAB

Rheims-Douay Version. Reprint of 1899 Benziger edition (No 2101). Approbations, frontispiece, Indulgences, Letter from Pope Pius VI, Prayer, Preface, and Order of Books precede text. Family Record follows OT. NT has frontispiece and Order of Books. Index, Tables, Selected Readings, and Order of Books at end. Added matter varies with copies. Illustrations and colored maps. Copyright 1914.

OC has copy issued by Benziger Bros. of New York, Chicago, Cincinnati, and San Francisco, with the imprimatur and approbation of Cardinal Farley, Archbishop of New York. Also issued by P. J. Kenedy and Sons, New York. Some copies were marketed by the John C. Winston Co., Philadelphia, with "Winston" printed on spine (copy on file at Winston Co.).

1914? The Holy Bible . . . A. J. Holman Co.: Philadelphia   **2218**

1 vol: (16) 9–968 (2) 971–1264; other matter var. paged.   20 cm   NNAB

Holman Pronouncing Edition appears at head of title page, which has device, *Let There be Light*. Large Bourgeois Octavo with references. Blank leaf for notes, colored illustration, and presentation page precede title page; Preface, Key to Pronunciation, and Order of Books follow title. Family Record in red and black follows OT. Plans for Reading the Bible Through in a Year (2 leaves), Treasury of Biblical Information by Peloubet (copyright 1913, 32 p), Bible Dictionary (copyright 1896, 128 p), Concordance (copyright 1901, 109 p), Four Thousand Questions and Answers (94 p), and Bible Atlas with Index (copyright 1914, 16 p) appear at end.

MnSJ has a similar Holman Pronouncing Edition (text paged as above, but size reported as 24 cm) which has been assigned the date of 1913? and contains the Treasury of Biblical Information, pictures with descriptions of oriental objects, Concordance, Questions and Answers, illustrations, and maps. See 1898?, No 2094.

1914 The Sacred Writings of the Apostles and Evangelists . . . New Testament . . . George Campbell, James MacKnight and Philip Doddridge . . . Alexander Campbell. Sixteenth Edition. Christian Board of Publication: St. Louis **2219**

26 cm   TNDC

Alexander Campbell Version; see 1826 NT, No 567. From the same plates as the 1870 edition (No 1862).

1914 The New Testament from the Greek Text as Established by Bible Numerics. Edited by Ivan Panin. [The Commonwealth Press, Printers, Worcester, Mass.] Bible Numerics Co.: New Haven   **2220**

1 vol: (xx) (665)   16 cm   DLC, NNAB

Printed in paragraph form with verse numbers in text. Alternative readings and renderings at foot of page. Copyright 1913, by Ivan Panin, Grafton, Mass.

Ivan Panin (1855–1942) was born in Russia, but his exile as a young man resulted in his eventually coming to the United States. He was graduated from Harvard University in 1882, and at about that time turned from agnosticism to Christianity. In 1890, Mr. Panin discovered a mathematical design underlying the Greek text of the NT. Subsequently he found that the OT had a similar structure. The above translation of the NT into English was in accordance with his system of Bible numerics. "The standard used for comparison was: for the Greek, the Revision of Westcott & Hort; and, for the English, the American Revised Version" (Preface).

In Panin's translation, every Greek word was rendered by the same English word, and each English word represented only one Greek word. Other literalisms were employed.

The second edition appeared in 1935 and was reprinted several times. Since 1935, it has been printed by the University Press at Oxford with varying imprints. In 1945 its distribution was transferred to the Book Society of Canada, Toronto. In the 1914 edition, the translation in Mark 14:27 appears as "all ye shall be stumbled"; in the 1935 edition, it reads "all ye shall stumble." Panin's edition of the Greek NT was published privately in 1934.

1915?   The Student's Bible . . . According to the Version of the 1911 Bible; with a New System of Connected Topical References . . . and a New System of Collected References . . . Oxford University Press, American Branch: New York   **2221**

Reported as (1152) (vii) 9–35 (134)   24 cm   DLC
Illustrations, some in color. Copyright 1915.

1915?   The Holy Bible, Translated from the Latin Vulgate . . . Published with the Approbation of His Eminence James Cardinal Gibbons, Archbishop of Baltimore. John Murphy Company, Publishers: Baltimore and New York   **2222**

21 cm   NNAB
Rheims-Douay Version. Reprint of 1914? edition (No 2217).

1915?   [The Holy Bible] "International" Series. Self-Pronouncing Edition. Containing Sixty Thousand Original References. The Precious Promise Holy Bible. The Authorized Version . . . with the "Exceeding Great and Precious Promises" Indexed and Marked in Red . . . Marked by J. G. Lawson . . . Glad Tidings Publishing Co.: Chicago   **2223**

21 cm   NNAB
Long Primer Octavo Clear Type Reference Edition. Text is similar to 1905? Christian Worker's Bible (No 2168) but with new system of marking. Preliminary matter includes frontispiece, Preface, Explanation of Markings, Precious Promises, Hurlbut's Preface, Order of Books, and Explanation of Pronouncing System. At end are List of Promises Marked (9 p), Bible Encyclopedia and Concordance by Hurlbut and McClure (with Winston imprint, 390 p), and maps. Illustrated. Copyright 1915, by John C. Winston; Entered 1915 at Stationers Hall.

1915   The Runner's Bible, compiled and annotated for the reading of him who runs, by Nora Holm. Houghton Mifflin Company: Boston and New York; The Riverside Press: Cambridge   **2224**

158 p   16 cm   NNAB
A compilation of passages arranged under various headings with some comment: Statements of Truth, The Divine Commands, and Promises. AV and ERV text prepared particularly for Christian Scientists. Many times reprinted over the years. Copyright 1913 and 1915, by Nora S. Holm.

1915?   [New Testament] The Greatest Book Ever Written; the New Testament in Its Inspired Literary Form, Authorized Version, by the Rev. S. Townsend Weaver . . . The University Literature Extension: Washington, D. C.   **2225**

Reported as (xxxiii) (692)   25 cm   DLC

1915   The New Testament . . . Printed for the New York Bible Society . . . American Bible Society: [New York]   **2226**

12 cm   NNAB
Reprint of the 1899 Agate 32mo (No 2106). Has dedication note, To the Defenders of Their Country! On inside cover is list of Selections For Your Emergency.

1916 The Emphasised Bible . . . By Joseph Bryant Rotherham . . . The Standard
Publishing Company: Cincinnati **2227**

4 vols in 1: (4) (32) 33–920 (4) (272)   23 cm   NNAB

Rotherham "Emphasised" Version; see 1878 NT, No 1930. Vol ɪ: Genesis-Ruth. Vol ɪɪ:
Samuel-Psalms. Vol ɪɪɪ: Proverbs-Malachi. Vol ɪv: NT. Each vol has separate title page. Preface
dated 1902; NT Preface dated 1897. Copyright 1897, by Joseph Bryant Rotherham; Reprinted
in the United States by the Standard Publishing Company, 1916.

NNAB also has separate NT (4, 272 p; 23 cm).

This version was reprinted a number of times by the Standard Publishing Company. In
1956 the plates were owned by James Raymond of Los Angeles, who had no plans for printing
at that time. However, the Faith Bible and Tract Society, Salem, West Virginia, had purchased
sheets and had them bound.

1916 The Twenty-Four Books of the Old Testament. Hebrew text and English
Version with Illustrations. Translation revised by Alexander Harkavy . . .
Hebrew Publishing Company: New York **2227A**

4 vols: (6) (1384) (6)   24 cm   DLC, NNJ

Four lines of Hebrew appear at head of title page. Hebrew and English text on facing
pages, double numbered 1–1384. Prefatory Note, List of Illustrations, and title to the Pentateuch precede text. Doré illustrations. Copyright 1916.

This is the first printing of the Alexander Harkavy revision. The English text is the AV
emended to make the language conform to modern usage; a few passages have been paraphrased.
"Among the passages emended are all those which have been mistranslated or colored to suit
Christian dogma. . . ."

Alexander Harkavy (1863–   ) was born in Nowogrudok, Russia, but came to America in
1882 where he took up residence except for a few years in Paris. His Yiddish dictionaries did
a good deal to secure the recognition of Yiddish as a literary language.

1916? The Soul Winners' Testament, Embodying in Concise Form Helps and
Connected Scriptural References, to the Clear Understanding of the Gospel's Teaching Regarding the Certainty and Security of a Believer's Salvation . . . A. J. Holman Company: Philadelphia **2228**

Reported as (x) (421)   12 cm   DLC

Holman Edition. The Self-Pronouncing New Testament . . . A. J. Holman . . . c1900 appears on added title page. See 1900 NT, No 2121.

1917? The Marginal Chain-Reference Bible. Revised Edition, Containing Thompson's New Condensed Cyclopedia . . . with . . . System of Topical Chain-
References . . . Self-Pronouncing Text. Compiled and Edited by Frank
Charles Thompson . . . Cambridge University Press: London; Chain-Reference Bible Publishing Co.: Mount Morris, New York **2229**

26 cm   DLC

Reprint of 1908? edition (No 2184).

1917? The Scofield Reference Bible . . . Authorized Version with a New System
of Connected Topical References . . . with Annotations, Revised Marginal
Renderings, Summaries, Definitions, Chronology, and Index, [etc.] . . . Edi-
ted by Rev. C. I. Scofield . . . [and Consulting Editors] . . . New and Improved
Edition . . . [Printed by the Abingdon Press, New York]. Oxford University
Press, American Branch: New York [etc.] **2230**

1 vol: (8) (1362) 151–378 (8) (12)   21 cm   MB, NN, NNAB, TU

A new edition (Facsimile Series No. 2) of the Scofield Bible; see 1909, No 2192. Introduction, Order of Books, How to Use the Subject References, and Introduction to the Pentateuch precede text. NT has Introduction to the Four Gospels and How to Use the Subject References. Indexes, Dictionary, Concordance, and colored maps at end. Copyright 1917, by Oxford University Press, American Branch.

NNAB also has a similar edition (Facsimile Series No. 1) reduced to 18 cm, first published in 1917. It does not contain the Dictionary, Subject Index, and Concordance.

The Rev. William L. Pettingill, D.D., was added to the list of contributing editors for this edition.

1917 The Holy Bible ... American Bible Society, Instituted ... : New York **2231**

1159 p   19 cm   NNAB

Army and Navy Edition, bound in blue or khaki. During World War I, the ABS supplied for the American forces a total of 4,920,543 volumes of Scriptures, most of them small Testaments (*ABS Report* 1920, p 18). "To expedite the printing and binding of a million Testaments for the Army and Navy two sets of electroplates were made from moulders and gauged for a certain imposition, from which four sets of steel plates were made for printing, amounting to 3,672 pages" (*ABS Report* 1918, p 39).

Other Army and Navy editions were printed from the 1855 Small Pica Octavo Bible (No 1587); the 1883 Minion 18mo Bible (No 1999); the 1887 Nonpareil 32mo NT (No 2029); and the 1899 Agate 32mo NT, with or without Psalms (No 2106). A Nonpareil Pocket NT (612 p, 10 cm) was issued in 1917. A 32mo NT (332 p, 13 cm) was issued in 1918 for the YMCA.

1917? The Holy Bible ... Nelson's Series. Thomas Nelson & Sons: New York **2232**

1 vol: (807) (248)   14 cm   NNAB

Ruby 32mo Army and Navy Edition, bound in khaki. A partial index, "A Prayer for a Soldier," spaces for addresses, and "The Star-Spangled Banner" appear on inside front cover and first leaf. Epistle Dedicatory and Order of Books precede text. "Onward Christian Soldiers" and "America" are printed on last leaf, with "Battle Hymn of the Republic" inside back cover.

1917? Holy Bible ... Nelson's Series. Thomas Nelson & Sons: New York **2233**

1 vol: (viii) (835)   13 cm   NNAB

Army and Navy Edition bound in khaki. Text paged same as 1913? Red Letter Edition (No 2214); no supplementary matter at end.

[5677] *1917* תורה נביאים וכתובים The Holy Scriptures According to the Masoretic Text. A New Translation with the Aid of Previous Versions and with Constant Consultation of Jewish Authorities ... The Jewish Publication Society of America: Philadelphia **2234**

1 vol: (xv) (1136)   18 cm   NNAB, OC

Jewish Publication Society Version; see 1903 Psalms, No 2151. Preface (dated September 27, 1916) and Table of Scriptural Readings precede text. Each of the three parts (The Law, The Prophets, The Writings) has its own title page. Printed in paragraph form, with poetical form in required places. Copyright 1917.

"The present translation is the first for which a group of men representative of Jewish learning among English-speaking Jews assume joint responsibility.... It aims to combine the spirit of Jewish tradition with the results of biblical scholarship, ancient, mediaeval, and modern" (Preface, p vii).

Professor Max L. Margolis prepared the manuscript of this version. His text was based on that of E. Baer, and for parts not completed by him, on the text of C. D. Ginsburg. The manuscript also made use of earlier translations which had been done for the Society, as well as ancient versions, other modern translations, and commentaries. In 1908, Prof. Margolis was elected Editor-in-Chief of a seven-member Board of Editors. The Board, sitting as a committee of the whole, considered this manuscript in sixteen sessions. At the last of these, in Oct – Nov of 1915, the revised proofs were accepted. (See Preface for a full account of the proceedings.) Psalms in this edition is a revision of the 1903 text.

This edition has been frequently reprinted with original date remaining on title page, but date of reprinting added on verso. A folio edition (34 cm) was produced in 1919 from a photographic enlargement of sheets of the 1917 edition. Abridgments were made for the armed forces of both World Wars: *Readings from the Holy Scriptures for Jewish Soldiers and Sailors* was published by The Jewish Publication Society of America in 1918 (iv, 276 p; 13 cm); a ninth impression of 20,000 copies was issued in 1941–42?, completing a total of 250,000 copies. *Readings from the Holy Scriptures prepared for use of Jewish Personnel of the Army of the United States* was published under the direction of the Chief of Chaplains by the United States Government Printing Office in 1942 (512 p, 14 cm). A peace-time abridgment, *The Holy Scriptures . . . for use in the Jewish School and Home*, was published by The Jewish Publication Society of America in 1931 (xxiv, 795 p; 22 cm). NNAB has copies of all of these.

1917?   The New Testament; a New Translation by James Moffatt . . . New Edition, Revised. [Printed in the United States of America.] Hodder and Stoughton, George H. Doran Company: New York   **2235**

1 vol: (xii) (395)   17 cm   NNAB

Moffatt's new translation of the NT was first printed by Hodder and Stoughton, Ltd., London, in 1913 (x, 327 p; 22 cm; NNAB). The publisher's records are incomplete because of war damage but the firm reports that "500 cancel titles" (with sheets?) were printed and an extra set of stereos sent to America about January 1914. The first royalties were received from the George H. Doran Company in July 1914; royalties for the same editions were later received in 1930 from Richard R. Smith and in 1933 from Harper and Brothers. NN, DLC, and other libraries have undated copies of the first edition imprinted *Hodder and Stoughton, George H. Doran Company* and copyright 1913. It seems impossible at this date to determine when the version was printed for the first time in America.

The New Edition, Revised, listed above, was purchased by NNAB in 1917 and may be the first American printing of the Moffatt Version. It is printed in paragraph form, single column. Sheets and then plates for this format were sent to Hodder and Stoughton in London in 1919.

NNAB has a reprint of the above dated 1930 and imprinted *Richard R. Smith, Inc.* NN and ViU have copies with *Everyday Life Edition* on title page, imprinted *Association Press, New York, 1917.* This was reprinted in 1941.

James Moffatt (1870–1944) was born in Scotland. He was Yates Professor of Greek at Mansfield College, Oxford, and later Professor of Church History at the United Free Church College, Glasgow. In 1927 he came to the United States and served as Washburn Professor of Church History at Union Theological Seminary, New York, 1927–1940. Dr. Moffatt made two different translations of the NT. The first preserved the language of the AV and was published in Edinburgh in 1901 under the title, *The Historical New Testament . . . A New Translation.* A second edition, somewhat revised, appeared in August of the same year. The second translation, based on the Greek text of von Soden, was first published in 1913 in England as noted above. It is a fresh translation in modern speech and not a revision of the 1901 edition (see Preface). This translation was published with the AV in a parallel edition in 1922 (No 2257).

Dr. Moffatt later translated the OT, which was first published in 1924–25 in 2 vols (No 2275). An edition of the complete Bible, incorporating the 1913 NT and the 1924–25 OT, was published in London in 1 vol in 1926; a revision was published in the United States by Harper & Bros. in 1935 (No 2350).

The Moffatt Version has been frequently reprinted in several formats. The NT text forms the basis of the Moffatt NT Commentary (17 vols). The text of the Gospels was also used in a continuous harmony arrangement with introductions and other comment in *Everyman's Life of Jesus, a Narrative in the words of the Four Gospels*, edited by James Moffatt, George H. Doran Company: New York, 1925 (242 p, 18 cm, NNAB).

1917   The New Testament . . . Emphasizing His Second Coming . . . Testament Publishing Corporation: New York   **2236**

383 p   14 cm   DLC, NNAB

Text of Acts 1:11 appears on title page. On verso are brief explanations of special features (emphasis by boldface type and colored ink — although there seem to be no examples of color) and statements that John Henry Troy has applied for copyright and that profits will go to worldwide missions.

1917? The New Testament . . . First Published . . . at Rheims . . . 1582. Special
  Edition for the Army and Navy, with a Foreword by . . . Cardinal Gibbons.
  Paulist Press for the Chaplains' Aid Association: New York   **2237**

1 vol: (vi) (554)   11 cm   NNAB, OC

Rheims Version. Has Imprimatur of Cardinal Farley, Foreword to the Soldiers and Sailors
of the United States (3 p), and Prayers (1 p).

1917? The New Testament . . . Nelson's Series . . . Thomas Nelson & Sons: New
  York   **2238**

10 cm   NNAB

This is the 1902? Ruby 32mo (No 2146) made up in an Army and Navy Edition. Presentation page has "The Governor's Salutation to the Soldier . . . Presented To [two lines for signa-
ture] by the Massachusetts Bible Society, Boston."
Also issued with Book of Psalms (177 p); also with national anthem, etc. on fly leaves
and inside covers.

1918? The Analytical Reference Bible Containing Four Valuable Aids to the
  Student of the Word of God. The Holy Bible with Marginal Notes and
  Analytical References; Comprehensive Bible Helps . . . Edited by Philip
  Schaff; The Whole Bible by Subjects . . . Edited by Roswell D. Hitchcock
  . . . and Cruden's Concordance, Edited by John Eadie . . . Funk & Wagnalls
  Company: New York and London   **2239**

27 cm   NNAB

Reprint of Wilmore's Analytical Reference Bible of 1891 (No 2043) in limp leather bind-
ing with thumb indexes. The Preface is undated. Copyright 1891, 1910, and 1918, by Funk
& Wagnalls Company.
DLC and TxDaM have 1921? reprint.

1918? The Holy Bible . . . Thomas Nelson & Sons: New York   **2240**

Reported as (806) (247)   15 cm   NNFM

This is a copy of one of the Nelson Ruby 32mo editions. There are four frontispieces
reproducing: (1) title page of Mark Baskett's Bible, London, 1767; (2) verso of title and cover,
"a reduced facsimile of the Bible upon which George Washington took the oath as First President of the United States The Bible was then, and has been ever since, the property of St.
John's Lodge, No. 1, Ancient York Masons, New York."; (3) presentation page; (4) portrait
of George II. The tooled leather cover is inscribed "God shall establish | St. John's lodge consti-
tuted | 5757 | burnt down the 8th of March | 5770 rebuilt and opened November 28 5770 | officers
then presiding Jonathan Hampton M | William Butler S W | Isaac Heron J W."

[*1918*] The Holy Bible . . . Thomas Nelson & Sons: New York   **2241**

Reported as (viii) (835)   13 cm   NNFM

Service edition with end papers containing Suggested Readings, "A Prayer for a Soldier,"
ownership page, "The Star-spangled Banner," "America," and "Battle Hymn of the Republic."
Presentation page inserted in front has "Sea and Field Lodge, No. 1, F.&A.M., State of New
York"; similar cover stamp. See 1917?, No 2233.

1918 The New Testament, translated and arranged by Charles Foster Kent . . .
  with the Collaboration of Charles Cutler Torrey . . . Henry A. Sherman . . .
  Frederick Harris . . . Ethel Cutler . . . Charles Scribner's Sons: New York
                                                                         2242

1 vol: (xix) (305)   18 cm   NNAB

Kent Version; see 1904–27 OT, No 2158. *The Shorter Bible* appears at head of title page;
see 1921, No 2253, for OT companion volume. The first three Gospels are printed in synoptic

form. Divisions in text are indicated by section numbers, with descriptive headings. In an endeavor to eliminate duplicated matter, about one-third of the NT text has been dropped. Contents give chapter and verse identification. Index of Biblical Passages at end.

NNAB also has a copy imprinted *The Woman's Press, New York,* and another marked Third Edition Revised (copyright 1922). OC has copy dated 1923.

1918? The New Testament. Translated from the Sinaitic Manuscript Discovered by Constantine Tischendorf at Mt. Sinai, by H. T. Anderson. . . . The Standard Publishing Company: Cincinnati   **2243**

320 p   18 cm   DLC, NN

Anderson Version; see 1864 NT, No 1785. Has Preface signed by Picket Anderson Timmins. This is Anderson's new translation, published posthumously.

1918 The New Testament. A New Translation by James Moffatt . . . Association Press: New York   **2244**

1 vol: (4) (340)   13 cm   NNAB

Moffatt Version; see 1917? NT, No 2235. *National War Work Council Young Men's Christian Association Edition* appears at head of title page. Issued through the courtesy of George H. Doran Company, New York, and printed in double column, paragraph form, probably from Doran's thin paper edition. However, this does not match the 1913 British format.

Hodder and Stoughton, Ltd. of London printed an edition in 1921 from Doran plates purchased in 1920.

1918? The New Testament and Catholic Prayer Book Combined . . . Benziger Brothers: New York, Cincinnati, [etc.]   **2245**

Reported as (36) (707)   12 cm   DLC

Rheims Version. *Edition for Soldiers and Sailors* appears at head of title. NT has separate title and frontispiece.

1918? The New Testament . . . first published . . . at Rheims . . . 1582. Special Edition for the Army and Navy with a Foreword by His Eminence James Cardinal Gibbons. Published by the Paulist Press . . . for the Chaplains' Aid Association: New York   **2246**

11 cm   DLC, NNAB, PLatS

Rheims Version. Reprint of 1917? edition (No 2237) with the addition of a page before title for name, etc., and at end, Tables of Subject References and Readings for Sundays and Holidays (p 555–565) and blank pages for notes (p 566–570). Copyright 1918, by The Missionary Society of St. Paul the Apostle in the State of New York.

NNAB has another copy imprinted *National Catholic War Council for the Chaplains' Aid Association, Washington, D.C.*

1919? The Holy Bible . . . [International Series. Self-Pronouncing. ClearNUType]. The John C. Winston Co.: Philadelphia   **2247**

995 p   20 cm   NNAB

Loose-leaf Bible with blank pages in front for notes. Inside binding is the statement: "Protected under United States Patent Rights of August 27, 1918, June 4, 1907; Dominion of Canada Patent Rights of June 24, 1919." For later edition with same format of text, see 1928?, No 2294.

1919 Simplified Edition of the Holy Bible . . . Indexing God's Promises . . . Also Simplified by an Extensive Series of Questions and Answers . . . S. A. Mullikin Co.: Marietta [Ohio]   **2248**

1 vol: (xxxii) (2) 7–1000 3–160 163–307 [1] (56)   20 cm   NNAB

Publisher's Preface (Marietta, 1919) states that the various helps will be of use to all readers. Preliminary matter includes God's Assurances of Spiritual and Temporal Blessings, Index to Leading Doctrines of the Bible, Contents of the Books, To Read the Bible Through in a Year, and the Dedication to King James. Text is printed from old plates in double column form with reference columns in outer margins. At end are The Bible Simplified by Questions and Answers, Concordance, and Subject Index, followed by 6 p for notes. 16 colored plates.

1919?   The Holy Bible . . . American Revision Committee A.D. 1901. Standard Edition. American Bible Society. Published by Thomas Nelson & Sons: New York   **2249**

19 cm   NNAB

ASV; see 1901, No 2124. This is the 1910? Brevier Duodecimo (No 2197) reprinted for the ABS. Prefaces are omitted. First listed in the *ABS Annual Report* for 1919.

1919–26?   [The New Testament] Concordant Version. The Sacred Scriptures. Designed to put the English reader in possession of all the vital facts of Divine revelation without a former knowledge of Greek by means of A Restored Greek Text with Various Readings, conforming, as far as possible, to the inspired autographs; A Consistent Sublinear, based upon a Standard English equivalent for each Greek Element, and An Idiomatic, Emphasized English Version with notes, which are linked together and correlated for the English reader by means of An English Concordance and Lexicon and a complementary list of The Greek Elements. The Concordant Publishing Concern: Los Angeles   **2250**

20 cm   NNAB

This consists of nine parts in a loose-leaf binder, with proof page numbers. Most of the parts are stapled in wrappers and printed on wartime paper. The Greek text and the annotated English version are on facing pages. Has six preliminary leaves, apparently issued as a prospectus, with copyright 1919, by A. E. Knoch on verso of title; Matthew's Account and Introduction has copyright 1926.

Cited copy lacks Concordance and other added matter.

Adolph E. Knoch was the editor of this version. His purpose was to give the Bible reader a means of interpreting the original text for himself through establishing a uniform English translation for each Greek form. To accomplish this work, Dr. Knoch and his assistants spent twenty-five years preparing a concordance in which the whole Greek vocabulary was analyzed and translated, along with a revision of the Greek grammar. This language system was the basis of the translation, which was made from the Textus Receptus with the addition of variations from the Alexandrinus, Vaticanus, and Sinaiticus codices. The translation was published in parts over the period 1921–26. It contains on one page the Greek text, including variations, with a sublinear English literal translation; and on the opposite page, the English idiomatic translation with notes.

A 1-vol reprint was issued in 1931 with proof page numbers removed (No 2323A). A pocket edition of the English idiomatic translation only was published in 1927? (No 2292).

1920?   Holman Home Bible . . . A. J. Holman Co.: Philadelphia   **2251**

Reported as (1246) (16) (4)   24 cm   CLSU

Has colored frontispiece. At end are A New Practical Course in Bible Reading, by Jos. V. Collins, and a Biblical Atlas with Index.

NNAB has a similar edition (Pica Octavo with references) which lacks general title page; NT title has Holman device and heading although it lacks imprint. The Bible Reading Course is also missing. Has Atlas (copyright 1898, 8 p) and 15 maps and charts.

1921?   The Holy Bible . . . [Composition by the Riverside Press, Cambridge, Mass.]. A. J. Holman Company: Philadelphia   **2252**

15 cm   NNAB

Reprint of 1895 edition (No 2065) but with chapter heads reset, and book and chapter indications extending to outer margin instead of centered between a split caption. *Holman Pronouncing Edition* appears at head of title. Colored maps at end. Copyright 1895, by A. J. Holman & Co.

1921   The Old Testament, translated and arranged by Charles Foster Kent . . . with the Collaboration of Charles Cutler Torrey . . . Henry A. Sherman . . . Frederick Harris . . . Ethel Cutler . . . Charles Scribner's Sons: New York
2253

1 vol: (xxxi) (622)   18 cm   NNAB
Kent Version; see 1904–27 OT, No 2158. *The Shorter Bible* appears at head of title page; for companion NT volume, see 1918, No 2242. About two-thirds of the text is omitted. Divisions in text are indicated by section numbers, with descriptive headings.

1921?   The New Testament . . . Printed by Rodeheaver Co.: Chicago and Philadelphia. [Jim Hicks Bible Society: Chicago]   **2254**

445 p   12 cm   NNAB
Has Foreword by the Publisher. At end are songs, The Anvil of God's Word, and letter from President Harding to Mr. Hicks.

1922?   The Holy Bible . . . [Printed by the Abingdon Press, New York]. Oxford University Press, American Branch: New York; Humphrey Milford: London
2255

1 vol: (1485) (15)   19 cm   NNAB
Long Primer 16mo. Has Epistle Dedicatory and Order of Books, Maps at end.

1922?   System Bible Study . . . Being an Effort to Give the Most Complete, the Most Concise and the Most Useful Book of Classified Bible Helps; the Gems, the Masterpieces, the Crown-Jewels, the Heart of the Bible by Many of the World's Greatest Bible Scholars . . . System Bible Co.: Chicago   **2256**

Reported as 786 p   23 cm   USl
This seems to be an early printing of Section II of the 1930 System Bible Study (No 2315).

1922?   The New Testament. A New Translation by James Moffatt . . . Together with the Authorized Version. Parallel Edition with Introduction . . . George H. Doran: New York   **2257**

1 vol: (xliii) (633)   20 cm   DLC, MB, NcD, NNAB
AV and Moffatt Version; see 1917? NT, No 2235. Copyright 1922, by George H. Doran Company; Printed in the U.S.A.
Hodder and Stoughton, Ltd., of London made two sets of molds for this NT in 1922, one of which was sent to New York. Royalties were received from Doran in 1923, from Smith in 1930, and from Harper in 1933. Harper must have begun publishing this NT in the older text early in 1933.
NNAB has 1930 reprint issued by Richard R. Smith, Inc., New York. Harper published a new parallel edition with the Moffatt text from the 1935 revised Bible; see 1935 NT, No 2352A.

1922   [New Testament] A Plainer Bible for Plain People in Plain American . . . from the Original Greek by Chaplain Ballentine . . . Plainer Bible Press: Jersey City   **2258**

461 p   19 cm   DLC, NN
Ballentine Version; see 1899–1901 NT, No 2102.

Simms (p 278) says that this edition is an improvement over previous editions. However, Cheek (p 150 f, note 2) says that "the two are quite obviously printed from the same plates and it is improbable that changes were made in the text. Obvious errors such as page numbers upside-down, omission of numbers and letters, badly broken and defaced type, and so on, are unchanged. Even the presswork is similar in such matters as poorly inked-pages and uncleaned type, which raises the question whether this was an attempt to dispose of the 7000 copies unsold from the poorly printed edition of 1909 [See No 2193]. In any case the 1922 edition is not to be considered a separate revision." Simms adds that the volumes were ruined by storage in a damp place before binding and only fifty or sixty copies were ever bound and given away.

1923   The New Indexed Bible ... Comprising Biblical Biography ... Revised and Enlarged from the Original Edition. John A. Dickson Publishing Company: Chicago   **2259**

1 vol: (ccxxxviii) (634) (507) (78)   25 cm   NNAB

Text uniform with the 1913 edition (No 2213) but with some variations in pagination, wording of title, and appended matter. Illustrated. Copyright 1901, 1909, 1913, and 1923.

1923   The New Testament. An American Translation by Edgar J. Goodspeed ... The University of Chicago Press: Chicago   **2260**

1 vol: (ix) (481)   21 cm   DLC, NcD, NN, NNAB, PPP

Preface and Contents precede text, which is printed in paragraph form, single column, without chapter and verse numbers. A key chapter and verse number appears at bottom of page. Poetical passages are in verse form, indented. Copyright 1923.

NNAB also has *The Student's Gospels ... arranged by Shailer Mathews, using The New Testament, An American Translation, By Edgar J. Goodspeed,* The University of Chicago Press: Chicago, 1927 (ix, 193 p; 17 cm), which has the synoptic Gospels printed in harmonized form, with the Gospel of John Following.

Dr. Edgar J. Goodspeed (1871–   ), professor of Biblical and Patristic Greek at the University of Chicago and one of the outstanding Biblical scholars of the country, translated the NT from the text of Westcott and Hort into "simple, straight-forward English of the everyday expression" for American readers. The Testament was well received and has been issued in numerous editions from 1923 to the present. The text has not been basically changed, though a few improvements were made in the Twenty-fifth Anniversary Edition of 1948. Dr. Goodspeed discusses many of his distinctive renderings in *Problems of New Testament Translation,* University of Chicago Press: Chicago, 1945. For a fascinating account of the reaction of the press, see Goodspeed's *As I Remember,* Harper and Bros.: New York, 1953. The NT was printed serially in the Chicago *Evening Post.* Early in October parts of it were read over radio station KYW.

In 1927 Dr. J. M. Powis Smith, in cooperation with other Biblical scholars, translated the OT from the Massoretic text into modern English as used by Americans, drawing on the latest scholarship in Hebrew and OT studies (see No 2290). In 1931 it was published together with the NT of Dr. Goodspeed under the title *The Bible, an American Translation* (see No 2321).

1923   The Riverside New Testament. A Translation from the Original Greek Into the English of To-Day by William G. Ballantine. The Riverside Press, [Cambridge] ... Houghton Mifflin Company: Boston and New York   **2261**

1 vol: (vii) 3–499   21 cm   CoD, CU, DLC, MB, NcD, NNAB, OC

Preface signed W. G. Ballantine and dated Springfield, Mass., January 1, 1923. Text printed in single column, paragraph form, without verse numbers. Copyright 1923.

William G. Ballantine (1848–1937), a Congregational minister and educator, was for many years associated with Oberlin Theological Seminary, serving as president from 1891–1906. His translation, based on Nestle's Greek text, is more literal than most modern speech versions. Ballantine states in the Preface that his NT aims "to serve as a plate glass window through which the man who does not read Greek will see in English what he would see if he did read Greek."

1923?   Simplified New Testament, Authorized Version; Black-Face Type — Self-Pronouncing in Part — Definitions of Hundreds of Words, Uncommon or Out of Use — Simplified Translations of Hundreds of Hard Passages — References on the Thought . . . and at the Beginning of Each Book is an Account of the Writer, the Ones Written to, and the Subject Written on; and an Important Outline of the Argument in the Book, with Carefully Prepared Headings . . . Edited by D. A. Sommer . . . "Simplified Bible" House: Indianapolis   **2262**

Reported as (viii) (475)   18 cm   DLC

1923   The New Testament . . . American Bible Society, Instituted . . . : New York
2263

1 vol: (452) (114)   13 cm   NNAB

This Nonpareil 32mo was one of the first editions issued by the ABS after the discontinuance of printing at the Bible House. Printing machinery had improved so much by this period that it was deemed no longer practical for the Society to do its own work. From 1853 to 1922 there had been printed and bound in the Bible House 76,051,112 volumes of Scripture in sixty-eight languages and six systems of embossed type for the blind. During 1921 the Society experimented with having some books printed and bound elsewhere. As of February 1, 1922, the pressroom and the composing and electrotyping departments were closed and the machinery sold. Contracts were let to outside firms which, by the use of large presses, were, for example, able to print and bind five sets of the Gospel of John at a time. An edition of 250,000 copies was printed in May 1922 to sell at 1¢ each. In 1923 the bindery was almost completely closed down and other arrangements were made for printing for the blind.

In 1923, an edition of 250,000 of the above NT was printed, sewed in 32-page signatures, and bound "two-up," and sold at 10¢ each in limp cloth, cut flush. A wire-stitched Testament printed from the same plates was issued in two forms: one on inferior paper with paper cover, selling at 5¢; and another with better binding and paper and containing the Psalms. These processes were much more practical for the large English editions the Society needed. While from 1850 to 1900 three or four English Bibles had been set up each decade, none were set from 1900 to 1920. With funds now available from more economical processes, new English Scriptures were planned. (See *ABS Reports* for 1922, p 32 and 36; 1923, p 41–44; 1924, p 41–43; and 1926, p 60.)

1923–25   [The New Testament] The Gospel according to St. Matthew, American Bible Society, Instituted . . . : New York   **2264**

11 parts   12 cm   NNAB

Above title taken from one of these 32mo portions of the NT, which are variously paged. These "penny portions" were published first with plain covers — some containing colored illustrations of places in the Holy Land — but later with picture covers — some with half-tones at end. They were originally issued at 1¢ each (2¢ with pictures); the price was raised to 2¢ in 1951, and to 3¢ in 1959.

1923   The New Testament . . . Rheims . . . 1582. Published by The Chaplains' Aid Association: New York   **2265**

11 cm   NNAB

Rheims Version. Reprint of 1917? edition (No 2237); has Tables and List of Readings at end, as in 1918? edition (No 2246). Has Imprimatur of Archbishop Hayes, 1923. Foreword by Pope Benedict xv, Sept 15, 1920. Copyright 1918.

1924?   The Holy Bible . . . [Hertel's New Standard Alphabetically Indexed Bible] . . . Alphabetical Arrangement of the Leading Doctrines, the Parables and Miracles, Harmony of the Gospels, Pictorial Pronouncing Dictionary . . . Red Letter Edition . . . The Only Family Bible Richly Illustrated with

1924?, continued

Beautiful Colored Plates of the Old Masters . . . Manufactured by the John
A. Hertel Co. for International Constructive Sunday School League: Chicago   **2266**

Reported as (xxxvi) (768) (41) (96)   34 cm   DLC
Illustrated.
DLC also has the following similar editions, all 30 cm, with titles same as above except for
omission of "Constructive" from imprint: 1931? (977 p), 1932? (1086 p), 1934? (198, 9–803,
96 p), 1942 Masonic edition with special matter (32, 254, 9–803, 96 p), and 1949 Masonic
edition.

1924? Holman Home Bible . . . A. J. Holman Company: Philadelphia   **2267**

24 cm   MB
Reprint of 1920? Home Bible (No 2251) with same added matter. Illustrated.

1924? [Holy Bible] The Living Word; the Bible Abridged for Public and Private
Reading; Edited and Arranged with Notes by H. H. Saunderson . . . The
Century Co.: New York   **2268**

1 vol: (xviii) (709)   23 cm   NNAB
The passages "which devoted readers love to mark" are printed in prose or poetry form
in large type, with an appendix containing notes, an index giving the references for passages
included in the order in which they appear, and another index giving the references in Biblical
order. A third index covers titles and topics. Copyright 1924.

1924? The Holy Bible . . . New York Bible Society: New York   **2269**

1 vol: (752) (239)   19 cm   NN
Family Record follows OT. Contains Wright's Bible Readers' Aids.

1924? The Holy Bible. The Great Light in Masonry . . . together with illuminated
frontispiece, presentation and Record Pages and Helps to the Masonic Student . . . A. J. Holman Co.: Philadelphia   **2270**

Reported as (16) (16) (827) (255) (14)   19 cm   NNFM
Masonic Edition appears at head of title page. Preliminary matter includes illuminated
altar and presentation pages and frontispieces; A Description of King Solomon's Temple, by
John Wesley Kelchner (copyright 1925, 16 p); Restoration of King Solomon's Temple, by
Kelchner (Helmle and Corbet, architects, N. Y. C., 16 plates); and The Great Light in Masonry, Bible Presentation, The Bible in Masonry by Joseph Fort Newton, Scriptural Quotations
and Allusions in the Masonic Ritual compiled by Sydney Morse, and Opening the Lodge (p 3–
16). Has New Practical Course in Bible Reading by Joseph V. Collins (14 p) at end.
    Scott G. Lamb, Executive Vice President of the A. J. Holman Company, states that prior
to March 1924 the firm did not have any Masonic editions although some Bibles may have been
issued with a special Masonic presentation page and with a Masonic emblem on the cover.
    NNFM also has copies bound with a variety of other material for Masons: One Hundred
and Sixty Questions and Answers Compiled from the Works of Albert G. Mackey and Many
Other Eminent Masonic Authorities, by C. E. Patterson (31 p); Index to Curious Facts, by
C. E. Patterson; Structure of Freemasonry, Newark, N. J., I. Bernard Edelstein (copyright
1931); A Masonic Creed; Ancient and Accepted Scottish Rite (Biblical references); Scriptural
Quotations and Allusions . . . York Rite . . . compiled by Ray V. Denslow; The Bible and King
Solomon's Temple (plates); History and Facts Concerning the Eastern Star, with Scriptural
Quotations and References prepared by Rev. W. Mark Sexson, revised 1941.

1924? The Holy Bible . . . Black Face 8vo Text . . . A. J. Holman Co.: Philadelphia
2271

1 vol: 5–827 3–255   19 cm   NNAB
The Holman Edition appears at head of title. Illustrated with maps.

1924 The Everyday Bible ... Edited by Charles M. Sheldon ... Thomas Y. Crowell Co.: New York   **2272**

1 vol: (x) (640)   18 cm   NN, NNAB

ASV; see 1901, No 2124. This is an abridgment which omits the Levitical Laws, genealogies, parts of the prophecies, and some other matter. The Gospels follow the Harmony of J. M. Fuller. Text is printed in prose and poetry form in sections, without chapter or verse indication. Subject Index at end. Copyright 1924.

DLC has second edition, published in 1939 (xiv, 640 p; 21 cm).

The Everyday Bible was edited over a period of some 25 years by Charles M. Sheldon (1857–1946). He served a long term as pastor of the Central Congregational Church, Topeka, Kansas, and from 1920 to 1925 was editor of the *Christian Herald*. Among his many writings was the world-famous *In His Steps* (Chicago, 1896).

1924 The Holy Bible ... A. J. Holman Company: Philadelphia   **2273**

14 cm   NNAB

Reprint of 1902 Agate 32mo (No 2138) with same supplementary matter. *Holman Pronouncing Edition* appears at head of title. Has Order of Books and Key to Pronunciation. Maps at end.

1924–28 [Old Testament] The Authentic Literature of Israel freed from the disarrangements, expansions and comments of early native editors, edited with an introduction by Elizabeth Czarnomska ... The Macmillan Company: New York   **2274**

2 vols: Part I, (xxxv) (2) (422); Part II, (xxxi) (1) (553)   24 cm   NN

Part I, From the Exodus to the Exile; Part II, From the Exile to the Recovery of Israel's Independence. Appendixes at end of each vol. The text is the AV with some modifications, notably the use of *Yahweh* for the Tetragrammaton. The arrangement of the text aims to show the results of the work of Driver, Haupt, Kent, et al, in simple form, without notes, and in chronological order beginning with the Decalogue. All the text is included at some point. Chapter and verse indication is given at the beginning of each section. Poetry is printed in broken lines, often attempting to show the parallelism of Hebrew poetry. The book is planned for the student and Bible reader to whom the longer and more elaborate works are not available.

1924–25 The Old Testament. A New Translation by James Moffatt ... George H. Doran Company: New York   **2275**

2 vols: Vol I, (xi) (560); Vol II, (x) 561–1031   20 cm   NNAB, OC

Moffatt Version; see 1917? NT, No 2235. Vol I (copyright 1924) has Preface dated Glasgow, 1924; Genesis-Esther. Vol II (copyright 1925) has Preface dated Glasgow, 1925; Job-Malachi. Printed in the U. S. A.

In the first six Books, Dr. Moffatt has indicated the several strata of texts by the use of italics and square brackets. Passages that are obscure in the Hebrew have been omitted, as indicated by dots.

1924 Centenary Translation of the New Testament Published to Signalize the Completion of the First Hundred Years of Work of the American Baptist Publication Society. Translated by Helen Barrett Montgomery ... The American Baptist Publication Society: Philadelphia   **2276**

Reported as 724 p   17 cm   PPABP

Dedication, Introduction, and Declaration of Discipleship precede text, which is printed in single column, paragraph form, with verse numbers in left margin.

NNAB has second printing, 1924 (same pagination and size as above). A 14th printing was issued in 1954. Title pages in current editions read *Centenary Translation, The New Testament in Modern English. Translated by Helen Barrett Montgomery, A.M., D.H.L., LL.D. The Judson Press: Philadelphia, Chicago, Kansas City, Los Angeles, and Seattle.*

NNAB also has separate printings of the Gospels (1924; 7, 308 p; 16 cm) and Acts (pamphlet subtitled *Acts of the Apostles, better entitled Acts of the Holy Spirit;* 2, 311–393 p; 16 cm).

Mrs. Helen Barrett Montgomery (1861–1934) lived in Rochester, New York, and was a licensed Baptist minister. She was the first woman to independently produce a translation of the NT in modern speech. It was based on the Greek text underlying the ERV.

1924? The "International" Christian Worker's New Testament, Indexed and Marked by the Best Methods of Bible Marking on all Subjects Connected with the Theme of Salvation . . . Edited by J. Gilchrist Lawson . . . The John C. Winston Company: Philadelphia, Chicago [etc.]   2277

Reported as 336 p   13 cm   DLC

1925? The Holy Bible . . . [Quiet Hour Edition]. Published for the United Society of Christian Endeavor . . . Oxford University Press, American Branch: Boston and New York   2278

Reported as (7) (1088)   18 cm   DLC
Has maps.
Several Masonic editions were printed with this same Bible text. DLC has one with The Bible and Masonry: the Great Light of the Lodge, by Joseph Fort Newton following text. NNFM has three with varying Masonic matter: one (vii, 1088, 132 p) with plates and maps, Introduction by Charles A. Conover, and The Sacred Volume of the Law in Royal Arch Masonry; a second published for the Board of General Activities, Grand Lodge, F. & A. M. (32, 1088, 132 p) with 19 plates and 12 maps, containing The Holy Bible in Freemasonry and other preliminary matter by James E. Craig (p 1–32) and The Oxford Bible Concordance for Masonic Use at end; and a third (1088, 8, 132 p) "with special helps for the student of Masonry."

1925? Concordia Junior Bible . . . Concordia Publishing House: St. Louis 2278A

1 vol: (10) 5–1081 (5) 3–334 (64) (12)   17 cm   NNAB
This is a pronouncing edition which has the Nelson Series device on NT title page. Presentation page precedes title; Epistle Dedicatory, Order of Books, Key to Pronunciation, and Bible Reading Plan by John Baer (4 p) precede text. Helps by P. Kretzmann (64 p) and 12 colored maps (copyright 1925) follow text.

1925? The Holy Bible . . . Oxford University Press, American Branch: New York, [etc.], [etc.]   2279

1276 p   15 cm   NN
S. S. *Scholars Edition* appears on cover. Contains The Sunday School Scholars Treasury of Practical Information, edited by F. N. Peloubet (copyright 1904). Illustrated.
NN also has 1926 edition.

1925? [New Testament] The People's New Covenant . . . Scriptural Writings Translated from the Meta-Physical Standpoint by Arthur E. Overbury. Being a Revision Unhampered by So-Called Ecclesiastical Authority. This Version Interprets the New Covenant . . . from a Spiritual or Meta-Physical Standpoint, and Recognizes Healing as Well as Teaching as a Component Part of True Christianity . . . [Didion & Company, New York, Hyatt & Lyon, Los Angeles, Printers]. Published and For Sale by Arthur E. Overbury: Monrovia, California   2280

1 vol: (53) (502) (229)   21 cm   CSmH, NcD, NN, NNAB
Preface setting forth the author's viewpoint precedes text. Subject Index at end, which contains statement that this version "is based on the premise of 'Scientific Statement of Being'

as given in 'Science and Health,' by Mary Baker Eddy" (p 7). Copyright 1925, by Arthur E. Overbury.

NNAB also has 1932 reprint (52, 502, 240 p; 21 cm) in which "change" becomes "deviation" in James 1:17 and some additional articles are included in the Explanatory Index Notes.

1925   The New Testament . . . Krusader Edition. N. C. Freeman: Philadelphia
2281

Reported as (7) 3–520   "12mo"   DLC

Preliminary matter includes References for Krusaders by Norris C. Freeman and frontispiece.

1925?   The New Testament . . . [International Series. Self-Pronouncing. Perfection
Type. Printed . . . at the International Press . . .]. The John C. Winston
Company: Philadelphia [etc.]   **2282**

1 vol: (476) (123)   19 cm   NNAB

Preliminary matter includes special page with illustration of printing of first English NT, "Commemorating the 400th Anniversary of the Printing of the First English New Testament, Translated by William Tyndale, 1525–1925"; Order of Books; and Key to Pronunciation. Has Book of Psalms at end.

Also issued without Psalms.

1925   The New Testament . . . American Bible Society, Instituted . . . : New York
2283

1 vol: (512) (126)   11 cm   NNAB

Nonpareil Pocket NT and Psalms with 300M, 1925 on verso of title, although pagination seems to differ from previous editions.

1926?   Standard Reference Indexed Bible . . . Self-Pronouncing. Words Spoken
by Christ Printed in Red; to Which is Added an Alphabetical and Cyclopedic
Index . . . Charts . . . Leading Doctrines, Alphabetically Arranged, An Alphabetical Bible Dictionary, a Practical Concordance, Harmony of the Gospels,
Parables and Miracles, etc., etc. A Hand Bible for Everyday Use . . . Published Exclusively by the John A. Hertel Co. for International Constructive
Sunday School League: Chicago   **2284**

Reported as (975) (295) (64) (144) (112)   24 cm   DLC

Has frontispiece, illustrations, and maps.

NNAB has a 1928? edition which contains Practical Instructions for Personal Workers, Helps to Bible Study, maps, and illustrations. DLC has the following later printings with similar title but varying contents: 1930?, 1937? ("This blue ribbon Bible . . . awarded the blue ribbon at the Texas Centennial Celebration, Dallas, Texas, 1936"), 1938 (with cover title, *Cyclopedic Indexed Bible;* 1865 p), 1941? (1865 p), and 1945? (with cover title, *Cyclopedic Indexed Bible, Good Shepherd Edition;* 1632 p). DLC and NNAB have copies of a 1948 edition copyright 1926, 1928, 1930, 1938, 1941, and 1948. The cover title is same as the 1945? edition, but title page adds after imprint, *Publishers of Blue Ribbon Bibles.* A section of Bible Helps (317 p) precedes text; at end are Bible Dictionary, Concordance, and maps; additional extra matter is scattered throughout. * indicates prophetic passages referring to Christ. Has many color plates dated 1945 and signed by Frank McDonough.

1926?   The Master Bible, the Master Bible Study Designed for Mastery of the
Bible Embracing the Studies of Biblical Archaeology, History, etc., Ency-
clopaedic Bible Dictionary . . . Systematized, Classified, Analytical, Topical
. . . By Many of the World's Most Eminent Bible Scholars . . . J. W. Dickson
& Co.: Chicago   **2285**

Reported as (xviii) (1821)   23 cm   DLC

This is somewhat similar to Dickson's Indexed Bible and Analytical Indexed Bible (see 1902?, No 2134, and 1931, No 2320), but not identical. Maps.

1926?   The Picture Bible. Self Pronouncing with Marginal References, Maps and
Numerous Helps. 583 Explanatory Illustrations Including 16 Color Plates
of the Famous Biblical Paintings by Tissot . . . Published by the Bible Corporation of America: New York   **2286**

20 cm   NNAB

Reprint of the 1898 New Illuminated Holy Bible (No 2093) with addition of 16 colored
plates from Tissot. Copyright 1897, 1898, 1924, and 1925, by Frank E. Wright, and 1926, by
the Bible Corporation of America.

1926?   The Holy Bible . . . Text conformable to that of the edition of 1611 . . . Bold
Black Type 16mo.   A. J. Holman and Company: Philadelphia   **2287**

1 vol: (1276) (4) (14) (256) (2)   18 cm   NNAB

Holman Pronouncing Edition appears at head of title page. Order of Books and A Key to
Pronunciation precede text, which is arranged with center references. Each chapter is consecu-
tively numbered 1–1189. At end are New Practical Course in Bible Reading by J. V. Collins
(copyright 1924), Holman's Inclusive Dictionary Concordance (copyright 1925), List of
Words Likely to be Misunderstood, and colored maps (copyright 1904, 12 p).
This book was first listed in Holman's 1926 Catalog.

1926   The Holy Bible . . . [Self-Pronouncing Edition] . . . National Bible Press:
Philadelphia   **2288**

Reported as (990) (303)   17 cm   ViU

Printed in 8 pt. Cushing Bold type. Illustrated.
DLC has 1927? Masonic edition with this text, which contains Freemasonry by J. Myron
Shimer, illustrations, and maps. NNAB has 1932 edition, many copies of which were distributed
through the Chicago Bible Society. The NT was also issued separately, with or without Psalms.

1926   The Twenty-Four Books of the Old Testament. Hebrew text and English
Version. Translation revised by Alexander Harkavy . . . Hebrew Publishing
Company: New York   **2289**

2 vols: (4) (1384) (6)   22 cm   NN

Harkavy revision; see 1916 OT, No 2227A. Hebrew and English text on facing pages,
double numbered 1–1384. Reprinted without illustrations.

1926   The New Testament, An American Translation by Edgar J. Goodspeed . . .
The University of Chicago Press: Chicago   **2289A**

1 vol: (x) (481) (5)   18 cm   NNAB, ViU

Goodspeed Version; see 1923 NT, No 2260. This thin-paper edition is marked fifth impression March 1926 and has small chapter and verse numbers added at inner margins.
NN has a copy with *Tyndale Edition* in center of title page. It contains a one-page Preface
by Dr. Goodspeed for the Tyndale Edition, dated Oct 1925; however, the list of printings on
verso of title has fifth impression February 1925 and sixth impression November 1925. As the
format is the same as above cited edition, there were possibly two sets of plates.

1927   The Old Testament. An American Translation. By J. M. Powis Smith, of the
University of Chicago; Theophile J. Meek, of the University of Toronto;
Alex. R. Gordon, of the United Theological College and McGill University;
and Leroy Waterman, of the University of Michigan. Edited by J. M. Powis
Smith. Chicago University Press: Chicago   **2290**

1 vol: (xii) (1713)   24 cm   NNAB, OC

Four parts in 1 vol: Part I — The Pentateuch, Part II — The Historical Books, Part III
— The Poetical Books, Part IV — The Books of the Prophets, followed by Appendix. Each part
has title page. Preface and Contents precede text. Printed in paragraph form, single column,

with verse and chapter numbers in margin. Appendix at end contains textual notes. Copyright 1927. For American Translation of NT by Edgar J. Goodspeed, see 1923, No 2260.

The Psalms, translated by J. M. Powis Smith, appeared in advance of the OT. It was published by The University of Chicago Press: Chicago, 1926 (xiii, 274 p; 24 cm; NNAB).

1927 [New Testament] The Emphatic Diaglott, containing the original Greek text . . . with an interlineary word for word English translation, a new Emphatic Version based on the interlineary translation . . . by Benjamin Wilson. Publishers: International Bible Students Association, Watch Tower Bible and Tract Society: Brooklyn, New York, U. S. A. [etc.]   *2291*

923 p   17 cm   NNAB

Benjamin Wilson Version; see 1865 NT, No. 1792.

Printing was begun in the organization's old plant but finished in their new one. Editions were printed every few years. NNAB was informed in 1933 that the plates had been acquired "about 40 years ago." The text has been reset, breathings and accents having been added to the Greek text.

1927? [New Testament] Concordant Version. The Sacred Scriptures. An Idiomatic, Consistent English Version, Conforming to the Basic Laws of Language, in that, as far as Possible Each English Expression Constantly Represents its Closest Greek Equivalent, and Each Greek Word is Translated by an Exclusive English Rendering . . . Concordant Publishing Concern: Los Angeles

2292

383 p   16 cm   NN, NNAB

Concordant Version; see 1919–26? NT, No 2250. A pocket edition containing reprint of the idiomatic English text found in the Complete Greek/English Edition of 1919–26. Foreword signed "The Compilers." Copyright 1927, by A. E. Knoch.

A "Revised, International Edition" was issued in 1944? with the title: *The Sacred Scriptures. "New Testament." An Idiomatic, Consistent, Emphasized Version, Conforming to the basic laws of language, in that, as far as feasible, each expression selected constantly represents its closest Greek equivalent, and each Greek word is given one, exclusive English rendering . . .* (319, 321–381 p; 20 cm). NNAB has a copy of this which includes A Practical Keyword Concordance at end (342 p).

1928 The Living Bible, being the Whole Bible in its fewest Words. Edited from the King James Version by Bolton Hall . . . Alfred A. Knopf: New York   *2293*

423 p   24 cm   NNAB

Preface, signed B. H., has statement: "The Living Bible attempts to present in condensed form the entire contents of the Scriptures, omitting only repetitions, ceremonial details, most genealogies, land-boundaries, and matter that is no longer of general interest. . . . The Order of the books is that of the King James Version, except for the Epistles and the Prophets, where the editor has followed nearly the order found in Moulton's Modern Reader's Bible." Printed in paragraph form with verse numbers in margin. Also divided into sections with topical headings. Copyright 1928, by Alfred A. Knopf, Inc.

Bolton Hall (1854–1938) was a lawyer, author, and advocate of single tax reform.

1928? The Marked Bible, Being the King James . . . Version . . . Marked by the Best Methods of Bible Marking on all Subjects Connected with the Themes of Salvation [Red], The Holy Spirit [Green], Temporal Blessings [Brown], Prophetic Subjects [Purple], so as to Enable Any Person to Turn Rapidly to Verses on any Subject Marked . . . Marked by J. Gilchrist Lawson . . . [Printed at the International Press.] The John C. Winston Company: Philadelphia, [etc.]   *2294*

1 vol: (12) (995) (24) (iv) (390)   21 cm   DLC, NNAB

A new device appears on verso of title page. Explanations, Introduction, Order of Books, and Pronunciation Key precede text. NT, marked ClearNUType Edition, has no imprint. At end are Summary of References, The International Teachers' Handy Bible Encyclopedia and Concordance (edited by Rev. Jesse Lyman Hurlbut and Rev. Alfred J. P. McClure), and colored maps. Copyright 1928, by The John C. Winston Co. The Encyclopedia is copyright 1908 by Winston and has the 1905 International device.

The color is added by over-printing. This text was also published with the words of Christ in red, and again in loose leaf form.

1928? The Holy Bible. Red Letter Edition . . . Large Type. Octavo. [Manufactured by The Commercial Bookbinding Company, Cleveland.] World Syndicate Company, Inc.: New York   **2295**

21 cm   NNAB

Reprint of 1901 Red Letter Edition (No 2126) but with a shorter note (dated 1913) after the Synopsis of Books. *Self-Pronouncing Helps and References* appears at head of title page. Copyright 1901, by Klopsch.

In 1928 the Commercial Bookbinding Company of Cleveland, which had previously printed books for other publishers, bought out the World Syndicate Publishing Company. All Bibles and Testaments with this imprint must have been published before 1946, when the word "Syndicate" was dropped from the imprint. Copyright dates cover various types of added matter and do not indicate when the books were actually published. See 1907? Bible, No 2179. For other editions published by the firm at this time, see No 2296, No 2297, No 2298, and No 2300.

1928? The Holy Bible . . . The World Syndicate Publishing Company: Cleveland and New York   **2296**

1 vol: 17–976 3–296; other matter var. paged   21 cm   NNAB

Self-pronouncing edition with center references and chronology. Has presentation page with colored picture on verso. Contains Synopsis of Books and note about * for Messianic OT prophecies. The note is shorter than in the Red Letter Editions of 1901 (No 2126) and 1928? (No 2295). Has Family Record. No imprint on NT title page. From the Fly-leaf of D. L. Moody's Bible, Order of Books, Bible Readers' Aids by Wright, and colored maps with index follow text. Colored illustrations and half-tones in NT.

1928? The Holy Bible . . . [Press of The Commercial Bookbinding Co., Cleveland]. World Syndicate Publishing Company: Cleveland and New York
2297

1 vol: (800) (246) (8) (28) (118)   20 cm   NNAB

Self-Pronouncing Edition appears at head of title page. Following NT are Some of the Passages Changed in the Revised Version (5 p), A Brief Summary of the Characteristics of the Books (2 p), The Bible Readers' Aids by Wright (without imprint or copyright, 28 p), Concordance (118 p), and colored maps (8 p).

IaU and ICN have entries for similar books with 64 p of Bible Aids by Wright, dated 19—? and 194–? respectively.

NNAB also has: (1) A separate NT of the cited edition. (2) An edition (17 cm) received in 1950 and imprinted *World Publishing Company*, evidently made by photographic reduction of the above Bible; contains text and A Brief Summary . . . , plus colored presentation page; printed after 1945. (3) Another undated copy (15 cm) imprinted *David C. Cook Publishing Company: Elgin, Illinois*, printed on very poor quality paper and bound in coated stock, which was evidently reduced from the cited entry.

For World Syndicate Publishing Co., see No 2295 of this year.

1928? The Holy Bible . . . [Press of the Commercial Bookbinding Co.: Cleveland]. World Syndicate Company, Inc.: New York   **2298**

1 vol: (752) (233) (68)   19 cm   DLC, NNAB

Order of Books precedes text. Bible Readers' Aids, and 8 p of half-tones and maps at end. Copyright 1922, by World Syndicate Co., Inc.

NNAB also has similar copy, copyright 1923, with imprint of *New York Bible Society* and half-tones bound in before title. NNAB has a Red Letter Edition in a zipper binding with imprint lacking the word "Syndicate"; it contains Wright's Aids (copyright 1924, 61 p), Concordance (118 p), Family Record before NT (4 p), and 8 p of colored maps (different from those in cited edition). PLatS has copy similar to this last edition but with "Syndicate" in imprint and no Concordance.

For World Syndicate Publishing Co., see No 2295 of this year.

1928?   The Holy Bible . . . [De Molay Edition]. Together with . . . Helps to the De Molay Student . . . A. J. Holman Company: Philadelphia   **2299**

Reported as (16) (1161) (121)   19 cm   DLC

Contains title page of Holman pronouncing editions, and Four Thousand Questions and Answers for the Use of Students and Sunday School Teachers. Has frontispiece, presentation page, and maps.

1928?   The Holy Bible . . . [Printed by the Commercial Bookbinding Company . . .] World Syndicate Company, Inc.: New York   **2300**

1 vol: (iv) (1203)   18 cm   NNAB

Bold Minion type with center references. A star following an OT passage indicates a prophetic reference to Christ. Copyright 1907 by Louis Klopsch, New York City.

NNAB also has a red letter edition without copyright but with Wright's Bible Reader's Aids (32 p), A New and Practical Plan of Self-Pronunciation (26 p), Calendar for Daily Reading of Scriptures by D. W. Whittle (4 p) and colored maps (8 p).

1928?   The Holy Bible . . . [Press of the Commercial Bookbinding Co.: Cleveland]. New York Bible Society: New York   **2301**

1 vol: (800) (300) (8)   15 cm   NNAB

Contains half-tone frontispiece, and Calendar for Daily Reading of Scriptures and Comment on the Lord's Prayer by the Rev. Hugh Macmillan. Copyright 1923, by World Syndicate Co., Inc.

Although this bears a 1923 copyright, it must have been published between 1928 and 1945. For World Syndicate Publishing Co., see No 2295 of this year.

NNAB has another copy with World Syndicate imprint only, containing same material but no copyright date. DLC has copy with World Syndicate imprint only.

1928   The Psalms Complete. Their Prayers, their Collects, their Praises, in three Books. Separated, arranged and translated by William Wallace Martin. Press of Marshall & Bruce Co.: Nashville, Tennessee   **2302**

3 parts: Part I, (14) 9–121; Part II, (14) 9–120; Part III, (14) 9–89   11 cm   NNAB

NNAB also has 1940? reprint with additional notes, issued by The Parthenon Press: Nashville (xiv, 365 p; 16 cm).

Other parts of the Martin translation were published as follows (all held by NNAB):

> 1929   The Book of Job in two Versions: a Judean Version, an Ephramæan Version; and The Book of Ecclesiastes. Reconstructive Studies. Separated, arranged, and translated by William Wallace Martin. Press of Methodist Publishing House: Nashville
> (191 p, 11 cm).

> 1940   Isaian Prophecies. Promises to Chosen People; Punishments to Chosen People; Promises to Other Peoples; Punishments to Other Peoples. Reconstructed, Retranslated and Annotated by William Wallace Martin. The Parthenon Press: Nashville
> (xi, 262 p, 16 cm).

1940   Jeremiah-Ezekiel Prophecies of Promises to Chosen People ... [etc., as
       above]. The Parthenon Press: Nashville
       (xii, 301 p, 16 cm).

1941   The Book of Genesis Complete. The Ephramean Version, its Author a De-
       scendant of the Northern Kingdom; the Judean Version, its Author a
       Descendant of the Southern Kingdom. Reconstructed and Retranslated by
       William Wallace Martin. The Parthenon Press: Nashville
       (x, 219 p, 16 cm).

1941   Twelve Minor Prophets, Complete . . . [as above]. Parthenon Press:
       Nashville
       (xi, 206 p, 16 cm).

William Wallace Martin (1851-1947) was a graduate of Wesleyan University who later
studied at Drew Seminary, Leipzig, and Bonn. For seven years he was professor of Hebrew
at Vanderbilt University. In 1909 he was "set aside" by the New York East Conference of the
Methodist Episcopal Church "to pursue investigations in the Old Testament." He had previously
published two books on the structure and documents of the Pentateuchal books, against the
dominant Wellhausen school: *Torah of Moses*, 1900 (339 p, octavo) and *Law and Covenant,
being a critical study of Deuteronomy, its separation into two versions*, 1902 (213 p, octavo).

In 1928 Martin began to publish the above parts under various imprints, at Nashville.
(Parthenon Press is the term used when the Methodist Publishing House in printing but not
publishing a work.) The work is of a highly original nature. The text is divided into brief sections with headings; the chapter number in the traditional order is noted at the end. So extensive
are the rearrangements that it is impossible to determine without a full collation whether the
entire text has been included, or whether some sections may not have been abbreviated or
removed. For New Testament see No 2360, 1937?.

1928   The Christian's Bible ** New Testament. A Translation from the Greek,
         Chiefly of the Codex Sinaiticus and Codex Vaticanus; These Being the
         Oldest and Most Complete MSS. of the New Testament. It is not Simply
         a Translation of Words, but Under the Guidance of the Holy Ghost, His
         Thoughts, as Recorded in Greek by His Specially Inspired Writers, are
         Made Known Unto Us. By a Servant of Christ. Published by George N.
         LeFevre: Strasburg, Pennsylvania   *2303*

Unpaged   23 cm   NNAB
Preface, Brief History of English Versions, and Table of Contents precede text, which is
in paragraph form, double column, with verse numbers in text. Footnotes. Material on codices
Sinaiticus and Vaticanus at end, with facsimiles. Blank pages for notes. Copyright 1928.

George LeFevre is considered the translator as well as the publisher of this Testament.
His aim was to make an English translation as close to the original as possible. The translation
is therefore dependent on the interpretation of the translator as to meaning, and it contains a
number of highly original changes. Simms (p 254) states that it is the last "immersion" version
to be published in America.

Union Catalog lists entry for DLC with date of 1929, [352] p. In NNAB folder describing
the translation, the title is reproduced with date 1929.

1928?   The New Testament [and Psalms] . . . [Press of The Commercial Book-
          binding Co., Cleveland]. World Syndicate Publishing Co., Inc.: New York
                                                                             2304

588 p   13 cm   NNAB
NNAB also has a copy without Psalms (457 p), which lacks the word "Publishing" in
imprint.

1929?   The New Indexed Bible . . . Comprising Biblical Biography . . . Illustrated
          with Photographs . . . Making a Sacred Album for Every Home . . . Revised

and Enlarged from the Original Edition . . . John A. Dickson Publishing
Company: Chicago **2305**

25 cm   DLC

Reprint of the 1923 edition (No 2259). For original Dickson Indexed Bible, see 1902?,
No 2134.

1929? The New Chain-Reference Bible . . . Second Revised Edition. Containing
Thompson's Chain-References and Text Cyclopedia . . . Complete System
of Bible Study . . . Self Pronouncing . . . Compiled and Edited by Frank
Charles Thompson . . . B. B. Kirkbride Bible Co.: Indianapolis **2306**

23 cm   DLC

This is the fifteenth reprint of the Marginal Chain-Reference Bible; see 1908?, No 2184.
Illustrated.

1929? The Holy Bible . . . Newly Edited by the American Revision Committee
A.D. 1901. Standard Edition . . . Thomas Nelson & Sons: New York **2307**

1 vol: (viii) (2) (1022) (v) [1] (291)   23 cm   NNAB

ASV; see 1901, No 2124. Pica Octavo, which includes only the American Prefaces. Has
Family Record between Testaments and 12 p of colored maps at end. Copyright 1901 by Nelson
and 1929 by the International Council of Religious Education which took over the expiring Nelson copyright.

1929? The Holy Bible . . . Being the version set forth A.D. 1611 . . . Revised
A.D. 1881–1885. Newly Edited by the American Revision Committee A.D.
1901. Standard Edition . . . Thomas Nelson & Sons: New York **2308**

21 cm   NNAB

ASV; see 1901, No 2124. Reprint of the 1901? edition (No 2125) but with A New Concordance combined with a Subject-Index and Pronouncing Dictionary (copyright 1903, 234 p)
at end. Copyright 1901, by Thomas Nelson & Sons, and 1929, by International Council of Religious Education.

1929? The Holy Bible . . . National Bible Press: Philadelphia **2309**

1 vol: (990) (303) (160) (72) (22)   19 cm   NNAB

Teachers' Self Pronouncing Reference Edition appears at head of title. Bold face type.
Text set page for page and often line for line with that of the 1926 edition (No 2288) but
has a center reference column with chronology and reference symbols in the text, making a
wider and longer page. Epistle Dedicatory, Order of Books, and Key to Pronunciation precede
text. Concordance, Practical Helps to Study, and Atlas at end. Date supplied from folder
announcing publication of this Bible Oct 1, 1929.

1929 The Holy Bible . . . American Revision Committee, 1901. American Standard Version . . . Thomas Nelson & Sons: New York **2310**

18 cm   DLC, ICU, NcD

ASV; see 1901, No 2124. Brevier Duodecimo reprinted from the 1910? edition (No 2197).
Copyright 1929, by International Council of Religious Education.

1929 The Holy Bible . . . Twentieth Century Edition . . . Co-operative Bible Publishers: Philadelphia **2311**

1 vol: (990) (303)   17 cm   DLC, NNAB

Text reprinted from the National Bible Press edition of 1926 (No 2288) but with considerable material omitted, a row of asterisks appearing in the blank spaces. Note on verso of title

page: "This Twentieth Century Edition . . . from which certain indicated deletions have been made." The omitted material, all in the OT, seems to consist mostly of genealogies and passages considered "indelicate." Has presentation page, ornate title, and Order of Books classified by subject but in normal order. Also Family Record. Three blank pages for notes at end. Several half-tones of famous paintings. Blue fabricoid cover has a gold seal with an open Bible inside the legend, *To read, to fear, to hope, to pray.*

1929   The New Testament in Blank Verse by Geo. W. Wolff. Becktold Company, Edition Binders: St. Louis   *2312*

1 vol: (8) (586)   24 cm   DLC, MB, NN, NNAB

Has Introduction. Text printed in blank verse form, single column, with regular verse numbers and chapter numbers in margin. Copyright 1929.

Mr. Wolff states that "a late authentic Bible" was used in his transposition of the text to blank verse (see Introduction). According to Cheek (p 156) this is only the AV in verse form, or as the Introduction states, "pentameter or so-called heroic or blank verse." Both italic and bold face type are used.

1929?   The New Testament; A New Translation, by James Moffatt . . . Hodder and Stoughton . . . George H. Doran Company: New York   *2313*

Reported as (x) (327)   21 cm   IU

Moffatt Version; see 1917? NT, No 2235.

The date was supplied by the IU cataloger. It would probably be one of the last with the Doran imprint.

1930?   The Holy Bible . . . [Indexed Self-Pronouncing Edition] . . . Including . . . Index . . . Edited and Revised by A. Dana Adams . . . A. J. Holman Company: Philadelphia   *2314*

Reported as 1071 p   30 cm   DLC

Contains The Life of Our Lord Jesus Christ, by Rev. James Stalker, and A New Self-Pronouncing Dictionary Compiled from the Latest Editions of William Smith (96 p). Illustrated.

1930   The System Bible Study, being an effort to give the most complete, the most concise, and the most useful book of classified Bible helps. The gems, the masterpieces — the crown-jewels, the heart of the Bible by many of the World's greatest Bible scholars. Revised and enlarged Edition of 1930. The System Bible Company: Chicago   *2315*

1 vol: (4) (426) (10) (786) (31)   23 cm   NNAB

Text is based on the AV and ASV. Section i: Historical and General Information (a sort of concordance or Bible dictionary with lists of miracles, prayers, and parables) and maps and photographs (half-tones). Section ii: Classified Scripture (text arranged by subject) followed by Laws, Prophecies, Gospels harmonized in parallel column (based on A. T. Robertson) and interwoven (by William M. Reese), Teachings of Jesus, Passages arranged by other subjects, Sayings of the Angels, Sayings of Satan, etc. Copyright 1922 and 1927. For earlier printing of Section ii only, see 1922?, No 2256.

The System Bible Company also published this year *The Bible in My Everyday Life*, edited by Eugene Franklin Reese (432 p, 20 cm, NNAB) which consists of passages from the AV arranged by subject. This is much less elaborate than the System Bible.

1930   The Holy Bible . . . Translated from the Latin Vulgate . . . Douay Version. Published with Approbation of His Eminence James Cardinal Gibbons, Archbishop of Baltimore . . . J. Murphy Company: Baltimore   *2316*

Reported as (991) (282)   18 cm   LU

Rheims-Douay Version. *Murphy Edition* appears at head of title page. Illustrations, maps, and plan.

1930? The Holy Bible . . . A. J. Holman: Philadelphia **2317**

Reported as (16) (916)   16 cm   DLC

Contains History and Facts Concerning the Order of the Eastern Star with Scriptural Quotations and References prepared by Rev W. Mark Sexson. Maps.

193–? Explanatory Notes Upon the New Testament. [with Text], by John Wesley, M.A., Late Fellow of Lincoln College, Oxford . . . Eaton & Mains: New York; Jennings & Graham: Cincinnati   **2318**

734 p   23 cm   NNAB

Wesley Version; see 1791 NT, No 35. *Wesley's Notes*. *The Methodist Book Concern* appears on cover. Preface (dated 1754) and List of Notes on the Gospel of St. Matthew precede text. Notes on lower part of page, and references at bottom of page. Explanatory notes also precede each Book. Index of Words Explained at end.

1930? The New Testament . . . National Home Library Foundation: Washington, [D. C.]   **2319**

Reported as 402 p   IaU

No further information reported.

1931 New Analytical Indexed Bible. Authorized Version, with More Accurate Renderings of the A.R.V. Placed in Brackets in the Text. A System of Helps Comprising Textual Revision, Analysis of the Entire Bible, Treatment of Outstanding Facts of Each Book, Forty-Two Charts, Contemporaneous History, A Specially Arranged Harmony of the Gospels, A Condensed Dictionary of the Bible, and Many Other Features . . . [Edited by James R. Kaye]. John A. Dickson Publishing Co.: Chicago   **2320**

1 vol: (6) (220) (6) (1639)   25 cm   NNAB

Preface, Dedication to King James, Outline, Introduction, Character Building, Index and Digest, Pronunciation Chart, and List of Books and Abbreviations precede text. Gospel Harmony follows John. At end are Chronology; Index to Hebrew Laws; Calendar, Weights, and Measures; Indexes to Lives, etc.; Topical Study; Concordance; Bible Atlas; and maps. Copyright 1931.

New copyrights were secured in 1938, 1941, and 1947, covering new supplementary material. For new edition, see 1950?, No 2485.

1931 The Bible. An American Translation. The Old Testament Translated by a Group of Scholars Under the Editorship of J. M. Powis Smith. The New Testament Translated by Edgar J. Goodspeed. The University of Chicago Press: Chicago   **2321**

1 vol: (xvii) (1619) (iv) (418)   22 cm   NN, NNAB

American Translation; see 1923 NT, No 2260, and 1927 OT, No 2290. Preface and Contents precede text. Prefaces to both Testaments. The NT has been reset but the OT seems the same as first published, except for a few changes in the text. Copyright 1931.

OC has seventh impression, 1946.

1931 The Holy Bible . . . Grosset & Dunlap, Publishers: New York   **2322**

1 vol: (8) (1080) (8)   19 cm   NNAB

Frontispiece; Epistle Dedicatory; Introduction by John H. Finley; Order of Books; Why and How to Read, What to Read, Quotations, etc., edited by Wilbert W. White; Biographical and Geographical Dictionary; and maps precede text. Illustrated.

This Bible was printed for Grosset and Dunlap by the Van Rees Press, which at that time owned the plates, having taken them over from a bankrupt previous owner.

1931–46   The Interpretation of the [New Testament] . . . R. C. H. Lenski. Lutheran
    Book Concern: Columbus, Ohio   **2323**

12 vols   23 cm   KyLoS

    Contains an independent translation by R. C. H. Lenski. Each vol has separate title and
pagination: Matthew, 1943, 1181 p. Mark, 1946, 775 p. Luke, 1946, 1212 p. John 1931, 1418 p.
Acts, 1934, 1126 p. Romans, 1936, 934 p. Corinthians, 1935, 1383 p. Galatians, Ephesians,
Philippians, 1937, 911 p. Colossians-Philemon, 1937, 986 p. Hebrews-James, 1938, 685 p.
i Peter-Jude, 1938, 662 p. Revelation, 1935, 686 p. Matthew, Mark, and Luke were published
by The Wartburg Press, Columbus.

    Richard Charles Henry Lenski (1864–1936) was born in Prussia but was brought up in
Michigan. He received an A.B. from Capital University in 1885 but he accepted a pastorate in
1887 before completing seminary training. For twenty years he was a professor at the Evangelical Lutheran Theological Seminary in Columbus, serving as Dean from 1919 to 1935. He was
also editor of the *Lutherische Kirchenzeitung* from 1904 to 1924. He was awarded an M.A.
from Capital in 1890 and a D.D. in 1915. His most extensive work was this commentary.

1931   [New Testament] Concordant Version of the Sacred Scriptures . . . A uni-
    form sublinear based upon an exclusive English equivalent for each Greek
    element and a consistent, emphasized English Version with notes . . . Com-
    pletely revised 1930 . . . The Concordant Publishing Company: Los Angeles
                                                                                  2323A

Unpaged   21 cm   NNAB

    Concordant Version; see 1919–26? NT, No 2250. The text is arranged in four columns on
facing pages: English explanation and literal translation on left and Greek text in two columns
on right; the interlinear translation is printed below text and variants of the MSS and papyri
above. At end are Lexicon and Concordance (378 p), Greek Elements consisting of Grammatical
Elements (42 p), Reverse Index of Greek Endings (4 p), The Greek Word Elements (98 p),
and Course in Sacred Greek (20 p). Copyright 1931, by A. E. Knoch.

1931   The New Testament . . . Translated from the Latin Vulgate . . . First Pub-
    lished . . . at Rheims . . . 1582: with Annotations, References and an His-
    torical and Chronological Index . . . Benziger Brothers: New York, Cin-
    cinnati, [etc.]   **2324**

Reported as (xiv) (195)   19 cm   DLC, ICU
Rheims Version. With maps.

1932?   The Holy Bible . . . [Self-Pronouncing]. [Masonic Edition] . . . Marginal
    References. 20th Century Edition . . . A. J. Holman Co.: Philadelphia **2325**

Reported as 1242 p   30 cm   DLC

    Includes material of interest in Masonry as well as numerous helps in the general study
of the Bible. Illustrated. See Holman's 20th Century Edition of 1903?, No 2147.

1932?   The Holy Bible . . . [Holman Pronouncing Edition] . . . A. J. Holman Co.:
    Philadelphia   **2326**

Reported as 1658 p   25 cm   DLC

    Contains a Bible Study Course, Treasury of Biblical Information arranged by Rev. F. N.
Peloubet, and Bible Dictionary by James P. Boyd. Illustrations and maps.

1932?   The Craftsman's Bible . . . The Great Light in Masonry, Containing the
    King James or Authorized Version . . . With the Words of Christ Printed in
    Red, and with Original Articles by Well Known Members of the Fraternity

... Including the International Bible Concordance and Encyclopedia...
T. H. Fellows: Des Moines, Iowa   **2327**

Reported as (32) (995) (ix) (390)   23 cm   DLC
This is a Red Letter edition of the 1928? Marked Bible (No 2294) but with added Masonic material. Concordance edited by Hurlbut and McClure and published by John C. Winston Co., 1908. Contains Family Record and Masonic Record pages. Illustrated.

1932 The Holy Bible... American Bible Society, Instituted...: New York
                                                                2328

1 vol: (vi) (848) (263)   21 cm   NNAB
First edition of a new ABS standard text, in preparation since 1923. Some changes were made in orthography to conform to American usage; pronunciation marks were placed on most proper names in consultation with the G. and C. Merriam Company, publishers of Webster's Dictionary; and the page headings were completely re-edited. An English bold monotype face was chosen for its suitability to enlargement or reduction without resetting for other size books (for examples, see 1933, No 2337; 1935, No 2346; and 1938, No 2367). Copies were available also with maps and Concordance. Text preceded by Order of Books (1 p), Table of Pronunciation Marks (1 p), and Alphabetical Index (1 p).

1932? The Holy Bible . . . [Self-Pronouncing Edition]. Chicago Bible Society: Chicago   **2329**

Reported as (990) (303)   19 cm   MiU
Printed by the National Bible Press, Philadelphia, and for many years carried by the Chicago Bible Society with their imprint.

1932 The Holy Bible . . . American Revision Committee A.D. 1901. Standard Edition. American Bible Society . . . Published by Thomas Nelson & Sons: New York   **2330**

16 cm   NNAB
ASV; see 1901, No 2124. Reprint of 1901? edition (No 2131). The footnote to John 9:38 has been omitted; see 1933?, No 2336. Although the date 1931 appears at the foot of the List of Books for the OT, the book was issued in the summer of 1932. The 1901 copyright is the only one given.

1932 The Holy Bible . . . Whitman Publishing Company: Racine, Wisconsin *2331*

14 cm   Not Located
One of the cheap editions issued by this publisher. According to the publisher, includes separate Lord's Prayer, text ends on p 179 (probably NT text). In print Jan 1959.

1932 The New Testament . . . King James Version . . . National Home Library Foundation: Washington   **2332**

402 p   17 cm   NNAB
The New Testament . . . Jacket Library appears as cover title. Facing title is a statement giving the aim of the Jacket Library, signed by Sherman F. Mittell, Editor: "To make available to all American Homes and Schools the best works of the world's literary masters, at a price within the reach of all." Bound in black suede paper. 100,000 copies were printed and 99,200 sold at 10¢ a copy from 1932 to 1941.

1932 The New Testament . . . American Bible Society, Instituted . . . : New York   **2333**

1 vol: (4) (376) (4)   13 cm   NNAB

Photographically reduced from the 1933 NT (No 2338) which had been set in type in 1932. Table of Pronunciation Marks and Order of Books (2 p) precede text; black and white maps (3 p) at end (copyright 1928).

The changes approved for the 1932 Bible (No 2328) were not made in this book; however, the type was corrected for the 1933 NT before it was printed (see note under No 2338).

1933 The Holy Bible ... Whitman Publishing Company: Racine, Wisconsin *2334*

21 cm   Not Located

One of the cheap editions issued by this publisher; see 1932, No 2331. According to information received from publisher, includes Pronouncing Guide, Calendar for Daily Reading, Bible Reader's Atlas, and 7 illustrations and 8 maps. Text (probably NT) ends on p 304. Not in print Jan 1959.

1933 The Short Bible, An American Translation. Edited by Edgar J. Goodspeed and J. M. Powis Smith. The University of Chicago Press: Chicago   *2335*

1 vol: (x) (549)   20 cm   NNAB

American Translation; see 1923 NT, No 2260, and 1927 OT, No 2290. An abridgment. The sections have short introductions and are not in the normal Biblical order, but verse numbers remain in inner margins.

NNAB also has 1940? reprint (same pagination, 19 cm) issued by the Modern Library, New York.

1933? The Holy Bible . . . American Revision Committee A.D. 1901. Standard Edition. Made Specially for the American Bible Society . . . Thomas Nelson & Sons: New York   *2336*

1 vol: (4) (996) (4) (288)   19 cm   NNAB

ASV; see 1901, No 2124. Reprint of 1919? ABS edition (No 2249) but with the 1929 copyright of the International Council of Religious Education.

In this and other ASV editions printed for the ABS after this date, the footnote to John 9:38 is omitted. Some members of the ABS Board of Managers had objected to the wording of this note in 1918 and the Board requested the publishers to omit the words "as here" from the note. However, the Nelson firm felt they were not at liberty to do so. After the copyright was taken over by the International Council, the question was again raised and the American Standard Bible Committee gave permission for the omission of the whole note.

1933 The Holy Bible ... American Bible Society, Instituted ... : New York *2337*

16 cm   NNAB

A smaller Bible produced page for page by photographic reduction from the 1932 edition (No 2328).

1933 The New Testament ... American Bible Society, Instituted ... : New York *2338*

1 vol: (4) (376) (4) (2) (94)   17 cm   NNAB

A 24mo Testament (with Psalms) in the 1932 ABS standard text; see No 2328. Has Table of Pronunciation Marks and Order of Books (2 p). Black and white maps (copyright 1928, 3 p) follow NT. The 1932 NT (No 2333) was photographed from type set for this. Later the type was corrected to include the following changes before the above edition was printed: *nowise* for *no wise* (Mat 5:18), *seaside* for *sea side* (Mat 13:1), *winefat* for *winevat* (Mark 12:1), *kinsfolks* for *kinsfolk* (Luke 21:16), *strake* for *struck* (Acts 27:17), and *God speed* for *God-speed* (2 John 10, 11).

Also issued without Psalms

1933 The Four Gospels, a New Translation. By Charles Cutler Torrey...Harper & Brothers, Publishers: New York and London **2339**

1 vol: (xii) (331)   20 cm   NNAB

Jesus and his disciples spoke and wrote Aramaic. His reported words and discourses, and the earliest accounts of his deeds, were written down and circulated in that language, as no one doubts. . . .

It is purposed here to show that the Gospels of Matthew, Mark, and John were composed in Aramaic on the basis of popular documents widespread in Palestine, and that they were by others translated into Greek without intended change. Also, that Luke employed only Semitic sources, assembling them into an especially complete Gospel, which he himself translated. (Preface, p ix)

An essay on The Origin of the Gospels and Notes on the New Readings follow text. NNAB also has second edition revised, 1947, with new preface (xx, 331 p; 20 cm).

Dr. Torrey (1863–1956) graduated from Bowdoin College in 1884 and studied at Andover Theological Seminary and the University of Strasburg (Ph.D., 1892). From 1900 he was for many years professor of Semitic languages at Yale University and had been a collaborator on the Kent Version (see 1904–27 OT, No 2158, and 1918 NT, No 2242).

1933 The Four Gospels according to the Eastern Version. Translated from the Aramaic by George M. Lamsa . . . A. J. Holman Company: Philadelphia **2340**

1 vol: (xxvi) (228) (4)   17 cm   NNAB

Dedication to Dr. and Mrs. W. E. Rollins, Introduction, and List of Words with Many Meanings precede text. Has footnotes and maps. Copyright 1933.

George M. Lamsa (1892–   ) was born in Kurdistan where Aramaic or ancient Syriac is the language of the Church. He studied at Urmiah and Van, and in 1916 came to the United States, where he attended Virginia Theological Seminary and Dropsie College. It is his belief that the entire NT was originally written in Aramaic and that the Syriac text, known as the Peshitta, is "written in the language in which Our Blessed Lord, His disciples and the early Christians spoke and wrote." For a review of his work, see W. D. McHardy's "A Translation of an Ancient Version," in *The Bible Translator* (vol 7, no 2, p 66–72).

The Psalms were published in 1939 (No 2377), the NT in 1940 (No 2389), and the Bible in 1957 (No 2568).

1934 The New Chain-Reference Bible. Third Improved Edition Containing Thompson's Original and Complete System of Bible Study Including Chain References, Text Cyclopedia, Analyses of Books, Outline Studies of Characters, And Unique Charts to Which Has Been Added a New and Valuable Series of Pictorial Maps Together with Other Features. Self-Pronouncing Text. Compiled and Edited by Frank Charles Thompson . . . [Printed by Chain-Reference Bible Publishing Co., Mt. Morris]. B. B. Kirkbride Bible Co.: Indianapolis **2341**

1 vol: (viii) (876) (270) (xxii) (293) (86)   23 cm   NNAB

The eighteenth reprint of the Marginal Chain Reference Bible; see 1908?, No 2184. Preface, Aids to Using the Chain Reference Bible, Key to Pronunciation, Diagram of Books, and Order of Books precede text. At end are General Index, New Comprehensive Bible Helps, Concordance, and maps. All NT references have serial numbers. This edition has been improved by the introduction of many new features, including new maps. Copyright 1908, 1917, 1929, 1934.

1934 The Holy Bible . . . Royal Purple Edition . . . Scott and Fellows: New York **2342**

Reported as (1109) (339) (5)   19 cm   DLC

With maps.

DLC also has copy imprinted *J. A. Fellows* and copyright 1935.

1934?   The Holy Bible . . . T. Nelson & Sons: New York   **2343**

Reported as (1322) (vi) (122) (307) (7)   18 cm   CtMW

References Self-Pronouncing. Teacher's Edition. Nelson's Series appears at head of title page. Contains The Concise Bible Dictionary. Illustrated.

1934   The Riverside New Testament. A Translation from the Original Greek into the English of To-day. By William G. Ballantine. Revised Edition . . . The Riverside Press, Cambridge. Houghton Mifflin Company: Boston and New York   **2344**

18 cm   NNAB

Ballantine Version; see 1923 NT, No 2261. Although a revised edition, pagination remains same as in the 1923 NT. Copyright 1923.

1934?   The Self-Pronouncing New Testament . . . National Bible Press: Philadelphia   **2345**

520 p   11 cm   NNAB

National Edition appears at head of title page. Nonpareil 32mo printed for the Million Testament Campaign with added statements about the Daily Bible Reading Society and MTC. Also issued without added matter.

George T. B. Davis (1873–   ) has been an evangelist since 1904. He was international secretary for the Pocket Testament League (see 1941? NT, No 2399) from 1912 to about 1924. He left to undertake special Million Testament campaigns in China (1925–28), Latin America (1928–31), among students in the U. S. and Canada (1931–34), the Philippines (1934–37), and since then especially among Jews, for whom the 1938? NT (No 2370) was planned.

1935   The Holy Bible . . . American Bible Society, Instituted . . . : New York **2346**

25 cm   NNAB

A larger book produced page for page by photographic enlargement from the 1932 edition (No 2328). Family Record pages precede NT.

1935–36   The King James Version of the Holy Bible . . . The Limited Editions Club: New York   **2347**

5 vols: 2575 p   24 cm   DLC, MB, NN, NNAB

The preliminary matter includes the Dedication to King James and The Translators to the Reader from the 1611 edition.

Vols i–iii contain the OT; Vols iv–v contain the Apocrypha and the NT. Printed from text of the ABS edition P53, 1932. Editor's note: "This edition is intended as a graceful and simple presentation, to bookish literary people, of the loveliest prose in English Literature." Colophon at end of Vol iii: "This edition . . . consists of fifteen hundred copies made for the members of the Limited Editions Club. It is designed for reading by George Macy. . . ." Printed over a period of more than a year at the Limited Editions Club's press in Westport. Vols iv and v, dated 1936, printed at Yale University Press. Text is in paragraph form without verse numbers. Initial letter of each Book in color. Psalms and Song of Solomon set in italics. Sold in "gold" box at $10 to members.

1935   The Bible. An American Translation. The Old Testament Translated by a Group of Scholars Under the Editorship of J. M. Powis Smith. The New Testament Translated by Edgar J. Goodspeed. The University of Chicago Press: Chicago   **2348**

1 vol: (16) (883) (5) (247)   22 cm   NNAB

American Translation; see 1923 NT, No 2260, and 1927 OT, No 2290. A new edition of the 1931 Bible (No 2321), printed in paragraph form, double columns, with verse numbers in the margins. Has original Prefaces to both Testaments and Publisher's Note (1935).

1935?   The Holy Bible . . . Self-Pronouncing . . . Whitman Publishing Company: Racine, Wisconsin **2349**

832 p   21 cm   NN, NNAB

Order of Books, Key to Pronunciation, Tables of Measure, etc. precede text. Chapters are numbered consecutively.

1935   A New Translation of the Bible Containing the Old and New Testaments. James Moffatt . . . Harper & Brothers, Publishers: New York and London **2350**

1 vol: (xlvii) (1039) (iii) (329)   19 cm   NNAB

Moffatt Version; see 1917? NT, No 2235. Preface dated December 1934. This is "the revised and final edition." The translator reviewed the entire work "in order to make the English more exact, more telling, or more idiomatic" (p vi). Copyright 1922, 1924, 1926, 1935.

Beginning in 1935, Harper & Brothers published the Moffatt Bible in the United States on short-term contract basis. About 1946, Harper was granted by Hodder and Stoughton, London, a "life-of-the-copyright contract" as the exclusive publishers of the Moffatt Bible in the United States.

NNAB also has a 1950 copy with Concordance and maps (160 and 16 p); and *The Book of Psalms. A New Translation, by James Moffatt,* Harper & Brothers, Publishers: New York, n. d. last copyright 1935, 192 p, 18 cm).

1935   The Holy Bible . . . Specially Bound for Church of Jesus Christ of Latter Day Saints . . . [Printed by the University Press, Cambridge]. Distributed by the Deseret Book Co.: Salt Lake City, Utah **2351**

Reported as (703) (112) 707–921 (160) 386–506   18 cm   MH

Although this edition was printed in England, it is listed here because it contains distinctive materials. A section of Ready References (A Compilation of Texts Subjectively Arranged with Annotations, Designed especially for the use of Missionaries and other students of the Scriptures, Published by the Church of Jesus Christ of Latter-day Saints; copyright 1917, by Joseph F. Smith) appears between OT and NT. A Concise Biblical Encyclopedia and A Concordance from *The Cambridge Companion to the Bible,* Index, and maps follow NT.

1935   The Holy Bible . . . American Revision Committee A.D. 1901. Standard Edition. Congregational Publishing Society, Pilgrim Press . . . : Boston and Chicago **2352**

1 vol: (18) (1002) (8) (288)   17 cm   NNAB

ASV; see 1901, No 2124. Minion Black-Faced Type edition. Colored frontispiece and presentation pages (printed in Great Britain), note for Special Commemoration (First English Bible, 1535) Edition, and Foreword by Dean Weigle of Yale Divinity School precede title. Note on maps and pronunciation system and Order of Books follow 1901 Preface. Consecutive Daily Bible Reading by John Willis Baer (4 p). At end are Helps to the Study of the Bible edited by Sidney A. Weston, Ph.D., International Council of Religious Education (copyright 1932 by Nelson, 64 p). Colored illustrations and 8 colored maps. Copyright 1901, by Nelson, and 1929, by International Council of Religious Education.

1935   The New Testament, A New Translation by James Moffatt together with the Authorized Version . . . New Edition, Revised. [Printed in the United States of America.] Harper & Brothers: New York and London **2352A**

1 vol: (xxxiv) (2) (657) (3)   21 cm   NNAB

AV and Moffatt Version; see 1917? NT, No 2235. A new edition of the Moffatt-AV NT of 1922 (No 2257) with the Moffatt text from the revised Bible of this year (No 2350). Copyright 1922 and 1935, by Harper & Brothers.

1935? The New Testament. A New Translation. By James Moffatt. New Edition, Revised. Harper & Brothers, Publishers: New York and London   **2353**

1 vol: (xi) (371)   14 cm   NNAB

Moffatt Version; see 1917? NT, No 2235. Has Preface to revised edition (dated December 31, 1934) and Preface to the original edition. Copyright 1922 and 1935.

1936? The New Standard Alphabetical Indexed Bible . . . School and Library Reference Edition . . . Alphabetical Arrangement of All Essential Subjects. King Solomon's Temple. Character Analysis. Also Authentic and Reliable Chronologic Historical Charts and History of the Bible. Pictorial Pronouncing Dictionary . . . Red Letter Edition . . . Plates of the Old Masters . . . The John A. Hertel Co.: Chicago   **2354**

Reported as (254) (762) (40) (96)   30 cm   DLC
Illustrated.

Also issued with added imprint of *International Sunday School League*. DLC also has the following similar editions: 1941 Masonic edition, printed for Washington Memorial Bible Associates, Inc., Atlanta, Georgia, 1188 p; 1948? edition with International Sunday School League imprint; 1951? Masonic edition; 1951 Blue Ribbon edition (see 1926?, No 2284); and 1955? Blue Ribbon edition.

1936 The Bible Designed to be Read as Living Literature . . . This Edition Arranged and Edited by Ernest Sutherland Bates. Simon and Schuster: New York   **2355**

1 vol: (xxiv) (1239)   25 cm   NN, NNAB

A preliminary note states: "In this edition the text of the King James Version is followed, except in the case of Proverbs, Job, Ecclesiastes, and the Song of Songs, where that of the Revised [ERV] Version is used. The arrangement of the books is by time and subject matter; prose passages are printed as prose, verse as verse, drama as drama, letters as letters; the spelling and punctuation are modernized; genealogies and repetitions are omitted, as well as the whole of Chronicles, the minor Epistles, and similar unimportant passages throughout, to the end that the Bible may be read as living literature." Printed in single column without verse or chapter indication. Subject heads and poetry are in italics. Introductions precede each Book. Copyright 1936.

This Bible was chosen as one of the fifty best books of the year by the American Institute of Graphic Arts. Distributed as a "book dividend" by the Book-of-the-Month Club, Inc. 85,000 copies printed in first run; priced at $3.75. For details of printing see *Publishers' Weekly* Nov. 7, 1936, p 2865–7. A similar edition in different format was issued in England in 1937 by Heinemann.

1936 The Junior Bible, An American Translation. Edited by Edgar J. Goodspeed. Illustrated by Frank Dobias. The Macmillan Company: New York   **2356**

1 vol: (xiv) (282)   23 cm   NNAB

American Translation; see 1923 NT, No 2260, and 1927 OT, No 2290. "The Bible Text is quoted from The Bible: An American Translation . . ." by permission of The University of Chicago Press. The text is printed in prose style with introductions in italics. Illustrated.

1936 [Old Testament] The Holy Scriptures. English Version. Revised by Alexander Harkavy . . . Hebrew Publishing Company: New York   **2357**

1 vol: (viii) (1272) (xvi)   18 cm   NNAB

Harkavy Version; see 1916 OT, No 2227A. Two lines in Hebrew appear at head of title page. Preface signed A. H.   English text only, printed in paragraph form, double columns, with verse numbers in text. At end are Index, Tables for the Readings of the Law and of the Haftaroth, and Tables for Family Record. Copyright 1936.

1936?   The New Testament, Red Letter Edition . . . The World Syndicate Publishing Co.: Cleveland and New York   **2358**

1 vol: (233) (16)   19 cm   NNAB

Issued, with a Foreword, by the Haskin Information Service, Washington, D. C. At end are 16 p of Harmony Outline of the Gospels; Lists of Parables, Miracles, Prayers, etc.; and 4 p of Interesting Facts (copyright 1936, by Frederick J. Haskin).

1937?   Self-Pronouncing . . . Holy Bible. With Self-Pronouncing Reference Dictionary Index, Revised and Newly Edited by W. C. Sanderson . . . A. J. Holman Company: Philadelphia   **2359**

Reported as 1212 p   30 cm   DLC

A 20th Century Edition which includes Masonic material and aids to Biblical study. Illustrated, some plates colored. See 1903?, No 2147.

1937?   The New Testament critically reconstructed and retrans-lated. by William Wallace Martin. Parthenon Press: Nashville, Tennessee   **2360**

1 vol: (viii) (244)   30 cm   NNAB

Martin Version; see 1928 Psalms, No 2302. Mr. Martin has reconstructed the twenty-one canonical Epistles into thirty-six, including as authors Apollos, Barnabas, and John, son of Zebedee (as the writer of part of the Epistle of James). Except for the Epistle to the Laodicaens, the destinations are not altered. Text is printed in double column format. The type already used for the parts was incorporated, without apparent change, into the completed work. Copyright 1937.

In 1929–30 the Epistles were issued in two volumes: Part I, Press of Marshall and Bruce Co.: Nashville, 1929 (6, 222 p; 11 cm); Part II, Press of Publishing House of the Methodist Episcopal Church: Nashville, 1930 (246 p, 11 cm). Reprinted in 1942 with many notes interspersed with text (xi, 191 p; 16 cm). In "An Important Distinction" in the 1942 reprint, Mr. Martin wrote: "I am fully aware that I am open to challenge from scholars when I affirm that we have Epistles of length from Paul, and Apollos, and Barnabas. And if I reproduce them and use only material found in the Scriptures of the New Testament, I prove my assertion" (p 3).

1937   The New Testament. A New Translation and Explanation Based on the Oldest Manuscripts by Johannes Greber. Part I, Translation . . . John Felsberg, Inc.: New York   **2361**

463 p   23 cm   NNAB

Text is printed in paragraph form, single column, with verse numbers in margin. Copyright 1937, by Johannes Greber.

Johannes Greber (18??–1944?) of Germany, was a former Roman Catholic priest who came to believe in communication with the world of divine spirits. He based his translation on Codex Bezae (D), which "most nearly approaches the truth." "In the rare instances in which a text pronounced correct by the divine spirits can be found in none of the manuscripts available today, I have used the text as it was given to me by those spirits." "In my German Translation I made it my chief concern to reproduce the exact meaning of the Greek text in good but simple German. . . . The translation of the German original into English was made by a professional translator, corrected by a committee of American clergymen . . . and thoroughly revised by a teacher. . . ." (p 15f.)

Part II, the Explanation, "is not so much intended to make the translation clearer as it is to offer reasons for the several truths contained therein. . . ." (p 16.) Part II was never published.

1937   The New Testament. A Translation in the Language of the People by
Charles B. Williams, Professor of Greek in Union University . . . Bruce
Humphries, Inc., Publishers: Boston   **2362**

575 p   21 cm   NNAB

Foreword and Contents precede text, which is printed in normal prose form without verse
numbers. Explanatory and critical notes. Copyright 1937.

Mr. Williams (1860–1952) was a Baptist who aimed in his translation to make the NT
readable and understandable by the plain people. It is based on the Westcott & Hort Greek
text, and where there have been conflicts in the Greek text, the Vatican manuscript was used.
The effort has been made to translate thoughts and not single words into idiomatic English.
The translator spent twenty years on the work. (See Preface.)

1937   The New Testament . . . Translated into English from the Original Greek
by The Very Reverend Francis Aloysius Spencer, O.P. Edited by Charles
J. Callan, O.P., and John A. McHugh, O.P. . . . [Nihil Obstat: Arthur J.
Scanlan, S.T.D., Censor Librorum. Imprimatur: ✠ Patrick Cardinal Hayes,
Archbishop of New York. Printed by the Stratford Press, Inc., New York.]
The Macmillan Company: New York   **2363**

1 vol: (xiv) (717)   20 cm   DLC, NN, NNAB, OC

Spencer Version; see 1898 Gospels, No 2099. Preface and Introduction, etc. precede text,
which is printed in paragraph form, single column, with verse numbers in margin. Bible Aids
and maps at end. Copyright 1937.

In his introduction to this edition, Fr. Vosté wrote: "The Vulgate, the authentic text of the
Latin Church, retains all its authority in the official acts of that Church; but it is desirable to
have a translation from the original languages which avails itself of the assured results and the
progress of textual criticism. . . ." (p ix.)

Reissued in 1940, 1941, etc.

1938   The New Analytical Bible and Dictionary of the Bible . . . with the Addition
in Many Instances, in Brackets, of the More Correct Renderings of the American Revised Version, Copyright 1929 by the International Council of Religious Education, and Used by Permission . . . John A. Dickson Publishing
Co.: Chicago   **2364**

26 cm   DLC

Reprint of the 1931 edition (No 2320) with some changes in the wording of title page.
Maps.

1938   The Living Bible; Being the Whole Bible in the Fewest Words. Edited from
the King James Version by Bolton Hall. Revised Edition . . . The World
Syndicate Publishing Co.: Cleveland and New York   **2365**

24 cm   CU, MH

Reprint of the 1928 Knopf edition (No 2293).

1938   The People's Bible; An Anthology, King James Version; arranged and edited
by Caradoc J. Morgan. Morgan Publishing Corp.: Minneapolis   **2366**

Reported as 368 p   21 cm   MnM

An anthology of Biblical passages arranged by topic instead of in the traditional order.

1938   The Holy Bible. . . American Bible Society, Instituted . . . : New York **2367**

19 cm   NNAB

A medium-sized Bible set line for line from the 1932 edition (No 2328). Contains 4 p of
new black and white maps at end. Number of copies printed and date of publication (50M–
1938) appear below Order of Books.

1938   The New Testament. A Translation. Rev. Edgar Lewis Clementson . . . The
Evangelization Society of the Pittsburgh Bible Institute: [Pittsburgh]   **2368**

1 vol: (16) (628) (6)   19 cm   DLC, NNAB

Introduction dated 1938. Text is printed in paragraph form, single column, with verse
numbers in left margin.

1938   John Wesley's New Testament Compared with the Authorized Version, with
an Introduction by George C. Cell, Late Professor in Boston University,
School of Theology. The John C. Winston Company: Chicago, Philadelphia, Toronto   **2369**

1 vol: (xiv) (391)   17 cm   NNAB

Wesley Version; see 1791 NT, No 35. The text is that of the standard edition, which
differs very little from the 1790 pocket edition. Preliminary matter includes fly title, illustration
of John Wesley reproduced from the 1755 edition, Dedication, To the Reader (signed Ella
Clark Cell), Introduction (signed George C. Cell), and facsimile of three pages from the
original edition including title page dated 1790. Text printed in paragraph form, single column,
with verse numbers in left margin; no notes or references. Explanatory note precedes each Book.
Deviations from the King James Version are indicated by italics; omissions from the King
James Version are indicated by two dots. Copyright 1938.

1938?   The New Testament with Old Testament References with many Verses
which are the fulfillment of Old Testament Prophecies regarding the Messiah, together with other verses that refer to the Old Testament Scriptures,
set in bold type. Million Testaments Campaigns, Inc.: Philadelphia   **2370**

1 vol: (x) (647)   12 cm   NN, NNAB

Planned especially for Jews; see note under 1934? NT, No 2345. *Old Testament Prophecy
Edition* appears as cover title. OT Prophecies (8 p) and Introduction (2 p) precede text. OT
references and quotations are printed in bold face type with reference indications at foot of page.
My Promise, etc., appears inside front cover; My Conviction and How to be Saved appears
inside back cover.

NNAB copy received in 1941. Material inside covers varies in different printings.

From 1938 until about 1955 these were printed at the Kingsport Press, Kingsport, Tenn.,
all undated. The MTC headquarters reported in July 1959 that "after running more than a
million testaments from the same plates, the plates were in need of repairs and for the last
three years our Testaments have been produced by the National Bible Press here in Philadelphia."

NNAB has undated copy with imprint of *New York Bible Society.*

1938?   The New Testament . . . at Rheims . . . 1582. Published by the Chaplains'
Aid Association: New York   **2371**

11 cm   NNAB

Rheims Version. Reprint of 1923 edition (No 2265).

1938?   [New Testament] Holy Bible Contains 224 Pages of the New Testament
of Our Lord Jesus Christ. Globe Novelty Company: Detroit   **2372**

224 p   4 cm   NNAB

The Lord's Prayer appears on verso of title page. Has the attached advertising matter:
"Midget — World's smallest Bible . . . Available in six different styles . . . with souvenir mailing
tag . . . DeLuxe Bibles with imitation leather cover, etc. . . . prices from 45¢ a dozen for plain
black to $200 per 1000 for gold edge edition." The type is almost unreadable.

Similar booklets appear from time to time attached to greeting cards, etc.

1939   The Bible of the World. Edited by Robert O. Ballou . . . Friedrich Spiegel-
berg . . . and Horace L. Friess . . . The Viking Press: New York   **2373**

1 vol: (xxii) (1415)   24 cm   NN

A collection of treasures of Hinduism, Buddhism, Confucianism, Taoism, Zoroastrianism,
Judaeo-Christian Scriptures, and Mohammedanism. The material from the Bible appears on
p 641–1246, which is almost half the text. It is printed in normal prose and poetry form without
source identification. The historical events of the Gospels are in chronological harmony form,
followed by a collection of the Sermons and Sayings of Jesus. There are also passages from
the apocryphal NT. At end are Notes (including chapter references for Bible passages), a
Bibliography, Glossary, and Index (p 1345–1415).

1939?   New-Style Family Bible. A New Convenient Edition, Large, Clear, Self-
Pronouncing Type. Sixty Thousand Marginal References. Brief but Com-
prehensive and Authoritative History and Description of Each Book . . .
Outline Harmony of the Gospels. Practical Concordance . . . New Five-
Color Maps of Bible Lands. Family Record Pages in Colors . . . The System
Bible Company: Kansas City, Missouri   **2374**

Reported as 1463 p   23 cm   DLC
Has maps.

1939   The Complete Bible. An American Translation. The Old Testament Translated by J. M. Powis Smith and a Group of Scholars. The Apocrypha and
the New Testament Translated by Edgar J. Goodspeed. University of Chicago Press: Chicago   **2375**

20 cm   DLC, NcD, OC, OGK

American Translation; see 1923 NT, No 2260, and 1927 OT, No 2290. Reprint of the
1935 edition (No 2348) but with Apocrypha included (202 p). *The Apocrypha, An American
Translation by Edgar J. Goodspeed* was first published in 1938 by the Univ. of Chicago Press
(ix, 493 p; 20 cm) with Allori's *Judith* as frontispiece. It has been reset here into the double
column format of this Bible.

1939?   The Holy Bible . . . Methodist Publishing House: Nashville   **2376**

Reported as (1081) (334) (64)   19 cm   DLC
Illustrated.

1939   The Book of Psalms according to the Eastern Version. Translated from Original Aramaic Sources by George M. Lamsa. A. J. Holman Company: Philadelphia   **2377**

1 vol: (xvi) (130)   18 cm   NNAB
Lamsa Version; see 1933 Gospels, No 2340. Has three facsimile leaves before text.

1939   The Book of Life. Volume One. Home Library. The Interwoven Gospels,
The Acts, Revelation, The Epistles, and Gems from Proverbs by Zed Hopeful Copp . . . The John C. Winston Company: Chicago, Philadelphia, Toronto   **2378**

1 vol: (xvi) (510)   21 cm   NNAB

Dedication, Introduction, Similitudes of the Lord, Note on the Bible, Hymn, Chapter
Synopsis, Order of Books, etc., Explanatory Notes, and title to Gospels precede text. Also con-
tains Gems from Proverbs, Key-Word Concordance, Genealogy of Jesus, Prominent Parables,
Index to Major Miracles, World Home Flag, and Pledges. According to the dust jacket, "The

text is the original Greek from the Tyndall translation, in the Cap and Gown language of the Church, and is modern only in the Interwoven Gospels, rearranged book order, and the omission of obsolete words and phrases." The text is basically the King James Version with some modification and a good deal of paraphrase in the interwoven Gospels.

1940? The Holy Bible . . . [Self-Pronouncing] [Masonic Edition] . . . Marginal References. 20th Century Edition . . . A. J. Holman Company: Philadelphia **2379**

Reported as 1356 p   30 cm   DLC

Contains Bible Helps and The First Authentic Restoration of King Solomon's Temple by John Wesley Kelchner. Illustrated. See 1903?, No 2147.

NNFM has copy with a great deal of added matter; copyright dates 1875 and 1888 to 1940.

1940 The Holy Bible . . . Whitman Publishing Company: Racine, Wisconsin **2380**

778 p   28 cm   Not Located

One of the cheap editions issued by this publisher; see 1932, No 2331, and 1933, No 2334. According to information received from publisher, contains center references, Tables and Indexes, and Family Register. In print Jan 1959.

1940? The New Indexed Bible . . . Comprising the Biography, Geography, History and Teachings of the Holy Bible, Giving Complete Helps . . . Revised and Enlarged from the Original Edition . . . John A. Dickson Publishing Company: Chicago **2381**

26 cm   DLC

Reprint of the 1923 edition (No 2259). Maps. For the original Indexed Bible, see 1902? No 2134.

1940? The Holy Bible . . . American Revision Committee A.D. 1901. Standard Edition . . . Thomas Nelson & Sons: New York **2382**

24 cm   NNAB

ASV; see 1901, No 2124 Long Primer Quarto reprinted from No 2124. Copyright 1901 by Nelson and 1929 by the International Council of Religious Education. Below copyright line, "To insure purity of text."

NNAB has another copy containing the ERV Apocrypha in smaller type, marked Nelson's Series, Minion Octavo (8, 176 p), and blue-lined pages for notes before and after text. Publisher's address listed as 385 Madison Ave.

1940? The Holy Bible . . . [Teacher's Edition, Self-Pronouncing]. Concordia Publishing House: St. Louis, Missouri **2383**

24 cm   DLC

Contains The Concordia Bible Dictionary, third edition, edited by T. C. Graebner.

1940 The Master Indexed Bible . . . The Master Bible Study, Designed for Mastery of the Bible Embracing the Studies of Biblical Archaeology, History, Biography, Chronology, Geography, Maps, Encyclopaedic Bible Dictionary . . . Systematized, Classified, Analytical, Topical . . . By many of the World's Most Eminent Bible Scholars . . . J. W. Dickson & Co.: San Antonio and Chicago **2384**

23 cm   DLC

Reprint of 1926? edition (No 2285).

1940?   The Holy Bible and International Bible Encyclopedia and Concordance
... Self-Pronouncing ... Garden City Publishing Co.: New York   **2385**

Reported as (995) (4) (390)   22 cm   DLC
De Luxe Library Edition appears on cover. Has Encyclopedia and Concordance edited by
Hurlbut and McClure. Illustrations and maps.

1940   [The Holy Bible] The Story of the Hamitic Peoples of the Old and New
Testaments Together with Original Subject Illustrations and Condensed
Concordance on the Hamitic Peoples and Their Lands . . . A. J. Holman
Company. Copyright 1940: Philadelphia   **2386**

1724 p   21 cm   DLC, NNAB
This is Holman's Bourgeois Octavo Self-Pronouncing Red Letter Edition with text on
p 9–1264 plus the following added matter: Family Record, Preface by R. R. Moton (with portrait), Synopsis of the Hamitic Peoples of Biblical Times (with bibliography), The Hamitic
Peoples of Bible Times by John Malcus Ellison (with portrait), Historical Notes, Chronology
of Events Bearing Upon the Origin and History of the Hamitic Peoples, and Condensed Concordance. Also has spirituals with music, maps, and Biblical scenes with Negro figures.
Hamitic Edition appears on the spine of this book. For many years reports have reached the
Bible Society of editions sold in the South with illustrations showing Negroes but this is the
first and only edition located. The publisher states that it has not been popular.

194–?   The Holy Bible . . . Watchtower Bible and Tract Society, Inc.: [Brooklyn]
                                                                           2387
19 cm   DLC
Minion 16mo. Illustrated.

1940   The New Covenant . . . American Revision Committee A.D. 1901. Standard
Edition. American Bible Society: [New York]   **2388**

1 vol: (5) 6–615 [1]   28 cm   NNAB
ASV; see 1901, No 2124. This wide margin Testament is unbound, with each stapled signature forming a complete unit. The text is from one of Nelson's Pica Octavo NTs and is printed
one column per page, leaving the rest blank. No running heads. Prepared at the request of the
National Association of Biblical Instructors and the Society of Biblical Literature and Exegesis,
and many times reprinted. Copyright 1901 and 1929.

1940   The New Testament According to the Eastern Text Translated from the
Original Aramaic Sources by George M. Lamsa . . . A. J. Holman Company:
Philadelphia   **2389**

1 vol: (xxv) (527) (3)   17 cm   NNAB
Lamsa Version; see 1933 Gospels, No 2340. *The Modern New Testament from Aramaic*
appears as cover title. First printing, October 1940.

1941?   The New Analytical Bible and Dictionary of the Bible. . . . A System of
Helps . . . John A. Dickson Publishing Company: Chicago   **2390**

26 cm   NN, NNAB
A reprint of 1938 edition, No 2364. Copyright 1941, also 1931 and 1938.

1941   The Bible for Today, Edited by John Stirling, Illustrated by Rowland
Hilder and Other Artists . . . [Printed in the United States of America].
Oxford University Press: London, New York, Toronto   **2391**

1 vol: (xix) (1255)   25 cm   NN, NNAB

Has Introduction signed by William Lyon Phelps and Preface with acknowledgments to Dr. A. S. Peake, Dr. J. E. M'Fayden, Dr. W. O. E. Oesterley, Dr. Bertram Lee Woolf, and Eric Partridge. Also Index and Order of Books. The text is printed without chapter or verse indication, in sections with introductions and headings. The illustrations — a bombed village, a modern observatory (reference to stars in Job), crowd going to work in a modern city — are designed to show the Bible's "peculiar and definite relevance to problems and to men and women of the twentieth century." Copyright 1941.

This was issued in England earlier in the year and published in America October 1941. By November of 1943, 50,000 copies had been sold.

1941   The Master Bible, The Master Indexed Bible . . . J. W. Dickson & Co.: Chicago and San Antonio   **2392**

Reported as 1810 p   24 cm   DLC

Published in 1926? as The Master Bible (No 2285) and in 1940 as The Master Indexed Bible (No 2384).

1941   The Illuminated Bible . . . Comprising the Biography, Geography, History and Teachings of the Holy Bible, Giving Complete Helps, Illustrated and Arranged in Such Simple Form that the Subjects of the Bible are Made Easily Accessible to Everyone. Published by John A. Dickson Publishing Co. for Columbia Educational Books, Inc.: Chicago   **2393**

1 vol: (220) (634) (10) (490) (34)   23 cm   NNAB

The Good Samaritan Bible appears as cover title. Verso of title has "Copyright 1941. Columbia Educational Books, Inc. Text of The Illuminated Bible previously published as the New Indexed Bible, Copyright 1901, 1909, 1913, 1929, 1940 [by] John A. Dickson Publishing Co." Text is uniform with the 1913 Dickson edition (No 2213) but with the addition of the Words of Christ in red, colored illustrations, photographs, and green and white illustrations. There is also some variation in appended material, paging, and wording of the title page. Illustrated.

1941   The Holy Bible . . . Translated from the Latin Vulgate . . . With Notes by Bishop Challoner and Also the Encyclical Letter "On the Study of the Holy Scriptures." . . . Preface by Rev. William H. McClellan . . . Also an Appendix . . . The Douay Bible House, C. Wilderman Co.: New York   **2394**

1 vol: (xxxii) (964) (2) (267) [1] (30)   21 cm   DLC, MH, NcD, NjMD, NNAB

Rheims-Douay Version. Imprimatur of Archbishop Spellman dated 1941. Preliminary matter includes Preface by Father McClellan, Encyclical of Pope Leo xiii, Order of Books, Abbreviations, and Prayers. Tables and Lists of Readings at end. Illustrations and maps. Copyright 1941.

Although this claims to be a Challoner edition, it is a reprint of the 1899 Benziger Bible (No 2101) which is based on the 1749 Challoner text (Pope, p 493). Most of the editions issued by the Douay Bible House were printed in Belgium, but this was printed in the United States.

NcC has 1942 edition, OCl has 1943 one, and IU has 1945? copy.

1941   The Holy Bible . . . [Red Letter Edition]. Self-Pronouncing . . . Simplified Reference Edition . . . Southern Bible House: Charlotte, North Carolina   **2395**

Reported as 1867 p   21 cm   DLC

Contains Aids for Bible Studies by V. M. Walker, and Encyclopedia and Concordance largely based upon articles prepared by C. H. H. Wright. Illustrated.

1941   The New Testament in Basic English . . . E. P. Dutton & Co., Inc., New York   **2396**

1 vol: (vi) (2) (548)   21 cm   DLC, NNAB

First edition, June 1941. Text printed in paragraph form, single column, with verse numbers in margin. Copyright 1941.

This Testament was reprinted from a Cambridge edition. It was prepared by a committee under the direction of S. H. Hooke (University of London), in collaboration with the Orthological Institute of Cambridge, using "Basic English," which is a simplified form of the English tongue developed by the English semanticist, Mr. C. K. Ogden of Cambridge. There had already been printed in England a book of selections in 1933, Micah and Habakkuk in 1934, Mark in 1945, and John in 1938.

Frequently reprinted. NNAB also has second printing, July 1941.

1941 The New Testament . . . Translated from the Latin Vulgate. A Revision of the Challoner-Rheims Version. Edited by Catholic Scholars Under the Patronage of the Episcopal Committee of the Confraternity of Christian Doctrine . . . St. Anthony Guild Press: Paterson, New Jersey   **2397**

1 vol: (viii) (762) (10)   20 cm   NcD, NN, NNAB, OC, OGK, ViU

Recommendation, excerpt from Encyclical of Pope Benedict xv, and Preface precede text, which is printed in paragraph form, single column, with verse numbers in left margin. Bible Helps at end. Maps. Copyright 1941.

This translation, known as the Confraternity Version, was prepared at the request of the Episcopal Committee of the Confraternity of Christian Doctrine, and approved by the Biblical Commission at Rome and by twenty-eight scholars of the Catholic Biblical Association under the chairmanship of the Rev. Edward P. Arbez. It is a revision of the Challoner-Rheims Version, taking advantage of advances in Greek scholarship but based on the Vulgate. Changes were also made in sentence structure and expression to "give a simple and clear modern version." After permission was granted by Pope Pius xii in 1943 for translations to be made from the original texts, a version of the whole Bible was begun under the same auspices and with the Rev. Louis F. Hartman, C.S.S.R., S.S.L., as chairman of the Editorial Board (see 1948–   , No 2470). Three sections of the OT have been published and it is understood that when the OT is completed a new revision of the NT will follow, based directly on the Greek text.

Many times reprinted in two sizes but with the same pagination. Also printed with the Challoner-Douay OT a number of times, to which was added in 1954 Genesis-Ruth in the Confraternity text. (See 1952, No 2508; 1954, No 2539; 1957, No 2570.)

1941 My Daily Reading from the New Testament, Gospels Unified, Epistles Unified . . . Confraternity of Christian Doctrine . . . arranged by Rev. Joseph F. Stedman . . . Confraternity of the Precious Blood . . . Brooklyn . . . Catholic Society of the Bible . . . : Montreal   **2398**

575 p   13 cm   NNAB

Confraternity Version; see previous entry, No 2397. This contains selections covering nearly all of the NT, arranged for daily reading with annotations. Approbation signed by Edwin V. O'Hara, Bishop of Kansas City.

1941? The New Testament . . . The Pocket Testament League, Incorporated . . . Printed in U. S. A., International Bible Press: New York   **2399**

568 p   11 cm   NNAB

Bound in blue cloth with cover title, *New Testament. U. S. Navy.* PTL membership card inside front cover. What Members Can Do precedes text. At end are How to Become a Christian, "Carry Your Bible" (hymn), and Origin and Aim of the PTL. Inside back cover has Decision. Colored illustrations.

Also issued in brown cloth binding and marked U. S. Army. NNAB also has NT with *Kingsport Press* imprint only but with PTL membership card inside front cover and "decision card" inside back cover. Received 1947 (515 p, 11 cm).

The Pocket Testament League was organized in New York in 1916 as a world-wide Bible movement uniting those who agree to read the Bible every day and to carry a Bible or Testament wherever they go. It combines evangelistic effort with Scripture distribution. The League originated in England, but has been active in the United States and other parts of the world. At least as early as 1938 the John C. Winston Company began printing at the Kingsport Press, Kingsport, Tenn. for the PTL. During 1941 and 1942 this firm printed a great many copies for the League for distribution to the Armed Forces. Their leather-bound Testaments have usually been printed in England by the Oxford University Press.

1941 The New Testament . . . American Scripture Gift Mission: Philadelphia
2400

512 p   11 cm   NNAB

Bold Face Vest Pocket Pronouncing Testament, with *National Edition* at head of title page. The Way of Life, Key to Pronunciation, and Order of Books precede text. Gospel Harmony at end. Half-tone illustrations. Copyright 1941, by National Publishing Co.

NNAB has another copy with *National Bible Press* imprint, which contains the Psalms (123 p) and an 8-page supplement, Helps to the Use . . . and Suggested Helps to Strength and Courage. Many copies of this edition were supplied by churches to men from their congregations entering military service, etc. Does not include SGM The Way of Life. NNAB and DLC also have an edition printed for the Gideons, with Psalms, a note about "Your Chaplain," a letter from President Roosevelt dated Jan 25, 1941, and a 12-page statement about the Gideons, with prayers, hymns, etc. NNAB has another copy with Proverbs and the Psalms, also for the Gideons.

1942 The Holy Bible . . . [Simplified Pronouncing Edition] . . . A. J. Holman Company: Philadelphia
2401

1 vol: (1280) (170) (20)   20 cm   NNAB

Reference Jewel 16mo, Clearface type. Presentation page, Explanation of References, and Order of Books precede text. Family Record follows OT. At end are Combined Dictionary-Concordance in a Single Alphabetical Arrangement, Index of Maps, and 15 maps and plans in color. Copyright 1942.

1942 [New Testament] The Emphatic Diaglott: Containing the Original Greek Text of What is Commonly Styled the New Testament, According to the Recension of Dr. J. J. Griesbach, with an Interlineary Word for Word English Translation; A New Emphatic Version, Based on the Interlineary Translation, on the Renderings of Eminent Critics, and on the Various Readings of the Vatican Manuscript, No. 1209 in the Vatican Library . . . By Benjamin Wilson . . . International Bible Students Association; Watch Tower Bible and Tract Society: Brooklyn, London, [etc.]
2402

19 cm   DLC, NNAB

Benjamin Wilson Version; see 1865 NT, No 1792. Reprint of the 1927 edition (No 2291).

1942 Concordia New Testament with Notes . . . Concordia Publishing House: St. Louis
2403

Reported as 800 p   17 cm   DLC

This is the old American Tract Society Family Annotated Testament (see 1862 NT, No 1762) edited and revised by Dr. John Theodore Mueller. With maps.

1942 The New Testament . . . Rheims . . . 1582. As revised by Dr. Challoner, London, A.D. 1752. With annotations and references by Dr. Challoner, Canon Haydock and Dr. H. J. Ganss and an historical and chronological index. With a preface by Rev. Robert I. Gannon . . . The Douay Bible House: New York
2404

Reported as (iv) (588) (12)   14 cm   DLC

Rheims Version. Pope (p 494) says "this edition is the best text in the American tradition." See note under 1941 Bible, No 2394.

1942   The New Testament . . . Prepared for Use of Protestant Personnel of the
Army of the United States. Published Under the Direction of the Chief of
Chaplains. United States Government Printing Office: Washington, [D. C.]
2405

607 p   14 cm   MBU–T, NNAB

Bound in brown cloth with cover title, *New Testament. Protestant Version. Presented by
the Army of the United States.* Statement by President Roosevelt, dated March 6, 1941, on fly
leaf. Verso has space for identification, etc. Article — Do You Know Your Chaplain?, signed by
W. R. Arnold, Chief of Chaplains, at end.

1942   My Daily Reading from the Four Gospels and the New Testament. Gospels
Unified, Epistles Unified. [Government Printing Office: Washington, D. C.]
2406

575 p   13 cm   NNAB

Confraternity Version; see 1941 NT, No 2397. Uniform with Father Stedman's 1941 edition of the NT (No 2398) although his name is omitted from the Introduction. Bound to match
editions of the AV NT and of the Jewish Publication Society's Scripture selections published
for the Armed Forces in World War II.

1942   The New Testament. An American Translation by Edgar J. Goodspeed. The
University of Chicago Press: Chicago   **2407**

1 vol: (ix) (481)   13 cm   NNAB

American Translation; see 1923 NT, No 2260. This has been photographed down from an
edition reset line for line from the 1923 Testament.

1942   The New Testament . . . American Bible Society, Instituted . . . : New
York   **2408**

1 vol: (512) (126) (xix)   11 cm   NNAB

Service Testament with text and Psalms reprinted from the 1925 NT (No 2283). Bound in
navy blue, brown, or light blue with the insignia of the various branches of the Armed Forces,
Nurses Corps, etc. Has Supplement printed on blue paper consisting of The Ten Commandments; Psalms 19, 23, 24, 27, 46, 51, 91, and 142; the Lord's Prayer; several prayers and
hymns including "America the Beautiful," "My Country, 'Tis of Thee," and the National
Anthem.

During World War II, 4,440,119 copies of this or similar Testaments in various bindings
were supplied to chaplains, churches, and individuals. Some were sealed in water-proof paper
and placed in survival kits on ships and planes — the only Scriptures issued by the Society
that it hoped would not be read. The total number of Bibles, Testaments, and Portions supplied
by the Society to service personnel was 7,419,366 copies.

1942?   The New Testament . . . The Pocket Testament League, Incorporated . . .
International Bible Press: New York   **2409**

11 cm   NNAB

An Army-Navy Edition with text reprinted from the 1941? edition (No 2399). Has Letter
to the Armed Forces, signed by Franklin D. Roosevelt, and Emergency Rations: What to Read
preceding text.

1943?   The Bible Designed to be Read as Living Literature . . . This Edition Arranged and Edited by Ernest Sutherland Bates . . . Simon and Schuster:
New York   **2410**

Reported as (xxviii) (1238)   25 cm   NNC

Contains A Glossary of Biblical Terms compiled by Wallace Brockway. Maps. See 1936,
No 2355.

1943?   The Holy Bible . . . With the Words of Christ Printed in Red. The Combination Bible Designed For the Use of Students and Teachers . . . [showing] Changes, Additions and Omissions that Appear in the Revised Version . . . Other Supplementary Data . . . The National Bible Press: Philadelphia **2411**

1 vol: (1380); other matter var. paged   21 cm   DLC, NNAB

Red Letter Combination Edition appears at head of title page. Binder's title, *Self Pronouncing. S. S. Teachers Edition.* Presentation page, frontispiece, Preface, Key to Pronunciation, Order of Books, Synopses of Books, and How to Use Your Combination Bible precede text. Has Family Record. At end are illustrations, Historical Notes by James C. Muir, Study Helps, Concordance, Questions and Answers, Dictionaries, Index to Maps, and maps. Chapters are numbered consecutively 1–1189. Has center references and ERV variations noted at bottom of page. Copyright 1895 and 1902 by J. R. Jones; 1926 and 1943 by National Publishing Co.

1943?   The Holy Bible . . . [Self-Pronouncing]. Illustrated by Fritz Kredel . . . The Modern Library: New York   **2412**

1 vol: (10) (1131)   19 cm   NN, NNAB

Fly title, Epistle Dedicatory, Alphabetical Order of Books, etc., and Key to Pronunciation precede text. Illustrated. Verso of title page has "Copyright 1943, by Random House, Inc. Printed by the Parkway Printing Co., and bound by H. Wolff. Published by A. S. Barnes & Co., Inc., and distributed by Random House, Inc."

1943?   The Holy Bible . . . Watchtower Bible and Tract Society, Inc.: [Brooklyn]
                                                                        2413

19 cm   DLC

Minion 16mo. Illustrated. See 194–?, No 2387.

1943   Psalms from the Jewish Holy Scriptures, prepared for emergency Use by Jewish Personnel in Air Force Life Rafts. Published under the direction of the Chief of Chaplains. United States Government Printing Office: Washington [D. C.]   **2414**

1 vol: (4) 3–102   13 cm   NNAB

Jewish Publication Society Version; see 1903 Psalms, No 2151, and 1917 OT, No 2234. P 101–102 contains space for log. Issued in a waterproof jacket with matching editions of Matthew for use by Protestant Personnel (AV; 4, 100 p) and for use by Roman Catholic Personnel (Douay; 1944; 4, 111 p). The packet is marked *Scriptures | Protestant | Catholic | Jewish.*

1943   The Goodspeed Parallel New Testament. The American Translation and the King James Version in Parallel Columns, with Introductions and Explanatory Notes by Edgar J. Goodspeed. The University of Chicago: Chicago   **2415**

1 vol: (viii) (600)   21 cm   DLC, MiHi, NcD, NN, NNAB, OC

American Translation; see 1923 NT, No 2260. Preface dated 1942. Text printed in parallel columns with the Goodspeed text on left and AV on right. Goodspeed translation is in paragraph form, with verse numbers in text. The AV text is from an ABS edition. The edition is dedicated "To My Colleagues in the New Testament Section of the American Standard Bible Revision Committee. . . ." Copyright 1943.

1943–45   [New Testament] . . . A Translation, Harmony and Annotations by Ervin Edward Stringfellow . . . Planographed by John S. Swift Co., Inc.: St. Louis
                                                                        2416

2 vols: Vol I, (8) (263); Vol II, (x) (301)   21 cm   NNAB

Vol I (1943) contains The Gospels. Vol II (1945) has Acts-Revelation and was published by Wm. C. Brown Co., Dubuque, Iowa. Each vol has frontispiece, Preface, Introduction, and Index. Gospels arranged in harmony form in parallel columns. Epistles interwoven with Acts. Copyright 1943.

Dr. Stringfellow was a professor of New Testament Language and Literature at Drake University. His translation is from the Greek text of Westcott & Hort, and emphasizes the literal significance of the Greek tenses. The Harmony is based on the work of Burton and Stevens.

1943 The New Testament . . . Confraternity of Christian Doctrine . . . St. Anthony
        Guild Press: Paterson, New Jersey   **2417**

Reported as (vii) (762)   16 cm   DLC
Confraternity Version; see 1941 NT, No 2397.

1943 The New Testament in Modern Speech. An Idiomatic Translation into
        Every Day English from the Text of the Resultant Greek Testament by the
        Late Richard Francis Weymouth . . . Newly Revised by James Alexander
        Robertson . . . with . . . Notes . . . Fifth Edition . . . The Pilgrim Press: Boston;
        James Clarke & Co., Ltd.: London   **2418**

1 vol: (xxii) (712)   15 cm   DLC, NNAB
American Pocket Edition printed in the United States in reduced size by photographic process from the London fifth edition of 1936. Copyright 1943, by The Pilgrim Press.

Also printed in a regular size edition.

This translation, first published in England in 1903, was the work of Richard Francis Weymouth (1822–1902), a Baptist layman who edited The Resultant Greek Testament in 1886. His aim was to express the Greek text in the form the inspired writers would have used if writing in our age and country, to serve as supplement and commentary to the versions in general use. The translation was completed in 1900 and seen through the press by the Rev. Ernest Hampden-Cook. It was issued with and without notes and has been very popular both in the British Isles and America. Earlier editions issued in the United States were actually printed in Great Britain. The text was revised in the 1924 edition by the Rev. S. W. Green, the Rev. Prof. A. J. D. Farrer, and the Rev. Prof. H. T. Andrews, and again in 1929 by the Rev. Prof. James Alexander Robertson.

1943? [New Testament] The Testament for Fishers of Men, Offering a Simple
         and Practical Method for Personal Work, with Selected Passages to Use in
         Soul-Winning. Also Suggested Outlines of Books and Divisions of Chapters
         which Aid in Daily Readings and the Devotional Study of the Word. John
         Knox Press: Richmond, Virginia   **2419**

Reported as (xxv) (467)   14 cm   DLC
Fishers of Men, by Wade C. Smith, appears on p i–xxv.

1943? The New Testament . . . [Self-Pronouncing]. Editor, William H. Ritchie . . .
         Co-editor, Philip E. Howard, Jr. . . . The World Publishing Company: Cleve-
         land and New York   **2420**

1 vol: (479) [1] (111) [1]   12 cm   NNAB
The "Paragraphed" Edition appears at head of title page. Editors' note about paragraphing dated March 1943 and copyright 1943 by World Publishing Co. Has Table of Pronunciation and List of Books. Questions Answered from the Word of God appears on last page. The text is printed in usual verse form, with italic subject heads inserted in the NT but not in the Psalms.

1943 The New Testament . . . Whitman Publishing Company: Racine, Wisconsin
2421

512 p   12 cm   NNAB

Has gilt metal cover applied to front cover with stamping, *May God Bless You.* A card is inserted inside front cover which has Presented To   , and imprint of the Know Your Bible Sales Co., Cincinnati. Order of Books precedes text.

The Know Your Bible Sales Company bought Testaments from other firms and added the shield to them. Some ABS regular service Testaments were purchased by them for this purpose. After September 1943, however, no more copies were sold by ABS for this purpose. The metal covers were no protection from a missile of any strength, nor were they worth the price. The company also used many Thomas Nelson Testaments for this purpose.

1944? The Holy Bible . . . Self-Pronouncing Reference Edition . . . [Printed, Bound, and Published in the U. S. A. by the National Bible Press, Philadelphia]. The National Bible Press: Philadelphia   **2422**

1 vol: (viii) (1462)   25 cm   NNAB

Printed in "Crystal-Clear Type." The trade mark is now NBP on an open Bible in front of a torch. Presentation page, Epistle Dedicatory, Daily Bible Readings, etc., Order of Books, and Key to Pronunciation precede text. Family Record follows OT. Maps with Index at end. Copyright 1944, by National Publishing Co.

CO has Family Altar Edition, Red Letter, dated 1949?.

1944? Gold Seal Holy Bible . . . Gold Seal Edition. Including an Encyclopedic Directory, Factual and Inspirational Material, and Many Other Simple Aids . . . The National Bible Press: Philadelphia   **2423**

Reported as 1914 p   25 cm   DLC

Home Edition appears on spine. Contains Dictionary of the Bible by William Smith (112 p). Illustrations ("new color renditions of . . . Carl Gottfried Pfanneschmidt") and maps.

1944? The Holy Bible . . . [International Series. Self-Pronouncing]. Universal Book and Bible House: Philadelphia   **2424**

Reported as (xxii) (1322)   23 cm   DLC

A Winston edition containing Bible Encyclopedia and Concordance (Hurlbut), Parallel Quotations from the Old Testament and the New Testament (Gray), and The Hour of Prayer. Illustrations and maps.

A similar edition was known as The New Home Bible. Also issued with the words of Christ in red letters. See 1946?, No 2447.

1944 [Holy Bible] The Holy Scriptures . . . An Inspired Revision of the Authorized Version by Joseph Smith, Junior. A New Corrected Edition. The Reorganized Church of Jesus Christ of Latter Day Saints. Herald Publishing House: Independence, Missouri   **2425**

1 vol: (1418) (159)   21 cm   MB, NNAB

Joseph Smith Version; see 1867, No 1817. *Inspired Version* appears at head of title page. "This corrected edition . . . was prepared under the direction of the First Presidency and the Board of Publication of the Reorganized Church. . . ." "The committee found some words and phrases transposed or improperly placed in the work done by Joseph Smith, Jr. These errors, together with others involving spelling, punctuation, and typographical or other omissions, were corrected . . ." (Preface, p 6). Has Concordance and Bible Helps at end. Copyright 1944, by the Board of Publication of the Reorganized Church of Jesus Christ of Latter Day Saints.

DLC has separate NT (1085–1418 p) dated 1949.

1944? The Holy Bible . . . Illustrated by Fritz Kredel . . . The Modern Library:
New York   **2426**

Reported as 1131 p   19 cm   MB
Self-Pronouncing appears at head of title page. Illustrated.

1944 The Holy Bible . . . Appointed to be read in churches . . . Cum Privilegio.
[Oxford University Press crest] Oxford: At the University Press. Humphrey
Milford, Amen House, E.C. 4: London; New York and Toronto   **2427**

1152 p   19 cm   CaOTP, NNAB
    Coral 16mo. Self-pronouncing, appears at bottom of title page. A special page before gen-
eral title page has "This is a copy of the first Bible printed and bound in Canada 1943–44."
Contains Dedication to King James. Colophon: Printed by the Ryerson Press — 30M — 43, publishing arm of the United Church of Canada. The dust jacket adds, "This, the first Bible printed
and bound in Canada, is printed from type set in England in 1936–7. Canadian paper and cloth
have been used in its manufacture."

1944 The Holy Bible. The Catholic Bible, Douay-Rheims Version . . . with notes
by Bishop Challoner . . . the Encyclical Letter "on the study of the Holy
Scriptures" by Pope Leo xiii. Also . . . the essence of the Encyclical letter
"on biblical studies," *Divino afflante Spiritu,* by Pope Pius xii. and an introduction by Vy. Rev. Charles J. Callan. The Douay Bible House: New York
                                                                            2428

Reported as (xxxi) (1309) (354) (xv)   16 cm   DLC
    Rheims-Douay Version. *Red Letter Edition* appears at head of title page. Imprimatur of
Cardinal Spellman dated 1943. The Introduction contains a "vigorous apologia" for the old
Challoner text. Among the errors corrected is that in ii Esdras 3:15, *guard* to *garden* (Pope
p 494). The Encyclical Letter of Pope Pius xii gives encouragement to translations made directly
from the Hebrew and Greek.
    Also issued by Benziger.

1944 The New Testament . . . Newly Translated from the Vulgate Latin at the
Request of Their Lordships, the Archbishops and Bishops of England and
Wales. Sheed & Ward: New York   **2429**

1 vol: (viii) (573)   22 cm   CtY, DLC, ICU, NcAS, NN, NNAB
    Imprimatur, etc., Archbishop Spellman, New York. Preface signed by R. A. Knox, 1943.
Text printed in paragraph form, single column, with verse numbers in margin. Notes and refer-
ences at foot of page. Copyright 1944.
    TxU has copy with statement: Fourth Printing, entered for 1944. MH has 1947 and 1949
editions.
    In the third and subsequent printings, the title was shortened to The New Testament of
Our Lord and Saviour Jesus Christ. A New Translation. (Pope, p 504.) The text follows the
British "trial" edition of 1944.
    Msgr. Ronald Arbuthnott Knox (1888–1957) was the fourth son of Dr. E. A. Knox, the
Anglican Bishop of Manchester. He received his education at Eton and Oxford (Balliol) and
took orders in the Church of England in 1912 but became a Roman Catholic in 1917. Msgr.
Knox was an eminent scholar, churchman, preacher, literary stylist, satirist, and writer of de-
tective stories. His translation of the Bible is based on the Latin Vulgate text, and he aimed at
a sort of timeless English. While his work has delightful literary style, he occasionally resorted
to paraphrase. The translation of the NT is probably more satisfactory from a scholarly point of
view, particularly in the Epistles, than of the OT. Professor Robert A. Dyson, S.J., says of his
work: "His translations will reach more people and influence more lives than anything else he
did." Some changes were made in a "final" edition (1945) printed in England. Among these
are *Lads* to *Friends* in John 21:5 and *It is within your knowledge* to *You yourselves can testify*
in Acts 20:18.

1944   The New Testament. Self-Pronouncing. [Pocket Books monogram] The John
C. Winston Company. Distributed by Pocket Books, Inc.: New York   **2430**

1 vol: (4) (340) (8)   17 cm   NNAB

Where to Look (by permission of the ABS), Order of Books, and Key to Pronunciation pre-
cede text. Calendar for Daily Reading and Publisher's List at end. Verso of title page has "The
New Testament Published by Pocket Books, Inc., March 1944. 1st Printing December, 1943.
Printed by arrangement with the John C. Winston Co."

1944?   The New Testament . . . with the Words of Christ Printed in Red . . . The
John C. Winston Co.: Philadelphia, Chicago, [etc.]   **2431**

Reported as (572) (147)   11 cm   DLC

New Testament and Psalms appears as cover title. Printed in "Clear type." Colored illustrations.
Also issued in Army and Navy bindings.

1945   [Holy Bible] A Commentary, Critical, Experimental and Practical, on the
Old and New Testaments, by the Rev. Robert Jamieson . . . Rev. A. R. Faus-
set . . . and the Rev. David Brown . . . Wm. B. Eerdmans Publishing Co.:
Grand Rapids, Michigan   **2432**

6 vols   24 cm   DLC

American edition, with a biographical sketch of the authors by Dr. Wilbur M. Smith. This
had first been published in England in 1871.

1945?   The Holy Bible . . . Translated from the Latin Vulgate . . . With Annotations, References, and an Historical and Chronological Table. Published
with the Approbation of His Eminence James Cardinal Gibbons, Archbishop of Baltimore . . . P. J. Kenedy & Sons: New York   **2433**

Reported as (1086) (306)   21 cm   Vi

Rheims-Douay Version. According to Pope (p 741), this is a reprint of the 1914? Murphy
edition (No 2217) with slight corrections in punctuation, etc. The date 1944 was supplied to
Pope by Mr. A. R. Kenedy. Illustrations by Gustave Doré and maps.

1945   The Holy Bible . . . The World Publishing Company: Cleveland and New
York   **2434**

1 vol: (1203) (26) (118) (6) (8)   21 cm   NNAB

The text has been reset page for page from the 1928? edition (No 2300) but in larger type.
Presentation page with red, blue, and gold design; colored frontispiece; and Order of Books
precede text. Family Record follows OT List of Proper Names. Concordance and maps with
Index at end. Verso of title page has How to use the Cross Reference Page Index, which includes
page as well as chapter and verse numbers. A star follows OT verses referring to Christ. Illustrations, some in color. Copyright 1945, by The World Publishing Company.

1945?   The Holy Bible . . . [International Series. Self-Pronouncing]. Universal Book
and Bible House: Philadelphia   **2435**

Reported as (xx) (939) (287)   15 cm   DLC

A Winston edition with text printed in Peerless type. No references. Contains The Hour
of Prayer and maps.

1945?   The New Testament . . . with Notes and Complete Index . . . The John C.
Winston Company: Philadelphia, Chicago, [etc.]   **2436**

Reported as (ix) (441) [1] (88)   17 cm   DLC

International Series, Self-Pronouncing Bold Face Testament first published in 1913. Section headings are cut into text. Has Index compiled by J. Gilchrist Lawson and colored illustrations.

1945   The Berkeley Version of the New Testament from the Original Greek with Brief Footnotes by Gerrit Verkuyl . . . James J. Gillick & Co.: Berkeley, California   **2437**

1 vol: (v) (672)   15 cm   DLC, NNAB

Preface signed G. V. Text printed in paragraph form, single column, with verse numbers in margin. Commentary below text. First printing, October 1945. Copyright 1945.

Dr. Verkuyl, a Presbyterian, was born in Holland in 1872. He was a New Testament fellow at Princeton and also studied at Leipzig and Berlin, receiving his Ph.D. from Leipzig. He based his modern speech translation on the Tischendorf and Nestle and Leusden Greek texts, on the Latin New Testament, and on some modern language versions. Words which could not be translated adequately are explained in footnotes. Dr. Verkuyl also worked out as far as possible the dates of events or sayings and of writings of the NT.

In 1946 the Gillick firm printed an edition in which forty-one errors were corrected; in 1947 they issued another edition with additional corrections. Zondervan published editions in 1950 and 1953 with corrected notes but the original text. The copyright was assigned to the Zondervan Publishing House in 1958.

A translation of the entire Bible was published in 1959 (x, 944, 2,289 p; 22 cm; NNAB). Dr. Verkuyl served as editor-in-chief for the OT, assisted by a large group of scholars and advisers. While this text is "in tune with the AV," it claims to be a fresh translation from Hebrew and Greek with reference to Aramaic and the Greek LXX.

1945?   The New Testament . . . Rheims . . . 1582, with Annotations and References by Dr. Challoner and Dr. H. J. Ganss; an Historical and Chronological Index. Index of Proper Names . . . and Preface by Rev. J. M. Lelen . . . [Catholic Book Publishing Company: New York]   **2438**

Reported as 670 p   14 cm   DLC

Rheims Version. Illustrated.

1946   The Holy Bible . . . Published as the Good Leader Bible. Easy-to-Use References, Complete Indexes and Charts, Colorful Illustrations, and Other Features Which Make this Bible More Enjoyable to Read, and Easier to Understand . . . Printed and Bound Especially for Goodwill Distributors. Published by John A. Dickson Publishing Company: Chicago   **2439**

1 vol: (xxvii) (268) (915) (5)   31 cm   NNAB

Presentation page, Epistle Dedicatory, Foreword, Introduction, Contents, List of Illustrations, Order of Books, Chronology, Events in the Life of Jesus, Key to Pronunciation, Encyclopedic Index, and Concordance and Dictionary edited by Gilbert James Brett precede text. An Account of the 400 Years Between Old and New Testaments follows OT. NT has the words of our Lord in red. At end are Gathering Together of Scripture, with Index; maps and Index; Teaching & Discourses of Christ; and List of Parables. The text is printed in three columns, each book preceded by a two-column line drawing by R. Winkler. Illustrated with half-tones of scenes in Bible Lands and color reproductions of H. Hoffman's paintings of the life of Jesus. "Illuminated" pages for the 23rd Psalm. The Encyclopedic Index includes definitions of such current terms as "atomic energy" (Gen 19:24, 28; Mic 1:4; Isa 24:20, 34:4) and "telephone" (Job 38:35).

Also published with other bindings and reproductions of famous Old Masters.

The publisher's name was "lent" temporarily for the publication of this Bible. Its permanent publisher was Consolidated Book Publishers, Chicago, a division of Book Production Industries, which owns, with Sears Roebuck and Company, the Spencer Press. The John A. Dickson Publishing Company, Columbia Educational Press, the Catholic Press, the Menorah Press, and others are also divisions of Consolidated Book Publishers.

1946? The Holy Bible . . . [National Masonic Edition] to Which has been Added Information of Great Value to all Masons . . . The National Bible Press: Philadelphia **2440**

Reported as (3) (96) (viii) (1462) (32)   25 cm   DLC

Contains The Bible in Masonry; The Influence of the Bible by Quotation and Allusion Upon the Ritual of the Blue Lodge (p 7–34, first group). Illustrations and maps. See 1944?, No 2422.

1946? The Holy Bible . . . The World Publishing Company: Cleveland and New York **2441**

1 vol: (6) 5–954 (2) 3–292 (8) (16)   24 cm   NNAB

Self-Pronouncing edition appears at head of title page. Printed in Jewel type and similar to a Holman edition set in Cushing Bold type, replacing Holman's old Pica Octavo Reference Bible. Contains presentation page before title, Epistle Dedicatory (2 p), Order of Books, and Key to Pronunciation. Also Family Record. Index and Atlas follow text. A few colored illustrations.

In 1946 the word "Syndicate" was officially dropped from the World imprint (see 1928?, No 2295) but it is omitted in many earlier editions. This may not have been issued until 1949.

1946 The Holy Bible . . . with the Words of Jesus Printed in Red and all Proper Names Self-Pronounced. Large-Type Edition . . . Consolidated Book Publishers: Chicago **2442**

Reported as (xv) (1442) (12)   24 cm   DLC

Contains Index to Biblical Place Names at end. Colored illustrations and maps.

1946 Christian Workers Bible . . . [International Series: Self Pronouncing. Good Shepherd Edition]. The John C. Winston Company: Philadelphia **2443**

Reported as (xiii) (1149) (160)   24 cm   DLC

Contains Gray's Index and The Hour of Prayer. Also Concordance. See 1905?, No 2168.

1946 The Scofield Reference Bible . . . New and Improved Edition . . . Oxford University Press: New York **2444**

1 vol: (vi) (2) 3–1353 1354–1362   21 cm   NNAB

Scofield Bible; see 1909, No 2192. Similar to 1917? edition (No 2230) with Indexed Atlas but without Dictionary and Concordance. 30M–46 appears on last page of Index. Copyright 1909 and 1917; copyright renewed 1937 and 1945.

1946? The Holy Bible, self-pronouncing . . . The World Publishing Company: Cleveland and New York **2445**

1 vol: (582) (179)   20 cm   NNAB

Has presentation page, colored frontispiece, and Order of Books (2 p).

1946? The Holy Bible . . . The World Publishing Company: Cleveland and New York **2446**

1 vol: (4) 5–627 (4) 3–194 (4)   20 cm   NNAB

A new setting with semi-Gothic chapter numbers and in condensed type. Has decorated presentation page, colored frontispiece, Order of Books, and Pronunciation.

1946? The Holy Bible . . . [International Series. Self-Pronouncing]. The John C. Winston Company: Philadelphia, Chicago, [etc.] **2447**

Reported as (xxii) (1322) (160)   20 cm   DLC

Contains Concordance, List of Proper Names, and maps.

[5707] *1946* [Old Testament] Pathways Through The Bible by Mortimer J. Cohen. Illustrations by Arthur Szyk. The Jewish Publication Society of America: Philadelphia   **2448**

1 vol: (xxv) (2) (548)   22 cm   NNAB

Jewish Publication Society Version; see 1903 Psalms, No 2151. An abridgment of the OT printed in regular prose form, with identification at end of each passage. Illustrated with 26 colored pictures by Arthur Szyk.

"A special committee advised with the author in planning this volume . . . as an editorial committee to represent various national institutions and organizations interested in the Bible and concerned with spreading knowledge and appreciation of it among the Jewish people" (Foreword, p ix). "While the Jewish Publication Society translation of the Bible has been used as the basic text, liberty has been taken occasionally to modernize that text" (p x).

1946 The Psalms, a Prayer Book. Also the Canticles of the Roman Breviary. New English Translation, with Ecclesiastical Approbation, including the new Latin version from the Hebrew by the Professors of the Pontifical Biblical Institute; also containing preface, explanatory introductions, verse summaries, reflections, commentaries and topical guides by Rev. William H. McClellan, S.J., Very Rev. John F. Rowan, D.D., L.S.S., Rev. James E. Coleran, S.J., Dom Bede Babo, O.S.B., Rev. Francis P. Le Buffe, S.J. Benziger Brothers: New York, [etc.]   **2449**

1 vol: (xvi) (416) (29)   18 cm   NNAB

Imprimatur of Francis Cardinal Spellman, Abp. of New York. The Latin text is printed in the left column, the English in the right. This new Latin version was first published in 1945 by the Pontifical Biblical Institute at Rome. Headings, numbers of Psalms, and initial capitals are printed in red. Glossary and Index at end.

The English text has been reprinted several times with the Rheims-Douay and Confraternity texts in complete Bibles; see 1949, No 2475, and 1950, No 2487.

NNAB has another translation from the new Latin Psalter, *My Daily Psalm Book*, the book of Psalms arranged for each day of the week . . . Rev. Joseph B. Frey, Director of the Confraternity of the Precious Blood . . . Brooklyn, copyright 1947 (xii, 368 p; 13 cm). Also contains some canticles. Illustrated by Ariel Agemian.

1946 The New Testament . . . A New Translation. A Chanticleer Edition, Published by Sheed and Ward: New York   **2450**

1 vol: (ix) [1] (502)   24 cm   DLC, NNAB

Knox Version; see 1944 NT, No 2429. Preface signed by R. A. Knox, 1943, Notes Concerning This Edition, Order of Books, and List of Illustrations precede text, which is printed in paragraph form, single column, with verse numbers in text. Illustrated with reproductions in color of famous paintings and woodcuts from the 1493 Italian Malermi Bible. Fifth printing of general edition. First printing of illustrated edition produced by Chanticleer Press, Inc. Copyright 1944.

1946? The Red Letter New Testament . . . The Words of Christ Printed in Red . . . The John C. Winston Company: Philadelphia, Chicago, [etc.]   **2451**

Reported as (xx) (378) (104)   19 cm   DLC

International Series, Self-Pronouncing Long Primer Testament. Contains Psalms, History of the Apostles by Rev. A. R. Fausset, Meditations on the Gospels by Joseph Howard Gray, and History of the Psalms by Joseph Howard Gray. Colored illustrations.

1946? The New Testament . . . Translated from the Latin Vulgate . . . First Published by the English College at Rheims . . . 1582. With Annotations and

References by Dr. Challoner and Dr. H. J. Ganss; an Historical and Chronological Index, Index of Proper Names . . . Preface by Rev. J. M. Lelen . . .
[Catholic Book Publishing Company: New York]   **2452**

Reported as 670 p   15 cm   DLC
Rheims Version. Contains *Imitatio Christi* in English. Illustrated.

1946 The New Covenant Commonly Called the New Testament . . . Revised
Standard Version . . . Being the Version Set Forth A.D. 1611. Revised 1881
and 1901 . . . and Revised 1946 . . . [Norwood Press, J. S. Cushing Co. —
Berwick & Smith Co., Norwood, Mass., Printers]. Thomas Nelson & Sons:
New York   **2453**

1 vol: (vi) (2) (553) (3)   19 cm   NcD, NNAB, OC, ViU

Has Preface. Text in paragraph form, single column, with verse numbers in text; references
and alternative readings and renderings at foot of page. Copyright 1901, by Thomas Nelson &
Sons; copyright renewed 1929, by the International Council of Religious Education; copyright
1946, by the International Council of Religious Education.

This is the first appearance of the Revised Standard Version, or RSV. When the copyright
to the American Standard Version was transferred in 1929 to the International Council of Religious Education, consideration was given to its further revision. In 1930 the American Standard
Bible Committee was set up, with Dean Luther A. Weigle, of the Yale University Divinity
School, as chairman. At meetings in 1930 and 1931 there was a good deal of discussion as to
how much revision was desirable. Although none of the members of the committee were to
receive salaries or honoraria, there would be considerable expenses for travel to meetings, etc.
In the early 1930s funds were difficult to secure for such a project but in 1936 satisfactory finan-
cial arrangements were made. New members were added to the original committee of thirteen
and in 1939 the Committee defined its task "to be that of revision of the present American
Standard Edition of the Bible in the light of the results of modern scholarship, this revision to be
designed for use in public and private worship and to be in the direction of the simple, classic
English style of the King James Version." Dr. James Moffatt, retiring from the faculty of Union
Theological Seminary in 1938, became the executive secretary until his death in 1944. Dr.
Weigle carried on this responsibility until the appointment in 1947 of Dr. Fleming James, dean
emeritus of the School of Theology, the University of the South, Sewanee, Tenn. Other members of the NT Committee: H. J. Cadbury (Harvard), E. J. Goodspeed (U of Chicago), W. R.
Bowie (Grace Church), F. C. Grant (Union), M. Burrows (Yale), C. T. Craig (Oberlin), and
A. R. Wentz (Lutheran). For fuller details as to personnel, procedures, etc., see the Prefaces
to the NT and Bible, and two pamphlets published by Thomas Nelson & Sons: *An Introduction
to the Revised Standard Version of the New Testament by Members of the Revision Committee, Luther A. Weigle, Chairman,* copyright 1946, and a similar one on the OT, copyright
1952.

The NT was published on Feb 11, 1946, and dedicated at a service of thanksgiving at a
session of the International Council in Columbus, Ohio. The OT (No 2514) and the complete
Bible (No 2510) were published in 1952. The RSV NT was widely welcomed but the publication of the OT in 1952 raised a storm of violent opposition on the part of a small group of con-
servatives who objected particularly to the translation of Isaiah 7:14. In spite of this the RSV
Bible has received constantly increasing acceptance as the best English Bible for general Protestant use.

1946? The New Testament and Psalms . . . The World Publishing Company:
Cleveland and New York   **2454, 2455**

1 vol: (428) (4) 3–111 [1]   12 cm   NNAB

World Pronouncing Edition appears at head of title page. Key to Pronunciation and Order
of Books (2 p). Questions Answered from the Word of God (1 p) follows NT. The Psalms
lacks imprint on title page.

1947   The Holy Bible . . . with the Words of Jesus Printed in Red . . . Large Type
         Edition . . . Distributed by Southeastern Distributors, Inc., Charlotte, N. C.
         Published by Spencer Press: [Chicago]   **2456**

1 vol: (xiv) (206) (1566)   27 cm   DLC, NNAB

Presentation page, Epistle Dedicatory, Contents, etc., List of Illustrations, Key to Pronunciation, Books of the Old and New Testaments Arranged Chronologically and Alphabetically,
and Readers' Guide (Concordance by Gilbert James Brett) precede text. Portraits and illustrations follow OT. At end are Harvest of Scriptural Truth, Bible Dates, Gospel Harmony, Family
Record, Character Building, Bible Promises, Children's Stories, Bible Curiosities, Pathways to
Wisdom, Index, and maps. Has drawings and colored plates by A. H. Winkler. Cover title:
Revelation. Copyright 1947.

A similar edition, copyright 1952, was called the Revelation Bible.

1947   The Inspirational Bible; . . . Containing Self-Pronunciation of all Proper
         Names, the Words of Jesus in Red Letters, Full-Color Illustrations of Many
         Biblical Events and Places, an Illustrated Life of Jesus, a Complete Index
         to All Biblical Facts, a Guide to Every Well-Known Scriptural Quotation,
         and an Unabridged Dictionary of the Bible. De Luxe Edition . . . Consoli-
         dated Book Publishers, Distributed by L. B. Price Mercantile Co.: Chicago
                                                                                  2457

Reported as (x) (640) (22) (45) 23–196 (522)   27 cm   DLC

"Text . . . previously published as the New Indexed Bible, copyright 1901 . . . 1940 [by]
John A. Dickson Publishing Co." Contains The Bible in Alphabet, by G. J. Brett, and other
matter specially prepared for this edition. Illustrations and maps.

DLC also has 1950? Golden Book Edition, distributed by L. B. Price Mercantile Co.

1947   The New Analytical Bible and Dictionary of the Bible. . . . with the Addi-
         tion in Many Instances, in Brackets, of the More Correct Renderings of the
         American Revised Version, Copyright 1929 . . . A System of Helps . . . and
         Many Other Features . . . to Facilitate the Study and Better Understanding
         of the Scriptures . . . J. A. Dickson Publishing Co.: Chicago   **2458**

Reported as (295) (1639)   26 cm   DLC
Reprint of 1931 edition (No 2320).

1947? The Concordia Bible, with Notes . . . Revised by John Theodore Mueller
         . . . Concordia Publishing House: St. Louis   **2459**

Reported as (1491) (16)   26 cm   DLC
Has maps. See 1952, No 2507

1947   The Holy Bible . . . with the Words of Jesus Printed in Red and All Proper
         Names Self-Pronounced. Large-Type Edition . . . Spencer Press: Chicago
                                                                                   2460

Reported as (xii) (1398)   25 cm   DLC

Contains Index to the Words and Wisdom of the Bible by Gilbert James Brett (p 1335–
1353). Illustrations and maps.

DLC has another copy without Index (1334 p).

1947   The Holy Bible . . . A. J. Holman Company: Philadelphia   **2461**

Reported as (954) (292) (24)   25 cm   DLC

Holman Home Bible appears at head of title page. Contains Selections for Today and Every
Day by P. Z. Strodach. Maps.

1947 The Holy Bible. Light of the World Edition. The Publishers Guild, Inc.: New York **2462**

1 vol: (1203); other matter var. paged   21 cm   NNAB

Light of the World Bible appears on front cover; *Holy Bible. Red Letter Edition* appears on spine. Text reprinted from the 1945 edition (No 2434). Presentation page, frontispiece, Condensed Bible Commentary and Difficult Bible Questions Answered (edited by Geo. H. Sandison, 75 p), List of Proper Names Pronounced (26 p), illustrations (half in color; 16, 32 p), Statement on References, and Order of Books precede text. NT illustrations (16, 32 p). NT has device of World Publishing Company on title page and is marked Red Letter Edition. At end are Biblical Encyclopedia and Concordance (410 p), Family Record, Record of Military Service, maps, and Geographical Index. "The Special Contents of this Book Copyright 1947, by The World Publishing Company."

DLC has an entry for 1947 that seems to be same, with text and Concordance printed by World but title and imprint appear as *Rock of Ages Edition . . . Lloyd Distributors: Charlotte, N. C.*

In 1942 the World Publishing Company advertised the World Master-Art Edition with much of the material of cited copy, including the Sandison Condensed Commentary often used by World. NNAB has a full-page advertisement from *This Week* for October 25, 1942, for this edition.

1947 The Psalms. A New Translation by Ronald Knox. Sheed and Ward: New York **2463**

1 vol: (6) (239)   18 cm   NNAB

Knox Version; see 1944 NT, No 2429. Includes the Canticles of the Roman Breviary. DLC has 1955 edition.

1947 The New Testament . . . Translated from the Greek text of Westcott and Hort. By Rev. George Swann . . . [Printed by the Pentecostal Publishing Company: Louisville, Kentucky] **2464**

1 vol: (vi) (262) (2)   24 cm   NNAB

A second edition was issued in 1949. NNAB has third edition imprinted *New Testament Publishers: Louisville, Kentucky* (vii, 262, v p; 23 cm).

George Swann (1882–   ) received his A.B. degree from Transylvania and College of the Bible, Lexington, Kentucky, in 1909 and since has served as pastor in Christian churches in Kentucky, being with the Edenside Christian Church in Louisville from 1928 to 1952. Ten years were spent in the preparation of this work. He has sought to avoid paraphrase and has enclosed added words in parentheses. He has retained the "thou" forms in the Gospels in about half of their occurrences, eliminating them elsewhere except in direct quotations. In the first two editions the traditional chapter and verse numbering is given only at the head of the page, a system of continuous versification (1–1782) being used instead. In the third edition the usual numbering is given at the right of the caption. A brief index, based on his numbering, follows the text. Mr. Swann has made changes in each edition.

1947 The New Testament . . . Confraternity of Christian Doctrine. St. Anthony Guild Press: Paterson, New Jersey **2465**

Reported as (viii) (762)   20 cm   MH

Confraternity Version; see 1941 NT, No 2397.

1948 The Holy Bible . . . In the Beloved King James Version with the Words of Christ in Red. Christian Home Edition . . . National Bible Press: Philadelphia **2466**

25 cm   DLC

Contains Dictionary of the Bible by William Smith (112 p). Illustrations and maps. See 1944?, No 2422.

1948?   The Westminster Study Edition of the Holy Bible . . . Arranged in Paragraphs and in Verses, Together with Introductory Articles and Prefaces, Explanatory Footnotes, a Concordance, and Maps . . . The Westminster Press: Philadelphia   **2467**

    1 vol: (xxvi) (1376) (x) (486) (103) (3) (6) (16)   25 cm   DLC, ICU, MB, MiU, NN, NNAB, OC, ViU

    Fly title, List of Aids, Preface, Contents, account: "God Has Spoken," History of the Bible, and Introductions precede text. Account: "From the Old to the New" follows OT. Introductions precede NT. At end are Concordance, Bible Atlas, and Index to maps. Maps and plans.

    This work was prepared by a group of scholars from several Protestant denominations. Introductions are provided for each Book and footnotes trace ideas, explain archaic words, and clarify difficult passages.

1948–49   [Holy Bible] The Book of Human Destiny . . . By Solomon Goldman. Publishers, Harper & Brothers: New York and London   **2468**

    2 vols: Vol I, (xiii) (459); Vol II, (xiv) (892)   24 cm   NNAB

    Vol I (1948), The Book of Books: An Introduction. Contains an evaluation of the Hebrew Bible and the impression it has made on the mind of Western man. Vol II (1949), Genesis. Contains selections from text, commentary, etc. The rather large amount of supplementary matter includes some useful material on the influence of the Bible on literature, entitled "Echoes and Allusions." Other volumes were planned but the project was discontinued.

    Rabbi Goldman (1893–1953) was born in Russia. He received an A.B. degree at New York University in 1917 and later studied at the Jewish Theological Seminary, Columbia University, and the University of Chicago.

1948   The Holy Bible . . . with Notes Especially Adapted for Young Christians . . . Pilgrim Edition. Oxford University Press: New York   **2469**

    1 vol: (xxii) (1721) (17)   20 cm   DLC, MB, NNAB

    An abridgment of the AV edited by a group of scholars, pastors, teachers, and editors, headed by E. Schuyler English, Litt.D. Planned originally for children, it developed into a text understandable "to any young Christians of any age, children included." With a somewhat "dispensational slant," it is related to the Scofield Bible (see 1909, No 2192). Some of the "literal or more accurate" translations of the revised versions are included in the notes. The footnotes also have definitions, refinements of translation, and sidelights from contemporary literature. Between the OT and NT is a History of the Intertestament Period. Has Introductions to each Book, maps, and plans. Ussher's Chronology is included and italics are employed for supplied words.

1948–   The Holy Bible. Translated from the Original Languages with Critical Use of All the Ancient Sources by Members of the Catholic Biblical Association of America. Sponsored by the Episcopal Committee of the Confraternity of Christian Doctrine . . . St. Anthony Guild Press: Paterson, New Jersey   **2470**

    Confraternity Version; see 1941 NT, No 2397. This work is still in progress. The volumes published to date are all 20 cm with notes and references at foot of page, and are located as follows:

    The Book of Genesis, 1948. (vi, 1, 2–129 p; NN, NNAB)

    The Book of Psalms and the Canticles of the Roman Breviary, 1950. (vi, 1, 2–301 p; NN, NNAB)

    [Volume One] Genesis to Ruth, 1952. (xii, 1, 2–664 p; OC)

        Genesis is reproduced without substantial difference from the 1948 edition. The following misprints have been noted: ". . . bdellium and onyx [are] there" (Gen 2:12, p 6) and ". . . the skunk (for skink), and the mole" (Lev 11:30, p 255).

These errors have been corrected and the textual notes reset in the 1953 reprint (x, 1, 2–662 p; NNAB).

[Volume Three] The Sapiential Books, Job to Sirach, 1955. (viii, 1, 2–712 p; NNAB)

[Volume Four] The Prophetic Books, Isaia-Malachia, 1961. (viii, 1–776; NNAB).

1948–50 The Old Testament newly translated from the Vulgate Latin by Msgr. Ronald Knox at the request of His Eminence The Cardinal Archbishop of Westminster. . . . Issued by Sheed & Ward, Inc.: New York   *2471*

2 vols: Vol I, (10) (737) (3); Vol II, (6) 741–1604   22 cm   NNAB

Knox Version; see 1944 NT, No 2429. This is the first American printing of the Knox OT. Vol I, Genesis-Esther. Vol II, Job-Machabees; also contains an alternative version of the Psalms based on the Latin text of the Pontifical Biblical Institute (Rome, 1945), printed in smaller type (p 1535–1604).

The alternative Knox version of the Psalms was also printed separately with the Pontifical Biblical Institute Latin text: *The Book of Psalms in Latin and English*, Sheed and Ward: New York, 1950 (451 p, 15 cm).

1948 The New Testament. An American Translation by Edgar J. Goodspeed. The University of Chicago Press: Chicago   *2472*

1 vol: (x) (373)   25 cm   NN, NNAB

American Translation; see 1923 NT, No 2260. Twenty-Fifth Anniversary Edition 1948. Dr. Goodspeed furnished materials for numerous changes to improve the translation. The format and type page were changed in an attempt to make this the most readable NT on the market. It is printed in paragraph form, double columns, with verse numbers in margin. Copyright 1923 and 1948.

ICU has 1951? edition (ix, 372 p).

1948 Letters to Young Churches. A Translation of the New Testament Epistles by J. B. Phillips, with an Introduction by C. S. Lewis . . . The Macmillan Company: New York   *2473*

1 vol: (xiv) (225)   21 cm   NNAB

Preliminary matter includes Order of Books, Introduction by C. S. Lewis, and Translator's Preface dated 1941–46. Text printed in paragraph form, single column, with section heads and chapter and verse indication. Copyright 1947.

This volume was followed by:

The Gospels, 1953. (ix, 2, 243 p; 21 cm)

The Young Church in Action. A translation of the Acts of the Apostles, 1955. (xvi, 2, 3–103 p; 21 cm)

The Book of Revelation, 1957. (xiv, 50 p; 21 cm)

Letters to Young Churches . . . Epistles, a corrected edition, 1957. (xiv, 225 p; 21 cm)

The New Testament in Modern English, translated by J. B. Phillips, 1958. (xiv, 575 p; 21 cm)

The Gospels, a corrected edition, 1958. (x, 252 p; 21 cm)

NNAB has all of these. All but the NT were printed first in England, usually a year before American publication, by Geoffrey Bles. The NT appeared in London two weeks after the American edition.

John Bertram Phillips (1906–   ) was born in London and returned there after taking a B.D. degree at Emmanuel College, Cambridge, and studying for the ministry at Cambridge. He was ordained a priest in the Church of England in 1930, but because of ill health served as a journalist between his first two curacies. In 1940 he became vicar of the Church of The Good Shepherd in London and remained in that much-blitzed section until nearly the end of the war. In 1955 he retired from parish work to devote himself to writing and speaking. It was during the War that he was impressed by the fact that young people in his parish could understand hardly a sentence of the AV. His translation is rather free but is based on somewhat conservative scholarship. The Letters to Young Churches has been extremely popular in Britain and America. By the end of 1957, over 400,000 copies of the cheap edition had been sold in England.

The following is from the Foreword to the NT: "... the translator's function is to understand as fully and deeply as possible what the New Testament writers had to say and then, after a process of what might be called reflective digestion, to write it down in the language of the people today.... Occasionally one is driven into what appears to be a paraphrase, simply because a literal translation of the original Greek would prove unintelligible."

1949   The Holy Bible . . . The World Publishing Company: Cleveland and New York   **2474**

1 vol: (xxiv) (942)   49 cm   CtY, DLC, MH, MnU, NN, NNAB

Has type ornaments on title page, and ornamental head and tail pieces and initial for each Book. Dedication to King James with border reflecting the English rose, Scottish thistle, fleur-delis, and harp of Ireland of the 1611 edition. Contains The Translators to the Reader (14 p). Printed in paragraph form, double columns, with poetry passages indented. NT title lacks border and imprint. Colophon reads "Printed by A. Colish from designs by Bruce Rogers for the World Publishing Company Cleveland and New York MCMXLIX nine hundred and seventy-five copies."

This is World's Bruce Rogers Bible. The type is based on that originally designed by Frederic Goudy (Newstyle) and considered by Rogers for the Oxford Lectern Bible. It was modified by Rogers and cast for Monotype composition. The type and the ornaments were thought to give a slightly oriental flavor to the volume, reflecting the Syriac and Hebrew sources. It was planned for memorial presentation to schools and churches, as well as for collectors and book lovers.

1949   The New Catholic Edition of the Holy Bible, Translated from the Latin Vulgate. The Old Testament, Douay Version, with Newly Edited Annotations of Bishop Challoner and a New Translation of the Book of Psalms from the New Latin Version Approved by Pope Pius XII and the New Testament Confraternity Edition, A Revision of the Challoner-Rheims Version Edited by Catholic Scholars under the Patronage of the Episcopal Committee of the Confraternity of Christian Doctrine . . . Catholic Book Publishing Co.: New York   **2475**

1 vol: (1086) (367)   21 cm   NN, NNAB

Imprimatur of Cardinal Spellman, 1948. Letter of Pope Pius XII, Preface by publisher, Prayers, Indulgences, List of Books, and Order of Books precede text. Family Record follows OT. Imprimaturs, etc., Order of Books, Permission to Use NT text, and copyright 1948 precede NT. At end are List of Committee Members of the Confraternity of Christian Doctrine, Indexes, Table, Miracles and Parables of Jesus, List of Readings, Bible Reading Guide, and Lilly's Topical Outline for Bible Reading. Maps. Copyright 1949.

For Confraternity Version, see 1941 NT, No 2397. The Psalms in this and other Bibles combining Douay and Confraternity texts is a new translation of the 1945 new Latin text prepared from the Hebrew by scholars of the Pontifical Biblical Institute (see 1946, No 2449).

1949? The Holy Bible . . . The World Publishing Company: Cleveland and New York   **2476**

1 vol: (8) 7–865 (3) 3–265 (2) 269–283 (8)   19 cm   NNAB

Self-pronouncing appears at head of title page. Printed in Nu-Bold Brevier type. Contains decorative presentation page, Wedding Certificate, and Family Record. Dedication to King James, Lists of Books, and Key to Pronunciation precede text. Bible Readers' Aids and Concordance at end. Illustrated.

1949–56 Harper's Annotated Bible. The Book of The Twelve Prophets . . . with introductions and critical notes by Julius A. Bewer . . . Harper and Brothers: New York   **2477**

Various paging   12 cm   ICU, NN, NNUT

No 1, Vol i, Amos, Hosea, and Micah, 1949.
No 2, Vol ii, completing the Minor Prophets, 1949.
No 3, Isaiah, Vol i, ch 1–39, 1950.
No 4, Isaiah, Vol ii, ch 40–66, 1950.
No 5, Jeremiah, Vol i, ch 1–25, 1951.
No 6, Jeremiah, Vol ii, ch 26–52, 1952.
No 7, The Gospel of Mark, 1952.
No 8, Ezekiel, Vol i, ch 1–24, 1954.
No 9, Ezekiel, Vol ii, ch 25–48, 1954.
No 10, The Gospel of Matthew, Vol i, ch 1–13:52, 1955.
No 11, The Gospel of Matthew, Vol ii, ch 13:53–28:20, 1955.
No 12, Daniel, 1955.
No 13, The Gospel of John, Vol i, ch 1–12, 1956.
No 14, The Gospel of John, Vol ii, ch 13–21, and the Epistles of John, 1956.
No 15, The Epistle to the Hebrews, 1956.
The OT portions were edited by Julius Bewer and the NT by Frederick C. Grant. No more were published. Although the AV is used as the basic text because of its place in the life of the English-speaking people, improved readings based on modern scholarship are given in the notes. Each Book has Introduction and considerable comment.
Nos 1–6, 8, 9, and 12 were printed in 1 vol: *The Prophets* ... with introduction and critical notes by Julius A. Bewer. Harper and Bros.: New York, 1956 (viii, 663 p; 25 cm; DLC, NNUT).

1949? The Holy Bible ... A. J. Holman Co.: Philadelphia   **2478**

Reported as 1131 p   OO
No further information reported.

1949? The New Covenant ... Revised Standard Version ... Thomas Nelson &
Sons: New York   **2479**

1 vol: (viii) (542)   17 cm   NNAB
RSV; see 1946 NT, No 2453. Has Preface. Copyrights same as in 1946 edition.

1949 The New Covenant ... Revised Standard Version ... Thomas Nelson &
Sons: New York   **2480**

1 vol: (vii) (670)   13 cm   NNAB
RSV; see 1946 NT, No 2453. Has Preface. No references. Copyrights same as in 1946 edition.

1950? The Holy Bible ... A Comprehensive Encyclopedic Guide to Biblical
Knowledge and Other Features, with the Words of Jesus Printed in Red and
Self Pronunciation of All Words. With Illustrations by Tissot. Good Saviour
Edition. Consolidated Book Publishers: Chicago   **2481**

1 vol: (xv) (894) (302)   30 cm   DLC, NN
Has Dictionary, Concordance, and Collation of Scriptures edited by Gilbert James Brett. Colored illustrations and maps.
DLC also has the following similar editions: (1) the Heritage Edition, with colored reproductions of paintings by celebrated old masters; (2) a 1954? copy of the Good Samaritan Edition, containing Brett's Dictionary, Concordance, and Collation (268 p); (3) a 1955? copy of the Good Saviour Edition, with Tissot illustrations and Brett's Dictionary, Concordance, and Collation; (4) a 1955? Masonic Edition, with Articles on the History and Philosophy of Masonry and an Alphabetical Dictionary of Masonic Knowledge by Curt A. Mundstock.

1950 The Bible for my grandchildren, arranged ... by Ruth Hornblower Greenough with illustrations from designs by William Blake and decorations by
Rudolph Ruzicka ... Privately Printed: [n. p.]   **2482**

2 vols: Vol i, (xiv) (350); Vol ii, (viii) (388)   27 cm   NNAB

Has Preface, Acknowledgments, Contents, and List of Illustrations. Text printed in prose and poetry form, single column, without chapter or verse indication. Subject heads appear in margin in blue, brown, or black, with small decoration toward bottom of many pages. Blake illustrations are full page. The frontispiece to Vol i is a color reproduction of Blake's *Creation;* the one in Vol ii is mosaic from St. Sophia. Index at end of each vol gives chapter and verse source for each passage. Copyright 1950, by Mrs. Greenough.

A 1-vol edition was issued in 1951 by Harper and Brothers as *The Home Bible: arranged for Family Reading.*

1950   The Holy Bible. Old Testament in the Douay-Challoner Text. New Testament and Psalms in the Confraternity Text. Edited by Reverend John P. O'Connell . . . With Illustrations by James Joseph Jacques Tissot. Published with the Approbation of His Eminence Samuel Cardinal Stritch, Archbishop of Chicago. [Cuneo Press] The Catholic Press, Inc.: Chicago   **2483**

1 vol: (lxi) (909) (308) (288)   26 cm   NNAB
Family Catholic Edition appears at head of title page. Illuminated title and presentation pages. Words of Our Lord are printed in red. The great variety of added matter includes Encyclical Letters, material on the Catholic Bible, Index, etc., Bible Dictionary and Collation of Texts, pictorial maps, and a variety of colored illustrations. Copyright 1950.
For Confraternity Version, see 1941 NT, No 2397.

1950   The New Chain-Reference Bible. Third Improved Edition . . . Compiled and Edited by Frank Charles Thompson . . . B. B. Kirkbride Bible Co.: Indianapolis   **2484**

23 cm   NNAB
Thirty-second reprint. Copyright 1934, by Frank Charles Thompson. Previous copyrights 1908, 1917, 1929. See 1908?, No 2184; also 1934, No 2341.

1950?   The New Analytical Bible and Dictionary of the Bible . . . with the Addition, in Brackets, of Renderings from the American Revised Version. Comprehensive Subject Index Edition . . . J. A. Dickson Publishing Co.: Chicago   **2485**

Reported as (xiii) (204) (1702)   23 cm   DLC
A new edition of the New Analytical Indexed Bible (see 1931, No 2320) with the Concordance set in more legible type, a New Index ("the most complete yet to be published for any Bible"), and an improved Bible Dictionary. Maps.

1950   The Dartmouth Bible, an Abridgment . . . with aids to its understanding as history and literature, and as a source of religious experience. Roy B. Chamberlin, D.D., Herman Feldman, Ph.D., Dartmouth College, with the counsel of an advisory board of Biblical scholars . . . [The Riverside Press, Cambridge] Houghton Mifflin Company: Boston   **2486**

1 vol: (xxxviii) (1257)   23 cm   NNAB
Preliminary matter includes dedication to Dartmouth College, Advisory Board, etc., Contents, list of maps, Authors' Preface and The Bible Through the Ages. The text is printed in paragraph and poetry form with verse numbers in the margins. About half the full text is omitted (repetitions, material of interest only to technical students), such omissions usually being indicated. Footnotes give readings of modern scholarship in addition to explanations. Ruth, Esther and Jonah are placed together, Proverbs is broken up into subject divisions, the Prophets and the Epistles arranged chronologically, and the Gospels harmonized. Has Key to Abbreviations, bibliography, and A Modern Reader's Index (45 p) at end. Colored maps of the OT and NT worlds are used as endpapers.

1950 The Holy Bible. Old Testament, Douay Version, With Psalms from the New Latin Version Authorized by Pope Pius xii. New Testament, Confraternity Edition, with the Encyclical Letter "On the Study of the Holy Scriptures" by Pope Leo xiii; Also a Presentation of the Essence of the Encyclical Letter "On Biblical Studies" by Pope Pius xii; and a Preface by William H. Mc-Clellan . . . Also an Appendix Containing an . . . Index, Table of References and Maps . . . Benziger Brothers, Inc.: New York, Boston, Cincinnati, Chicago, San Francisco   **2487**

1 vol: (xxxii) (964) (288)   21 cm   NN, NNAB

New American Catholic Edition appears at head of title page. Imprimatur of Francis Cardinal Spellman, 1950. Copyright 1950, by Benziger Brothers, Inc.
For Confraternity Version, see 1941 NT, No 2397. For the Psalms see 1946, No 2449.

1950 The Basic Bible containing the Old and New Testaments in Basic English. E. P. Dutton Co., Inc.: New York   **2488**

1 vol: (10) 11–910   21 cm   NN, NNAB

Basic English Version; see 1941 NT, No 2396. This is the first American edition of the whole Bible in Basic English, first printed in England in 1949 by the Cambridge University Press.

195–? The Holy Bible . . . 1901. Standard Edition. [Printed by the Watchtower Bible and Tract Society, Inc.: Brooklyn]   **2489**

1 vol: (viii) (4) (1002) (vi) (288) (96)   19 cm   NNAB

ASV; see 1901, No 2124. Nelson's Minion Black-Faced Type edition. Has the usual authorization, copyrights, and Prefaces of earlier editions. Text followed by Concordance with a list of the Chief Office and official address of the Watch Tower Bible and Tract Society and branch offices on last page. Two maps in black and white and green.
Title page lacks imprint. A set of plates was sold to the Watchtower Bible and Tract Society after the 1929 copyright ran out.

1950 The Holy Bible . . . New York Bible Society: New York   **2490**

19 cm   NNAB

10,000 copies printed from plates of the 1938 ABS edition (No 2367) for placing in New York hotels. Has maps.

1950 The New Testament . . . Confraternity . . . Special Student Edition. Catholic Book Publishing Co.: New York   **2491**

Reported as 379 p   26 cm   DLC

Confraternity Version; see 1941 NT, No 2397. Has colored illustrations and maps.

1950 The New Testament . . . Confraternity . . . Catholic Book Publishing Co.: New York   **2492**

Reported as 383 p   21 cm   DLC

Confraternity Version; see 1941 NT, No 2397. Red Letter Edition with colored maps and illustrations.

1950 The New Testament; a Translation in the Language of the People, by Charles B. Williams . . . Moody Press: Chicago   **2493**

Reported as 575 p   21 cm   DLC, MB

C. B. Williams Version; see 1937 NT, No 2362. In this edition verse numbers have been inserted in the text. Moody first issued this in October 1949, and by November 1958 had issued eight editions in paper binding, twelve in cloth, and five in leather.

1950 [New Testament] New World Translation of the Christian Greek Scriptures Rendered from the Original Language by the New World Bible Translation Committee ... [Publishers: Watchtower Bible and Tract Society, Inc.; International Bible Students Association: Brooklyn]   **2494**

1 vol: (792) (8)   19 cm   DLC, NN, NNAB, OC

Foreword and other explanatory material precede text, which is printed in paragraph form, single column, with verse numbers in text and references in margin. Has textual interpretations in footnotes. Appendix, Bible Helps, and maps at end. Copyright 1950.

NNAB also has 1951 reprint with additional notes and minor changes.

The New World Translation Committee, an organization of the Jehovah's Witnesses, based its translation largely on the Greek text of Westcott and Hort, supplemented by the texts of Nestle and the Jesuit scholars Bover and Merk. Variations from Westcott and Hort are shown in the footnotes. The translators aimed to dispose of archaic language and "to give as literal a translation as possible.... To each major word we have assigned one meaning and have held to that meaning as far as the context permitted ..." (Foreword, p 9). The Foreword (p 25) contains an extended vindication of the rendering "Jehovah" in place of "the Lord" in cases of quotations from or apparent allusions to the Hebrew. The translators would have preferred "Yah·weh" but kept the form "Jehovah" because of its familiarity.

For New World Translation of the Hebrew Scriptures, see 1953–60 OT, No 2527.

1950 The New Testament of Our Messiah and Saviour Yahshua. Sacred Name Version. Critically compared with ancient authorities and divers manuscripts. The Scripture Research Association: Irvington, New Jersey   **2495**

566 p   18 cm   DLC, NN, NNAB

Copyright 1950, by The Scripture Research Association, Inc.

This translation is understood to have been made by Mr. A. B. Traina and printed at his expense. At the end of the Preface, signed Scripture Research Association, Philip B. Wisman ... April, 1950, acknowledgment is made of "the work of Pastor A. B. Traina ... whose many years of extensive scriptural research have given continuity to our efforts and has brought them to successful completion" (p 13). The work attempts to restore Semitic proper names to their Aramaic or Hebrew form and to clear up difficulties in the text in the light of possible Semitic background. The text of the AV is used as the framework for this version.

1950? The New Testament and the Psalms; ... James Moffatt ... Harper: New York   **2496**

561 p   11 cm   DLC

Moffatt Version; see 1917? NT, No 2235. Contains the Psalms. Copyright 1950.

1950? The New Testament ... [and Psalms]. Harper and Brothers: New York   **2497**

1 vol: (iv) (567)   10 cm   NNAB

Times-Ruby Vest Pocket edition, self-pronouncing.

1951 The Devotional Family Bible ... Self-Pronouncing ... Red Letter Edition. Dictionary-Concordance and ... Useful Aids ... Dixie Bibles: Wichita, Kansas   **2498**

Reported as 1088 p   30 cm   DLC

Illustrations and maps.
DLC also has 1954 edition.

1951 The Holy Bible ... edited by John P. O'Connell. Holy Trinity Edition. Catholic Press: Chicago   **2499**

27 cm   DLC

Rheims-Douay Version. Illustrated.

1951–57 The Interpreter's Bible . . . in the King James and Revised Standard Versions with general articles and introduction for each book of the Bible. In twelve volumes . . . [Printed and bound by the Parthenon Press, Nashville, Tenn.]. Abingdon-Cokesbury Press: New York and Nashville **2500**

12 vols   26 cm   DLC, NN, NNAB, OC

Vol I, Genesis and Exodus, 1952. (xxx, 1099 p)
Vol II, Leviticus-2 Samuel, 1953. (x, 1176 p)
Vol III, Kings-Job, 1954. (xi, 1198 p)
Vol IV, Psalms-Proverbs, 1955. (ix, 959 p)
Vol V, Ecclesiastes-Jeremiah, 1956. (x, 1142 p)
Vol VI, Lamentations-Malachi, 1956. (xii, 1144 p)
Vol VII, Matthew-Mark, 1951. (xxiv, 917 p)
Vol VIII, Luke-John, 1952. (x, 811 p)
Vol IX, Acts-Romans, 1954. (x, 668 p)
Vol X, 1 and 2 Corinthians, Galatians, Ephesians, 1953. (x, 749 p)
Vol XI, Philippians-Hebrews, 1955. (ix, 763 p)
Vol XII, James-Revelation, 1957. (xi, 818 p)
In Vols III–VI, XI, and XII the imprint is *Abingdon Press.*

AV and RSV (see 1946 NT, No 2453) printed side by side with alternative readings and renderings and exegesis and exposition below, often taking up most of the page. There are also many special articles by well-known British and American scholars. The Editorial Board consisted of George Arthur Buttrick, Walter Russell Bowie, Paul Scherer, John Knox, Samuel Terrien, and Nolan B. Harmon. The preliminary pages list the editors, consulting editors, and contributors, who represent many denominations and theological points of view. Published simultaneously in the U. S., Canada, and Great Britain. Copyright 1951, by Pierce and Smith; copyright acknowledgments cover RSV, ASV, Moffatt, and the Smith-Goodspeed versions.

1951 The Bible . . . Designed to be Read as Living Literature . . . This Edition Arranged and Edited by Ernest Sutherland Bates . . . Simon and Schuster: New York   **2501**

Reported as (xxvi) (1285)   25 cm   NNC

Contains A Glossary of Biblical Terms compiled by Wallace Brockway at end and colored maps on end-paper. See 1936, No 2355.

NNAB has 1951 paper-back abridgment, with a Preface by Cyril C. Richardson, Professor of Church History, Union Theological Seminary, published by Pocket Books, Inc., A Cardinal Edition (xviii, 461 p; 17 cm). It was sold in the King Supermarkets, New Jersey.

1951 The New Testament . . . in Modern English translated from the original Greek and supplied with an outline by Olaf Morgan Norlie. [Published by the Author: Northfield: Minnesota]   **2502**

Various paging   28 cm   NNAB

Mimeographed by Mr. Norlie. Each Book separately paged.

Mr. Norlie, a professor at St. Olaf College, Northfield, Minn., author of a number of books on the Bible, and a Lutheran pastor, had earlier translated the Gospel of John (Life Builders Press: San Antonio, Texas, 1943; 152 p; 13 cm). The NT was mimeographed in the unsuccessful hope of finding a publisher.

1951 The Sacred Writings of the Apostles and Evangelists of Jesus Christ, Commonly Styled the New Testament. Translated from the Original Greek, by George Campbell, James Macknight and Philip Doddridge. With Prefaces, Various Emendations and an Appendix, by Alexander Campbell: Hardinger Book Club: Nashville   **2503**

Reported as (452) (80)   22 cm   CtY

Alexander Campbell Version; see 1826 NT, No 567. Imprint covered by label with *Grand Rapids, Baker Book House. The Living Oracles* appears as binder's title. Printed from the 1870 plates or by offset.

Reprinted 1954 by the Gospel Advocate Company.

1951   The New Testament of Our Lord and Savior Jesus Christ. The Authentic Version Published by Brotherhood Authentic Bible Society: Plattsburg, Missouri   *2504*

475 p   18 cm   DLC, NNAB

Has Preface. Copyright 1951.

The Brotherhood Authentic Bible Society is a non-profit organization, organized "to bring the true Word of God to the world." The anonymous translator writes, "Believing that I have been given divine authority through the Holy Spirit to bring the true translation of the original Greek text, and that which has been given me through the inspiration of the Holy Spirit, I have diligently and carefully compared with the original Greek text by the use of the best Greek dictionaries and former translations, some out of the Greek and some Latin; and find that what the Spirit has given me is according to the original Greek." It is a modern speech version.

1951?   The New Testament . . . with a guide to the parables and an index to the words and wisdom of Jesus as applied to everyday problems of life. Spencer Press: Chicago   *2505*

Reported as (x) (308)   12 cm   DLC

Self-pronouncing edition.

1952   The Holy Bible . . . with Illustrations by Celebrated Old Masters, Easy To Use References, Complete Indexes and Charts . . . and Other Features. Consolidated Book Publishers: Chicago   *2506*

30 cm   DLC

Reprint of the 1946 Dickson edition (No 2439). *The Good Leader Bible* appears on spine. Has Encyclopedic Index, Concordance, and Dictionary edited by Gilbert James Brett at end. Illustrations (some in color) and 4 colored maps.

1952   The Concordia Bible with notes. Introduction, Explanations, Instructions, and References at the bottom of every Page. Revised by John Theodore Mueller, Th.D., Professor of Doctrinal and Exegetical Theology, Concordia Seminary, St. Louis, Mo. Concordia Publishing House: St. Louis   *2507*

1 vol: (1491) [1] (12) (14)   26 cm   NNAB

This is "a modern revision of the . . . Self-Explaining Bible edited by Dr. J. Wilbur Chapman and published by the American Tract Society"; see 1906?, No 2175. Has Preface (2 p), Names and Order of the Books (1 p, verso blank), and The Harmony and Perfection of the Holy Scriptures From the Preface to the Polyglot Bible, signed T. C. (6 p). At end are Synopsis of Kerr's Harmony of the Gospels (based on the ASV) and Tables, etc. (12 p), followed by New Biblical Atlas with Index and maps (copyright 1914, by A. J. Holman Company; 14 p). Copyright 1947.

10,000 copies printed. 4400 copies of the Concordia Bible were printed in 1947? (see No 2459).

1952   The Holy Bible. Old Testament in the Douay-Challoner Text. New Testament and Psalms in the Confraternity Text. Edited by Reverend John P. O'Connell . . . With Illustrations by Celebrated Old Masters . . . Approbation . . . Samuel Cardinal Stritch, Archbishop of Chicago. [Cuneo Press] The Catholic Press, Inc.: Chicago   *2508*

26 cm   NNAB

Reprint of the 1950 Family Edition (No 2483) with the addition of reproductions of colored photographs of Rome, the Vatican, various Popes, and American Cardinals. *Papal Edition* appears at head of title page
For Confraternity Version, see 1941 NT, No 2397.

1952? The Holy Bible . . . Harper and Brothers: New York   **2509**

1 vol: (vi) 7–1546   23 cm   NNAB

Set in Imperial Pica type. Includes presentation page, Family Record, Epistle Dedicatory, Order of Books, and ABS maps.
First printed in 1952. Copies printed in 1956 and later also include an Index of the Women of the Bible by E. Deen (16 p).

1952 The Holy Bible. Revised Standard Version . . . Being the Version Set Forth A.D. 1611. Revised . . . 1881–1885 and . . . 1901 . . . and Revised A.D. 1952. Thomas Nelson & Sons: Toronto, New York, Edinburgh   **2510**

1 vol: (xxii) (2) (997) (7) (294) [1]   22 cm   DLC, NN, NNAB, OC

RSV; see 1946 NT, No 2453. The RSV Bible was published simultaneously in New York, Toronto, and Edinburgh. Contains Preface and Key to Abbreviations. Alternative readings and renderings and references at foot of page. Text printed in paragraph form, double columns, with verse numbers in text. Poetical sections in poetry form. OT copyright 1952 and NT 1946, by the Division of Christian Education of the National Council of the Churches of Christ in the U. S. A.

The addresses of the Nelson offices in various parts of the world are listed on the last page, followed by the statement: "The text for this book was set in 9 point Linotype Electra on a 9½ point body with short descenders by: H. Wolff Book Mfg. Co., Inc., New York, N. Y. Paper supplied by: Central Paper Company, Inc., Muskegon, Mich. Buckram and imitation leather for binding supplied by: The Holliston Mills, Inc., Norwood, Mass. Stamped in 24 karat genuine gold supplied by: M. Swift and Sons, Hartford, Conn. Buckram edition manufactured by: American Book-Stratford Press, Inc., New York, N. Y."

NNAB has another copy for which the paper was supplied by Crocker, Burbank Papers, Inc., Fitchburg, Mass., and the printer of both buckram and leather editions was the Riverside Press, Cambridge, Mass., bound by Thomas Nelson & Sons, Camden, N. J. In later printings p 294 is not numbered. NNAB also has an edition printed in 1953 in which certain errors in the NT have been corrected: "has" to "hast" (Luke 2.31) and "kill" to "killed" (Acts 3:15). At Mat 1:16 occurs a note that was later eliminated. (See 1952 NT, No 2517).

In addition to Dr Weigle, Dr Moffatt, and Dr Burrows, the following scholars were active on the OT Committee: W. R. Taylor (Toronto), G. Dahl (Yale), W. A. Irwin (U of Chicago), W. L. Sperry (Harvard Divinity), L. Waterman (U of Chicago), K. M. Yates (So. Baptist), W. F. Albright (Johns Hopkins), J. P. Hyatt (Vanderbilt), J. Muilenburg (Pacific), and H. M. Orlinsky (Jewish Institute of Religion).

Thomas Nelson and Sons were granted the exclusive rights to publish this Bible for ten years. In 1962 other publishers will be granted rights to publish. The Apocrypha was published in 1957 (see No 2573). An edition of the Bible with references and concordance was published in 1959. By 1960 more than eight million copies of the RSV Bible had been sold.

The Standard Bible Committee, a Standing Committee of the Division of Christian Education of the National Council of the Churches of Christ in the U. S. A., continues to exist, having charge of the text. It has recommended (1959) that no revision of the RSV be undertaken at present but an edition published by Nelson in Nov 1960 had certain corrections in punctuation, capitalization or footnotes but with a few changes in wording: "from," Job 19:26; "bread," Mat 7:9 and 1 Cor 10:17; "the husband of one wife," I Tim 3:2, 12; 5:9 and Titus 1:6 and a few others. These changes will appear in editions issued by other publishers in 1962.

1952 The Living Bible, a Shortened Version for Modern Readers . . . edited by Robert O. Ballou. The Viking Press: New York   **2511**

1 vol: (xviii) (726)   22 cm   NN, NNAB

An abridgment printed in normal prose and poetry form with sources at the end of sections and in a Reference Index. In general, the arrangement follows Moulton. Contains some Apocrypha selections, Gospels in harmony form, and Introductions to each section. Copyright 1952.

1952   The Holy Bible . . . [Printed by the World Publishing Company, Cleveland].
         American Bible Society, Instituted . . . : New York   **2512**

1 vol: (4) 5–627 (3) 3–194   20 cm   NNAB
Order of Books, Alphabetic Order, and Key to Pronunciation precede text.

1952   The Bible, selections from the old and new Testaments with an introduc-
         tion and notes by Allan J. Chester . . . Rinehart and Company: New York
                                                                                2513

Reported as (xxxi) (415)   19 cm   CaOTV
Printed in normal prose and poetry form with Book and chapter identification after subject
heads. Aims to present the Bible as literature. Copyright 1952, by A. J. Chester.

1952   The Old Testament . . . Revised Standard Version . . . Being the Version
         Set Forth 1611. Revised 1885 and 1901 . . . and Revised 1952 . . . Thomas
         Nelson & Sons: New York, [etc.]   **2514**

2 vols: Vol ɪ, (xiv) (969); Vol ɪɪ, (iv) 971–1957   19 cm   NNAB
RSV; see 1946 NT, No 2453. Vol ɪ, Genesis-Nehemiah. Vol ɪɪ, Esther-Malachi. The format
matches that for the NT. Copyright 1952.

1952   Olive Pell Bible condensed from the King James Version. [Text of Psalm
         26:6, 7] Exposition Press: New York   **2515**

1 vol: (xii) (381)   17 cm   NNAB
An abridgment eliminating long historical and biographical sections but retaining the
inspirational passages with vital and spiritual messages. Has Editor's Preface and Publisher's
Note. Frontispiece is from a crayon drawing of the head of Christ by Mrs. Herbert Pell (known
as an artist as Olive Bigelow). Text printed in verse form, single column. Copyright 1952, by
Olive Pell.
Mrs. Pell had marked many Bibles for friends who urged her to publish this text.

1952   The New Testament . . . Confraternity . . . Holy Land Edition. C. Wilder-
         mann Co.: New York   **2516**

Reported as (x) (310)   23 cm   DLC
Confraternity Version; see 1941 NT, No 2397. Contains illustrations (some colored), maps,
and a Study Outline of the NT (used by permission of the Benedictine Fathers of St. Meinard's
Abbey) on p 256–310. Words of Our Lord printed in red.

1952   The New Covenant . . . Revised Standard Version. Translated from the
         Greek. Being the Version Set Forth A.D. 1611. Revised 1881 and 1901 . . .
         and Revised 1946 . . . Thomas Nelson & Sons: New York, [etc.]   **2517**

1 vol: (ix) [1] (523)   19 cm   NNAB
RSV; see 1946 NT, No 2453. Copyright 1946, by Division of Christian Education of the
National Council of the Churches of Christ in the United States of America.
    The Division of Christian Education, etc. took over the work of the International Council of
Religious Education in 1950. The text was reset by linotype from the 1946 edition with a number
of corrections. One of the most frequent changes was substituting "Other" for "Some" or
"Many" in the identification of alternative readings; i.e., "Other authorities read. . . ." Other
changes include "thou" to "you" (Mat 2:6, etc.) and "consecration" to "holiness" (ɪ Thess 4:7)
and to "sanctification" (ɪɪ Thess 2:13). The error in Luke 2:31, "has" for "hast," still stands.
In this edition a footnote was added at Mat 1:16: "Other ancient authorities read *Joseph, to
whom was betrothed the virgin Mary, was the father of Jesus who is called Christ.*" This was
eliminated later.
    NNAB has a copy of the 1946 NT which contains all the changes and corrections marked by
the Nelson proofreader.

1952 The New Testament . . . with Notes Intended to Point out the Essential Truths it Contains, by Fernand Faivre. Notes Translated from the Fifth French Edition by Alice Fontannaz, L. L. A. Third Edition. The Higley Press: Butler, Indiana   **2518**

480 p   17 cm   NNAB

The Faivre Annotated New Testament appears as cover title. Order of Books, Introduction to the First English Edition (dated Chicago 1935), Preface to Second English Edition (dated Chicago 1936), and Preface to the Third English Edition — Preface to the Sixth French Edition, 1931, all precede text. Index to Principal Passages, etc. at end. Copyright 1952.

1952? The New Covenant . . . Revised Standard Version. . . . Thomas Nelson & Sons: New York, [etc.]   **2519**

1 vol: (xii) (666)   13 cm   NNAB

RSV; see 1946 NT, No 2453. This is another corrected edition of the 1946 NT (see also No 2517 of this year). Copyright 1946, by Division of Christian Education of the National Council of the Churches of Christ in the United States of America.

1953? The Holy Bible . . . Self-pronouncing . . . words spoken by Christ . . . in red. To which is added an alphabetical and cyclopedia index, a unique set of charts from Adam to Christ, leading doctrines, harmony . . . parables and miracles, Bible dictionary; all alphabetically arranged for practical and everyday use . . . J. A. Hertel Co.: Chicago   **2520**

Reported as (317) (1504)   26 cm   DLC

Has illustrations (some colored) and colored maps.

1953 The Holy Bible. Edited by Reverend John P. O'Connell . . . Approbation of . . . Samuel Cardinal Stritch, Archbishop of Chicago. [Cuneo Press] Catholic Press, Inc.: Chicago   **2521**

26 cm   DLC, NNAB

Reprint of 1950 Family Edition (No 2483) with some of the colored material of the 1952 Papal Edition (No 2508) and some new supplementary matter. *The Family Rosary Edition* appears at head of title page.

For Confraternity Version, see 1941 NT, No 2397.

1953 The Holy Bible. Catholic Action Edition. Confraternity Text: Genesis to Ruth, Psalms, New Testament. Douay-Challoner Text: remaining books of Old Testament. Published with the approbation of Vincent George Taylor . . . Abbot-Ordinary, Diocese of Belmont Abbey Nullius. Good Will Publishers: Gastonia, North Carolina   **2522**

1 vol: (xlviii) (912) (2) (302) (80)   26 cm   DLC, NNAB

Confraternity and Douay Versions; see 1941 NT, No 2397, and 1948–   Bible, No 2470. An elaborately illustrated edition bound in gold fabricoid in gold box, prepared by the monks of the Benedictine Belmont Abbey, Belmont, N. C. Preliminary matter includes acknowledgments for illustrations, etc., Catholic Action and the Bible, Table of Contents, This Bible and Belmont Abbey ("It is a fine thing that a Catholic Bible should come out of the *Bible Belt* . . ."), Catholics and the Bible, A Background to the Bible, Manual of Prayers, and Order of Books. Illustrative matter in the OT includes photogravure pictures of Bible Lands (32 p), illuminated plates with text passages for various Holy Days, and Family Record (24 p); inserted in the NT are colored pictures illustrating the Mass (32 p), The Way of the Cross (16 p), The Holy Rosary (36 p), and The Seven Sacraments (8 p). Catholic Doctrinal Guide at end (79 p). Copyright 1953, by Catholic Books, Inc.

1953   Young's Literal Translation of the Holy Bible, by Robert Young . . . Revised
        Edition. [Photolithographed by Cushing-Malloy, Inc.: Ann Arbor, Mich-
        igan.] Baker Book House: Grand Rapids   **2523**

Reported as (16) (586) (3) (178)   23 cm   MH–AH
Contains Preface to the 1898 Edinburgh edition.
This is the first American edition of Young's Literal Translation. Robert Young (1822–88),
a Presbyterian, was a lay theologian and orientalist who took up printing and book selling in
1847. He spent the years 1857–61 in India as superintendent of the Mission Press at Surat. His
literal translation, first published in Edinburgh in 1863, was intended to help "the reader think,
see, feel and reason" as does the writer of the text. Even more famous than this frequently-
reprinted translation was *The Analytical Concordance of the Bible,* 1879. He also prepared
A Concise Commentary on the Holy Bible, which was published in 1865.
DLC has a 1956 edition of the Bible.

1953? Catholic Family Edition of the Holy Bible. The first eight books and the
        book of Psalms . . . entire New Testament . . . Confraternity of Christian
        Doctrine text; the remaining books . . . Challoner-Douay text. John J. Craw-
        ley & Co., Inc.: New York   **2524**

Reported as (xii) (1186) (381)   22 cm   OC
Confraternity and Douay Versions; see 1941 NT, No 2397, and 1948–   Bible, No 2470.
Contains colored maps and illustrations.

1953   The Holy Bible . . . Revised Standard Version . . . Thomas Nelson & Sons:
        Toronto, New York, Edinburgh   **2525**

1 vol: (viii) (2) (750) (6) 757–981   20 cm   DLC, NN, NNAB
RSV; see 1946 NT, No 2453, and 1952 Bible, No 2510. A new edition, in smaller type, with
decorative initial letters for each Book, twelve full-page colored illustrations by various artists
(mostly unsigned), and, at the end, twelve colored maps and plans (Jerome S. Kates, Cartog-
rapher; Research Editors: Herbert May [8] and Chester C. McCown [4]; copyright 1951, by
Nelson). The footnote at Mat 1:16 is omitted; errors in Luke 2:31 and Acts 3:15 are corrected.
    Also issued without illustrations. The DLC copy has Bible Helps (63 p). NNAB has an-
other copy imprinted *Whittemore Associates, Inc., Boston,* containing a section of Bible Helps
(copyright 1955, by Nelson; 64 p). DLC has another copy imprinted *Massachusetts Bible
Society* and dated 1956?; on the title to the Helps, Sidney A. Weston appears as editor. DLC
also has 1956 edition printed for the Augustana Book Concern, Rock Island, Ill.

1953? The Holy Bible . . . Harper and Brothers: New York   **2526**

1 vol: (xii) (1140) 1141–1144   19 cm   NNAB
Brevier Self-Pronouncing Bible, Red Letter Edition. Presentation page precedes title;
Epistle Dedicatory with alphabetical List of Books, Order of Books, Helps to Pronunciation,
and Table of Daily Bible Readings precede text. Family Record follows OT (4 p). At end is
An Outline of the Life of Jesus (4 p), followed by 8 maps in color (C. S. Hammond).
    First printed in the U. S. in 1953 and since issued in various bindings and with various
added matter. Not all Red Letter editions.

1953–60 [Old Testament] New World Translation of the Hebrew Scriptures.
          Rendered from the Original Languages by the New World Bible Transla-
          tion Committee . . . Publishers: Watchtower Bible and Tract Society, Inc.:
          International Bible Students Association: Brooklyn   **2527**

5 vols   19 cm   NNAB
New World Version; see 1950 NT, No 2494. The basic Hebrew text is the seventh edition
of Kittel's Biblica Hebraica, 1951. Issued in five vols: [Vol i], Genesis-Ruth, 1953 (853 p, with
maps and plan); Vol ii, i Samuel-Esther, 1955 (705 p, with maps and plans); Vol iii, Job-Song

of Solomon, 1957 (511 p, including 1 plan); Vol IV, Isaiah-Lamentations, 1958 (398 p, with maps and figures) and Vol v, Ezekiel-Malachi, 1960 (472 p with 8 maps and plans).

All the volumes issued are inscribed "First Edition" on the verso of title, with the date of first issue. Mr. Glass of the Brooklyn Office has reported that the number of copies in print is increased with each new run, but that the book is to be considered first edition until major revisions are made.

1953/54? The New Testament. A New, Independent, Individual Translation from the Greek, by George Albert Moore, Colonel, USA., Rtd. Issued Serially. The Country Dollar Press: Chevy Chase, Maryland   **2528**

1 vol: (14) (353)   29 cm   DLC, NNAB

Has Preface and biographical material. Text in paragraph form, single column, with verse numbers in margin. "This collector's edition is limited to 250 copies signed and numbered." Stencils cut and mimeographing done by Country Dollar Press. Copyright 1953.

Using Souter's 1950 Greek text, Colonel Moore made a line for line comparison with the edition of the Latin Vulgate printed at Tournai, 1894; Martin Luther's German translation, Halle edition of 1741; the French translation of the Bible Society of France of 1918; and the English translations of Lattey, the Confraternity of Christian Doctrine, R. A. Knox, and the AV. The translator states in the Preface, "The reason for this translation is that I want to do it, that there is none that exactly suits me, and that, since it is absolutely mine, and mine only, independent, individual, unsponsored, and dedicated solely to accuracy, clarity, and simplicity, it is possible that it may induce more individuals to read the Scriptures."

NNAB has separate issue of the Gospels, 1953.

1953? The People's New Testament. The common and revised versions, with references and colored maps. With explanatory notes by B. W. Johnson . . . Gospel Advocate Company: Nashville   **2529**

2 vols   24 cm   TNDC

ERV; see 1881 NT, 1953. Pagination same as in 1889–91 edition (No 2032).

A 1-vol edition was published in 1960 by the Firm Foundation Publishing House, Austin, Texas.

1953 The New Testament . . . Translated from the Latin Vulgate . . . Confraternity of Christian Doctrine. St. Anthony Guild Press: Paterson, New Jersey **2530**

1 vol: (viii) (762) (10)   20 cm   NNAB

Confraternity Version; see 1941 NT, No 2397. Third edition, 1953 printing. Copyright 1941.

1953? The New Testament in Modern Speech. An Idiomatic Translation into Every-Day English from the Text of the Resultant Greek Testament by the Late Richard Francis Weymouth . . . Newly Revised by James Alexander Robertson . . . with . . . Notes . . . Harper & Brothers, Publishers: New York
2531

1 vol: (xxii) (712)   19 cm   NNAB

Weymouth Version; see 1943 NT, No 2418. Reprinted from London fifth edition of 1936. Has Preface to fifth edition, dated 1929, and Preface to first edition, signed R.F.W., 1902. Appendix at end.

Printed in the U. S. by special arrangement with James Clarke and Company, Ltd., London.

1953 The New Testament in Modern Speech . . . Richard Francis Weymouth . . . Sixth Edition. Harper and Brothers: New York   **2532**

Reported as 456 p   19 cm   DLC

Weymouth Version; see 1943 NT, No 2418. Printed without notes, first American printing. Has maps on lining papers.

1953? John Wesley's New Testament Compared with the Authorized Version,
with an Introduction by Bishop Corson . . . The John C. Winston Company:
Chicago, Philadelphia, Toronto   **2533**

17 cm   MBU–T
Wesley Version; see 1791 NT, No 35. Reprint of 1938 Winston edition (No 2369) except
the Introduction by George C. Cell is replaced with one by Bishop Corson, with no credit given
to Mr. Cell.

1953– New Testament Commentary . . . William Hendricksen. Baker Book House:
Grand Rapids, Michigan   **2534**

16 cm   KyLoS
The following vols have been published to date: Gospel of John, 1953/54 (2 vols, 250 and
507 p); 1 and 2 Thessalonians, 1955 (214 p); The Pastoral Epistles, 1957 (404 p).
William Hendricksen (1900–   ), Th.D. from Princeton Theological Seminary, has
served as pastor and as professor of New Testament Literature at Calvin Seminary.

1953 The Epistles and Gospels For Sundays and Holydays, translation and commentary by Ronald A. Knox. Sheed & Ward: New York   **2535**

1 vol: (vii) (374)   22 cm   NNAB
Knox Version; see 1944 NT, No 2429. First issued in 1946. Imprimatur of Francis Cardinal
Spellman, Archbishop of New York. Commentary in smaller type follows each section of text.

1954 The Holy Bible . . . Revised Standard Version . . . Thomas Nelson & Sons:
Toronto, New York, Edinburgh   **2536**

1 vol: (xii) (1303) (7) (358)   32 cm   NNAB
RSV; see 1946 NT, No 2453, and 1952 Bible, No 2510. A pulpit Bible set in 18-point
Plantin type. At the beginning of each Book is a small woodcut initial. Special paper that is not
expected to become brittle has been used.

1954? The Holy Bible; Old Testament in the Douay-Challoner text, New Testament and Psalms in the Confraternity text. Edited by John P. O'Connell.
With illustrations by celebrated old masters. Published with the approbation of Samuel Cardinal Stritch. Catholic Press: Chicago   **2537**

Various paging   30 cm   DLC
Confraternity and Douay Versions; see 1941 NT, No 2397, and 1948–   Bible, No 2470.
Has Catholic Home Encyclopedia at end (288 p). Illustrations, portraits, and maps (partly
colored).

1954 The Holy Bible . . . with Illustrations by Celebrated Old Masters . . . A Comprehensive Encyclopedic Guide to Biblical Knowledge, and Other Features,
with the Words of Jesus Printed in Red, and Self-Pronunciation of all
Proper Names. Consolidated Book Publishers: Chicago   **2538**

1 vol: (xvi) (689) (2) (302)   26 cm   NNAB
The Holy Bible, Heritage Edition appears on spine. This Bible is printed from special type,
and illustrations are reproductions made from copyright kodachromes of the original paintings.
Colored presentation page, Epistle Dedicatory, Note on the Old Masters, Order of Books, Mile-
stones of the Bible, Incidents in the Life of Jesus, Index to Teachings of Jesus, and Key to
Pronunciation precede text. At end are Military Record pages, Dictionary, Concordance, and
Collation of Scriptures. Also maps with Index, Parables of Jesus, and Family Record. Colored
and sepia illustrations; maps. Illuminated Sermon on the Mount. Copyright 1954, by Book Production Industries, Inc.

1954 New Catholic Edition of the Holy Bible. The Old Testament. Confraternity Douay Version with the New Confraternity of Christian Doctrine Translation of the First Eight Books, and a New Translation of the Book of Psalms from the New Latin Version. Approved by Pope Pius XII. And the New Testament Confraternity Edition. A Revision of the Challoner-Rheims Version Edited by Catholic Scholars under the Patronage of the Episcopal Committee of the Confraternity of Christian Doctrine. Catholic Book Publishing Company: New York   **2539**

1 vol: (1118) (383)   21 cm   DLC, NN, NNAB

Confraternity and Douay Versions; see 1941 NT, No 2397, and 1948–   Bible, No 2470. Imprimatur signed by Francis Cardinal Spellman, 1953. Each Testament has Preface and Contents, etc. Text printed in paragraph form, double columns, with verse numbers in text. Family Record follows OT. At end are List of Committee Members, Bible Helps, etc., and maps. New Edition copyright 1954; previous copyrights 1952, 1951, 1949; NT copyright 1948.

DLC copy is dated 1953 but seems the same otherwise.

1954 [Old Testament] The Septuagint Bible. The Oldest Version of the Old Testament in the Translation of Charles Thomson, Secretary of the Continental Congress of the United States of America, 1774–1789, as Edited, Revised and Enlarged by C. A. Muses . . . Falcon's Wing Press: Indian Hills, Colorado   **2540**

1 vol: (xxvi) (1426)   22 cm   NNAB, OC

Charles Thomson Version; see 1808, No 153. Does not include Apocrypha. Fly title, Dedication, Acknowledgments, Foreword to the Reader, Introduction, Order of Books, and half title precede text, which is printed in paragraph form, single column, with verse numbers in brackets in text. Square brackets indicate material added by the editor to make the meaning clear, while parentheses indicate a parenthetical expression in the text itself. Footnotes are those of Thomson, except for linguistic notes by the editor. Copyright 1954, by the Falcon's Wing Press.

According to the Foreword, the editor confined himself to changing Thomson's work only where the facts of the text required it, or where another translation was called for preferentially by the oldest manuscript tradition. The editor added that portion of the Greek version of the Book of Esther (from 10:4) which did not appear in the Thomson text.

1954 The New Covenant . . . Revised Standard Version. American Bible Society . . . : New York   **2541**

615 p   28 cm   NNAB

RSV; see 1946 NT, No 2453. Wide margin Testament similar in format to the ASV NT of 1940 (No 2388). Type set from the 1952 edition (No 2517) but adjusted so that each column ends with a complete sentence or phrase.

In 1951 the constitution of the ABS was changed to permit distribution of the 1946 RSV NT. However, arrangements with Thomas Nelson and Sons and the National Council of Churches of Christ in the U. S. A. would permit the publication of a complete NT only in a bi-lingual form, for missionary purposes. The above edition, prepared especially for students, was an exception.

1954 The New Testament in Cadenced Form. Designed by Morton C. Bradley, Jr. The Bradley Press, Cambridge [Mass.]. Distributed by Rinehart & Co., Inc.: New York   **2542**

1 vol: (viii) (675)   24 cm   NN, NNAB, OC

Fly title, A Note on Cadenced Form, Order of Books, and half title precede text, which is printed in single column form with uneven lines and no verse numbers. Paragraphs and sentences are broken up according to sense and emotional content. OT quotations appear in italics. At end is A Note on Design and Production: "The second book composed on a Higonnet-

Moyroud or Photon photographic type composing machine and the first printed letterpress from such composition. Magnesium plates etched by the Dow process by the Wright Company and the book manufactured by the Riverside Press." Copyright 1954, by Morton C. Bradley, Jr.

1954 The New Testament Rendered from the Original Greek with Explanatory Notes. Part One, the Four Gospels, Translated by James A. Kleist . . . Part Two, Acts of the Apostles, Epistles and Apocalypse, Translated by Joseph L. Lilly . . . The Bruce Publishing Company: Milwaukee   **2543**

1 vol: (xii) (690)   23 cm   NNAB

Imprimatur of Moyses E. Kiley, Archbishop of Milwaukee. General Foreword (dated 1948), Preface, Contents, and List of Abbreviations of the Books of the NT precede text, which is printed in paragraph form, single column, with verse numbers in margin. Each Book has Introduction. Notes at foot of page. List of Readings at end. Maps. Copyright 1954.

DLC has edition copyright 1956, but same pagination, etc.

This is the Kleist-Lilly Version, a translation from the 1943 Bover Greek text into modern popular English. James A. Kleist, S.J. (1873–1949) was born in Germany. He became Professor of Classical languages at St. Louis University in 1928, and for many years edited the *Classical Bulletin*. He was the author of a Greek grammar and made a translation of the Apostolic Fathers. Father Kleist translated *The Memoirs of St. Peter, or the Gospel according to St. Mark, translated into English sense-lines* . . . (Bruce Publishing Co., Milwaukee, 1932; xvi, 216 p; 22 cm). Another edition was published in 1936 (xxii, 266 p). Joseph L. Lilly, C.M. (1893–1952) was Assistant Professor of NT Exegesis at the Catholic University of America and served on the editorial boards of the NT Revision Committee (Confraternity) and of the *Catholic Biblical Quarterly*. The work of these two men was brought together by the late Joseph Husslein, S.J., of St. Louis University. Father Kleist died before he had completed the notes to the Four Gospels; they were largely composed by the Rev. Henry Willmering, S.J. Father Lilly had completed the notes for his division at the time of his death.

The Psalms in Rhythmic Prose, translated by Father Kleist and Thomas James Lynam, S.J. (1887–   ), was published in 1954 by the Bruce Publishing Company (xii, 236 p; 22 cm). This is based on the 1945 Latin text of the Pontifical Biblical Institute in Rome.

1954 The Student's New Testament. The Greek Text and the American Translation. Edgar J. Goodspeed. The University of Chicago Press: Chicago   **2544**

1 vol: (x) (1055)   20 cm   NNAB

American Translation; see 1923 NT, No 2260. Has Preface. English and Greek text printed on facing pages, in paragraph form, single column. The Greek text is that of Westcott and Hort, which Goodspeed's translation follows very closely. The Greek text is photographed from a blow-up of the 1885 Cambridge edition and the English is photographed from the sheets of the 1948 NT (No 2472) pasted to fit the Greek text. Copyright 1948 and 1954.

1954 The New Testament . . . Translated by Ronald Knox. Sheed & Ward: New York   **2545**

1 vol: (xvi) (2) (697)   16 cm   NNAB

Knox Version; see 1944 NT, No 2429. Pocket edition with Preface by Bernard, Archbishop of Westminster, and brief introductions to each Book (p vii–xv). Text followed by Pronunciation of Difficult Names (1 p) and The Epistles and Gospels (p 693–697).

1955 The Holy Bible; Old Testament in the Douay-Challoner text, New Testament and Psalms in the Confraternity text. Edited by John P. O'Connell. With illustrations by . . . Tissot, Published with the approbation of Samuel Cardinal Stritch. Catholic Press: Chicago   **2546**

Various paging   30 cm   DLC

Confraternity and Douay Versions; see 1941 NT, No 2397, and 1948–   Bible, No 2470. *The Martin de Porres edition of the Catholic Bible* appears as cover title. Contains A Practical

Dictionary of Biblical and General Catholic Information (288 p). Illustrations, portraits, and maps, some in color. Copyright 1955.

1955 The Holy Scriptures According to the Masoretic Text. A New Translation with the Aid of Previous Versions and with Constant Consultation of Jewish Authorities . . . [New Edition]. The Jewish Publication Society of America: Philadelphia. [Distributed by the World Publishing Company: Cleveland] **2547**

1 vol: (x) (1270)   22 cm   NN, NNAB, OC

Jewish Publication Society Version; see 1903 Psalms, No 2151. Preface to first edition is followed by note about format of this edition, which explains that no changes were made in the text except for typographical errors and identification of "haftarot." Copyright 1917 and 1955.

1955 The Holy Bible, Teachers' Edition . . . Spencer Press, Inc.: Chicago   **2548**

1 vol: (xiv) 15–1303 (5) (278) (2)   21 cm   NNAB

Includes Dedication to King James, Order of Books and Abbreviations, and Key to Pronunciation. Red Letter Bible with center references and chronology. Has Family Record pages. The illustrations include color reproductions of paintings by Paul Laune, Lilstrom, and others; maps and half-tones covering life in Palestine. Illuminated insert on the Sermon on the Mount (20 p). Helps to an Understanding and Use of the Bible at end. Copyright 1955.

1955 The Holy Bible . . . Douay Version; Genesis to Ruth and the Book of Psalms . . . and the New Testament . . . Confraternity . . . Apostolate of the Press: Alexandria, [Louisiana]   **2549**

Reported as (1280) (382)   21 cm   DLC

Confraternity and Douay Versions; see 1941 NT, No 2397, and 1948–   Bible, No 2470. *Daughters of St. Paul* appears on spine. Illustrations and maps, some colored.

1955 The Holy Bible . . . The Gideons, International: Chicago   **2550**

1 vol: (8) (870)   21 cm   NNAB

A 2 p note, explaining the organization and containing a list of suggested readings, precedes title.

For the Gideons, see note under 1900?, No 2110.

1955 The Compact Bible . . . edited for easy reading by Margaret Nicholson. Hawthorn Books, Inc.: New York   **2551**

1 vol: (vi) (504)   20 cm   NNAB

An abridged text printed in verse form, single column, with chapter and verse indication for each section. Aims to include "essential material" known, loved, and quoted since 1611. "Published by arrangement with Pyramid Books in association with Samuel Curl, with acknowledgment to Louis M. Notkin, editor of the Quotable Bible. . . ." Copyright 1955, by Almat Publishing Corporation. (The Quotable B. was an abridged edition, 1941, NNAB.)

1955? The Holy Bible . . . Self-Pronouncing Edition. The World Publishing Company: Cleveland and New York   **2552**

1 vol: (800) (246) (2) (8)   17 cm   NNAB

This is known as the Rainbow Bible, with full color illustration cloth binding, illustrated Lord's Prayer and 23rd Psalm on end papers, and colored illustrations. Presentation page, Order of Books, and Key to Pronunciation precede text. At end are A Brief Summary of the Characteristics of Books, and Spiritual Memory Gems (printed in colored border, 8 p). While the text is paged same as the 1928? edition (No 2297), this has been reset page for page, without a center rule and with rearranged running heads.

1955 The Holy Bible . . . Harper and Brothers: New York   *2553*

    1140 p   13 cm   NNAB

Printed in Diamond type from plates made by reducing the 1953? Brevier Bible (No 2526). Preceding title page are Epistle Dedicatory, alphabetical Order of Books, regular Order of Books, and Pronunciation Helps. Table of Daily Bible Readings (4 p) follows text.

1955 The New Testament . . . in eight 32-page Portions, with over 500 illustra-
    tions and with 14 maps [followed by list of titles of each portion and page
    references]. The King James Version is used unless * indicates the use of
    the Revised Standard Version. The American Bible Society . . . : New York
                                                                                                    2554

    28 cm   NN, NNAB

The Good News, The New Testament with over 500 illustrations and maps appears as cover title. Reproductions in color of photographs of River Jordan and Sea of Galilee on front cover, and of Athens, Corinth, Rome, and Island of Patmos on back cover. Each of the portions is available separately and has its own title:

    The Light of the World: Matthew.
    Sowing the Seed: Mark.
    The Good News: Luke.
    He gave His Only Son: John.
    Into All the World: Acts.
    More than Conquerors: Romans-Corinthians.
    A Cloud of Witnesses: Galatians-Hebrews.
    Out of Death into Life: James-Revelation.

Matthew, Mark, and John are RSV and were first printed in 1953; Rom-Cor and Jas-Rev are also RSV and were first printed in 1955. Luke, Acts, and Gal-Heb are in the AV and were first printed in 1950, 1951, and 1955 respectively. An Index of Pictures was added to a second printing late in 1955, and a key letter identifying each portion was added to the page number.

The pictures were carefully selected by the Rev. Gilbert Darlington, D.D., for many years Treasurer of the ABS and in charge of its Publication Department, to show as much as possible of the life and atmosphere of the places and things mentioned in the NT. The captions and historical introductions were checked with Dr. F. W. Albright and other scholars. The text is printed without chapter or verse numbers except for identification at the end of the section headings.

A similar edition has been printed in German, and several of the sections have appeared in Arabic, Chinese, Danish, Dutch, French, Modern Greek, Japanese, Korean, Indonesian, Norwegian, Portuguese, Spanish, and Swahili.

1955 The New Testament for English Readers . . . marginal corrections of read-
    ings and renderings; Marginal References; and a critical and Explanatory
    commentary. By Henry Alford . . . Moody Press: Chicago   *2555*

    1 vol: (viii) (1952)   23 cm   NNAB

This is the first American edition of Alford's NT, first published in London in 1863. Henry Alford (1810–71) was an English churchman and writer, Dean of Canterbury, and one of the original members of the ERV NT committee. His edition of the Greek NT was well-known and from that grew the above. He also prepared a revised English NT (1869). In the cited NT, in the Gospels and Acts passages translated by Dean Alford are printed in italics in the notes; but in the remainder of the NT the AV appears in italics, separated from the new translation by a rule. A publisher's note states that the long Introduction, referred to in the notes, is omitted from this edition.

1956?   The Holy Bible . . . [with] approximately 9,000 informative parallel renderings from the American Standard Version and the Revised Standard Version . . . the words of Jesus . . . in red . . . a comprehensive encyclopedic guide . . . many other features. Clarified Edition. Consolidated Book Publishers: Chicago   **2556**

Reported as (xviii) (1328)   31 cm   DLC

Good Samaritan Edition, with Brett's Encyclopedic Index, etc. on p [1009]–[1228]. The parallel renderings from the ASV and RSV are printed in smaller type in the text line. Colored illustrations and maps.

1956   The Holy Bible . . . Good Counsel Publishing Co.: Chicago   **2557**

Reported as (96) (958) (292) (94) (96)   30 cm   DLC

Good Book Edition appears on spine. Contains Illustrated Story of the Bible for Young and Old (94 p) and The Scriptural Directory (96 p). Illustrations, some in color.

1956   The Holy Bible . . . Family Circle Edition. Universal Book and Bible House: Philadelphia   **2558**

Various paging   26 cm   DLC

500th Anniversary (of Gutenberg?) appears on cover. Includes various Bible Helps. Illustrations (some colored) and maps.

1956   The Holy Bible. Sacred Heart Edition. Confraternity text: Genesis to Ruth, Psalms, New Testament; Douay-Challoner text: remaining books of the Old Testament. Published with the approbation of John George Bennett, Bishop of the Diocese of Lafayette in Indiana. Good Counsel Publishing Co.: Chicago   **2559**

Reported as (xxxii) (912) (302) (96)   26 cm   DLC

Confraternity and Douay Versions: see 1941 NT, No 2397, and 1948–   Bible, No 2470. Illustrations, some in color.

DLC has another edition of 1956, with the Approbation of Vincent George Taylor, published by C. Wildermann Co., New York (same pagination).

1956   The Bible for Family Reading with introductions and Notes . . . by Joseph Gaer . . . and Chester C. McCown . . . Little, Brown and Company: Boston **2560**

1 vol: (xxv) (752)   24 cm   NN, NNAB

While the text is essentially the AV, the Hebrew and Greek have been carefully compared with it and some changes made. Obscurities and archaisms are eliminated. The text is printed in prose and poetry form, single column, without verse numbers, and is divided into sections. Omitted passages are listed in an Index. The Gospels are printed in harmony form, based on Huck and Lietzmann. Copyright 1956, by Gaer.

1956   Catholic Family Edition of the Holy Bible. J. J. Crawley: New York   **2561**

Reported as (xii) (1186) (381)   23 cm   DLC

Confraternity and Douay Versions; see 1941 NT, No 2397, and 1948–   Bible, No 2470. The first eight books, the Psalms and the Sapiental books Job to Sirach, and the NT are from the Confraternity Version.

1956 The Holy Bible. A Translation from the Latin Vulgate in the Light of the Hebrew and Greek Originals Authorized by the Hierarchy of England and Wales and the Hierarchy of Scotland. [By Ronald A. Knox.] Sheed & Ward: New York   **2562**

1 vol: (viii) (4) (914) (2) (286)   22 cm   NNAB, OC
Knox Version; see 1944 NT, No 2429. Table of Contents, Preface by Cardinal Griffin (1954), and Dedication to Cardinal Griffin precede text, which is printed in paragraph form, double columns, with verse numbers in margins. Bible Helps and maps at end. Copyright 1944, 1948, and 1950.

1956–59 Wuest's Expanded Translation of the Greek New Testament . . . Kenneth S. Wuest, Litt.D., Teacher of New Testament Greek, the Moody Bible Institute. Wm. B. Eerdmans Publishing Company: Grand Rapids, Michigan   **2563**

3 vols: Vol ɪ, 320 p; Vol ɪɪ, 248 p; Vol ɪɪɪ, 284 p   22 cm   NNAB,OC
Vol ɪ (1956) The Gospels, Vol ɪɪ (1958) Acts through Ephesians, and Vol ɪɪɪ (1959) Philippians through Revelation. Preliminary matter in Vol ɪ includes The Advantages of an Expanded Translation (p 11–24), The Supreme Importance of the Doctrine of Verbal Inspiration, in the Translation of the Greek New Testament (p 25–30), and A Personal Word to the Reader (p 31–37). A Personal Word also precedes text in Vol ɪɪ (1 p) and in Vol ɪɪɪ (2 p). Vols ɪɪ and ɪɪɪ each contain Definitions of Terms and a Bibliography at the end. Text is printed in paragraph form, single column, with introductions to each Book. Verse numbers appear only at beginning of paragraphs. The added words are not indicated by differences in type, but through them the translator seeks "to bring out the richness, force, and clarity of the Greek text." He also tries to follow the Greek word order and to reflect other peculiarities of Greek grammar, etc., still using modern English.

1956? The New Testament and the Book of Psalms . . . World Publishing Company: Cleveland   **2564**

636 p   19 cm   DLC, NNAB
Large type Red Letter Edition, Plates, some colored.

1956 The New Testament . . . Confraternity of Christian Doctrine. Image Books . . . Doubleday & Company, Inc.: Garden City, New York   **2565**

1 vol: (x) (549) [1]   18 cm   NNAB
Confraternity Version; see 1941 NT, No 2397. *Official Catholic Edition, Complete and unabridged* appears on paper cover.
Image Books is the name for Doubleday's series of the "world's finest Catholic literature."

1957 Holy Bible . . . The Divine Healing Edition with helps on healing, salvation, miracles. Barrett: Dallas   **2566**

Reported as (xii) (1270) (156)   25 cm   DLC
Red Letter self-pronouncing edition with colored illustrations.

1957 The Holy Bible. Spiritual Harvest Edition . . . with the words of Jesus in red . . . proper names self-pronounced . . . page reference index, a directory of subject headings, laws of the Bible and other clarifying features. The supplementary material in this Bible was conceived by and produced under the direction of Melbourne I. Feltman . . . Consolidated Book Publishers Division of Book Publishing Industries, Inc.: Chicago   **2567**

1 vol: (xxviii) (1158)   22 cm   Not Located

1957 The Holy Bible from Ancient Eastern Manuscripts, containing the Old and New Testaments, Translated from the Peshitta, The Authorized Bible of the Church of the East. By George M. Lamsa. A. J. Holman Company: Philadelphia **2568**

1 vol: (xix) (1243)   22 cm   NN, NNAB, OC
Lamsa Version; see 1933 Gospels, No 2340. Contains Publisher's Preface, Introduction, and Words Resembling One Another with comparisons of Lamsa and AV renderings. Copyright 1933, 1939, 1940, and 1957.

1957 The Holy Bible . . . Being the version set forth A.D. 1611 . . . and revised A.D. 1881–1885 newly edited by the American Revision Committee A.D. 1901. Standard Edition. Thomas Nelson & Sons: New York   **2569**

1 vol: (viii) (4) (814) (vi) (252) (2) (viii) (118) (2) (234) (6) (8) (12)   21 cm
NNAB
ASV; see 1901, No 2124. Revisers' Prefaces, Key to Pronunciation, Order of Books, and Consecutive Daily Bible Reading by J. W. Baer precede text. At end are Bible Dictionary (copyright 1900) and Concordance (combined for AV and ASV). Set in Onyx type, with center references and alternative readings and renderings at foot of page. Title appears at outer corner and chapter and verse index at head of each column. Copyright 1901 and 1929.
Although cited copy was actually published in 1957, this format was probably printed before 1925 as it appears in Nelson's catalog for that year.

1957? New Catholic Edition of the Holy Bible. The Old Testament. Confraternity-Douay Version with the New Confraternity of Christian Doctrine Translation of the First Eight Books, and the Seven Sapiential Books of the Old Testament and the New Testament Confraternity Edition . . . Catholic Book Publishing Company: New York   **2570**

Reported as (1150) (383)   21 cm   OC
Confraternity and Douay Versions; see 1941 NT, No 2397, and 1948–   Bible, No 2470. Reprint of the 1954 edition (No 2539) but with more OT books in the Confraternity text.

1957 [Old Testament] The Holy Scriptures, a Jewish Family Bible according to the Massoretic text. Complete with inspirational and informational features, including a most comprehensive, encyclopedic dictionary of the Bible and religious terms . . . plus magnificent full color reproductions of paintings of people in the Bible and their stories . . . Menorah Press: Chicago   **2571**

Reported as (xvi) (942)   27 cm   DLC
Jewish Publication Society Version; see 1903 Psalms, No 2151. Edited by Morris A. Gutstein and David Graubart; Editorial Coordinator, Gilbert J. Brett; Executive Director, Melbourne I. Feltman. Copyright 1957, by Leonard S. Davidow.

1957 In a Beginning — Genesis. Concordant Version. International Edition. The Sacred Scriptures. An Idiomatic, Consistent, Emphasized Version . . . Concordant Publishing Concern . . . : Los Angeles   **2572**

128 p   19 cm   NNAB
Concordant Version; see 1919–26? NT, No 2250. Has half-title with *Concordant Version of the Hebrew Scriptures. In a Beginning, commonly called "Genesis."*

1957   The Apocrypha. Revised Standard Version . . . Revised A.D. 1957. Thomas
         Nelson & Sons: Toronto, New York, Edinburgh   *2573*

        1 vol: (vi) (250)   22 cm   NNAB

        RSV; see 1946 NT, No 2453, and 1952 Bible, No 2510. The Preface lists the scholars on
the Committee and gives a short history of the Apocrypha. Format matches that of the 1952
Bible. In addition to Dr Burrows, Dr Cadbury, Dr Craig, Dr Grant, and Dr Weigle, the following
served on this Committee: F. W. Filson (McCormick), B. M. Metzger (Princeton), R. H. Pfeiffer
(Harvard), and A. P. Wikgren (U of Chicago).

INDICES

GEOGRAPHICAL INDEX OF PUBLISHERS AND PRINTERS

UNITED STATES

ALABAMA

Mobile
Kellogg, J. S.

Tuscaloosa
Woodruff, D.

CALIFORNIA

Berkeley
Gillick, James J. and Co.

Los Angeles
Concordant Publishing Concern
Hyatt and Lyon

San Francisco
Whitaker and Ray Co.

COLORADO

Denver
Collier and Cleaveland

Indian Hills
Falcon's Wing Press

CONNECTICUT

Bridgeport
Baldwin, J. B. & S.
Baldwin, Josiah B.
Lockwood, L.

Hartford
American Publishing Company [3]
Andrus and Judd
Andrus, Judd & Franklin
Andrus, S. and Son
Andrus, Silas
Andrus, William
Brainard & Sampson
Burr, J. B. Publishing Co.
Canfield, P.
Case, Lockwood and Company
Case, Tiffany and Burnham
Case, Tiffany and Company
Cooke, Oliver D.
Cooke, Oliver D. and Sons
Day, E. T.
Gilman and McKillip
Goodman, A. C. and Co.
Goodrich, Samuel G.
Goodwin, George
Goodwin, George and Sons

Hudson and Co.
Hudson and Goodwin
Hudson, Goodwin, and Co.
Hudson, H.
Hudson, W. and Skinner, L.
Hunt, E.
Hutchison and Dwier
Judd and Franklin
Judd, Loomis and Co.
Lincoln and Gleason
Loomis, S. L., Hart and Lincoln
Loomis, Simeon L.
Palmer, S.
Robins and Smith
Robinson, D. F.
Sheldon and Goodrich
Summer and Goodman
Sumner, H. F.
Wells, J. G.
White, R. and Co.
Worthington, Dustin and Co.

Middletown
Hunt, E. and Co.
Niles, William H.
Noyes, E.
Reynolds, Charles

New Haven
Babcock, S.
Bible Numerics Co.
Durrie & Peck & Co.
Howe and Deforest
Howe, Hezekiah and Co.
Morse, Abel
O'Brien, Edward
Webster, N.
Yale University Press

New London
Green, Samuel

Norwich
Bill, Henry Publishing Company

Westport
Limited Editions Club

DELAWARE

Wilmington
Adams, James
Andrews, Samuel
Bonsal & Niles
Brynberg, Peter
Porter, Robert
Porter, Robert and Son

DISTRICT OF COLUMBIA

Georgetown
Duffy, W.

Washington
Jewell, L. W. and Co.
National Home Library Foundation
United States Government Printing Office
University Literature Extension

GEORGIA

Atlanta
Martin and Hoyt Co.
Washington Memorial Bible Associates, Inc.
Wood, Hanleiter & Co.

Augusta
Confederate States Bible Society

Savannah
Seymour and Williams

ILLINOIS

Carbondale
Egyptian Publishing Company

Chicago
America Publishing Co.
Book Production Industries Inc.
Catholic Press Inc.
Central Book Concern
Chicago Bible Society
Columbia Educational Books, Inc.
Columbia Educational Press
Conkey, W. B. Company
Consolidated Book Publishers
Cuneo Press
Dickson, J. W. & Co.
Dickson, John A. Publishing Company
Gideons International
Glad Tidings Publishing Co.
Good Counsel Publishing Co.
Goodman, J. S. and Company
Hertel, John A. Co.
Hicks, Jim Bible Society
International Constructive Sunday School League
International Sunday School League
Lakeside Installment Co.
McClurg, A. C. Co.
Menorah Press
Moody Press
Ogilvie, Geo. W. & Co.
Peerless Bible Company
Potter, John E. Ltd.
Price, L. B. Mercantile Co.
Rodeheaver Co.
Sears Roebuck and Company
Spencer Press, Inc.
Spiegel, May, Stern Company
System Bible Co.
U. S. Publishing House

University of Chicago Press
Western Publishing House
Wilcox and Follett Company
Winona Publishing Company
Ziegler, J. S. and Co.

Elgin
Brethren Publishing House
Cook, David C. Publishing Company

Geneva
Wilson, Benjamin

Plano
Church of Jesus Christ of Latter-Day Saints

Rock Island
Augustana Book Concern

INDIANA

Butler
Higley Press

Evansville
Indexed Bible Publishing Co.

Indianapolis
Kirkbride, B. B. Bible Co.
Marrow, S. L. & Co.
"Simplified Bible" House

IOWA

Des Moines
Fellows, T. H.

Dubuque
Brown, Wm. C. Co.

Lamoni
Reorganized Church of Jesus Christ of Latter Day Saints

Muscatine
Cooperative Bible and Publishing Co.

KANSAS

Wichita
Dixie Bibles

KENTUCKY

Lexington
Hunt, William G.
Kentucky Auxiliary Bible Society

Louisville
Morton, John P. and Company
New Testament Publishers
Noble and Dean
Pentecostal Publishing Company
Worrell, A. S.

LOUISIANA

Alexandria
Apostolate of the Press

New Orleans
Duncan, Hurlbutt & Co.

MAINE

Brunswick
Nelson, James, Jr.
Richardson, George F.

Gardiner
Sheldon, P.

Hallowell
Goodale, E.

Portland
Blake and Carter
Colesworthy, S. H.
Foster, N. A.
Hallett, H.
Hyde, Lord and Duren
Sanborn and Carter
Sanborn, O. L.
Sanborn, Sherburne and Co.
Thurston & Co.
Thurston, Ilsley and Co.

Wiscasset
Babson, J.

MARYLAND

Baltimore
Armstrong & Berry
Armstrong and Plaskitt
Baltimore Publishing Company
Bible Society at Baltimore
Cathers, John & Co.
Cushing and Bailey
Cushing & Jewett
Cushing, John & Co.
Edes
Fry, John D.
Hagerty, John
Harrod, J. J.
Herrod
Hill and Harvey
Kelly, Hedian and Piet
Lewis and Coleman
Lewis, Joseph N.
Lucas Brothers
Lucas, Fielding, Jr.
Medairy and Musselman
Methodist Protestant Church
Murphy, John and Co.
Neal, Joseph
Neal, W. and J.
Plaskitt and Co.
Sower, Brook W.

Sower, Brook W. and Co.
Stockton, T. H.
Thomas, Andrews and Butler
Toy, John D.
Walker and Medairy
Wallace, John
Whiting, Cushing and Comstock
Wood, Phoenix N. and Co.
Wood, Samuel S. and Co.

Chevy Chase
Country Dollar Press

Hagerstown
Bell, Edwin
Stewart, William

MASSACHUSETTS

Amherst
Adams, J. S. and C.
Boltwood, L.
McFarland, Charles

Andover
Flagg and Gould
Gould and Newman

Belchertown
Wilson, S.

Boston
Adams, Benjamin
Adams, J. Q. and Co.
Alden, Charles F. and Company
Allen and Farnham
American Tract Society
American Unitarian Association
Andrews and Cummings
Andrews, William
Armstrong, Samuel T.
Baker & Greele
Ballard, J. A.
Bannister, R.
Beacon Press
Bedlington, Timothy
Bedlington, Timothy and Ewer, Charles
Blake, W. P.
Boston Daily Advertiser
Boston Press
Boston Type and Stereotype Foundry
Bowen, Charles
Boyle, J.
Bradford & Read
Bradley
Brattleboro' Power Press
Brown
Buckingham, J. T.
Carter, Hendee, & Co.
Carter, T. & C.
Carter, T. H. and C.
Carter, T. H. & Co.

White, J. and Co.
Whiting, Charles H.
Whittemore Associates, Inc.
Williams, A. and Company
Williams, R. P. and C.
Young, Alexander

Brookfield
Merriam, E. and Co.

Cambridge
Folsom, Wells and Thurston
Hilliard and Brown
Hilliard and Metcalf
Hilliard, Metcalf and Co.
Houghton, H. O. and Company
Manson and Grant
Riverside Press
University Press [3]
Wilson, John and Co.
Wilson, John and Son

Charlestown
Brown, Asahel
Etheridge, Samuel
Etheridge, Samuel, Junior

Greenfield
Merriam, W. and H. [1]

Groton
Richardson, Alpheus

Haverhill
Allen, H. G.
Allen, W. B. & G.

Lancaster
Shepard, Oliver, Lancaster and Co.

Leicester
Brown, Hori

Lowell
Billings, Thomas
Wolcott, J., Jr.

Lunenburg
Cushing, Edmund
Greenough, W. [2]
Greenough, W. and Son

New Bedford
Sherman, A., Jr.

Newburyport
Allen, E. W. and W. B.
Allen, E. W., Wm. B. and H. G.
Allen, William B. and Co.
Mycall, John
Nason, William W.
Parker and Robinson

Thomas and Whipple
Tilton, John G.

Northampton
Butler, J. H.
Hopkins, Bridgman and Co.

Norwood
Berwick and Smith Co.
Cushing, J. S. Co.
Norwood Press
Plimpton Press

Plymouth
Avery, J.

Salem
Cushing and Appleton
Dabney, J.
Ives, W. and S. B.
Whipple, Henry

Springfield
Bridgman, Chapin and Co.
Holland, W. J. and Co.
Merriam, George and Charles

Taunton
Brewer, David, Jun.

Westfield
Fitch, John

Worcester
Andrews, Ebenezer and Thomas, Isaiah
Baker, Z. & Co.
Commonwealth Press
Thomas, Isaiah
Thomas, Isaiah, Jun.

MICHIGAN

Ann Arbor
Cushing-Malloy, Inc.

Detroit
Globe Novelty Company

Grand Rapids
Baker Book House
Eerdmans, Wm. B. Publishing Company
Zondervan Publishing House

MINNESOTA

Minneapolis
Morgan Publishing Corp.

MISSOURI

Independence
Herald Publishing House
Reorganized Church of Jesus Christ of Latter
Day Saints

Missouri, continued

  Kansas City

Richards, H. J. and Co.
Smart, J. H. and Co.
System Bible Co.

  Plattsburg

Brotherhood Authentic Bible Society

  St Louis

Becktold Company
Bible Educational Society
Christian Board of Publication
Christian Publishing Company
Concordia Publishing House
Hutchinson, F. A. and Co.
Jones, G. I. and C.
Nafis, Cornish & Co.
Scammell and Company
Swift, John S. Co., Inc.
Thompson, N. D. and Co.
Thompson, N. D. Publishing Co.

NEBRASKA

  Lincoln

Alpha Publishing Co. [1]
Chain-Reference Bible Co.
Topical Bible Publishing Company

NEW HAMPSHIRE

  Amherst

Roby, Luther

  Claremont

Claremont Manufacturing Company's Power
    Press
Ide, Simeon [1]
Stevens and Blake

  Concord

Allison and Foster
Atwood, Moses G.
Brown, John F.
Coffin, Roby, Hoag & Co.
Cooledge, Daniel
Hill, Horatio and Co.
Hill, Isaac and W. R.
Hoag, C. and A.
Hoag, Charles
Hough, George
Moore, Jacob B.
Morrill, Silsby, and Company
Perkins, Jacob
Putnam, John H.
Roby, Kimball and Merrill
Roby, Luther
Sanborn, Oliver L.
Wallis, Henry and Roby, Luther

  Dover

Bragg, Samuel, Jun'r.
Mann, John

Stevens, S. C.
Varney and Co.

  Exeter

Derby, James
Norris, C.
Odiorne, Thomas, Jun.
Parker, Samuel
Ranlet, Henry
Stearns, William
Williams, J. and B.
Williams, John I.

  Franklin

Kimball, D.
Peabody and Daniell

  Hopkinton

Long, Isaac, Jun.

  Keene

Morrison, S. A. and Co.
Prentiss, J. and J. W.

  New Ipswich

Ide, Simeon [2]

  Sandbornton

Lane, Charles

  Walpole

Thomas and Co.
Whipple, Anson

NEW JERSEY

  Delaware

Subject Reference Co.

  Elizabethtown

Austin, David
Brookfield, B. F.
Hale, Mervin
Kollock, Shepard
Sanderson, Edward
Sanderson, J.

  Irvington

Scripture Research Association

  Jersey City

Plainer Bible Press

  Morristown

Mann and Douglass

  Newark

Dennis, Alfred L.
Olds, Benjamin

  New Brunswick

Elliot, William

New York, continued

Carvill, G. & C.
Catholic Book Publishing Company
Catholic Publication Society
Caxton Press
Century Co.
Chandler, A.
Chanticleer Press, Inc.
Chaplains' Aid Association
Christian Herald
Clark, Austin, Maynard & Co.
Clark, Austin & Smith
Clark & Maynard
Clark & Mead
Class, D. G. F.
Coddington, Robert
Colby, Lewis
Collier, P. F.
Collins
Collins, B. and J.
Collins & Brother
Collins and Co.
Collins and Hannay
Collins, Perkins, and Co.
Collins, Robert R.
Collord, James
Colman, S.
Conner, James
Conner, James and Cooke, William R.
Cooledge, Daniel
Cooper, Ezekiel and Wilson, John
Corey and Fairband
Cornish, Lamport & Co.
Crane, B.
Crawley, John J. and Co., Inc.
Cross Reference Bible Company
Crowell, Thomas Y. and Co.
Cunningham, James
Current Literature Publishing Co.
Davis, M. L. & W. A.
Davison, C. & Company
Dean, W. E.
Dearborn, George
Delisser & Proctor
Didion and Company
Dillingham, Charles T.
Dodd, Mead and Co.
Dodge and Sayre
Doran, George H. Company
Douay Bible House
Doyle, John
Drummond, Robert
Dunham, David
Dunigan, Edward
Dunigan, Edward & Brother
Dunning, T. and Hyer, W. W.
Durell, William
Dutton, E. P. and Co., Inc.
Duyckinck, Evert
Duyckinck, Evert and Mesier, Peter A.
Duyckinck and Miller

Eastburn, Kirk & Co.
Eaton and Mains
Emmins and Co.
Emory, J.
Emory, J. and Waugh, B.
Emory, J. and Waugh, B. for the Methodist
    Episcopal Church
European Publishing Company
Excelsior Catholic Publishing House
Exposition Press
Fanshaw, Daniel
Fay, Joseph D.
Fellows, J. A.
Felsberg, John, Inc.
Felt, Joseph P.
Flanagan, C.
Fords, Howard and Hulbert
Fowler and Wells
Fraser, Donald
Funk, I. K. and Co.
Funk and Wagnalls
Funk, Wilfred, Inc.
Gaine, Hugh
Gaine and Ten Eyck
Garden City Publishing Co.
Gateley, M. R. and Company
Gay Bros. and Co.
Giere, H. F.
Gilman, J. S.
Gomez, Benjamin
Goodspeed, H. S.
Gould, S. and Co.
Gray, John
Gray and Bunce
Grolier Society
Grosset and Dunlap
Harper and Brothers
Harper, J. and J.
Harrison, J.
Haven, John P.
Hawthorn Books
Hebrew Publishing Co.
Herrick, J. K.
Hewett and Spooner
Hiller, Ira R.
Hinds, Arthur and Company
Hinds, Noble and Eldredge
Hinds and Noble
Hitt, Daniel
Hitt, Daniel and Paul, Abraham
Hitt, Daniel and Ware, Thomas
Hodge and Campbell
Holman, Thomas
Hopkins, George F.
Hopkins and Seymour
Howe, J.
Hoyt, Azor
Hueston, Samuel
International Bible Agency
International Bible Press
Ivison, Blakeman, Taylor, and Company

New York, continued

Sears, J. H. and Co. Inc.
Sears, Robert
Seymour, J.
Sheed and Ward, Inc.
Sheldon and Company
Sheldon, Lamport and Blakeman
Simon and Schuster
Sinclair, G.
Sleight, Henry C.
Smith, Daniel D.
Smith and Forman
Smith and McDougal
Smith, Richard R., Inc.
Smith, T. B.
Smith, T. B. and Son
Smith and Valentine
Smith, W.
Soule, J. and Mason, T.
Spingler Institute
Stanford and Swords
Stansbury, S.
Starr, Charles
Stebbins, L.
Stephens, S.
Stevens, S.
Stratford Press, Inc.
Strong, T. W.
Swan, W. and Allinson, S.
Swords and Stanford and Company
Swords, T. and J.
Syndicate Publishing Company
Tallis, Willoughby and Co.
Tegg, T. and Son and Washbourne, H.
Testament Publishing Corporation
Thompson, Hart and Co.
Tibballs, N. and Sons
Tiebout, J.
Totten, John C.
Tripp, E. H.
Trow, John F.
Turner, Hughes and Hayden
Turney, John H.
Valentine, Richard C.
Van Rees Press
Vent, C. F.
Viking Press
Virtue and Company
Virtue, Emmins and Roberts
Virtue, George
Virtue and Yorston
Waite, G. B.
Waite, G. and R.
Walker, S. and Co. [1]
Wallis, H. and H.
Wallis, Hammond
Ward, M.
Waugh, B. and Mason, T.
Waugh, B. and Mason, T., for the Methodist
    Episcopal Church

Wells, G.
Wells, Samuel R.
White, E.
White, E. and Bliss, E.
White, E. and J.
White, Gallaher and White
White and Hagar
White, N. and J.
Whiting, Samuel and Co.
Whiting and Watson
Whittaker, Thomas
Wilderman, C. Co.
Wiley, John and Sons
Williams, E.
Williams and Whiting
Wilmore-Andrews Publishing Co.
Wilmore, J. A. and Co.
Wilson, John
Wolff, H. Book Mfg. Co., Inc.
Woman's Press
Wood, Richard and George S.
Wood, Samuel
Wood, Samuel and Sons
Worthington, R.
Wynkoop and Hallenbeck
Young, William H. and Company

Rochester

Darrow, E. & Bro.
Wanzer, Beardsley and Co.
Wanzer, Foote and Co.

Sagharbor, L. I.

Wickham, O. O.

Saratoga Springs

Davison, G. M.

Syracuse

Burnham, W. A.
Hall, Mills and Co.
Mills, Hopkins and Co.

Troy

Adancourt, J.
Merriam, Moore and Co.
Merriam, W. and H. [2]

Utica

Davis, Thomas
Fuller, John W. & Co.
Griffith, T. J.
Tiffany, I.
Williams, William

Watertown

Knowlton and Rice

Whitesboro

Sawyer, Rev. Leicester A.

NORTH CAROLINA

Charlotte

Lloyd Distributors
Southeastern Distributors, Inc.
Southern Bible House

Gastonia

Goodwill Distributors

OHIO

Cincinnati

Ames, A. T.
Applegate, H. S. & J. & Co.
Benton, F. S.
Bloch Publishing and Printing Co.
Bosworth, H. S.
Buckley, T.
Central Book Concern
Clarke, Robert and Co.
Cranston and Stowe
Elm Street Printing Company
Ely, J. W.
Ernst, Jacob
Franklin & Rice
Franklin Type Foundry
Gately & Co.
Guilford
Guilford, N. and G.
Hannaford, E. and Co.
Hitchcock and Walden
James, A. C.
James, J. A.
James, J. A. and U. P.
James, U. P.
Jennings and Graham
Jones Brothers and Co.
Knapp, M. W.
Know Your Bible Sales Co.
Longley Bros.
Longley, Elias
Moore, Anderson and Co.
Moore, Wilstach, Keys and Company
Moore, Wilstach, Keys and Overend
Morgan, E. and Co.
Morgan and Sanxay
National Publishing Company [1]
Rice, G. W.
Roff, A. B.
Ruter, Martin
Sphar, Henry
Standard Publishing Co.
Walden and Stowe
Western Methodist Book Concern Press

Cleveland

Commercial Bookbinding Company
Jewett, Henry P. B.
World Publishing Company
World Syndicate Company, Inc.

Columbus

Garretson, William and Co.
Kerins, S. H. and Co.
Lutheran Book Concern
Wartburg Press

Dayton

More, E. A. and T. T.
United Brethren in Christ, Printing Establishment of
United Brethren Concern
United Brethren Publishing House

Marietta

Mullikin, S. A. Co.

Mount Union

Snead, L. U. and Company

Toledo

Browning, O. A. and Co.
Buckmaster, J. H.

Xenia

Arbogust, C. E. and Co.

Zanesville

Lippitt, J. R. and A.

PENNSYLVANIA

Chambersburg

Shyrock, John

Harrisburg

General Eldership of the Church of God
Gospel Publisher

Lancaster

Bailey, F.
Bailey, J.
Bailey, J. and Dickson, W. & R.
Dickson, W.

Octorara

Bailey, F.
Steele, J.

Perkiomen

Perkiomen Press

Philadelphia

Adams, H.
Adams, John
Aitken, Jane
Aitken, R.
Alexander C. and Co.
Altemus, Henry
American Baptist Publication Society
American Publishing Company [1]
American Scripture Gift Mission

Pennsylvania, continued

American Sunday School Union
Amies, William T.
Ashmead, I. Co.
Bailey, Francis
Ball, John
Barrington, Ed. and Haswell, Geo. D.
Bartram, A.
Bernard, David
Berriman and Co.
Berriman, Jacob R.
Bible Association of Friends in America
Bible Committee of the Society of the Protes-
    tant Episcopal Church for the Advance-
    -ment of Christianity in Pennsylvania
Bible Society of Philadelphia
Biddle
Biddle, E. C. & J.
Bill, James A.
Booksellers
Bouvier, J.
Bradford, Samuel F.
Bradley, Garretson and Co.
Bradley, J. W.
Brinkloe, C. E. P. and Co.
Brown and Sinquet
Brown, Wm.
Bruce, D. G. [2]
Burlock, Samuel D. and Co.
Butler, E. H. & Co.
Butler and Williams
Buzby, Benjamin C.
Campbell, J. M.
Campbell, Robert
Carey, H. C. & Lea I.
Carey, Lea and Blanchard
Carey, Mathew
Carey, Mathew & Son
Carey, Stewart and Co.
Carr, Robert
Catholic Bible House
Charless, Joseph
Christman, J. C. D. & Co.
Cist, Charles
Clark & Hesser
Claxton, E. and Co.
Claxton, Remsen & Haffelfinger
Cochran, Robert
Collins, T. K., Jr.
Collins, T. K. & P. G.
Comstock, A.
Co-operative Bible Publishers
Crolius & Gladding
Crukshank, Joseph
Cummiskey, Eugene
Davis, Charles H. & Co.
Davis, Thomas
Desilver, Charles
Desilver, Jr. & Thomas
Desilver, Robert P.

Desilver, Thomas
Desilver, Thomas and Co.
Dickins, J.
Dickinson, Abel
Dickinson, Abel J.
Dobson, Thomas
Eckendorff, G.
Fagan, J.
Fagan, J. & Son
Ferguson Bros. and Co.
Finley, A.
Flint, William
Foster, C. Publishing Co.
Freeman, N. C.
Fry, William
Gately and Fitzgerald
Geddes, William F.
George, R. S. H.
Gihon, J.
Great Eastern Publishing Co.
Griffith, Harvey
Griffith and Simon
Grigg and Elliot
Grigg, Elliot and Co.
Griggs and Co.
Griggs and Dickinsons
Hall and Sellers
Hancock, William
Harding, Jesper
Harding, Jesper and Sons
Harding, William W.
Harmstead, J.
Haswell and Barrington
Haswell, Barrington and Haswell
Hogan and Co.
Hogan, M.
Hogan and Thompson
Hogan and Towers
Hollowbush and Carey
Holman, A. J. and Company
Howe, J.
Hubbard, A. H.
Hubbard Bros.
Hunt, Uriah and Son
International Press
Jewish Publication Society of America
Johnson, Benjamin
Johnson, Benjamin and Jacob
Johnson, Jacob
Johnson, Jacob and Co.
Johnson, L.
Johnson, L. and Co.
Johnson and Warner
Judson Press
Kay and Brothers
Kelly, J. and Sons
Kelly, John
Key and Meilke
Kilner, H. L. and Co.
Kimber and Conrad
Kimber, Conrad and Co.

Pennsylvania, continued

Scranton
Good News Publishing Co.

Strasburg
LeFevre, George N.

Sunbury
Alpha Publishing Co. [2]

Whitehall
Dickinson, Abel
Young, William

RHODE ISLAND

Providence
Brewer, J.
Miller and Hammond
Miller and Hutchens

SOUTH CAROLINA

Charleston
Babcock, S. and Co.
Morford, E. and Mill, John

Columbia
Evans & Cogswell

TENNESSEE

Kingsport
Kingsport Press

Knoxville
Ogden Brothers & Company

Nashville
Bible Board of the Southern Baptist Convention
Gospel Advocate Company
Graves, Marks and Co.
Hardinger Book Club
Marshall and Bruce Co.
Methodist Episcopal Church, Publishing House
   of the
Methodist Episcopal Church, South, Publish-
   ing House of the
Methodist Publishing House
Parthenon Press
Redford, A. H.
Southern Methodist Publishing House
Southwestern Company
Tennessee Bible Society

TEXAS

Austin
Firm Foundation Publishing House
Dickson, J. W. and Co.

Dallas
Barrett

San Antonio
Life Builders Press

UTAH

Salt Lake City
Deseret Book Co.

VERMONT

Bellows Falls
Blake, Cutler & Co.
Cook & Taylor
Cutler, James I. and Co.

Bennington
Clark, Darius

Bradford
Hildreth, A. B. F.
Low, A.

Brattleboro
Brattleboro Bible Company
Brattleboro Power Press
Brattleboro' Typographic Co.
Fessenden & Co.
Holbrook and Fessenden
Holbrook, John
Peck, Steen and Co.
Peck and Wood
Salisbury, G. H.
Steen, Joseph and Co.

Burlington
Mills, E. and T.
Wells

Castleton
Denison, H. C., Jr.

Middlebury
Colton, A.

Montpelier
Vermont Bible Society
Walton, E. P. and Co.

Wells River
White, Ira

Windsor
Cochran, Jesse
Cunningham, John
Ide and Goddard's Power Press
Ide, Simeon [3]
Merrifield and Cochran

Woodstock
Chase, J. B. and S. L. & Co.
Colton, R. and Seeley, G. W.
Colton, R. and Smith, G. W.
Colton, Rufus

Haskell, Nahum
Watson, David

VIRGINIA

Bethany, Brooke County
Campbell, Alexander [2]
M'Vay and Ewing

Buffaloe
Campbell, Alexander [1]

Richmond
John Knox Press
Johnson, B. F. and Co.

WISCONSIN

Milwaukee
Bruce Publishing Company

Racine
Whitman Publishing Company

CANADA

NEW BRUNSWICK

St Johns
McMillan, J. & A.

NOVA SCOTIA

Halifax
White, John H.

ONTARIO

Brantford
Bradley, Garretson and Co.

Guelph
Lyon, J. W. [1]
World Publishing Company

Hamilton
Campbell, Sherrill & Co.

Hollowell
Wilson, Joseph

Kingston
Macfarland, James and Co.

Toronto
Book Society of Canada
Briggs, William
Mackenzie, William Lyon
Oxford University Press
Ryerson Press

York [Toronto]
Stanton, R.
Thompson, S.

QUEBEC

Montreal
Catholic Society of the Bible

GREAT BRITAIN

Berwick
Taylor, John

Cambridge
University Press [2]

Edinburgh
Clark, T. and T.

Glasgow
Collins, William & Co.
Collins, William and Son

London
Bagster, Samuel
Bagster, Samuel and Sons
Bell, Allan & Co.
Chapman Brothers
Clarke, James and Co., Ltd.
Frowde, Henry
Hodder and Stoughton Ltd.
Low, Sampson, Son and Company
McGowan, J.
Rutt, T.
Trübner and Co.
Virtue, Emmins and Company
Virtue, James S.

Oxford
University Press [3]

INDEX OF PUBLISHERS AND PRINTERS

Numbers refer to items, not pages (or years). Figures in parentheses
refer to instances in which a printer or firm is referred to in relation
to a publication which does not bear his or its name.

Abbey, Richard, 1670
Abingdon Press, 2230, 2255, (2500)
Abingdon-Cokesbury Press, 2500
Adams, Benjamin, 1121, 1275
Adams, H., 640
Adams, J. S. and C., 658, 837, 878, 948, 954, 984
Adams, James, 9, 15
Adams, John, 102, 104, 112
Adams, J. Q. and Co., (2070)
Adancourt, J., 652
Aitken, R., 1, 2, 3, 10, 11
Aitken, Jane, 153
Alden, Beardsley and Co., (439), 1488, 1576, 1594, 1626, 1675
Alden, Charles F. and Company, 2007
Alden, James M., 1462, 1512
Alexander and Co., C., 865
Allen, E. W. & W. B., 247
Allen, E. W., Wm. B. & H. G., 234
Allen, H. G., (268)
Allen, T., 39
Allen, W. B. & G., 221
Allen, William B. and Co., 268, 278, 324
Allen and Farnham, 1687
Allison and Foster, (951)
Almat Publishing Corporation, (2551)
Alpha Publishing Co., [1], 2188
Alpha Publishing Co., [2], 2141
Altemus, Henry, (439), 2037, 2057
Alvord, C. A., 1646, 1685
America Publishing Co., 2148
American Baptist Publication Society, 1794, 1958, (1972), 1992, 2009, 2048, (2065), (2073), 2120, 2159, 2209, 2161, 2276
American Bible House, 2075, 2093
American Bible Publishing Co., 1950, (2036)
American Bible Society, (303), 304, (330), 332, 337, 347, 351, 362, 375, 376, 377, 378, 383, 388, 398, 399, 401, 408, 412, 417, 420, 443, 466, 479, 493, 503, 543, 565, 598, 604, 625, 626, 673, 707, 708, 724, 764, 822, 857, 869, 953, 986, 1018, 1040, 1063, 1083, 1136, 1209, 1281, 1303, 1304, 1380, 1382, 1393, 1408, 1443, 1467, 1480, 1482, 1483, 1504, 1505, 1533, 1536, 1587, 1602, 1628, 1633, 1643, 1660, 1661, 1666, 1689, 1724, 1736, 1739, 1747, 1748, 1754, 1758, 1759, 1760, 1769, 1770, 1776, 1783, 1801, 1810, 1812, 1814, 1818, 1824, 1830, 1832A, 1834, 1836, 1837, 1861, 1881, 1894, 1906, 1908, 1911, 1919, 1926, 1932, 1935, 1981, 1999, 2029, 2033, 2058,

2062, 2079, 2106, 2169, 2172, 2206, 2210, 2226, 2231, 2249, 2263, 2264, 2283, 2328, 2330, 2333, 2336, 2337, 2338, 2346, 2367, 2388, 2408, 2512, 2541, 2554
American Bible Union, 1764, 1773, 1787, 1791, 1793, 1804, 1806, 1808, 1820, 1835, 1863, 1907
American Book Exchange, (1972), 1976, 1978
American Book — Stratford Press, Inc., (2510)
American and Foreign Bible Society, 1007, 1024, 1027, 1042, 1137, 1171, 1185, 1202, 1234, 1258, 1259, 1262, 1274, 1279, 1280, 1284, 1298, 1325, 1338, 1347, 1353, 1355, 1366, 1367, 1376, 1379, 1391, 1407, 1412, 1436, 1553, 1615, 1682, 1746, 1755, 1782, (1808), 1826
American Publishing Company, [1], 1884
American Publishing Company, [2], 1889, 1928
American Publishing Company, [3], 1918
American Scripture Gift Mission, 2400
American Sunday School Union, 559, 572, 574, 627, 635, 657, 684, 698, 808
American Tract Society, 676, 677, 1476, 1530, 1656, 1742, 1762, 1816, 1972, 2104, 2171, 2175, 2181, (2507)
American Unitarian Association, 1803, 1819, 1833, 1845
Ames, A. T., 1389
Amies, William T., (1949) 1959, 1996
Andrews and Cummings, 165
Andrews, Ebenezer and Thomas, Isaiah, (97)
Andrews, Samuel, 49
Andrews, William, 191, 192
Andrus and Judd, 706, 770, (797), 830, 831, 834, 851, 868, 876, 892, 906, 910, 920, 921
Andrus, Judd, & Franklin, 969, 998, 1011, 1014, 1016, 1029, 1044
Andrus, S. and Son, (499), 1096, 1169, 1170, 1175, 1177, 1194, 1203, 1214, 1216, 1224, 1230, 1246, 1248, 1260, 1261, 1264, 1265, 1285, 1295, 1299, 1300, 1305, 1307, 1324, 1333, 1334, 1377, 1381, 1395, 1420, 1454, 1508, 1516
Andrus, Silas, 499, 513, 558, 573, 588, 591, 609, 634, 637, 638, 666, 679, 681, 688, 700, 716, 725, 751, 754, 761, 787, 791, 797, 806, 1126, 1160, 1192, 1430
Andrus, William, (499), 1109, 1110, 1115, 1128, 1138, 1140, 1141, 1159, 1173
Apostolate of the Press, 2549
Applegate, H. S. & J. & Co., 1446, 1461
Arbogust, C. E. and Co., 2042
Arden, T. S., 78, (89), 103, 111

INDEX OF TRANSLATIONS AND OF TRANSLATORS
AND REVISERS

Asterisk (*) indicates a name included also on the Index of Editors and Commentators

Abbot, Ezra*, 1953
Aiken, C. A., 1953
Albright, W. F.*, 2510
Alford, Henry, 2555
American Bible Union, (ABU), 1764, 1773, 1787, 1791, 1793, 1794, 1804, 1806, 1808, 1820, 1835, 1863, 1907, 2048, 2209
American Standard Version (ASV), 2124, 2125, 2130, 2131, 2132, 2154, 2163, 2169, 2172, 2183, 2186, 2187, 2196, 2197, 2199, 2200, 2201, 2202, 2207, 2208, 2212, 2249, 2272, 2296, 2307, 2308, 2310, 2315, 2320, 2330, 2336, 2352, 2364, 2382, 2388, 2458, 2485, 2489, 2500, 2556, 2569
An American Translation, 2209, 2260, 2289A, 2290, 2321, 2335, 2348, 2356, 2375, 2407, 2415, 2472, 2500, 2544
Anderson, H. T., 1785, 1805, 1807, 2243
Andrews, H. T., 2418
Arbez, Edward P., 2397
Authentic Version, 2504
Authorized Version, xi

Ballantine, Wm. G., 2261, 2344
Ballentine, Frank S., 2102, 2143, 2193, 2258
Basic English, 2396, 2488
Bayley, J. R., 1485
Belsham, Thomas, 171
Benson, Egbert, 726
Berkeley Version, 2437
Bernard, David, 1134
Bliss, George Ripley*, 1134, 1764
Body, W. E., 2149
Bowie, W. R.*, 2453
Bradford, Alden, 253, 956
Broadus, John A.*, 2048
Burr, J. K., 1953
Burrows, Millar, 2453, 2510, 2573

Cadbury, H. J., 2453, 2573
Callan, Charles J.*, 2363
Campbell, Alexander, 567, 647, 796, 854, 915, 1058, 1737, 1764, 1862, 1982, 2219, 2503
Campbell, George, 56, 71, 207, 517, 997, 1286. See also Alexander Campbell entries.
Centenary Translation, 2276
Chambers, T. W., 1953
Chase, T., 1953
Clementson, Edgar Lewis, 2368
Conant, Thomas J., 1764, 1953, 2048
Concordant Version, 2250, 2292, 2323A, 2572
Cone, Spencer H., 1027, 1444
Confraternity Version, 2397, 2398, 2406, 2417, 2465, 2470, 2491, 2492, 2516, 2528, 2530, 2565

Confraternity Version with Douai Version: 2475, 2483, 2487, 2508, 2521, 2522, 2524, 2537, 2539, 2546, 2549, 2559, 2561, 2570
Copp, Zed Hopeful, 2378
Corrected English NT, 2170
Craig, Clarence T., 2453, 2573
Crooks, G. R., 1953
Crosby, H.*, 1953
Cutler, Ethel, 2242, 2253

Dahl, G., 2510
Day, G. E., 1953, 2124
DeWitt, J., 1953
Dickinson, Rodolphus, 839, 987
Dillard, W. D., 2023
Doddridge, Philip, 147, 148, 311, 837, 954, 984, 1056. See also Alexander Campbell
Dwight, T., 1953

English Revised Version (ERV), 1953, 1955–1957, 1959–1970, 1972–1977, 1979, 1980, 1983–1985A, 1988–1990, 1993–1997, 2004, 2005, 2007, 2010, 2012–13, 2015–17, 2019–2021, 2023A, 2025, 2026, 2032, 2036, 2037, 2040, 2042, 2049, 2050, 2053, 2060, 2063, 2066, 2087, 2091, 2092, 2108, 2135, 2178, 2183, 2186, 2207, 2224, 2355, 2382, 2411, 2529
Expanded Translation, 2563

Farrer, A. J. D., 2418
Filson, F. W., 2573
Folsom, Nathaniel S., 1846
Frey, Joseph B., 2449

General Convention of the Protestant Episcopal Church, 2149
Godbey, W. B., 2142, 2260
Goodspeed, Edgar J.*, 2453. See also An American translation
Gordon, Alex. R., 2290
Grant, Frederick C.*, 2453, 2573
Grant, Frederick W., 2044
Greber, Johannes, 2361
Green, S. W., 2418
Green, W. H., 1953

Hackett, Horatio B.*, 1764, 1953
Hadley, J., 1953
Hall, Arthur C. A., 2149
Hampden-Cook, Ernest, 2418
Hanson, John Wesley, 2008
Hare, G. E., 1953

INDEX OF EDITORS AND COMMENTATORS

Asterisk (*) indicates a name included also an the Index of Translators and Revisers

INDEX OF EDITION TITLES

GENERAL INDEX

ERRATA

No 38   *Symbol* OCIW *should read* OClW

No 208   *Symbol* KKB *should read* KBB

No 523   *Reference to* No 486 *should be to* No 490

No 689   *Symbol* CtMW *should read* CtW

No 867   *Pagination given as* 569 *should be* 869

No 885   *Symbol* CaQ,MBM *should read* CaQMBM

No 964   A . . . B . . . S . . . *should read* American Bible Society

No 1122   King Baird *should read* King & Baird

No 1156   Daniel *should read* Daniell

No 1166   "   "   "   "

No 1201   *In last line,* Kennedy *should read* Kenedy

No 1333   *In last line, symbol* CtMW *should be* CtW

No 1645   *The date should be* 1835, *not* 1857 (*as erroneously reported to DLC*)

No 1687   *In the note, second paragraph,* (No 2048) *should read* (No 2047)

                  Final paragraph, No 2001 *should read* No 2000

No 1930   *Dates for* J. B. Rotherham *should be* 1828–1910

No 2053   *In first line of note,* 1855 OT *should be* 1885 OT

No 2067   *In note, third paragraph,* This Bible *should read* This "Bible"

No 2070   Josiah I. Porter *should read* Josiah L. Porter

No 2075   American Bible Union *should read* American Bible House

No 2090   *In last line,* J. Little and Co. *should read* J. J. Little and Co.

No 2323A   The Concordant Publishing Company *should be* Publishing Concern